Fifth Edition

ALBERT B. HAKIM
Seton Hall University

PEARSON
Prentice
Hall

UPPER SADDLE RIVER, NEW JERSEY 07458

Hakim, Albert
   Historical introduction to philosophy / Albert B. Hakim.—5th ed.
     p. cm.
   Includes bibliographical references (p.   ) and index.
   ISBN 0-13-190005-6
   1. Philosophy—Introductions. 2. Philosophy—History. I. Title.
   BD21.H22

Editorial Director: *Charlyce Jones Owen*
Editorial Assistant: *Carla Worner*
Marketing Assistant: *Jennifer Lang*
Managing Editor: *Joanne Riker*
Production Liaison: *Jan Schwartz*
Permissions Researcher: *Margaret Gorenstein*
Manufacturing Buyer: *Christina Helder*
Cover Director: *Jayne Conte*
Cover Designer: *Bruce Kenselaar*
Composition / Full Service Project Management: *Jaya Nilamani/Integra*

Pearson Prentice Hall™ is a trademark of Pearson Education, Inc.
Pearson® is a registered trademark of Pearson plc
Prentice Hall® is a registered trademark of Pearson Education, Inc.

Pearson Education Ltd.
Pearson Education Singapore, Pte. Ltd.
Pearson Education Canada, Ltd.
Pearson Education—Japan

Pearson Education Australia Pty, Limited
Pearson Education North Asia Ltd.
Pearson Educación de Mexico, S.A. de C.V.
Pearson Education Malaysia, Pte. Ltd.

PEARSON
Prentice
Hall

10 9 8 7 6 5 4 3

ISBN 0-13-190005-6

Dedicated with affection to my wife and family

Contents

PART TWO: THE MEDIEVAL PERIOD

The Spirit of Medieval Philosophy: Philosophy Meets Theology   149

PART THREE: THE MODERN PERIOD

The Spirit of Modern Philosophy:
Philosophy and the Rise of Science   235

Table of Problems: Readings

III. RELIGION

IV. THE HUMAN BEING

V. ETHICS, MORALITY, AND POLITICAL PHILOSOPHY

Preface

The format of the fifth edition of *Historical Introduction to Philosophy* remains the same as the previous ones. The text material spans 2,500 years of Western philosophy, extending from the predecessors of Socrates to the present day. Introductions to each of the four periods—ancient, medieval, modern, and contemporary—provide a synopsis of each age, describe its intellectual milieu, and trace the development of philosophy throughout the period. For the most part, each chapter is devoted to a single philosopher and begins with a presentation of his life and work. The readings offer a representative selection of the philosopher's work. This substantial and broad-ranging anthology gives students the flavor of the philosopher's writings and allows professors to tailor the material to their courses. Questions for discussion or review come at the end of each chapter. At the end of the book, a glossary of key terms and a detailed index are to be found for ready reference. An alternate table of contents—the Table of Problems—provides a separate reference to the problems discussed in the readings and can be used to pursue a particular theme or subject of interest. *Historical Introduction to Philosophy* thus lends itself as a practical and pliable text to instructors in a variety of teaching styles, course objectives, and classroom contexts.

But in light of the recommendations made by reviewers of the text, there are enough changes to warrant a fifth edition. A section on Jacques Derrida has been added and a chapter on St. Anselm has been revived. Portions of the readings were dropped, but none in their entirety. The text has been enriched by a map of the philosophic world at the time of Plato and Aristotle, as well as several pertinent illustrations. Sub-headings have been inserted into the introductory portions of the text to highlight the material presented. A significant amount of text has been reworked for greater clarity or further explanation. Commensurate changes were made in the bibliographies, glossary, and index.

Acknowledgment

Thanks to my colleagues in the Department of Philosophy at Seton Hall University, and to the many others, already gratefully mentioned for their help in preparing the previous editions of this text, and especially to David O'Connor who has graciously supported it from the beginning with perceptive suggestions and critical readings of many of its chapters, including the section on Derrida for the present edition.

In addition, I'd like to thank Terence Hoyt of Tulane University, and Frank Schalow of University of New Orleans for their comments and helpful critiques of the manuscript.

ABH

Introduction

The purpose of this book is to introduce you, as a beginning student, to philosophy. By the time you reach the end, you will have seen philosophers at work, discussed their ideas, and developed a feeling for the spirit of philosophical inquiry—which feeling is by far the best introduction to philosophy you can have. But even now it would be useful to have some basic notion of the ways in which philosophy differs from other areas of knowledge. Often, in undertaking a new study, a start can be made with a definition; in this case, however, a definition does not immediately come to hand, for there is none to be found which states absolutely and simply what philosophy is. But we can develop a sense for what takes place when we "philosophize" or "do philosophy," and accordingly describe it.

Philosophy as Reflection on Experience

First, let's look at the kind of question we ask when we think about things, for the kind of question is in itself a key to the truth we seek. Take the simple example of an apple. We can ask questions like, What is its shape? its color? its taste? How much does it cost? How much does it weigh? Where does it grow? How is it shipped? What is its best perspective for a painting? and so on. But we can also ask questions of another kind: Why does the apple exist rather than not? Is it caused, or is it just there? What's in its makeup to distinguish it from a stone, a dog, a man? Is there a reason why it exists? a purpose? an end? The questions of the first kind differ from those of the second in that they are questions of fact. They are questions we ask as merchants, farmers, or artists. They arise from experience, but they are not an inquiry into the experience itself. The questions of the second kind, however, ask for more than a mere statement of fact, for things not given in the experience; they arise from experience, but they invite us to probe the possibility as to whether there is more in experience than what we first meet. They summon us to reflect on what, if anything, is required beyond the experience to warrant our having it to begin with. Thus, *reflection on experience* is a good description of what philosophy is.

Take the following example of an experience you might well have had. You are a spectator in an art gallery, attracted by a painting you never saw before. You call it beautiful; you enjoy it; you experience it. You don't have to ask yourself *why* it is beautiful, yet if you do, you are asking a question which opens up further understanding of the experience. Thus, given the experience of this work of art as beautiful, the effort to discover why this is so is what the philosophy of art is all about.

An example of an entirely different texture is had in language—our ordinary everyday use of words. Our experience is generally one of satisfaction that by the words we use and the sentences we fashion we can communicate with others in speech and writing. The questions we raise usually refer to grammar or style. But further questions can be raised, like those pertaining to the relationship between language and the world of facts, or how words stand to each other in a sentence; an inquiry of this kind, which occupied many British philosophers of the recent past, goes by the name of the philosophy of language, or language analysis.

If we switch our attention to humanity, more specific questions naturally arise. What do human beings, as living things, have in common with other living things? What do they not have in common? Or, given two people, what differentiates one from the other, making each one an individual? Or, are human activities, such as thinking and willing, radically different from the activities of animals or a computer solving an engineering problem? Is there some kind of life after death? Do we have a destiny? Why are some actions of ours called good, and others not? A list like this can go on indefinitely, but the point made here is that they are philosophical questions because they initiate a search for the deeper meaning of human life. They are questions all of us can and must ask at the risk of running foul of Socrates' time-honored dictum: "the unexamined life is not worth living."

Examples of experience abound, every one of them giving us further entrée into reality. They can come from natural science, mathematics, psychology, anthropology; from our self-understanding as knowing and willing beings; from our inward consciousness of our selves, our emotions, our choices; from fears of loneliness, alienation, despair; from love, friendship, desire, joy; from laughter, sorrow; from social life; from privacy; from government, law; from history and religion; in short, from all those experiences whereby reality as a whole makes itself known to the human mind in the course of time.

Philosophy as Pursuit of Truth

Another helpful way of getting to understand the nature of philosophy is to look at the derivation of the word. The word *philosophy* is of Greek origin and signifies "love of wisdom" (*philia*, love; *sophia*, wisdom). Once again, wisdom stands for more than the kind of knowledge a pilot has, who knows how to set a compass for direction or by the sociologist who knows the right sampling device for making a survey. We do not call the pilot or the sociologist "wise" because each knows how to use the appropriate device. Wisdom looks for more; it touches a level where separate things can be seen in unity or disparate things in interrelatedness. Perhaps this is something like what Aristotle had in mind when he said that wisdom deals with "first causes and the principles of things."

The pursuit of truth is not the domain of any one person, as though any one person's mind were ample enough to embrace all; the pursuit of truth belongs to many and stretches over long periods of human history. This continual pursuit is often expressed in the phrase *perennial philosophy*, which bespeaks the love of wisdom as it characterizes humanity's search in the course of time. Perennial philosophy does not refer to an unassailable body of truth handed on from generation to generation, for, even though there may be agreement on many things, philosophers do not agree on everything. Augustine, for example, holds to the immortality of the soul, Sartre does not; Aristotle says that cause and effect is an extramental relationship, Hume says it's mental; Descartes asserts that knowledge begins with innate ideas, Locke flatly denies it; Aquinas maintains that man is social by nature, which Hobbes rejects; Kierkegaard insists on individuality as his primary concern, Marx insists on society; and thus it goes. As Hume observed, "There is nothing which is not the subject of debate, and in which men of learning are not of contrary opinions."

The difficulty in achieving certainty does not point to the impoverishment of philosophy; it points to the *nature of reality* whose very depth and mystery are veritable magnets to the inquiring mind and preclude philosophers from abandoning their common search for meaning. Granted there are differences among them, philosophers are called philosophers because of their concern for investigating questions implied in their experience. Their concern is precisely with the problems of reality that, because of their significance, easily lead to disagreement: knowledge, morality, selfhood, cause and effect, language, art, law, happiness, good, love, virtue, determinism, freedom, and so on. This common search and common concern is what unites philosophers as philosophers, generating thereby a "unity of philosophical experience."

The Plan of this Book

It follows from what has been said that beginning students, to get into the spirit of philosophy, do well to study philosophical problems in historical context; here they will observe philosophers at work and come to grips with the problems themselves in the historical setting which nurtured them; the history of philosophy will become for them what the laboratory is for students of science.

The historical span of philosophy in the West, which is the scope of this book, is about 2,500 years, extending from the predecessors of Socrates to our own day. This text covers the four main periods: ancient, medieval, modern, and contemporary. The first period, for the most part Greek, runs from the earliest Greek philosophers in the sixth century B.C. to the third century A.D.; here we shall see the pre-Socratics, Socrates, Plato, Aristotle, Epicurus, and the Stoics. The medieval period extends from the beginning of Christian philosophy around the fourth century to the early part of the fifteenth century, with the coming of the Renaissance; in this period we shall particularly meet St. Augustine, St. Anselm, St. Thomas Aquinas, and William of Ockham, but we shall make the acquaintance of Nicholas of Cusa, Maimonides, and Duns Scotus as well. The modern period, also referred to as "classical" modern, begins in the early seventeenth century and goes to the middle of the nineteenth; the philosophers to be studied here are Descartes, Spinoza, Leibniz, Hobbes, Locke, Berkeley, Hume, Kant, Hegel, and Mill. The contemporary period covers philosophers living today or in the recent past, from the middle of the nineteenth century, inasmuch as a great deal of contemporary thought has its origin in the second half of that century; here we shall read chapters on Kierkegaard, Nietzsche, Marx, Bergson, James, Husserl, Heidegger, Sartre, Russell, Wittgenstein, and a final chapter on Langer, Quine, Searle, Rawls, Singer, and Derrida.

In a book dealing with two and a half millennia of Western philosophy, clearly not every philosopher can be discussed, nor every problem, lest it become an encyclopedia instead of a textbook. So some selection had to be made with all the perils of choice. The guiding principle has been to select philosophers who are representative, whose contributions are arguably major, and whose inclusion therefore would be more defensible than their exclusion. Selection hardly means that excluded philosophers are not important, nor their insights without merit; it simply means that the philosophers included serve, in the opinion of the author, as admirable historical profiles in the adventure of Western philosophy.

SUGGESTIONS FOR FURTHER READING

Copleston, F. *A History of Philosophy*, 9 vols. New York, Doubleday Image, 1946 sqq.

Edwards, P., ed. *Encyclopedia of Philosophy*, 8 vols. in 4. New York, Free Press, 1973.

Honderich, Ted, ed. *The Oxford Companion to Philosophy*. New York, Oxford University Press, 1995.

Kenny, Anthony. *The Oxford History of Western Philosophy*. New York, Oxford University Press, 1994.

Warnock, M. *Women Philosophers* (Everyman). Boston, C. E. Tuttle, 1996.

PART ONE

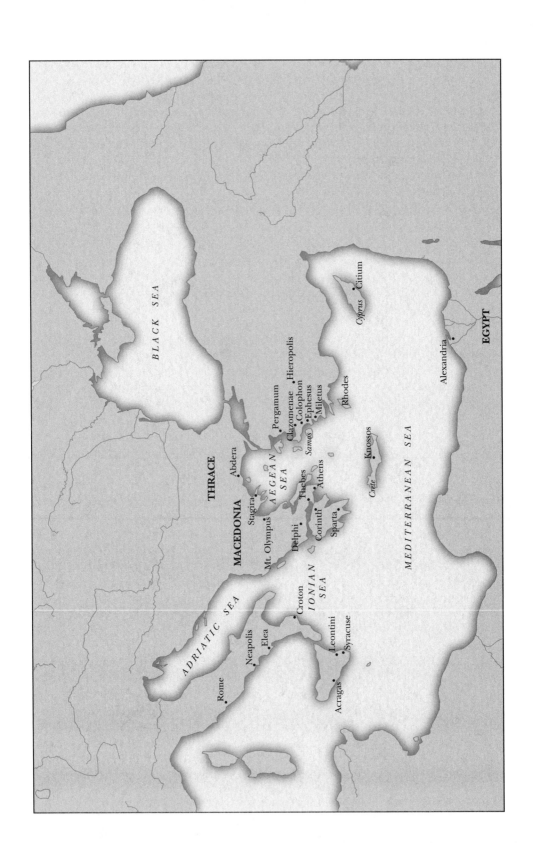

THE ANCIENT PERIOD

The Spirit of Greek Philosophy

Just as it is impossible to think of a Renaissance figure without recalling the vibrant intellectual environment of that incredible epoch or of a seventeenth-century savant apart from the mathematical enthusiasm of the time, or of a contemporary scientist isolated from the whirlwind of technology, it is also impossible to think of philosophy without considering the history, heritage, ancestry, or culture in which it germinated. This does not mean that there was always a hand-in-glove relationship between philosophy and the prevailing culture, because often it was the prevailing culture that philosophers opposed; nevertheless, philosophers, like the rest of us, are children of their time.

The Greek world, where philosophy was born, included not only present-day Greece but extended east to the shores of Asia Minor (present-day Turkey) and the many islands in the Aegean, and west to Sicily and southern Italy; though not a political entity, it was united by race, language, custom, religious feeling, and tradition. In this Greek world, long before the first recognized philosopher appeared, a culture already existed: Civic life existed in city-states like Athens, Sparta, Thebes, and Corinth; the rich literature of Homer and Hesiod prevailed, filled with myths, heroes, and legends; and religion suffused the

Greeks' daily life, though it was fragmented into countless beliefs and rites proper to the gods and goddesses who lorded it over all. Subsequently, Greek culture was enriched with the poetry of Solon (c. 640–558 B.C.), as well as by the wise measures he took as a respected statesman. Some one hundred to two hundred years later, in its flowering as the dominant city-state, Athens saw the rise of its three great tragedians, Aeschylus, Sophocles, and Euripides, and two of its great historians, Herodotus and Thucydides. The genius of Greece created such a climate of poetry, drama, religion, music, science, polity, and even sport that the total Greek experience was unparalleled in the history of the West. Part of this experience was philosophy itself as it unfolded from its beginnings with Thales, through the golden age of Socrates, Plato, and Aristotle in the fifth and fourth centuries B.C. to the Stoics and Epicureans in the late fourth and early third centuries B.C.

If we ask what kinds of things the early philosophers thought about, we find the classic response in the opening pages of Aristotle's *Metaphysics:* "For it is owing to their wonder that men both now and at first began to philosophize; they wondered originally at the obvious difficulties, then advanced little by little and stated difficulties about greater matters, for example, about the phenomena of the moon and those of the sun and of the stars, and about the genesis of the universe." Indeed, the first philosophers of Greece were awed by the world of nature, a world offering an endless variety of activity, of elements, of shapes, of movement, of bodily things both living and nonliving. Such a world inspired wonder—wonder both in the sense of admiration and in the sense of responding to an invitation to inquire why things are the way they are. This same spirit inspired the later philosophers too as they broadened the horizons of their predecessors, culminating in the achievements of Plato and Aristotle, who between them inaugurated two distinct, but complementary, traditions in the history of philosophy.

In a sense, Greek philosophy never died, for it continued to nourish generation after generation of thinkers. Of course, not every aspect of Greek philosophy produced its counterpart in subsequent thought, but allowing for the vagaries of history, its influence has been pervasive. For many Christian philosopher-theologians in the age that was its direct inheritor, Greek philosophy was the vehicle of reason (and, for some, providentially appointed) for conveying revealed truth, whether in claiming the existence of the very God who revealed, or in establishing the framework for temporal man's imaging the eternal, or in providing rational support for the immortality of the soul. Further indebtedness to Greek philosophy is seen in every subsequent inquiry, down to our day, into the meaning of life, ethics, psychology, knowledge, death, destiny, cosmos, law, government, society, and happiness; indeed, two great Greek themes, the one and the many (unity in reality) and being and becoming (permanence in change), are so basic that they emerge in different guises throughout philosophy and can be used as guidelines in writing its history. Specific instances of influence aside, the priceless bequest of Greek philosophy to its heirs is its spirit of wonder in the face of reality. All else is derived from this spirit. To study this period is both a privilege and a necessity; it is its own reward.

SUGGESTIONS FOR FURTHER READING

Armstrong, A. H. *An Introduction to Ancient Philosophy*. Lanham, MD, Littlefield, 1981.

Barnes, J. *Early Greek Philosophy*. New York, Penguin, 2002.

Guthrie, W. R. C. *A History of Greek Philosophy*, 6 vols. Cambridge, Cambridge University Press, 1962–1981.

Jaeger, W. *Paideia: The Ideals of Greek Culture*. New York, Oxford University Press, 1965.

1

The Predecessors
of Socrates

The Pre-Socratics

The philosophers preceding Socrates lived in the sixth and early fifth centuries B.C. and are collectively called the *pre-Socratics*. Their original writings suffered the fate of many works of antiquity and do not exist today, so that we do not have direct access to their thought. Nevertheless, through quotations and references to their work by later authors who either did have access to them or were in a position to pass on received information, some of their ideas have come down to us. By painstaking research, scholars have been able to reconstruct something of their background and to develop a picture of the main lines of their thought.

Philosophy began in that part of the Greek world known as Ionia, roughly corresponding to the western part of present-day Turkey and some nearby islands. Why philosophy originated in Ionia is a matter of conjecture, but it is certainly true that philosophy thrives along with other refinements of civilization, and the land whose creative impulse inaugurated the Greek epics inaugurated philosophy as well. The coastal cities of Asia Minor, having developed as sea and land termini joining east and west, tended to become active intellectual centers too and such a one was Miletus. It counted among its citizens Thales, Anaximander, and Anaximenes, the first three Greek philosophers who are presumed to have had a successive teacher–student relationship. Because of the region, they are referred to as *Ionians*; because of their citizenship, they are referred to as *Milesians*; and because of their primary concern with the natural world, or cosmos, they are often referred to as *cosmologists*.

Thales of Miletus: The Problem of the One and the Many

The philosopher generally recognized as the first in Western philosophy was *Thales*, who was born in the last quarter of the seventh century B.C. and who flourished in Miletus in the early part of the sixth century. Though he apparently wrote little, he was acknowledged as a man of great wisdom, displaying an enormous range of knowledge as an astronomer, a mathematician, and a statesman. He was accorded the honor of being listed among the Seven Sages of Greece. In converting his theoretical knowledge into practice, he seemed to have little trouble: he gave ship pilots the means of charting their course by the stars; he made recommendations for the establishment of effective governing bodies; and once, when the soldiers of King Croesus could not cross a river running in front of them, he is said to have diverted the flow so that the river ran behind them. His practical sense took an economic turn too when, on one occasion, having predicted a large olive crop, he cornered the market on olive presses so that the growers had to rent them from him—a story to which Aristotle wryly adds that Thales demonstrated how easy it was for philosophers to become rich if they so wanted. But not even his renown, Plato writes, prevented a servant girl from laughing at him when he "was looking up to study the stars and tumbled down a well. She scoffed at him for being so eager to know what was happening in the sky that he could not see what lay at his feet."

From his observation of the all-pervading presence of water in the growth and nourishment of living things, and from his belief that the earth rests on water, Thales concluded that all things derive in some way from water. In terms of the one and the many previously mentioned, the many things of the natural world are held together as one, as a universe, because water is their underlying principle and the source of their unity. We must not be put off by the seeming naiveté of Thales; he clearly saw that, where there are many things, no unity is possible unless there is a basis for it, unless the many share it. In his view of *water as the primal element*, Thales discovered what, for him, was the substrate of unity in the cosmos and the basic reason why the cosmos was able to render itself shareable in the manifold of physical things.

He was making sure that reality as a whole did not rob the individual of its individuality. In fact, the relationship between the one and the many is reciprocal, and it is an enduring insight that the very uniqueness of the individual flows from its relationship to reality as a whole. Philosophers have to maintain a delicate balance: not to emphasize the one (reality as a whole) at the expense of the many (as individuals), or the many at the expense of the one. The reciprocal relationship is what supports both the individual and the whole.

Add to this notion of cosmic unity the belief, for Thales, that all things are "full of gods." Now there is no notion in Greek literature that has a meaning more variegated than that of "god" as it fluctuates from sublime divinity to barely more than human, yet, it is consistent with what we have seen already that Thales was trying to express the vitality, the life of the cosmos, which, as god-filled, commands our wonder and our reverence all the more.

The naming of someone as the "first philosopher" is a highly privileged designation, especially when you consider the bounteous culture of early Greece. We can be sure that others philosophized long before Thales, but he is the first one we have a record of; that is, the first in the *recorded history* of the West to be so recognized. By the same token if the goal of philosophy is to seek the explanations of things, hasn't the human mind sought them since the beginning of time? What is there so distinctive about Thales in virtue of which we call him a philosopher, let alone the first? The term *philosopher* refers to one who looks for a *rational* explanation of his experience of reality, who tries to grasp the real as a matter of *understanding*, as opposed, let us say, to a magical, mythical, fictional, or even a revealed explanation of things. Despite the fact that Thales was wrong-headed about the physical role of water in unifying the cosmos, he was right-headed in the way he sought for a rational explanation.

Faithful to the central thought of Thales, the other Milesians sought elsewhere for the unifying factor of the cosmos. *Anaximander*, relying perhaps on the notion that things are generated only by their opposites, believed that the common origin of all things was completely unlike that which was generated; if that which was generated was finite and bounded and many, then that which generated it was Infinite and Boundless and One. For *Anaximenes* the unifying substrate was air, from which, by its properties of condensation and rarefaction, the many were formed.

Pythagoras of Croton: The Adaptability of Mathematics

In his enthusiasm for geometry, Thales proved to be a herald of the love affair the Greeks had with mathematics. Wherever there is an intellectual ferment in the natural sciences, there is bound to be one in mathematics as well. This was true of Greece, where all the cultural ingredients were present for science and mathematics to grow. We can ask what there is about mathematics which makes for the incredible fascination it has over the human mind. Perhaps it is because mathematics extends the mind and leads it to unassailable conclusions or because it produces order, organizing things under the umbrella of unity, thereby doing precisely what the mind naturally yearns to do. At any rate, mathematics is the favorite language of the sciences in its capacity to express their findings, to unify them, and to open up new avenues of discovery.

There was every reason then for *Pythagoras*, the sixth-century mathematician-philosopher who spent his early years on the island of Samos and his later years at Croton in southern Italy, in his inquiry into unity, to think that real things and their relationships are somehow expressible by number, if indeed they are not actual numbers themselves. There must be a profound analogy between the unity of numbers and the unity of the universe. Though there are many numbers, they are still one, for no number is conceivable without 1; further, every number other than 1 is generated by 1. So, without surrendering the difference between a given number and all other numbers, or differences like odd and even, all numbers must be seen as belonging to the unity of their common origin in 1. And if many numbers are the expression of a basic harmonious unity, there is no reason why the many things of the universe cannot be the expression of a basic unity as well. That at least seemed to be Pythagoras' hope, and he received some encouragement from his interest in music when he discovered that the interval between notes on the musical scale can be expressed numerically, depending on the length of the string required to produce them; if physical length and tone are so easily expressed by number, perhaps the rest of the universe is too.

For an ardent thinker like Pythagoras, mathematics became the touchstone for a deeper vision of cosmic unity; for if the number 1 is found in the composition of every other number, and if all numbers share the unity of 1, then can we not envision that at the head of all reality stands the One, Unity, and that all things share it? It is the culmination of man's desire to rest in a transcendent peace. The possibility of sharing the One was, for Pythagoras, the *mystical aspect* of mathematics. There is a level of reality that man is drawn to, that he does not truly comprehend, yet is convinced that reaching it is his calling as a human being. This idea may not be found explicitly in the works of Pythagoras, but it is the only way in which our knowledge of his teaching and his life fit together.

An anecdote informs us that Pythagoras believed in the *transmigration* of souls; that is, the soul does not cease to exist when the body dies but is reembodied in another: "And once, they saw him passing by when a puppy was being beaten, he pitied it, and spoke as follows: 'Stop! Cease your beating, because this is really the soul of a man who was my friend: I recognized it as I heard it cry aloud.'" Another fragment from a later Pythagorean, in referring to the doctrines of Pythagoras, states, "The ancient theologians and seers also bear witness that because of certain punishments the soul is yoked to the body and buried in it as in a tomb." Release from the body and from the cycle of *reincarnation* indicates Pythagoras' belief in the immortality of the soul and the care that must be taken to wean oneself gradually from the body by a lifelong process of purification. To this end, he established a community of men and women. It was a secret society and apparently had a full program of study, dietary rules, prohibitions, and permissions. It was established mainly for the pursuit of holiness, which in turn meant the pursuit of purification whereby the soul was released from the body. Final perfection, then, comes when the soul is freed from the body and united or reunited, with the One.

Heraclitus of Ephesus: The Problem of Change

While Thales and Pythagoras struggled with the problem of *the one and the many* (unity in plurality), Heraclitus and Parmenides struggled with the kindred problem of *being and becoming* (permanence in change). These two great problems, as already noted, arose among the Pre-Socratics from diverse ways of reading reality, each with its own enduring insight. About *Heraclitus* very little is known, but he can be situated at the turn of the sixth and fifth centuries at Ephesus, a seaport town just north of Miletus; he was probably a member of one of its more influential families. Whether he ever wrote a book is not known, but what has come down to us is a fairly generous collection of short, pithy statements, rather like aphorisms or epigrams, whose language is obscure but whose content is thought-provoking. Perhaps Heraclitus wanted to imitate the oracle at Delphi: "The lord whose oracle is at Delphi neither speaks nor conceals, but indicates." Heraclitus too never "said" anything; he only "indicated." Even among the ancients he was referred to as the "obscure one."

Among all the phenomena, or manifestations, of reality, the one that struck Heraclitus most forcefully was that of *change*. Nothing remains permanent or static; everything changes in a sea of change. It is as though in the very same moment we notice a thing is, we also notice that it has become something else. The leaves change, animals change, humans change, the heavens change, and even if a thing appears unchanging, we suddenly realize that as everything else about it changes, so does the thing itself because its relationships change. As another philosopher would say many centuries later, there is "more" in becoming than in being. The image Heraclitus uses is "All things flow." That is, all things exist as though they are part of a stream, continually flowing, running, changing, always different; so much so that, as Plato records, Heraclitus maintained that it was "impossible to step into the same river twice."

Yet universal change does not mean disorder or chance togetherness like that of a heap of stones. No, the many changing things, or the "manifold" of change, despite their seeming randomness, are disposed in orderly fashion. The mind has to undergo a reengagement with reality; we are dealing with reality for sure, but a reality on the move, a literal "universe" in which all things turn around as one. So, for Heraclitus, two main questions arise: What is the source of this unified motion, and what is the agency whereby movement is provided?

In answer to the first question Heraclitus says, "Listening not to me but to the Logos it is wise to agree that all things are one." This fragment, together with others, suggests that movement is not self-originated, but originates on a higher level, and that the originator also presides over this movement and ensures its unity. Movement means not only natural or physical activity, but human activity as well. In another fragment Heraclitus states that "It is necessary to follow the common; but although the Logos is common the many live as though they had a private understanding." There is a distinct moral dimension in Heraclitus' work, centering on the unity that human actions should have with the Logos. Human actions are as manifold as any others; they are in flux, and they change in a never-ending stream of action; thus there is a great risk of dispersion, of meaninglessness, unless they too share a higher focus of unity. To see this unity is a large part of the search for wisdom expressed by Heraclitus in the words "I sought out myself," a motif to become traditional in Greek philosophy.

The term *logos* has an extremely revealing and valuable history. Its basic meaning in Greek is word or discourse, but it takes on, according to the historical context, a host of other meanings as well such as law, reason, intelligence, and wisdom. As Greek philosophy, at a much later date, interacted with Hebrew and Christian thought, logos came to mean person inasmuch as the spoken word projects the person speaking. In the New Testament, John refers to Christ personified as the Word spoken by God. Obviously, we cannot say precisely what Heraclitus means, but a good guess is that he is using a play on words: when you hear *my* logos (word, discourse, message), I trust you hear *the* Logos (orderer, law, reason).

In answer to the second question, the Greeks came to recognize four elements as basic: earth, air, fire, and water, each a primitive contributor to the stuff of the world. But fire, life-giving in its warmth and long revered for its sacred character, took on a special power in the form of lightning as it accompanies the thunderbolt: it "steers the universe." Couple this saying with "The mixed drink separates if it is not stirred," and the image is that of the universe turning as it is constantly being struck by lightning, thus achieving unity in movement or unity in becoming. Whether fire, for Heraclitus, is somehow endowed with intelligence is hard to say, but that it effects the work of intelligence in producing unity is clear.

Heraclitus sums up his prophetic pronouncements by rebuking those who are indifferent to the transcendent vision, who fail to respond to the call of the highest wisdom. "Of the Logos, which is as I describe it, men always prove to be uncomprehending, both before they have heard it and when once they have heard it. For although all things happen according to this Logos men are like people of no experience, even when they experience such words and deeds as I explain, when I distinguish each thing according to its constitution and declare how it is; but the rest of men fail to notice what they do after they wake up just as they forget what they do when asleep."

Parmenides of Elea: The Problem of Permanence

If being and becoming are the two sides of reality's coin, and if Heraclitus chose becoming as the more promising side, it was not long before *Parmenides*, in seeing profound problems in reading reality chiefly in terms of change, came down strongly on the side of *being*. A late contemporary of Heraclitus, he flourished in the first decade of the fifth century. He lived in Elea, a city on the southwestern coast of Italy, was active in political life, and in his early days was probably a Pythagorean. He made at least one trip to Athens, where he and his disciple Zeno met a budding young philosopher by the name of Socrates.

As a literary style well suited for expressing wonder, poetry can hardly be surpassed; Parmenides uses it to usher his listeners into the mystery of being. In a poem he tells of a vision in which he was swept upward in a carriage to the domain of light, where the "goddess of light" was to unfold for him the way of Truth as compared with the way of opinion. The way of opinion is the way human beings normally look at reality, but it is deceptive. Men are accustomed to see things in opposition to each other, such as light–dark or dense–rare, and then they proceed to put not-being opposite being, as though not-being were a real thing. The goddess enlightens Parmenides with the Truth, that *only* being is and it is impossible for it not to be: "Being has no coming-into-being and no destruction, for it is whole . . . without motion, and without end. And it never Was, nor Will Be, because it Is now, a Whole all together, One, continuous; for what creation of it will you look for? How, whence could it have sprung? Nor shall I allow you to speak or think of it as springing from Not-Being; for it is neither expressible nor thinkable that What-Is-Not Is . . . Thus it must Be absolutely, or not at all."

We can appreciate the difficulty Parmenides had. When we affirm *being* of a thing, there is no problem: it *is*, it has existence, it has being. But the moment we say a thing *changes*—a piece of wood burns, an acorn grows, a bird flies— we are saying that it *becomes* what it *is not*. "Is" turns into "is not," "being" into "not-being." In this analysis, not-being is equivalent to being, and for Parmenides a contradiction so blatant that the only remaining course was to deny that change ever really occurs. So the change-saturated world about us has only the appearance of truth; it is not real, and the statements we make based on it only *seem* to be true. What is based on seeming cannot be truth, only *opinion*.

Followers of Parmenides tried to draw out further implications of their master's teaching by means of examples calculated to demonstrate the absurdity of change. In a series of paradoxes for which he is famous, Zeno of Elea hoped to show that the idea of motion is self-contradictory. One such paradox concerns the runner trying to run the length of a stadium. He can never really get to the other end, because, before he reaches it, he must go halfway first, and then halfway again, and so on ad infinitum. In another paradox, Achilles will never catch up with the tortoise because, by the time he gets to the point where the tortoise is, it has moved on to another point, and so on ad infinitum.

But what Parmenides is saying is that being designates the real, and if we want the truth we have to rely on being that is unchanging, permanent. Heraclitus, on the other hand, is saying that becoming designates the real, and if we want the truth we have to rely on a thing's change or activity to reveal it to us. It is not as though these two philosophers have nothing in common, for both, one holding to being and the other to becoming, insist on the unity of the cosmos, and thus centralize the problem of being and becoming, together with that of one and many, as companion issues that emerge at all times whenever thinkers attempt to understand the real world.

The Atomists

Reaction to these positions was not long in coming. Though the next generation of philosophers saw the profound truth in the views of both Parmenides and Heraclitus, it also saw that there was something unforgiving in the extreme way in which they were presented. They realized that they had to say "yes" to the assertion that "what is, is" and "yes" to the assertion that "all things flow"; but they also realized that they had to say "no" to any assertion that denied the obviousness of either change or permanence. The next generation, in the second half of the fifth century, included *Empedocles* of Acragas in Sicily, *Anaxagoras* of Clazomenae (just north of Miletus), *Leucippus* of Miletus, and a little later, *Democritus* of Abdera (in Thrace on the northern shore of the Aegean). What these four had in common was their search for a way to affirm the being of the physical cosmos (it always was, is, and will be the same) and not to betray their experience of change in the cosmos. So they all agreed on the idea of a cosmos composed of small particles, ultimate in nature, constantly in motion to allow for changing configurations without undergoing change themselves, and eternally existing so that they never come to be, but always are.

Empedocles, whose worldview was widely influential and who seems to have had a respectable grasp of medicine, was the first philosopher to propound the classical four elements of earth, air, fire, and water, which he referred to as the "roots of all"; the ultimate particles were each composed of these elements. But in their midst there were two great forces at work, Love and Strife; when Love prevailed there was harmony because the mixture of elements was properly balanced, but when Strife prevailed there was disharmony because the mixture was unbalanced. Empedocles apparently held that Love and Strife were physical forces, though their names suggest more.

Anaxagoras differed from Empedocles in two significant ways. First, the ultimate particles did not consist of earth, air, fire, and water, but of an indefinite variety; and since "in everything there is a portion of everything," the objects configured in the world differ because one kind of particle dominates all others. Second, the force whereby the particles moved had to be outside the particles and independent of them, and therefore completely unlike them. This force is Mind, or Nous, described in the famous fragment no. 12 as infinite, self-ruling, the finest, the purest, omniscient. Even if we cannot be sure that Anaxagoras took Mind to be spiritual and transcendent, by introducing it to account for motion as an unmoved mover, he already marks a revolutionary departure from the past.

But it fell to Leucippus and Democritus to follow the cosmology of ultimate particles to its extreme implications and, since, it is often impossible to unravel the individual contributions of each, both are credited as founding philosophical *atomism* in its classical dress. Like Empedocles and Anaxagoras, they remained true to the Eleatic notion of unchanging being and called for unchanging ultimate particles; these particles, they maintained, were extended in space, unlimited in number, and, though perhaps mathematically divisible, were physically indivisible, for this reason they were called *atoms*, from *atomon*, that which cannot be cut or divided. Unlike Empedocles and Anaxagoras, they arrived at a completely mechanistic explanation of motion and rejected any agency even vaguely suggestive of the noncorporeal, like Love and Strife, or Mind, invoked to cause motion in particles; there was no need to "begin" motion, it was always there. Democritus seems to have held that all movements and configurations of atoms are brought about not by chance but by a necessity natural to the atoms themselves. Apart from his cosmological views, Democritus believed that the conduct of life should be based on happiness, which, in turn, meant "well-being" or "cheerfulness;" that is, the capacity to make balanced judgments with regard to choosing goods of the soul over goods of the body: "He who chooses the advantages of the soul chooses things more divine, but he who chooses those of the body, chooses things human."

In this brief study we have seen in the pre-Socratics the first effort in the West to explore the real rationally, based on what was given by way of wonder through experience. It was perfectly natural that the first questions they pondered were those raised by the cosmos, the physical world, and that in the beginning little distinction was made between natural science and philosophy; but philosophy soon began to sort itself out by facing such problems as unity in plurality, and being and becoming. These were accompanied by corollary questions about the stuff of the universe, particles, atoms, basic elements, source of motion, and so on, and also by parallel questions such as the meaning of knowledge, wisdom, human behavior, and human destiny. In all, a profound and fertile start for the subsequent growth of philosophy.

READING

Selected Fragments from the Pre-Socratics

(Note: Since no writings of the Pre-Socratics are extant, what we know of their teaching has come from references made to them by later writers. If the references are seen as direct quotations, they are called *fragments*; otherwise, they are called *testimonies* or simply *statements* about the philosopher in question. The fragments have been gathered together in a work accepted as the standard reference by Diels, whose numbering is followed, as shown. Sources in English as indicated.)

THALES

Testimonies

1. Thales is traditionally the first to have revealed the investigation of nature to the Greeks; he had many predecessors, as also Theophrastus thinks, but so far surpassed them as to blot out all who came before him. He is said to have left nothing in the form of writings except the so-called *Nautical star-guide*.

2. Yet they do not agree as to the number and the nature of these principles. Thales, the founder of this type of philosophy, says the principle is water (for which reason he declared that the earth rests on water), getting the notion perhaps from seeing that the nutriment of all things is moist, and that heat itself is generated from the moist and kept alive by it (and that from which they come to be is a principle of all things). He got his notion from this fact, and from the fact that the seeds of all things have a moist nature, and that water is the origin of the nature of moist things.

3. For moist natural substance, since it is easily formed into each different thing, is accustomed to undergo very various changes: that part of it which is exhaled is made into air, and the finest part is kindled from air into aither, while

when water is compacted and changes into slime it becomes earth. Therefore Thales declared that water, of the four elements, was the most active, as it were, as a cause.

4. Certain thinkers say that soul is intermingled in the whole universe, and it is perhaps for that reason Thales came to the opinion that all things are full of gods.

5. Some think he (Thales) was the first to study the heavenly bodies and to foretell eclipses of the sun and solstices, as Eudemus says in his history of astronomy; for which reason both Xenophanes and Herodotus express admiration; and both Heraclitus and Democritus bear witness for him.

6. Hieronymus says that he (Thales) actually measured the pyramids by their shadow, having observed the time when our own shadow is equal to our height.

7. Eudemus in the *History of geometry* refers this theorem to Thales; for the method by which they say demonstrated the distance of ships out at seas must, he says, have entailed the use of this theorem.

PYTHAGORAS

Testimonies

1. Empedocles too bears witness to this, writing of him: 'And there was among them a man of rare knowledge, most skilled in all manner of wise works, a man who had won the utmost wealth of wisdom; for whensoever he strained with all his mind, he easily saw everything of all the things that are, in ten, yes, twenty lifetimes of men.'

2. Pythagoras wrote nothing . . .

3. None the less the following became universally known; first, that he maintains that the soul is immortal; next, that it changes into other kinds of living things; also that events recur in certain cycles, and that nothing is ever absolutely new; and finally, that all living things should be regarded as akin. Pythagoras seems to have been the first to bring these beliefs into Greece.

4. If one were to believe the Pythagoreans, with the result that the same individual things will recur, then I shall be talking to you again sitting as you are now, with this printer in my hand, and everything else will be just as it is now, and it is reasonable to suppose that the time then is the same as now.

5. Let the rules to be pondered be these: When you are going out to a temple, worship first, and on your way neither say nor do anything else connected with your daily life. . . . Sacrifice and worship without shoes on. . . . Follow the gods and restrain your tongue above all else. . . . Speak not of Pythagorean matters without light. . . . Disbelieve nothing strange about the gods or about religious beliefs. . . . Be not possessed by irrepressible mirth. . . . Abstain from beans. . . . Abstain from living things.

6. So Pythagoras turned geometrical philosophy into a form of liberal education by seeking its first principles in a higher realm of reality. . . .

7. Life, he said, is like a festival; just as some come to the festival to compete, some to ply their trade, but the best people come as spectators, so in life the slavish men go hunting for fame or gain, the philosophers for the truth.

8. The Pythagoreans, according to Aristoxenus, practised the purification of the body by medicine, that of the soul by music.

9. Ten is the very nature of number. . . . And again, Pythagoras maintains, the power of the number ten lies in the number four, the tetrad. This is the reason: if one starts at the unit and adds the successive numbers up to four, one will make up the number ten. . . . If, that is, one takes the unit, adds two, then three and then four, one will make up the number ten. . . . And so the Pythagoreans used to invoke the tetrad as their most binding oath: 'Nay, by him that gave to our generation the tetractys, which contains the fount and root of eternal nature.'

10. Contemporaneously with these philosophers and before them, the so-called Pythagoreans, who were the first to take up mathematics, not only advanced this study, but also having been brought up in it they thought its principles were the principles of all things. Since of these principles numbers are by nature the first, and in numbers they seemed to see many resemblances to the things that exist and come into being—more than in fire and earth and water (such and such a modification of numbers being justice, another being soul and reason, another being opportunity—and similarly almost all other things being numerically expressible); since, again, they saw that the modifications and the ratios of the musical scales were expressible in numbers;—since, then, all other things seemed in their whole nature to be modelled on numbers, and numbers seemed to be the first things in the whole of nature, they supposed the elements of numbers to be the elements of all things, and the whole heaven to be a musical scale and a number. And all the properties of numbers and scales which they could show to agree with the attributes and parts and the whole arrangement of the heavens, they collected and fitted into their scheme; and if there was a gap anywhere, they readily made additions so as to make their whole theory coherent. E.g. as the number 10 is thought to be perfect and to comprise the whole nature of numbers, they say that the bodies which move through the heavens are ten, but as the visible bodies are only nine, to meet this they invent a tenth—the 'counter-earth'. We have discussed these matters more exactly elsewhere.

HERACLITUS

Fragments

1. Of the Logos which is as I describe it men always prove to be uncomprehending, both before they have heard it and when once they have heard it. For although all things happen according to this Logos men are like people of no experience, even when they experience such words and deeds as I explain, when I distinguish each thing according to its constitution and declare how it is; but the rest of men fail to notice what they do after they wake up just as they forget what they do when asleep.

2. Therefore it is necessary to follow the common; but although the Logos is common the many live as though they had a private understanding.

8. That which is in opposition is in concert, and from things that differ comes the most beautiful harmony.

12. Upon those that step into the same rivers different and different waters flow. . . . It scatters and . . . gathers . . . it comes together and flows away . . . approaches and departs.

18. If one does not expect the unexpected one will not find it out, since it is not to be searched out, and difficult to compass.

19. Men who do not know how to listen or how to speak.

26. A man in the night kindles a light for himself when his vision is extinguished; living, he is in contact with the dead, when asleep, and with the sleeper, when awake.

27. There await men after they are dead things which they do not expect or imagine.

30. This ordered universe (cosmos), which is the same for all, was not created by any one of the gods or of mankind, but it was ever and is and shall be ever-living Fire, kindled in measure and quenched in measure.

36. For souls it is death to become water, for water it is death to become earth; from earth water comes-to-be, and from water, soul.

40. Much learning does not teach one to have intelligence. . . .

41. That which is wise is one; to understand the purpose which steers all things through all things.

47. Let us not conjecture at random about the greatest things.

49a. In the same river, we both step and do not step, we are and we are not.

50. Listening not to me but to the Logos it is wise to agree that all things are one.

51. They do not understand how that which differs with itself is in agreement: harmony consists of opposing tension, like that of the bow and the lyre.

60. The way up and the way down is one and the same.

64. The thunder-bolt (i.e., Fire) steers the universe.

65. Similarly, a living man, when his vision is extinguished in death, flares into flame on achieving the state of death.

67. God is day night, winter summer, war peace, satiety hunger, (all the opposites; this is the meaning); he undergoes alteration in the way that fire, when it is mixed with spices, is named according to the scent of each of them.

73. We must not act and speak like men asleep.

90. There is an exchange: all things for Fire and Fire for all things, like goods for gold and gold for goods.

91. It is not possible to step twice into the same river.

93. The lord whose oracle is that at Delphi neither speaks nor conceals, but indicates.

101. I searched into myself.

102. To God, all things are beautiful, good and just; but men have assumed some things to be unjust, others just.

112. Moderation is the greatest virtue, and wisdom is to speak the truth and to act according to nature, paying heed (thereto).

116. All men have the capacity of knowing themselves and acting with moderation.

123. Nature likes to hide.

125. The 'mixed drink' (i.e., mixture of wine, grated cheese and barley-meal) also separates if it is not stirred.

Testimonies

1. According to Heraclitus we become intelligent by drawing in this divine reason (logos) through breathing, and forgetful when asleep, but we regain our senses when we wake up again. For in sleep, when the channels of perception are shut, our mind is sundered from its kinship with the surrounding, and breathing is the only point of attachment to be preserved, like a kind of root; being sundered, our mind casts off its former power of memory. But in the waking state it again peeps out through the channels of perception as though through a kind of window, and meeting with the surrounding it puts on its power of reason. . . .*

2. Coming to his particular tenets, we may state them as follows: fire is the element, all things are exchange for fire and come into being by rarefaction and condensation; but of this he gives no clear explanation. All things come into being by conflict of opposites, and the sum of things flows like a stream. Further, all that is is limited and forms one world. And it is alternately born from fire and again resolved into fire in fixed cycles to all eternity, and this is determined by destiny. Of the opposites that which tends to birth or creation is called war and strife, and that which tends to destruction by fire is called concord and peace.

Change he called a pathway up and down, and this determines the birth of the world. For fire by contracting turns into moisture, and this condensing turns into water; water again when congealed turns into earth. This process he calls the downward path. Then again earth is liquefied, and thus gives rise to water, and from water the rest of the series is derived. He reduces nearly everything to exhalation from the sea. This process is the upward path.

Exhalations arise from earth as well as from sea; those from sea are bright and pure, those from earth dark. Fire is fed by the bright exhalations, the moist element by the others.

He does not make clear the nature of the surrounding element. He says, however, that there are in it bowls with their concavities turned toward us, in which the bright exhalations collect and produce flames. These are the heavenly bodies.

The flame of the sun is the brightest and hottest; and other stars are further from the earth and for that reason give it less light and heat. The moon, which is nearer to the earth, traverses a region which is not pure. The sun, however, moves in a clear and untroubled region, and keeps a proportionate distance from us. That is why it gives us more heat and light. Eclipses of the sun and moon occur when the bowls are turned upwards; the monthly phases of the moon are due to the bowl turning round in its place little by little.

Day and night, months, seasons and years, rains and winds and other similar phenomena are accounted for by the various exhalations. Thus the bright exhalation, set aflame in the hollow orb of the sun, produces day, the opposite exhalation when it has got the mastery causes night; the increase of warmth due to the bright exhalation produces summer, whereas the preponderance of moisture due to the dark exhalation brings about winter. His explanations of other phenomena are in harmony with this.

He gives no account of the nature of the earth, nor even of the bowls.

These, then, were his opinions.

PARMENIDES

1. The mares which carry me conveyed me as far as my desire reached, when the goddesses who were driving had set me on the famous highway which bears a man who has knowledge through all the cities. Along this way I was carried; for by this way the exceedingly intelligent mares bore me, drawing the chariot, and the maidens directed the way. The axle in the naves gave forth a pipe-like sound as it glowed (for it was driven round by the two whirling circles *(wheels)* at each end) whenever the maidens, daughters of the Sun, having left the Palace of Night, hastened their driving towards the light, having pushed back their veils from their heads with their hands.

There *(in the Palace of the Night)* are the gates of the paths of Night and Day, and they are enclosed with a lintel above and a stone threshold below. The gates themselves are filled with great folding doors; and of these Justice, might to punish, has the interchangeable keys. The maidens, skilfully cajoling her with soft words, persuaded her to push back the bolted bar without delay from the gates; and these, flung open, revealed a wide gaping space, having swung their jambs, richly-wrought in bronze, reciprocally in their sockets. This way, then straight through them went the maidens, driving chariot and mares along the carriage-road.

And the goddess received me kindly, and took my right hand in hers, and thus she spoke and addressed me:

'Young man, companion of immortal charioteers, who comest by the help of the steeds which bring thee to our dwelling: welcome!—since no evil fate has despatched thee on thy journey by this road (for truly it is far from the path trodden by mankind); no, it is divine command and Right. Thou shalt inquire into everything: both the motionless heart of well-rounded Truth, and also the opinions of mortals, in which there is no true reliability. But nevertheless thou shalt learn these things *(opinions)* also—how one should go through all the things-that-seem, without exception, and test them.

2. Come, I will tell you—and you must accept my word when you have heard it—the ways of inquiry which alone are to be thought: the one that IT IS, and it is not possible for IT NOT TO BE, is the way of credibility, for it follows Truth; the other, that IT IS NOT, and that IT is bound NOT TO BE: this I tell you is a path that cannot be explored; for you could neither recognise that which is NOT, nor express it.

3. For it is the same thing to think and to be.

4. Observe nevertheless how things absent are securely present to the mind; for it will not sever Being from its connection with Being, whether it is scattered everywhere utterly throughout the universe, or whether it is collected together.

5. It is all the same to me from what point I begin, for I shall return again to this same point.

6. One should both say and think that Being Is; for To Be is possible, and Nothingness is not possible. This I command you to consider; for from the latter way of search first of all I debar you. But next I debar you from that way along which wander mortals knowing nothing, two-headed, for perplexity in their bosoms steers their intelligence astray, and they are carried along as deaf as they are blind, amazed, uncritical hordes, by whom To Be and Not To Be are regarded as the same and not the same, and *(for whom)* in everything there is a way of opposing stress.

7, 8. For this *(view)* can never predominate, that That Which Is Not exists. You must debar your thought from this way of search, nor let ordinary experience in its variety force you along this way, *(namely, that of allowing)* the eye, sightless as it is, and the ear, full of sound, and the tongue, to rule; but *(you must)* judge by means of the Reason *(Logos)* the much-contested proof which is expounded by me.

There is only one other description of the way remaining, *(namely)*, that *(What Is)* Is. To this way there are very many sign-posts: that Being has no coming-into-being and no destruction, for it is whole of limb, without motion, and without end. And it never Was, nor Will Be, because it Is now, a Whole all together, One, continuous; for what creation of it will you look for? How, whence *(could it have)* sprung? Nor shall I allow you to speak or think of it as springing from Not-Being; for it is neither expressible nor thinkable that What-Is-Not Is. Also, what necessity impelled it, if it did spring from Nothing, to be produced later or earlier? Thus it must Be absolutely, or not at all. Nor will the force of credibility ever admit that anything should come into being, beside Being itself, out of Not-Being. So far as that is concerned, Justice has never released *(Being)* in its fetters and set it free either to come into being or to perish, but holds it fast. The decision on these matters depends on the following: IT IS, or IT IS NOT. It is therefore decided—as is inevitable—*(that one must)* ignore the one way as unthinkable and inexpressible (for it is no true way) and take the other as the way of Being and Reality. How could Being perish? How could it come into being? If it came into being, it Is Not; and so too if it is about-to-be at some future time. Thus Coming-into-Being is quenched, and Destruction also into the unseen.

Nor is Being divisible, since it is all alike. Nor is there anything *(here or)* there which could prevent it from holding together, nor any lesser thing, but all is full of Being. Therefore it is altogether continuous; for Being is close to Being.

But it is motionless in the limits of mighty bonds, without beginning, without cease, since Becoming and Destruction have been driven very far away, and true conviction has rejected them. And remaining the same in the same place, it rests by itself and thus remains there fixed; for powerful Necessity holds it in the bonds of a Limit, which constrains it round about, because it is decreed by divine law that Being shall not be without boundary. For it is not lacking; but if it were *(spatially infinite)*, it would be lacking everything.

To think is the same as the thought that It Is; for you will not find thinking without Being, in *(regard to)* which there is an expression. For nothing else either is or shall be except Being, since Fate has tied it down to be a whole and motionless; therefore all things that mortals have established, believing in their truth, are just a name: Becoming and Perishing, Being and Non-Being, and Change of position, and alteration of bright colour.

But since there is a *(spatial)* Limit, it is complete on every side, like the mass of a well-rounded sphere, equally balanced from its centre in every direction; for it is not bound to be at all either greater or less in this direction or that; nor is there Not-Being which could check it from reaching to the same point, nor is it possible for Being to be more in this direction, less in that, than Being, because it is an inviolate whole. For, in all directions equal to itself, it reaches its limits uniformly.

EMPEDOCLES

Fragments

8. And I shall tell you another thing: there is no creation of substance in any one of mortal existences, nor any end in execrable death, but only mixing and exchange of what has been mixed; and the name 'substance' *(Phusis, 'nature')* is applied to them by mankind.

11. Fools!—for they have no long-sighted thoughts, since they imagine that what previously did not exist comes into being, or that a thing dies and is utterly destroyed.

17. I shall tell of a double *(process):* at one time it increased so as to be a single One out of Many; at another time again it grew apart so as to be Many out of One. There is a double creation of mortals and a double decline: the union of all things causes the birth and destruction of the one *(race of mortals)*, the other is reared as the elements grow apart, and then flies asunder. And these *(elements)* never cease their continuous exchange, sometimes uniting under the influence of Love, so that all become One, at other times again each moving apart through the hostile force of Hate. Thus in so far as they have the power to grow into One out of Many, and again, when the One grows apart and Many are formed, in this sense they come into being and have no stable life; but in so far as they never cease their continuous exchange, in this sense they remain always unmoved *(unaltered)* as they follow the cyclic process.

But come, listen to my discourse! For be assured, learning will increase your understanding. As I said before, revealing the aims of my discourse, I shall tell you of a double process. At one time it increased so as to be a single One out of Many; at another time it grew apart so as to be Many out of One—Fire and Water and Earth and the boundless height of Air, and also execrable Hate apart from these, of equal weight in all directions, and Love in their midst, their equal in length and breadth. Observe her with your mind, and do not sit with wondering eyes! She it is who is believed to be implanted in mortal limbs also; through her they think friendly thoughts and perform harmonious actions, calling her Joy and Aphrodite. No mortal man has perceived her as she moves in and out among them. But you must listen to the undeceitful progress of my argument.

All these *(Elements)* are equal and of the same age in their creation; but each presides over its own office, and each has its own character, and they prevail in turn in the course of Time. And besides these, nothing else comes into being, nor does anything cease. For if they had been perishing continuously, they would Be no more; and what could increase the Whole? And whence could it have come? In what direction could it perish, since nothing is empty of these things? No, but these things alone exist, and running through one another they become different things at different times, and are ever continuously the same.

ANAXAGORAS

Fragments

1. *(Opening sentences from his book 'On Natural Science'):* All Things were together, infinite in number and in smallness. For the Small also was infinite. And since all were together, nothing was distinguishable because of its smallness. For Air and Aether dominated all things, both of them being infinite. For these are the most important *(Elements)* in the total mixture, both in number and in size.

4. Conditions being thus, one must believe that there are many things of all sorts in all composite products, and the seeds of all Things, which contain all kinds of shapes and colours and pleasant savours. And men too were fitted together, and all other creatures which have life. And the men possessed both inhabited cities and artificial works just like ourselves, and they had sun and moon and the rest, just as we have, and the earth produced for them many and diverse things, of which they collected the most useful, and now use them for their dwellings. This I say concerning Separation, that it must have taken place not only with us, but elsewhere.

Before these things were separated off, all things were together, nor was any colour distinguishable, for the mixing of all Things prevented this, *(namely)* the mixing of moist and dry and hot and cold and bright and dark, and there was a great quantity of earth in the mixture, and seeds infinite in number, not at all like one another. For none of the other things either is like any other. And as this was so, one must believe that all Things were present in the Whole.

6. And since there are equal *(quantitative)* parts of Great and Small, so too similarly in everything there must be everything. It is not possible *(for them)* to exist apart, but all things contain a portion of everything. Since it is not possible for the Least to exist, it cannot be isolated, nor come into being by itself; but as it was in the beginning, so now, all things are together. In all things there are many things, and of the things separated off, there are equal numbers in *(the categories)* Great and Small.

12. Other things all contain a part of everything, but Mind is infinite and self-ruling, and is mixed with no Thing, but is alone by itself. If it were not by itself, but were mixed with anything else, it would have had a share of all Things, if it were mixed with anything; for in everything there is a portion of everything, as I have said before. And the things mixed *(with Mind)* would have prevented it, so that it could not rule over any Thing in the same way as it can being alone by itself. For it is the finest of all Things, and the purest, and has complete understanding of everything,

and has the greatest power. All things which have life, both the greater and the less, are ruled by Mind. Mind took command of the universal revolution, so as to make *(things)* revolve at the outset. And at first things began to revolve from some small point but now the revolution extends over a greater area, and will spread even further.And the things which were mixed together, and separated off, and divided, were all understood by Mind.And whatever they were going to be, and whatever things were then in existence that are not now, and all things that now exist and whatever shall exist—all were arranged by Mind, as also the revolution now followed by the stars, the sun and moon, and the Air and Aether which were separated off. It was this revolution which caused the separation off. And dense separated from rare, and hot from cold, and bright from dark, and dry from wet.There are many portions of many things. And nothing is absolutely separated off or divided the one from the other except Mind. Minds all alike, both the greater and the less. But nothing else is like anything else, but each individual thing is and was most obviously that which it contains the most.

(From *Ancilla to the Pre-Socratic Philosophers*. Trans. Kathleen Freeman, Oxford: Basil Blackwell, 1947. Reprinted by permission of Basil Blackwell.)

LEUCIPPUS AND DEMOCRITUS

Fragments

303. And further, they (*sc.* Leucippus and Democritus) say that since the atomic bodies differ in shape, and there is an infinity of shapes, there is an infinity of simple bodies. But they have never explained in detail the shapes of the various elements, except so far as to allot the sphere to fire.Air, water, and the rest they dintinguished by the relative size of the atom, assuming that the atomic substance was a sort of master-seed for each and every element.

For they (*sc.* Leucippus and Democritus) say that their primary magnitudes are infinite in number and indivisible in magnitude; the many does not come from one nor one from many, but rather all things are generated by the intertwining and scattering around of these primary magnitudes.

295. . . . As they (*sc.* the atoms) move they collide and become entangled in such a way as to cling in close contact to one another, but not so as to form one substance of them in reality of any kind whatever; for it is very simpleminded to suppose that two or more could ever become one. The reason he gives for atoms staying together for a while is the intertwining and mutual hold of the primary bodies; for some of them are angular, some hooked, some concave, some convex, and indeed with countless other differences; so he thinks they cling to each other and stay together until such time as some stronger necessity comes from the surrounding and shakes and scatters them apart.

242. . . . these atoms move in the infinite void, separate one from the other and differing in shapes, sizes, position and arrangement; overtaking each other they collide, and some are shaken away in any chance direction, while others, becoming intertwined one with another according to the congruity of their shapes, sizes, positions and arrangements, stay together and so effect the coming into being of compound bodies.

34. Man is a universe in little *(Microcosm).*

37. He who chooses the advantages of the soul chooses things more divine, but he who chooses those of the body, chooses things human.

191. Cheerfulness is created for men through moderation of enjoyment and harmoniousness of life. Things that are in excess or lacking are apt to change and cause great disturbance in the soul. Souls which are stirred by great divergences are neither stable nor cheerful. Therefore one must keep one's mind on what is attainable, and be content with what one has, paying little heed to things envied and admired, and not dwelling on them in one's mind. Rather must you consider the lives of those in distress, reflecting on their intense sufferings, in that your own possessions and condition may seem great and enviable and you may, by ceasing to desire more, cease to suffer in your soul. For he who admires those who have, and who are called happy by other mortals, and who dwells on them in his mind every hour, is constantly compelled to undertake something new and to run the risk, through his desire, of doing something irretrievable among those things which the laws prohibit. Hence one must not seek the latter, but must be content with the former, comparing one's own life with that of those in worse cases, and must consider oneself fortunate, reflecting on their sufferings, in being so much better off than they. If you keep to this way of thinking, you will live more serenely, and will expel those not-negligible curses in life, envy, jealousy and spite.

Review Questions

1. How does philosophy begin in wonder?
2. Discuss the importance of the one and the many, and of being and becoming, for the early Greek philosophers.
3. Describe the efforts to achieve unity that underlay the thought of Thales, Pythagoras, Heraclitus, and Parmenides.
4. What kind of opposition exists between being and not-being? Between being and becoming?
5. What is the meaning of atomism? How do the atomists respond to the problem of being and becoming?

Suggestions for Further Reading

Barnes, J., ed. and tr. *Early Greek Philosophy.* New York, Penguin, 1987.

Jaeger, W. *The Theology of the Early Greek Philosophers.* Tr. Robertson, E. S. Westport, CT, Greenwood Press, 1980.

Kirk, G. S., Raven, J., and Schofield, M. *The Pre-Socratic Philosophers,* 2nd ed. Cambridge, Cambridge University Press, 1984.

Waterfield, R. (tr.), *The First Philosophers: The Pre-Socratics and Sophists.* Oxford University Press, 2000.

2

Socrates
(469–399 B.C.)

The three great Greek philosophers, Socrates, Plato, and Aristotle, appeared in a relatively short space of time in the fifth and fourth centuries, with Socrates enormously influencing the young Plato, and Plato enormously influencing the young Aristotle. They stand for the value of knowledge, the worth of virtue, and the unflagging pursuit of human meaning. They represent one of the most sustained efforts of the human mind to work its way into the mystery of reality, into the rich diversity of the real world and its overarching unity. Western philosophy has been in their enduring debt ever since.

Socrates was a fifth-century person. He was the son of a sculptor and is said to have done some sculpting himself. He lived in Athens, leaving it only a few times on military expeditions. Though never a political candidate, he was very much involved in city affairs. It was as a thinker and teacher that he gained his reputation.

Socrates as Teacher

Though institutions of learning as they exist today were not part of the Greek world at that time, for a certain segment of society, a kind of formal education could be gained from a group of teachers who traveled from place to place, taking payment for their services. They were known as *sophists* because their profession was to instruct in *sophia*, or wisdom. Earlier no opprobrium had been associated with this term, which not infrequently was applied to a number of eminent learned men. As time went on, however, it came to be used pejoratively and even scornfully because sophists were looked upon not as purveyors of wisdom but as pretenders; not as seekers of the truth but as artists of persuasion. Hence, the word *sophistry* became attached to an argument that on first hearing sounds cogent but on analysis is seen to be fallacious.

Socrates can be thought of as belonging to this class of teacher, but inasmuch as he supported the highest ideals of education, he cannot be thought of as contributing to the disesteem into which the sophists fell. He never took payment for teaching; he was acknowledged to be skillful in pedagogy; as a familiar figure in Athens, he was always to be found in earnest dialogue with others. Ironically, while he was thus garnering respect for himself, he was also suffering ridicule as an outspoken political critic and as a practitioner of sophistry. One of the charges brought against him was that he made "the weaker argument defeat the stronger," not therefore by logic but by sophistry; it's not the truth that counts, but victory. On the Greek stage the playwright Aristophanes satirized him in a comedy, *The Clouds*, in which he was lampooned as the Master of the Thinking Factory.

The portrait given by Plato, as well as by Xenophon, shows Socrates to have been a man thoroughly set against the pretensions of knowledge. Plato records that, far from pretending to know, he even prized his ignorance, for when he was informed by a friend that the oracle at Delphi had referred to him as the wisest man in Athens, Socrates, after diligently seeking to learn how this could be true, finally decided that it was because he was aware of his ignorance, whereas others were not aware of theirs: "I am better off than he is,—for he knows nothing and thinks that he knows; I neither know nor think that I know." His encouragement of youth to think things through for themselves, his own search for the meaning of wisdom, and his willingness to die out of fidelity to his convictions are not characteristics of a person interested in argument for the sake of argument, but rather as a means of submitting life to an examination. This estimate of Socrates is supported by Xenophon, who writes, "For myself, I have described him as he was—so religious that he did nothing without counsel from the gods; so just that he did no injury, however small, to any man, but conferred the greatest benefit on all who dealt with him; so self-controlled that he never chose the pleasanter rather than the better course; so wise that he was unerring in his judgment of the better and the worse. . . . To me then he seemed to be all that a truly good and happy man must be."

Socrates was not handsome or imposing; he never wrote a recorded word. Yet he was an inspiration. That is, he was a seeker after truth in a personally attractive way, a consequence perhaps of his attitude that friendship is suited to the finding of truth. At any rate, love and wisdom were not far apart, but joined together in a truth–person context. The truth formed a link with the person: a deeper grasp of the truth meant a deeper grasp of the person, and a deeper grasp of the person meant a deeper grasp of the truth. The high regard Socrates had for his students as human beings and thinkers in their own right prompted him to draw out answers from them rather than to supply them—the so-called *Socratic method* of teaching. His concern for ethical principles, his integrity vis-à-vis a state-imposed religion, his composure in the face of a final verdict from his judges, all bear out the authenticity of Phaedo's testimony: "Such was the end of our comrade, who was, we may fairly say, of those whom we knew in our time, the bravest and also the wisest and most upright man."

Ethical Wisdom

The main feature of Socrates' thought, and the one on which all other aspects of his philosophy depend, is that of *ethical wisdom*—the recognition of the fundamental importance of the ethical in the life of man and of doing good as the basic principle of human activity. Socrates gave the concepts of virtue and goodness insistent attention, first by acknowledging myriad good acts, such as acts of courage, piety, and justice, and then by trying to discover their inward unity—that is, their essence, nature, or definition. Aristotle praised Socrates as the first philosopher who, in "seeking the universal in these ethical matters, fixed thought for the first time on definitions." But clearly Socrates' focal point was the personal, for the notion he was always trying to clarify was that of a virtuous person: what it was, in the last analysis, that could rightly be called wisdom.

Two considerations converge in Socrates' analysis of wisdom: that virtue is knowledge and that happiness resides in the possession of such knowledge. The first of these ideas seems contrary to our expectations, for we have ample experience that a person, with full knowledge, can do wrong. So, how is it, then, that virtue is knowledge? What Socrates had in mind is that knowledge, such as the knowledge of courage, piety, or justice, by its very nature flows immediately into active, practical life so that a person is morally compelled to become courageous, pious, or just—in short, to become virtuous; if he does not become virtuous, he does not really know—he is not really wise. Hence, in the *Phaedo*, Socrates says, "In fact, it is wisdom that makes possible courage and self-control and integrity or, in a word, true goodness."

With regard to the second consideration, Socrates was well aware that there is no such thing as a perfect definition of happiness, for happiness is a matter of continuing personal experience and is not easily open to definition. Yet happiness is the quest of all—a sense of satisfaction or fulfilment that occurs when our actions are right or good. This is certainly Socrates' meaning in one of Plato's minor dialogues called *Charmides*, in which Socrates and some of his friends are discussing the relationship between knowledge and happiness. Though it is clear that by acting according to knowledge, "we shall act well and be happy," not just any kind of knowledge, for example, knowledge of medicine, or ship piloting, or winning battles, or shoemaking, or playing checkers—important as it may otherwise be—is destined to make us happy. No, it is the knowledge of good and evil that holds the key. And granted that the dialogue portends some uncertainties for the young Charmides, Socrates reassures him that wisdom is a great good: "for wisdom and temperance I believe to be really a great good. And happy are you, Charmides, if you possess it . . . rest assured that the more wise and temperate you are, the happier you will be."

To what extent Socrates was committed to wisdom can be seen at the moment of greatest personal intensity: the moment of his death. He viewed death as a life event, pregnant with philosophical importance, for in death, as in a prism, life can be seen as the unity of happiness, goodness, truth, and all the other characteristics identified with humanity. Though this is true for everyone, it is especially true for Socrates, who, under the sentence of death, was able to convert his last days into a privileged stillpoint for contemplating the meaning of life and life's values. Without a doubt, the most important problem a philosopher has to face is the problem of death. Indeed, Socrates offered no more arresting description of philosophy than that philosophy is "practicing death."

The "practice of death" refers to what one does with his life, the way one lives, the ideals he holds, the convictions he has, the practice in which he externalizes what is internal: Death is a life-directing reality. That is why, for those who have led a good life, a life of "holiness," the future holds no fears and death can be thought of only as a blessing. The Pythagorean element of purification is evidently at work in Socrates' thinking, for the soul must be cleansed of all attachments to the body, all those enticements of the bodily world which draw us away from the spiritual world at the risk of putting off, through another period of this life's restlessness, the time of enduring peace. The fulfillment of life is surely what Socrates sought, but such fulfillment, achievable here only inchoately, is achievable finally in the hereafter. Among the last words Socrates uttered before taking the poison cup were: "There is one way, then, in which a man can be free from all anxiety about the fate of his soul—if in life he has abandoned bodily pleasures and adornments, as foreign to his purpose and likely to do more harm than good, and has devoted himself to the pleasures of acquiring knowledge, and so by decking his soul not with a borrowed beauty but with its own—with self-control, and goodness, and courage, and liberality, and truth—has fitted himself to await his journey to the next world."

READINGS

The Trial of Socrates
(Plato's *Apology*)

How you, O Athenians, have been affected by my accusers, I cannot tell; but I know that they almost made me forget who I was—so persuasively did they speak; and yet they have hardly uttered a word of truth. But of the many falsehoods told by them, there was one which quite amazed me;—I mean when they said that you should be upon your guard and not allow yourselves to be deceived by the force of my eloquence. To say this, when they were certain to be detected as soon as I opened my lips and proved myself to be anything but a great speaker, did indeed appear to me most shameless—unless by the force of eloquence they mean the force of truth; for if such is their meaning, I admit that I am eloquent. But in how different a way from theirs! Well, as I was saying, they have scarcely spoken the truth at all; but from me you shall hear the whole truth: not, however, delivered after their manner in a set oration duly ornamented with words and phrases. No, by heaven! but I shall use the words and arguments which occur to me at the moment; for I am confident in the justice of my cause: at my time of life I ought not to be appearing before you, O men of Athens, in the character of a juvenile orator—let not one expect it of me. And I must beg of you to grant me a favour:—If I defend myself in my accustomed manner, and you hear me using the words which I have been in the habit of using in the agora, at the tables of the moneychangers, or anywhere else, I would ask you not to be surprised, and not to interrupt me on this account. For I am more than seventy years of age, and appearing now for the first time in a court of law, I am quite a stranger to the language of the place; and therefore I would have you regard me as if I were really a stranger, whom you would excuse if he spoke in his native tongue, and after the fashion of his country:—Am I making an unfair request of you? Never mind the manner, which may or may not be good; but think only of the truth of my words, and give heed to that: let the speaker speak truly and the judge decide justly.

And first, I have to reply to the older charges and to my first accusers, and then I will go on to the later ones. For of old I have had many accusers, who have accused me falsely to you during many years; and I am more afraid of them than of Anytus and his associates, who are dangerous, too, in their own way. But far more dangerous are the others, who began when you were children, and took possession of your minds with their falsehoods, telling of one Socrates, a wise man, who speculated about the heaven above, and searched into the earth beneath, and made the worse appear the better cause. The disseminators of this tale are the accusers whom I dread; for their hearers are apt to fancy that such enquirers do not believe in the existence of the gods. And they are many, and their charges against me are of ancient date, and they were made by them in the days when you were more impressible than you are now—in childhood, or it may have been in youth—and the cause when heard went by default, for there was none to answer. And hardest of all, I do not know and cannot tell the names of my accusers; unless in the chance case of a Comic poet. All who from envy and malice have persuaded you—some of them having first convinced themselves—all this class of men are most difficult to deal with; for I cannot have them up here, and cross-examine them, and therefore I must simply fight with shadows in my own defence, and argue when there is no one who answers. I will ask you then to assume with me, as I was saying, that my opponents are of two kinds; one recent, the other ancient: and I hope that you will see the propriety of my answering the latter first, for these accusations you heard long before the others, and much oftener.

Well, then, I must make my defence, and endeavor to clear away in a short time, a slander which has lasted a long time. May I succeed, if to succeed be for my good and yours, or likely to avail me in my cause! The task is not an easy one; I quite understand the nature of it. And so leaving the event with God, in obedience to the law I will now make my defence.

I will begin at the beginning, and ask what is the accusation which has given rise to the slander of me, and in fact has encouraged Meletus to prefer this charge against me. Well, what do the slanderers say? They shall be my prosecutors, and I will sum up their words in an affidavit: 'Socrates is an evil-doer, and a curious person, who searches into things under the earth and in heaven, and he makes the worse appear the better cause; and he teaches the aforesaid doctrines to others.' Such is the nature of the accusation: it is just what you have yourselves seen in the comedy of Aristophanes, who has introduced a man whom he calls Socrates, going about and saying that he walks in air, and talking a deal of nonsense concerning matters of which I do not pretend to know either much or little—not that I mean to speak disparagingly of any one who is a student of natural philosophy. I should be very sorry if Meletus could bring so grave a charge against me. But the simple truth is, O Athenians, that I have nothing to do with physical speculations. Very many of those here present are witnesses to the truth of this, and to them I appeal. Speak then, you who have heard me, and tell your neighbours whether any of you have ever known me hold forth in few words or in many upon such matters. . . . You hear their answer. And from what they say of this part of the charge you will be able to judge of the truth of the rest.

As little foundation is there for the report that I am a teacher, and take money; this accusation has no more truth in it than the other. Although, if a man were really able to instruct mankind, to receive money for giving instruction would, in my opinion, be an honour to him. There is Gorgias of Leontium, and Prodicus of Ceos, and Hippias of Elis, who go the round of the cities, and are able to persuade the young men to leave their own citizens by whom they might be taught for nothing, and come to them whom they not only pay, but are thankful if they may be allowed to pay them. There is at this time a Parian philosopher residing in Athens, of whom I have heard; and I came to hear of him in this way:—I came across a man who has spent a world of money on the Sophists, Callias, the son of Hipponicus, and knowing that he had sons, I asked him: 'Callias,' I said, 'if your two sons were foals or calves, there would be no difficulty in finding some one to put over them; we should hire a trainer of horses, or a farmer probably, who would improve and perfect them in their own proper virtue and excellence; but as they are human beings, whom are you thinking of placing over them? Is there any one who understands human and political virtue? You must have thought about the matter, for you have sons; is there any one?' 'There is,' he said. 'Who is he?' I said; 'and of what country? and what does he charge?' 'Evenus the Parian,' he replied; 'he is the man, and his charge is five minae.' Happy is Evenus, I said to myself, if he really has this wisdom, and teaches at such a moderate charge. Had I the same, I should have been very proud and conceited; but the truth is that I have no knowledge of the kind.

I dare say, Athenians, that some of you will reply, 'Yes, Socrates, but what is the origin of these accusations which are brought against you; there must have been something strange which you have been doing? All these rumours and this talk about you would never have arisen if you had been like other men: tell us, then, what is the cause of them, for we should be sorry to judge hastily of you.' Now I regard this as a fair challenge, and I will endeavour to explain to you the reason why I am called wise and have such an evil fame. Please to attend then. And although some of you may think that I am joking, I declare that I will tell you the entire truth. Men of Athens, this reputation of mine has come of a certain sort of wisdom which I possess. If you ask me what kind of wisdom, I reply, wisdom such as may perhaps be attained by man, for to that extent I am inclined to believe that I am wise; whereas the persons of whom I was speaking have a superhuman wisdom, which I may fail to describe, because I have it not myself; and he who says that I have, speaks falsely, and is taking away my character. And here, O men of Athens, I must beg you not to interrupt me, even if I seem to say something extravagant. For the word which I will speak is not mine. I will refer you to a witness who is worthy of credit; that witness shall be the God of Delphi—he will tell you about my wisdom, if I have any, and of what sort it is. You must have known Chaerephon; he was early a friend of mine, and also a friend of yours, for he shared in the recent exile of the people, and returned with you. Well, Chaerephon, as you know, was very impetuous in all his doings, and he went to Delphi and boldly asked the oracle to tell him whether—as I was saying, I must beg you not to interrupt—he asked the oracle to tell him whether any one was wiser than I was, and the Pythian prophetess answered, that there was no man wiser. Chaerephon is dead himself; but his brother, who is in court, will confirm the truth of what I am saying.

Why do I mention this? Because I am going to explain to you why I have such an evil name. When I heard the answer, I said to myself, What can the god mean? and what is the interpretation of his riddle? for I know that I have no wisdom, small or great. What then can he mean when he says that I am the wisest of men? And yet he is a god, and cannot lie; that would be against his nature. After long consideration, I thought of a method of trying the question. I reflected that if I could only find a man wiser than myself, then I might go to the god with a refutation in my hand. I should say to him, 'Here is a man who is wiser than I am; but you said that I was the wisest.' Accordingly I went to one who had the reputation of wisdom, and observed him—his name I need not mention; he was a politician whom I selected for examination—and the result was as follows: When I began to talk with him, I could not help thinking that he was not really wise, although he was thought wise by many, and still wiser by himself; and thereupon I tried to explain to him that he thought himself wise, but was not really wise; and the consequence was that he hated me, and his enmity was shared by several who were present and heard me. So I left him, saying to myself, as I went away: Well, although I do not suppose that either of us knows anything really beautiful and good, I am better off than he is,—for he knows nothing, and thinks that he knows; I neither know nor think that I know. In this latter particular, then, I seem to have slightly the advantage of him. Then I went to another who had still higher pretensions to wisdom, and my conclusion was exactly the same. Whereupon I made another enemy of him, and of many others besides him.

Then I went to one man after another, being not unconscious of the enmity which I provoked, and I lamented and feared this: But necessity was laid upon me,—the word of God, I thought, ought to be considered first. And I said to myself, Go I must to all who appear to know, and find out the meaning of the oracle. And I swear to you, Athenians, by the dog I swear!—for I must tell you the truth—the result of my mission was just this: I found that the men most in repute were all but the most foolish; and that others less esteemed were really wiser and better. I will tell you the tale of my wanderings and of the 'Herculean' labours, as I may call them, which I endured only to find at last the oracle irrefutable. After the politicians, I went to the poets; tragic, dithyrambic, and all sorts. And there, I said to myself, you will be instantly detected; now you will find out that you are more ignorant than they are. Accordingly, I took them some of the most elaborate passages in their own writings, and asked what was the meaning of them—thinking that they would teach me something. Will you believe me? I am almost ashamed to confess the truth, but I must say that there is hardly a person present who would not have talked better about their poetry than they did themselves. Then I knew that not by wisdom do poets write poetry, but by a sort of genius and inspiration; they are like diviners or soothsayers who also say many fine things, but do not understand the meaning of them. The poets appeared to me to be much in the same case; and I further observed that upon the strength of their poetry they believed themselves to be the wisest of men in other things in which they were not wise. So I departed, conceiving myself to be superior to them for the same reason that I was superior to the politicians.

At last I went to the artisans, for I was conscious that I knew nothing at all, as I may say, and I was sure that they knew many fine things; and here I was not mistaken, for they did know many things of which I was ignorant, and in this they certainly were wiser than I was. But I observed that even the good artisans fell into the same error as the poets;—because they were good workmen they thought that they also knew all sorts of high matters, and this defect in them overshadowed their wisdom; and therefore I asked myself on behalf of the oracle, whether I would like to be as I was, neither having their knowledge nor their ignorance, or like them in both; and I made answer to myself and to the oracle that I was better off as I was.

This inquisition has led to my having many enemies of the worst and most dangerous kind, and has given occasion also to many calumnies. And I am called wise, for my hearers always imagine that I myself possess the wisdom which I find wanting in others: but the truth is, O men of Athens, that God only is wise; and by his answer he intends to show that the wisdom of men is worth little or nothing; he is not speaking of Socrates, he is only using my name by way of illustration, as if he said, He, O men, is the wisest, who, like Socrates, knows that his wisdom is in truth worth nothing. And so I go about the world, obedient to the god, and search and make enquiry into the wisdom of any one, whether citizen or stranger, who appears to be wise; and if he is not wise, then in vindication of the oracle I show him that he is not wise; and my occupation quite absorbs me, and I have no time to give either to any public matter of interest or to any concern of my own, but I am in utter poverty by reason of my devotion to the god.

There is another thing:—young men of the richer classes, who have not much to do, come about me of their own accord; they like to hear the pretenders examined, and they often imitate me, and proceed to examine others; there are plenty of persons, as they quickly discover, who think that they know something, but really know little or nothing; and then those who are examined by them instead of being angry with themselves are angry with me: This confounded Socrates, they say; this villainous misleader of youth!—and then if somebody asks them, Why, what evil does he practice or teach? they do not know, and cannot tell; but in order that they may not appear to be at a loss, they repeat the ready-made charges which are used against all philosophers about teaching things up in the clouds and under the earth, and having no gods, and making the worse appear the better cause; for they do not like to confess that their pretence of knowledge has been detected—which is the truth; and as they are numerous and ambitious and energetic, and are drawn up in battle array and have persuasive tongues, they have filled your ears with their loud and inveterate calumnies. And this is the reason why my three accusers, Meletus and Anytus and Lycon, have set upon me; Meletus, who has a quarrel with me on behalf of the poets; Anytus, on behalf of the craftsmen and politicians; Lycon, on behalf of the rhetoricians: and as I said at the beginning, I cannot expect to get rid of such a mass of calumny all in a moment. And this, O men of Athens, is the truth and the whole truth; I have concealed nothing, I have dissembled nothing. And yet, I know that my plainness of speech makes them hate me, and what is their hatred but a proof that I am speaking the truth?—Hence has arisen the prejudice against me; and this is the reason of it, as you will find out either in this or in any future enquiry.

I have said enough in my defence against the first class of my accusers; I turn to the second class. They are headed by Meletus, that good man and true lover of his country, as he called himself. Against these, too, I must try to make a defence:—Let their affidavit be read: it contains something of this kind: It says that Socrates is a doer of evil, who corrupts the youth; and who does not believe in the gods of the state, but has other new divinities of his own. Such is the charge; and now let us examine the particular counts. He says that I am a doer of evil, and corrupt the youth; but I say, O men of Athens that Meletus is a doer of evil, in that he pretends to be in earnest when he is only in jest, and is so eager to bring men to trial from a pretended zeal and interest about matters in which he really never had the smallest interest. And the truth of this I will endeavour to prove to you.

Come hither, Meletus, and let me ask a question of you. You think a great deal about the improvement of youth?

Yes, I do.

Tell the judges, then, who is their improver; for you must know, as you have taken the pains to discover their corrupter, and are citing and accusing me before them. Speak, then, and tell the judges who their improver is.—Observe, Meletus, that you are silent, and have nothing to say. But is not this rather disgraceful, and a very considerable proof of what I was saying, that you have no interest in the matter? Speak up, friend, and tell us who their improver is.

The laws.

But that, my good sir, is not my meaning. I want to know who the person is, who, in the first place, knows the laws.

The judges, Socrates, who are present in court.

What, do you mean to say, Meletus, that they are able to instruct and improve youth?

Certainly they are.

What, all of them, or some only and not others?

All of them.

By the goddess Here, that is good news! There are plenty of improvers, then. And what do you say of the audience,—do they improve them?

Yes, they do.

And the senators?

Yes, the senators improve them.

But perhaps the members of the assembly corrupt them?—or do they too improve them.

They improve them.

Then every Athenian improves and elevates them; all with the exception of myself; and I alone am their corrupter? Is that what you affirm?

That is what I stoutly affirm.

I am very unfortunate if you are right. But suppose I ask you a question: How about horses? Does one man do them harm and all the world good? Is not the exact opposite the truth? One man is able to do them good, or at least not many;—the trainer of horses, that is to say, does them good, and others who have to do with them rather injure them? Is not that true, Meletus, of horses, or of any other animals? Most assuredly it is; whether you and Anytus say yes or no. Happy indeed would be the condition of youth if they had one corrupter only, and all the rest of the world were their improvers. But you, Meletus, have sufficiently shown that you never had a thought about the young; your carelessness is seen in your not caring about the very things which you bring against me.

And now, Meletus, I will ask you another question—by Zeus I will: Which is better, to live among bad citizens, or among good ones? Answer, friend, I say; the question is one which may easily be answered. Do not the good do their neighbours good, and the bad do them evil?

Certainly.

And is there any one who would rather be injured than benefited by those who live with him? Answer, my good friend, the law requires you to answer—does any one like to be injured?

Certainly not.

And when you accuse me of corrupting and deteriorating the youth, do you allege that I corrupt them intentionally or unintentionally?

Intentionally, I say.

But you have just admitted that the good do their neighbours good, and evil do them evil. Now, is that a truth which your superior wisdom has recognized thus early in life, and am I, at my age, in such darkness and ignorance as not to know that if a man with whom I have to live is corrupted by me, I am very likely to be harmed by him; and yet I corrupt him, and intentionally, too—so you say, although neither I nor any other human being is ever likely to be convinced by you. But either I do not corrupt them, or I corrupt them unintentionally; and on either view of the case you lie. If my offence is unintentional, the law has no cognizance of unintentional offences: you ought to have taken me privately, and warned and admonished me; for if I had been better advised, I should have left off doing what I only did unintentionally—no doubt I should; but you would have nothing to say to me and refused to teach me. And now you bring me up in this court, which is a place not of instruction, but of punishment.

It will be very clear to you, Athenians, as I was saying, that Meletus has no care at all, great or small, about the matter. But still I should like to know, Meletus, in what I am affirmed to corrupt the young. I suppose you mean, as I infer from your indictment, that I teach them not to acknowledge the gods which the state acknowledges, but some other new divinities or spiritual agencies in their stead. These are the lessons by which I corrupt the youth, as you say.

Yes, that I say emphatically.

Then, by the gods, Meletus, of whom we are speaking, tell me and the court, in somewhat plainer terms, what you mean! For I do not as yet understand whether you affirm that I teach other men to acknowledge some gods, and therefore that I do believe in gods, and am not an entire atheist—this you do not lay to my charge,—but only you say that they are not the same gods which the city recognizes—the charge is that they are different gods. Or, do you mean that I am an atheist simply, and a teacher of atheism?

I mean the latter—that you are a complete atheist.

What an extraordinary statement! Why do you think so, Meletus? Do you mean that I do not believe in the godhead of the sun or moon, like other men?

I assure you, judges, that he does not: for he says that the sun is stone, and the moon earth.

Friend Meletus, you think that you are accusing Anaxagoras: and you have but a bad opinion of the judges, if you fancy them illiterate to such a degree as not to know that these doctrines are found in the books of Anaxagoras the Clazomenian, which are full of them. And so, forsooth, the youth are said to be taught them by Socrates, when there are not unfrequently exhibitions of them at the theatre (price of admission one drachma at the most); and they might pay their money, and laugh at Socrates if he pretends to father these extraordinary views. And so, Meletus, you really think that I do not believe in any god?

I swear by Zeus that you believe absolutely in none at all.

Nobody will believe you, Meletus, and I am pretty sure that you do not believe yourself. I cannot help thinking, men of Athens, that Meletus is reckless and impudent, and that he has written this indictment in a spirit of mere wantonness and youthful bravado. Has he not compounded a riddle, thinking to try me? He said to himself:—I shall see whether the wise Socrates will discover my facetious contradiction, or whether I shall be able to deceive him and the rest of them. For he certainly does appear to me to contradict himself in the indictment as much as if he said that Socrates is guilty of not believing in the gods, and yet of believing in them—but this is not like a person who is in earnest.

I should like you, O men of Athens, to join me in examining what I conceive to be his inconsistency; and do you, Meletus, answer. And I must remind the audience of my request that they would not make a disturbance if I speak in my accustomed manner:

Did ever man, Meletus, believe in the existence of human things, and not of human beings? . . . I wish, men of Athens, that he would answer, and not be always trying to get up an interruption. Did ever any man believe in horseman-ship, and not in horses? or in flute-playing, and not in flute-players? No, my friend; I will answer to you and to the court, as you refuse to answer for yourself. There is no man who ever did. But now please to answer the next question: Can a man believe in spiritual and divine agencies, and not in spirits or demigods?

He cannot.

How lucky I am to have extracted that answer, by the assistance of the court! But then you swear in the indictment that I teach and believe in divine or spiritual agencies (new or old, no matter for that); at any rate, I believe in spiritual agencies,— so you say and swear in the affidavit; and yet if I believe in divine beings, how can I help believing in spirits or demigods;—must I not? To be sure I must; and therefore I may assume that your silence gives consent. Now what are spirits or demigods? Are they not either gods or the sons of gods?

Certainly they are.

But this is what I call the facetious riddle invented by you: the demigods or spirits are gods, and you say first that I do not believe in gods, and then again that I do believe in gods; that is, if I believe in demigods. For if the demigods are the illegitimate sons of gods, whether by the nymphs or by any other mothers, of whom they are said to be the sons—what human being will ever believe that there are no gods if they are the sons of gods? You might as well affirm the existence of mules, and deny that of horses and asses. Such nonsense, Meletus, could only have been intended by you to make trial of me. You have put this into the indictment because you had nothing real of which to accuse me. But no one who has a particle of understanding will ever be convinced by you that the same men can believe in divine and superhuman things, and yet not believe that there are gods and demigods and heroes.

I have said enough in answer to the charge of Meletus: any elaborate defence is unnecessary; but I know only too well how many are the enmities which I have incurred, and this is what will be my destruction if I am destroyed;—not Meletus, nor yet Anytus, but the envy and detraction of the world, which has been the death of many good men, and will probably be the death of many more; there is no danger of my being the last of them.

Some one will say: And are you not ashamed, Socrates, of a course of life which is likely to bring you to an untimely end? To him I may fairly answer: There you are mistaken: a man who is good for anything ought not to calculate the charge of living or dying; he ought only to consider whether in doing anything he is doing right or wrong—acting the part of a good man or of a bad. Whereas, upon your view, the heroes who fell at Troy were not good for much, and the son of Thetis above all, who altogether despised danger in comparison with disgrace; and when he was so eager to slay Hector, his goddess mother said to him, that if he avenged his companion Patroclus, and slew Hector, he would die himself—'Fate,' she said, in these or the like words, 'waits for you next after Hector'; he, receiving this warning, utterly despised danger and death, and instead of fearing them, feared rather to live in dishonour, and not to avenge his friend. 'Let me die forthwith,' he replies, 'and be avenged of my enemy, rather than abide here by the beaked ships, a laughing-stock and a burden of the earth.' Had Achilles any thought of death and danger? For wherever a man's place is, whether the place which he has chosen or that in which he has been placed by a commander, there he ought to remain in the hour of danger; he should not think of death or of anything but of disgrace. And this, O men of Athens, is a true saying.

Strange, indeed, would be my conduct, O men of Athens, if I who, when I was ordered by the generals whom you chose to command me at Potidaea and Amphipolis and Delium, remained where they placed me, like any other man, facing death—if now, when, as I conceive and imagine, God orders me to fulfil the philosopher's mission of searching into myself and other men, I were to desert my post through fear of death, or any other fear; that would indeed be strange, and I might justly be arraigned in court for denying the existence of the gods, if I disobeyed the oracle because I was afraid of death, fancying that I was wise when I was not wise. For the fear of death is indeed the pretence of wisdom, and not real wisdom, being a pretence of knowing the unknown; and no one knows whether death, which men in their fear apprehend to be the greatest evil, may not be the greatest good. Is not this ignorance of a disgraceful sort, the ignorance which is the conceit that man knows what he does not know? And in this respect only I believe myself to differ from men in general, and may perhaps claim to be wiser than they are:—that whereas I know but little of the world below, I do not suppose that I know: but I do know that injustice and disobedience to a better, whether God or man, is evil and dishonourable, and I will never fear or avoid a possible good rather than a certain evil. And therefore if you let me go now, and are not convinced by Anytus, who said that since I had been prosecuted I must be put to death (or if not that I ought never to have been prosecuted at all); and that if I escape now, your sons will all be utterly ruined by listening to my words—if you say to me, Socrates, this time we will not mind Anytus, and you shall be let off, but upon one condition, that you are not to enquire and speculate in this way any more, and that if you are caught doing so again you shall die;—if this was the condition on which you let me go, I should reply: Men of Athens, I honour and love you; but I shall obey God rather than you, and while I have life and strength I shall never cease from the practice and teaching of philosophy, exhorting any one whom I meet and saying to him after my manner: You, my friend,—a citizen of the great and mighty and wise city of Athens,—are you not ashamed of heaping up the greatest amount of money and honour and reputation, and caring so little about wisdom and truth and the greatest improvement of the soul, which you never regard or heed at all? And if the person with whom I am arguing, says: Yes, but I do care; then I do not leave him or let him go at once; but I proceed to interrogate and examine and cross-examine him, and if I think that he has no virtue in him, but only says that he has, I reproach him with undervaluing the greater, and overvaluing the less. And I shall repeat the same words to every one whom I meet, young and old, citizen and alien, but especially to the citizens, inasmuch as they are my brethren. For know that this is the command of God; and I believe that no greater good has ever happened in the state than my service to the God. For I do nothing but go about persuading you all, old and young alike, not to take thought for your persons or your properties, but first and chiefly to care about the greatest improvement of the soul. I tell you that virtue is not given by money, but that from virtue comes money and every other good of man, public as well as private. This is my teaching, and if this is the doctrine which corrupts the youth, I am a mischievous person. But if any one says that this is not my teaching, he is speaking an untruth. Wherefore, O men of Athens, I say to you, do as Anytus bids or not as Anytus bids, and either acquit me or not; but whichever you do, understand that I shall never alter my ways, not even if I have to die many times.

Men of Athens, do not interrupt, but hear me; there was an understanding between us that you should hear me to the end: I have something more to say, at which you may be inclined to cry out; but I believe that to hear me will be good for you, and therefore I beg that you will not cry out. I would have you know, that if you kill such an one as I am, you will injure yourselves more than you will injure me. Nothing will injure me, not Meletus nor yet Anytus—they cannot, for a bad man is not permitted to injure a better than himself. I do not deny that Anytus may, perhaps, kill him, or drive him into exile, or deprive him of civil rights; and he may imagine, and others may imagine, that he is inflicting a great injury upon him: but there I do not agree. For the evil of doing as he is doing—the evil of unjustly taking away the life of another—is greater far.

And now, Athenians, I am not going to argue for my own sake, as you may think, but for yours, that you may not sin against the God by condemning me, who am his gift to you. For if you kill me you will not easily find a successor to me, who, if I may use such a ludicrous figure of speech, am a sort of gadfly, given to the state by God; and the state is a great and noble steed who is tardy in his motions owing to his very size, and requires to be stirred into life. I am that gadfly which God has attached to the state, and all day long and in all places am always fastening upon you, arousing and persuading and reproaching you. You will not easily find another like me, and therefore I would advise you to spare me. I dare say that you may feel out of temper (like a person who is suddenly awakened from sleep), and you think that you might easily strike me dead as Anytus advises, and then you would sleep on for the remainder of your lives, unless God in his care of you sent you another gadfly. When I say that I am given to you by God, the proof of my mission is this:—if I had been like other men, I should not have neglected all my own concerns or patiently seen the neglect of them during all these years, and have been doing yours, coming to you individually like a father or elder brother, exhorting you to regard virtue; such conduct, I say, would be unlike human nature. If I had gained anything, or if my exhortations had been paid, there would have been some sense in my doing so; but now, as you will perceive, not even the impudence of my accusers dares to say that I have ever exacted or sought pay of any one; of that they have no witness. And I have a sufficient witness to the truth of what I say—my poverty.

Some one may wonder why I go about in private giving advice and busying myself with the concerns of others, but do not venture to come forward in public and advise the state. I will tell you why. You have heard me speak at sundry times and in diverse places of an oracle or sign which comes to me, and is the divinity which Meletus ridicules in the indictment. This sign, which is a kind of voice, first began to come to me when I was a child; it always forbids but never commands me to do anything which I am going to do. This is what deters me from being a politician. And rightly, as I think. For I am certain, O men of Athens, that if I had engaged in politics, I should have perished long ago, and done no good either to you or to myself. And do not be offended at my telling you the truth: for the truth is, that no man who goes to war with you or any other multitude, honestly striving against the many lawless and unrighteous deeds which are done in a state, will save his life; he who will fight for the right, if he would live even for a brief space, must have a private station and not a public one.

I can give you convincing evidence of what I say, not words only, but what you value far more—actions. Let me relate to you a passage of my own life which will prove to you that I should never have yielded to injustice from any fear of death, and that 'as I should have refused to yield' I must have died at once. I will tell you a tale of the courts, not very interesting perhaps, but nevertheless true. The only office of state which I ever held, O men of Athens, was that of senator: the tribe Antiochis, which is my tribe, had the presidency at the trial of the generals who had not taken up the bodies of the slain after the battle of Arginusae; and you proposed to try them in a body, contrary to law, as you all thought afterwards; but at the time I was the only one of the Prytanes who was opposed to the illegality, and I gave my vote against you; and when the orators threatened to impeach and arrest me, and you called and shouted, I made up my mind that I would run the risk, having law and justice with me, rather than take part in your injustice because I feared imprisonment and death. This happened in the days of the democracy. But when the oligarchy of the Thirty was in power, they sent for me and four others into the rotunda, and bade us bring Leon the Salaminian from Salamis, as they wanted to put him to death. This was a specimen of the sort of commands which they were always giving with the view of implicating as many as possible in their crimes; and then I showed, not in word only but in deed, that, if I may be allowed to use such an expression, I cared not a straw for death, and that my great and only care was lest I should do an unrighteous or unholy thing. For the strong arm of that oppressive power did not frighten me into doing wrong; and when we came out of the rotunda the other four went to Salamis and fetched Leon, but I went quietly home. For which I might have lost my life, had not the power of the Thirty shortly afterwards come to an end. And many will witness to my words.

Now do you really imagine that I could have survived all these years, if I had led a public life, supposing that like a good man I had always maintained the right and had made justice, as I ought, the first thing? No indeed, men of Athens, neither I nor any other man. But I have been always the same in all my actions, public as well as private, and never have I yielded any base compliance to those who are slanderously termed my disciples, or to any other. Not that I have any regular disciples. But if any one likes to come and hear me while I am pursuing my mission, whether he be young or old, he is not excluded. Nor do I converse only with those who pay; but any one, whether he be rich or poor, may ask and answer me and listen to my words; and whether he turns out to be a bad man or a good one, neither result can be justly imputed to me; for I never taught or professed to teach him anything. And if any one says that he has ever learned or heard anything from me in private which all the world has not heard, let me tell you that he is lying.

But I shall be asked, Why do people delight in continually conversing with you? I have told you already, Athenians, the whole truth about this matter: they like to hear the cross-examination of the pretenders to wisdom; there is amusement in it. Now this duty of cross-examining other men has been imposed upon me by God; and has been signified to me by oracles, visions, and in every way in which the will of divine power was ever intimated to any one. This is true, O Athenians; or, if not true, would be soon refuted. If I am or have been corrupting the youth, those of them who are now grown up and become sensible that I gave them bad advice in the days of their youth should come forward as accusers, and take their revenge; or if they do not like to come themselves, some of their relatives, fathers, brothers, or other kinsmen, should say what evil their families have suffered at my hands. Now is their time. Many of them I see in the court. There is Crito, who is of the same age and of the same deme with myself, and there is Critobulus his son, whom I also see. Then again there is Lysanias of Sphettus, who is the father of Aeschines—he is present; and also there is Antiphon of Cephisus, who is the father of Epigenes; and there are the brothers of several who have associated with me. There is Nicostratus the son of Theosdotides, and the brother of Theodotus (now Theodotus himself is dead, and therefore he, at any rate, will not seek to stop him); and there is Paralus the son of Demodocus, who had a brother Theages; and Adeimantus the son of Ariston, whose brother Plato is present; and Aeantodorus, who is the brother of Apollodorus, whom I also see. I might mention a great many others, some of whom Meletus should have produced as witnesses in the course of his speech; and let him still produce them, if he has forgotten—I will make way for him. And let him say, if he has any testimony of the sort which he can produce. Nay, Athenians, the very opposite is the truth. For all these are ready to witness on behalf of the corrupter, of the injurer of their kindred, as Meletus and Anytus call me; not the corrupted youth only—there might have been a motive for that—but their uncorrupted elder relatives. Why should they too support me with their testimony? Why, indeed, except for the sake of truth and justice, and because they know that I am speaking the truth, and that Meletus is a liar.

Well, Athenians, this and the like of this is all the defence which I have to offer. Yet a word more. Perhaps there may be some one who is offended at me, when he calls to mind how he himself on a similar, or even a less serious occasion, prayed and entreated the judges with many tears, and how he produced his children in court, which was a moving spectacle, together with a host of relations and friends; whereas I, who am probably in danger of my life, will do none of these things. The contrast may occur to his mind, and he may be set against me, and vote in anger because he is displeased at me on this account. Now if there be such a person among you,—mind, I do not say that there is,—to him I may fairly reply: My friend, I am a man, and like other men, a creature of flesh and blood, and not 'of wood or stone' as Homer says; and I have a family, yes, and sons, O Athenians, three in number, one almost a man, and two others who are still young; and yet I will not bring any of them hither in order to petition you for an acquittal. And why not? Not from any self-assertion or want of respect for you. Whether I am or am not afraid of death is another question, of which I will not now speak. But, having regard to public opinion, I feel that such conduct would be discreditable to myself, and to you, and to the whole state. One who has reached my years, and who has a name for wisdom, ought not to demean himself. Whether this opinion of me be deserved or not, at any rate the world has decided that Socrates is in some way superior to other men. And if those among you who are said to be superior in wisdom and courage, and any other virtue, demean themselves in this way, how shameful is their conduct! I have seen men of reputation, when they have been condemned, behaving in the strangest manner: they seemed to fancy that they were going to suffer something dreadful if they died, and that they could be immortal if you only allowed them to live; and I think that such are a dishonour to the state, and that any stranger coming in would have said of them that the most eminent men of Athens, to whom the Athenians themselves give honour and command, are no better than women. And I say that these things ought not to be done by those of us who have a reputation; and if they are done, you ought not to permit them; you ought rather to show that you are far more disposed to condemn the man who gets up a doleful scene and makes the city ridiculous, than him who holds his peace.

But, setting aside the question of public opinion, there seems to be something wrong in asking a favour of a judge, and thus procuring an acquittal, instead of informing and convincing him. For his duty is, not to make a present of justice, but to give judgment; and he has sworn that he will judge according to the laws, and not according to his own good pleasure; and we ought not to encourage you, nor should you allow yourself to be encouraged, in this habit of perjury—there can be no piety in that. Do not then require me to do what I consider dishonourable and impious and wrong, especially now, when I am being tried for impiety on the indictment of Meletus. For if, O men of Athens, by force of persuasion and entreaty I could overpower your oaths, than I should be teaching you to believe that there are no gods, and in defending should simply convict myself of the charge of not believing in them. But that is not so—far otherwise. For I do believe that there are gods, and in a sense higher than that in which any of my accusers believe in them. And to you and to God I commit my cause, to be determined by you as is best for you and me.

There are many reasons why I am not grieved, O men of Athens, at the vote of condemnation. I expected it, and am only surprised that the votes are so nearly equal; for I had thought that the majority against me would have been far larger; but now, had thirty votes gone over to the other side, I should have been acquitted. And I may say, I think, that I have escaped Meletus. I may say more; for without the assistance of Anytus and Lycon, any one may see that he would not have had a fifth part of the votes, as the law requires, in which case he would have incurred a fine of a thousand drachmae.

And so he proposes death as the penalty. And what shall I propose on my part, O men of Athens? Clearly that which is my due. And what is my due? What return shall be made to the man who has never had the wit to be idle during his whole life; but has been careless of what the many care for—wealth, and family interests, and military offices, and speaking in the assembly, and magistracies, and plots, and parties. Reflecting that I was really too honest a man to be a politician and live, I did not go where I could do no good to you or to myself; but where I could do the greatest good privately to every one of you, thither I went, and sought to persuade every man among you that he must look to himself, and seek virtue and wisdom before he looks to his private interests, and look to the state before he looks to the interests of the state; and that this should be the order which he observes in all his actions. What shall be done to such an one? Doubtless some good thing, O men of Athens, if he has his reward; and the good should be of a kind suitable to him. What would be a reward suitable to a poor man who is your benefactor, and who desires leisure that he may instruct you? There can be no reward so fitting as maintenance in the Prytaneum, O men of Athens, a reward which he deserves far more than the citizen who has won the prize at Olympia in the horse or chariot race, whether the chariots were drawn by two horses or by many. For I am in want, and he has enough; and he only gives you the appearance of happiness, and I give you the reality. And if I am to estimate the penalty fairly, I should say that maintenance in the Prytaneum is the just return.

Perhaps you think that I am braving you in what I am saying now, as in what I said before about the tears and prayers. But this is not so. I speak rather because I am convinced that I never intentionally wronged any one, although I cannot convince you—the time has been too short; if there were a law at Athens, as there is in other cities, that a capital cause should not be decided in one day, then I believe that I should have convinced you. But I cannot in a moment refute great slanders; and, as I am convinced that I never wronged another, I will assuredly not wrong myself. I will not say of myself that I deserve any evil, or propose any penalty. Why should I? Because I am afraid of the penalty of death which Meletus proposes? When I do not know whether death is a good or an evil, why should I propose a penalty which would certainly be an evil? Shall I say imprisonment? And why should I live in prison, and be the slave of the magistrates of the year—of the Eleven? Or shall the penalty be a fine, and imprisonment until the fine is paid? There is the same objection. I should have to lie in prison, for money I have none, and cannot pay. And if I say exile (and this may possibly be the penalty which you will affix), I must indeed be blinded by the love of life, if I am so irrational as to expect that when you, who are my own citizens, cannot endure my discourses and words, and have found them so grievous and odious that you will have no more of them, others are likely to endure me. No indeed, men of Athens, that is not very likely. And what a life should I lead, at my age, wandering from city to city, ever changing my place of exile, and always being driven out! For I am quite sure that wherever I go, there, as here, the young men will flock to me; and if I drive them away, their elders will drive me out at their request; and if I let them come, their fathers and friends will drive me out for their sakes.

Some one will say: Yes, Socrates, but cannot you hold your tongue, and then you may go into a foreign city, and no one will interfere with you? Now I have great difficulty in making you understand my answer to this. For if I tell you that to do as you say would be a disobedience to the God, and therefore that I cannot hold my tongue, you will not believe that I am serious; and if I say again that daily to discourse about virtue, and of those other things about which you hear me examining myself and others, is the greatest good of man, and that the unexamined life is not worth living, you are still less likely to believe me. Yet I say what is true, although a thing of which it is hard for me to persuade you. Also, I have never been accustomed to think that I deserve to suffer any harm. Had I money I might have estimated the offence at what I was able to pay, and not have been much the worse.

But I have none, and therefore I must ask you to proportion the fine to my means. Well, perhaps I could afford a mina, and therefore I propose that penalty: Plato, Crito, Critobulus, and Apollodorus, my friends here, bid me say thirty minae, and they will be the sureties. Let thirty minae be the penalty; for which sum they will be ample security to you.

Not much time will be gained, O Athenians, in return for the evil name which you will get from the detractors of the city, who will say that you killed Socrates, a wise man; for they will call me wise, even although I am not wise, when they want to reproach you. If you had waited a little while, your desire would have been fulfilled in the course of nature. For I am far advanced in years, as you may perceive, and not far from death. I am speaking now not to all of you, but only to those who have condemned me to death. And I have another thing to say to them: You think that I was convicted because I had no words of the sort which would have procured my acquittal—I mean, if I had thought fit to leave nothing undone or unsaid. Not so; the deficiency which led to my conviction was not of words—certainly not. But I had not the boldness or impudence or inclination to address you as you would have liked me to do, weeping and wailing and lamenting, and saying and doing many things which you have been accustomed to hear from others, and which, as I maintain, are unworthy of me. I thought at the time that I ought not to do anything common or mean when in danger: nor do I now repent of the style of my defence; I would rather die having spoken after my manner, than speak in your manner and live. For neither in war nor yet at law ought I or any man to use every way of escaping death. Often in battle there can be no doubt that if a man will throw away his arms, and fall on his knees before his pursuers, he may escape death; and in other dangers there are other ways of escaping death, if a man is willing to say and do anything. The difficulty, my friends, is not to avoid death, but to avoid unrighteousness; for that runs faster than death. I am old and move slowly, and the slower runner has overtaken me, and my accusers are keen and quick, and the faster runner, who is unrighteousness, has overtaken them. And now I depart hence condemned by you to suffer the penalty of death,—they too go their ways condemned by the truth to suffer the penalty of villainy and wrong; and I must abide by my award—let them abide by theirs. I suppose that these things may be regarded as fated,—and I think that they are well.

And now, O men who have condemned me, I would fain prophesy to you; for I am about to die, and in the hour of death men are gifted with prophetic power. And I prophesy to you who are my murderers, that immediately after my departure punishment far heavier than you have inflicted on me will surely await you. Me you have killed because you wanted to escape the accuser, and not to give an account of your lives. But that will not be as you suppose: far otherwise. For I say that there will be more accusers of you than there are now; accusers whom hitherto I have restrained: and as they are younger they will be more inconsiderate with you, and you will be more offended at them. If you think that by killing men you can prevent some one from censuring your evil lives, you are mistaken; that is not a way of escape which is either possible or honourable; the easiest and the noblest way is not to be disabling others, but to be improving yourselves. This is the prophecy which I utter before my departure to the judges who have condemned me.

Friends, who would have acquitted me, I would like also to talk with you about the thing which has come to pass, while the magistrates are busy, and before I go to the place at which I must die. Stay then a little, for we may as well talk with one another while there is time. You are my friends, and I should like to show you the meaning of this event which has happened to me. O my judges—for you I may truly call judges—I should like to tell you of a wonderful circumstance. Hitherto the divine faculty of which the internal oracle is the source has constantly been in the habit of opposing me even about trifles, if I was going to make a slip or error in any matter; and now as you see there has come upon me that which may be thought, and is generally believed to be, the last and worst evil. But the oracle made no sign of opposition, either when I was leaving my house in the morning, or when I was on my way to the court, or while I was speaking, at anything which I was going to say; and yet I have often been stopped in the middle of a speech, but now in nothing I either said or did touching the matter in hand has the oracle opposed me. What do I take to be the explanation of this silence? I will tell you. It is an intimation that what has happened to me is a good, and that those of us who think that death is an evil are in error. For the customary sign would surely have opposed me had I been going to evil and not to good.

Let us reflect in another way, and we shall see that there is great reason to hope that death is a good; for one of two things—either death is a state of nothingness and utter unconsciousness, or, as men say, there is a change and migration of the soul from this world to another. Now if you suppose that there is no consciousness, but a sleep like the sleep of him who is undisturbed even by dreams, death will be an unspeakable gain. For if a person were to select the night in which his sleep was undisturbed even by dreams, and were to compare with this the other days and nights of his life, and then were to tell us how many days and nights he had passed in the course of his life better and more pleasantly than this one, I think that any man, I will not say a private man, but even the great king will not find many such days or nights, when compared with the others. Now if death be of such a nature, I say that to die is gain; for eternity is then only a single night. But if death is the journey to another place, and there, as men say, all the dead abide, what good, O my friends and judges, can be greater than this? If indeed when the pilgrim arrives in the world below, he is delivered from the professors of justice in this world, and finds the true judges who are said to give judgment there, Minos and Rhadamanthus and Aeacus and Triptolemus, and other sons of God who were righteous in their own life, that pilgrimage will be worth making. What would not a man give if he might converse with Orpheus and Musaeus and Hesiod and Homer? Nay, if this be true, let me die again and again. I myself, too, shall have a wonderful interest in there meeting and conversing with Palamedes, and Ajax the son of Telamon, and any other ancient hero who has suffered death through an unjust judgment; and there will be no small pleasure, as I think, in comparing my own sufferings with theirs. Above all, I shall then be able to continue my search into true and false knowledge; as in this world, so also in the next; and I shall find out who is wise, and who pretends to be wise, and is not. What would not a man give, O judges, to be able to examine the leader of the great Trojan expedition; or Odysseus or Sisyphus, or numberless others, men and women too! What infinite delight would there be in conversing with them and asking them questions! In another world they do not put a man to death for asking questions: assuredly not. For besides being happier than we are, they will be immortal, if what is said is true.

Wherefore, O judges, be of good cheer about death, and know of a certainty, that no evil can happen to a good man, either in life or after death. He and his are not neglected by the gods; nor has my own approaching end happened by mere chance. But I see clearly that the time had arrived when it was better for me to die and be released from trouble; wherefore the oracle gave no sign. For which reason, also, I am not angry with my condemners, or with my accusers; they have done me no harm, although they did not mean to do me any good; and for this I may gently blame them.

Still I have a favour to ask of them. When my sons are grown up, I would ask you, O my friends, to punish them; and I would have you trouble them, as I have troubled you, if they seem to care about riches, or anything, more than about virtue; or if they pretend to be something when they are really nothing,—then reprove them, as I have reproved you, for not caring about that for which they ought to care, and thinking that they are something when they are really nothing. And if you do this, both I and my sons will have received justice at your hands.

The hour of departure has arrived, and we go our ways—I to die, and you to live. Which is better God only knows.

The Death of Socrates
(from Plato's *Phaedo*)

We will do our best, said Crito: And in what way shall we bury you?

In any way that you like; but you must get hold of me, and take care that I do not run away from you. Then he turned to us, and added with a smile:—I cannot make Crito believe that I am the same Socrates who has been talking and con-ducting the argument; he fancies that I am the other Socrates whom he will soon see, a dead body—and he asks, How shall he bury me? And though I have spoken many words in the endeavour to show that when I have drunk the poison I shall leave you and go to the joys of the blessed,—these words of mine, with which I was comforting you and myself, have had, as I perceive, no effect upon Crito. And therefore I want you to be surety for me to him now, as at the trial he was surety to the judges for me: but let the promise be of another sort; for he was surety for me to the judges that I would remain, and you must be my surety to him that I shall not remain, but go away and depart; and then he will suffer less at my death, and not be grieved when he sees my body being burned or buried. I would not have him sorrow at my hard lot, or say at the burial, Thus we lay out Socrates, or, Thus we follow him to the grave or bury him; for false words are not only evil in themselves, but they infect the soul with evil. Be of good cheer then, my dear Crito, and say that you are burying my body only, and do with that whatever is usual, and what you think best.

When he had spoken these words, he arose and went into a chamber to bathe; Crito followed him and told us to wait. So we remained behind, talking and thinking of the subject of discourse, and also of the greatness of our sorrow; he was like a father of whom we were being bereaved, and we were about to pass the rest of our lives as orphans. When he had taken his bath his children were brought to him—(he had two young sons and an elder one); and the women of his family also came, and he talked to them and gave them a few directions in the presence of Crito; then he dismissed them and returned to us.

Now the hour of sunset was near, for a good deal of time had passed while he was within. When he came out, he sat down with us again after his bath, but not much was said. Soon the jailer, who was the servant of the Eleven, entered and stood by him, saying:—To you, Socrates, whom I know to be the noblest and gentlest and best of all who ever came to this place, I will not impute the angry feelings of other men, who rage and swear at me, when, in obedience to the authorities, I bid them drink the poison—indeed, I am sure that you will not be angry with me; for others, as you are aware, and not I, are to blame. And so fare you well, and try to bear lightly what must needs be—you know my errand. Then bursting into tears he turned away and went out.

Socrates looked at him and said: I return your good wishes, and will do as you bid. Then turning to us, he said, How charming the man is: since I have been in prison he has always been coming to see me, and at times he would talk to me, and was as good to me as could be, and now see how generously he sorrows on my account. We must do as he says, Crito; and therefore let the cup be brought, if the poison is prepared: if not, let the attendant prepare some.

Yet, said Crito, the sun is still upon the hill-tops, and I know that many a one has taken the draught late, and after the announcement has been made to him, he has eaten and drunk, and enjoyed the society of his beloved; do not hurry—there is time enough.

Socrates said: Yes, Crito, and they of whom you speak are right in so acting, for they think that they will be gainers by the delay; but I am right in not following their example, for I do not think that I should gain anything by drinking the poison a little later; I should only be ridiculous in my own eyes for sparing and saving a life which is already forfeit. Please then to do as I say, and not refuse me.

Crito made a sign to the servant, who was standing by; and he went out, and having been absent for some time, returned with the jailer carrying the cup of poison. Socrates said: You, my good friend, who are experienced in these matters, shall give me directions how I am to proceed. The man answered: You have only to walk about until your legs are heavy, and then to lie down, and the poison will act. At the same time he handed the cup to Socrates, who in the easiest and gentlest manner, without the least fear or change of colour or feature, looking at the man with all his eyes, Echecrates, as his manner was, took the cup and said: What do you say about making a libation out of this cup to any god? May I, or not? The man answered: We only prepare, Socrates, just so much as we deem enough. I understand, he said: but I may and must ask the gods to prosper my journey from this to the other world—even so—and so be it according to my prayer. Then raising the cup to his lips, quite readily and cheerfully he drank off the poison. And hitherto most of us had been able to control our sorrow; but now when we saw him drinking, and saw too that he had finished the draught, we could no longer forbear, and in spite of myself my own tears were flowing fast; so that I covered my face and wept, not for him, but at the thought of my own calamity in having to part from such a friend. Nor was I the first; for Crito, when he found himself unable to restrain his tears, had got up, and I followed; and at that moment, Apollodorus, who had been weeping all the time, broke out in a loud and passionate cry which made cowards of us all. Socrates alone retained his calmness: What is this strange outcry? he said. I sent away the women mainly in order that they might not misbehave in this way, for I have been told that a man should die in peace. Be quiet then, and have patience. When we heard his words we were ashamed, and refrained our tears; and he walked about until, as he said, his legs began to fail, and then he lay on his back, according to the directions, and the man who gave him the poison now and then looked at his feet and legs; and after a while he pressed his foot hard, and asked him if he could feel; and he said, No; and then his leg, and so upwards and upwards, and showed us that he was cold and stiff. And he felt them himself, and said: When the poison reaches the heart, that will be the end. He was beginning to grow cold about the groin, when he uncovered his face, for he had covered himself up, and said—they were his last words—he said: Crito, I owe a cock to Asclepius; will you remember to pay the debt? The debt shall be paid, said Crito; is there anything else? There was no answer to this question; but in a minute or two a movement was heard, and the attendants uncovered him; his eyes were set, and Crito closed his eyes and mouth.

Such was the end, Echecrates, of our friend; concerning whom I may truly say, that of all the men of his time whom I have known, he was the wisest and justest and best.

Except where noted all translations of Plato are by Benjamin Jowett.

Review Questions

1. In what way does Socrates identify wisdom with virtue?
2. What does Socrates mean by his stunning description of philosophy as "practicing death"?
3. What possibility of immortality do you find in Socratic thought?
4. What constitutes a good person for Socrates?
5. Centuries later, Kierkegaard will refer to Socrates as a "tragic hero." Do you consider this an apt characterization?
6. How does Socrates justify his defiance of authority?

SUGGESTIONS FOR FURTHER READING

Brickhouse, T. C. and Smith, N. D. *Plato's Socrates*. New York, Oxford University Press, 1995.

Guardini, R. *The Death of Socrates*. New York, Sheed and Ward, 1948.

Guthrie, W. K. *Socrates*. New York, Cambridge University Press, 1972.

Taylor, A. E. *Socrates*. Westport, CT, Hyperion Press, 1986.

Vlastos, G., ed. *The Philosophy of Socrates*. South Bend, University of Notre Dame Press, 1980.

3

---•❦•---

Plato
(427–347 B.C.)

❧

The second of the great trinity of Greek philosophers was born in Athens in 428/27 B.C.; according to an ancient account, he was later called Plato because of his broad forehead. He came from a family that was, by all reports, educated, aristocratic, and politically influential. It was no doubt assumed that he would enter political life, but his disaffection from the ineptness and injustice of Athenian "democracy," especially on the execution of Socrates, turned him to the pursuit of philosophy with the cherished hope that someday philosophy and politics would combine to bring about a happier life: "the human race will not see better days" until philosophers become politicians or politicians become philosophers. He was a formal student of Socrates for perhaps a year or so as a late teenager, but he resonated to the spirit of the Master for his entire life.

At the Academy

For the next ten or eleven years after the death of Socrates, Plato traveled throughout Greece, going as far as southern Italy and Sicily to various centers of intellectual activity. During this time he began some lifelong friendships, intensified a philosophic cast of mind, and wrote his early works, which were known, because of their central figure, as the "Socratic dialogues," such as the *Apology, Gorgias, Meno,* and *Crito.* These and several other works were done before Plato's most significant work was even begun—the founding of the Academy.

When Plato was about forty years of age, and after this period of travel, reflection, and writing, he founded a school just outside Athens which became known as the Academy. It was a quiet retreat where teachers and students could be together daily; where, despite a rigorous intellectual discipline and a fairly formal administrative structure, respect and friendship flourished. It was a place, in Plato's eyes, that provided an opportunity for the pursuit of pure, disinterested knowledge, particularly scientific knowledge with mathematics at its core, so that students devoted to the truth could become true public servants. The students came from all over Greece; they came to share the adventure of learning, to experience growth toward wisdom, and to receive a spark of life from the revered founder of the Academy. Given the Academy's influence and its status as the forerunner of the modern university, it is not surprising that, for some historians, its founding was one of the outstanding intellectual events in the history of the West.

Plato and the Academy were to become inseparable until his death in 347 B.C.; except for the time when he returned to Sicily, his life was spent there, and daily his voice was heard within its walls. He seems to have lectured without notes, yet his words were precise. He focused on dialectic as the primary educational method; it was the method of question and answer, with every attempt made to satisfy the rigors of reason and clarity uniquely achievable in the form of a dialogue; in this form, Plato's works were delivered to the public. Among the dialogues of Plato's middle life were the *Phaedo, Symposium,* and *Republic;* later, the *Parmenides, Timaeus,* and lastly the *Laws.*

Permanence vs. Change: Perfection vs. Imperfection

We can be sure, because it pervades his writings, that one of the ongoing dialogues Plato conducted with his students related to the even then traditional question of being and becoming—the search for the permanent element in things subject, as they all are, to change; this was a continuation of the Socratic search for the *essence* of things. Once we realize that, for Plato, the pressing question was how to escape the ever-changing world of Heraclitus, we also realize why he leaned toward the permanent, and why he emphasized being rather than becoming. It is all too obvious, Plato held, that changing things are not as important as permanent things and therefore occupy a lower rank in the hierarchy of the real; they are not "really real." Things-as-becoming can never have the same value as things-as-being. So Plato's search for the permanent, for essences, is also a search for the higher and nobler. The oak is a tree, the maple is a tree, the spruce is a tree; yet the individual oak, maple, and spruce change, but not the *meaning of tree.* Further, if individual trees perish, where do we find the essence of tree that does not perish? Surely there must be a place where the tree exists in all its perfection—the ideal tree, the essential tree. Plato, of course, does not mean a physical tree, since that, as an individual, would be subject to the same problem he is trying to solve. What he means is that the tree stripped of all its changing features—akin to the idea we have in our minds—must exist somewhere, unchanging, in a permanent, perfect *world of ideas.* And what is said of tree can be said of anything else: dog, man, wisdom, and virtue.

The distinction between changing and lower on one hand, and unchanging and higher on the other, is borne out in the famous allegory of the cave, a parable in which Plato summarizes a number of his main doctrines. He asks us to imagine a subterranean cave, lightless except for a fire that casts its light over a low mid-wall to the end-wall of the cave. When figures and shapes of all sorts are moved along the mid-wall, their shadows are reflected on the end-wall, as though it were a screen. Further, imagine a group of men situated with their backs to the mid-wall who have, since childhood, been chained like prisoners so that they continually face the end-wall. The only things they ever see, then, are shadows—their own and those of the objects moved along the mid-wall behind them, and the only sounds they ever hear are the cave's echoes of real sounds.

If one of these men is suddenly freed and walks around to see the whole affair in light of the fire, he is jolted into the awareness that the real is utterly different from what he had taken to be real—the difference between truth and illusion. If he then struggles to the mouth of the cave and sees the sun in all its brightness, he marvels at beholding light itself and all other things in that light. He then reaches the highest point in his understanding that there are things more real than the things he previously knew, and that the difference between opinion and true knowledge is forever fixed. Thus the distinction made by Parmenides receives ardent support from Plato, that is, the more our grasp of things tends toward the unchanging, the more right it has to be called *knowledge*, and true knowledge is knowledge of the eternal and higher world. Imprisoned in the world of opinion, men have become too blind to see and too deaf to hear the logos of the higher world whose truth would set them free.

The blazing light of that vision does not remain on a speculative level. On realizing that the Light—eternal, permanent, and unchanging—can be nothing less than the Idea of Good, which, as the highest of all Forms, is the cause of all things "right and beautiful," the beholder is drawn to translate the dynamism of that vision into a life of practical goodness for others, a life of ethical and political wisdom. Truth, untranslated into action is not truth at all.

Participation

To acquire a fuller picture of the relationship between the changing and the unchanging, it is necessary to underscore Plato's view that although the two worlds are opposites, they are nonetheless correlatives. Essence is indeed found in changing things, but in a vague and imperfect way; better, as it is found in this world, it is a pointer to the world beyond, where it is found in its perfect form. Yet the relationship involves more than mere pointing; there is an inner bond between the two worlds. Essence in the unchanging world is immanent in the changing one, so that the changing world shares the unchanging world, participates in it. The changing world exists in time, and in the beautiful phrase of the *Timaeus*, "time is the moving image of eternity." Put differently, essence has two dimensions, one found in the unchanging world of the perfect and the other in the changing world of the imperfect; but the only explanation for the imperfect is that it shares the perfect in a limited way. The doctrine of *participation*, as it is sometimes called, eventually became a favorite of later Christian philosophers, who employed it to show how the created world is one with the uncreated world.

Plato's Epistemology . . . Extreme Realism

Because of the continuity of this world with the higher world, Plato was consistent in concluding that knowledge does not come to us anew, as though with an absolute beginning, but it is somehow always possessed by us. Following Socrates, he takes learning to be a *process of recalling.* Learning occurs not because a teacher conveys new ideas to the student, but because the teacher supplies the conditions necessary to draw forth from the student the knowledge he already possesses. This concept is exemplified in an episode in which Socrates invites a slave boy, therefore untaught, to join a group of friends in order to ask him a series of questions about mathematics. Though the boy is given none of the answers, Socrates successfully draws him out. Socrates infers that the answers already rest within the boy, unrecognized because they are latent but recognized when they are summoned forth under the proper conditions. Plato's final view is that the boy, like all of us, must have been endowed with knowledge in a previous state and transported it, forgotten, into this one. The knowledge we have as we *preexisted* in the world of ideas, with its pure intelligibility, becomes obscured in this world of physical things; that is why, like the prisoners in the cave, we have to make a renewed effort to see reality in the eternal light.

Plato's emphasis on the eternal world vis-à-vis the changing world discloses, very early in the history of philosophy, one of the fundamental problems in epistemology: the ontological status of what we know. The question is whether or not ideas refer to objects outside the mind; do they refer to real existences? If so, to what do they actually refer? We have already seen Plato's response to this question: Inasmuch as the individual material thing changes whereas its meaning does not— the tree perishes but not the idea of it—there must be some real thing "out there" that answers to our idea of it; otherwise the knowledge we say we have is not knowledge at all. Sometimes this position is referred to as *realism*, and since there are no hard and fast rules governing the use of the terms *realism* and *idealism*, we have to readjust our understanding of them according to the contexts in which they are used. Believing as he does that there *are* in extra-mental reality things answering precisely to our ideas of them, Plato's epistemological stance is referred to as *extreme realism*. Ideas for him are universal, essential, formal, and detached from matter, corresponding to these characteristics, then, is the existence of a real world of universals, essences, forms, and immaterial things; otherwise, ideas would refer to nothing and be completely devoid of meaning. The position contrary to extreme realism is *extreme idealism,* which means that nothing exists but mind and mental things, and that matter and material things are somehow subsumed under ideas, as will be seen later in Berkeley and Hegel.

If, however, a philosopher begins with the opposite belief, that because only individual things exist, our knowledge is only individual, then common knowledge is impossible. This extreme position coincides with the philosophical outlook of the pre-Socratic atomists, for whom, since atoms are the only real things, knowledge had to be equally "atomic" to be called real. For Democritus, for example, there could be no genuine distinction between thought and sensation; for him, the senses say to the intellect: "Miserable Mind, you get your evidence from us, and do you try to overthrow us? The overthrow will be your downfall."

Two widely divergent views then, are as follows: There are, or are not, real things outside the mind called essences, forms, Ideas, or universals that correspond to the concepts in our minds. Is there any other option? Looking ahead to Plato's student and friend, Aristotle thought so. He argued against his master's doctrine on the real existence of Ideas, pointing out the contradiction he said it implied: A universal could never be a substance, for then you could never call it a "this," which is the designation used of existing things. Still, for Aristotle, universal knowledge is real knowledge even though there are no universals as such existing outside the mind. For him only *individual* things exist, yet it is possible for me to have knowledge of an individual *in common* with other individual things, and this commonality is in fact rooted in their existence. In Aristotle's view, therefore, when I say "Socrates is a man" and "Plato is a man," I mean that they are both *really* men; humanity is *realized* in each. To deny this common, or universal, feature would be to deny what I mean. Ideas, in their formal, essential, general, or universal aspects, have real content, but not in the extreme sense spoken of by Plato. Likewise, abstractions like justice and honesty have objective content because they refer to individual acts that have a moral character in common. The history of philosophy shows the reemergence of this same issue, although in various forms: in the Middle Ages in the controversy between realism and nominalism, in the context of seventeenth-century rationalism and empiricism, and in the recent problem of what makes scientific knowledge possible.

. . . *Dualism*

The phrase *platonic dualism* is often used in reference to the distinction Plato made between permanent and passing, unchanging and changing, higher and lower, being and becoming, knowledge and opinion, real and not as real. This overall dualism is part of the heritage of most religious traditions because the notions of higher and lower are a fundamental reading of reality. In the West, it is woven, along with other elements from the East, into the fabric of the Christian worldview and, in its extreme form, displays the remarkable trait of reappearing in particular projects of Christian piety under the rubric of matter as evil and spirit as good.

That same insistence on the superiority of permanence, unchange, the formal, the essential, and the intellectualist comes down with special force on another problem, that of the relationship between soul and body. It is clear that the body of man is subject to change and impermanence, so if there is a part of man not subject to change and impermanence, it must be the part that knows the unchanging and the permanent; whatever knows the permanent must itself be permanent in some way; whatever knows essences must itself somehow be an essence. In man, this is the soul. Strictly speaking, then, for Plato the soul is not a "part" of man; it is the *whole* man; by nature *man is soul* only. The relationship of soul to body is not, as it would be for Aristotle, two principles metaphysically united to form one being or two vectors constituting one force; it is more like the relationship of a captain to his ship or a rider to his horse—two separate beings maintaining their distinction even while cooperating with each other. This is what is meant by *Platonic dualism,* and as a dualistic approach to man it draws with it, as the history of philosophy shows, a host of problems touching on the meaning of experience that were not directly addressed by Plato. But very much in keeping with the ethical side of his patrimony, from Pythagoras to Socrates, Plato saw man's task as freeing himself from the body. This can be done only by riveting our attention on the eternal world of Forms and acting according to its summonses. This is a duty particularly incumbent on the philosopher, the lover of wisdom, who understands the role of purification, of overcoming the weight of the body, of seeing man's eternal goal in the separation of soul from body, and in the return to the higher world in which he pre-existed; in this sense, the philosopher lives day by day with his mind's eye on death, and "makes dying a profession."

Wisdom, Love, and the Affairs of State

That's why the perfection of the permanent and unchanging has special relevance for Plato in the practical realms of ethics and politics too. Here Plato, along with Socrates, tries to find what is common to all types of human action and thereby to unveil the pure form of each virtue as a guide to doing good. Inasmuch as knowledge in the highest degree is knowledge of what *is* in the highest degree—the essences in the world of Ideas—then perfect knowledge of the Good should beget actions that are good; if it does not, our knowledge is not yet perfect: perfect knowledge means perfect virtue. But in this, our embodied life, such knowledge and such virtue, are not possible. Imperfection enters in because of the body and all its trappings. What the philosopher, indeed, what everyone has to do is to work at getting beyond the trappings and then to perceive the perfect by a steady, contemplative effort. In this sense, a higher degree of knowledge means a higher degree of virtue, and the rightful name of knowledge-virtue is *wisdom.*

But wisdom is never divorced from love. If wisdom is one with virtue, and the essence of virtue is one with good, that is, the practice of virtue is the doing of good, then *love* is the pursuit and possession of good. There are countless instances of love in this life because there are countless objects worthy of love, but the vast array of good and beautiful things has to be understood as lifting us, as it were, bit by bit, to higher levels of good until its everlasting possession is achieved. This ascent is movingly described by Plato in the *Symposium* in which Diotima, Socrates' teacher in the philosophy of love, says to him, "And the true order of going, or being led by another, to the things of love, is to begin from the beauties of earth and mount upwards for the sake of that other beauty, using these as steps only, and from one going on to two, and from two to all fair forms, and from fair forms to fair practices, and from fair practices to fair notions, until from fair notions he arrives at the notion of absolute beauty, and at last he knows what the essence of beauty is. This, my dear Socrates ... is that life above all others which man should live, in the contemplation of beauty absolute."

Wisdom, however, is not a matter just for the individual; it is a matter for the entire state which, in turn, should be governed by the highest principles. The state should somehow be the incarnation of justice, so much so that if any citizen were incapable of understanding the meaning of justice for himself, he would come to understand it by seeing it "writ large" in the state. The shape of the state, entrusted to its rulers, is modeled after the eternal Forms; it is, therefore, as perfect as it can be in the world of human affairs, a Utopia, an Ideal state based on the Ideas. Plato's perception of such a state is minutely detailed; he specifies, for example, the exact number of citizens, the stratification of classes, the treatment of slaves, marriage, child rearing, and other precise features bearing on his overall purpose of showing that the state is a natural society intended for the good of man. The state exists for its citizens, not the other way around.

The proper education of potential rulers is of special concern and importance; it is to be given in particular areas and over a long period of time to allow for the candidate's development. In Plato's own words, "those who have survived the tests and approved themselves altogether the best in every task and form of knowledge must be brought at last to the goal. We shall require them to turn upward the vision of their souls and fix their gaze on that which sheds light on all, and when they have thus beheld the good itself, they shall use it as a pattern for the right ordering of the state and the citizens and themselves throughout the remainder of their lives, each in his turn, devoting the greater part of their time to the study of philosophy." Much is at stake; humanity itself is at stake: "Unless either philosophers become kings in our states or those whom we call our kings and rulers take to the pursuit of philosophy seriously and adequately, and there is a conjunction of these two things, political power and philosophical intelligence ... there can be no cessation of troubles for our states, nor, I fancy, for the human race either."

READINGS

Doctrine of Forms
(General statement, from *Parmenides*)

Socrates, he said, your eagerness for discussion is admirable. And now tell me. Have you yourself drawn this distinction you speak of and separated apart on the one side forms themselves and on the other the things that share in them? Do you believe that there is such a thing as likeness itself apart from the likeness that we possess, and so on with unity and plurality and all the terms in Zeno's argument that you have just been listening to?

Certainly I do, said Socrates.

And also in cases like these, asked Parmenides, is there, for example, a form of rightness or of beauty or of goodness, and of all such things?

Yes.

And again, a form of man, apart from ourselves and all other men like us—a form of man as something by itself? Or a form of fire or of water?

I have often been puzzled about those things, Parmenides, whether one should say that the same thing is true in their case or not.

Are you also puzzled, Socrates, about cases that might be thought absurd, such as hair or mud or dirt or any other trivial and undignified objects? Are you doubtful whether or not to assert that each of these has a separate form distinct from things like those we handle?

Not at all, said Socrates. In these cases, the things are just the things we see; it would surely be too absurd to suppose that they have a form. All the same, I have sometimes been troubled by a doubt whether what is true in one case may not be true in all. Then, when I have reached that point, I am driven to retreat, for fear of tumbling into a bottomless pit of nonsense. Anyhow, I get back to the things which we were just now speaking of as having forms, and occupy my time with thinking about them.

That, replied Parmenides, is because you are still young, Socrates, and philosophy has not yet taken hold of you so firmly as I believe it will someday. You will not despise any of these objects then, but at present your youth makes you still pay attention to what the world will think. However that may be, tell me this. You say you hold that there exist certain forms, of which these other things come to partake and so to be called after their names; by coming to partake of likeness or largeness or beauty or justice, they become like or large or beautiful or just?

Certainly, said Socrates.

Then each thing that partakes receives as its share either the form as a whole or a part of it? Or can there be any other way of partaking besides this?

No, how could there be?

Do you hold, then, that the form as a whole, a single thing, is in each of the many, or how?

Why should it not be in each, Parmenides?

If so, a form which is one and the same will be at the same time, as a whole, in a number of things which are separate, and consequently will be separate from itself.

No, it would not, replied Socrates, if it were like one and the same day, which is in many places at the same time and nevertheless is not separate from itself. Suppose any given form is in them all at the same time as one and the same thing in that way.

I like the way you make out that one and the same thing is in many places at once, Socrates. You might as well spread a sail over a number of people and then say that the one sail as a whole was over them all. Don't you think that is a fair analogy?

Perhaps it is.

Then would the sail as a whole be over each man, or only a part over one, another part over another?

Only a part.

In that case, Socrates, the forms themselves must be divisible into parts, and the things which have a share in them will have a part for their share. Only a part of any given form, and no longer the whole of it, will be in each thing.

Evidently, on that showing.

Are you, then, prepared to assert that we shall find the single form actually being divided? Will it still be one?

Certainly not.

No, for consider this. Suppose it is largeness itself that you are going to divide into parts, and that each of the many large things is to be large by virtue of a part of largeness which is smaller than largeness itself. Will not that seem unreasonable?

It will indeed.

And again, if it is equality that a thing receives some small part of, will that part, which is less than equality itself, make its possessor equal to something else.

No, that is impossible.

Well, take smallness. Is one of us to have a portion of smallness, and is smallness to be larger than that portion, which is a part of it? On this supposition again smallness itself will be larger, and anything to which the portion taken is added will be smaller, and not larger, than it was before.

That cannot be so.

Well then, Socrates, how are the other things going to partake of your forms, if they can partake of them neither in part nor as wholes?

Really, said Socrates, it seems no easy matter to determine in any way.

Doctrine of Forms
(Creation Myth, from *Timaeus*)

CRITIAS: Let me proceed to explain to you, Socrates, the order in which we have arranged our entertainment. Our intention is that Timaeus, who is the most of an astronomer among us, and has made the nature of the universe his special study, should speak first, beginning with the generation of the world and going down to the creation of man; next, I am to receive the men whom he has created, and of whom some will have profited by the excellent education which you have given them; and then, in accordance with the tale of Solon, and equally with his law, we will bring them into court and make them citizens, as if they were those very Athenians whom the sacred Egyptian record has recovered from oblivion, and thenceforward we will speak of them as Athenians and fellow citizens.

SOCRATES: I see that I shall receive in my turn a perfect and splendid feast of reason. And now, Timaeus, you, I suppose, should speak next, after duly calling upon the gods.

TIMAEUS: All men, Socrates, who have any degree of right feeling at the beginning of every enterprise, whether small or great, always call upon God. And we, too, who are going to discourse of the nature of the universe, how created or how existing without creation, if we be not altogether out of our wits, must invoke the aid of gods and goddesses and pray that our words may be above all acceptable to them and in consequence to ourselves. Let this, then, be our invocation of the gods, to which I add an exhortation of myself to speak in such manner as will be most intelligible to you, and will most accord with my own intent.

First then, in my judgment, we must make a distinction and ask, what is that which always is and has no becoming, and what is that which is always becoming and never is? That which is apprehended by intelligence and reason is always in the same state, but that which is conceived by opinion with the help of sensation and without reason is always in a process of becoming and perishing and never really is. Now everything that becomes or is created must of necessity be created by some cause, for without a cause nothing can be created. The work of the creator, whenever he looks to the unchangeable and fashions the form and nature of his work after an unchangeable pattern, must necessarily be made fair and perfect, but when he looks to the created only and uses a created pattern, it is not fair or perfect. Was the heaven then or the world, whether called by this or by any other more appropriate name—assuming the name, I am asking a question which has to be asked at the beginning of an inquiry about anything—was the world, I say, always in existence and without beginning, or created, and had it a beginning? Created, I reply, being visible and tangible and having a body, and therefore sensible, and all sensible things are apprehended by opinion and sense, and are in a process of creation and created. Now that which is created must, as we affirm, of necessity be created by a cause. But the father and maker of all this universe is past finding out, and even if we found him, to tell of him to all men would be impossible. This question, however, we must ask about the world. Which of the patterns had the artificer in view when he made it—the pattern of the unchangeable or of that which is created? If the world be indeed fair and the artificer good, it is manifest that he must have looked to that which is eternal, but if what cannot be said without blasphemy is true, then to the created pattern. Everyone will see that he must have looked to the eternal, for the world is the fairest of creations and he is the best of causes. And having been created in this way, the world has been framed in the likeness of that which is apprehended by reason and mind and is unchangeable, and must therefore of necessity, if this is admitted, be a copy of something. Now it is all-important that the beginning of everything should be according to nature. And in speaking of the copy and the original we may assume that words are akin to the matter which they describe; when they relate to the lasting and permanent and intelligible, they ought to be lasting and invincible—nothing less. But when they express only the copy or likeness and not the eternal things themselves, they need only be likely and analogous to the former words. As being is to becoming, so is truth to belief. If then, Socrates, amidst the many opinions about the gods and the generation of the universe, we are not able to give notions which are altogether and in every respect exact and consistent with one another, do not be surprised. Enough if we adduce probabilities as likely as any others, for we must remember that I who am the speaker and you who are the judges are only mortal men, and we ought to accept the tale which is probable and inquire no farther.

SOCRATES: Excellent, Timaeus, and we will do precisely as you bid us. The prelude is charming and is already accepted by us—may we beg of you to proceed to the strain?

TIMAEUS: Let me tell you then why the creator made this world of generation. He was good, and the good can never have any jealousy of anything. And being free from jealousy, he desired that all things should be as like himself as they could be. This is in the truest sense the origin of creation and of the world, as we shall do well in believing on the testimony of wise men. God desired that all things should be good and nothing bad, so far as this was attainable. Wherefore also finding the whole visible sphere not at rest, but moving in an irregular and disorderly fashion, out of disorder he brought order, considering that this was in every way better than the other. Now the deeds of the best could never be or have been other than the fairest, and the creator, reflecting on the things which are by nature visible, found that no unintelligent creature taken as a whole could ever be fairer than the intelligent taken as a whole, and again that intelligence could not be present in anything which was devoid of soul. For which reason, when he was framing the universe, he put intelligence in soul, and soul in body, that he might be the creator of a work which was by nature fairest and best. On this wise, using the language of probability, we may say that the world came into being—a living creature truly endowed with soul and intelligence by the providence of God.

When the father and creator saw the creature which he had made moving and living, the created image of the eternal gods, he rejoiced, and in his joy determined to make the copy still more like the original, and as this was an eternal living being, he sought to make the universe eternal, so far as might be. Now the nature of the ideal being was everlasting, but to bestow this attribute in its fullness upon a creature was impossible. Wherefore he resolved to have a moving image of eternity, and when he set in order the heaven, he made this image eternal but moving according to number, while eternity itself rests in unity, and this image we call time. For there were no days and nights and months and years before the heaven was created, but when he constructed the heaven he created them also. They are all parts of time, and the past and future are created species of time, which we unconsciously but wrongly transfer to eternal being, for we say that it 'was,' or 'is,' or 'will be,' but the truth is that 'is' alone is properly attributed to it, and that 'was' and 'will be' are only to be spoken of becoming in time, for they are motions, but that which is immovably the same forever cannot become older or younger by time, nor can it be said that it came into being in the past, or has come into being now, or will come into being in the future, nor is it subject at all to any of those states which affect moving and sensible things and of which generation is the cause. These are the forms of time, which imitates eternity and revolves according to a law of number. Moreover, when we say that what has become is become and what becomes is becoming, and that what will become is about to become and that the nonexistent is nonexistent—all these are inaccurate modes of expression. But perhaps this whole subject will be more suitably discussed on some other occasion.

Knowledge: The Allegory of the Cave
(from *The Republic*, Book VII)

And now, I said, let me show in a figure how far our nature is enlightened or unenlightened:—Behold! human beings living in an underground den, which has a mouth open towards the light and reaching all along the den; here they have been from their childhood, and have their legs and necks chained so that they cannot move, and can only see before them, being prevented by the chains from turning round their heads. Above and behind them a fire is blazing at a distance, and between the fire and the prisoners there is a raised way; and you will see, if you look, a low wall built along the way, like the screen which marionette players have in front of them, over which they show the puppets.

I see.

And do you see, I said, men passing along the wall carrying all sorts of vessels, and statues and figures of animals made of wood and stone and various materials, which appear over the wall? Some of them are talking, others silent.

You have shown me a strange image, and they are strange prisoners.

Like ourselves, I replied; and they see only their own shadows, or the shadows of one another, which the fire throws on the opposite wall of the cave?

True, he said; how could they see anything but the shadows if they were never allowed to move their heads?

And of the objects which are being carried in like manner they would only see the shadows?

Yes, he said.

And if they were able to converse with one another, would they not suppose that they were naming what was actually before them?

Very true.

And suppose further that the prison had an echo which came from the other side, would they not be sure to fancy when one of the passers-by spoke that the voice which they heard came from the passing shadow?

No question, he replied.

To them, I said, the truth would be literally nothing but the shadows of the images.

That is certain.

And now look again, and see what will naturally follow if the prisoners are released and disabused of their error. At first, when any of them is liberated and compelled suddenly to stand up and turn his neck round and walk and look towards the light, he will suffer sharp pains; the glare will distress him, and he will be unable to see the realities of which in his former state he had seen the shadows; and then conceive some one saying to him, that what he saw before was an illusion, but that now, when he is approaching nearer to being and his eye is turned towards more real existence, he has a clearer vision,—what will be his reply? And you may further imagine that his instructor is pointing to the objects as they pass and requiring him to name them,—will he not be perplexed? Will he not fancy that the shadows which he formerly saw are truer than the objects which are now shown to him?

Far truer.

And if he is compelled to look straight at the light, will he not have a pain in his eyes which will make him turn away to take refuge in the objects of vision which he can see, and which he will conceive to be in reality clearer than the things which are now being shown to him?

True, he said.

And suppose once more, that he is reluctantly dragged up a steep and rugged ascent, and held fast until he is forced into the presence of the sun himself, is he not likely to be pained and irritated? When he approaches the light his eyes will be dazzled, and he will not be able to see anything at all of what are now called realities.

Not all in a moment, he said.

He will require to grow accustomed to the sight of the upper world. And first he will see the shadows best, next the reflections of men and other objects in the water, and then the objects themselves; then he will gaze upon the light of the moon and the stars and the spangled heaven; and he will see the sky and the stars by night better than the sun or the light of the sun by day?

Certainly.

Last of all he will be able to see the sun, and not mere reflections of him in the water, but he will see him in his own proper place, and not in another; and he will contemplate him as he is.

Certainly.

He will then proceed to argue that this is he who gives the season and the years, and is the guardian of all that is in the visible world, and in a certain way the cause of all things which he and his fellows have been accustomed to behold?

Clearly, he said, he would first see the sun and then reason about him.

And when he remembered his old habitation, and the wisdom of the den and his fellow-prisoners, do you not suppose that he would felicitate himself on the change, and pity them?

Certainly, he would. . . .

This entire allegory, I said, you may now append, dear Glaucon, to the previous argument; the prison-house is the world of sight, the light of the fire is the sun, and you will not misapprehend me if you interpret the journey upwards to be the ascent of the soul into the intellectual world according to my poor belief, which, at your desire, I have expressed—whether rightly or wrongly God knows. But, whether true or false, my opinion is that in the world of knowledge the idea of good appears last of all, and is seen only with an effort; and, when seen, is also inferred to be the universal author of all things beautiful and right, parent of light and of the lord of light in this visible world, and the immediate source of reason and truth in the intellectual; and that this is the power upon which he who would act rationally either in public or private life must have his eye fixed.

Learning as Recollection

(from *Meno*)

MENO: Yes, Socrates; but what do you mean by saying that we do not learn, and that what we call learning is only a process of recollection? Can you teach me how this is?

SOCRATES: I told you, Meno, just now that you were a rogue, and now you ask whether I can teach you, when I am saying that there is no teaching, but only recollection; and thus you imagine that you will involve me in a contradiction.

MENO: Indeed, Socrates, I protest that I had no such intention. I only asked the question from habit; but if you can prove to me that what you say is true, I wish that you would.

SOCRATES: It will be no easy matter, but I will try to please you to the utmost of my power. Suppose that you call one of your numerous attendants, that I may demonstrate on him.

MENO: Certainly. Come hither, boy.

SOCRATES: He is Greek, and speaks Greek, does he not?

MENO: Yes, indeed; he was born in the house.

SOCRATES: Attend now to the questions which I ask him, and observe whether he learns of me or only remembers.

MENO: I will.

SOCRATES: Tell me, boy, do you know that a figure like this is a square?

BOY: I do.

SOCRATES: And you know that a square figure has these four lines equal?

BOY: Certainly.

SOCRATES: And these lines which I have drawn through the middle of the square are also equal?

BOY: Yes.

SOCRATES: A square may be of any size?

BOY: Certainly.

SOCRATES: And if one side of the figure be of two feet, and the other side be of two feet, how much will the whole be? Let me explain: if in one direction the space was of two feet, and in the other direction of one foot, the whole would be of two feet taken once?

BOY: Yes.

SOCRATES: But since this side is also of two feet, there are twice two feet?

BOY: There are.

SOCRATES: Then the square is of twice two feet?

BOY: Yes.

SOCRATES: And how many are twice two feet? count and tell me.

BOY: Four, Socrates.

SOCRATES: And might there not be another square twice as large as this, and having like this the lines equal?

BOY: Yes.

SOCRATES: And of how many feet will that be?

BOY: Of eight feet.

SOCRATES: And now try and tell me the length of the line which forms the side of that double square: this is two feet—what will that be?

BOY: Clearly, Socrates, it will be double.

SOCRATES: Do you observe, Meno, that I am not teaching the boy anything, but only asking him questions; and now he fancies that he knows how long a line is necessary in order to produce a figure of eight square feet; does he not?

MENO: Yes.

SOCRATES: And does he really know?

MENO: Certainly not.

SOCRATES: He only guesses that because the square is double, the line is double.

MENO: True.

SOCRATES: Observe him while he recalls the steps in regular order. (*To the boy*.) Tell me, boy, do you assert that a double space comes from a double line? Remember that I am not speaking of an oblong, but of a figure equal every way, and twice the size of this—that is to say of eight feet: and I want to know whether you still say that a double square comes from a double line?

BOY: Yes.

SOCRATES: But does not this line become doubled if we add another such line here?

BOY: Certainly.

SOCRATES: And four such lines will make a space containing eight feet?

BOY: Yes.

SOCRATES: Let us describe such a figure: Would you not say that this is the figure of eight feet?

BOY: Yes.

SOCRATES: And are there not these four divisions in the figure, each of which is equal to the figure of four feet?

BOY: True.

SOCRATES: And is not that four times four?

BOY: Certainly.

SOCRATES: And four times is not double?

BOY: No, indeed.

SOCRATES: But how much?

BOY: Four times as much.

SOCRATES: Therefore, the double line, boy, has given a space, not twice, but four times as much.

BOY: True.

SOCRATES: Four times four are sixteen—are they not?

BOY: Yes.

SOCRATES: What line would give you a space of eight feet, as this gives one of sixteen feet;—do you see?

BOY: Yes.

SOCRATES: And the space of four feet is made from this half line?

BOY: Yes.

SOCRATES: Good; and is not a space of eight feet twice the size of this, and half the size of the other?

BOY: Certainly.

SOCRATES: Such a space, then, will be made out of a line greater than this one, and less than that one?

BOY: Yes; I think so.

SOCRATES: Very good; I like to hear you say what you think. And now tell me, is not this a line of two feet and that of four?

BOY: Yes.

SOCRATES: Then the line which forms the side of eight feet ought to be more than this line of two feet, and less than the other of four feet?

BOY: It ought.

SOCRATES: Try and see if you can tell me how much it will be.

BOY: Three feet.

SOCRATES: Then if we add a half to this line of two, that will be the line of three. Here are two and there is one; and on the other side, here are two also and there is one: and that makes the figure of which you speak?

BOY: Yes.

SOCRATES: But if there are three feet this way and three feet that way, the whole space will be three times three feet?

BOY: That is evident.

SOCRATES: And how much are three times three feet?

BOY: Nine.

SOCRATES: And how much is the double of four?

BOY: Eight.

SOCRATES: Then the figure of eight is not made out of a line of three?

BOY: No.

SOCRATES: But from what line?—tell me exactly; and if you would rather not reckon, try and show me the line.

BOY: Indeed, Socrates, I do not know.

SOCRATES: Do you see, Meno, what advances he has made in his power of recollection? He did not know at first, and he does not know now, what is the side of a figure of eight feet: but then he thought that he knew, and answered confidently as if he knew, and had no difficulty; now he has a difficulty, and neither knows nor fancies that he knows.

MENO: True.

SOCRATES: Is he not better off in knowing his ignorance?

MENO: I think that he is.

SOCRATES: If we have made him doubt, and given him the 'torpedo's shock,' have we done him any harm?

MENO: I think not.

SOCRATES: We have certainly, as would seem, assisted him in some degree to the discovery of the truth: and now he will wish to remedy his ignorance, but then he would have been ready to tell all the world again and again that the double space should have a double side.

MENO: True.

SOCRATES: But do you suppose that he would ever have enquired into or learned what he fancied that he knew, though he was really ignorant of it, until he had fallen into perplexity under the idea that he did not know, and had desired to know?

MENO: I think not, Socrates.

SOCRATES: Then he was the better for the torpedo's touch?

MENO: I think so.

SOCRATES: Mark now the farther development. I shall only ask him, and not teach him, and he shall share the enquiry with me: and do you watch and see if you find me telling or explaining anything to him, instead of eliciting his opinion. Tell me, boy, is not this a square of four feet which I have drawn?

BOY: Yes.

SOCRATES: And now I add another square equal to the former one?

BOY: Yes.

SOCRATES: And a third, which is equal to either of them?

BOY: Yes.

SOCRATES: Suppose that we fill up the vacant corner?

BOY: Very good.

SOCRATES: Here, then, there are four equal spaces?

BOY: Yes.

SOCRATES: And how many times larger is this space than this other?

BOY: Four times.

SOCRATES: But it ought to have been twice only, as you will remember.

BOY: True.

SOCRATES: And does not this line, reaching from corner to corner, bisect each of these spaces?

BOY: Yes.

SOCRATES: And are there not here four equal lines which contain this space?

BOY: There are.

SOCRATES: Look and see how much this space is.

BOY: I do not understand.

SOCRATES: Has not each interior line cut off half of the four spaces?

BOY: Yes.

SOCRATES: And how many spaces are there in this section?

BOY: Four.

SOCRATES: And how many in this?

BOY: Two.

SOCRATES: And four is how many times two?

BOY: Twice.

SOCRATES: And this space is of how many feet?

BOY: Of eight feet.

SOCRATES: And from what line do you get this figure?

BOY: From this.

SOCRATES: That is, from the line which extends from corner to corner of the figure of four feet?

BOY: Yes.

SOCRATES: And that is the line which the learned call the diagonal. And if this is the proper name, then you, Meno's slave, are prepared to affirm that the double space is the square of the diagonal?

BOY: Certainly, Socrates.

SOCRATES: What do you say of him, Meno? Were not all these answers given out of his own head?

MENO: Yes, they were all his own.

SOCRATES: And yet, as we were just now saying, he did not know?

MENO: True.

SOCRATES: But still he had in him those notions of his—had he not?

MENO: Yes.

SOCRATES: Then he who does not know may still have true notions of that which he does not know?

MENO: He has.

SOCRATES: And at present these notions have just been stirred up in him, as in a dream; but if he were frequently asked the same questions, in different forms, he would know as well as any one at last?

MENO: I dare say.

SOCRATES: Without any one teaching him he will recover his knowledge for himself, if he is only asked questions?

MENO: Yes.

SOCRATES: And this spontaneous recovery of knowledge in him is recollection?

MENO: True.

SOCRATES: And this knowledge which he now has must he not either have acquired or always possessed?

MENO: Yes.

SOCRATES: But if he always possessed this knowledge he would always have known; or if he has acquired the knowledge he could not have acquired it in this life, unless he has been taught geometry: for he may be made to do the same with all geometry and every other branch of knowledge. Now, has any one ever taught him all this? You must know about him, if, as you say, he was born and bred in your house.

MENO: I am certain that no one ever did teach him.

SOCRATES: And yet he has the knowledge?

MENO: The fact, Socrates, is undeniable.

SOCRATES: But if he did not acquire the knowledge in this life, then he must have had and learned it at some other time?

MENO: Clearly he must.

SOCRATES: Which must have been the time when he was not a man?

MENO: Yes.

SOCRATES: And if there have been always true thoughts in him, both at the time when he was and was not a man, which only need to be awakened into knowledge by putting questions to him, his soul must have always possessed this knowledge, for he always either was or was not a man?

MENO: Obviously.

SOCRATES: And if the truth of all things always existed in the soul, then the soul is immortal. Wherefore be of good cheer, and try to recollect what you do not know, or rather what you do not remember.

MENO: I feel, somehow, that I like what you are saying.

SOCRATES: And I, Meno, like what I am saying. Some things I have said of which I am not altogether confident. But that we shall be better and braver and less helpless if we think that we ought to enquire, than we should have been if we indulged in the idle fancy that there was no knowing and no use in seeking to know what we do not know;—that is a theme upon which I am ready to fight, in word and deed, to the utmost of my power.

MENO: There again, Socrates, your words seem to me excellent.

Socrates' Dinner-Party Speech
(from Symposium)

(At a dinner-party given by the poet Agathon, each of the invited guests, Socrates among them, speaks to the others on the subject of love.)

And now, taking my leave of you, I will rehearse a tale of love which I heard from Diotima of Mantineia, a woman wise in this and in many other kinds of knowledge, who in the days of old, when the Athenians offered sacrifice before the coming of the plague, delayed the disease ten years. She was my instructress in the art of love, and I shall repeat to you what she said to me, beginning with the admissions made by Agathon, which are nearly if not quite the same which I made to the wise woman when she questioned me: I think that this will be the easiest way, and I shall take both parts myself as well as I can. As you, Agathon, suggested, I must speak first of the being and nature of Love, and then of his works. First I said to her in nearly the same words which he used to me, that Love was a mighty god, and likewise fair; and she proved to me as I proved to him that, by my own showing, Love was neither fair nor good. 'What do you mean, Diotima,' I said, 'is love then evil and foul?' 'Hush,' she cried; 'must that be foul which is not fair?' 'Certainly,' I said. 'And is that which is not wise, ignorant? do you not see that there is a mean between wisdom and ignorance?' 'And what may that be?' I said. 'Right opinion,' she replied; 'which, as you know, being incapable of giving a reason, is not knowledge (for how can knowledge be devoid of reason? nor again, ignorance, for neither can ignorance attain the truth), but is clearly something which is a mean between ignorance and wisdom.' 'Quite true,' I replied. 'Do not then insist,' she said, 'that what is not fair is of necessity foul, or what is not good evil; or infer that because love is not fair and good he is therefore foul and evil; for he is in a mean between them.' 'Well,' I said, 'Love is surely admitted by all to be a great god.' 'By those who know or by those who do not know?' 'By all.' 'And how, Socrates,' she said with a smile, 'can Love be acknowledged to be a great god by those who say that he is not a god at all?' 'And who are they?' I said. 'You and I are two of them,' she replied. 'How can that be?' I said. 'It is quite intelligible,' she replied; 'for you yourself would acknowledge that the gods are happy and fair—of course you would—would you dare to say that any god was not?' 'Certainly not,' I replied. 'And you mean by the happy, those who are the possessors of things good or fair?' 'Yes.' 'And you admitted that Love, because he was in want, desires those good and fair things of which he is in want?' 'Yes, I did.' 'But how can he be a god who has no portion in what is either good or fair?' 'Impossible.' 'Then you see that you also deny the divinity of Love.'

'What then is Love?' I asked: 'Is he mortal?' 'No.' 'What then?' 'As in the former instance, he is neither mortal nor immortal, but in a mean between the two.' 'What is he, Diotima?' 'He is a great spirit (δαίμων), and like all spirits he is intermediate between the divine and the mortal.' 'And what,' I said, 'is his power?' 'He interprets,' she replied, 'between gods and men, conveying and taking across to the gods the prayers and sacrifices of men, and to men the commands and replies of the gods; he is the mediator who spans the chasm which divides them, and therefore in him all is bound together, and through him the arts of the prophet and the priest, their sacrifices and mysteries and charms, and all prophecy and incantation, find their way. For God mingles not with man; but through Love all the intercourse and converse of god with man, whether awake or asleep, is carried on. The wisdom which understands this is spiritual; all other wisdom, such as that of arts and handicrafts, is mean and vulgar. Now these spirits or intermediate powers are many and diverse, and one of them is Love.' 'And who,' I said, 'was his father, and who his mother?' 'The tale,' she said, 'will take time; nevertheless I will tell you. On the birthday of Aphrodite there was a feast of the gods, at which the god Poros or Plenty, who is the son of Metis or Discretion, was one of the guests. When the feast was over, Penia or Poverty, as the manner is on such occasions, came about the doors to beg. Now Plenty, who was the worse for nectar (there was no wine in those days), went into the garden of Zeus and fell into a heavy sleep; and Poverty considering her own straitened circumstances, plotted to have a child by him, and accordingly she lay down at his side and conceived Love, who partly because he is naturally a lover of the beautiful, and because Aphrodite is herself beautiful, and also because he was born on her birthday, is her follower and attendant. And as his parentage is, so also are his fortunes. In the first place he is always poor, and anything but tender and fair, as the many imagine him; and he is rough and squalid, and has no shoes, nor a house to dwell in; on the bare earth exposed he lies under the open heaven, in the streets, or at the doors of houses, taking his rest; and like his mother he is always in distress. Like his father too, whom he also partly resembles, he is always plotting against the fair and good; he is bold, enterprising, strong, a mighty hunter, always weaving some intrigue or other, keen in the pursuit of wisdom, fertile in resources; a philosopher at all times, terrible as an enchanter, sorcerer, sophist. He is by nature neither mortal nor immortal, but alive and flourishing at one moment when he is in plenty, and dead at another moment, and again alive by reason of his father's nature. But that which is always flowing in is always flowing out, and so he is never in want and never in wealth: and, further, he is in a mean between ignorance and knowledge. The truth of the matter is this: No god is a philosopher or seeker after wisdom, for he is wise already; nor does any man who is wise seek after wisdom. Neither do the ignorant seek after wisdom. For herein is the evil of ignorance, that he who is neither good nor wise is nevertheless satisfied with himself: he has no desire for that of which he feels no want.' 'But who then, Diotima,' I said, 'are the lovers of wisdom, if they are neither the wise nor the foolish?' 'A child may answer that question,' she replied; 'they are those who are in a mean between the two; Love is one of them. For wisdom is a most beautiful thing, and Love is of the beautiful; and therefore Love is also a philosopher or lover of wisdom, and being a lover of wisdom is in a mean between the wise and the ignorant. And of this too his birth is the cause; for his father is wealthy and wise, and his mother poor and foolish. Such, my dear Socrates, is the nature of the spirit Love. The error in your conception of him was very natural, and as I imagine from what you say, has arisen out of a confusion of love and the beloved, which made you think that love was all beautiful. For the beloved is the truly beautiful, and delicate, and perfect, and blessed; but the principle of love is of another nature, and is such as I have described.'

I said: 'O thou stranger woman, thou sayest well; but, assuming Love to be such as you say, what is the use of him to men?' 'That, Socrates,' she replied, 'I will attempt to unfold: of his nature and birth I have already spoken; and you acknowledge that love is of the beautiful. But some one will say: Of the beautiful in what, Socrates and Diotima?—or rather let me put the question more clearly, and ask: When a man loves the beautiful, what does he desire?' I answered her, 'That the beautiful may be his.' 'Still,' she said, 'the answer suggests a further question: What is given by the possession of beauty?' 'To what you have asked,' I replied, 'I have no answer ready.' 'Then,' she said, 'let me put the word "good" in the place of the beautiful, and repeat the question once more: If he who loves loves the good, what is it then that he loves?' 'The possession of the good,' I said. 'And what does he gain who possesses the good?' 'Happiness,' I replied; 'there is less difficulty in answering that question.' 'Yes,' she said, 'the happy are made happy by the acquisition of good things. Nor is there any need to ask why a man desires happiness; the answer is already final.' 'You are right,' I said. 'And is this wish and this desire common to all? and do all men always desire their own good, or only some men?—what say you?' 'All men,' I replied; 'the desire is common to all.' 'Why, then,' she rejoined, 'are not all men, Socrates, said to love, but only some of them? whereas you say that all men are always loving the same things.' 'I myself wonder,' I said, 'why this is.' 'There is nothing to wonder at,' she replied; 'the reason is that one part of love is separated off and receives the name of the whole, but the other parts have other names.' 'Give an illustration,' I said. She answered me as follows: 'There is poetry, which, as you know, is complex and manifold. All creation or passage of non-being into being is poetry or making, and the processes of all art are creative; and the masters of art are all poets or makers.' 'Very true.' 'Still,' she said, 'you know that they are not called poets, but have other names; only that portion of the art which is separated off from the rest, and is concerned with music and metre, is termed poetry, and they who possess poetry in this sense of the word are called poets.' 'Very true,' I said. 'And the same holds of love. For you may say generally that all desire of good and happiness is only the great and subtle power of love; but they who are drawn towards him by any other path, whether the path of moneymaking or gymnastics or philosophy, are not called lovers—the name of the whole is appropriated to those whose affection takes one form only—they alone are said to love, or to be lovers.' 'I dare say,' I replied, 'that you are right.' 'Yes,' she added, 'and you hear people say that lovers are seeking for their other half: but I say that they are seeking neither for the half of themselves, nor for the whole, unless the half or the whole be also a good. And they will cut off their own hands and feet and cast them away, if they are evil; for they love not what is their own, unless perchance there be some one who calls what belongs to him the good, and what belongs to another the evil. For there is nothing which men love but the good. Is there anything?' 'Certainly, I should say, that there is nothing.' 'Then,' she said, 'the simple truth is, that men love the good.' 'Yes,' I said. 'To which must be added that they love the possession of the good?' 'Yes, that must be added.' 'And not only the possession, but the everlasting possession of the good?' 'That must be added too.' 'Then love,' she said, 'may be described generally as the love of the everlasting possession of the good?' 'That is most true.'

'Then if this be the nature of love, can you tell me further,' she said, 'what is the manner of the pursuit? what are they doing who show all this eagerness and heat which is called love? and what is the object which they have in view? Answer me.' 'Nay, Diotima,' I replied, 'if I had known, I should not have wondered at your wisdom, neither should I have come to learn from you about this very matter.' 'Well,' she said, 'I will teach you:—The object which they have in view is birth in beauty, whether of body or soul.' 'I do not understand you,' I said; 'the oracle requires an explanation.' 'I will make my meaning clearer,' she replied. 'I mean to say, that all men are bringing to the birth in their bodies and in their souls. There is a certain age at which human nature is desirous of procreation—procreation which must be in beauty and not in deformity; and this procreation is the union of man and woman, and is a divine thing; for conception and generation are an immortal principle in the mortal creature, and in the inharmonious they can never be. But the deformed is always inharmonious with the divine, and the beautiful harmonious. Beauty, then, is the destiny or goddess of parturition who presides at birth, and therefore, when approaching beauty, the conceiving power is propitious, and diffusive, and benign, and begets and bears fruit: at the sight of ugliness she frowns and contracts and has a sense of pain, and turns away, and shrivels up, and not without a pang refrains from conception. And this is the reason why, when the hour of conception arrives, and the teeming nature is full, there is such a flutter and ecstasy about beauty whose approach is the alleviation of the pain of travail. For love, Socrates, is not, as you imagine, the love of the beautiful only.' 'What then?' 'The love of generation of birth in beauty.' 'Yes,' I said. 'Yes, indeed,' she replied. 'But why of generation?' 'Because to the mortal creature, generation is a sort of eternity and immortality,' she replied; 'and if, as has been already admitted, love is of the everlasting possession of the good, all men will necessarily desire immortality together with good: Wherefore love is of immortality.' . . .

'Those who are pregnant in the body only, betake themselves to women and beget children—this is the character of their love; their offspring, as they hope, will preserve their memory and give them the blessedness and immortality which they desire in the future. But souls which are pregnant—for there certainly are men who are more creative in their souls than in their bodies—conceive that which is proper for the soul to conceive or contain. And what are these conceptions?—wisdom and virtue in general. And such creators are poets and all artists who are deserving of the name inventor. But the greatest and fairest sort of wisdom by far is that which is concerned with the ordering of states and families, and which is called temperance and justice. And he who in youth has the seed of these implanted in him and is himself inspired, when he comes to maturity desires to beget and generate. He wanders about seeking beauty that he may beget offspring—for in deformity he will beget nothing—and naturally embraces the beautiful rather than the deformed body; above all when he finds a fair and noble and well-nurtured soul, he embraces the two in one person, and to such an one he is full of speech about virtue and the nature and pursuits of a good man; and he tries to educate him; and at the touch of the beautiful which is ever present to his memory, even when absent, he brings forth that which he had conceived long before, and in company with him tends that which he brings forth; and they are married by a far nearer tie and have a closer friendship than those who beget mortal children, for the children who are their common offspring are fairer and more immortal. Who, when he thinks of Homer and Hesiod and other great poets, would not rather have their children than ordinary human ones? Who would not emulate them in the creation of children such as theirs, which have preserved their memory and given them everlasting glory? Or who would not have such children as Lycurgus left behind him to be the saviours, not only of Lacedaemon, but of Hellas, as one may say? There is Solon, too, who is the revered father of Athenian laws; and many others there are in many other places, both among Hellenes and barbarians, who have given to the world many noble works, and have been the parents of virtue of every kind; and many temples have been raised in their honour for the sake of children such as theirs; which were never raised in honour of any one, for the sake of his mortal children.

'These are the lesser mysteries of love, into which even you, Socrates, may enter; to the greater and more hidden ones which are the crown of these, and to which, if you pursue them in a right spirit, they will lead, I know not whether you will be able to attain. But I will do my utmost to inform you, and do you follow if you can. For he who would proceed aright in this matter should begin in youth to visit beautiful forms; and first, if he be guided by his instructor aright, to love one such form only—out of that he should create fair thoughts; and soon he will of himself perceive that the beauty of one form is akin to the beauty of another; and then if beauty of form in general is his pursuit, how foolish would he be not to recognize that the beauty in every form is one and the same! And when he perceives this he will abate his violent love of the one, which he will despise and deem a small thing, and will become a lover of all beautiful forms; in the next stage he will consider that the beauty of the mind is more honourable than the beauty of the outward form. So that if a virtuous soul have but a little comeliness, he will be content to love and tend him, and will search out and bring to the birth thoughts which may improve the young, until he is compelled to contemplate and see the beauty of institutions and laws, and to understand that the beauty of them all is of one family, and that personal beauty is a trifle; and after laws and institutions he will go on to the sciences, that he may see their beauty, being not like a servant in love with the beauty of one youth or man or institution, himself a slave mean and narrow-minded, but drawing towards and contemplating the vast sea of beauty, he will create many fair and noble thoughts and notions in boundless love of wisdom; until on that shore he grows and waxes strong, and at last the vision is revealed to him of a single science, which is the science of beauty everywhere. To this I will proceed; please to give me your very best attention:

'He who has been instructed thus far in the things of love, and who has learned to see the beautiful in due order and succession, when he comes toward the end will suddenly perceive a nature of wondrous beauty (and this, Socrates, is the final cause of all our former toils)—a nature which in the first place is everlasting, not growing and decaying, or waxing and waning; secondly, not fair in one point of view and foul in another, or at one time or in one relation or at one place fair, at another time or in another relation or at another place foul, as if fair to some and foul to others, or in the likeness of a face or hands or any other part of the bodily frame, or in any form of speech or knowledge, or existing in any other being, as for example, in an animal, or in heaven, or in earth, or in any other place; but beauty absolute, separate, simple, and everlasting, which without diminution and without increase, or any change, is imparted to the ever-growing and perishing beauties of all other things. He who from these ascending under the influence of true love, begins to perceive that beauty, is not far from the end. And the true order of going, or being led by another, to the things of love, is to begin from the beauties of earth and mount upwards for the sake of that other beauty, using these as steps only, and from one going on to two, and from two to all fair forms, and from fair forms to fair practices, and from fair practices to fair notions, until from fair notions he arrives at the notion of absolute beauty, and at last knows what the essence of beauty is. This, my dear Socrates,' said the stranger of Mantineia, 'is that life above all others which man should live, in the contemplation of beauty absolute; a beauty which if you once beheld, you would see not to be after the measure of gold, and garments, and fair boys and youths, whose presence now entrances you; and you and many a one would be content to live seeing them only and conversing with them without meat or drink, if that were possible—you only want to look at them and to be with them. But what if man had eyes to see the true beauty—the divine beauty, I mean, pure and clear and unalloyed, not clogged with the pollutions of mortality and all the colours and vanities of human life—thither looking, and holding converse with the true beauty simple and divine? Remember how in that communion only, beholding beauty with the eye of the mind, he will be enabled to bring forth, not images of beauty, but realities (for he has hold not of an image but of a reality), and bringing forth and nourishing true virtue to become the friend of God and be immortal, if mortal man may. Would that be an ignoble life?'

Such, Phaedrus—and I speak not only to you, but to all of you—were the words of Diotima; and I am persuaded of their truth. And being persuaded of them, I try to persuade others, that in the attainment of this end human nature will not easily find a helper better than love. And therefore, also, I say that every man ought to honour him as I myself honour him, and walk in his ways, and exhort others to do the same, and praise the power and spirit of love according to the measure of my ability now and ever.

The words which I have spoken, you, Phaedrus, may call an encomium of love, or anything else which you please.

Virtue and the Highest Good
(from *Laws*, Book IV)

ATHENIAN: 'Friends,' we say to them,—'God, as the old tradition declares, holding in His hand the beginning, middle, and end of all that is, travels according to His nature in a straight line towards the accomplishment of His end. Justice always accompanies Him, and is the punisher of those who fall short of the divine law. To justice, he who would be happy holds fast, and follows in her company with all humility and order; but he who is lifted up with pride, or elated by wealth or rank, or beauty, who is young and foolish, and has a soul hot with insolence, and thinks that he has no need of any guide or ruler, but is able himself to be the guide of others, he, I say, is left deserted of God; and being thus deserted, he takes to him others who are like himself, and dances about, throwing all things into confusion, and many think that he is a great man, but in a short time he pays a penalty which justice cannot but approve, and is utterly destroyed, and his family and city with him. Wherefore, seeing that human things are thus ordered, what should a wise man do or think, or not do or think'?

CLEINIAS: Every man ought to make up his mind that he will be one of the followers of God; there can be no doubt of that.

ATH: Then what life is agreeable to God, and becoming in His followers? One only, expressed once for all in the old saying that 'like agrees with like, with measure measure,' but things which have no measure agree neither with themselves nor with the things which have. Now God ought to be to us the measure of all things, and not man[1], as men commonly say (Protagoras): the words are far more true of Him. And he who would be dear in God must, as far as is possible, be like Him and such as He is. Wherefore the temperate man is the friend of God, for he is like Him; and the intemperate man is unlike Him, and different from Him, and unjust. And the same applies to other things; and this is the conclusion, which is also the noblest and truest of all sayings,— that for the good man to offer sacrifice to the Gods, and hold converse with them by means of prayers and offerings and every kind of service, is the noblest and best of all things, and also the most conducive to a happy life, and very fit and meet. But with the bad man, the opposite of this is true: for the bad man has an impure soul, whereas the good is pure; and from one who is polluted, neither a good man nor God can without impropriety receive gifts. Wherefore the unholy do only waste their much service upon the Gods, but when offered by any holy man, such service is most acceptable to them. This is the mark at which we ought to aim. But what weapons shall we use, and how shall we direct them? In the first place, we affirm that next after the Olympian Gods and the Gods of the State, honour should be given to the Gods below; they should receive everything in even numbers, and of the second choice, and ill omen, while the odd numbers, and the first choice, and the things of lucky omen, are given to the Gods above, by him who would rightly hit the mark of piety. Next to these Gods, a wise man will do service to the demons or spirits, and then to the heroes, and after them will follow the private and ancestral Gods, who are worshipped as the law prescribes in the places which are sacred to them. Next comes the honour of living parents, to whom, as is meet, we have to pay the first and greatest and oldest of all debts, considering that all which a man has belongs to those who gave him birth and brought him up, and that he must do all that he can to minister to them, first, in his property, secondly, in his person, and thirdly, in his soul, in return for the endless care and travail which they bestowed upon him of old, in the days of his infancy, and which he is now to pay back to them when they are old and in the extremity of their need. And all his life long he ought never to utter, or to have uttered, an unbecoming word to them; for of light and fleeting words the penalty is most severe; Nemesis, the messenger of justice, is appointed to watch over all such matters. When they are angry and want to satisfy their feelings in word or deed, he should give way to them; for a father who thinks that he has been wronged by his son may be reasonably expected to be very angry. At their death, the most moderate funeral is best, neither exceeding the

customary expense, nor yet falling short of the honour which has
been usually shown by the former generation to their parents. And let
a man not forget to pay the yearly tribute of respect to the dead, hon-
ouring them chiefly by omitting nothing that conduces to a perpetual
remembrance of them, and giving a reasonable portion of his fortune
to the dead. Doing this, and living after this manner, we shall receive
our reward from the Gods and those who are above us [i.e. the
demons]; and we shall spend our days for the most part in good hope.
And how a man ought to order what relates to his descendants and
his kindred and friends and fellow-citizens, and the rites of hospitality
taught by Heaven, and the intercourse which arises out of all these
duties, with a view to the embellishment and orderly regulation of his
own life—these things, I say, the laws, as we proceed with them, will
accomplish, partly persuading, and partly when natures do not yield
to the persuasion of custom, chastising them by might and right, and
will thus render our state, if the Gods co-operate with us, prosperous
and happy.

Laying the Groundwork for Justice
(from *The Republic*, Book II)

(In this portion of the dialogue Plato, through the persona of Socrates, has
Glaucon and Adeimantus deliberately make a case for injustice. The unjust man,
as in the following legend of Gyges, gets away with it, prospers in the real
world, whereas the just man is not even recognized. Plato has them draw
Socrates out so that the entire dialogue, as Socrates' response, is Plato's "writing
large" the role of justice in human affairs. The true meaning of justice is more
clearly seen through a large lens rather than a small one, through the State
rather than the individual—whence the Republic. *ABH*)

(Here Glaucon is the main speaker.) I want to hear justice praised in respect of
itself; then I shall be satisfied, and you are the person from whom I think that I am
most likely to hear this; and therefore I will praise the unjust life to the utmost of my
power, and my manner of speaking will indicate the manner in which I desire to
hear you too praising justice and censuring injustice. Will you say whether you
approve of my proposal?

Indeed I do; nor can I imagine any theme about which a man of sense would
oftener wish to converse.

I am delighted, he replied, to hear you say so, and shall begin by speaking, as
I proposed, of the nature and origin of justice.

They say that to do injustice is, by nature, good; to suffer injustice, evil; but
that the evil is greater than the good. And so when men have both done and suffered injustice and have had experience of both, not being able to avoid the one
and obtain the other, they think that they had better agree among themselves to
have neither; hence there arise laws and mutual covenants; and that which is

ordained by law is termed by them lawful and just. This they affirm to be the origin and nature of justice;—it is a mean or compromise, between the best of all, which is to do injustice and not be punished, and the worst of all, which is to suffer injustice without the power of retaliation; and justice, being at a middle point between the two, is tolerated not as a good, but as the lesser evil, and honoured by reason of the inability of men to do injustice. For no man who is worthy to be called a man would ever submit to such an agreement if he were able to resist; he would be mad if he did. Such is the received account, Socrates, of the nature and origin of justice.

Now that those who practise justice do so involuntarily and because they have not the power to be unjust will best appear if we imagine something of this kind: having given both to the just and the unjust power to do what they will, let us watch and see whither desire will lead them; then we shall discover in the very act the just and unjust man to be proceeding along the same road, following their interest, which all natures deem to be their good, and are only diverted into the path of justice by the force of law. The liberty which we are supposing may be most completely given to them in the form of such a power as is said to have been possessed by Gyges the ancestor of Croesus the Lydian. According to the tradition, Gyges was a shepherd in the service of the king of Lydia; there was a great storm, and an earthquake made an opening in the earth at the place where he was feeding his flock. Amazed at the sight, he descended into the opening, where, among other marvels, he beheld a hollow brazen horse, having doors, at which he stooping and looking in saw a dead body of stature, as appeared to him, more than human, and having nothing on but a gold ring; this he took from the finger of the dead and reascended. Now the shepherds met together, according to custom, that they might send their monthly report about the flocks to the king; into their assembly he came having the ring on his finger, and as he was sitting among them he chanced to turn the collet of the ring inside his hand, when instantly he became invisible to the rest of the company and they began to speak of him as if he were no longer present. He was astonished at this, and again touching the ring he turned the collet outwards and reappeared; he made several trials of the ring, and always with the same result—when he turned the collet inwards he became invisible, when outwards he reappeared. Whereupon he contrived to be chosen one of the messengers who were sent to the court; where as soon as he arrived he seduced the queen, and with her help conspired against the king and slew him, and took the kingdom. Suppose now that there were two such magic rings, and the just put on one of them and the unjust the other; no man can be imagined to be of such an iron nature that he would stand fast in justice. No man would keep his hands off what was not his own when he could safely take what he liked out of the market, or go into houses and lie with any one at his pleasure, or kill or release from prison whom he would, and in all respects be like a god among men. Then the actions of the just would be as the actions of the unjust; they would both come at last to the same point. And this we may truly affirm to be a great proof that a man is just, not willingly or because he thinks that justice is any good to him individually, but of necessity, for wherever any one thinks that he can safely be unjust, there he is unjust. For all men believe in their hearts that injustice is far more profitable to the individual than justice, and he who argues as I have been supposing, will say that they are right. If you could imagine any one obtaining this power of becoming invisible, and never doing any wrong or touching what was another's, he would be thought by the lookers-on to be a most wretched idiot, although they would praise him to one another's faces, and keep up appearances with one another from a fear that they too might suffer injustice. Enough of this.

Now, if we are to form a real judgment of the life of the just and unjust, we must isolate them; there is no other way; and how is the isolation to be effected? I answer: Let the unjust man be entirely unjust, and the just man entirely just; nothing is to be taken away from either of them, and both are to be perfectly furnished for the work of their respective lives. First, let the unjust be like other distinguished masters of craft; like the skilful pilot or physician, who knows intuitively his own powers and keeps within their limits, and who, if he fails at any point, is able to recover himself. So let the unjust make his unjust attempts in the right way, and lie hidden if he means to be great in his injustice (he who is found out is nobody): for the highest reach of injustice is, to be deemed just when you are not. Therefore I say that in the perfectly unjust man we must assume the most perfect injustice; there is to be no deduction, but we must allow him, while doing the most unjust acts, to have acquired the greatest reputation for justice. If he have taken a false step he must be able to recover himself; he must be one who can speak with effect, if any of his deeds come to light, and who can force his way where force is required by his courage and strength, and command of money and friends. And at his side let us place the just man in his nobleness and simplicity, wishing, as Aeschylus says, to be and not to seem good. There must be no seeming, for if he seem to be just he will be honoured and rewarded, and then we shall not know whether he is just for the sake of justice or for the sake of honours and rewards; therefore, let him be clothed in justice only, and have no other covering; and he must be imagined in a state of life the opposite of the former. Let him be the best of men, and let him be thought the worst; then he will have been put to the proof; and we shall see whether he will be affected by the fear of infamy and its consequences. And let him continue thus to the hour of death; being just and seeming to be unjust. When both have reached the uttermost extreme, the one of justice and the other of injustice, let judgment be given which of them is the happier of the two.

Heavens! my dear Glaucon, I said, how energetically you polish them up for the decision, first one and then the other, as if they were two statues.

I do my best, he said. And now that we know what they are like there is no difficulty in tracing out the sort of life which awaits either of them. This I will proceed to describe; but as you may think the description a little too coarse, I ask you to suppose, Socrates, that the words which follow are not mine.—Let me put them into the mouths of the eulogists of injustice: They will tell you that the just man who is thought unjust will be scourged, racked, bound—will have his eyes burnt out; and, at last, after suffering every kind of evil, he will be impaled: Then he will understand that he ought to seem only, and not to be, just; the words of Aeschylus may be more truly spoken of the unjust than of the just. For the unjust is pursuing a reality; he does not live with a view to appearances—he wants to be really unjust and not to seem only:—

"His mind has a soil deep and fertile,
Out of which spring his prudent counsels."

In the first place, he is thought just, and therefore bears rule in the city; he can marry whom he will, and give in marriage to whom he will; also he can trade and deal where he likes, and always to his own advantage, because he has no misgivings about injustice; and at every contest, whether in public or private, he gets the better of his antagonists, and gains at their expense, and is rich, and out of his gains he can benefit his friends, and harm his enemies; moreover, he can offer sacrifices, and dedicate gifts to the gods abundantly and magnificently, and can honour the gods or any man whom he wants to honour in a far better style than the just, and therefore he is likely to be dearer than they are to the gods. And thus, Socrates, gods and men are said to unite in making the life of the unjust better than the life of the just.

(Here Adeimantus is the main speaker.) On what principle, then, shall we any longer choose justice rather than the worst injustice? when, if we only unite the latter with a deceitful regard to appearances, we shall fare to our mind both with gods and men, in life and after death, as the most numerous and the highest authorities tell us. Knowing all this, Socrates, how can a man who has any superiority of mind or person or rank or wealth, be willing to honour justice; or indeed to refrain from laughing when he hears justice praised? And even if there should be some one who is able to disprove the truth of my words, and who is satisfied that justice is best, still he is not angry with the unjust, but is very ready to forgive them, because he also knows that men are not just of their own free will; unless, peradventure, there be some one whom the divinity within him may have inspired with a hatred of injustice, or who has attained knowledge of the truth—but no other man. He only blames injustice who, owing to cowardice or age or some weakness, has not the power of being unjust. And this is proved by the fact that when he obtains the power, he immediately becomes unjust as far as he can be.

The cause of all this, Socrates, was indicated by us at the beginning of the argument, when my brother and I told you how astonished we were to find that of all the professing panegyrists of justice—beginning with the ancient heroes of whom any memorial has been preserved to us, and ending with the men of our own time—no one has ever blamed injustice or praised justice except with a view to the glories, honours, and benefits which flow from them. No one has ever adequately described either in verse or prose the true essential nature of either of them abiding in the soul, and invisible to any human or divine eye; or shown that of all the things of a man's soul which he has within him, justice is the greatest good, and injustice the greatest evil. Had this been the universal strain, had you sought to persuade us of this from our youth upwards, we should not have been on the watch to keep one another from doing wrong, but every one would have been his own watchman, because afraid, if he did wrong, of harbouring in himself the greatest of evils. I dare say that Thrasymachus and others would seriously hold the language which I have been merely repeating, and words even stronger than these about justice and injustice, grossly, as I conceive, perverting their true nature. But I speak in this vehement manner, as I must frankly confess to you, because I want to hear from you the opposite side; and I would ask you to show not only the superiority which justice has over injustice, but what effect they have on the possessor of them which makes the one to be a good and the other an evil to him. And please, as Glaucon requested of you, to exclude reputations; for unless you take away from each of them his true reputation and add on the false, we shall say that you do not praise justice, but the appearance of it; we shall think that you are only exhorting us to keep injustice dark, and that you really agree with Thrasymachus in thinking that justice is another's good and the interest of the stronger, and that injustice is a man's own profit and interest, though injurious to the weaker. Now as you have admitted that justice is one of that highest class of goods which are desired indeed for their results, but in a far greater degree for their own sakes—like sight or hearing or knowledge or health, or any other real and natural and not merely conventional good—I would ask you in your praise of justice to regard one point only: I mean the essential good and evil which justice and injustice work in the possessors of them. Let others praise justice and censure injustice, magnifying the rewards and honours of the one and abusing the other; that is a manner of arguing which, coming from them, I am ready to tolerate, but from you who have spent your whole life in the consideration of this question, unless I hear the contrary from your own lips, I expect something better. And therefore, I say, not only prove to us that justice is better than injustice, but show what they either of them do to the possessor of them, which makes the one to be a good and the other an evil, whether seen or unseen by gods and men.

I had always admired the genius of Glaucon and Adeimantus, but on hearing these words I was quite delighted, and said: Sons of an illustrious father, that was not a bad beginning of the Elegiac verses which the admirer of Glaucon made in honour of you after you had distinguished yourselves at the battle of Megara:—

"Sons of Ariston," he sang, "divine offspring of an illustrious hero."

The epithet is very appropriate, for there is something truly divine in being able to argue as you have done for the superiority of injustice, and remaining unconvinced by your own arguments. And I do believe that you are not convinced—this I infer from your general character, for had I judged only from your speeches I should have mistrusted you. But now, the greater my confidence in you, the greater is my difficulty in knowing what to say. For I am in a strait between two; on the one hand I feel that I am unequal to the task; and my inability is brought home to me by the fact that you were not satisfied with the answer which I made to Thrasymachus, proving, as I thought, the superiority which justice has over injustice. And yet I cannot refuse to help, while breath and speech remain to me; I am afraid that there would be an impiety in being present when justice is evil spoken of and not lifting up a hand in her defence. And therefore I had best give such help as I can.

Glaucon and the rest entreated me by all means not to let the question drop, but to proceed in the investigation. They wanted to arrive at the truth, first, about the nature of justice and injustice, and secondly, about their relative advantages. I told them, what I really thought, that the enquiry would be of a serious nature, and would require very good eyes. Seeing then, I said, that we are no great wits, I think that we had better adopt a method which I may illustrate thus; suppose that a short-sighted person had been asked by some one to read small letters from a distance; and it occurred to some one else that they might be found in another place which was larger and in which the letters were larger—if they were the same and he could read the larger letters first, and then proceed to the lesser—this would have been thought a rare piece of good fortune.

Very true, said Adeimantus; but how does the illustration apply to our enquiry?

I will tell you, I replied; justice, which is the subject of our enquiry, is, as you know, sometimes spoken of as the virtue of an individual, and sometimes, as the virtue of a State.

True, he replied.

And is not a State larger than an individual?

It is.

Then in the larger the quantity of justice is likely to be larger and more easily discernible. I propose therefore that we enquire into the nature of justice and injustice, first as they appear in the State, and secondly in the individual, proceeding from the greater to the lesser and comparing them.

That, he said, is an excellent proposal.

And if we imagine the State in process of creation, we shall see the justice and injustice of the State in process of creation also.

I dare say.

When the State is completed there may be a hope that the object of our search will be more easily discovered.

Yes, far more easily.

But ought we to attempt to construct one? I said; for to do so, as I am inclined to think, will be a very serious task. Reflect therefore.

I have reflected, said Adeimantus, and am anxious that you should proceed.

The Philosopher King
(from *Republic*, Book V)

Next, it seems, we must try to discover and point out what it is that is now badly managed in our cities, and that prevents them from being so governed, and what is the smallest change that would bring a state to this manner of government, preferably a change in one thing, if not, then in two, and, failing that, the fewest possible in number and the slightest in potency.

By all means, he said.

There is one change, then, said I, which I think that we can show would bring about the desired transformation. It is not a slight or an easy thing but it is possible.

What is that? he said.

I am on the very verge, said I, of what we likened to the greatest wave of paradox. But say it I will, even if, to keep the figure, it is likely to wash us away on billows of laughter and scorn. Listen.

I am all attention, he said.

Unless, said I, either philosophers become kings in our states or those whom we now call our kings and rulers take to the pursuit of philosophy seriously and adequately, and there is a conjunction of these two things, political power and philosophical intelligence, while the motley horde of the natures who at present pursue either apart from the other are compulsorily excluded, there can be no cessation of troubles, dear Glaucon, for our states, nor, I fancy, for the human race either. Nor, until this happens, will this constitution which we have been expounding in theory ever be put into practice within the limits of possibility and see the light of the sun. But this is the thing that has made me so long shrink from speaking out, because I saw that it would be a very paradoxical saying. For it is not easy to see that there is no other way of happiness either for private or public life.

REVIEW QUESTIONS

1. What are Plato's reasons for holding that a world of ideas, separate from this world, exists?
2. Explain the difference between truth and illusion in Plato's epistemology.
3. Why do both Plato and Socrates describe learning as a process of recollection?
4. Explain what is meant by Platonic dualism. How does this concept apply to human nature?
5. What is the meaning of creation for Plato? Of participation?
6. What is the role of civil society for Plato?

SUGGESTIONS FOR FURTHER READING

Grube, I. M. *Plato's Thought*, 2nd ed. Indianapolis, Hackett, 1980.

The Collected Dialogues of Plato. Hamilton, E. and Cairns, H., ed. Princeton, Princeton University Press, 1961.

Kraut, R., ed. *Cambridge Companion to Plato*. New York, Cambridge University Press, 1992.

Hare, R. M. *Plato*. New York, Oxford University Press, 1983.

Taylor, A. E. *Plato, The Man and His Work*. New York, Methuen, 1960.

4

Aristotle
(384–322 B.C.)

Aristotle was born in Stagira, a town that lay between Thrace and Macedonia, in 384 B.C. He was the son of a physician, and because his father was a friend of the king of Macedonia, he lived at the royal court and shared its cultural life and social status. He acquired an interest in the art of medicine and dissection from his father, who no doubt laid down a firm basis for his son's scientific bent and lifelong sense of careful observation. Orphaned as a boy, and now growing into young manhood, Aristotle went to Athens at the age of seventeen to enroll at the Academy, where his guardians knew he would get the best education available in Greece.

Plato and Aristotle

Though we have no detailed reports on the relationship between teacher and student, we know Aristotle respected and admired Plato, with whom he lived for twenty years, until the time of Plato's death. Aristotle's experience at the Academy was an exercise in friendship as well as in learning, for Plato was, to him, not only a revered philosopher but also a friend. In his writings, Aristotle's regard for Plato is shown at every turn, even while he is criticizing his master's views. In a famous passage, in which he feels obliged to reject the doctrine of Ideas, he acknowledges that it was introduced by friends of his, yet "it would perhaps be thought to be better, indeed to be our duty, for the sake of maintaining the truth even to destroy what touches us closely, especially as we are philosophers or lovers of wisdom; for, while both are dear, piety requires us to honour truth above our friends."

After Plato's death, Aristotle left Athens for Assos, a town on the northern coast of present-day Turkey, probably having been invited there by Hermias, a former fellow student at the Academy; he had risen from the status of slave to king and was still committed to the ideal of politician-philosopher. From the island of Lesbos, where he had gone after Assos, Aristotle was requested by King Philip of Macedon to become the tutor of his thirteen-year-old son, Alexander, later known as Alexander the Great. Aristotle stayed at the court for eight years, until Alexander became the ruler of Macedonia after the assassination of his father in 336. During these years, Aristotle's interest in biology was heightened; he spent endless hours in the collection and study of marine life while at the seacoast and of the flora and fauna of Macedonia.

He returned to Athens in 335–34 to begin the most productive period of his life. He established a school, just to the northeast of Athens, at a place with buildings and gardens called the *Lyceum,* after the god Apollo, one of whose titles was Lyceus. The spot was mentioned by Plato as the favorite haunt of Socrates. At the Lyceum the pattern of the Academy was duplicated—a close community, friendly, intent on learning, given to much dialogu particularly while strolling along the garden path, the *peripatos,* whence the followers of Aristotle were called *Peripatetics.* Aristotle amassed an invaluable collection of manuscripts for the school's library, which became the exemplar for subsequent great libraries of the West, especially that of Alexandria. Many of Aristotle's writings, done before the founding of Lyceum, have been lost, but most of his extant writings were completed there. His numerous writings include treatises on logic (*Categories, Prior and Posterior Analytics*), physical treatises (*Physics, On the Heavens, On the Soul*), the *Metaphysics,* moral and political treatises (*Nicomachean Ethics, Politics*), and the *Rhetoric* and *Poetics.*

When Alexander the Great died in 323, a strong anti-Macedonian feeling arose in Athens, and because he was known to have had long-standing Macedonian ties, Aristotle, fearing a false charge of "impiety," left Athens so that, in his words, the Athenians would not "sin twice against philosophy." He went to Chalcis, his mother's native city, where he died in 322.

In his thought, Aristotle was agile, well balanced, and unprejudiced; his first approach was to let things speak for themselves. We saw earlier the danger of labeling any philosopher as a rationalist or an empiricist, but as a general rule, for the former, the process of knowing moves from the mind to things, as though, by examining the mind, we know what things are; for the latter, the process of knowing moves from things to the mind; the mind, that is, knows only what things tell it. Philosophers often emphasize one direction over the other. In this sense, Plato favored the rationalist, spiritualist, mathematical, universal side, whereas Aristotle favored the empirical, experiential, individual side. His scientific bent would not allow him to depart from the evidence: we learn what human beings are by observing what they do; we learn rhetoric by hearing persuasive people speak; we learn the habits of animals by watching them in action; we learn the rules of correct thinking by studying ourselves thinking correctly.

Primer of Logic

Perhaps as good an example as any of Aristotle's systematic, thorough work is his treatises on logic, known collectively as the *Organon,* which are traditionally grouped together and presented first in the body of his works. Granted that there are many truths we know directly, such as things we know by experience (e.g., the stove is hot, I want to sit down) or by intuition (e.g., the whole is greater than any of its parts; whatever is wrong ought not be done), there are many other truths we know indirectly, among which are those we arrive at by argumentation, that is, by *reasoning,* the process whereby we go from what we know to what we do not know. To reason correctly is a prime requisite for a thinker, and the study of correct thinking, generally called *logic* today but called *analytic* by Aristotle, is an indispensable tool for making headway in any branch of knowledge. The purpose of logic is to investigate the *form* reasoning takes when we pass from "certain things being stated" (called *premises*) to "something other than what is stated" (called *conclusion*), which follows of necessity. Logic, then, deals with *words* and *propositions* with which reasoning, in the form of a *syllogism,* is expressed; to these factors Aristotle gives detailed consideration.

Basically, a word (or term) is a symbol: "Spoken words are the symbols of mental experience and written words are the symbols of spoken words." There are two major divisions of terms, among many made by Aristotle: a division into univocal and equivocal, and into universal and particular. A term is *univocal* if it is used in several sentences with the same meaning. In the sentences "Man is an animal" and "An ox is an animal," the word *animal* is used with the same meaning. In the sentences "The riverside is a bank" and "The savings institution is a bank," the word *bank* is used in different senses and is therefore *equivocal*. A term is *universal* when it refers to all the members of a class, as in "all men" or, negatively, "no man." But a term is *particular* when it does not refer to all members of a class, as in "some men," which indicates its less than universal usage. It should be clear that the precise meaning of the term comes from the way it is actually used in a sentence.

Terms are used in propositions, which are sentences affirming or denying one thing of another. Propositions, like terms, are universal or particular: universal if the predicate refers to all the members of a class, as in "All men are wise"; particular if it refers only to some, as in "Some men are wise." They are affirmative if they affirm the predicate of the subject, negative if they deny it. Two propositions having the same subject and predicate can differ from each other in a number of ways; the difference is called *opposition*. The principal kind of opposition is called *contradiction,* wherein the difference is so strong that the two propositions cannot be both true and false at the same time: "All men are wise" and "Some men are not wise" cannot both be true or false together.

The syllogism is the heart of Aristotelian logic, and "it belongs to the philosopher, i.e., to him who is studying the nature of all substance, to inquire also into the principles of syllogism." The syllogism helps the philosopher extend his knowledge because it makes explicit what was implicit in the premises. If premises are given as true, then the conclusion necessarily follows as true; for example, if "All Athenians are Greek" and "Some philosophers are Athenians," then it is necessarily true that "Some philosophers are Greek." There are three terms in the premises, which yield only two in the conclusion, because one term (Athenians) is in the "middle" term against which the others are measured and is excluded in the conclusion. The kind of reasoning expressed in the syllogism is known as *deductive* reasoning, inasmuch as it moves from the general to the particular (or less general).

There is a second kind of reasoning, called *inductive,* to which Aristotle did not give the same thorough examination as he gave to deductive reasoning; broadly speaking, induction moves from the particular to the universal: "Induction is a passage from individuals to universals." How this movement takes place depends, it seems, upon the context in which the particular-universal relationship arises: a different configuration, or status, of particulars gives rise to a different kind of particular-universal relationship. For example, you can simply enumerate every case and then collect them in a universal statement by saying "All." Or, on seeing one three-sided plane figure called a *triangle,* you can state that "All triangles are three-sided" because you have grasped the nature of the triangle and expressed it in its definition. When Aristotle avers that there is no induction without sense perception, he perhaps comes close to the modern notion that induction is the approach of the natural sciences in that generalizations are based on positive observation, because somehow the universal "is elicited from the several groups of singulars." If you drop zinc into acid, a chemical reaction takes place, and this happens a second and a third time, you have no doubt that it will happen again and always; that is, you have scientific certitude.

Aristotle's works on logic represent a tremendous effort to analyze how the human mind proceeds in doing logical thinking; it is all the more astonishing when we realize that he had no predecessors in logic. Indeed, he was aware of breaking new ground; whereas in other areas of knowledge one builds on previous contributions, in this case there were none: "Of this inquiry, on the other hand, it was not the case that part of the work had been thoroughly done before, while part had not. Nothing existed at all." Once the work was begun, however, and the foundation laid, Aristotle would have been the first to applaud the complements to his logic provided by the later Greek Stoics, by the logicians of the Middle Ages, and by modern logicians using symbolic logic. The very last sentence of his logical treatises captures both his confidence and his humility: if after inspecting the work and finding it satisfactory, he says, "there must remain for all of you, or for our students, the task of extending us your pardon for the shortcomings of the inquiry, and for the discoveries thereof your warm thanks."

Metaphysics and Epistemology: Co-dependent

If logic is the instrument for philosophical thinking, what the philosopher thinks about is the main concern and, for Aristotle, at the very center of his thought was the question of *being.* The word *metaphysics,* traditionally used to designate the philosophy of being, was not supplied by Aristotle but probably by his later disciples, although, according to a widely held story, despite its unreliability, it was supplied by an ancient cataloguer, thought to be Andronicus of Rhodes in the first century B.C., who, in assembling the works of Aristotle, placed an untitled work after the *Physics* and simply called it the "Work After the Physics" (in Greek, *meta-ta-physica*), or *Metaphysics*. In any case, metaphysics is the science which goes "beyond physics" because it goes beyond what is given in sense experience; it reaches to what is highest, separated from matter, divine, whence Aristotle is prompted to call this kind of inquiry "wisdom," or "first philosophy," or even "theology." Aristotle further defines metaphysics as the study that "investigates being as being and the attributes which belong to this in virtue of its own nature." The object of metaphysics, then, is *being as being* or *being as such*. These phrases seem rather awkward at first until we realize that we actually use similar ones, as in the "President as President" when we want to strip away every other consideration to get to the meaning of "President" itself. So, with *being as being* or *being as such* Aristotle is bringing attention to the fact that among all the characteristics of a thing, there is one without which none of the others would be possible: its existence. It would be a strange commentary indeed if all the other characteristics of a thing were inquired into, but not this one.

Metaphysics then raises questions such as these: Why do things exist, rather than not? What is there about the nature of being that allows it to change? Are things caused? What does causality mean? Why are there many things? Or are they really one? Do things have to be? If so, why? Why are some things independent, others not? Is there a being so necessary that without it nothing else would be? Questions like these are the staple of traditional metaphysics, and they are so basic that they form the philosopher's primary orientation, often leading to an entirely new worldview, as in the case of Spinoza, Hegel, Bergson, and Whitehead. There is a strong human need for unity, a natural tendency to look for patterns drawing things together. The scientist looks for laws governing discrete phe-nomena. The economist searches for the causes controlling the ebb and flow of economic well-being. The conductor tries to orchestrate disparate sounds into harmony. The reasonable person wants his actions to express a coherent life. The metaphysician, too, faced with the dizzying plurality of things in reality, is eager to find out why we call them by a common name, *being*.

The analysis of being seems doomed to frustration because it involves, at the very outset, the investigation of truth and the difficulties attached thereto; in Aristotle's words: "The investigation of the truth is in one way hard, in another easy. An indication of this is found in the fact that no one is able to attain the truth adequately, while, on the other hand, we do not collectively fail. . . . Therefore, since the truth seems to be like the proverbial door, which no one can fail to hit, in this respect it must be easy, but the fact that we can have a whole truth and not the particular part we aim at shows the difficulty of it."

At stake here is the fundamental question, what does our knowledge refer to, to be called *truth?* There is no doubt that, for Aristotle, truth is the name we give to the relationship between our intellect and what the intellect considers, between knowing and what is known, between knowledge and reality. In Aristotelian terms, we do not know a truth unless we know its cause; and what a thing *is,* its very *being,* is the cause of our knowing it, that is, the cause of truth: "as each thing is in respect of being, so it is in respect of truth." This statement underscores Aristotle's doctrine that whatever is, is knowable, and therefore "the soul is in a way all things"—not that the soul knows everything, but that the soul, in knowing "being," knows "Being."

Immediately upon our knowing that a being is we also know that it cannot not be. What Aristotle said in logic, that contradictory propositions cannot both be true and cannot both be false, is said here with regard to being itself: there is no intermediary, no middle ground, between being and non-being; is and is not, being and non-being, be-ing and not be-ing are mutually exclusive; in this respect, Aristotle certainly agrees with Parmenides. When Aristotle writes, "To say of what is that it is not, or of what is not that it is, is false," he is stating what, for him, is the most basic truth of metaphysics, for without it no other truth would be possible, no judgment would stand because affirmation and negation would have the same meaning. In later centuries this principle would be referred to as the *principle of contradiction,* or better, the *principle of noncontradiction.*

The Disclosing Power of Change: . . . Its Nature

In early Greek philosophy, we should recall, Parmenides was so overwhelmed by the nature of being (permanence, stability) that anything hinting at nonbeing was under suspicion. Heraclitus, on the other hand, saw a universe on the move and tried to avoid any reading of reality that would make it static; in that sense, being was under suspicion. These two positions represent historical extremes in reaction to a phenomenon as immediate to us as it was to them, the *phenomenon of change.*

After Plato's effort to resolve reality into the changing and the changeless, Aristotle took his turn in facing the problem of change. He never thought that change was something to get around, as though it were unreal or stood in the way of knowing reality. Rather, it was the high road for getting to the heart of things. Every change, however slight, reveals some facet of the way a thing *is*, for a thing must *be* such as to allow the change to take place. In the broadest terms, a thing ready to undergo a change is not yet what it will become: The chunk of marble, ready to become a statue, is still a chunk; the boy, ready to become a man, is still a boy; the arrow, ready to hit the target, is still in the bow; the unknowing intellect, ready to know, is still unknowing. What the thing becomes, it is not now; it would be a contradiction to state that a thing is what it will become, for then it would both be and not be at the same time. The marble cannot be both a chunk and a statue at the same time; nor the boy, both a boy, and a man; nor the arrow both in the target and in the bow; nor the intellect both unknowing and knowing.

. . . Act and Potency

Yet no change would occur *in the thing* unless the thing was of such a nature as to permit it; in other words, there must be some factors or principles within the thing to allow for the change. Although the principles involved vary according to the kind of change involved, in general they can be referred to as the *principle of actuality* and the *principle of potentiality,* or the *actual principle* and the *potential principle,* or simply, *act* and *potency.* They are the counterparts of each other in such a way that act imparts to potency all the concrete determinations found in a given being; act "perfects" potency. As applied to physical things, Aristotle calls these principles *form* (act) and *matter* (potency), whence his teaching on this subject is called the *hylomorphic* doctrine, from the Greek words *hyle* (matter) and *morphe* (form). Matter, with no innate determination, has its actuality in a being precisely because it is determined by form, as the actualizing principle, to be this individual: "by matter I mean that which, not being a 'this' actually, is potentially a 'this.'"

. . . *Substance and Accidents*

Another aspect of being whose existence is confirmed in the phenomenon of change is that of *substance.* Substance is the factor that continues to exist in a changing thing while other factors like shape, color, movement, and health cease to exist. It has therefore a permanence, a relatively independent existence, and a primary claim on the meaning of being. This claim is another fundamental concept in the history of philosophy. For Plato, as an example, the changing nature of this world required the unchanging nature of the world of ideas as the true substance of the real. St. Thomas saw in substance the primary reality that, if destroyed, would destroy all reality as well. The notion of independence of substance, renewed in modern times by Descartes, was brought to its apex by Spinoza, for whom substance is that which *is* in itself and *conceived* through itself, and is therefore applicable only to all of reality taken as a whole. In later times, substance suffered a setback in the attack on metaphysics, first advanced by Locke and Berkeley, and then propounded by Hume, who set the pace for the empirical tradition, in which substance is either passed over or denied entirely as outside our experience.

But for Aristotle, substance is knowable in and through *accidents,* or *qualities,* such as shape, color, movement, and health, which do not exist on their own but *in* that which is shaped, colored, moving, healthy—namely, substance. The word *substance* has had a varied career, but as used here it is of later Latin coinage and means literally "that which stands under," that is, under the changing factors, under the accidents. So, relative to substance, accidents are knowable inasmuch as they exist in something else; and substance, relative to accidents, is knowable inasmuch as it exists on its own and is therefore the prime reason for designating a thing as an individual entity. As Aristotle writes: " 'white' is accidental to man, because though he is white, whiteness is not his essence. But if *all* statements are accidental, there will be nothing primary about which they are made. . . . There must be something which denotes substance." It is this fact that separates the ingrained empiricist from the metaphysician: the empiricist holds that shape, color, movement, and health are knowable in themselves and do not lead to any further conclusion; the metaphysician, beginning with these qualities, insists that they are knowable indeed, but *as existing in something else*, called substance.

. . . *Soul and Body*

Substance of a special kind exists in *living* things, in which the principles of form and matter are called *soul* and *body*. The living thing is an organism, that is, a body organized to live, but its life does not come about because it is a body—there are many things made of matter that are not alive. Since, however, the body is living, its life must come about because of another principle, called *soul,* which enlivens it: "the soul is the . . . actuality of a natural body having life potentially within it. The body so described is a body which is organized." Whence Aristotle refers to living things as *besouled,* or *animate (anima,* Latin for soul).

In applying this principle to man, we can see not only how original was Aristotle's view on the nature of man but also how radically different it was from Plato's and from the tradition behind him. For Aristotle, soul and body are not separate entities in man, but correlative constituents of *one* being; man is neither body alone nor soul alone, but a single substance composed of both. The unity of man is a matter of experience and common sense, which is "why we can wholly dismiss as unnecessary the question of whether the soul and body are one." Aristotle's view, that man is a unitary being composed of body and soul, and Plato's view, that man is spirit only, embody the profound difference between two opposing traditions on the definition of man for centuries to come. This difference generates far-reaching consequences in the way we understand the deliverances of the senses, our inward experience, knowledge, the approach we take toward mental health or psychosomatic medicine, and our attitude toward pain, suffering, and the social ills of this world. The problem of body and soul is another classical problem in the history of philosophy.

. . . *Causality*

If we see a marble statue, in our mind is the vision of the chunk from which it came, and we ask who made it. Or if we see the stones at Stonehenge, large and mysteriously arranged, we ask how this arrangement came about. Or, in this age of environmental concerns, we ask what causes acid rain. These questions arise naturally because they seem to follow the natural expectation that something traditionally called *causality* is at work.

It takes a great effort to dampen that expectation, but it has been done. Parmenides, we will recall, led the way for those who would not countenance the reality of change because it would have meant a coming-to-be from not-being, which was, they maintained, impossible. The problem here, as Aristotle avers, is very difficult, but it is not solved by either wishing it away or giving it up. As he sees it, it was by failing to make the proper qualification that "these thinkers gave the matter up . . . thus doing away with all becoming." Aristotle himself solves the problem by going about it another way; he does not begin a priori, but from the *experienced* fact that change *does* occur. He does not say that because change is unthinkable, it does not take place; rather, change does take place, therefore it can. In terms we have previously discussed, whatever changes had the potentiality (potency) within itself to become what it was not; therefore, potency must be a constitutive factor within it. Aristotle does not disagree in absolute terms with those who deny change but rather in qualified terms: "We ourselves are in agreement with them in holding that nothing can be said without qualification to come from what is not. But nevertheless we maintain that anything may 'come to be from what is not'—that is, in a qualified sense."

It follows that whatever comes-to-be cannot be now and therefore must be brought about: It is the "bluing" of the red litmus paper that, as the coming-to-be in question, must be brought about. It is brought about by that which is called a cause. It's a clear contradiction if that which comes-to-be were the cause of its own coming-to-be, for then it would have to be and not be at the same time; that is, it would have to be in order to act, and not to be in order to be acted upon. Put another way, a cause is, as Aristotle states, that "from which the change or the resting from change first begins." So the connection between cause and effect is inherent in the very nature of being; it is a necessary connection, for Aristotle, at the center of metaphysics. Centuries later, David Hume would prove right in holding that the undoing of the principle of causality entails the undoing of metaphysics, which was precisely the consequence of his insistence on a chronological or temporal conjunction between cause and effect rather than a necessary conjunction between them. Aristotle's view, in contrast to Hume's, is that chronology is simply a calendar and of itself supplies no explanation for the change taking place. However, once we establish the causal order, the chronology makes sense.

Aristotle calls for four different kinds of causes, inasmuch as there are four different kinds of connection between cause and effect: material, formal, efficient and final. The basic meanings can be outlined as follows. The *material* cause is the "stuff" or matter, from which a physical thing is brought into being, as the marble from which the statue comes-to-be, or the matter that comes-to-be alive, as the body of an animal. Neither the statue nor the animal could have become one without the contribution made by matter. The *formal* cause is the factor within a thing that imparts, or determines, the "whatness" under consideration, such as the actual shape of the statue, or the soul that enlivens the body of the animal. The *efficient* (or agent, or active) cause is that which, by its activity, brings about a change, as the sculptor who works the marble, or the soul which makes the body actually living. The *final* cause is the purpose, or end, "for the sake of which a thing is." It's easiest to think of final cause as a function of intelligence that gives purpose to an action, as the sculptor's purpose is to sculpt a statue of George Washington. It's clear, though, that a sequence of purposes subordinated to one another is often, if not always, called for to achieve a primary end, as the sculptor buys the marble to make the statue to sell it to make a living. It's less clear, however, when you are not thinking directly of an intelligence at work but an action on the part of a non-thinking thing, such as a magnet and its attraction for iron filings. The magnet would not achieve the end of attracting iron filings if it were not able to do so, unless there were some kind of power embedded in it ordered to that end. Consider whether the dart in your favorite pub is on the way to the bull's eye on its own ordering!

. . . The Uncaused Cause

Using the principle of causality, Aristotle is able to analyze the unity of the cosmos. It is obvious that things are not thrown together in a haphazard heap in which nothing has any relationship to anything else. An unmistakable unity is there to begin with, an orderly movement of things that accounts for their being called a *world* or a *cosmos*. The arguments Aristotle offers in the *Metaphysics* and the *Physics* complement each other regarding his well-known doctrine on the origin of motion. Given that all physical things of our experience move, no one of them can move itself; movement requires that a thing *be moved* by another. But this process of being moved by another cannot go on ad infinitum, so here must be a mover by whose influence all motion takes place. This is the *Prime Mover*, whose first attribute must be to move everything without itself being moved; therefore, an *unmoved* mover. But there are other attributes with which such a being must be endowed, attributes including life, activity, thought, goodness, and eternity. Book Twelve of the *Metaphysics* is the culmination of Aristotle's reflection on the kind of being the Prime Mover must be, and Chapter Seven contains the following passage: "The first mover, then, exists of necessity; and it is in this sense a first principle. . . . And life also belongs to God; for the actuality of thought is life, and God is that actuality; and God's self-dependent actuality is life most good and eternal. We say therefore that God is a living being, eternal, most good, so that life and duration continuous and eternal belong to God; for this *is* God."

Virtue, the Good, and Human Happiness

We are left with the question of whether or not there is a relationship between the divine being and the human being. To answer this question is the purpose of the *Nicomachean Ethics*, in which Aristotle, already disposed to think in terms of ultimates, proposes to seek an ultimate function for man: "Have the carpenter, then, and the tanner certain functions or activities, and has man none? Is he born without a function? . . . What then can this be?" Aristotle focuses on human activity in its two aspects, the activity itself and the good at which it aims; he announces his project in the opening lines of the *Ethics*: "Every art and every inquiry, and similarly every action and pursuit, is thought to aim at some good; and for this reason the good has rightly been declared to be that at which all things aim."

The human activity involved is not any activity a human being is capable of, but that which is human activity at its highest point, whose proper name is virtue, and precisely moral virtue. Moral virtue, though not easy to define, focuses on the concrete actions a person performs and the measured sense he has regarding them: "to feel them at the right times, with reference to the right objects, towards the right people, with the right motive, and in the right way." A good action thus exhibits due proportion, neither excessive nor defective, but midway between them; this is Aristotle's doctrine of the *mean*. A virtuous action is one that lies between the extremes of too much and too little, excess or defect, both of which are vices; so, for example, in regard to the feeling of confidence, courage is the mean between the excess of rashness and the defect of cowardice; in regard to the feeling of shame, modesty is the mean between bashfulness and shamelessness.

Not every virtue, however, is a mean, and so not every action is to be measured in this way; but every action is to be measured—measured in its rightness by *prudence* or, in a larger sense, by "practical wisdom," the wisdom whose field is moral practice. Practical wisdom is the sense of governance we have in directing our free and voluntary choices to ends befitting us as human beings; it is, in Aristotle's words, "a true and reasoned state of capacity to act with regard to the things that are good or bad for men."

Good is the aim of every action but, given the fact that goods can be ordered in relation to one another, there must be a highest good to which practical wisdom directs us. And if the possession of any good is what makes us happy to some extent, the possession of the highest good is the highest happiness, the ultimate goal of all our actions. At this point there are some unclear elements in Aristotle's presentation, but this much is clear: Happiness, which is the possession of the good, is ultimately an act of contemplating, or of beholding, the good; but to contemplate the good is to enter into union with it; so, if contemplating God means entering into union with the life of God, this is the highest activity of man and his ultimate happiness. The conclusion of the *Ethics* is one with the *Metaphysics,* in which the "divine element" in a man coincides with the "possession" of God by an act of thought, called *contemplation,* which is the "most pleasant and best" we can perform. This is perhaps best said by Aristotle in the last lines of one of his earlier ethical works, the *Eudemian Ethics:* "What choice, then, or possession of the natural goods—whether bodily goods, wealth, friends, or other things—will most produce the contemplation of God, that choice or possession is best; this is the noblest standard, but any that through deficiency or excess hinders one from the contemplation and service of God is bad; this man possesses in his soul, and this is the best standard for the soul."

Human beings, for Aristotle, are not compelled to achieve their end totally on their own. Indeed, if society has a function, it is to move each of its individual members toward their end along with the entire community, the family as the first community a person is born into, but primarily society in its organization as a state. Perhaps this is a testimony to Aristotle's consistent concern in maintaining the balance between the whole and its parts, the one and the many, the individual and the universal, the human cosmos and the individual human beings composing it. The state, of course, has multiple levels on which it operates to satisfy the needs of each member in developing a full human life. Aristotle was as much interested in the ideal state as Plato was but, following the lines of practical wisdom, he turned more to the empirical aspects of human living and, in observing the anguish of everyday life as a reality, sought the upbuilding of a state for the best life possible for its citizens, always aiming at a system of politics that would never lose sight of the highest of human goods, for, in the words of a renowned student of Aristotle, "the spiritual and moral value of the state is based on its citizens."

Readings

Toward a Definition of Wisdom
(from Metaphysics, Book I)

1. All men by nature desire to know. An indication of this is the delight we take in our senses; for even apart from their usefulness they are loved for themselves; and above all others the sense of sight. For not only with a view to action, but even when we are not going to do anything, we prefer seeing (one might say) to everything else. The reason is that this, most of all the senses, makes us know and brings to light many differences between things.

By nature animals are born with the faculty of sensation, and from sensation memory is produced in some of them, though not in others. And therefore the former are more intelligent and apt at learning than those which cannot remember; those which are incapable of hearing sounds are intelligent though they cannot be taught, e.g. the bee, and any other race of animals that may be like it; and those which besides memory have this sense of hearing can be taught.

The animals other than man live by appearances and memories, and have but little of connected experience; but the human race lives also by art and reasonings. Now from memory experience is produced in men; for the several memories of the same thing produce finally the capacity for a single experience. And experience seems pretty much like science and art, but really science and art come to men through experience; for 'experience made art', as Polus says, 'but inexperience luck'. Now art arises when from many notions gained by experience one universal judgement about a class of objects is produced. For to have a judgement that when Callias was ill of this disease this did him good, and similarly in the case of Socrates and in many individual cases, is a matter of experience; but to judge that it has done good to all persons of a certain constitution, marked off in one class, when they were ill of this disease, e.g. to phlegmatic or bilious people when burning with fever—this is a matter of art.

With a view to action experience seems in no respect inferior to art, and men of experience succeed even better than those who have theory without experience. (The reason is that experience is knowledge of individuals, art of universals, and actions and productions are all concerned with the individual; for the physician does not cure man, except in an incidental way, but Callias or Socrates or some other called by some such individual name, who happens to be a man. If, then, a man has the theory without the experience, and recognizes the universal but does not know the individual included in this, he will often fail to cure; for it is the individual that is to be cured.) But yet we think that knowledge and understanding belong to art rather than to experience, and we suppose artists to be wiser than men of experience (which implies that Wisdom depends in all cases rather on knowledge); and this because the former know the cause, but the latter do not. For men of experience know that the thing is so, but do not know why, while the others know the 'why' and the cause. Hence we think also that the master-workers in each craft are more honourable and know in a truer sense and are wiser than the manual workers, because they know the causes of the things that are done (we think the manual workers are like certain lifeless things which act indeed, but act without knowing what they do, as fire burns—but while the lifeless things perform each of their functions by a natural tendency, the labourers perform them through habit); thus we view them as being wiser not in virtue of being able to act, but of having the theory for themselves and knowing the causes. And in general it is a sign of the man who knows and of the man who does not know, that the former can teach, and therefore we think art more truly knowledge than experience is; for artists can teach, and men of mere experience cannot.

Again, we do not regard any of the senses as Wisdom; yet surely these give the most authoritative knowledge of particulars. But they do not tell us the 'why' of anything—e.g. why fire is hot; they only say that it is hot.

At first he who invented any art whatever that went beyond the common perceptions of man was naturally admired by men, not only because there was something useful in the inventions, but because he was thought wise and superior to the rest. But as more arts were invented, and some were directed to the necessities of life, others to reaction, the inventors of the latter were naturally always regarded as wiser than the inventors of the former, because their branches of knowledge did not aim at utility. Hence when all such inventions were already established, the sciences which do not aim at giving pleasure or at the necessities of life were discovered, and first in the places where men first began to have leisure. This is why the mathematical arts were founded in Egypt; for there the priestly caste was allowed to be at leisure.

We have said in the Ethics what the difference is between art and science and the other kindred faculties; but the point of our present discussion is this, that all men suppose what is called Wisdom to deal with the first causes and the principles of things; so that, as has been said before, the man of experience is thought to be wiser than the possessors of any sense-perception whatever, the artist wiser than the men of experience, the master-worker than the mechanic, and the theoretical kinds of knowledge to be more of the nature of Wisdom than the productive. Clearly then Wisdom is knowledge about certain principles and causes.

2. Since we are seeking this knowledge, we must inquire of what kind are the causes and the principles, the knowledge of which is Wisdom. If one were to take the notions we have about the wise man, this might perhaps make the answer more evident. We suppose first, then, that the wise man knows all things, as far as possible, although he has not knowledge of each of them in detail; secondly, that he who can learn things that are difficult, and not easy for man to know, is wise (sense-perception is common to all, and therefore easy and no mark of Wisdom); again, that he who is more exact and more capable of teaching the causes is wiser, in every branch of knowledge; and that of the sciences, also, that which is desirable on its own account and for the sake of knowing it is more of the nature of Wisdom than that which is desirable on account of its results, and the superior science is more of the nature of Wisdom than the ancillary; for the wise man must not be ordered but must order, and he must not obey another, but the less wise must obey him.

Such and so many are the notions, then, which we have about Wisdom and the wise. Now of these characteristics that of knowing all things must belong to him who has in the highest degree universal knowledge; for he knows in a sense all the instances that fall under the universal. And these things, the most universal, are on the whole the hardest for men to know; for they are farthest from the senses. And the most exact of the sciences are those which deal most with first principles; for those which involve fewer principles are more exact than those which involve additional principles, e.g., arithmetic than geometry. But the science which investigates causes is also instructive, in a higher degree, for the people who instruct us are those who tell the causes of each thing. And understanding and knowledge pursued for their own sake are found most in the knowledge of that which is most knowable (for he who chooses to know for the sake of knowing will choose most readily that which is most truly knowledge, and such is the knowledge of that which is most knowable); and the first principles and the causes are most knowable; for by reason of these, and from these, all other things come to be known, and not these by means of the things subordinate to them. And the science which knows to what end each thing must be done is the most authoritative of the sciences, and more authoritative than any ancillary science; and this end is the good of that thing, and in general the supreme good in the whole of nature. Judged by all the tests we have mentioned, then, the name in question falls to the same science; this must be a science that investigates the first principles and causes; for the good, i.e., the end, is one of the causes.

That it is not a science of production is clear even from the history of the earliest philosophers. For it is owing to their wonder that men both now begin and at first began to philosophize; they wondered originally at the obvious difficulties, then advanced little by little and stated difficulties about the greater matters, e.g. about the phenomena of the moon and those of the sun and of the stars, and about the genesis of the universe. And a man who is puzzled and wonders thinks himself ignorant (whence even the lover of myth is in a sense a lover of Wisdom, for the myth is composed of wonders); therefore since they philosophized in order to escape from ignorance, evidently they were pursuing science in order to know, and not for any utilitarian end. . . .

Hence also the possession of it might be justly regarded as beyond human power; for in many ways human nature is in bondage, so that according to Simonides 'God alone can have this privilege,' and it is unfitting that man should not be content to seek the knowledge that is suited to him. . . .

For the most divine science is also most honourable; and this science alone must be, in two ways, most divine. For the science which it would be most meet for God to have is a divine science, and so is any science that deals with divine objects; and this science alone has both these qualities; for (1) God is thought to be among the causes of all things and to be a first principle, and (2) such a science either God alone can have, or God above all others. All the sciences, indeed, are more necessary than this, but none is better.

Yet the acquisition of it must in a sense end in something which is the opposite of our original inquiries. For all men begin, as we said, by wondering that things are as they are, as they do about self-moving marionettes, or about the solstices or the incommensurability of the diagonal of a square with the side; for it seems wonderful to all who have not yet seen the reason, that there is a thing which cannot be measured even by the smallest unit. But we must end in the contrary and, according to the proverb, the better state, as is the case in these instances too when men learn the cause; for there is nothing which would surprise a geometer so much as if the diagonal turned out to be commensurable.

We have stated, then, what is the nature of the science we are searching for, and what is the mark which our search and our whole investigation must reach.

(From *The Works of Aristotle Translated into English*, ed. W. D. Ross. Trans. by W. D. Ross. Oxford: Oxford University Press, 1924. Reprinted by permission of Oxford University Press.)

The Prime Mover: One and Eternal
(from *Physics*, Books I and VIII)

1. Everything that is in motion must be moved by something. For if it has not the source of its motion in itself it is evident that it is moved by something other than itself, for there must be something else that moves it. If on the other hand it has the source of its motion in itself, let AB be taken to represent that which is in motion essentially of itself and not in virtue of the fact that something belonging to it is in motion. Now in the first place to assume that AB, because it is in motion as a whole and is not moved by anything external to itself, is therefore moved by itself—this is just as if, supposing that JK is moving KL and is also itself in motion, we were to deny that JL is moved by anything on the ground that it is not evident which is the part that is moving it and which the part that is moved. In the second place that which is in motion without being moved by anything does not necessarily cease from its motion because something else is at rest, but a thing must be moved by something if the fact of something else having ceased from its motion causes it to be at rest. Thus, if this is accepted, everything that is in motion must be moved by something. For AB, which has been taken to represent that which is in motion, must be divisible, since everything that is in motion

is divisible. Let it be divided, then, at C. Now if CB is not in motion, then AB will not be in motion: for if it is, it is clear that AC would be in motion while BC is at rest, and thus AB cannot be in motion essentially and primarily. But ex hypothesi AB is in motion essentially and primarily. Therefore if CB is not in motion AB will be at rest. But we have agreed that that which is at rest if something else is not in motion must be moved by something. Consequently, everything that is in motion must be moved by something: for that which is in motion will always be divisible, and if a part of it is not in motion the whole must be at rest.

Since everything that is in motion must be moved by something, let us take the case in which a thing is in locomotion and is moved by something that is itself in motion, and that again is moved by something else that is in motion, and that by something else, and so on continually: then the series cannot go on to infinity, but there must be some first movent. . . .

6. Since there must always be motion without intermission, there must necessarily be something, one thing or it may be a plurality, that first imparts motion, and this first movent must be unmoved. Now the question whether each of the things are unmoved but impart motion is eternal is irrelevant to our present argument: but the following considerations will make it clear that there must necessarily be some such thing, which, while it has the capacity of moving something else, is itself unmoved and exempt from all change, which can affect it neither in an unqualified nor in an accidental sense. Let us suppose, if any one likes, that in the case of certain things it is possible for them at different times to be and not to be, without any process of becoming and perishing (in fact it would seem to be necessary, if a thing that has not parts at one time is and at another time is not, that any such thing should without undergoing any process of change at one time be and at another time not be). And let us further suppose it possible that some principles that are unmoved but capable of imparting motion at one time are and at another time are not. Even so, this cannot be true of *all* such principles, since there must clearly be something that *causes* things that move themselves at one time to be and at another not to be. For, since nothing that has not parts can be in motion, that which moves itself must as a whole have magnitude, though nothing that we have said makes this necessarily true of every movent. So the fact that some things become and others perish, and that this is so continuously, cannot be caused by any one of those things that, though they are unmoved, do not always exist: nor again can it be caused by any of those which move certain particular things, while others move other things. The eternity and continuity of the process cannot be caused either by any one of them singly or by the sum of them, because this causal relation must be eternal and necessary, whereas the sum of these movents is infinite and they do not all exist together. It is clear, then, that though there may be countless instances of the perishing of some principles that are unmoved but impart motion, and though many things that move themselves perish and are succeeded by others that come into being, and though one thing that is unmoved moves one thing while another moves another, nevertheless there is something that comprehends them all, and that as something apart from each one of them, and this it is that is the cause of the fact that some things are and others are not and of the continuous process of change: and this causes the motion of the other movents, while they are the causes

of the motion of other things. Motion, then, being eternal, the first movent, if there is but one, will be eternal also: if there are more than one, there will be a plurality of such eternal movents. We ought, however, to suppose that there is one rather than many, and a finite rather than an infinite number. When the consequences of either assumption are the same, we should always assume that things are finite rather than infinite in number, since in things constituted by nature that which is finite and that which is better ought, if possible, to be present rather than the reverse: and here it is sufficient to assume only one movent, the first of unmoved things, which being eternal will be the principle of motion to everything else.

The following argument also makes it evident that the first movent must be something that is one and eternal. We have shown that there must always be motion. That being so, motion must also be continuous, because what is always is continuous, whereas what is merely in succession is not continuous. But further, if motion is continuous, it is one: and it is one only if the movent and the moved that constitute it are each of them one, since in the event of a thing's being moved now by one thing and now by another the whole motion will not be continuous but successive.

Moreover a conviction that there is a first unmoved something may be reached not only from the foregoing arguments, but also by considering again the principles operative in movents. Now it is evident that among existing things there are some that are sometimes in motion and sometimes at rest. This fact has served above to make it clear that it is not true either that all things are in motion or that all things are at rest or that some things are always at rest and the remainder always in motion: on this matter proof is supplied by things that fluctuate between the two and have the capacity of being sometimes in motion and sometimes at rest. The existence of things of this kind is clear to all: but we wish to explain also the nature of each of the other two kinds and show that there are some things that are always unmoved and some things that are always in motion. In the course of our argument directed to this end we established the fact that everything that is in motion is moved by something, and that the movent is either unmoved or in motion, and that, if it is in motion, it is moved either by itself or by something else and so on throughout the series: and so we proceeded to the position that the first principle that directly causes things that are in motion to be moved is that which moves itself, and the first principle of the whole series is the unmoved. Further it is evident from actual observation that there are things that have the characteristic of moving themselves, e.g. the animal kingdom and the whole class of living things. This being so, then, the view was suggested that perhaps it may be possible for motion to come to be in a thing without having been in existence at all before, because we see this actually occurring in animals: they are unmoved at one time and then again they are in motion, as it seems. We must grasp the fact, therefore, that animals move themselves only with one kind of motion, and that this is not strictly originated by them. The cause of it is not derived from the animal itself: it is connected with other natural motions in animals, which they do not experience through their own instrumentality, e.g. increase, decrease, and respiration: these are experienced by every animal while it is at rest and not in motion in respect of the motion set up by its own agency: here the motion is caused by the atmosphere and by many things that enter into the animal: thus in some cases the cause is nourishment: when it is being digested animals sleep, and when it is being distributed through the system they awake and move themselves, the first principle of this motion being thus originally derived from outside. Therefore animals are not always in continuous motion by their own agency: it is something else that moves them, itself being in motion and changing as it comes into relation with each several thing that moves itself. (Moreover in all these self-moving things the first movent and cause of their self-motion is itself moved by itself, though in an accidental sense: that is to say, the body changes its place, so that that which is in the body changes its place also and is a self-movent through its exercise of leverage.) Hence we may confidently conclude that if a thing belongs to a class of unmoved movents that are also themselves moved accidentally, it is impossible that it should cause continuous motion. So the necessity that there should be motion continuously requires that there should be a first movent that is unmoved even accidentally, if, as we have said, there is to be in the world of things an unceasing and undying motion, and the world is to remain permanently self-contained and within the same limits: for if the first principle is permanent, the universe must also be permanent, since it is continuous with the first principle. (We must distinguish, however, between accidental motion of a thing by itself and such motion by something else, the former being confined to perishable things, whereas the latter belongs also to certain first principles of heavenly bodies, of all those, that is to say, that experience more than one locomotion.)

And further, if there is always something of this nature, a movent that is itself unmoved and eternal, then that which is first moved by it must be eternal. Indeed this is clear also from the consideration that there would otherwise be no becoming and perishing and no change of any kind in other things, which require something that is in motion to move them: for the motion imparted by the unmoved will always be imparted in the same way and be one and the same, since the unmoved does not itself change in relation to that which is moved by it. But that which is moved by something that, though it is in motion, is moved directly by the unmoved stands in varying relations to the things that it moves, so that the motion that it causes will not be always the same: by reason of the fact that it occupies contrary positions or assumes contrary forms at different times it will produce contrary motions in each several thing that it moves and will cause it to be at one time at rest and at another time in motion.

The foregoing argument, then, has served to clear up the point about which we raised a difficulty at the outset—why is it that instead of all things being either in motion or at rest, or some things being always in motion and the remainder always at rest, there are things that are sometimes in motion and sometimes not? The cause of this is now plain: it is because, while some things are moved by an eternal unmoved movent and are therefore always in motion, other things are moved by a movent that is in motion and changing, so that they too must change. But the unmoved movent, as has been said, since it remains permanently simple and unvarying and in the same state, will cause motion that is one and simple.

(From *The Works of Aristotle Translated into English*, ed. W. D. Ross. Trans. by R. P. Hardie and R. K. Gaye. Oxford: Oxford University Press, 1930. Reprinted by permission of Oxford University Press.)

Thought, Contemplation, and the Life of God
(from *Metaphysics*, Book XII)

Now if something is moved it is capable of being otherwise than as it is. Therefore if its actuality is the primary form of spatial motion, then in so far as it is subject to change, in *this* respect it is capable of being otherwise—in place, even if not in substance. But since there is something which moves while itself unmoved, existing actually, this can in no way be otherwise than as it is. For motion in space is the first of the kinds of change, and motion in a circle the first kind of spatial motion; and this the first mover *produces*. The first mover, then, exists of necessity; and in so far as it exists by necessity, its mode of being is good, and it is in this sense a first principle. For the necessary has all these senses—that which is necessary perforce because it is contrary to the natural impulse, that without which the good is impossible, and that which cannot be otherwise but can exist only in a single way.

On such a principle, then, depend the heavens and the world of nature. And it is a life such as the best which we enjoy, and enjoy for but a short time (for it is ever in this state, which we cannot be), since its actuality is also pleasure. (And for this reason are waking, perception, and thinking most pleasant, and hopes and memories are so on account of these.) And thinking in itself deals with that which is best in itself, and that which is thinking in the fullest sense with that which is best in the fullest sense. And thought thinks on itself because it shares the nature of the object of thought; for it becomes an object of thought in coming into contact with and thinking its objects, so that thought and object of thought are the same. For that which is *capable* of receiving the object of thought, i.e. the essence, is thought. But it is *active* when it *possesses* this object. Therefore the possession rather than the receptivity is the divine element which thought seems to contain, and the act of contemplation is what is most pleasant and best. If, then, God is always in that good state in which we sometimes are, this compels our wonder; and if in a better this compels it yet more. And God *is* in a better state. And life also belongs to God; for the actuality of thought is life, and God is that actuality; and God's self-dependent actuality is life most good and eternal. We say therefore that God is a living being, eternal, most good, so that life and duration continuous and eternal belong to God; for this *is* God.

Those who suppose, as the Pythagoreans and Speusippus do, that supreme beauty and goodness are not present in the beginning, because the beginnings both of plants and of animals are causes, but beauty and completeness are in the *effects* of these, are wrong in their opinion. For the seed comes from other individuals which are prior and complete, and the first thing is not seed but the complete being; e.g. we must say that before the seed there is a man—not the man produced from the seed, but another from whom the seed comes.

It is clear then from what has been said that there is a substance which is eternal and unmovable and separate from sensible things. It has been shown also that this substance cannot have any magnitude, but is without parts and indivisible (for it produces movement through infinite time, but nothing finite has infinite power; and, while every magnitude is either infinite or finite, it cannot, for the above reason, have finite magnitude, and it cannot have infinite magnitude because there is not infinite magnitude at all). But it has also been shown that it is impassive and unalterable; for all the other changes are posterior to change of place.

9. The nature of the divine thought involves certain problems; for while thought is held to be the most divine of things observed by us, the question how it must be situated in order to have that character involves difficulties. For if it thinks of nothing, what is there here of dignity? It is just like one who sleeps. And if it thinks, but this depends on something else, then (since that which is its substance is not the act of thinking, but a potency) it cannot be the best substance; for it is through thinking that its value belongs to it. Further, whether its substance is the faculty of thought or the act of thinking, what does it think of? Either of itself or of something else; and if of something else, either of the same thing always or of something different. Does it matter, then, or not, whether it thinks of the good or of any chance thing? Are there not some things about which it is incredible that it should think? Evidently, then, it thinks of that which is most divine and precious, and it does not change; for change would be change for the worse, and this would be already a movement. First, then, if 'thought' is not the act of thinking but a potency, it would be reasonable to suppose that the continuity of its thinking is wearisome to it. Secondly, there would evidently be something else more precious than thought, viz. that which is thought of. For both thinking and the act of thought will belong even to one who thinks of the worst thing in the world, so that if this ought to be avoided (and it ought, for there are even some things which it is better not to see than to see), the act of thinking cannot be the best of things. Therefore it must be of itself that the divine thought thinks (since it is the most excellent of things), and its thinking is a thinking on thinking.

But evidently knowledge and perception and opinion and understanding have always something else as their object, and themselves only by the way. Further, if thinking and being thought of are different, in respect of which does goodness belong to thought? For to be an act of thinking and to *be* an object of thought are not the same thing. We answer that in some cases the knowledge is the object. In the productive sciences it is the substance or essence of the object, matter omitted, and in the theoretical sciences the definition or the act of thinking is the object. Since, then, thought and the object of thought are not different in the case of things that have not matter, the divine thought and its object will be the same, i.e. the thinking will be one with the object of its thought.

A further question is left—whether the object of the divine thought is composite; for if it were, thought would change in passing from part to part of the whole. We answer that everything which has not matter is indivisible—as human thought, or rather the thought of composite beings, is in a certain period of time (for it does not possess the good at this moment or at that, but at its best, being something *different* from it, is attained only in a whole period of time), so throughout eternity is the thought which has *itself* for its object.

(From *The Works of Aristotle Translated into English*, ed. W. D. Ross. Trans. by W. D. Ross. Oxford: Oxford University Press, 1924. Reprinted by permission of Oxford University Press.)

Happiness and Man's Good
(from *Nicomachean Ethics*, Book I)

1. EVERY art and every scientific inquiry, and similarly every action and purpose, may be said to aim at some good. Hence the good has been well defined as that at which all things aim. But it is clear that there is a difference in the ends; for the ends are sometimes activities, and sometimes results beyond the mere activities. Also, where there are certain ends beyond the actions, the results are naturally superior to the activities.

As there are various actions, arts, and sciences, it follows that the ends are also various. Thus health is the end of medicine, a vessel of shipbuilding, victory of strategy, and wealth of domestic economy. It often happens that there are a number of such arts or sciences which fall under a single faculty, as the art of making bridles, and all such other arts as make the instruments of horsemanship, under horsemanship, and this again as well as every military action under strategy, and in the same way other arts or sciences under other faculties. But in all these cases the ends of the architectonic arts or sciences, whatever they may be, are more desirable than those of the subordinate arts or sciences, as it is for the sake of the former that the latter are themselves sought after. It makes no difference to the argument whether the activities themselves are the ends of the actions, or something else beyond the activities as in the above mentioned sciences.

If it is true that in the sphere of action there is an end which we wish for its own sake, and for the sake of which we wish everything else, and that we do not desire all things for the sake of something else (for, if that is so, the process will go on *ad infinitum*, and our desire will be idle and futile) it is clear that this will be the good or the supreme good. Does it not follow then that the knowledge of this supreme good is of great importance for the conduct of life, and that, *if we know it*, we shall be like archers who have a mark at which to aim, we shall have a better chance of attaining what we want? But, if this is the case, we must endeavour to comprehend, at least in outline, its nature, and the science or faculty to which it belongs.

It would seem that this is the most authoritative or architectonic science or faculty, and such is evidently the political; for it is the political science or faculty which determines what sciences are necessary in states, and what kind of sciences should be learnt, and how far they should be learnt by particular people. We perceive too that the faculties which are held in the highest esteem, e.g. strategy, domestic economy, and rhetoric, are subordinate to it. But as it makes use of the other practical sciences, and also legislates upon the things to be done and the things to be left undone, it follows that its end will comprehend the ends of all the other sciences, and will therefore be the true good of mankind. For although the good of an individual is identical with the good of a state, yet the good of the state, whether in attainment or in preservation, is evidently greater and more perfect. For while in an individual by himself it is something to be thankful for, it is nobler and more divine in a nation or state.

These then are the objects at which the present inquiry aims . . .

5. But leaving this subject for the present let us revert to the good of which we are in quest and consider what its nature may be. For it is clearly this description, as we always desire happiness for its own sake and never as a means to something else, whereas we desire honour, pleasure, intellect, and every virtue, partly for their own sakes (for we should desire them independently of what might result from them) but partly also as being means to happiness, because we suppose they will prove the instruments of happiness. Happiness, on the other hand, nobody desires for the sake of these things, nor indeed as a means to anything else at all.

We come to the same conclusion if we start from the consideration of self-sufficiency, if it may be assumed that the final good is self-sufficient. But when we speak of self-sufficiency, we do not mean that a person leads a solitary life all by himself, but that he has parents, children, wife, and friends, and fellow-citizens in general, as man is naturally a social being. But here it is necessary to prescribe some limit; for if the circle be extended so as to include parents, descendants, and friends' friends, it will go on indefinitely. Leaving this point, however, for future investigation, we define the self-sufficient as that which, taken by itself, makes life desirable, and wholly free from want, and this is our conception of happiness.

Again, we conceive happiness to be the most desirable of all things, and that not merely as one among other good things. If it were one among other good things, the addition of the smallest good would increase its desirableness; for the accession makes a superiority of goods, and the greater of two goods is always the more desirable. It appears then that happiness is something final and self-sufficient, being the end of all action.

6. Perhaps, however, it seems a truth which is generally admitted, that happiness is the supreme good; what is wanted is to define its nature a little more clearly. The best way of arriving at such a definition will probably be to ascertain the function of Man. For, as with a flute-player, a sculptor, or any artisan, or in fact anybody who has a definite function and action, his goodness, or excellence seems to lie in his function, so it would seem to be with Man, if indeed he has a definite function. Can it be said then that, while a carpenter and a cobbler have definite functions and actions, Man, unlike them, is naturally functionless? The reasonable view is that, as the eye, the hand, the foot, and similarly each several part of the body has a definite function, so Man may be regarded as having a definite function apart from all these. What then, can this function be? It is not life; for life is apparently something which man shares with the plants; and it is something peculiar to him that we are looking for. We must exclude therefore the life of nutrition and increase. There is next what may be called the life of sensation. But this too, is apparently shared by Man with horses, cattle, and all other animals. There remains what I may call the practical life of the rational part *of Man's being*. But the rational part is twofold; it is rational partly in the sense of being obedient to reason, and partly in the sense of possessing reason and intelligence. The practical life too may be conceived of in two ways, *viz., either as a moral state, or as a moral activity:* but we must understand by it the life of activity, as this seems to be the truer form of the conception.

The function of Man then is an activity of soul in accordance with reason, or not independently of reason. Again the functions of a person of a certain kind, and of such a person who is good of his kind e.g. of a harpist and a good harpist, are in our view generically the same, and this view is true of people of all kinds without exception, the superior excellence being only an addition to the function; for it is the function of a harpist to play the harp, and of a good harpist to play the harp well. This being so, if we define the function of Man as a kind of life, and this life as an activity of soul, or a course of action in conformity with reason, if the function of a good man is such activity or action of a good and noble kind, and if everything is successfully performed when it is performed in accordance with its proper excellence, it follows that the good of Man is an activity of soul in accordance with virtue or, if there are more virtues than one, in accordance with the best and most complete virtue. But it is necessary to add the words "in a complete life." For as one swallow or one day does not make a spring, so one day or a short time does not make a fortunate or happy man.

(Ethics tr. by. J. E. C. Welldon)

Moral Virtue and the Mean
(from *Nicomachean Ethics*, Book II)

5. The nature of virtue has been now generically described. But it is not enough to state merely that virtue is a moral state, we must also describe the character of that moral state.

It must be laid down then that every virtue or excellence has the effect of producing a good condition of that of which it is a virtue or excellence, and of enabling it to perform its function well. Thus the excellence of the eye makes the eye good and its function good, as it is by the excellence of the eye that we see well. Similarly, the excellence of the horse makes a horse excellent and good at racing, at carrying its rider and at facing the enemy.

If then this is universally true, the virtue or excellence of man will be such a moral state as makes a man good and able to perform his proper function well. We have already explained how this will be the case, but another way of making it clear will be to study the nature or character of this virtue.

Now in everything, whether it be continuous or discrete, it is possible to take a greater, a smaller, or an equal amount, and this either absolutely or in relation to ourselves, the equal being a mean between excess and deficiency. By the mean in respect of the thing itself, or the absolute mean, I understand that which is equally distinct from both extremes; and this is one and the same thing for everybody. By the mean considered relatively to ourselves I understand that which is neither too much nor too little; but this is not one thing, nor is it the same for everybody. Thus if 10 be too much and 2 too little we take 6 as a mean in respect of the thing itself; for 6 is as much greater than 2 as it is less than 10, and this is a mean in arithmetical proportion. But the mean considered relatively to ourselves must not be ascertained in this way. It does not follow that if 10 pounds *of meat* be too much and 2 be too little for a man to eat, a trainer will order him 6 pounds, as this may itself be too much or too little for the person who is to take it; it will be too little e.g. for Milo, but too much for a beginner in gymnastics. It will be the same with running and wrestling; *the right amount will vary with the individual.* This being so, everybody who understands his business avoids alike excess and deficiency; he seeks and chooses the mean, not the absolute mean, but the mean considered relatively to ourselves.

Every science then performs its function well, if it regards the mean and refers the works which it produces to the mean. This is the reason why it is usually said of successful works that it is impossible to take anything from them or to add anything to them, which implies that excess or deficiency is fatal to excellence but that the mean state ensures it. Good[1] artists too, as we say, have an eye to the mean in their works. But virtue, like Nature herself, is more accurate and better than any art; virtue therefore will aim at the mean;—I speak of moral virtue, as it is moral virtue which is concerned with emotions and actions, and it is these which admit of excess and deficiency and the mean. Thus it is possible to go too far, or not to go far enough, in respect of fear, courage, desire, anger, pity, and pleasure and pain generally, and the excess and the deficiency are alike wrong; but to experience these emotions at the right times and on the right occasions and towards the right persons and for the right causes and in the right manner is the mean or the supreme good, which is characteristic of virtue. Similarly there may be excess, deficiency, or the mean, in regard to actions. But virtue is concerned with emotions and actions, and here excess is an error and deficiency a fault, whereas the mean is successful and landable, and success and merit are both characteristics of virtue.

It appears then that virtue is a mean state, so far at least as it aims at the mean.

Again, there are many different ways of going wrong; for evil is in its nature infinite, to use the Pythagorean figure, but good is finite. But there is only one possible way of going right. Accordingly the former is easy and the latter difficult; it is easy to miss the mark but difficult to hit it. This again is a reason why excess and deficiency are characteristics of vice and the mean state a characteristic of virtue.

"For good is simple, evil manifold."

6. Virtue then is a state of deliberate moral purpose consisting in a mean that is relative to ourselves, the mean being determined by reason, or as a prudent man would determine it.

It is a mean state *firstly as lying* between two vices, the vice of excess on the one hand, and the vice of deficiency on the other, and secondly because, whereas the vices either fall short of or go beyond what is proper in the emotions and actions, virtue not only discovers but embraces the mean.

Accordingly, virtue, if regarded in its essence or theoretical conception, is a mean state, but, if regarded from the point of view of the highest good, or of excellence, it is an extreme.

But it is not every action or every emotion that admits of a mean state. There are some whose very name implies wickedness, as e.g. malice, shamelessness, and envy, among emotions, or adultery, theft, and murder, among actions. All these, and others like them, are censured as being intrinsically wicked, not merely the excesses or deficiencies of them. It is never possible then to be right in respect of them; they are always sinful. Right or wrong in such actions as adultery does not depend on our committing them with the right person, at the right time or in the right manner; on the contrary it is sinful to do anything of the kind at all. It would be equally wrong then to suppose that there can be a mean state or an excess or deficiency in unjust, cowardly or licentious conduct; for, if it were so, there would be a mean state of an excess or of a deficiency, an excess of an excess and a deficiency of a deficiency. But as in temperance and courage there can be no excess or deficiency because the mean is, in a sense, an extreme, so too in these cases there cannot be a mean or an excess or deficiency, but, however the acts may be done, they are wrong. For it is a general rule that an excess or deficiency does not admit of a mean state, nor a mean state of an excess or deficiency.

7. But it is not enough to lay down this as a general rule; it is necessary to apply it to particular cases, as in reasonings upon actions general statements, although they are broader, are less exact than particular statements. For all action refers to particulars, and it is essential that our theories should harmonize with the particular cases to which they apply.

We must take particular virtues then from the catalogue *of virtues*.

In regard to feelings of fear and confidence, courage is a mean state. On the side of excess, he whose fearlessness is excessive has no name, as often happens, but he whose confidence is excessive is foolhardy, while he whose timidity is excessive and whose confidence is deficient is a coward.

In respect of pleasures and pains, although not indeed of all pleasures and pains, and to a less extent in respect of pains than of pleasures, the mean state is temperance, the excess is licentiousness. We never find people who are deficient in regard to pleasures; accordingly such people again have not received a name, but we may call them insensible.

As regards the giving and taking of money, the mean state is liberality, the excess and deficiency are prodigality and illiberality. Here the excess and deficiency take opposite forms; for while the prodigal man is excessive in spending and deficient in taking, the illiberal man is excessive in taking and deficient in spending.

(For the present we are giving only a rough and summary account *of the virtues*, and that is sufficient for our purpose; we will hereafter determine their character more exactly.)

In respect of money there are other dispositions as well. There is the mean state which is magnificence; for the magnificent man, as having to do with large sums of money, differs from the liberal man who has to do only with small sums; and the excess *corresponding to it* is bad taste or vulgarity, the deficiency is meanness. These are different from the excess and deficiency of liberality; what the difference is will be explained hereafter.

In respect of honour and dishonour the mean state is highmindedness, the excess is what is called vanity, the deficiency littlemindedness. Corresponding to liberality, which, as we said, differs from magnificence as having to do *not with great but* with small sums of money, there is a moral state which has to do with petty honour and is related to high-mindedness which has to do with great honour; for it is possible to aspire to honour in the right way, or in a way which is excessive or insufficient, and if a person's aspirations are excessive, he is called ambitious, if they are deficient, he is called unambitious, while if they are between the two, he has no name. The dispositions too are nameless, except that the disposition of the ambitious person is called ambition. The consequence is that the extremes lay claim to the mean or intermediate place. We ourselves speak of one who observes the mean sometimes as ambitious, and at other times as unambitious; we sometimes praise an ambitious, and at other times an unambitious person. The reason for our doing so will be stated in due course, but let us now discuss the other virtues in accordance with the method which we have followed hitherto.

Anger, like other emotions, has its excess, its deficiency, and its mean state. It may be said that they have no names, but as we call one who observes the mean gentle, we will call the mean state geutleness. Among the extremes, if a person errs on the side of excess, he may be called passionate and his vice passionateness, if on that of deficiency, he may be called impassive and his deficiency impassivity.

There are also three other mean states with a certain resemblance to each other, and yet with a difference. For while they are all concerned with intercourse in speech and action, they are different in that one of them is concerned with truth in such intercourse, and the others with pleasantness, one with pleasantness in amusement and the other with pleasantness in the various circumstances of life. We must therefore discuss these states in order to make it clear that in all cases it is the mean state which is an object of praise, and the extremes are neither right nor laudable but censurable. It is true that these mean and extreme states are generally nameless, but we must do our best here as elsewhere to give them a name, so that our argument may be clear and easy to follow.

In the matter of truth then, he who observes the mean may be called truthful, and the mean state truthfulness. Pretence, if it takes the form of exaggeration, is boastfulness, and one who is guilty of pretence is a boaster; but if it takes the form of depreciation it is irony, and he who is guilty of it is ironical.

As regards pleasantness in amusement, he who observes the mean is witty, and his disposition wittiness; the excess is buffoonery, and he who is guilty of it a buffoon, whereas he who is deficient in wit may be called a boor and his moral state boorishness.

As to the other kind of pleasantness, viz. pleasantness in life, he who is pleasant in a proper way is friendly, and his mean state friendliness; but he who goes too far, if he has no ulterior object in view, is obsequious, while if his object is self interest, he is a flatterer, and he who does not go far enough and always makes himself unpleasant is a quarrelsome and morose sort of person.

There are also mean states in the emotions and in the expression of the emotions. For although modesty is not a virtue, yet a modest person is praised as if he were virtuous; for here too one person is said to observe the mean and another to exceed it, as e.g. the bashful man who is never anything but modest, whereas a person who has insufficient modesty or no modesty at all is called shameless, and one who observes the mean modest.

Righteous indignation, again, is a mean state between envy and malice. They are all concerned with the pain and pleasure which we feel at the fortunes of our neighbours. A person who is righteously indignant is pained at the prosperity of the undeserving; but the envious person goes further and is pained at anybody's prosperity, and the malicious person is so far from being pained that he actually rejoices *at misfortunes*.

We shall have another opportunity however of discussing these matters. But in regard to justice, as the word is used in various senses, we will afterwards define those senses and explain how each of them is a mean state. And we will follow the same course with the intellectual virtues.

(Tr. J. E. C. Welldon)

The End of Human Nature: Happiness
(from *Nicomachean Ethics*, Book X)

6. After this discussion of the kinds of virtue and friendship and pleasure it remains to give a sketch of happiness, since we defined happiness as the end of human things. We shall shorten our account of it if we begin by recapitulating our previous remarks.

We said that happiness is not a moral state; for, if it were, it would be predicable of one who spends his whole life in sleep, living the life of a vegetable, or of one who is utterly miserable. If then we cannot accept this view if we must rather define happiness as an activity of some kind, as has been said before, and if activities are either necessary and desirable as a means to something else or desirable in themselves, it is clear that we must define happiness as belonging to the class of activities which are desirable in themselves, and not desirable as means to something else; for happiness has no want, it is self-sufficient.

Again, activities are desirable in themselves, if nothing is expected from them beyond the activity. This seems to be the case with virtuous actions, as the practice of what is noble and virtuous is a thing desirable in itself. It seems to be the case also with such amusements as are pleasant, we do not desire them as means to other things; for they often do us harm rather than good by making us careless about our persons and our property. Such pastimes are generally the resources of those whom the world calls happy. Accordingly people who are clever at such pastimes are generally popular in the courts of despots, as they make themselves pleasant to the despot in the matters which are the objects of his desire, and what he wants is to pass the time pleasantly.

The reason why these things are regarded as elements of happiness is that people who occupy high positions devote their leisure to them. But such people are not, I think, a criterion. For a high position is no guarantee of virtue or intellect, which are the sources on which virtuous activities depend. And if these people, who have never tasted a pure and liberal pleasure, have recourse to the pleasures of the body, it must not be inferred that these pleasures are preferable; for even children suppose that such things as are valued or honoured among them are best. It is only reasonable then that, as men and children differ in their estimate of what is honourable, so should good and bad people.

As has been frequently said, therefore, it is the things which are honourable and pleasant to the virtuous man that are really honourable and pleasant. But everybody feels the activity which accords with his own moral state to be most desirable, and accordingly[1] the virtuous man regards the activity in accordance with virtue as most desirable.

Happiness then does not consist in amusement. It would be paradoxical to hold that the end of human life is amusement, and that we should toil and suffer all our life for the sake of amusing ourselves. For we may be said to desire all things as means to something else except indeed happiness, as happiness is the end *or perfect state*.

It appears to be foolish and utterly childish to take serious trouble and pains for the sake of amusement. But to amuse oneself with a view to being serious seems to be right, as Anacharsis says; for amusement is a kind of relaxation, and it is because we cannot work for ever that we need relaxation.

Relaxation then is not an end. We enjoy it as a means to activity; but it seems that the happy life is a life of virtue, and such a life is serious, it is not one of mere amusement. We speak of serious things too *(for serious things are virtuous)* as better than things which are ridiculous and amusing, and of the activity of the better part of man's being or of the better man as always the more virtuous. But the activity of that which is better is necessarily higher and happier. Anybody can enjoy bodily pleasures, a slave can enjoy them as much as the best of men; but nobody would allow that a slave is capable of happiness unless he is capable of life[2]; for happiness consists not in such pastimes as I have been speaking of, but in virtuous activities, as has been already said.

7. If happiness consists in virtuous activity, it is only reasonable to suppose that it is the activity of the highest virtue, or in other words, of the best part of our nature. Whether it is the reason or something else which seems to exercise rule and authority by a natural right, and to have a conception of things noble and divine, either as being itself divine or as relatively the most divine part of our being, it is the activity of this part in accordance with its proper virtue which will be the perfect happiness. . . . to be realized in this activity. This then will be the perfect happiness of Man, if a perfect length of life is given it, for there is no imperfection in happiness. But such a life will be too good for Man. He will enjoy such a life not in virtue of his humanity but in virtue of some divine element within him, and the superiority of this activity to the activity of any other virtue will be proportionate to the superiority of this divine element in man to his composite *or material* nature.

If then the reason is divine in comparison with *the rest of* Man's nature, the life which accords with reason will be divine in comparison with human life in general. Nor is it right to follow the advice of people who say that the thoughts of men should not be too high for humanity or the thoughts of mortals too high for mortality; for a man, as far as in him lies, should seek immortality and do all that is in his power to live in accordance with the highest part of his nature, as, although that part is insignificant in size, yet in power and honour it is far superior to all the rest.

It would seem too that this is the true self of everyone, if a man's true self is his supreme or better part. It would be absurd then that a man should desire not the life which is properly his own but the life which properly belongs to some other being. The remark already made will be appropriate here. It is what is proper to everyone that is in its nature best and pleasantest for him. It is the life which accords with reason then that will be best and pleasantest for Man, as a man's reason is in the highest sense himself. This will therefore be also the happiest life.

8. It is only in a secondary sense that the life which accords with other, *i.e. non-speculative,* virtue can be said to be happy; for the activities of such virtue are human, *they have no divine element.* Our just or courageous actions or our virtuous actions of any kind we perform in relation to one another, when we observe the law of propriety in contracts and mutual services and the various moral actions and in our emotions. But all these actions appear to be human affairs. It seems too that moral virtue is in some respects actually the result of physical organization and is in many respects closely associated with the emotions. Again, prudence is indissolubly linked to moral virtue, and moral virtue to prudence, since the principles of prudence are determined by the moral virtues, and moral rectitude is determined by prudence. But the moral virtues, as being inseparably united with the emotions, must have to do with the composite *or material* part *of our nature,* and the virtues of the composite part *of our nature* are human, *and not divine,* virtues. So too therefore is the life which accords with these virtues; so too is the happiness *which accords with them.*

But the happiness *which consists in the exercise* of the reason is separated *from these emotions.* It must be enough to say so much about it; for to discuss it in detail would take us beyond our present purpose. It would seem too to require external resources only to a small extent or to a less extent than moral virtue. It may be granted that both will require the necessaries of life and will require them equally, even if the politician devotes more trouble to his body and his bodily welfare than the philosopher; for the difference will not be important. But there will be a great difference in respect of their activities. The liberal man will want money for the practice of liberality, and the just man for the requital of services which have been done him; for our wishes, *unless they are manifested in actions,* must always be obscure, and even people who are not just pretend that it is their wish to act justly. The courageous man too will want physical strength if he is to perform any virtuous action, and the temperate man liberty, as otherwise it will be impossible for him or for anybody else to show his character.

But if the question be asked whether it is the purpose or the performance that is the surer determinant of virtue, as virtue implies both, it is clear that both are necessary to perfection. But action requires various conditions, and the greater and nobler the action, the more numerous will the conditions be.

In speculation on the other hand there is no need of such conditions, at least for its activity; it may rather be said that they are actual impediments to speculation. It is as a human being and as living in society that a person chooses to perform virtuous actions. Such conditions then will be requisite if he is to live as a man.

9. Man, as being human, will require external prosperity. His nature is not of itself sufficient for speculation, it needs bodily health, food, and care of every kind. It must not however be supposed that, because it is impossible to be fortunate without external goods, a great variety of such goods will be necessary to

happiness. For neither self-sufficiency nor moral action consists in excess; it is possible to do noble deeds without being lord of land and sea, as moderate means will enable a person to act in accordance with virtue. We may clearly see that it is so; for it seems that private persons practise virtue not less but actually more than persons in high place. It is enough that such a person should possess as much as is requisite for virtue; his life will be happy if he lives in the active exercise of virtue. Solon[1] was right perhaps in his description of the happy man as one "who is moderately supplied with external goods, and yet has performed the noblest actions,"—such was his opinion[2]—"and had lived a temperate life," for it is possible to do one's duty with only moderate means. It seems too that Anaxagoras did not conceive of the happy man as possessing wealth or power when he said that he should not be surprised if the happy man proved a puzzle in the eyes of the world; for the world judges by externals alone, it has no perception of anything that is not external.

The opinions of philosophers then seem to agree with our theories. Such opinions, it is true, possess a sort of authority; but it is the facts of life that are the tests of truth in practical matters, as they possess a supreme authority. It is right then to consider the doctrines which have been already advanced in reference to the facts of life, to accept them if they harmonize with those facts, and to regard them as mere theories if they disagree with them.

Again, he whose activity is directed by reason and who cultivates reason, and is in the best, *i.e. the most rational,* state of mind is also, as it seems, the most beloved of the Gods. For if the Gods care at all for human things, as is believed, it will be only reasonable to hold that they delight in what is best and most related to themselves, i.e. in reason, and that they requite with kindness those who love and honour it above all else, as caring for what is dear to themselves and performing right and noble actions.

It is easy to see that these conditions are found preeminently in the wise man. He will therefore be most beloved of the Gods. We may fairly suppose too that he is most happy; and if so, this is another reason for thinking that the wise man is preeminently happy.

(Tr. J. E. C. Welldon)

Wisdom and Virtue as the Basis of Society
(from *Politics*, Book VII)

1. He who would duly inquire about the best form of a state ought first to determine which is the most eligible life; while this remains uncertain the best form of the state must also be uncertain; for, in the natural order of things, those may be expected to lead the best life who are governed in the best manner of which their circumstances admit. We ought therefore to ascertain, first of all, which is the most generally eligible life, and then whether the same life is or is not best for the state and for individuals.

Assuming that enough has been already said in discussions outside the school concerning the best life, we will now only repeat what is contained in them. Certainly no one will dispute the propriety of that partition of goods which separates them into three classes, viz. external goods, goods of the body, and goods of the soul, or deny that the happy man must have all three. For no one would maintain that he is happy who has not in him a particle of courage or temperance or justice or prudence, who is afraid of every insect which flutters past him, and will commit any crime, however great, in order to gratify his lust of meat or drink, who will sacrifice his dearest friend for the sake of half-a-farthing, and is as feeble and false in mind as a child or a madman. These propositions are almost universally acknowledged as soon as they are uttered, but men differ about the degree or relative superiority of this or that good. Some think that a very moderate amount of virtue is enough, but set no limit to their desires of wealth, property, power, reputation, and the like. To whom we reply by an appeal to facts, which easily prove that mankind do not acquire or preserve virtue by the help of external goods, but external goods by the help of virtue, and that happiness, whether consisting in pleasure or virtue, or both, is more often found with those who are most highly cultivated in their mind and in their character, and have only a moderate share of external goods, than among those who possess external goods to a useless extent but are deficient in higher qualities; and this is not only matter of experience, but, if reflected upon, will easily appear to be in accordance with reason. For, whereas external goods have a limit, like any other instrument, and all things useful are of such a nature that where there is too much of them they must either do harm, or at any rate be of no use, to their possessors, every good of the soul, the greater it is, is also of greater use, if the epithet useful as well as noble is appropriate to such subjects. No proof is required to show that the best state of one thing in relation to another corresponds in degree of excellence to the interval between the natures of which we say that these very states are states: so that, if the soul is more noble than our possessions or our bodies, both absolutely and in relation to us, it must be admitted that the best state of either has a similar ratio to the other. Again, it is for the sake of the soul that goods external and goods of the body are eligible at all, and all wise men ought to choose them for the sake of the soul, and not the soul for the sake of them.

Let us acknowledge then that each one has just so much of happiness as he has of virtue and wisdom, and of virtuous and wise action. God is a witness to us of this truth, for he is happy and blessed, not by reason of any external good, but in himself and by reason of his own nature. And herein of necessity lies the difference between good fortune and happiness; for external goods come of themselves, and chance is the author of them, but no one is just or temperate by or through chance. In like manner, and by a similar train of argument, the happy state may be shown to be that which is best and which acts rightly; and rightly it cannot act without doing right actions, and neither individual nor state can do right actions without virtue and wisdom. Thus the courage, justice, and wisdom of a state have the same form and nature as the qualities which give the individual who possesses them the name of just, wise, or temperate.

Thus much may suffice by way of preface: for I could not avoid touching upon these questions, neither could I go through all the arguments affecting them; these are the business of another science.

Let us assume then that the best life, both for individuals and states, is the life of virtue, when virtue has external goods enough for the performance of good actions. If there are any who controvert our assertion, we will in this treatise pass them over, and consider their objections hereafter.

The Civil Society
(from *Politics*, Book I)

1. Every state is a community of some kind, and every community is established with a view to some good; for mankind always act in order to obtain that which they think good. But, if all communities aim at some good, the state or political community, which is the highest of all, and which embraces all the rest, aims at good in a greater degree than any other, and at the highest good.

Some people think that the qualifications of a statesman, king, householder, and master are the same, and that they differ, not in kind, but only in the number of their subjects. For example, the ruler over a few is called a master; over more, the manager of a household; over a still larger number, a statesman or king, as if there were no difference between a great household and a small state. The distinction which is made between the king and the statesman is as follows: When the government is personal, the ruler is a king; when, according to the rules of the political science, the citizens rule and are ruled in turn, then he is called a statesman.

But all this is a mistake; for governments differ in kind, as will be evident to any one who considers the matter according to the method which has hitherto guided us. As in other departments of science, so in politics, the compound should always be resolved into the simple elements or least parts of the whole. We must therefore look at the elements of which the state is composed, in order that we may see in what the different kinds of rule differ from one another, and whether any scientific result can be attained about each one of them.

2. He who thus considers things in their first growth and origin, whether a state or anything else, will obtain the clearest view of them. In the first place there must be a union of those who cannot exist without each other; namely, of male and female, that the race may continue (and this is a union which is formed, not of deliberate purpose, but because, in common with other animals and plants, mankind have a natural desire to leave behind them an image of themselves), and of natural ruler and subject, that both may be preserved. For that which can foresee by the exercise of mind is by nature intended to be lord and master, and that which can with its body give effect to such foresight is a subject, and by nature a slave; hence master and slave have the same interest. Now nature has distinguished between the female and the slave. For she is not niggardly, like the smith

who fashions the Delphian knife for many uses; she makes each thing for a single use, and every instrument is best made when intended for one and not for many uses. But among barbarians no distinction is made between women and slaves, because there is no natural ruler among them: they are a community of slaves, male and female. Wherefore the poets say—

'It is meet that Hellenes should rule over barbarians';

as if they thought that the barbarian and the slave were by nature one.

Out of these two relationships between man and woman, master and slave, the first thing to arise is the family, and Hesiod is right when he says—

'First house and wife and an ox for the plough,'

for the ox is the poor man's slave. The family is the association established by nature for the supply of men's everyday wants, and the members of it are called by Charondas 'companions of the cupboard,' and by Epimenides the Cretan, 'companions of the manger.' But when several families are united, and the association aims at something more than the supply of daily needs, the first society to be formed is the village. And the most natural form of the village appears to be that of a colony from the family, composed of the children and grandchildren, who are said to be 'suckled with the same milk.' And this is the reason why Hellenic states were originally governed by kings; because the Hellenes were under royal rule before they came together, as the barbarians still are. Every family is ruled by the eldest, and therefore in the colonies of the family the kingly form of government prevailed because they were of the same blood. As Homer says:

'Each one gives law to his children and to his wives.'

For they lived dispersedly, as was the manner in ancient times. Wherefore men say that the Gods have a king, because they themselves either are or were in ancient times under the rule of a king. For they imagine, not only the forms of the Gods, but their ways of life to be like their own.

When several villages are united in a single complete community, large enough to be nearly or quite self-sufficing, the state comes into existence, originating in the bare needs of life, and continuing in existence for the sake of a good life. And therefore, if the earlier forms of society are natural, so is the state, for it is the end of them, and the nature of a thing is its end. For what each thing is when fully developed, we call its nature, whether we are speaking of a man, a horse, or a family. Besides, the final cause and end of a thing is the best, and to be self-sufficing is the end and the best.

Hence it is evident that the state is a creation of nature, and that man is by nature a political animal. And he who by nature and not by mere accident is without a state, is either a bad man or above humanity; he is like the

'Tribeless, lawless, heartless one,'

whom Homer denounces—the natural outcast is forthwith a lover of war; he may be compared to an isolated piece at draughts.

Now, that man is more of a political animal than bees or any other gregarious animals is evident. Nature, as we often say, makes nothing in vain, and man is the only animal whom she has endowed with the gift of speech. And whereas mere voice is but an indication of pleasure or pain, and is therefore found in other animals (for their nature attains to the perception of pleasure and pain and the intimation of them to one another, and no further), the power of speech is intended to set forth the expedient and inexpedient, and therefore likewise the just and the unjust. And it is a characteristic of man that he alone has any sense of good and evil, of just and unjust, and the like, and the association of living beings who have this sense makes a family and a state.

Further, the state is by nature clearly prior to the family and to the individual, since the whole is of necessity prior to the part; for example, if the whole body be destroyed, there will be no foot or hand, except in an equivocal sense, as we might speak of a stone hand; for when destroyed the hand will be no better than that. But things are defined by their working and power; and we ought not to say that they are the same when they no longer have their proper quality, but only that they have the same name. The proof that the state is a creation of nature and prior to the individual is that the individual, when isolated, is not self-sufficing; and therefore he is like a part in relation to the whole. But he who is unable to live in society, or who has no need because he is sufficient for himself, must be either a beast or a god: he is no part of a state. A social instinct is implanted in all men by nature, and yet he who first founded the state was the greatest of benefactors. For man, when perfected, is the best of animals, but, when separated from law and justice, he is the worst of all; since armed injustice is the more dangerous, and he is equipped at birth with arms, meant to be used by intelligence and virtue, which he may use for the worst ends. Wherefore, if he have not virtue, he is the most unholy and the most savage of animals, and the most full of lust and gluttony. But justice is the bond of men in states, for the administration of justice, which is the determination of what is just, is the principle of order in political society.

Review Questions

1. Compare rationalism and empiricism, using Plato and Aristotle as points of departure.
2. What, for Aristotle, is the role of logic?
3. What does Aristotle mean by defining metaphysics as the science of *being as such?*
4. Is there, for Aristotle, a contradiction between being and nonbeing?
5. In Aristotle's analysis, what is there in being that allow change, or becoming, to take place?
6. What does Aristotle mean by *cause?*

7. How does Aristotle come to the conclusion that living things have a soul or are "besouled"?

8. Outline Aristotle's argument for a Prime Mover.

9. What need does Aristotle see for a governed society?

SUGGESTIONS FOR FURTHER READING

Ackrill, J. L. *Aristotle the Philosopher*. New York, Oxford University Press, 1981.

Barnes, J. *Aristotle*. New York, Oxford University Press, 1982.

Höffe, O. *Aristotle*. SUNY PRESS, 2003.

McKeon, R. P., ed. *Introduction to Aristotle* (Modern Library). New York, Random House, 1992.

Ross, W. D. *Aristotle*. New York, Meridian, 1959.

5

Epicurus
(341–270 B.C.)

Epicureans and Stoics

The death of Aristotle brought the golden age of Greek philosophy to a close and with it, as we have seen, the end of one of the most intense periods of sustained intellectual efforts in Western thought. Yet there were many generations of Greek philosophy still to come. The generation immediately following, for example, saw the rise of two groups, the Stoics and the Epicureans; the former, whose founder was Zeno of Cition, were named after the *stoa,* or porch, where he taught; the latter after their founder Epicurus. Though the Stoics were in large part taken up with logic and the Epicureans with physical science, both groups tended to move away from the speculative interests of their predecessors toward the practical concerns of life, essaying thereby to shape an ethical stance for coping with the troubles of human existence. Both groups maintained that the main purpose of virtue was to control oneself so as to be undisturbed by those personal troubles. Both groups professed unconcern about goods and possessions. Epicurus, whose logo can be found in his pronouncement that "Vain is the word of the philosopher which does not heal some suffering in man," will serve as an example of a firmly stated philosophy of ethical value based strictly, as we shall see, on a physical view of reality. His was a basically simple philosophy and preached with such open-armed welcome that it attracted adherents well into the centuries ahead.

The Garden

Epicurus, whose parents were Athenians, was born in 341 B.C. and, in all probability, brought up on the island of Samos; though he was in Athens for a short time as a young man, after some political disturbances following the death of Alexander, he removed to Colophon in Asia Minor. For some time he had been developing an interest in the philosophy of Democritus, several of whose followers he was able to meet, and gave early evidence of his teaching skills and his ability to create a community of students and disciples. Later, around 307 or 306, he went to Athens, his home until his death, and established another community just outside the city at a place which became known as the Garden. Here for the next thirty-five years he lived a simple, communal life with like-minded followers, apart from the distracting bustle of daily life and political turmoil, trying to cultivate a sense of genuine friendship among them and welcoming into their company a broad spectrum of society including courtesans and slaves. By all accounts he was an affable and friendly person, though he came down heavily on other philosophers whom he disagreed with. He had little use for traditional knowledge and culture because he felt they gave a false view of reality and accordingly encouraged the study of nature because it was only our knowledge of physical reality that could free us from unfounded fears and give our minds the measure of peace and tranquillity they sorely needed. He is renowned for having been a prolific writer, though almost all of his writings have been lost; among those extant are three letters and a catalog of his principal teachings. He died in 270 B.C.

Atomism

There is no doubt that the very physicality of the world has an unyielding hold on knowledge and try as we might we can never dismiss it, although in the history of philosophy some few philosophers have done so. The earliest of Greek philosophers, as we will recall, addressed the wonders of the natural world and even though they hankered after supramaterial forces, it was the cosmos in its materiality they were seeking to explain. What Epicurus was heir to, as were the pre-Socratic atomists, was a real world in which there were two basic substances: body and soul, matter and spirit. And just like his philosophical progenitors, Leucippus and Democritus, Epicurus' focus was on matter; it was there, it demanded attention, it could not be willed away, and so much did it commandeer his mind that he felt there was no warrant for anything as implausible as soul.

The first striking fact about matter requiring further investigation on Epicurus' part was the fact of change, whose beguiling nature underlay all Greek philosophy. As did Leucippus and Democritus, Epicurus believed that change cannot be denied and that, if it is genuine change, there must be something permanent remaining throughout the process: being and becoming, once again. Epicurus reasoned that matter could not be a monolithic, solid mass; it had to be composed of exceedingly small particles of matter, with enough ambient space to allow movement, so that change in a thing presenting itself as solid could be accounted for. In addition to their infinitesimal size, following the dictum that "nothing comes from nothing," these particles always had to be, they were being forever, eternal; they were indeed permanent. Epicurus, then, holding both permanence and change to be undeniable, located permanence in the eternity of the atoms and change in the way they continually rearranged themselves into new configurations.

A word more about Epicurus' atoms. Atoms are indivisible: "the first beginnings are indivisible corporeal existences," and though limitless in number they are limited in variety. In themselves, atoms have no sensible qualities, but in their aggregates they do. So Epicurus, starting with his premises, has everything he needs to explain reality, whether in this world or in the other worlds he insists exist. The body of man, of course, is composed of physical atoms, but so is his soul; atoms of the body are of a less refined variety than those of the soul, which are "fine particles distributed throughout the whole structure and most resembling mind with a certain admixture of heat." Atoms pervade all reality, all entities whether substances or actions, and Epicurus' unswerving commitment to this view gives his philosophy a consistency for whose sake some glaring questions are simply overlooked.

This consistency naturally extends to our knowledge, especially sensation. Sense data are immediate; our knowledge then is true because the immediacy of sense knowledge is its own warrant; it is true because it is self-evident. There is no room here for the scepticism of some of Epicurus' contemporaries, against which he offers his position as an antidote. If, however, sense knowledge involves its own justification, there is no other source of knowledge similarly justified: ". . . we must keep all our investigations in accord with our sensations, and in particular with the immediate apprehensions." The activity of sensation is accomplished in a strictly mechanical way: The atom dispatches a gossamerlike image (idol) of itself through the body's channels to be received by an inner receptacle thus matching the inner with the outer.

This position represents the opposite pole from Plato. Recalling our discussion of Plato's epistemology, the object known takes its shape from the way the mind knows it, but for Epicurus the mind takes its shape from the object known; if the object known is atomic, the mind must be just as atomic because of the immediacy of sense knowledge: The particulate aggregate must be known by a particulate mind, so the conclusion must be, which Epicurus does not make, that the mind is a collection of particles just as the object is, the overall point being that Epicurus never really accounts for how the mind, not really a self, can know the particulate atoms constellated as a whole.

Responses to sense objects are not confined to epistemology strictly so-called, for the feelings of pleasure and pain are authentic, basic responses as well and just as "truthful" as knowledge. We have an immediate awareness of pleasure and at the same time an awareness that pleasure is our good and that pain is its enemy: ". . . we recognize pleasure as the first good innate in us, and from pleasure we begin every act of choice." When pleasure is absent, we feel pain. Pleasure then is "the beginning and end of the blessed life." Every pleasure is good, yet there is a hierarchy. Immediate pleasures may not be, in the long run, the ones to satisfy us, so that intelligent choices guided by practical wisdom (*phronesis*) must be made. Peace of mind, the undisturbed evenness of soul that gives us a mastery over our fears, is the ultimate good and all those dispositions traditionally called virtues like justice, temperateness, courage, prudence are to be looked on as the means to a happy life.

Peace of Mind and the Fear of Death

We can begin to see clearly how Epicurus will employ his worldview to put to rest popular fears with regard to unknown assailants on our peace of mind, for even a person who, following the Epicurean canon, has mastered his life with temperateness, there still remains the dread of death and the valley of doom to destroy him. But Epicurus' philosophy of materialism allays such fears, for the existence of a human being is the same as the existence of everything else, a mere configuration of atoms, so that when the configuration ceases, so does the total existent—that is the meaning of death. After death, therefore, there is no human being to suffer, and this fact alone should bring comfort to the person fearful of punishment after death.

One other fear for such a person, however, has to be put to rest, and that is the possibility that the gods, angered by some unconscious transgression on his part, would mete out punishment after death as a matter of justice. On this point, Epicurus, wishing to give the gods their due, admonishes us to recognize their existence, their immortality, their blessedness, and their worthiness of honor. If men fear the gods, it is only because they have a false view of them, but ". . . they are not such as the many believe them to be." Gods exist, but their activities pertain to their own domain; they do not influence the affairs of men. On neither count then is there anything to fear from death: on the one count there is the truth of physical reality, and on the other the noninterference of the gods in the lives of human beings: "So death, the most terrifying of ills, is nothing to us, since so long as we exist death is not with us; but when death comes, then we do not exist."

We can now understand why Epicurus, though well versed in the philosophers of his time and of his great predecessors, Plato and Aristotle, basically circumvented them; though they might bring more satisfaction to the educated and trained philosopher, they offered nothing to the average person who, of little sophistication, needed help and guidance to get on with his life. Epicureanism was a direct, coherent, simple philosophy, which made it attractive to a vast number of people looking for that guidance and, suffused with the cultivation of friendship as it was, it became an invitation to a way of life. This appeal made it one of the most widespread and enduring philosophies of the Greek period, extending into the early centuries of the Christian period.

The Letter of Epicurus to Herodotu

For those who are unable, Herodotus, to work in detail through all that I have written about nature, or to peruse the larger books which I have composed, I have already prepared at sufficient length an epitome of the whole system, that they may keep adequately in mind at least the most general principles in each department, in order that as occasion arises they may be able to assist themselves on the most important points, in so far as they undertake the study of nature. But those also who have made considerable progress in the survey of the main principles ought to bear in mind the scheme of the whole system set forth in its essentials. For we have frequent need of the general view, but not so often of the detailed exposition. Indeed it is necessary to go back on the main principles, and constantly to fix in one's memory enough to give one the most essential comprehension of the truth. And in fact the accurate knowledge of details will be fully discovered, if the general principles in the various departments are thoroughly grasped and borne in mind; for even in the case of one fully initiated the most essential feature in all accurate knowledge is the capacity to make a rapid use of observation and mental apprehension, and this can be done if everything is summed up in elementary principles and formulae. For it is not possible for any one to abbreviate the complete course through the whole system, if he cannot embrace in his own mind by means of short formulae all that might be set out with accuracy in detail. Wherefore since the method I have described is valuable to all those who are accustomed to the investigation of nature, I who urge upon others the constant occupation in the investigation of nature, and find my own peace chiefly in a life so occupied, have composed for you another epitome on these lines, summing up the first principles of the whole doctrine.

First of all, Herodotus, we must grasp the ideas attached to words, in order that we may be able to refer to them and so to judge the inferences of opinion or problems of investigation or reflection, so that we may not either leave everything uncertain and go on explaining to infinity or use words devoid of meaning. For this purpose it is essential that the first mental image associated with each word should be regarded, and that there should be no need of explanation, if we are really to have a standard to which to refer a problem of investigation or reflection or a mental inference. And besides we must keep all our investigations in accord with our sensations, and in particular with the immediate apprehensions whether of the mind or of any one of the instruments of judgement, and likewise in accord with the feelings existing in us, in order that we may have indications whereby we may judge both the problem of sense-perception and the unseen.

Having made these points clear, we must now consider things imperceptible to the senses. First of all, that nothing is created out of that which does not exist: for if it were, everything would be created out of everything with no need of seeds. And again, if that which disappears were destroyed into that which did not exist, all things would have perished, since that into which they were dissolved would not exist. Furthermore, the universe always was such as it is now, and always will be the same. For there is nothing into which it changes; for outside the universe there is nothing which could come into it and bring about the change.

Moreover, the universe is bodies and space: for that bodies exist, sense itself witnesses in the experience of all men, and in accordance with the evidence of sense we must of necessity judge of the imperceptible by reasoning, as I have already said. And if there were not that which we term void and place and intangible existence, bodies would have nowhere to exist and nothing through which to move, as they are seen to move. And besides these two nothing can even be thought of either by conception or on the analogy of things conceivable such as could be grasped as whole existences and not spoken of as the accidents or properties of such existences. Furthermore, among bodies some are compounds, and others those of which compounds are formed. And these latter are indivisible and unalterable (if, that is, all things are not to be destroyed into the non-existent, but something permanent is to remain behind at the dissolution of compounds): they are completely solid in nature, and can by no means be dissolved in any part. So it must needs be that the first-beginnings are indivisible corporeal existences.

Moreover, the universe is boundless. For that which is bounded has an extreme point: and the extreme point is seen against something else. So that as it has no extreme point, it has no limit; and as it has not limit, it must be boundless and not bounded. Furthermore, the infinite is boundless both in the number of the bodies and in the extent of the void. For if on the one hand the void were boundless, and the bodies limited in number, the bodies could not stay anywhere, but would be carried about and scattered through the infinite void, not having other bodies to support them and keep them in place by means of collisions. But if, on the other hand, the void were limited, the infinite bodies would not have room wherein to take their place.

Besides this the indivisible and solid bodies, out of which too the compounds are created and into which they are dissolved, have an incomprehensible number of varieties in shape: for it is not possible that such great varieties of things should arise from the same atomic shapes, if they are limited in number. And so in each shape the atoms are quite infinite in number, but their differences of shape are not quite infinite, but only incomprehensible in number.

And the atoms move continuously for all time, some of them falling straight down, others swerving, and others recoiling from their collisions. And of the latter, some are borne on, separating to a long distance from one another, while others again recoil and recoil, whenever they chance to be checked by the interlacing with others, or else shut in by atoms interlaced around them. For on the one hand the nature of the void which separates each atom by itself brings this about, as it is not able to afford resistance, and on the other hand the hardness which belongs to the atoms makes them recoil after collision to as great a distance as the interlacing permits separation after the collision. And these motions have no beginning, since the atoms and the void are the cause.

These brief sayings, if all these points are borne in mind, afford a sufficient outline for our understanding of the nature of existing things.

Furthermore, there are infinite worlds both like and unlike this world of ours. For the atoms being infinite in number, as was proved already, are borne on far out into space. For these atoms, which are of such nature that a world could be created out of them or made by them, have not been used up either on one world or on a limited number of worlds, nor again on all the worlds which are alike, or on those which are different from these. So that there nowhere exists an obstacle to the infinite number of the worlds.

Moreover, there are images like in shape to the solid bodies, far surpassing perceptible things in their subtlety of texture. For it is not impossible that such emanations should be formed in that which surrounds the objects, nor that there should be opportunities for the formation of such hollow and thin frames, nor that there should be effluences which preserve the respective position and order which they had before in the solid bodies: these images we call idols.

Next, nothing among perceptible things contradicts the belief that the images have unsurpassable fineness of texture. And for this reason they have also the unsurpassable speed of motion, since the movement of all their atoms is uniform, and besides nothing or very few things hinder their emission by collisions, whereas a body composed of many or infinite atoms is at once hindered by collisions. Besides this, nothing contradicts the belief that the creation of the idols takes place as quick as thought. For the flow of atoms from the surface of bodies is continuous, yet it cannot be detected by any lessening in the size of the object because of the constant filling up of what is lost. The flow of images preserves for a long time the position and order of the atoms in the solid body, though it is occasionally confused. Moreover, compound idols are quickly formed in the air around, because it is not necessary for their substance to be filled in deep inside: and besides there are certain other methods in which existences of this sort are produced. For not one of these beliefs is contradicted by our sensations, if one looks to see in what way sensation will bring us the clear visions from external objects, and in what way again the corresponding sequences of qualities and movements.

Now we must suppose too that it is when something enters us from external objects that we not only see but think their shapes. For external objects could not make on us an impression of the nature of their own colour and shape by means of the air which lies between us and them, nor again by means of the rays of effluences of any sort which pass from us to them—nearly so well as if models, similar in colour and shape, leave the objects and enter according to their respective size either into our sight or into our mind; moving along swiftly, and so by this means reproducing the image of a single continuous thing and preserving the corresponding sequence of qualities and movements from the original object as the result of their uniform contact with us, kept up by the vibration of the atoms deep in the interior of the concrete body.

And every image which we obtain by an act of apprehension on the part of the mind or of the sense-organs, whether of shape or of properties, this image is the shape or the properties of the concrete object, and is produced by the constant repetition of the image or the impression it has left. Now falsehood and error always lie in the addition of opinion with regard to what is waiting to be confirmed or not contradicted, and then is not confirmed or is contradicted. For the similarity between the things which exist, which we call real and the images received as a likeness of things and produced either in sleep or through some other acts of apprehension on the part of the mind or the other instruments of judgement, could never be, unless there were some effluences of this nature actually brought into contact with our senses. And error would not exist unless another kind of movement too were produced inside ourselves, closely linked to the apprehension of images, but differing from it; and it is owing to this, supposing it is not confirmed, or is contradicted, that falsehood arises; but if it is confirmed or not contradicted, it is true. Therefore we must do our best to keep this doctrine in mind, in order that on the one hand the standards of judgement dependent on the clear visions may not be undermined, and on the other error may not be as firmly established as truth and so throw all into confusion.

Moreover, hearing, too, results when a current is carried off from the object speaking or sounding or making a noise, or causing in any other way a sensation of hearing. Now this current is split up into particles, each like the whole, which at the same time preserve a correspondence of qualities with one another and a unity of character which stretches right back to the object which emitted the sound: this unit it is which in most cases produces comprehension in the recipient, or, if not, merely makes manifest the presence of the external object. For without the transference from the object of some correspondence of qualities, comprehension of this nature could not result. We must not then suppose that the actual air is moulded into shape by the voice which is emitted or by other similar sounds—for it will be very far from being so acted upon by it—but that the blow which takes place inside us, when we emit our voice, causes at once a squeezing out of certain particles, which produce a stream of breath, of such a character as to afford us the sensation of hearing.

Furthermore, we must suppose that smell too, just like hearing, could never bring about any sensation, unless there were certain particles carried off from the object of suitable size to stir this sense-organ, some of them in a manner disorderly and alien to it, others in a regular manner and akin in nature. . . .

Next, referring always to the sensations and the feelings, for in this way you will obtain the most trustworthy ground of belief, you must consider that the soul is a body of fine particles distributed throughout the whole structure, and most resembling wind with a certain admixture of heat, and in some respects like to one of these and in some to the other. There is also the part which is many degrees more advanced even than these in fineness of composition, and for this reason is more capable of feeling in harmony with the rest of the structure as well. Now all this is made manifest by the activities of the soul and the feelings and the readiness of its movements and its processes of thought and by what we lose at the moment of death. Further, you must grasp that the soul possesses the chief cause of sensation: yet it could not have acquired sensation, unless it were in some way enclosed by the rest of the structure. And this in its turn having afforded the soul this cause of sensation acquires itself too a share in this contingent capacity from the soul. Yet it does not acquire all the capacities which the soul possesses: and therefore when the soul is released from the body, the body no longer has sensation. For it never possessed this power in itself, but used to afford opportunity for it to another existence, brought into being at the same time with itself: and this existence, owing to the power now consummated within itself as a result of motion, used spontaneously to produce for itself the capacity of sensation and then to communicate it to the body as well, in virtue of its contact and correspondence of movement, as I have already said. Therefore, so long as the soul remains in the body, even though some other part of the body be lost, it will never lose sensation; nay more, whatever portions of the soul may perish too, when that which enclosed it is removed either in whole or in part, if the soul continues to exist at all, it will retain sensation. On the other hand the rest of the structure, though it continues to exist either as a whole or in part, does not retain sensation, if it has once lost that sum of atoms, however small it be, which together goes to produce the nature of the soul. Moreover, if the whole structure is dissolved, the soul is dispersed and no longer has the same powers nor performs its movements, so that it does not possess sensation either. For it is impossible to imagine it with sensation, if it is not in this organism and cannot effect these movements, when what encloses and surrounds it is no longer the same as the surroundings in which it now exists and performs these movements. Furthermore, we must clearly comprehend as well, that the incorporeal in the general acceptation of the term is applied to that which could be thought of as such as an independent existence. Now it is impossible to conceive the incorporeal as a separate existence, except the void: and the void can neither act nor be acted upon, but only provides opportunity of motion through itself to bodies. So that those who say that the soul is incorporeal are talking idly. For it would not be able to act or be acted on in any respect, if it were of this nature. But as it is, both these occurrences are clearly distinguished in respect of the soul. Now if one refers all these reasonings about the soul to the standards of feeling and sensation and remembers what was said at the outset, he will see that they are sufficiently embraced in these general formulae to enable him to work out with certainty on this basis the details of the system as well....

Moreover, we must suppose that human nature too was taught and constrained to do many things of every kind merely by circumstances; and that later on reasoning elaborated what had been suggested by nature and made further inventions, in some matters quickly, in others slowly, at some epochs and times making great advances, and lesser again at others. And so names too were not at first deliberately given to things, but men's natures according to their different nationalities had their own peculiar feelings and received their peculiar impressions, and so each in their own way emitted air formed into shape by each of these feelings and impressions, according to the differences made in the different nations by the places of their abode as well. And then later on by common consent in each nationality special names were deliberately given in order to make their meanings less ambiguous to one another and more briefly demonstrated. And sometimes those who were acquainted with them brought in things hitherto unknown and introduced sounds for them, on some occasions being naturally constrained to utter them, and on others choosing them by reasoning in accordance with the prevailing mode of formation, and thus making their meaning clear.

Furthermore, the motions of the heavenly bodies and their turnings and eclipses and risings and settings, and kindred phenomena to these, must not be thought to be due to any being who controls and ordains or has ordained them and at the same time enjoys perfect bliss together with immortality (for trouble and care and anger and kindness are not consistent with a life of blessedness, but these things come to pass where there is weakness and fear and dependence on neighbours). Nor again must we believe that they, which are but fire agglomerated in a mass, possess blessedness, and voluntarily take upon themselves these movements. But we must preserve their full majestic significance in all expressions which we apply to such conceptions, in order that there may not arise out of them opinions contrary to this notion of majesty. Otherwise this very contradiction will cause the greatest disturbance in men's souls. Therefore we must believe that it is due to the original inclusion of matter in such agglomerations during the birth-process of the world that this law of regular succession is also brought about.

Furthermore, we must believe that to discover accurately the cause of the most essential facts is the function of the science of nature, and that blessedness for us in the knowledge of celestial phenomena lies in this and in the understanding of the nature of the existences seen in these celestial phenomena, and of all else that is akin to the exact knowledge requisite for our happiness: in knowing too that what occurs in several ways or is capable of being otherwise has no place here, but that nothing which suggests doubt or alarm can be included at all in that which is naturally immortal and blessed. Now this we can ascertain by our mind is absolutely the case. But what falls within the investigation of risings and settings and turnings and eclipses, and all that is akin to this, is no longer of any value for the happiness which knowledge brings, but persons who have perceived all this, but yet do not know what are the natures of these things and what are the essential causes, are still in fear, just as if they did not know these things at all: indeed, their fear may be even greater, since the wonder which arises out of the observation of these things cannot discover any solution or realize the regulation of the essentials. . . .

And besides all these matters in general we must grasp this point, that the principal disturbance in the minds of men arises because they think that these celestial bodies are blessed and immortal, and yet have wills and actions and motives inconsistent with these attributes; and because they are always expecting or imagining some everlasting misery, such as is depicted in legends, or even fear the loss of feeling in death as though it would concern them themselves; and, again, because they are brought to this pass not by reasoned opinion, but rather by some irrational presentiment, and therefore, as they do not know the limits of pain, they suffer a disturbance equally great or even more extensive than if they had reached this belief by opinion. But peace of mind is being delivered from all this, and having a constant memory of the general and most essential principles.

Wherefore we must pay attention to internal feelings and to external sensations in general and in particular, according as the subject is general or particular, and to every immediate intuition in accordance with each of the standards of judgement. For if we pay attention to these, we shall rightly trace the causes whence arose our mental disturbance and fear, and, by learning the true causes of celestial phenomena and all other occurrences that come to pass from time to time, we shall free ourselves from all which produces the utmost fear in other men.

Here, Herodotus, is my treatise on the chief points concerning the nature of the general principles, abridged so that my account would be easy to grasp with accuracy. I think that, even if one were unable to proceed to all the detailed particulars of the system, he would from this obtain an unrivalled strength compared with other men. For indeed he will clear up for himself many of the detailed points by reference to our general system, and these very principles, if he stores them in his mind, will constantly aid him. For such is their character that even those who are at present engaged in working out the details to a considerable degree, or even completely, will be able to carry out the greater part of their investigations into the nature of the whole by conducting their analysis in reference to such a survey as this. And as for all who are not fully among those on the way to being perfected, some of them can from this summary obtain a hasty view of the most important matters without oral instruction so as to secure peace of mind.

Review Questions

1. Give an account of the human concerns in Epicurus's philosophy.
2. Using Epicurus as your example, what role does friendship play in the context of teaching and learning?
3. In what senses would you call Epicurus a materialist? an atomist? a naturalist?
4. What is the meaning of death for Epicurus?

Suggestions for Further Reading

Bailey, C. *The Greek Atomists and Epicurus.* Oxford University Press, 1928.
Gaskins, J. C. A. *The Epicurean Philosophers* (Everyman). London, C. E. Tuttle, 1995.
Lillegard, N. *On Epicurus.* California, Wadsworth, 2002.
Oates, W. J., ed. *The Stoic and Epicurean Philosophers.* New York, Random House, 1940.

6

The Stoics: Epictetus and Marcus Aurelius (A.D. 50–138) (A.D. 121–180)

Stoicism

Stoicism thrived as a philosophy alongside Epicureanism and exerted a widespread influence in Greece and Rome for over 500 years. Any long-standing philosophy such as this, holding its own through vast changes on the political and cultural horizon, is bound not to be doctrinally consistent in every respect throughout its career. Yet, with changes in emphasis and with positions sometimes conflicting, there remains a permanent philosophical spirit that identifies Stoicism as a community of thought or as exhibiting a "family resemblance" in the diverse periods of its history. You will find, for example, continual references to the world as eternal, physical, subject to a never-ending cycle of change, and though the Stoics were not generally given to the metaphysical speculations of Aristotle and Plato, metaphysics and logic were looked upon as ultimately indispensable for understanding the world. But these are not the considerations finally characterizing Stoicism as a family of thought; it was their insistent concern with ethical considerations, with the course of human behavior that would make living in the world an enterprise worthy of rational nature.

Historians identify three periods in the long reign of Stoicism—early, middle and late. The early period counts among its major figures *Zeno of Citium* (c.335-263 B.C., acknowledged to be the founder of Stoicism, a name taken from the school he established at the Stoa Poikile (painted porch or colonnade). As the generations passed and the power center of the Mediterranean began to shift from Greece to Rome, the Romans themselves took the opportunity to absorb Greek culture, not least of which was the philosophy of Stoicism. This was particularly true of Cicero, Roman philosopher and statesman, who was attracted to it by his studies on the Greek island of Rhodes and naturally committed himself to spreading his adopted view of life. The latest period of Stoicism thus became Roman in the first and second centuries A.D. and, in keeping with the Roman bent toward the practical, leaned on the Stoic injunctions for the predominance of self-control and the elusive prize of personal consolation.

Before considering Epictetus and Marcus Aurelius, the two best-known representatives of the Stoic philosophy, it would be worthwhile to look at the traditional "orthodox" core as we know it, both from the philosophers' own writings or from reports on what the earlier Stoics held.

The oneness of the cosmos is the foundation of all understanding of reality and of everything in it. Order is its keynote, and the harmony resounding in all things is brought about by the active presence of a power—God, logos, world soul, law of nature—so that God and the universe are effectively one, in a unity that can only be called *monistic pantheism*. Indebted to Heraclitus, the early Stoics held fire to be the ultimate physical element permeating all reality and, as delivered of God, binding all things together.

Following the traditional Greek notion that the universe never came to be, but always was, the Stoics held that the course of the universe is eternal and, given that "course" means "change," change also is eternal, thus rendering the universe, not linear in its unfolding, but cyclical and subject to eternal return. Lastly, because there is no "outside" the universe, that is, no "outside" God or "outside" Nature, all change is "within," immanent, natural; and if to humans things appear as crooked, straight, or chaotic, to the Eternal, things are totally otherwise; in his poem, Cleanthes writes, ". . . thou knowest to make crooked straight: Chaos to thee is order." In turn, this means that change is one-with-God, and is so by necessity, by the law of Nature. We shall see this notion of change as immanent in philosophers yet to come like Nicholas of Cusa, Spinoza, Hegel, and Bergson, indicating how profound must our understanding of change be for a proper reading of reality.

The Stoics, along with the Epicureans, were committed to the priority of sense knowledge and even to its exclusivity, so that an unyielding sense empiricism was their pathway to the real world. Whatever is, is individual and particular; no place for universals, neither the transcendental universal in Plato's world of ideas nor the concrete universal of Aristotle expressing the commonness really found in individuals of the same class; the best to be hoped for was a commonness of name, nominalism therefore. The generation of knowledge for the Stoic required that the mind be impressed by the object as wax is impressed by a seal, one on one, with its directness guaranteeing its truth.

Since the syllogism of Aristotle demanded a universal to begin with, and for the Stoic a universal is no place to be found, the standard syllogism was not a favorite device for the Stoic. Stoic logic focused on propositions whose truth or falsity follows from the immediacy of sense perception. And the fact that a proposition has to be either true or false allows it to become in turn the basis of a series of inferences. Take the type: if the first, then the second; but the first, therefore the second. For example, if there is a lighted candle under it, my hand gets hot; but there is a lighted candle under it, therefore my hand gets hot. In this fashion, the Stoics were able to develop insights into the logic of hypothetical, or conditional, propositions thus extending the inventive work of Aristotle.

As important as the earlier Stoics' views on logic and cosmology may be in their own right, the reputation enjoyed by Stoic philosophy in general rests on its *ethical teaching*, and this primarily through the guiding principles of life as propounded by its two best-known representatives, Epictetus and Marcus Aurelius, paradoxically one a slave and the other an emperor.

Epictetus

Epictetus of Hierapolis in Asia Minor (c. A.D. 50–138) was a slave (*epictetus* in Greek means "newly acquired property") and a member of Nero's bodyguard. Slaves were often themselves or through their parents spoils of war and therefore had no rights; but in many instances their talents were acknowledged, as in the case of Epictetus. He was given a liberal education, the education of a "free" man, by his master, and after actually becoming a freedman himself he lived in Rome, took up the study of Stoicism, and acquired a reputation as a philosopher. He was compelled to go into exile, however, when the tyrant Emperor Domitian forced the "philosophers" out of Rome, believing they were sympathetic to the political opposition. He traveled to northwest Greece, to the city of Nicopolis in Epiris, where he founded a school.

Though the course of studies at the school called for instruction in logic and physics, Epictetus himself was primarily concerned with developing standards for human behavior and was recognized in this capacity as a superb teacher. His classroom was a lively theater of interactive teaching and learning in which he would have the students read aloud passages from Stoic masters and then comment on them, all the while soliciting student response in the style of Socrates. What did the students hear from the master? Certainly admonitions of self-control, evenness of judgment, respect for Nature and the wisdom of following Nature's (God's) will; how to judge good and evil; and the use of reason to temper the power of impressions. They were given practical advice on how to soften anxiety, how to please the gods, how to develop friendships; why one should keep the body clean: if you come to learn, come with your hair trim and not "dishevelled and dirty"; why one should not get angry over another's mistakes; and why we should not stubbornly hold on to our judgments. These are the lessons Epictetus never put to writing, so the *Discourses* must be seen as lecture-comments of the master as written down by one of his students, Arrian, who also prepared a résumé of them for general use called the *Manual*, which was promptly adopted by the military for the guidance of its soldiers.

Achieving Peace of Mind

For anyone living a day-by-day human existence, open to the joys and pleasures of the world and, on the same account subject to its caprices, uncertainties, and even violence, the ultimate goal of life is *peace of mind*—an internal serenity brought about by equanimity, constancy, rational balance—achievable, in Epictetus' view, by the only coping device man has, *self-control*. What is it that tells you how to act? what not to fear? what is right? It is our reason, standing as mediator between God and His purposes in this world: "What will tell you then? That faculty which takes cognizance of itself and of all things else. What is this? The reasoning faculty: for this alone of the faculties we have received is created to comprehend even its own nature; that is to say, what it is and what it can do, and with what precious qualities it has come to us, and to comprehend all other faculties as well."

By looking at the downward side, we see a confusion of good and evil, right and wrong, crooked and straight, chaos and order; but looking at the upward side we see the all-provident God who cunningly insures that His purposes are observed. Our part in them? A person must "attach" himself to God to pass safely through this world: "What do you mean by 'attach' himself? That what God wills, he may will too, and what God wills not, he may not will either. How then is this to be done? How else, but by examining the purposes of God and His governance of the world."

Thus, virtue—the doing of what we know to be right—is within everyone's capacity. We can train our wills to manage what is "in our power" and to reject what "is not in our power"; to "bear" or endure what we can control and to "forbear" or renounce what we cannot. This distinction is found at every turn through Epictetus' pages of ethical advice. Can Caesar put me in prison? . . . outside my control; bear it. Can sickness bring me down? . . . outside my control; bear it. Can I lose all my goods? . . . outside my control; bear it. But to grieve or despair over those things, or to grow anxious about them is within my control, so I am bound to renounce them; succumbing to them is evil, but maintaining my serenity despite them is good. Man's good and evil then is really found, not in things, but in the faculty of reason: "Where then is man's good and man's evil, in the true sense, to be found? In that faculty which makes men different from all else."

It may be argued that no Greek philosopher had so profound a personal conception of God as did Epictetus: God is all-wise, all-provident; in Him is found the wholeness of reality, and in this wholeness all things are to be seen, or they are not seen at all. Each one of us is urged to see our actions as God sees them, and if we find ourselves in a dilemma we are bidden to ask, "What would Zeus have me do?", thus expressing a deep personal concern for moral direction. It's no wonder that some early Christians held that Stoic principles must have been leavened by Christian belief.

Yet the hope that Epictetus seems to have entertained, to make a seamless garment out of reality, has many difficulties: how to resolve the age-old problem of the one and the many, in this case the One and the many; how to give a spiritual overtone to the physicality of the world; how to reconcile personal freedom with an overriding determinism; how to hold the option of suicide against the moral imperative of a deterministic Nature; how to speak of eternity and yet hold to the absolute dissolution of the human being; how to hold monotheism as consistent with polytheism. These persistent and friction-laden dichotomies belong to the mystery of reality that Epictetus appointed "peace of mind" to overrule.

Marcus Aurelius

Marcus Aurelius (C. A.D. 121–180) was the adopted son of the Emperor Antoninus Pius, his uncle and father-in-law, who groomed him as his successor; he became Emperor in 161 and ruled for 19 years until 180, when he died of the plague on a military expedition against the northern barbarians along the Danube.

The Emperor was by all accounts a gentle, forgiving, and peace-minded man, but he had to invoke the Stoic principles he learned as a young man to maintain an even keel through the troubles in the empire he inherited. Rome was experiencing economic disaster and civil strife, along with insurrection, disease, earthquakes, and attacks on her northern and eastern frontiers, pressure from which eventually wore him down. His forbearance throughout was remarkable for an emperor, especially an emperor besieged, as the following example bears out. His commander for the east, Avidius Cassius, rebelled against him, initiated civil war, and proclaimed himself Emperor, though he was subsequently assassinated by his own men. Yet, so remarkable was Marcus Aurelius' forbearance that in a speech to his soldiers purported to be authentic he spoke of being deprived of a great "prize": "And what is that? To forgive a man who has done wrong, to be still a friend to one who had trodden friendship underfoot, to continue faithful to one who has broken faith . . . and show to all the world that even civil war can be dealt with on right principles." But the Emperor did the next best thing by pardoning the dead Cassius and his family as well.

In a far different situation, whether Marcus Aurelius departed from his storied forbearance or not depends on how much credit you are willing to assign to hindsight. It is quite well-founded that he sanctioned the persecution of Christians, at least those living in Lyons, but, say his defenders, this willingness to persecute must be seen in the prevailing context. The practice of Christians suffered misrepresentation, especially their refusal to worship the gods of the state, which made them liable to be looked upon as enemies of the state and to be treated as such. It's understandable then, if not excusable, that the Emperor's forbearance was not to be forthcoming. Still, say those who admire him, from the evidence of his personal lifestyle, from the internal spirit of the *Meditations*, and from the way he ruled the empire, Marcus Aurelius had all the qualities of Plato's philosopher-king, or, in the words of Matthew Arnold, ". . . perhaps the most beautiful figure in history."

The *Meditations* were written by Marcus Aurelius expressly for himself, not for publication, a kind of diary of his soul, reflections on the problems of life: divine providence, Nature, virtue, the good life, fame, earthly things, happiness, ingratitude, treatment of others, pain, death, self-reliance, tranquillity. He yearned for quiet and peace but, on not finding such an oasis in the real world outside, he had to create it within; his mind became his garden. He wrote his thoughts down wherever he could, many of them on his campaigns; later, to give these occasional reflections a sense of unity, he probably wrote the first book last, as an introduction.

On the Ordering of Life

As we've seen previously, whether he begins from the bottom and works up or from the top and works down, the mark of a true philosopher is his sense of unity. Marcus Aurelius is a top-down thinker, one who begins with totality, the whole, the all-in-all; and then particular things and actions make sense. If a Christian were asked what is man for, what is his destiny, the response would be in terms of man's ultimate personal fulfilment in some kind of return to the God from whence he came. If a Stoic, if Marcus Aurelius, were asked the same question, he would say that the question from one point of view is unreal because if we cannot meaningfully ask what the Universe is "for"—as though the Universe works toward a goal outside itself—then we cannot ask what man is for either because he is at-one-with-Nature. But from another point of view, the Stoic would say, the question makes eminent sense because to be at-one-with-Nature *is* the main goal of the human being: "All things are implicated with one another, and the bond is holy; and there is hardly anything unconnected with any other thing. For things have been co-ordinated, and they combine to form the same universe (order). For there is one universe made up of all things, and one God who pervades all things, and one substance, and one law, one common reason in all intelligent animals. . . ." *Live according to Nature* is the chief maxim for human activity.

The mediatorship of reason is called for precisely at this point. Possessing intelligence, the human being is different from all other beings and can knowingly grasp the law of the universe. There is within each of us a spark of divinity, a spirit to guide us, which is our share of the intelligence that pervades Nature and nourishes our willingness to accept its ordering: The one who walks with the gods is the one ". . . who lets them see his soul invariably satisfied with its lot and carrying out the will of the 'genius,' a particle of himself, which Zeus has given to every man as his captain and guide—and this is none other than each man's intelligence and reason." Life according to Reason duplicates the wonder of the universe in one's own soul; harmony is the goal set before us.

All the urgings to virtue, all the exhortations to do good, and all the admonitions to avoid evil make sense only if man is free to act upon them. So a problem is immediately created because, for the Stoic, activity in the universe, of which human activity is a part, is determined. How then can what is free be determined at the same time? The contradiction between the two is one of the knotty problems that have tried philosophers for centuries and is hardly about to disappear. But it does not sit very well to hold that the Stoics, especially Epictetus and Marcus Aurelius, were unaware of the contradiction, or simply unfazed by it; they were much too clear-headed for that. So there must be another kind of explanation, one allowing for some compatibility between the two extremes. Later on, even the Christian moralists will insist that it is *necessary* for intelligent creatures to *will* what God wants, that is, freely doing what is necessary; freedom, in this sense, is governed by necessity. Perhaps the Stoics, even though they did not formulate the tension between freedom and determinism in this way, were heading toward the conclusion which, centuries later, Spinoza found inescapable, that in God (Universe, Nature) necessity and freedom are one and the same.

The choices a person makes in the Stoic scheme of things take on the ethical shape imposed by the ordering of nature and filtered through reason as an imperative for the human being; in turn, this imperative is seen as the goal of life. But it's possible for this goal to be stonewalled, for the Stoic, as a distant echo against Camus' view that suicide is unacceptable because it is a repudiation of life's absurdity, held to the permissibility of suicide in certain cases like incurable illness or senility. Though not high on their agenda, Epictetus and Marcus Aurelius both allow it. Epictetus suggests that if life becomes unbearable, imitate the child who opts out of a game: "Children, when things do not please them, say 'I will not play anymore'; so, when things seem to you to reach that point, just say, 'I will not play anymore,' and so depart. . . ." And Marcus Aurelius, for whom the true life is of all-consuming importance, invites the person who cannot sustain the striving to be good, modest, true, rational, even-minded, magnanimous, to consider departing ". . . at once from life, not in passion, but with simplicity and freedom and modesty, after doing this one laudable thing at least in thy life, to have gone out of it thus."

Death

Death itself, however, is looked upon as a natural event, in rhythm with all the other events of nature; in this sense, it is beyond our control and should cause no disturbance of mind. It is not an evil, it is "a good, since it is seasonable and profitable to and congruent with the universal." Just as life brings youth and old age, so it brings its dissolution, yet "Do not despise death, but be well content with it, since this too is one of those things which nature wills." There is nothing to fear from death: It is either extinction or change. If it is the former, there is nothing in the future to fear; if it is the latter, the goodness of the universe insures no harm. It is not death, says Epictetus, that is to be feared, but the fear of death. Death is a "bogy," regarded as harmful when it is not, thereby causing a baseless fear.

Since life after death is not unmistakably written in the order of nature, no Stoic holds it to be so, though some maintain that a soul may exist after death until the next conflagration when it merges once again with the Universe as Primary Being. Marcus Aurelius is clearer. When he reflects on the possibility of a person who has lived devoutly in scrupulously following the divine will, he records his quandary that after death such a person may have "no second existence" but is "wholly extinguished." To resolve the quandary he turns again to the order of nature; if nature ordered immortality, it would be so, and it would be just; if nature has not ordered it, it would not be so, and it would still be just: "But if this is so (i.e., when they have once died they should never exist again), be assured that if it ought to have been otherwise, the gods would have done it. For if it were just, it would also be possible; and if it were according to nature, nature would have had it so. But because it is not so, if in fact it is not so, be thou convinced that it ought not to have been so . . . but if this is so, they would not have allowed anything in the ordering of the universe to be neglected unjustly and irrationally."

Just as with Epicureanism, the Stoicism of Epictetus and Marcus Aurelius made no demands on high speculation whereas it attempted to fashion a coherent philosophy that its practitioners could embrace as ennobling and humanizing. It matched to a tee the practical style of the Romans and contributed to Christian writers' trying to forge a pattern of life commensurate with Christian ideals. The melding of waning ancient with dawning Christian thought was accomplished not only by the philosophies of Epicureanism and Stoicism but also by the philosophy of Plato, whose great themes were rethought in a Christian setting by another Greek philosopher, Plotinus, in the third century A.D. This re-thinking of Plato resulted in a philosophic doctrine known as *Neoplatonism*. Inspired by Plato's overarching doctrines of the superiority of the eternal to the temporal, the world of Ideas as the world of pure being, the nature of man's participation in the Ideal world, and man's purification and return to the eternal, Plotinus constructed a pyramid of reality in which the very being of the One overflows, or emanates, into the formation of every other being, particularly into those with intelligence. And if this is the route whereby man comes from God, it is also the route he takes back. This is a mysticism of the highest order in which all distinctions are transcended and the soul recognizes that it is one with the One. Plotinus in his own right, but even more Plato through him, had a profound influence on the early Christian thinkers, the Fathers of the Church, to whom we will turn in the next chapter.

READINGS

The Hymn of Cleanthes

O God most glorious, called by many a name,
Nature's great King, through endless years the same;
Omnipotence, who by thy just decree
Controllest all, hail, Zeus, for unto thee
Behoves thy creatures in all lands to call.

We are thy children, we alone, of all
On earth's broad ways that wander to and fro,
Bearing thine image wheresoe'er we go.
Wherefore with songs of praise thy power I will forth show.
Lo! yonder Heaven, that round the earth is wheeled,
Follows thy guidance, still to thee doth yield
Glad homage; thine unconquerable hand
Such flaming minister, the levin brand,
Wieldeth, a sword two-edged, whose deathless might
Pulsates through all that Nature brings to light;
Vehicle of the universal Word, that flows
Through all, and in the light celestial glows
Of stars both great and small. A King of Kings
Through ceaseless ages, God, whose purpose brings
To birth, whate'er on land or in the sea
Is wrought, or in high heaven's immensity;
Save what the sinner works infatuate.
Nay, but thou knowest to make crooked straight:
Chaos to thee is order: in thine eyes
The unloved is lovely, who didst harmonize
Things evil with things good, that there should be
One Word through all things everlastingly.
One Word—whose voice alas! the wicked spurn;
Insatiate for the good their spirits yearn:
Yet seeing see not, neither hearing hear
God's universal law, which those revere,
By reason guided, happiness who win.
The rest, unreasoning, diverse shapes of sin
Self-prompted follow: for an idle name
Vainly they wrestle in the lists of fame:
Others inordinately riches woo,
Or dissolute, the joys of flesh pursue.
Now here, now there they wander, fruitless still,
For ever seeking good and finding ill.
Zeus the all-bountiful, whom darkness shrouds,
Whose lightning lightens in the thunder-clouds;
Thy children save from error's deadly sway:
Turn thou the darkness from their souls away:
Vouchsafe that unto knowledge they attain;
For thou by knowledge art made strong to reign
O'er all, and all things rulest righteously.
So by thee honoured, we will honour thee,
Praising thy works continually with songs,
As mortals should; nor higher meed belongs
E'en to the gods, than justly to adore
The universal law for evermore.

(Trans. James Adam)

The Manual of Epictetus

1. There are things which are within our power, and there are things which are beyond our power. Within our power are opinion, aim, desire, aversion, and, in one word, whatever affairs are our own. Beyond our power are body, property, reputation, office, and, in one word, whatever are not properly our own affairs.

Now the things within our power are by nature free, unrestricted, unhindered; but those beyond our power are weak, dependent, restricted, alien. Remember, then, that if you attribute freedom to things by nature dependent and take what belongs to others for your own, you will be hindered, you will lament, you will be disturbed, you will find fault both with gods and men. But if you take for your own only that which is your own and view what belongs to others just as it really is, then no one will ever compel you, no one will restrict you; you will find fault with no one, you will accuse no one, you will do nothing against your will; no one will hurt you, you will not have an enemy, nor will you suffer any harm.

Aiming, therefore, at such great things, remember that you must not allow yourself any inclination, however slight, toward the attainment of the others; but that you must entirely quit some of them, and for the present postpone the rest. But if you would have these, and possess power and wealth likewise, you may miss the latter in seeking the former; and you will certainly fail of that by which alone happiness and freedom are procured.

Seek at once, therefore, to be able to say to every unpleasing semblance, "You are but a semblance and by no means the real thing." And then examine it by those rules which you have; and first and chiefly by this: whether it concerns the things which are within our own power or those which are not; and if it concerns anything beyond our power, be prepared to say that it is nothing to you.

5. Men are disturbed not by things, but by the views which they take of things. Thus death is nothing terrible, else it would have appeared so to Socrates. But the terror consists in our notion of death, that it is terrible. When, therefore, we are hindered or disturbed, or grieved, let us never impute it to others, but to ourselves—that is, to our own views. It is the action of an uninstructed person to reproach others for his own misfortunes; of one entering upon instruction, to reproach himself; and one perfectly instructed, to reproach neither others nor himself.

8. Demand not that events should happen as you wish; but wish them to happen as they do happen, and you will go on well.

9. Sickness is an impediment to the body, but not to the will unless itself pleases. Lameness is an impediment to the leg, but not to the will; and say this to yourself with regard to everything that happens. For you will find it to be an impediment to something else, but not truly to yourself.

13. If you would improve, be content to be thought foolish and dull with regard to externals. Do not desire to be thought to know anything; and though you should appear to others to be somebody, distrust yourself. For be assured, it is not easy at once to keep your will in harmony with nature and to secure externals; but while you are absorbed in the one, you must of necessity neglect the other.

19. You can be unconquerable if you enter into no combat in which it is not in your own power to conquer. When, therefore, you see anyone eminent in honors or power, or in high esteem on any other account, take heed not to be bewildered by appearances and to pronounce him happy; for if the essence of good consists in things within our own power, there will be no room for envy or emulation. But, for your part, do not desire to be a general, or a senator, or a consul, but to be free; and the only way to this is a disregard of things which lie not within our own power.

21. Let death and exile, and all other things which appear terrible, be daily before your eyes, but death chiefly; and you will never entertain an abject thought, nor too eagerly covet anything.

25. Is anyone preferred before you at an entertainment, or in courtesies, or in confidential intercourse? If these things are good, you ought to rejoice that he has them; and if they are evil, do not be grieved that you have them not. And remember that you cannot be permitted to rival others in externals without using the same means to obtain them.

26. The will of nature may be learned from things upon which we are all agreed. As when our neighbor's boy has broken a cup, or the like, we are ready at once to say, "These are casualties that will happen"; be assured, then, that when your own cup is likewise broken, you ought to be affected just as when another's cup was broken. Now apply this to greater things. Is the child or wife of another dead? There is no one who would not say, "This is an accident of mortality." But if anyone's own child happens to die, it is immediately, "Alas! how wretched am I!" It should be always remembered how we are affected on hearing the same thing concerning others.

30. Duties are universally measured by relations. Is a certain man your father? In this are implied taking care of him, submitting to him in all things, patiently receiving his reproaches, his correction. But he is a bad father. Is your natural tie, then, to a *good* father? No, but to a father. Is a brother unjust? Well, preserve your own just relation toward him. Consider not what *he* does, but what *you* are to do to keep your own will in a state conformable to nature, for another cannot hurt you unless you please. You will then be hurt when you consent to be hurt. In this manner, therefore, if you accustom yourself to contemplate the relations of neighbor, citizen, commander, you can deduce from each the corresponding duties.

31. Be assured that the essence of piety toward the gods lies in this—to form right opinions concerning them, as existing and as governing the universe justly and well. And fix yourself in this resolution, to obey them, and yield to them, and willingly follow them amidst all events, as being ruled by the most perfect wisdom. For thus you will never find fault with the gods, nor accuse them of neglecting you. . . .

35. When you do anything from a clear judgment that it ought to be done, never shrink from being seen to do it, even though the world should misunderstand it; for if you are not acting rightly, shun the action itself; if you are, why fear those who wrongly censure you?

38. As in walking you take care not to tread upon a nail, or turn your foot, so likewise take care not to hurt the ruling faculty of your mind. And if we were to guard against this in every action, we should enter upon action more safely.

42. When any person does ill by you, or speaks ill of you, remember that he acts or speaks from an impression that it is right for him to do so. Now it is not possible that he should follow what appears right to you, but only what appears so to himself. Therefore, if he judges from false appearances, he is the person hurt, since he, too, is the person deceived. For if anyone takes a true proposition to be false, the proposition is not hurt, but only the man is deceived. Setting out, then, from these principles, you will meekly bear with a person who reviles you, for you will say upon every occasion, "It seemed so to him."

51. The first and most necessary topic in philosophy is the practical application of principles, as, *We ought not to lie*; the second is that of demonstrations as, *Why it is that we ought not to lie*; the third, that which gives strength and logical connection to the other two, as, *Why this is a demonstration*. For what is demonstration? What is a consequence? What a contradiction? What truth? What falsehood? The third point is then necessary on account of the second; and the second on account of the first. But the most necessary, and that whereon we ought to rest, is the first. But we do just the contrary. For we spend all our time on the third point and employ all our diligence about that, and entirely neglect the first. Therefore, at the same time that we lie, we are very ready to show how it is demonstrated that lying is wrong.

Upon all occasions we ought to have these maxims ready at hand:

> Conduct me, Zeus, and thou, O Destiny,
> Wherever your decrees have fixed my lot.
> I follow cheerfully; and, did I not,
> Wicked and wretched, I must follow still.[1]

> Who'er yields properly to Fate is deemed
> Wise among men, and knows the laws of Heaven.[2]

And this third:

> "O Crito, if it thus pleases the gods, thus let it be."[3]
> "Anytus and Melitus may kill me indeed; but hurt me they cannot."[4]

(Trans. by Thomas Wentworth Higginson)

The Meditations of Marcus Aurelius

BOOK IV

That which rules within, when it is according to nature, is so affected with respect to the events which happen, that it always easily adapts itself to that which is possible and is presented to it. For it requires no definite material, but it

[1]Cleanthes, *Hymn to Zeus*.
[2]Euripides.
[3]Plato, *Crito*.
[4]Plato, *Apology*.

moves towards its purpose, under certain conditions however; and it makes a material for itself out of that which opposes it, as fire lays hold of what falls into it, by which a small light would have been extinguished: but when the fire is strong, it soon appropriates to itself the matter which is heaped on it, and consumes it, and rises higher by means of this very material.

2. Let no act be done without a purpose, nor otherwise than according to the perfect principles of art.

3. Men seek retreats for themselves, houses in the country, sea-shores, and mountains: and thou too art wont to desire such things very much. But this is altogether a mark of the most common sort of men, for it is in thy power whenever thou shalt choose to retire into thyself. For nowhere either with more quiet or more freedom from trouble does a man retire than into his own soul, particularly when he has within him such thoughts that by looking into them he is immediately in perfect tranquillity; and I affirm that tranquillity is nothing else than the good ordering of the mind. Constantly then give to thyself this retreat, and renew thyself; and let thy principles be brief and fundamental, which, as soon as thou shalt recur to them, will be sufficient to cleanse the soul completely, and to send thee back free from all discontent with the things to which thou returnest. For with what art thou discontented? With the badness of men? Recall to thy mind this conclusion, that rational animals exist for one another, and that to endure is a part of justice, and that men do wrong involuntarily; and consider how many already, after mutual enmity, suspicion, hatred, and fighting, have been stretched dead, reduced to ashes; and be quiet at last.—But perhaps thou art dissatisfied with that which is assigned to thee out of the universe.—Recall to thy recollection this alternative: either there is providence or atoms, fortuitous concurrence of things; or remember the arguments by which it has been proved that the world is a kind of political community, and be quiet at last.—But perhaps corporeal things will still fasten upon thee.—Consider then further that the mind mingles not with the breath, whether moving gently or violently, when it has once drawn itself apart and discovered its own power, and think also of all that thou hast heard and assented to about pain and pleasure, and be quiet at last.—But perhaps the desire of the thing called fame will torment thee.—See how soon everything is forgotten, and look at the chaos of infinite time on each side of the present, and the emptiness of applause, and the changeableness and want of judgment in those who pretend to give praise, and the narrowness of the space within which it is circumscribed, and be quiet at last. For the whole earth is a point, and how small a nook in it is this thy dwelling, and how few are there in it, and what kind of people are they who will praise thee.

This then remains: Remember to retire into this little territory of thy own, and above all do not distract or strain thyself, but be free, and look at things as a man, as a human being, as a citizen, as a mortal. But among the things readiest to thy hand to which thou shalt turn, let there be these, which are two. One is that things do not touch the soul, for they are external and remain immovable; but our perturbations come only from the opinion which is within. The other is that all these things, which thou seest, change immediately and will no longer be; and constantly bear in mind how many of these changes thou hast already witnessed. The universe is transformation: life is opinion.

5. Death is such as generation is, a mystery of nature; a composition out of the same elements, and a decomposition into the same; and altogether not a thing of which any man should be ashamed, for it is not contrary to the nature of a reasonable animal, and not contrary to the reason of our constitution.

6. It is natural that these things should be done by such persons, it is a matter of necessity; and if a man will not have it so, he will not allow the fig-tree to have juice. But by all means bear this in mind, that within a very short time both thou and he will be dead; and soon not even your names will be left behind.

9. The nature of that which is universally useful has been compelled to do this.

10. Consider that everything which happens, happens justly, and if thou observest carefully, thou wilt find it to be so. I do not say only with respect to the continuity of the series of things, but with respect to what is just, and as if it were done by one who assigns to each thing its value. Observe then as thou hast begun; and whatever thou doest, do it in conjunction with this, the being good, and in the sense in which a man is properly understood to be good. Keep to this in every action.

11. Do not have such an opinion of things as he has who does thee wrong, or such as he wishes thee to have, but look at them as they are in truth.

12. A man should always have these two rules in readiness; the one, to do only whatever the reason of the ruling and legislating faculty may suggest for the use of men: the other, to change thy opinion, if there is any one at hand who sets thee right and moves thee from any opinion. But this change of opinion must proceed only from a certain persuasion, as of what is just or of common advantage, and the like, not because it appears pleasant or brings reputation.

17. Do not act as if thou wert going to live ten thousand years. Death hangs over thee. While thou livest, while it is in thy power, be good.

18. How much trouble he avoids who does not look to see what his neighbour says or does or thinks, but only to what he does himself, that it may be just and pure; or as Agathon says, look not round at the depraved morals of others, but run straight along the line without deviating from it.

23. Everything harmonizes with me, which is harmonious to thee, O Universe. Nothing for me is too early nor too late, which is in due time for thee. Everything is fruit to me which thy seasons bring, O Nature: from thee are all things, in thee are all things, to thee all things return. The poet says, Dear city of Cecrops; and wilt not thou say, Dear city of Zeus?

31. Love the art, poor as it may be, which thou hast learned, and be content with it; and pass through the rest of life like one who has intrusted to the gods with his whole soul all that he has, making thyself neither the tyrant nor the slave of any man.

40. Constantly regard the universe as one living being, having one substance and one soul; and observe how all things have reference to one perception, the perception of this one living being; and how all things act with one movement; and how all things are the co-operating causes of all things which exist; observe too the continuous spinning of the thread and the contexture of the web.

41. Thou art a little soul bearing about a corpse, as Epictetus used to say.

43. Time is like a river made up of the events which happen, and a violent stream; for as soon as a thing has been seen, it is carried away, and another comes in its place, and this will be carried away too.

44. Everything which happens is as familiar and well known as the rose in spring and the fruit in summer; for such is disease, and death, and calumny, and treachery, and whatever else delights fools or vexes them.

48. Think continually how many physicians are dead after often contracting their eyebrows over the sick; and how many astrologers after predicting with great pretensions the deaths of others; and how many philosophers after endless discourses on death or immortality; how many heroes after killing thousands; and how many tyrants who have used their power over men's lives with terrible insolence as if they were immortal; and how many cities are entirely dead, so to speak. Helice and Pompeii and Herculaneum, and others innumerable. Add to the reckoning all whom thou hast known, one after another. One man after burying another has been laid out dead, and another buries him; and all this in a short time. To conclude, always observe how ephemeral and worthless human things are, and what was yesterday a little mucus to-morrow will be a mummy or ashes. Pass then through this little space of time conformably to nature, and end thy journey in content, just as an olive falls off when it is ripe, blessing nature who produced it, and thanking the tree on which it grew.

49. Be like the promontory against which the waves continually break, but it stands firm and tames the fury of the water around it.

Unhappy am I, because this has happened to me.—Not so, but happy am I, though this has happened to me, because I continue free from pain, neither crushed by the present nor fearing the future. For such a thing as this might have happened to every man; but every man would not have continued free from pain on such an occasion. Why then is that rather a misfortune than this a good fortune? And dost thou in all cases call that a man's misfortune, which is not a deviation from man's nature? And does a thing seem to thee to be a deviation from man's nature, when it is not contrary to the will of man's nature? Well, thou knowest the will of nature. Will then this which has happened prevent thee from being just, magnanimous, temperate, prudent, secure against inconsiderate opinions and falsehood; will it prevent thee from having modesty, freedom, and everything else, by the presence of which man's nature obtains all that is its own? Remember too on every occasion which leads thee to vexation to apply this principle: not that this is a misfortune, but that to bear it nobly is good fortune.

REVIEW QUESTIONS

1. Discuss the primacy of ethics in the philosophy of Stoicism.
2. Compare the styles of Epictetus and Marcus Aurelius.
3. Why is the notion of control, as in "self-control" and "beyond one's control," so important to Epictetus?
4. For Marcus Aurelius, what is the meaning of being at-one-with-Nature?
5. For Epictetus and Marcus Aurelius, what is the role of reason in the philosophy of morality?
6. Compare the view of death held by Epictetus and Marcus Aurelius with that of Socrates.

SUGGESTIONS FOR FURTHER READING

Gill, C., ed. *The Discourses of Epictetus* (Everyman). London, C. E. Tuttle, 1995.

Inwood, B. and Gerson, L. P. *Hellenistic Philosophy: Introductory Readings.* Indianapolis, Hackett, 1988.

Long, A. A. and Sedley, D., eds. *Hellenistic Philosophy*, 2 vols. New York, Cambridge University Press, 1987–89.

Marcus Aurelius, *Meditations* (tr. G. Harp), New York, Modern Library, Random House, 2003.

PART TWO

THE MEDIEVAL PERIOD

The Spirit of Medieval Philosophy: Philosophy Meets Theology

Earlier we saw that the major divisions of the history of philosophy are usually given as ancient, medieval, modern, and contemporary, knowing that dates cannot be assigned as the absolute beginning or end of cultural eras. The Greek period, for example, extends well into the Christian era, and the Christian era was well underway before it could be identified as a culture. Establishing chronology varies according to the end the historian has in mind, so it is reasonable to designate the beginning of the medieval period around the time of St. Augustine, who would be the leading figure in anyone's presentation of the early part of the period in the fourth century A.D. Augustine was one of many Christian writers who were known as *Fathers of the Church*, a term which, in its usually accepted meaning, refers to all Christian writers of the early Church. In Latin the word for father is *pater*, the root from which the words used in referring to this early period are derived: *patrology, patristics, patristic age*. The earlier Church Fathers of the second and third centuries had as their main concern the defense of the fledgling Church and are therefore called *apologists*, from *apology*, the customary word for a defense tract. If they wrote in Greek, like Justin Martyr and Irenaeus they are called *Greek apologists*; if in Latin, like Tertullian and Lactantius did, *Latin apologists*. The later

Fathers, like Augustine, Basil the Great, Gregory of Nyssa, John Damascene, and Gregory the Great, were intellectual believers who tried to incorporate insights from various areas of knowledge, especially philosophy, into the texture of belief in order to develop an explanation of faith that would satisfy the demands of human reason.

Christianity as a religion did not become widespread until several centuries after its founding, having had to go underground in many places in the Roman Empire to save itself. But as it gradually became accepted, it became identified with the life of the people, so that during the Middle Ages there were no clear boundaries among religion, culture, and society; they evolved as one. The term *Christian Middle Ages* is the label that many historians use in referring to this period, although no one can say that it is *the* definitive Christian period. Yet, allowing for the substantial contributions of thinkers representing the Jewish and Islamic faiths, the period in Europe is identifiable as Christian. Belief in Christ, membership in the Church, the supremacy of the pope, the use of the sacraments, and acceptance of the Bible were all part of daily life. Architecture, painting, sculpture, music, education, and a host of other human activities were fashioned into expressions of belief. It was the age of faith.

Since every kind of experience invites reflection, reflection on faith experience must be most compelling for the believer because it is for him the fundamental vision of reality. As William James put it, at a single stroke, belief in God ". . . changes the dead blank *it* of the world into a living *thou*, with whom the whole man may have dealings." The analysis of faith, because of its nature, can proceed in several different directions depending on what is stressed. For example, if stress is placed on the rational, that is, if an attempt is made to satisfy primarily the demands of the intellect while bracketing what theologians call *revealed data*, the analysis emphasizes the philosophical aspects of faith. This approach, if pushed to the extreme, tends to make the act of faith a sort of conclusion to a logical process and to negate the suprarational character of faith. If, on the other hand, stress is placed on revealed data, that is, if an attempt is made to establish these data as revealed while bracketing the demands of the intellect, the analysis favors the nonrational aspects of faith. This approach tends to separate the act of faith from any kind of rational content, thus making the act of faith so utterly suprarational that any attempt to penetrate it by human understanding would be futile. During the Middle Ages, for the main line of Christian thinkers who avoided tipping the scales to either extreme, faith was explicated in the context of a theology that tried to blend philosophical insights with the scholarly exegesis of revealed data.

The imperative of faith to explain itself is announced in St. Anselm's phrase "faith seeking to be understood" or "faith seeking understanding" (*fides quaerens intellectum*), which, as a constant medieval theme, underlines the effort required in formulating its truths; it employs ideas from any discipline if they help to probe its meaning or to show that, whatever personal commitment to the suprarational it entails, faith is nonetheless reasonable.

Described in this way, medieval philosophy worked within theology to focus on questions that dealt with God and humans: God's existence; what He must be like in His inner life and what this means for people; what an individual's relationship to God is; man's destiny; the goal of human behavior; and countless other questions that show historically how Christian thought either developed ideas inherited from Greek thinkers or discovered radically new ones unfathomed in a Greek context. For example, though Aristotle wrote some insightful and beautiful pages on God and His inner life, it was the Christian thinkers, using what they learned from the Scriptures, who delineated a new understanding of the relationship between the divine and the human as one of love. Not only is God the Transcendent, the Creator, the Almighty, the Immense, but He is also Love. In saying "God is love," St. John is saying that God's very transcendence, power, and presence are, as far as man is concerned, *for the sake of man*. The world is not God's plaything; it is His cherished creation coming forth freely from His measureless abundance. The sacred character of creation, the meaning of personhood, the completion of one's mortal life here by immortal life hereafter, and the feeling that man can finally defeat evil are all indications of a new opening for human understanding as the Greek tradition passed into the Christian.

The long *medieval period*, extending from the fourth to the fifteenth century, is remarkable not only for its length of time but also for being able to nourish profound differences in the same family of thought. St. Thomas Aquinas, writing eight hundred years after St. Augustine, would still recognize in him a pursuit of truth similar to his own; and Nicholas of Cusa, writing in the fifteenth century, could resonate with the work of St. Thomas. Besides those representatives profiled in this section of the text, the list of philosopher-theologians is endless, attesting to a variety of problems, a plurality of styles, and independence of thought. Indeed, Anselm, Augustine and Thomas would all appreciate the stunning insights of Nicholas of Cusa who, in his doctrine of the *reconciliation of opposites*, would try to show that the contradiction between finite and infinite is dissolved in the mystery of God.

The texture of Europe of the Middle Ages was certainly Christian, but the intense intellectual activity dominated by the concerns of Christian theology must not obscure a similar activity among Islamic and Jewish thinkers. All three religions were religions "of the book," religions for which revelation was conveyed in a text, thus becoming the sacred core of a living tradition. There is no theologian who does not have to search out the problem of how reason relates to revelation, and the twelfth-century scholar, Moses Maimonides (1135–1204), exemplifies that search from a profound commitment to the Jewish faith. In his best-known work, *The Guide for the Perplexed*, he lauds philosophy as more than a mere aid to religion, more than a companion; it is a constituent of religion, internal to it, the essential key for appropriating its contents. In the end, the relationship of philosophy and religion is one of identity. Taking the spirit of Aristotle as his own guide, Maimonides covers a broad philosophical spectrum: the creation of the world in time or in eternity; divine omnipotence and human causality; divine justice and human freedom; proof of God's existence; God's attributes; essence and existence; God's goodness and evil in the world; natural knowledge and prophecy; the soul and immortality.

The Middle Ages, then, became a time of rich diversity as it turned theology and religious experience over and over again in philosophical reflection. Let us go on now to meet several outstanding examples of the philosopher-theologian at work.

SUGGESTIONS FOR FURTHER READING

Bosley, R. N. and Tweedale, M. M. *Basic Issues in Medieval Philosophy*. New York, Orchard Park, 1999.

Gilson, E. *History of Christian Philosophy in the Middle Ages*. New York, Random House, 1955. *The Spirit of Medieval Philosophy*. Tr. Downes, A. New York, Scribners, 1936.

Knowles, D. *The Evolution of Medieval Thought*, 2nd ed. London, Longman, 1988.

Leff, G. *Medieval Thought, St. Augustine to Ockham*. Baltimore, Penguin, 1958.

Schoedinger, A. B., ed. *Readings in Medieval Philosophy*. New York, Oxford University Press, 1996.

7

St. Augustine
(354–430)

St. Augustine is the Christian thinker *par excellence*; he combines the intellectual and personal forces previously described to create a profound commitment to religious life, and he typifies the anxiety endured by one who is torn between the appeal of God's revelation and fidelity to his own intellect, between his longing to lead a quiet life and the call to the busyness of a bishop's office. Having found himself in so many different situations, and having generated respect as a man of learning, he was obliged to address a wide variety of contemporary problems both practical and academic; but because his theology is personal and open-ended, it never fails to shed light on the problems of any given time; he is always contemporaneous—a theologian for all seasons.

The son of a Christian mother and a pagan father Aurelius Augustinus was a Roman, born in 354 in North Africa in the small town of Thagaste, the present-day Souk-Ahras in Algeria. The area, known as Numidia, was a province of the Roman Empire and thoroughly Latin in culture; it contained the city of Carthage, held to be the greatest city of the West after Rome. Augustine's birth and education made him a true heir of Latin antiquity. His early formal education was completed at Carthage; it was a literary education emphasizing the art of rhetoric, with some attention paid to philosophy. Rhetoric, the art of speaking and writing persuasively according to rigorous rules of presentation, was a highly prized talent, and Augustine's commitment to it contributed to his persuasiveness in years to come. Philosophy was not particularly exciting, except for one work, Cicero's *Hortensius*, now lost, which inspired him to a love of the discipline that never abated.

Following the not unusual practice of the time, Augustine lived for years with a woman who was not his legal wife; they had a son, Adeodatus ("God-given"), who died a young man. At the age of twenty, after his father died, Augustine turned to teaching to support his family. In 383 he went to Rome, where he became a professor of rhetoric, and in the same year he received an appointment as the public orator of Milan. Just outside Milan, at Cassiciacum, he established a retreat for himself and some friends where he could devote himself to reflection, study, and writing.

Until then, Augustine had never considered himself a Christian. He deemed Christianity a religion for simple folk, for the uneducated and unlettered. He, whose Latin usage was exquisitely classical, was put off by the Bible because he found it primitive in style and contradictory; the basic problem for him was that conversion meant full acceptance of the Christian life, and this he was not prepared to do. However, whether it was the example of his mother, Monica, later to be honored as a saint, or the influence of St. Ambrose, the bishop of Milan, whose sermons Augustine attended for the sheer force of his rhetoric, or the attractiveness of the Christian saints whose lives he had read is not clear, nevertheless, like many other famous figures whose future life crystallized in a single moment, Augustine experienced an instant of explosive clarity in which he knew, without doubt, that he was called to become a Christian.

Augustine's "conversion"

In a poignant description in the *Confessions,* Augustine recounts how, having long been absorbed in the things of the spirit but unwilling to take a decisive step, he heard a child's voice admonishing him to "take and read." He put his hands on the New Testament he had been reading and, in his own words, "I snatched it up, opened it and in silence read the passage upon which my eyes fell: 'Not in rioting and drunkenness, not in chambering and impurities, not in contention and envy, but put ye on the Lord Jesus Christ and make not provision for the flesh in its concupiscences.' I had no wish to read further, and no need. For in that instant, with the very ending of the sentence, it was as though a light of utter confidence shone in all my heart, and all the darkness of uncertainty vanished away." Augustine, with his son and some friends, was baptized the following year by St. Ambrose.

After his conversion, Augustine's life was never the same. If he had delayed conversion because it involved the full acceptance of the Christian life, full acceptance was now upon him. What he wanted, first and foremost, was to think out the God-man relationship, and this could be done only in solitude. As an echo of Socrates' injunction to "know thyself," Augustine knew that the experience of God had to come from within; to ignore the self is to ignore God who dwells there: "Too late have I loved You, O Beauty ever ancient and ever new. Too late have I loved You! For behold You were within me, and I without . . . You were with me, but I was not with You." So, a short while after his baptism, Augustine prepared to leave Milan for his native Thagaste, where he would resume his quiet way of life. But his retreat was not to last, for, one day when he was visiting the church in nearby Hippo, the most important city after Carthage, the people cried out for him to become their priest. Augustine finally yielded to their insistence, became a priest, and then later the Bishop of Hippo; yet, even after giving up his contemplative life for the active ministry, he still cherished the ideal of a peaceful, contemplative life and tried, insofar as he could, to follow it while busily engaged in ecclesiastical affairs.

Augustine's influence spread far and wide. His advice was sought from all quarters and from all sorts of petitioners. He preached and wrote incessantly; he traveled considerably. His sermons were eagerly attended, his books and letters anxiously awaited. He once wrote a letter to the great biblical scholar St. Jerome, and because the messenger allowed it to be copied, its contents were known to everyone long before Jerome himself received it! What can be said of an active contemplative who wrote 113 books, 218 letters, and 500 sermons? Uneven at times, unclear at times, ambiguous at times, it is true; but in so vast an undertaking, even Augustine knew that failings were to be expected. Thus, toward the end of his life, he felt compelled to review all his works in his *Reconciliations* and to publish his final comments. Augustine's most famous work is his *Confessions,* perhaps the first autobiography of its kind. To this must be added his work *On the Trinity,* and his last great work, *The City of God,* in which he used the sack of Rome by the Visigoths in 410 to demonstrate the passing nature of temporal power in contrast to another power that does not pass.

Theological Controversies

Though much of Augustine's thought grew from within, and in the undisturbed peace of solitude, much of it was forged in a climate of controversy, in which he emerged as the protector of orthodoxy against those theologies that, in his eyes, would distort the true Christian message. Two such theologies, which had become the centers of distinctly religious movements, stood out. The first of these was founded by a third-century Persian named Mani, who proclaimed himself an Apostle of Jesus Christ and the Paraclete (Holy Spirit) as well; thus *Manicheism* presented itself as the perfect form of Christianity. It made pretentious promises for a spiritual life without surrendering one's own reason, thus making it attractive to the young Augustine. One of its basic doctrines was that of extreme dualism between matter and spirit, to the extent that matter was considered evil and spirit good. But as Augustine came to see, this view of matter can go in two directions: Either the Christian must avoid every contact with the material world—which can lead to a life of severe asceticism, or the Christian can do anything he or she pleases in the material world, because it would make no difference to one's spiritual life, which can lead to a life of dissolute behavior. Mainly because he was led by what he thought was the exemplary life of its practitioners, Augustine was enthusiastic about Manicheism at first, but as time went on he came to realize the fantasy it really was and began to polemicize against it.

The second theology that Augustine challenged, presented a much more intricate problem, for it had to do with man's relationship with God vis-à-vis the need for grace. The monk Pelagius had for some time maintained that the divine gift of grace was not necessary for salvation and that man possessed within himself all the ingredients required; if grace meant anything, it meant simply a sign of adoption by God.

Perhaps Pelagius arrived at this conclusion in order to underscore that man has an indispensable role in his own salvation. At any rate, Augustine, whose dramatic conversion must be recalled, reacted against this notion, for it seemed to belittle, if not remove entirely, God's role in salvation, making salvation a completely human event to the exclusion of God's saving action. In one form or another, now original sin, now predestination, now free will, the polemic against Pelagianism was to continue until Augustine's death. Without trying to write finis to the delicate questions interwoven in this polemic, it shows Augustine's unequivocal contention that man's "ascending" to God can be accomplished only with God's "condescending" to man.

Wisdom: Ultimate Truth as Personal

God and man. God and myself. That was all Augustine wanted to know. He was not demeaning other kinds of knowledge, but his purpose was to go directly to that ultimate knowledge by which all other knowledge stands or falls, and without which no other knowledge has any importance. Knowledge without bearing on either God or man is not worthy of the name because it has no personal significance and, to that extent, is "depersonalized." When Augustine uses the word *science* he means knowledge dealing with the practical, the many, and, in general, temporal things; such knowledge is necessary, for without it the virtues needed for right living cannot be obtained. *Wisdom*, however, tends to draw the many to unity. It is concerned with the contemplation of eternal and immutable truth. All truth, for Augustine, has a personal dimension, and once the characteristics of eternity and immutability are touched, truth must be seen as Truth, and the ultimate Truth as Personal in the God who is Truth. Hence, the search for truth is, in essence, the search for the Person to whom we can relate as persons, to whom we can commit ourselves, confident that in reality He commits Himself to us first.

With this orientation, Augustine took the inward path to discover that the existence of God is confirmed by the very nature of truth. The inward path discloses ascending levels of knowledge, and at the highest level, that of reason, truth is beheld as immutable and eternal. It is not so much the content of a truth, such as seven and three are ten, that is its prime characteristic, but its very incorruptibility: That seven and three are ten is *incorruptibly* true, and incorruptibility cannot emanate from what is mutable and temporal, only from what is immutable and eternal.

Man, the Image of God

The discovery of God in ourselves sets forth the kind of linkage we have with Him. When called upon for a definition of man, rather than offering one like "rational animal," Augustine offers "image of God," a description carried down through the Middle Ages. Man is like God, yes; and this likeness is already a badge of honor; but man's crowning glory resides in his being God's *image*—a unique likeness because it is produced by the original as an expression of itself. Two things can have a likeness to each other without having any further relationship; two samples of handwriting can be like each other, but the relationship stops there. Image adds to the notion of likeness the fact of a resemblance to the original, made by the original, much like the image in a mirror. As the image of God, man bears a profound resemblance to the original. He is brought into being by God the Creator; all his perfections are participations of the uncreated and unlimited perfection of God the Exemplar; his growth in freedom is a growth unto God, who is infinitely free. Further, in His inmost being, God is triune, which, to use classical Christian terminology, means a trinity of persons in one nature. Whatever else this may signify for Augustine, the ruling idea is that plurality-unity pervades all reality because at the head of it, there is a Trinity of Persons acting within One Nature; and by an extension of the very activity "generating" the Trinity, all other things are also generated. Everything, then, bears an impression of the Trinity, but it is man, God's image, in whom the clearest resemblance is to be found. At man's inmost point, at that point of the soul where the unity of man is concentrated, there are three recognizable vectors into which this unity is resolved: mind, knowledge, and love. Though they are separate from one another, they are still one with each other, for the mind in knowing knows itself, and in knowing itself loves itself: "When the mind knows and loves itself, there is a trinity of mind, love and knowledge . . . wonderfully, these three are inseparable from each other yet, while each is a single thing unto itself, they are all one when considered relatively to each other."

In addition to the image-of-God relationship, there is still another dimension of human nature: the *societal* dimension. Of course, man is aware of what society is, and his experience of living in society demonstrates both its need and its appropriateness. It is this very life in society that is revealed as having a transcendent richness, for inasmuch as God is the supreme unity and yet triune, He is the perfect exemplar of society as unity, a community of Three Persons sharing a common life. As the image of God, man must translate this divine unity-in-society into a human reality by working toward a society unified by love. Even though we are all individual units, we are encompassed by the larger unity of human society, and we are drawn to see in each person the "neighbor" of the Gospel: "You ask, 'who is my neighbor?' Why, every person is your neighbor!"

The Perfecting of Love

It should be clear by now that Augustine's philosophy is a *philosophy of love*. For him, love is a principle of unity, of completion, of meaning. The myriad aspects of reality would lapse into incomprehensible fragmentation unless some way were found to hold them all together. Beyond the sources of unity supplied by mechanics and mathematics, so significantly essayed by the Greek philosophers, for Augustine, in keeping with his personalist outlook, the only successful way is the way of love. We know from our experience that love draws us into unity with the one we love; and we know that love draws all other things into it, thus becoming the center of a new world. So it is with the bond between God and man, a bond of love that gives humanity its meaning. It cannot be otherwise; man, by his very being, is drawn to God; or, in Augustine's phrase, borrowing from the physics of the ancient world in which objects tend to move toward the places assigned to them by nature and, once there remaining at rest, man *gravitates* toward Him: "A body, by its weight, is borne to its proper place . . . but my love is my weight, and I am borne to wherever I should be borne"—a sentiment that is reechoed in Augustine's writings and encapsulated in his most often quoted saying, "My heart is restless until it rest in Thee, My God."

Yet our relationship with God is not given all at once; it is subject to growth, as is true of all organic things. Our relationship is a gradual growing unto God, a growth by degrees. To outline this growth, spiritual writers talk of "steps" or "stages" in the approach to God; Augustine does the same, but the number of stages makes no difference—sometimes he speaks of three, sometimes four or five or seven. In his book *On Nature and Grace*, he presents a scale of four degrees based on charity; in *The Magnitude of the Soul* he discusses seven stages in the ascent of the soul to the contemplation of God. The number of stages toward fulfillment is not important, but the idea of growth is. Using the generally accepted threefold division of one's journey to God into the purgative, illuminative, and unitive ways, Augustine sees, in the first place, that we must free ourselves from the hold the world has on us. Love of the world connotes the sway that material and sensual things have over the mind and will; it includes the obvious gross vices, as well as the more subtler and less tangible. Augustine continually speaks of fleeing from the world, which does not mean condemnation, for the world is a good creature of God; it means, rather, a detachment from the world whereby we view created goods as means to the end, and not as ends in themselves. In the illuminative way, the soul quickens in its response to God; we take up more consciously the life of virtue and pursue cleanness of heart, moved by the light of God's truth in us. This stage is marked by an abiding awareness of God's presence in the life of the soul, an awareness Augustine calls "sensing God"; the more one senses God, the more one lives in His presence, becoming like Him, abounding in charity. The final stage Augustine conceives to be the most intimate union we have with God, brought about by contemplative knowledge, at once intuitive and experiential, wherein God is perceived as *the* transcendent reality and the soul is correspondingly flooded with love. In its fullest meaning, this stage is the happiness of the blessed in heaven, but on earth it can be experienced from time to time as a mystical experience, a perception of Something Unchangeable, filling the beholder with indescribable joy.

Freedom and the Problem of Evil

But the fulfillment of our humanity is hardly accomplished without our cooperation, a lifelong reaching out for those things that nourish our humanity and a rejection of those destructive of it. Therefore, the key to this growth is *freedom*, the personal dimension of the human being that is at the same time its grandeur and its misery. Whatever theological controversy Augustine's discussion of freedom occasioned in later centuries, he was never satisfied with a determinism of any kind because, by destroying man's power of self-definition, it made genuine growth impossible; personal control would be surrendered to the impersonal forces of the world.

That I am free is obvious to Augustine: "I hold nothing so firmly or surely as that I have a will by which I am moved to the enjoyment of things: what could I possibly call mine if the will, by which I choose or refuse, is not mine." The freedom Augustine speaks of is not only the possibility of free choice but the deeper question of how free choice is used—what is freedom for? Real freedom is the freedom to make choices befitting our humanity, in acts of charity, honesty, justice, respect, trust, acceptance, and so on; so used, freedom is the engine for the enlargement of our humanity. But if freedom is used to make choices unbecoming our humanity, such as acts of injustice, hatred, distrust, meanness, and unconcern, then it is not real freedom at all but its perversion; it is inhuman, it is wrong, it is sin. In a word, human nature is destined for the good; and this destiny is achieved only with man's free participation, for freedom is the glory of human nature.

It is precisely at this point that a huge problem looms for Augustine: the *problem of evil*. Evil creates an impasse for free will and a roadblock in the path to God. The problem was a long-standing one for Augustine, going back to his pre-Christian days when he was a Manichean. Though evil is a problem for all mankind, it is a special one for Augustine, who, having committed himself to Christianity, also committed himself to the God who is good and who acts out of love. He clearly poses the problem when he writes: "If the activity of the will in turning away from God is without doubt a sin, can we say that God is the cause of sin?" In a larger framework, the problem is as follows: God is good, and whatever is created by Him is good; but there is evil in the world—natural disasters, physical defects, accidental destruction, suffering, sin. How, in a world created by the good God, can there be evil? In facing the challenge of this once and forever problem, the Bishop of Hippo assumed the role of God's protector. He could not allow evil in the world to be charged against God as though it were the result of impotence, lack of compassion, or malevolence on His part. In trying to solve the problem radically, Augustine's view can be called metaphysical in that evil attaches to the very nature of the created being. Once we understand that God is the only perfect being, and not lacking in any good, it follows that any being less than God is not fully perfect and in some respect is lacking in good; imperfection is rooted in its very being. Imperfection, in the form of privation, defectiveness, or lack, is called evil and can be found only in that which is—only, therefore, in what is good. You cannot speak of God as the cause of that which is not, or the cause of the absence of good; therefore, you cannot speak of God as the author of evil, any more than you can speak of an artist, having painted his flowers yellow, as the cause of their not being red.

It is not difficult to see how Augustine concluded that moral evil in a human act is essentially a privation of what that act ought to be. Somehow the finite nature of the will explains why it is able to initiate a "defective" movement: "A wicked will is the cause of all evils." Or as Augustine put it in *The City of God*,

"No one ought to wonder whether an evil will has an 'efficient' cause,—rather its cause is not 'efficient' but 'deficient' because an evil will is not an 'effect' but a 'defect.'"True freedom, then, does not lie in the choice between good and evil; it lies only in the choice of the good. Freedom is found in the practice of virtue, in the pursuit of justice, in the doing of God's will; only the good are free. As expressed in Augustine's simple formula,"The law of freedom is the law of love."

Though with Augustine the problem of evil is not solved, his reflections on the nature of evil have become a permanent fixture in Western Christian thought inasmuch as he tried to show that God's bidding for the world will be done and that nothing, not even evil, can overcome the goodness that suffuses His creation.

READINGS

Augustine's Conversion
(from *Confessions*, Book Eight: vii, viii, xii)

But now, the more ardently I loved those whose healthful affections I heard tell of, that they had given up themselves wholly to Thee to be cured, the more did I abhor myself when compared with them. For many of my years (perhaps twelve) had passed away since my nineteenth, when, on the reading of Cicero's *Hortensius*, I was roused to a desire for wisdom; and still I was delaying to reject mere worldly happiness, and to devote myself to search out that whereof not the finding alone, but the bare search, ought to have been preferred before the treasures and king-doms of this world, though already found, and before the pleasures of the body, though encompassing me at my will. But I, miserable young man, supremely miser-able even in the very outset of my youth, had entreated chastity of Thee, and said, "Grant me chastity and continency, but not yet." For I was afraid lest Thou shouldest hear me soon, and soon deliver me from the disease of concupiscence, which I desired to have satisfied rather than extinguished. And I had wandered through per-verse ways in a sacrilegious superstition; not indeed assured thereof, but preferring that to the others, which I did not seek religiously, but opposed maliciously.

But when a profound reflection had, from the secret depths of my soul, drawn together and heaped up all my misery before the sight of my heart, there arose a mighty storm, accompanied by as mighty a shower of tears. Which, that I might pour forth fully, with its natural expressions, I stole away from Alypius; for it suggested itself to me that solitude was fitter for the business of weeping. So I retired to such a distance that even his presence could not be oppressive to me. Thus was it with me at that time, and he perceived it; for something, I believe, I had spoken, wherein the sound of my voice appeared choked with weeping, and in that state had I risen up. He then remained where we had been sitting, most completely astonished. I flung myself down, how, I know not, under a certain fig-tree, giving free course to my tears, and the streams of mine eyes gushed out, an acceptable sacrifice unto Thee. And, not indeed in these words, yet to this effect, spake I much unto Thee,—"But Thou, O Lord, how long?""How long, Lord? Wilt Thou be angry for ever? Oh, remember not against us former iniquities;"[7] for I felt that I was enthralled by them. I sent up these sorrowful cries,—"How long, how long? Tomorrow, and to-morrow? Why not now? Why is there not this hour an end to my uncleanness?"

I was saying these things and weeping in the most bitter contrition of my heart, when, lo, I heard the voice as of a boy or girl, I know not which, coming from a neighbouring house, chanting, and oft repeating, "Take up and read; take up and read." Immediately my countenance was changed, and I began most earnestly to consider whether it was usual for children in any kind of game to sing such words; nor could I remember ever to have heard the like. So, restraining the torrent of my tears, I rose up, interpreting it no other way than as a command to me from Heaven to open the book, and to read the first chapter I should light upon. . . . So quickly I returned to the place where Alypius was sitting; for there had I put down the volume of the apostles, when I rose thence. I grasped, opened, and in silence read that paragraph on which my eyes first fell,—"Not in rioting and drunkenness, not in chambering and wantonness, not in strife and envying; but put ye on the Lord Jesus Christ, and make not provision for the flesh, to fulfil the lusts thereof." No further would I read, nor did I need; for instantly, as the sentence ended,—by a light, as it were, of security infused into my heart,—all the gloom of doubt vanished away.

(*Confessions* tr. J. G. Pilkington)

On Love of God
(from *Confessions*, chap. Book Ten: vi, xxvii, xxviii)

Not with uncertain, but with assured consciousness do I love Thee, O Lord. Thou hast stricken my heart with Thy word, and I loved Thee. And also the heaven, and earth, and all that is therein, behold, on every side they say that I should love Thee; nor do they cease to speak unto all, "so that they are without excuse." But more profoundly wilt Thou have mercy on whom Thou wilt have mercy, and compassion on whom Thou wilt have compassion, otherwise do both heaven and earth tell forth Thy praises to deaf ears. But what is it that I love in loving Thee? Not corporeal beauty, nor the splendour of time, nor the radiance of the light, so pleasant to our eyes, nor the sweet melodies of songs of all kinds, nor the fragrant smell of flowers, and ointments, and spices, not manna and honey, not limbs pleasant to the embracements of flesh. I love not these things when I love my God; and yet I love a certain kind of light, and sound, and fragrance, and food, and embracement in loving my God, who is the light, sound, fragrance, food, and embracement of my inner man—where that light shineth unto my soul which no place can contain, where that soundeth which time snatcheth not away, where there is a fragrance which no breeze disperseth, where there is a food which no eating can diminish, and where that clingeth which no satiety can sunder. This is what I love, when I love my God.

And what is this? I asked the earth; and it answered, "I am not He;" and whatsoever are therein made the same confession. I asked the sea and the deeps, and the creeping things that lived, and they replied, "We are not thy God, seek higher than we." I asked the breezy air, and the universal air with its inhabitants answered, "Anaximenes was deceived, I am not God." I asked the heavens, the sun, moon, and stars: "Neither," say they, "are we the God whom thou seekest." And I answered unto all these things which stand about the door of my flesh, "Ye have told me concerning my God, that ye are not He; tell me something about Him." And with a loud voice they exclaimed, "He made us." My questioning was my observing of them; and their beauty was their reply. And I directed my thoughts to myself, and said, "Who art thou?" And I answered, "A man." And lo, in me there appear both body and soul, the one without, the other within. By which of these should I seek my God, whom I had sought through the body from earth to heaven, as far as I was able to send messengers—the beams of mine eyes? But the better part is that which is inner; for to it, as both president and judge, did all these my corporeal messengers render the answers of heaven and earth and all things therein, who said, "We are not God, but He made us." These things was my inner man cognizant of by the ministry of the outer; I, the inner man, knew all this—I, the soul, through the senses of my body. I asked the vast bulk of the earth of my God, and it answered me, "I am not He, but He made me."

Is not this beauty visible to all whose senses are unimpaired? Why then doth it not speak the same things unto all? Animals, the very small and the great, see it, but they are unable to question it, because their senses are not endowed with reason to enable them to judge on what they report. But men can question it, so that "the invisible things of Him . . . are clearly seen, being understood by the things that are made;" but by loving them, they are brought into subjection to them; and subjects are not able to judge. Neither do the creatures reply to such as question them, unless they can judge; nor will they alter their voice (that is, their beauty), if so be one man only sees, another both sees and questions, so as to appear one way to this man, and another to that; but appearing the same way to both, it is mute to this, it speaks to that—yea, verily, it speaks unto all; but they only understand it who compare that voice received from without with the truth within. For the truth declareth unto me, "Neither heaven, nor earth, nor any body is thy God." This, their nature declareth unto him that beholdeth them. "They are a mass; a mass is less in part than in the whole." Now, O my soul, thou art my better part, unto thee I speak; for thou animatest the mass of thy body, giving it life, which no body furnishes to a body; but thy God is even unto thee the Life of life. . . .

Too late have I loved Thee, O Beauty ever ancient and ever new! Too late have I loved Thee! For behold, Thou wert within, and I without, and there did I seek Thee; I, unlovely, rushed heedlessly among the things of beauty Thou madest. Thou wert with me, but I was not with Thee. Those things kept me far from Thee, which, unless they were in Thee, were not. Thou calledst, and criedst aloud, and forcedst open my deafness. Thou didst gleam and shine, and chase away my blindness. Thou didst exhale odours, and I drew in my breath and do pant after Thee. I tasted, and do hunger and thirst. Thou didst touch me, and I burned for Thy peace. . . .

When I shall cleave unto Thee with all my being, then shall I in nothing have pain and labour; and my life shall be a real life, being wholly full of Thee. But now since he whom Thou fillest is the one Thou liftest up, I am a burden to myself, as not being full of Thee. Joys of sorrow contend with sorrows of joy; and on which side the victory may be I know not. Woe is me! Lord, have pity on me. My evil sorrows contend with my good joys; and on which side the victory may be I know not. Woe is me! Lord, have pity on me. Woe is me! Lo, I hide not my wounds; Thou art the Physician, I the sick; Thou merciful, I miserable. Is not the life of man upon earth a temptation? Who is he that wishes for vexations and difficulties? Thou commandest them to be endured, not to be loved. For no man loves what he endures, though he may love to endure. For notwithstanding he rejoices to endure, he would rather there were naught for him to endure. In adversity, I desire prosperity; in prosperity, I fear adversity. What middle place, then, is there between these, where human life is not a temptation? Woe unto the prosperity of this world, once and again, from fear of misfortune and a corruption of joy! Woe unto the adversities of this world, once and again, and for the third time, from the desire of prosperity; and because adversity itself is a hard thing, and makes shipwreck of endurance! Is not the life of man upon earth a temptation, and that without intermission?

The Problem of Human Freedom
(from *On Free Choice of the Will*)

BOOK TWO

I.
Why did God give freedom of the will to men,
since it is by this that men sin?

EVODIUS: Now, if possible, explain to me why God gave man free choice of the will, since if he had not received it he would not be able to sin.

AUGUSTINE: Are you perfectly sure that God gave to man what you think ought not to have been given?

E: As far as I seem to understand the discussion in the first book, we have freedom of will, and could not sin if we were without it.

A: I, too, remember that this was made clear to us. But I just asked you whether you know that it was God who gave us that which we possess, through which it is clear that we commit sin.

E: No one else. For we are from Him, and whether we sin or whether we do right, we earn reward or punishment from Him.

A: I want to ask, as well: do you know this clearly, or do you believe it willingly without really knowing it, because you are prompted by authority?

E: I admit that at first I trusted authority on this point. But what can be more true than that all good proceeds from God, that everything just is good, and that it is just to punish sinners and to reward those who do right? From this it follows that through God sinners are afflicted with unhappiness, and those who do right endowed with happiness.

A: I do not object, but let me ask another question: how do you know that we are from God? You did not answer that; instead, you explained that we merit punishment and reward from God.

E: The answer to *that* question, too, is clear, if for no other reason than the fact that, as we have already agreed, God punishes sins. All justice is from God, and it is not the role of justice to punish foreigners, although it is the role of goodness to bestow benefits on them. Thus it is clear that we belong to God, since He is not only most generous in bestowing benefits upon us, but also most just in punishing us. Also, we can understand that man is from God through the fact, which I proposed and you conceded, that every good is from God. For man himself, insofar as he is a man, is a good, because he can live rightly when he so wills.

A: If this is so, the question that you proposed is clearly answered. If man is a good, and cannot act rightly unless he wills to do so, then he must have free will, without which he cannot act rightly. We must not believe that God gave us free will so that we might sin, just because sin is committed through free will. It is sufficient for our question, why free will should have been given to man, to know that without it man cannot live rightly. That it was given for this reason can be understood from the following: if anyone uses free will for sinning, he incurs divine punishment. This would be unjust if free will had been given not only that man might live rightly, but also that he might sin. For how could a man justly incur punishment who used free will to do the thing for which it was given? When God punishes a sinner, does He not seem to say, "Why have you not used free will for the purpose for which I gave it to you, to act rightly"? Then too, if man did not have free choice of will, how could there exist the good according to which it is just to condemn evildoers and reward those who act rightly? What was not done by will would be neither evil-doing nor right action. Both punishment and reward would be unjust if man did not have free will. Moreover, there must needs be justice both in punishment and in reward, since justice is one of the goods that are from God. Therefore, God must needs have given free will to man.

II.
If freedom is a good, given for good use,
why can it be turned to evil uses?

E: I concede now that God gave free will. But I beg you, don't you think that, if free will was given so that man might act rightly, it should not be possible to use it to sin? For example, justice itself was given so that man might live well. No one can live in evil through his own justice, can he? In the same way, no one could sin through his will, if the will is given for acting rightly.

A: I hope that God will give me the power to answer you, or rather that He will give you power to find the answer yourself through that very thing which is the highest teacher of all—the truth within which teaches us. Please tell me briefly: if you acknowledge as certain what I questioned you about, namely that God gave us free will, tell me whether we ought to say that God should not have given what we concede He did give. If it is uncertain whether He gave free will, we may properly ask whether it was a good gift, so that if we should discover that it is a good gift, we would discover also that it was given by Him who gave the soul of all good gifts. If, on the other hand, we should discover that free will is not a good gift, we would know that He whom it is wicked to blame did not give it. Yet if it is certain that God Himself gave free will, however it was given, we must acknowledge that it neither ought not to have been given, nor has been given in any other way than it was given; for God gave free will and His deed can in no wise be justly condemned.

E: Although I believe this with unshaken faith, nevertheless I do not understand it. Therefore, let us take up our investigation as though everything were uncertain. From the fact that it is uncertain whether free will was given so that man might live rightly, since we can sin through free will, it follows that it becomes uncertain whether free will ought to have been given. If we do not know that it was given so that man might live rightly, we also do not know that it ought to have been given. In consequence of this, it is uncertain whether God gave free will. For if it is uncertain that free will ought to have been given, it is also uncertain that free will was given by God, since it is wicked to believe that God gave anything that should not have been given.

A: At least you are certain that God exists.

E: I accept even this by faith, and not by reason.

A: If any fool who has said in his heart, "There is no God," should say this to you and be unwilling to believe with you what you believe, but should want to know whether your belief was true—would you walk away from the man, or would you think that he should be persuaded of what you firmly believe, especially if he was eager to know, and not just to argue stubbornly?

E: Your last question gives me a good hint as to how I should answer him. Surely, however unreasonable he might be, he would concede that I ought not to dispute with a sly and stubborn man about anything at all, let alone such an important thing. After he granted this, we should first hold a discussion so that I might believe that he raised the question in the right spirit, and that nothing which would affect the argument, like trickery or stubborness, lay hidden in him. Then I would prove to him what I think is very easily proven: how much fairer it is, when he wants another who does not know to believe him concerning the secrets of his own spirit which he himself knows—how much fairer it is to believe that God exists by the authority of the books of those great men who left written testimony that they lived with the Son of God, since they wrote that they saw things which could not have happened if God did not exist. He would be foolish indeed if he, who wanted me to believe him, were to blame me for believing them. A man could find no reason why he should not be willing to imitate what he cannot justly blame.

A: If you think that it is sufficient to judge that we have not been rash in believing such great men on the question of God's existence, why then, I beg you, don't you think that we can likewise believe these same men's authority in the other matters into whose investigations we entered assuming them to be uncertain and obscure? Then we would have to toil no further in investigating them.

E: But we want to know and understand what we believe.

A: You remember rightly; we cannot abandon the position we adopted at the beginning of the first discourse. Unless believing is different from understanding, and unless we first believe the great and divine thing that we desire to understand, the prophet has said in vain, "Unless you believe, you shall not understand." Our Lord Himself, by His words and deeds, first urged those whom He called to salvation to believe. Afterwards, when He spoke about the gift He was to give to those who believed, He did not say, "This is life eternal so that they may believe." Instead He said, "This is life eternal that they may know Thee, the one true God and Him whom Thou didst send, Jesus Christ." Then, to those who believed, He said, "Seek and you shall find." For what is believed without being known cannot be said to have been found, and no one can become fit for finding God unless he believes first what he shall know afterwards. Therefore, in obedience to the teachings of our Lord, let us seek earnestly. That which we seek at God's bidding we shall find when He Himself shows us—as far as it can be found in this life and by such men as we are. We must believe that these things are seen and grasped more clearly and fully by better men even while they dwell in this world, and surely by all good and devout men after this life. So we must hope and, disdaining worldly and human things, must love and desire divine things.

XIII.
Man's enjoyment of the truth.

A: But I promised, if you remember, that I would show you something higher than our mind and reason. Behold, it is truth itself. If you can, embrace it, enjoy it; "Be glad in the Lord, and He will grant you the prayers of your heart." What more do you ask than that you be happy? And what is more blessed than the man who enjoys unshaken, immutable, and most excellent truth? Men declare that they are happy when they embrace beautiful bodies that they have ardently desired, whether of their wives or of prostitutes; do we doubt that we are happy in the embrace of truth? Men exclaim how happy they are when, with throats parched from the heat, they come to a flowing and healthful spring; or when they are hungry and find a plentiful supper or dinner prepared. Shall we deny that we are happy when we are given the food and drink of truth? We usually hear voices of men declaring that they are happy if they rest among roses and other flowers or if they enjoy fragrant perfumes. What is more fragrant or more pleasant than the breath of truth? Do we hesitate to say that we are happy when we breathe the truth? Many think that the life lived amid the music of voice, stringed instrument, or flute is happy, and when they lack this, they think themselves unhappy; when they have it, they are elated with joy. Do we ask for any other happy life, when, so to speak, the silent eloquence of truth glides noiselessly into our minds? Do we not then enjoy a happiness that is sure, and near at hand? Men think themselves happy and want to live forever when they are delighted by the brightness of gold, silver, gems, colors; or by the light of their eyes themselves; or by the fires of the earth, the stars, the moon, or the sun. They are delighted by brightness and joy, as long as trouble or poverty do not separate them from this happiness. Are we afraid to place the happy life in the light of truth?

Furthermore, because the highest good is known and grasped by truth, and because this truth is wisdom, let us, by our wisdom, see and grasp the highest good, and enjoy it. Happy indeed is the man who enjoys the highest good. It is this truth that reveals all true goods, and every man in accordance with his capacity chooses them, either individually or together, for his enjoyment. Men choose by the light of the sun what they wish to see, and they rejoice in the sight. If they are by chance endowed with strong, keen, and healthy eyes, they look at nothing more willingly than at the sun which lights up even the other things by which men with weak eyes are delighted. In the same way, when the rapier edge of the mind cuts through the many true and immutable things with its sure reason, it steers toward the very truth, by which all things are revealed; clinging to truth as if forgetful of all else, it enjoys everything at once in its enjoyment of truth. Whatever is delightful in other truths derives its delightfulness from truth itself.

Our freedom then consists in submission to the truth. It is our God Himself who frees us from death, that is, from the state of sin. Truth itself, when it speaks as a man, says to those who believe in Him, "If you remain in My word, you shall be My disciples indeed, and you shall know the truth and the truth will make you free." The soul enjoys nothing with freedom, unless it enjoys it securely.

BOOK THREE

XVI.
God is not responsible for human sin.

A: But God owes nothing to anyone, for He freely maintains the universe. Even if someone should say that God owes him something for his merits, surely God is under no obligation for having given the man existence; it is not to the man that something is owing. Besides, what is the merit in turning to God, from whom you have your existence, since you do so to better yourself through Him who gave you your existence? What then do you ask—as if you were demanding payment of a debt? If you do not will to turn to Him, what loss is it to God? It is your loss, for you would be nothing without Him who made you something. Unless you turn to Him and repay the existence that He gave you, you won't be "nothing"; you will be wretched. All things owe to God, first of all, what they are insofar as they are natures. Then, those who have received a will owe to Him whatever better thing they can will to be, and whatever they ought to be. No man is ever blamed for what he has not been given, but he is justly blamed if he has not done what he should have done; and if he has received free will and sufficient power, he stands under obligation. When a man does not do what he ought, God the Creator is not at fault. It is to His glory that a man suffers justly; and by blaming a man for not doing what he should have done, you are praising what he ought to do. You are praised for seeing what you ought to do, even though you see this only through God, who is immutable Truth; how much more, then, should God be praised, since He has taught you to will, has given you the power to will, and has not allowed unwillingness to go unpunished! If every man owes what he has received, and if man was made so that he must necessarily sin, then he is obliged to sin. Therefore, when he sins, he does what he ought. But if it is wicked to say this, then no one is forced to sin by his own nature; nor is he forced to sin by any other nature. Indeed, no one sins when he suffers what he has not willed. If he suffers justly, his sin lies, not in the fact that he suffers unwillingly, but in the fact that he willingly acted in such a way as to suffer justly what he did not will. If he suffers unjustly, how does he sin? For to sin is not to suffer something unjustly, but to do something unjust. But if no one is forced to sin, either by his own nature or by that of another, it follows that he sins of his own will. If you wish to attribute his sin to the Creator, you will acquit the sinner of his sin. If the sinner is rightly defended, he has not sinned, and there is nothing to be imputed to the Creator. Let us, therefore, praise the Creator if the sinner can be defended, and let us praise Him if he cannot. For if he is justly defended, he is not a sinner—therefore, praise the Creator. If he cannot be defended, he is a sinner insofar as he turned away from his Creator—therefore, praise the Creator.

I cannot find, and I assert that there cannot be found, any way in which to attribute our sins to God the Creator. I find that He is to be praised in these very sins, because He punishes them, and because they occur when we turn from His truth.

E: I willingly accept and approve, and I agree that our sins cannot properly be attributed to our Creator.

(Trans. by A. S. Benjamin and L. H. Hackstaff. New York: Macmillan Pub. Co., 1964.)

The Problem of Evil: 1
(from *Confessions*, Book Seven)

III

But I also, as yet, although I said and was firmly persuaded, that Thou our Lord, the true God, who madest not only our souls but our bodies, and not our souls and bodies alone, but all creatures and all things, wert uncontaminable and inconvertible, and in no part mutable; yet understood I not readily and clearly what was the cause of evil. And yet, whatever it was, I perceived that it must be so sought out as not to constrain me by it to believe that the immutable God was mutable, lest I myself should become the thing that I was seeking out. I sought, therefore, for it free from care, certain of the untruthfulness of what these asserted, whom I shunned with my whole heart; for I perceived that through seeking after the origin of evil, they were filled with malice, in that they liked better to think that Thy Substance did suffer evil than that their own did commit it.[1]

And I directed my attention to discern what I now heard, that free will was the cause of our doing evil, and Thy righteous judgment of our suffering it. But I was unable clearly to discern it. So, then, trying to draw the eye of my mind from that pit, I was plunged again therein, and trying often, was as often plunged back again. But this raised me towards Thy light, that I knew as well that I had a will as that I had life: when, therefore, I was willing or unwilling to do anything, I was most certain that it was none but myself that was willing and unwilling; and immediately I perceived that there was the cause of my sin. But what I did against my will I saw that I suffered rather than did, and that judged I not to be my fault, but my punishment; whereby, believing Thee to be most just, I quickly confessed myself to be not unjustly punished. But again I said: "Who made me? Was it not my God, who is not only good, but goodness itself? Whence came I then to will to do evil, and to be unwilling to do good, that there might be cause for my just punishment? Who was it that put this in me, and implanted in me the root of bitterness, seeing I was altogether made by my most sweet God? If the devil were the author, whence is that devil? And if he also, by his own perverse will, of a good angel became a devil, whence also was the evil will in him whereby he became a devil, seeing that the angel was made altogether good by that most good Creator?" By these reflections was I again cast down and stifled; yet not plenged into that hell of error (where no man confesseth unto Thee), to think that Thou dost suffer evil, rather than that man doth it.

IV

For I was so struggling to find out the rest, as having already found that what was incorruptible must be better than the corruptible; and Thee, therefore, whatsoever Thou wert, did I acknowledge to be incorruptible. For never yet was, nor will be, a soul able to conceive of anything better than Thou, who art the highest and best good. But whereas most truly and certainly that which is incorruptible is to be preferred to the corruptible (like as I myself did now prefer it), then, if

Thou were not incorruptible, I could in my thoughts have reached unto something better than my God. Where, then, I saw that the incorruptible was to be preferred to the corruptible, there ought I to seek Thee, and there observe "whence evil itself was," that is, whence comes the corruption by which Thy substance can by no means be profaned. For corruption, truly, in no way injures our God,—by no will, by no necessity, by no unforeseen chance,—because He is God, and what He wills is good, and Himself is that good; but to be corrupted is not good. Nor art Thou compelled to do anything against Thy will in that Thy will is not greater than Thy power. But greater should it be wert Thou Thyself greater than Thyself; for the will and power of God is God Himself. And what can be unforeseen by Thee, who knowest all things? Nor is there any sort of nature but Thou knowest it. And what more should we say "why that substance which God is should not be corruptible," seeing that if it were so it could not be God?

<h2 style="text-align:center">V</h2>

And I sought "whence is evil?" And sought in an evil way; nor saw I the evil in my very search. And I set in order before the view of my spirit the whole creation, and whatever we can discern in it, such as earth, sea, air, stars, trees, living creatures; yea, and whatever in it we do not see, as the firmament of heaven, all the angels, too, and all the spiritual inhabitants thereof. But these very beings, as though they were bodies, did my fancy dispose in such and such places, and I made one huge mass of all Thy creatures, distinguished according to the kinds of bodies,—some of them being real bodies, some what I myself had feigned for spirits. And this mass I made huge,—not as it was, which I could not know, but as large as I thought well, yet every way finite. But Thee, O Lord, I imagined on every part environing and penetrating it, though every way infinite; as if there were a sea everywhere, and on every side through immensity nothing but an infinite sea; and it contained within itself some sponge, huge, though finite, so that the sponge would in all its parts be filled from the immeasurable sea. So conceived I Thy creation to be itself finite, and filled by Thee, the Infinite. And I said, Behold God, and behold what God hath created; and God is good, yea, most mightily and incomparably better than all these; but yet He, who is good, hath created them good, and behold how He encircleth and filleth them. Where, then, is evil, and whence, and how crept it in hither? What is its root, and what its seed? Or hath it no being at all? Why, then, do we fear and shun that which hath no being? Or if we fear it needlessly, then surely is that fear evil whereby the heart is unnecessarily pricked and tormented,—and so much a greater evil, as we have naught to fear, and yet do fear. Therefore either that is evil which we fear, or the act of fearing is in itself evil. Whence, therefore, is it, seeing that God, who is good, hath made all these things good? He, indeed, the greatest and chiefest Good, hath created these lesser goods; but both Creator and created are all good. Whence is evil? Or was there some evil matter of which He made and formed and ordered it, but left something in it which He did not convert into good? But why was this? Was He powerless to change the whole lump, so that no evil should remain in it, seeing that He is omnipotent? Lastly, why would He make anything at all of it, and not rather by the same omnipotency cause it not to be at all? Or could it indeed exist contrary to His will? Or if it were from eternity, why did He permit it so to be for infinite spaces of times in the past, and was pleased so long after to make something out of it? Or if He wished now all of a sudden to do something, this rather should the Omnipotent have accomplished, that this evil matter should not be at all, and that He only should be the whole, true, chief, and infinite Good. Or if it were not good that He, who was good, should not also be the framer and creator of what was good, then that matter which was evil being removed, and brought to nothing, He might form good matter, whereof He might create all things. For He would not be omnipotent were He not able to create something good without being assisted by that matter which had not been created by Himself. Such like things did I revolve in my miserable breast, overwhelmed with most gnawing cares lest I should die ere I discovered the truth; yet was the faith of Thy Christ, our Lord and Saviour, as held in the Catholic Church, fixed firmly in my heart, unformed, indeed, as yet upon many points, and diverging from doctrinal rules, but yet my mind did not utterly leave it, but every day rather drank in more and more of it.

XII

And it was made clear unto me that those things are good which yet are corrupted, which, neither were they supremely good, nor unless they were good, could be corrupted; because if supremely good, they were incorruptible, and if not good at all, there was nothing in them to be corrupted. For corruption harms, but, unless it could diminish goodness, it could not harm. Either, then, corruption harms not, which cannot be; or, what is most certain, all which is corrupted is deprived of good. But if they be deprived of all good, they will cease to be. For if they be, and cannot be at all corrupted, they will become better, because they shall remain incorruptibly. And what more monstrous than to assert that those things which have lost all their goodness are made better? Therefore, if they shall be deprived of all good, they shall no longer be. So long, therefore, as they are, they are good; therefore whatsoever is, is good. That evil, then, which I sought whence it was, is not any substance; for were it a substance, it would be good. For either it would be an incorruptible substance, and so a chief good, or a corruptible substance, which unless it were good it could not be corrupted. I perceived, therefore, and it was made clear to me, that Thou didst make all things good, nor is there any substance at all that was not made by Thee; and because all that Thou hast made are not equal, therefore all things are; because individually they are good, and altogether very good, because our God made all things very good.

XIII

And to Thee is there nothing at all evil, and not only to Thee, but to Thy whole creation; because there is nothing without which can break in, and mar that order which Thou hast appointed it. But in the parts thereof, some things, because they harmonize not with others, are considered evil; whereas those very things harmonize with others, and are good, and in themselves are good. And all these things which do not harmonize together harmonize with the inferior part which we call earth, having its own cloudy and windy sky concordant to it. Far be it from me, then, to say, "These things should not be." For should I see nothing but these, I should indeed desire better; but yet, if only for these, ought I to praise Thee; for that Thou art to be praised is shown from the "earth, dragons, and all deeps; fire, and hail; snow, and vapours; stormy winds fulfilling Thy word; mountains, and all hills; fruitful trees, and all cedars; beasts, and all cattle; creeping things, and flying fowl; kings of the earth, and all people; princes, and all judges of the earth; both young men and maidens; old men and children," praise Thy name. But when, "from the heavens," these praise Thee, praise Thee, our God, "in the heights," all Thy "angels," all Thy "hosts," "sun and moon," all ye stars and light, "the heavens of heavens," and the "waters that be above the heavens," praise Thy name. I did not now desire better things, because I was thinking of all; and with a better judgment I reflected that the things above were better than those below, but that all were better than those above alone.

The Problem of Evil: 2
(from *Enchiridion*)

CHAP. 12.—ALL BEINGS WERE MADE GOOD, BUT NOT BEING MADE PERFECTLY GOOD, ARE LIABLE TO CORRUPTION.

All things that exist, therefore, seeing that the Creator of them all is supremely good, are themselves good. But because they are not, like their Creator, supremely and unchangeably good, their good may be diminished and increased. But for good to be diminished is an evil, although, however much it may be diminished, it is necessary, if the being is to continue, that some good should remain to constitute the being. For however small or of whatever kind the being may be, the good which makes it a being cannot be destroyed without destroying the being itself. An uncorrupted nature is justly held in esteem. But if, still further, it be incorruptible, it is undoubtedly considered of still higher value. When it is corrupted, however, its corruption is an evil, because it is deprived of some sort of good. For if it be deprived of no good, it receives no injury; but it does receive injury, therefore it is deprived of good. Therefore, so long as a being is in process of corruption, there is in it some good of which it is being deprived; and if a part of the being should remain which cannot be corrupted, this will certainly be an incorruptible being, and accordingly the process of corruption will result in the manifestation of this great good. But if it do not cease to be corrupted, neither can it cease to possess good of which corruption may deprive it. But if it should be thoroughly and completely consumed by corruption, there will then be no good left, because there will be no being. Wherefore corruption can consume the good only by consuming the being. Every being, therefore, is a good; a great good, if it can not be corrupted; a little good, if it can: but in any case, only the foolish or ignorant will deny that it is a good. And if it be wholly consumed by corruption, then the corruption itself must cease to exist, as there is no being left in which it can dwell.

CHAP. 13.—THERE CAN BE NO EVIL WHERE THERE IS NO GOOD; AND AN EVIL MAN IS AN EVIL GOOD.

Accordingly, there is nothing of what we call evil, if there be nothing good. But a good which is wholly without evil is a perfect good. A good, on the other hand, which contains evil is a faulty or imperfect good; and there can be no evil where there is no good. From all this we arrive at the curious result: that since every being, so far as it is a being, is good, when we say that a faulty being is an evil being, we just seem to say that what is good is evil, and that nothing but what is good can be evil, seeing that every being is good, and that no evil can exist except in a being. Nothing, then, can be evil except something which is good. And although this, when stated, seems to be a contradiction, yet the strictness of reasoning leaves us no escape from the conclusion. We must, however, beware of incurring the prophetic condemnation: "Woe unto them that call evil good, and good evil: that put darkness for light, and light for darkness: that put bitter for sweet, and sweet for bitter."[1] And yet our Lord says: "An evil man out of the evil treasure of his heart bringeth forth that which is evil."[2] Now, what is an evil man but an evil being? for a man is a being. Now, if a man is a good thing because he is a being, what is an evil man but an evil good? Yet, when we accurately distinguish these two things, we find that it is not because he is a man that he is an evil, or because he is wicked that he is a good; but that he is a good because he is a man, and an evil because he is wicked. Whoever, then, says, "To be a man is an evil," or, "To be wicked is a good," falls under the prophetic denunciation: "Woe unto them that call evil good, and good evil!" For he condemns the work of God, which is the man, and praises the defect of man, which is the wickedness. Therefore every being, even if it be a defective one, in so far as it is a being is good, and in so far as it is defective is evil.

CHAP. 14.—GOOD AND EVIL ARE AN EXCEPTION TO THE RULE THAT CONTRARY ATTRIBUTES CANNOT BE PREDICATED OF THE SAME SUBJECT. EVIL SPRINGS UP IN WHAT IS GOOD, AND CANNOT EXIST EXCEPT IN WHAT IS GOOD.

Accordingly, in the case of these contraries which we call good and evil, the rule of the logicians, that two contraries cannot be predicated at the same time of the same thing, does not hold. No weather is at the same time dark and bright: no food or drink is at the same time sweet and bitter: no body is at the same time and in the same place black and white: none is at the same time and in the same place deformed and beautiful. And this rule is found to hold in regard to many, indeed nearly all, contraries, that they cannot exist at the same time in any one thing. But although no one can doubt that good and evil are contraries, not only can they exist at the same time, but evil cannot exist without good, or in anything that is not good. Good, however, can exist without evil. For a man or an angel can exist without being wicked; but nothing can be wicked except a man or an angel: and so far as he is a man or an angel, he is good; so far as he is wicked, he is an evil. And these two contraries are so far co-existent, that if good did not exist in what is evil, neither could evil exist; because corruption could not have either a place to dwell in, or a source to spring from, if there were nothing that could be corrupted; and nothing can be corrupted except what is good, for corruption is nothing else but the destruction of good. From what is good, then, evils arose, and except in what is good they do not exist; nor was there any other source from which any evil nature could arise. For if there were, then, in so far as this was a being, it was certainly a good: and a being which was incorruptible would be a great good; and even one which was corruptible must be to some extent a good, for only by corrupting what was good in it could corruption do it harm.

CHAP. 15.—THE PRECEDING ARGUMENT IS IN NO WISE INCONSISTENT WITH THE SAYING OF OUR LORD: "A GOOD TREE CANNOT BRING FORTH EVIL FRUIT."

But when we say that evil springs out of good, let it not be thought that this contradicts our Lord's saying: "A good tree cannot bring forth evil fruit."[3] For, as He who is the Truth says, you cannot gather grapes of thorns,[4] because grapes do not grow on thorns. But we see that on good soil both vines and thorns may be grown. And in the same way, just as an evil tree cannot bring forth good fruit, so an evil will cannot produce good works. But from the nature of man, which is good, may spring either a good or an evil will. And certainly there was at first no source from which an evil will could spring, except the nature of angel or of man, which was good. And our Lord Himself clearly shows this in the very same place where He speaks about the tree and its fruit. For He says: "Either make the tree gond, and his fruit good; or else make the tree corrupt, and his fruit corrupt," —clearly enough warning us that evil fruits do not grow on a good tree, nor good fruits on an evil tree; but that nevertheless the ground itself, by which He meant those whom He was then addressing, might grow either kind of trees.

(Tr. J. F. Shaw)

The Mystery of Time
(from *Confessions*, Book Eleven)

X

Lo, are they not full of their ancient way, who say to us, "What was God doing before He made heaven and earth? For if," say they, "He were unoccupied, and did nothing, why does He not for ever also, and from henceforth, cease from working, as in times past He did? For if any new motion has arisen in God, and a new will, to form a creature which He had never before formed, however can that be a true eternity where there ariseth a will which was not before? For the will of God is not a creature, but before the creature; because nothing could be created unless the will of the Creator were before it. The will of God, therefore, pertaineth to His very Substance. But if anything hath arisen in the Substance of God which was not before, that Substance is not truly called eternal. But if it was the eternal will of God that the creature should be, why was not the creature also from eternity?"

XI

Those who say these things do not as yet understand Thee, O Thou Wisdom of God, Thou light of souls; not as yet do they understand how these things be made which are made by and in Thee. They even endeavour to comprehend things eternal; but as yet their heart flieth about in the past and future motions of things, and is still wavering. Who shall hold it and fix it, that it may rest a little, and by degrees catch the glory of that ever-standing eternity, and compare it with the times which never stand, and see that it is incomparable; and that a long time cannot become long, save from the many motions that pass by, which cannot at the same instant be prolonged; but that in the Eternal nothing passeth away, but that the whole is present; but no time is wholly present; and let him see that all time past is forced on by the future, and that all the future followeth from the past, and that all, both past and future, is created and issues from that which is always present? Who will hold the heart of man, that it may stand still, and see how the still-standing eternity, itself neither future nor past, uttereth the times future and past? Can my hand accomplish this, or the hand of my mouth by persuasion bring about a thing so great?

XII

Behold, I answer to him who asks, "What was God doing before He made heaven and earth?" I answer not, as a certain person is reported to have done facetiously (avoiding the pressure of the question), "He was preparing hell," saith he, "for those who pry into mysteries." It is one thing to perceive, another to laugh,—these things I answer not. For more willingly would I have answered, "I know not what I know not," than that I should make him a laughing-stock who asketh deep things, and gain praise as one who answereth false things. But I say that Thou, our God, art the Creator of every creature; and if by the term "heaven and earth" every creature is understood, I boldly say, "That before God made heaven and earth, He made not anything. For if He did, what did He make unless the creature?" And would that I knew whatever I desire to know to my advantage, as I know that no creature was made before any creature was made.

XIII

But if the roving thought of any one should wander through the images of bygone time, and wonder that Thou, the God Almighty, and All-creating, and All-sustaining, the Architect of heaven and earth, didst for innumerable ages refrain from so great a work before Thou wouldst make it, let him awake and consider that he wonders at false things. For whence could innumerable ages pass by which Thou didst not make, since Thou art the Author and Creator of all ages? Or what times should those be which were not made by Thee? Or how should they pass by if they had not been? Since, therefore, Thou art the Creator of all times, if any time was before Thou madest heaven and earth, why is it said that Thou didst refrain from working? For that very time Thou madest, nor could times pass by before Thou madest times.

But if before heaven and earth there was no time, why is it asked, What didst Thou then? For there was no "then" when time was not.

Nor dost Thou by time precede time; else wouldest not Thou precede all times. But in the excellency of an ever-present eternity, Thou precedest all times past, and survivest all future times, because they are future, and when they have come they will be past; but "Thou art the same, and Thy years shall have no end."[1] Thy years neither go nor come; but ours both go and come, that all may come. All Thy years stand at once since they do stand; nor were they when departing excluded by coming years, because they pass not away; but all these of ours shall be when all shall cease to be. Thy years are one day, and Thy day is not daily, but to-day; because Thy to-day yields not with to-morrow, for neither doth it follow yesterday. Thy to-day is eternity; therefore didst Thou beget the Co-eternal, to whom Thou saidst, "This day have I begotten Thee."[2] Thou hast made all time; and before all times Thou art, nor in any time was there not time.

XIV

At no time, therefore, hadst Thou not made anything, because Thou hadst made time itself. And no times are co-eternal with Thee, because Thou remainest for ever; but should these continue, they would not be times. For what is time? Who can easily and briefly explain it? Who even in thought can comprehend it, even to the pronouncing of a word concerning it? But what in speaking do we refer to more familiarly and knowingly than time? And certainly we understand when we speak of it; we understand also when we hear it spoken of by another. What, then, is time? If no one ask of me, I know; if I wish to explain to him who asks, I know not. Yet I say with confidence, that I know that if nothing passed away, there would not be past time; and if nothing were coming, there would not be future time; and if nothing were, there would not be present time. Those two times, therefore, past and future, how are they, when even the past now is not, and the future is not as yet? But should the present be always present, and should it not pass into time past, time truly it could not be, but eternity. If, then, time present—if it be time—only comes into existence because it passes into time past, how do we say that even this is, whose cause of being is that it shall not be—namely, so that we cannot truly say that time is, unless because it tends not to be?

XV

And yet we say that "time is long and time is short;" nor do we speak of this save of time past and future. A long time past, for example, we call a hundred years ago; in like manner a long time to come, a hundred years hence. But a short time past we call, say, ten days ago: and a short time to come, ten days hence. But in what sense is that long or short which is not? For the past is not now, and the future is not yet. Therefore let us not say, "It is long;" but let us say of the past, "It hath been long," and of the future, "It will be long." O my Lord, my light, shall not even here Thy truth deride man? For that past time which was long, was it long when it was already past, or when it was as yet present? For then it might be long when there was that which could be long, but when past it no longer was; wherefore that could not be long which was not at all. Let us not, therefore, say, "Time past hath been long;" for we shall not find what may have been long, seeing that since it was past it is not; but let us say "that present time was long, because when it was present it was long." For it had not as yet passed away so as not to be, and therefore there was that which could be long. But after it passed, that ceased also to be long which ceased to be.

Let us therefore see, O human soul, whether present time can be long; for to thee is it given to perceive and to measure periods of time. What wilt thou reply to me? Is a hundred years when present a long time? See, first, whether a hundred years can be present. For if the first year of these is current, that is present, but the other ninety and nine are future, and therefore they are not as yet. But if the second year is current, one is already past, the other present, the rest future. And thus, if we fix on any middle year of this hundred as present, those before it are past, those after it are future; wherefore a hundred years cannot be present. See at least whether that year itself which is current can be present. For if its first month be current, the rest are future; if the second, the first hath already passed, and the remainder are not yet. Therefore neither is the year which is current as a whole present; and if it is not present as a whole, then the year is not present. For twelve months make the year, of which each individual month which is current is itself present, but the rest are either past or future. Although neither is that month which is current present, but one day only: if the first, the rest being to come, if the last, the rest being past; if any of the middle, then between past and future.

Behold, the present time, which alone we found could be called long, is abridged to the space scarcely of one day. But let us discuss even that, for there is not one day present as a whole. For it is made up of four-and-twenty hours of night and day, whereof the first hath the rest future, the last hath them past, but any one of the intervening hath those before it past, those after it future. And that one hour passeth away in fleeting particles. Whatever of it hath flown away is past, whatever remaineth is future. If any portion of time be conceived which cannot now be divided into even the minutest particles of moments, this only is that which may be called present; which, however, flies so rapidly from future to past, that it cannot be extended by any delay. For if it be extended, it is divided into the past and future; but the present hath no space. Where, therefore, is the time which we may call long? Is it future? Indeed we do not say, "It is long," because it is not yet, so as to be long; but we say, "It will be long." When, then, will it be? For if even then, since as yet it is future, it will not be long, because what may be long is not as yet; but it shall be long, when from the future, which as yet is not, it shall already have begun to be, and will have become present, so that there could be that which may be long; then doth the present time cry out in the words above that it cannot be long.

XVI

And yet, O Lord, we perceive intervals of times, and we compare them with themselves, and we say some are longer, others shorter. We even measure by how much shorter or longer this time may be than that; and we answer, "That this is double or treble, while that is but once, or only as much as that." But we measure times passing when we measure them by perceiving them; but past times, which now are not, or future times, which as yet are not, who can measure them? Unless, perchance, any one will dare to say, that that can be measured which is not. When, therefore, time is passing, it can be perceived and measured; but when it has passed, it cannot, since it is not.

XVII

I ask, Father, I do not affirm. O my God, rule and guide me. "Who is there who can say to me that there are not three times (as we learned when boys, and as we have taught boys), the past, present, and future, but only present, because these two are not? Or are they also; but when from future it becometh present, cometh it forth from some secret place, and when from the present it becometh past, doth it retire into anything secret? For where have they, who have foretold future things, seen these things, if as yet they are not? For that which is not cannot be seen. And they who relate things past could not relate them as true, did they not perceive them in their mind. Which things, if they were not, they could in no wise be discerned. There are therefore things both future and past.

XVIII

Suffer me, O Lord, to seek further; O my Hope, let not my purpose be confounded. For if there are times past and future, I desire to know where they are. But if as yet I do not succeed, I still know, wherever they are, that they are not there as future or past, but as present. For if there also they be future, they are not as yet there; if even there they be past, they are no longer there. Wheresoever, therefore, they are, whatsoever they are, they are only so as present. Although past things are related as true, they are drawn out from the memory,—not the things themselves, which have passed, but the words conceived from the images of the things which they have formed in the mind as footprints in their passage through the senses. My childhood, indeed, which no longer is, is in time past, which now is not; but when I call to mind its image, and speak of it, I behold it in the present, because it is as yet in my memory. Whether there be a like cause of foretelling future things, that of things which as yet are not the images may be perceived as already existing, I confess, my God, I know not. This certainly I know, that we generally think before on our future actions, and that this premeditation is present; but that the action whereon we premeditate is not yet, because it is future; which when we shall have entered upon, and have begun to do that which we were premeditating, then shall that action be, because then it is not future, but present.

In whatever manner, therefore, this secret preconception of future things may be, nothing can be seen, save what is. But what now is is not future, but present. When, therefore, they say that things future are seen, it is not themselves, which as yet are not (that is, which are future); but their causes or their signs perhaps are seen, the which already are. Therefore, to those already beholding them, they are not future, but present, from which future things conceived in the mind are foretold. Which conceptions again now are, and they who foretell those things behold these conceptions present before them. Let now so multitudinous a variety of things afford me some example. I behold daybreak; I foretell that the sun is about to rise. That which I behold is present; what I foretell is future,—not that the sun is future, which already is; but his rising, which is not yet. Yet even its rising I could not predict unless I had an image of it in my mind, as now I have while I speak. But that dawn which I see in the sky is not the rising of the sun, although it may go before it, nor that imagination in my mind; which two are seen as present, that the other which is future may be foretold. Future things, therefore, are not as yet; and if they are not as yet, they are not. And if they are not, they cannot be seen at all; but they can be foretold from things present which now are, and are seen.

XX

But what now is manifest and clear is, that neither are there future nor past things. Nor is it fitly said, "There are three times, past, present and future;" but perchance it might be fitly said, "There are three times; a present of things past, a present of things present, and a present of things future." For these three do somehow exist in the soul, and otherwise I see them not: present of things past, memory; present of things present, sight; present of things future, expectation. If of these things we are permitted to speak, I see three times, and I grant there are three. It may also be said, "There are three times, past, present and future," as usage falsely has it. See, I trouble not, nor gainsay, nor reprove; provided always that which is said may be understood, that neither the future, nor that which is past, now is. For there are but few things which we speak properly, many things improperly; but what we may wish to say is understood.

XXVIII

But how is that future diminished or consumed which as yet is not? Or how doth the past, which is no longer, increase, unless in the mind which enacteth this there are three things done? For it both expects, and considers, and remembers, that that which it expecteth, through that which it considereth, may pass into that which it remembereth. Who, therefore, denieth that future things as yet are not? But yet there is already in the mind the expectation of things future. And who denies that past things are now no longer? But, however, there is still in the mind the memory of things past. And who denies that time present wants space, because it passeth away in a moment? But yet our consideration endureth, through which that which may be present may proceed to become absent. Future time, which is not, is not therefore long; but a "long future" is "a long expectation of the future." Nor is time past, which is now no longer, long; but a long past is "a long memory of the past."

I am about to repeat a psalm that I know. Before I begin, my attention is extended to the whole; but when I have begun, as much of it as becomes past by my saying it is extended in my memory; and the life of this action of mine is divided between my memory, on account of what I have repeated, and my expectation, on account of what I am about to repeat; yet my consideration is present with me, through which that which was future may be carried over so that it may become past. Which the more it is done and repeated, by so much (expectation being shortened) the memory is enlarged, until the whole expectation be exhausted, when that whole action being ended shall have passed into memory. And what takes place in the entire psalm, takes place also in each individual part of it, and in each individual syllable: this holds in the longer action, of which that psalm is perchance a portion; the same holds in the whole life of man, of which all the actions of man are parts; the same holds in the whole age of the sons of men, of which all the lives of men are parts.

Confession trans. J.M. Pilkington, 1876
Enchiridion tr. J.F. Shaw, 1883

REVIEW QUESTIONS

1. Discuss St. Augustine as typical of the medieval theologian in working insights from philosophy into theology.
2. Is it true that St. Augustine took a narrow view of knowledge because all he wanted to know was God and himself?
3. Why is the concept of the unchangeability of truth so important to St. Augustine?
4. What dimension does St. Augustine add to our understanding of human nature by describing man as God's image?
5. What does Augustine mean by the *ascent to God?*
6. In Augustine's view, what relation is there between freedom and sin?
7. Explain how Augustine attempts to reconcile evil in the world with the goodness of God.
8. For Augustine, what is time and how does it relate to eternity?

SUGGESTIONS FOR FURTHER READING

Augustine of Hippo, Selected Writings. Tr. Clark, M. Ramsey. NJ, Paulist Press, 1984.
Confessions. Tr. F. J. Sheed, intro. by Peter Brown. Indianapolis, Hackett, 1993.
Brown, P. *Augustine of Hippo.* Berkeley, University of California Press, 2000.
Gilson, E. *The Christian Philosophy of Saint Augustine.* Tr. Lynch, L. New York, Random House, 1961.
Wills, Garry. *St. Augustine.* New York: Viking Penguin, 1999.

8

St. Anselm
(1033–1109)

What rhetoric was for St. Augustine, dialectics was for St. Anselm. Both of these activities deal with words. Rhetoric's strength comes from style—the moving, personal, emotional, telling use of words; dialectics' strength comes from the argument itself—the unadorned, unimpassioned, public, suprapersonal use of reasoning, to the extent that, if the argument is rejected, reason itself is rejected.

Dialectics as the Centerpiece of Education

How the centerpiece of education changed from rhetoric in the time of Augustine to dialectics in the time of Anselm is an engaging story. From the early Middle Ages down to the mid-eleventh century, education, limited as in classical times to the few, was inherited from the Greek and Roman civilizations. Some time after the radical innovations in education wrought by Plato, his colleague Isocrates, and Aristotle, rhetoric became the goal of the educated man. This goal was handed down to Roman civilization and reached its high point in Cicero in the first century B.C. After struggling for its life in its formative years, the Church became more and more independent and self-assured; in the matter of learning, Christian writers came to rely on Christian literature alone and to look upon non-Christian literature as pagan and therefore unfit for Christian consumption. There were adumbrations of this attitude even in St. Augustine and St. Jerome; in a well-known anecdote. Jerome tells of a vision he had in which he was turned out at the Judgment with the words. "You are a Ciceronian, not a Christian; for where your treasure is, there is your heart also." Histor-

ically symbolic was the year 529 A.D., for in that year the Emperor Justinian, a
Christian, closed Plato's Academy, which had survived as an educational center
for nine hundred years; in the same year the first abbey was founded by St.
Benedict at Monte Cassino, presaging the remarkable role Benedictine monastic schools were to have in the future.

For a variety of reasons, intellectual activity was subdued in the seventh and
eight centuries, a situation that Charlemagne set about to remedy in the ninth century when education became more available through cathedral and monastic
schools and the good offices of the village priest. The program of studies was both
an inheritance and a bequest, for it drew upon the so-called seven liberal arts from
Greek and Roman antiquity and, in the later Middle Ages, became consecrated as
the *trivium* (grammar, logic, and rhetoric) and *quadrivium* (arithmetic, geometry,
astronomy, and music). The Carolingian renaissance saw a revival of interest in classical authors, which meant a revival of interest in rhetoric, not as a formal goal but,
together with grammar, as a basis for a literary education, while logic temporarily
marked time. But as the eleventh century neared, the century of Anselm, logic or
dialectics burgeoned. In the service of the Christian faith, dialectics was seen to
have countless applications, from the rational grasp of the existence of God to the
meaning of the Eucharist. This approach made such bold inroads as to make a
number of theologians apprehensive, fearful that the mysteries of faith would be
negated by rationalizing them.

St. Anselm was one of those who felt called upon to explore faith by means
of dialectics. This decision disturbed his teacher Lanfranc, who reproached him
with writing theological treatises without even quoting Holy Scripture. Contention, however, was the furthest thing from Anselm's mind, bent, as he was, on
leading the life of a monk. He is one of those personalities who, like his master
Augustine six centuries before him, "instantaneously win our affection before
they have won our admiration." He was born of a noble family in Aosta, Italy, in
1033 but repudiated the kind of life expected of him to pursue a monastic life of
learning. As a young man he made his way to Bec, in Normandy, where a recently
established Benedictine abbey was achieving fame and respect under its abbott,
Lanfranc. Anselm lived the life of a monk—prayed, taught, wrote, and worked—
for thirty-three years, the last fifteen of which he served as abbott, attracting, by
his example, monks from all over Europe. In 1078 he was called to England to
become archbishop of Canterbury, a post that, through many a stormy and violent
episode, he held until his death in 1109.

Faith Seeking Understanding

As with Augustine, Anselm's consuming interest was theology, yet he hoped to
satisfy the demands of his intellect in trying to *understand* the truths he already
held by faith, whence the title of one of his main works, *Proslogion*, bears the subtitle, actually the original title, of *Faith Seeking Understanding;* we have already
seen this as one of the characteristics of the Middle Ages. "I desire," he writes, "to

understand, if only a little, the truth of Yours which my heart already believes and loves. Indeed I do not seek to understand that I may believe; no, I believe so that I may understand."

The Ontological Argument for the Existence of God

Such was Anselm's mind in pondering the problem of God's existence. Philosophically, Anselm is the originator of a mode of arguing to the existence of God called the *ontological argument,* a name, for better or worse, attached to it since the time of Kant. Two of Anselm's works, the *Monologion* (a soliloquy) and the *Proslogion* (a discourse), were responses to the request he had received from some of his monks for a meditation on the meaning of faith; both of these works deal with God and His attributes. In the *Monologion* he argues the existence of God from several data of experience, showing how these data are inexplicable without God as their cause. These arguments are not original with Anselm and are therefore not the ones for which he is remembered. But the ontological argument in the *Proslogion* follows an entirely different route because, though it is presented as an argument, it is actually an explication of what is immediately evident and therefore takes on the shape of an intuition. This approach explains both its beguiling attractiveness and its total rejection by many subsequent philosophers. The brevity of the argument is matched only by the incredibly large number of commentaries written on it down through the centuries.

The argument of the Proslogion runs as follows: there is a thought in our minds of a being so great that no other being greater than it can be thought of; but it would be impossible for this being not to exist outside our minds, for the simple reason that to exist outside our minds is greater than to exist inside our minds only; therefore such a being, called God, exists. In Anselm's own words: "We believe that You are something than which no greater can be conceived. But can it be that such a nature does not exist, since 'the fool said in his heart, there is no God'? For sure, even this fool, when he hears the very thing I am saying 'something than which nothing greater can be conceived' understands what he hears; and what he understands is in his intellect, even though he does not understand that it exists. For it is one case for a thing to be in the understanding, it is another to understand a thing to be. . . . Even the fool is convinced that there exists at least in the intellect that than which nothing greater can be conceived. . . . And certainly that than which nothing greater can be conceived cannot exist in the mind only. If it exists only in the mind, it can also be conceived of in reality, which is greater. This would be a clear contradiction: if 'that than which nothing greater can be conceived' exists only in the mind, the very same 'that than which nothing greater can be conceived' is also that than which a greater can be conceived. Therefore, there exists without doubt a being than which nothing greater can be conceived, both in the mind and in reality."

A monk named Gaunilo seems to have spoken on behalf of all those who would like to have cautioned Anselm to stop because something did not quite add up. What Gaunilo said, in effect, was that if you can affirm the existence of God from the concept of God, you can affirm the existence of anything from its concept. And then Gaunilo proceeded to make a famous case for the concept of an island, in a sense a "lost island," which is a place of "inestimable wealth of all manner of riches and delicacies"; this island, following Anselm's logic, really exists. The point here is that the nonexistence of a thing does not mean that I cannot have an idea of it; so, in having an idea of an island, I cannot tell whether it exists or not. But Anselm, who charmingly declares that he would love to give back to the distraught monk "his lost island, not to be lost again," responds to the objection by averring that the concept of God is unique because it is greater than anything else we can think of; this is not so of the concept of the island, nor of any other concept but God. So the argument still stands.

If Anselm had lived in the seventeenth century, his argument would have been referred to as *rationalistic;* that is, the argument does not begin with experience, which would have anchored it in reality; rather, it begins with the idea, or concept, of the all-perfect being, and in the idea of the all-perfect being the idea of existence is necessarily included. The argument therefore does not appeal to those who think that it short-circuits experience, which is why it is rejected by Thomas Aquinas and others in the Thomistic-Aristotelian tradition, as well as by the whole range of empirically bound philosophers such as Locke, Hume, and Kant. It does, however, appeal to Bonaventure and others of the Augustinian tradition in the Middle Ages, as well as to Descartes, Leibniz, Spinoza, and Hegel, all of whom recognize in it a claim validated by its directness. At any rate, it is clear that the ontological argument never lets go, for it always has its adherents. So it can never be thought of as part of a philosopher's dream world; it cannot be dismissed out of hand. It remains as a challenge, as a sticking point for philosophers who ask whether God exists.

READINGS

Faith Seeking Understanding
(from *Proslogion*)

PREFACE

After I had published, at the solicitous entreaties of certain brethren, a brief work (the *Monologion*) as an example of meditation on the grounds of faith, in the person of one who investigates, in a course of silent reasoning with himself, matters of which he is ignorant; considering that this book was knit together by the linking of many arguments, I began to ask myself whether there might be found a single argument which would require no other for its proof than itself alone; and alone would suffice to demonstrate that God truly exists, and that there is a supreme good requiring nothing else, which all other things require for their existence and well-being; and whatever we believe regarding the divine Being.

Although I often and earnestly directed my thought to this end, and at some times that which I sought seemed to be just within my reach, while again it wholly evaded my mental vision, at last in despair I was about to cease, as if from the search for a thing which could not be found. But when I wished to exclude this thought altogether, lest, by busying my mind to no purpose, it should keep me from other thoughts, in which I might be successful; then more and more, though I was unwilling and shunned it, it began to force itself upon me, with a kind of importunity. So, one day, when I was exceedingly wearied with resisting its importunity, in the very conflict of my thoughts, the proof of which I had despaired offered itself, so that I eagerly embraced the thoughts which I was strenuously repelling.

Thinking, therefore, that what I rejoiced to have found, would, if put in writing, be welcome to some readers, of this very matter, and of some others, I have written the following treatise, in the person of one who strives to lift his mind to the contemplation of God, and seeks to understand what he believes. In my judgment, neither this work nor the other, which I mentioned above, deserved to be called a book, or to bear the name of an author; and yet I thought they ought not to be sent forth without some title by which they might, in some sort, invite one into whose hands they fell to their perusal. I accordingly gave each a title, that the first might be known as, An Example of Meditation on the Grounds of Faith, and its sequel as, Faith Seeking Understanding. But, after both had been copied by many under these titles, many urged me, and especially Hugo, the reverend Archbishop of Lyons, who discharges the apostolic office in Gaul, who instructed me to this effect on his apostolic authority—to prefix my name to these writings. And that this might be done more fitly, I named the first, *Monologion,* that is, A Soliloquy; but the second, *Proslogion,* that is, A Discourse.

CHAPTER I
EXHORTATION OF THE MIND TO THE CONTEMPLATION OF GOD

Up now, slight man! flee, for a little while, thy occupations; hide thyself, for a time, from thy disturbing thoughts. Cast aside, now, thy burdensome cares, and put away thy toilsome business. Yield room for some little time to God; and rest for a little time in him. Enter the inner chamber of thy mind; shut out all thoughts save that of God, and such as can aid thee in seeking him; close thy door and seek him. Speak now, my whole heart! speak now to God, saying, I seek thy face; thy face, Lord, will I seek (Psalms xxvii. 8). And come thou now, O Lord my God, teach my heart where and how it may seek thee, where and how it may find thee. . . .

Be it mine to look up to thy light, even from afar, even from the depths. Teach me to seek thee, and reveal thyself to me, when I seek thee, for I cannot seek thee, except thou teach me, nor find thee, except thou reveal thyself. Let me seek thee in longing, let me long for thee in seeking; let me find thee in love, and love thee in finding. Lord, I acknowledge and I thank thee that thou hast created me in this thine image, in order that I may be mindful of thee, may conceive of thee, and love thee; but that image has been so consumed and wasted away by vices, and obscured by the smoke of wrong-doing, that it cannot achieve that for which it was made, except thou renew it, and create it anew. I do not endeavor, O Lord, to penetrate thy sublimity, for in no wise do I compare my understanding with that; but I long to understand in some degree thy truth, which my heart believes and loves. For I do not seek to understand that I may believe, but I believe in order to understand. For this also I believe,—that unless I believed, I should not understand.

The "Ontological Argument" for the Existence of God

(from *Proslogion*)

CHAPTER II
THAT GOD TRULY EXISTS

And so, Lord, do thou, who dost give understanding to faith, give me, so far as thou knowest it to be profitable, to understand that thou art as we believe; and that thou art that which we believe. And, indeed, we believe that thou art a being than which nothing greater can be conceived. Or is there no such nature, since the fool hath said in his heart, there is no God? (Psalms xiv. I). But, at any rate, this very fool, when he hears of this being of which I speak—*a being than which nothing greater can be conceived*—understands what he hears, and what he understands is in his understanding; although he does not understand it to exist.

For, it is one thing for an object to be in the understanding, and another to understand that the object exists. When a painter first conceives of what he will afterwards perform, he has it in his understanding, but he does not yet understand it to be, because he has not yet performed it. But after he has made the painting, he both has it in his understanding, and he understands that it exists, because he has made it.

Hence, even the fool is convinced that something exists in the understanding, at least, *than which nothing greater can be conceived.* For, when he hears of this, he understands it. And whatever is understood, exists in the understanding. And assuredly that, *than which nothing greater can be conceived,* cannot exist in the understanding alone. For, suppose it exists in the understanding alone: then it *can* be conceived to exist in reality; which is greater.

Therefore, if that, *than which nothing greater can be conceived,* exists in the understanding alone, the very being, *than which nothing greater can be conceived,* is one, than which a greater can be conceived. But obviously this is impossible. Hence, there is no doubt that there exists a being, than which nothing greater can be conceived, and it exists both in the understanding and in reality.

CHAPTER III
THAT GOD CANNOT BE THOUGHT NOT TO EXIST

And it assuredly exists so truly, that it cannot be conceived not to exist. For, it is possible to conceive of a being which cannot be conceived not to exist; and this is greater than one which can be conceived not to exist. Hence, if that, than which nothing greater can be conceived, can be conceived not to exist, it is not that, than which nothing greater can be conceived. But this is an irreconcilable contradiction. There is, then, so truly a being than which nothing greater can be conceived to exist, that it cannot even be conceived not to exist; and this being thou art, O Lord, our God.

So truly, therefore, dost thou exist, O Lord, my God, that thou canst not be conceived not to exist; and rightly. For, if a mind could conceive of a being better than thee, the creature would rise above the Creator; and this is most absurd. And, indeed, whatever else there is, except thee alone, can be conceived not to exist. To thee alone, therefore, it belongs to exist more truly than all other beings, and hence in a higher degree than all others. For, whatever else exists does not exist so truly, and hence in a less degree it belongs to it to exist. Why, then, has the fool said in his heart, there is no God (Psalms xiv. I), since it is so evident, to a rational mind, that thou dost exist in the highest degree of all? Why, except that he is dull and a fool?

CHAPTER IV
HOW 'THE FOOL SAID IN HIS HEART' WHAT CANNOT BE THOUGHT

But how has the fool said in his heart what he could not conceive; or how is it that he could not conceive what he said in his heart? since it is the same to say in the heart, and to conceive.

But, if really, nay, since really, he both conceived, because he said in his heart; and did not say in his heart, because he could not conceive; there is more than one way in which a thing is said in the heart or conceived. For, in one sense, an object is conceived, when the word signifying it is conceived; and in another, when the very entity, which the object is, is understood.

In the former sense, then, God can be conceived not to exist; but in the latter, not at all. For no one who understands what fire and water are can conceive fire to be water, in accordance with the nature of the facts themselves, although this is possible according to the words. So, then, no one who understands what God is can conceive that God does not exist; although he says these words in his heart, either without any or with some foreign, signification. For, God is that than which a greater cannot be conceived. And he who thoroughly understands this, assuredly understands that this being so truly exists, that not even in concept can it be non-existent. Therefore, he who understands that God so exists, cannot conceive that he does not exist.

I thank thee, gracious Lord, I thank thee; because what I formerly believed by thy bounty, I now so understand by thine illumination, that if I were unwilling to *believe* that thou dost exist, I should not be able not to *understand* this to be true.

(Tr. Sidney Norton Deane)

REVIEW QUESTIONS

1. Describe the relationship between Christian and non-Christian thought at the time of St. Anselm that made the introduction of dialectics suspect to orthodox theology.
2. What is the meaning of *faith seeking understanding?*
3. To argue from the idea of God to the existence of God is called the *ontological argument;* discuss its validity.

SUGGESTIONS FOR FURTHER READING

Anselm of Canterbury, *Complete Philosophical and Theological Treatises,* tr. J. Hopkins and H. Richardson. Minneapolis, MN, Banning, 2000. *Major Works,* tr. B. Davies and G. R. Evans. Oxford University Press, 2000. *Proslogion,* tr. M.J. Charlesworth, Oxford University Press, 1965.
Evans, G. R. *Anselm and Talking about God.* Oxford, Clarendon Press, 1978.
Southern, R. W. *Saint Anselm.* New York, Cambridge University Press, 1992.

9

St. Thomas Aquinas (1225–1274)

The High Middle Ages and the Revival of Learning

The eleventh century saw an intellectual rebirth that continued unabated for several hundred years, bringing new life to dormant areas of knowledge and to an increasing number of students who desired to learn. It was an age of great excitement in which art, architecture, music, and literature, as well as philosophy and theology, were eagerly pursued. In the realms of philosophy and theology, those who gave a distinctive coloring to the times were people such as Peter Abelard, John of Salisbury, St. Bernard of Clairvaux, Roger Bacon, William of Auvergne, Alexander Hales, Albert the Great, St. Bonaventure, and St. Thomas Aquinas. The works of the Arabian philosophers Avicenna and Averroes and the Jewish theologian Moses Maimonides were so impressive that the Christian West would not have been the same without them. Many of the scholastic centers established in the ninth and tenth centuries, during the following three hundred or four hundred years, developed into university centers that, together with a number of newly founded universities, transformed the educational landscape of Western Europe. In cities like Salerno, Bologna, Paris, Oxford, Cambridge, Padua, Naples, Salamanca, Prague, Vienna, Heidelberg, and Cologne, thousands of students and their masters came together to pursue learning under the title of *universitas*.

Aristotle Rediscovered

Philosophically, history took a dramatic turn with the rediscovery of the works of Aristotle. Except for some of his logical works, translated by Boethius, the writings of the Stagirite were all but unknown in the West; even during the patristic age, Aristotle was seldom more than a name. Of the Greek philosophers, it was Plato who was known to the early Christian thinkers; they saw in his philosophy a heralding of the Christian message. But now, principally as a result of the expansion of Islamic culture westward through North Africa into Spain and Portugal, Aristotle's writings were made available to the West through the texts and commentaries of the Arabian philosophers already mentioned. A new and refreshing breeze therefore blew among the early thirteenth-century scholars, owing largely to the good sense of Albert the Great and Thomas Aquinas, who recognized the stature of Aristotle and had his works translated into Latin. Many theologians felt that theology could be articulated anew with the help of Aristotle; for St. Thomas, Aristotle was "the Philosopher." However, there were other theologians who felt that, since Aristotle represented only the "natural" mind at work, his philosophy could never be helpful to theology and might even be inimical to it. These opposing attitudes hardened until the anti-Aristotelian faction succeeded in having a final ecclesiastical condemnation issued in 1277 against a mixed bag of propositions, authentically Aristotelian or presumed to be so, which included a number held by the now deceased Thomas Aquinas, though he was not mentioned by name. Despite this reversal, the philosophy of Aristotle and Thomas continued to gain adherence, but damage was certainly done to the acceptance of a synthesis that St. Thomas had tried to create.

St. Thomas was immersed in this academic ferment. He was a university student and professor; he wrote his works mainly for use in the university; an academic quality permeates his writings. Inasmuch as he was the complete academic, his personality never, or very seldom, spoke through his writings; he was content to let the argument speak for itself. Though he was academically rigorous, we know from his biographers that there was a warmth and an emotional side to the Angelic Doctor; we know this too from the hymns and poetry he composed.

It follows that the life of St. Thomas was basically uneventful, and the main points are simply told. He was born in 1224 or 1225 in the small town of Aquino, near Naples, and was educated as a youngster by the Benedictines at the monastery of Monte Cassino. Later he became a student at the newly founded University of Naples. He subsequently entered the Dominican Order, the center of a swirling controversy, and six or seven years later was ordained a priest. From 1245 to 1252 he carried on his studies at the universities of Paris and Cologne, and finally received his license to teach at Paris in 1256. He taught at various places including Paris, Rome, and Naples. In 1274 he died as a result of an accident while en route to the Council of Lyons, to which he had been invited.

As with all great personages, certain stories or legends reveal his character. While he was studying under Albert in Cologne, his colleagues called him "the dumb ox," apparently in reference to both his size and his reserved personality, whereupon Albert is supposed to have proclaimed that, despite the name he was dubbed with, his bellowing would be heard throughout the world. Another story tells of his dining at a banquet with King St. Louis IX of France when he became so abstracted that, with a sudden outburst, he slammed his fist on the table, exclaiming, "I have it! At last I can beat the Manicheans!" The king quickly summoned a scribe to take down Thomas' thoughts. Finally, several months before he died, Thomas was often wrapped in contemplation; he stopped writing and confided to his companion of many years that, because of the illuminating visions vouchsafed him, everything he had written seemed like straw.

St. Thomas is often presented as a great synthesizer, which indeed he was. But even though he had committed the entire Bible to memory and was able to dictate to six or seven secretaries at one time, it would be unfair to think of him as a kind of pretechnological computer. His reputation as a synthesizer is based instead on his coherent view of reality, in which he weaves together truths from reason and revelation so that the completed tapestry is interwoven with ideas inherited from his predecessors, a fresh understanding of Aristotle, the believing acceptance of the Bible, and his own insights. Every philosopher has a view of reality, assumed if not stated, in which the parts and the whole are so related as to become mutually self-defining, and in St. Thomas' view the principal relationship is between God and man so that whatever we know about God is a humanizing truth for man, and whatever we know about man enlarges our knowledge of God.

Thus, the architectonic of Aquinas's work is bold and clear, but its working out is complex. *Three main clusters* of problems indicate the nature of his thought: epistemology and its correlation with the unity of man, the mystery of existence, and the perfectibility of man.

The First Cluster of Problems: Epistemology

With regard to the *first,* man is an intelligent being, his highest power is his intellect, and it is this that separates him from all other material beings. There is, consequently, a tendency to define man *only* in terms of the intellect, a tendency with an ample tradition down to St. Thomas' day and far beyond. We have seen this in the early Greek philosophers, particularly Plato, as well as in the early Christian writers who were inclined to identify man as spirit, for spirit has greater nobility than matter. If this is true, it follows that the body is merely an accompaniment to the soul; it is, depending on one's outlook, an instrument, an ally, a close friend, a burden, or a tomb, but in no case does it constitute *one being* with soul. This "spiritualistic" view of man is held by its partisans to be corroborated by the intellect's mode of knowing things in their *general* or *universal* character it knows *man, tree,* or *animal.* This must be a higher kind of knowledge because the *idea* of man, tree, or animal does not change, whereas the individual man, tree, or animal does. So the intellect must be in *direct contact* with these objects and has no essential need of the body to know them. Further, matter is inimical to this mode of knowing and is inferior to spirit; this is why, in the Platonic tradition, the *really real* world is the world of ideas, which man, as spirit, somehow shares.

For St. Thomas, sharing Aristotle's radical position, there is too much here contrary to experience. Of course, man knows material things in a universal way, but he also knows them in particular; of course, he knows them in a general way, but he also knows them as individuals; of course, he knows them in a nonsensible way, but he also knows them in a sensible way. The same person, the one person, possesses both kinds of knowledge, one consciousness attaching to different aspects of reality. The human being is aware of its own unity so that, although there is a distinction between body and soul, there is no separation of them in the being of man. As St. Thomas writes in the beginning of his treatise on man, "Since, then, sensation is an operation of man, but not proper to the soul, it is clear that man is not only a soul, but something composed of soul and body."

In more detail, man has the privilege of self-knowledge and can testify to his own experience of unity. Man is *aware* that it is he, the same person, who understands, and wills, and loves, and hates, and desires; the same being who wakes up as went to sleep, the same being whose hand was burned on the stove who performs an act of charity. There is a chain of unity running from sense knowledge of the highest functions of the intellect. If anyone, then, as Aquinas puts it, denies that the intellect is one with the body, "he must explain how it is that this action of understanding is the action of this particular man; for each one is conscious that it is he himself who understands." Whatever man is, he is one. His very being is living; his very existence is to-be-living-with-this-kind-of-life.

Acknowledging the fact of man's unity, the question can be changed from "Is man one?" to "Why is man one?" What St. Thomas is really looking for is the *radical reason* for life in this living, material thing called man. Man cannot be what he is without matter, but that fact does not make matter the radical reason for life. Matter cannot be the radical reason for life because then everything endowed with matter would be alive, which is contrary to fact. Nor can it be that a thing is alive because of the way matter is disposed or arranged in patterns of functional unity because, as previously noted, that does not account for the unity of existence of the total living being. So, if there is a living unity among the material components of man's being, it must be because of some factor beyond them. How all the physical activities taking place in the body are integrated into a unitary life is one of the mysteries of life, but that they are so integrated is beyond doubt, especially in man, in the center of whose consciousness unity is unimpeachable.

If man possesses life, but does not possess it because of a material principle, he must possess it because of a principle that is not material, or immaterial, called *soul.* The words *besouled* and *animate* (from *anima,* the Latin word for soul) refer to the living thing composed of matter and that which enlivens it. Since the meaning of *immaterial* is not given to us directly, St. Thomas approaches it indirectly by way of negation; this is his favorite way of saying something positive in the absence of direct, experiential knowledge. What he is saying is that the soul *is* without matter in its makeup. Man therefore is not body alone, nor soul alone, nor any combination of these in which body and soul are thought of as two independent beings in a functional unity, like rider and horse, or pilot and ship, to use the appropriate Platonic images. They are metaphysically related to each other, forming one being in which the soul enlivens the body.

In addition to immateriality, or simplicity, there is a further characteristic of the soul designated by the word *spirituality.* Strictly speaking, *simplicity* means, for St. Thomas, without matter, and, of itself, does not necessarily mean the ability to function independently of matter; spirituality adds to the notion of simplicity the notion of independence of matter. A thing may be independent of another, but not in every respect; or dependent on another, but not in every respect. A painter, for example, is independent of (or dependent on) his brush, but not in every respect. A builder is independent of (or dependent on) his ladder, but not in every respect. So the human soul can be independent of (or dependent on) matter, though not in every respect. But can it be shown that the soul is actually *independent* of matter in *any* respect? St. Thomas holds that the soul does function in some respects independently of matter; therefore, the soul *is* in some respects independent of matter, that is, spiritual.

St. Thomas holds to the independence of the soul on many counts, but in the context of epistemology he maintains that it can be shown in at least two ways. The first is based on *universal knowledge,* which, as we have seen, is a constant theme in the history of philosophy. In reality, only individual things exist, such as this tree, this dog, this man; however, we not only know *this* tree in its individuality, we know "tree" in general; we know what a tree is in all cases. Further, this tree is this tree for any number of reasons, one of them being the matter of which it is composed. If the act of knowing were composed of matter, it would be limited in the same way to this one and only tree, and knowledge of tree in general would be impossible; but since our knowledge of tree is universal as well, the intellect cannot be material: Whatever acts without matter must *be* without matter.

The act of *reflection* is another indication of the intellect's independence of matter. Reflection here does not mean "thinking inwardly," or quiet meditation, but the "bending back" of a thing on itself, its reflection. Take the action of touch, proper to the hand. The hand can touch itself if the fingertips touch the palm, but the whole hand cannot touch the whole hand, that is, the whole hand cannot bend back on the whole hand. The reason is that the hand is composed of matter; one part can touch another part, but the whole cannot touch itself. Likewise, the eye cannot see itself; it cannot bend back on itself because it is blocked by the very matter of which it is made. But the act of knowing is entirely different, for the act of knowing *knows itself:* We, as knowers, know that we know. The intellect, then, knows itself in the act of knowing—a perfect example of reflection, of bending back. This act of the intellect must, therefore, be independent of matter.

So here, for St. Thomas, is a clear instance of dependence–independence. In knowing, the soul (intellect) depends on the body for access to material things, that is, for sense knowledge: Nothing is in the intellect unless it is first in the sense. But it does not follow that the intellect is dependent on matter for every one of its activities, as in the instances of universal knowledge and reflection just discussed.

The Second Cluster of Problems: The Mystery of Existence

The *second* cluster of problems St. Thomas faced was that concerning the mystery of existence. Any feature that determines a thing to be, what it actually is, is called a *perfection*, and the highest of all perfections is *existence*. At one and the same time, a thing is this *individual* kind of thing, and is this individual *kind* of thing, and *is* this individual kind of thing; in a sequence measured by understanding and not by time, it cannot be called *this*, or this *kind*, unless it first *is*. Now any one of these aspects is a mystery—a cause for wonder. That a thing is a tree, and not a dog, is cause for wonder; that it is *this* tree, and not that, is cause for wonder; but that a tree *is* in the first place is cause for the highest wonder. Existence is the perfection, the determination, that makes a thing real: To *be* is to be *real*. That is why things of our imagination remain fantasies, and though they have some relation to existence, they are not real because they do not exist; so, the flying horse, the golden mountain, and the lost island can somehow be conceptualized, inasmuch as their components are real, but they themselves are not real.

The mystery of existence, like all mysteries, is only partially open to reason, for although much of it is penetrable by reason, much more remains impenetrable. Existence is a question whose answer generates other questions; one question answered leaves many others unanswered. Perhaps that is why Democritus forbade his students to ask where his atoms came from. But St. Thomas, in a far different tradition, was compelled to ask such a question. How do things come to exist? The things St. Thomas is asking about are things that *do not have to be:* The tree, which came into existence anew, is cut down and ceases to be; a human being, who did not exist before now comes into existence. If they do not need to be, and yet they are, there must be an explanation of why they are, why they came to be. So, either–or: Either all these things cause themselves to be or they are caused to be by an uncaused being. But is impossible for anything to cause itself to be, for then it would have to be and not be at the same time. Because one side of a contradiction has to stand, it follows that an uncaused being exists. This is a simple statement of the well-known "five ways" of St. Thomas to demonstrate the existence of God, all of which begin empirically from five different facts of experience as different starting points but coalesce into the argument from causality.

The *first* argument is from motion; with Aristotle, St. Thomas takes local motion as the experienced event but sees it as applicable to change of any kind inasmuch as any change is a "reduction" from potentiality to actuality. Since it is a contradiction that a thing be mover and moved (changer and changed) at the same time in the same respect, any motion (change) ultimately demands a mover that is unmoved, an unmoved mover (or an unchanged changer). The *second* argument is from efficient causality; we observe that one thing is cause of another, which in turn raises the question as to whether that cause is itself caused or not. It is clearly seen, for St. Thomas, that if it is caused the question comes up again, creating a series of caused causes; but this cannot go on indefinitely for the simple reason that an explanation indefinitely postponed is no explanation at all, so that ultimately there must be a cause which itself is uncaused, an uncaused cause. The *third* argument is from possibility and necessity, or, from contingency; we observe that the things around us need not be, they do not have to exist, and yet they are; things that need not be, and yet are, must then have their existence of something else, and since this process cannot go on indefinitely, there must be a being that has existence in and of itself, that does not have the possibility of not being; it is a necessary being. The *fourth* argument is from the degrees of perfection, that is, of some quality or other; we recognize, for example, wise and less wise, bright and brighter, fast and faster, and so on. In recognizing that the perfection is degreed, we recognize that it is limited and, as limited, caused. The ultimate cause of limited perfection must be of unlimited perfection; it is an all-perfect being. The *fifth* argument is from the governance of the world, that is, from finality; every act is for an end (Latin for end is *finis,* hence, finality), that is, every act accomplishes something; every act has its end, or "term"-ination. The arrow, for example, hits the bull's-eye, not merely because it is an arrow, but because it is targeted; it does not have the trajectory toward the bull's-eye of itself, otherwise every arrow would hit the bull's-eye; therefore the targeting must be had of another. But this process "of another" cannot go on indefinitely; therefore, there must be a being that is an end unto itself and on which all finality, or acting for an end, depends.

As stated above, St. Thomas holds that an infinite series cannot be invoked to explain why any given thing exists when it does not have to. If A requires cause B, which in turn requires cause C, which in turn requires cause D, and so on, even if the number of causes were infinite, the entire series, taken together, would still be insufficient to explain why A exists in the first place, for each cause in the series would itself be caused; insufficiency added to insufficiency can never add up to sufficiency. The cause has to be *totally* different from what it is called on to explain, and therefore an *uncaused* cause whose very existence is necessary.

To those who would hold that an infinite series is not impossible and therefore does not require a *first* cause, St. Thomas would answer that the force of the argument is *existential,* not numerical. A thing that does not have to be (sometimes called *contingent*), and yet is, means that its very *is-ness* is caused here and now by the being that has to be (sometimes called *necessary*), just as the sounding of the trumpet requires a trumpeter: being points to Be-ing, exist-ence points to Existence. This is basically why St. Thomas could not accept the ontological argument as he knew it from St. Anselm: The idea of the all-perfect is not based on existence, that is, on extra-mental reality; it begins in the mind and must stay there.

The Third Cluster of Problems: The Perfectibility of Man

It is obvious, as we turn to perfectibility as the *third* main characteristic of Thomas' thought, that man bears a special relationship to God: He depends on Him for his existence; he is the highest visible creation; he has a natural tendency toward Him, a tendency whose satisfaction is man's ultimate fulfillment and completion of his humanity: "Man has a natural tendency to be completed in goodness." Nevertheless, the human being is subject to the growth pattern of all living things, but as befitting an intelligent and free nature. The "unfinished" dimension of the human being is a typical Christian stance in which "finishing" is the growth of one's humanity toward fulfillment in God.

But with Aquinas there is an emphasis on those ingredients of growth that answer the question, Why do we call a person good? We do not call a person good because he or she is a good doctor, carpenter, musician, or gas station attendant, for we know full well that a person can be a good doctor, carpenter, musician, or gas station attendant and still be a bad person; by the same token, a person can be a bad doctor, carpenter, musician, or gas station attendant and still be a good person. As Thomas says, "moral acts and human acts are the same." That is, they are human not only because they are done freely but also because they shape humanity to its end—they make a person human; in a sense, by them a person creates himself as a person.

Yet, with the full array of possibilities before us, how can we know which actions are right, and therefore good, and which ones we ought to do? Are they the ones that would give us the most pleasure? Not necessarily. Are they the ones that would be most useful? Not necessarily. The ones that most people would do? Not necessarily. The ones most satisfying to us emotionally? Not necessarily. Standing squarely on his rigorous intellectualism, St. Thomas holds that the moral quality of an action is grasped by our *reason,* that is, by our *understanding* of the action in its full context, which prompts us to say, "this is right, and to be done." Sometimes the moral quality of an action can be grasped directly; at other times, because of many complexities, we may have to reflect on it, research it, consult on it before we *see* it. And though we realize that there is an aspect of morality that is universal, or general, because of a human nature common to all human beings, we also realize that there is a subjective aspect as well, because any action is done in concrete, specific circumstances by an individual. St. Thomas comments approvingly on Aristotle when he writes: "Disquisitions on general morality are not entirely trustworthy, and the ground becomes more uncertain when one wishes to descend to individual cases in detail. The factors are infinitely variable and cannot be settled either by art or precedent. Judgment should be left to the people concerned. Each must set himself to act according to the immediate situation and the circumstances involved. The decision may be unerring in the concrete, despite the uneasy debate in the abstract. Nevertheless, the moralist can provide some help and direction in such cases." Conscience is precisely what reason says or dictates; to reject it is to reject the voice of God: "To disparage the dictate of reason is equivalent to condemning the command of God."

In terms of law, then, God's eternal plan is participated in by man in and through reason, a process referred to by St. Thomas as the *natural law.* It underscores the fact that every human action is done for an end (is *teleological*) and that the ultimate end is God's ultimate purpose for rational creation. Consequently, the moral man is the one who does the *right* thing, the one who respects the law within him summoning him to act in accordance with his humanity. This is the sense of *justice* (*jus* meaning both right and law), a sense not founded on duty for duty's sake but on love—the principle of life in every human action. In this way, the human being who in this life experiences love in so many fleeting instances perceives his gradual movement toward God as the All-Good whom he is called to love in the final stage of his unfolding.

Right along with the notion of gradual growth in goodness is the notion of gradual growth in love. Love, for St. Thomas, is not to be thought of as a virtue distinct from others as though you had temperance, honesty, sympathy, helpfulness, and then, in addition, love. Love, cannot be thought of as a stand-alone virtue. Rather, love is a virtue suffused throughout everything we do, every act we place, and gives all other virtues their distinctive *personal* character, enlivens them as though it were a soul animating them to a new level of life. In this sense, the primacy of love undergirds the entire thomistic philosophical structure so that even divine omnipotence and divine omniscience are ciphers without divine love. Infinite love is the engine that drives the action of the Infinite. God is love.

There is a naturalness in things that moves them toward each other, even inanimate things, so that Thomas, in company with Aristotle and Augustine, can refer to it as *natural love,* as with the stone that "desires" to fall because it seeks the center where it can find its place of rest. Analogously there is a naturalness in the human being in its openness to the good which, when known, is loved. Inasmuch as God is the highest good which, upon being known, or "contemplated" in Thomas' vocabulary, is the natural place of rest for the human heart, so that Thomas can aver with Augustine that "My heart is restless until it rest in Thee, O Lord."

READINGS

On the Existence of God
(from *Summa theologiae*, Part I)

QUESTION II

(The *Summa theologiae* is divided into three parts, I, II, and III; part II is itself divided into two parts, designated as I-II and II-II. Part I deals with God and creation; II with morality; and III the sacraments. Each part is subdivided into questions and then articles. A question refers to the larger treatment of a topic, while an article refers to the specific treatment of a topic. A typical citation is thus: I, 12, 1: part I, question 12, article 1. St. Thomas prefaces the body of each article with a series of objections to the sense of the article and ends, after his own explanation in the body, by answering those objections.)

FIRST ARTICLE
WHETHER THE EXISTENCE OF GOD IS SELF-EVIDENT?

We proceed thus to the First Article:—

Objection 1. It seems that the existence of God is self-evident. Now those things are said to be self-evident to us the knowledge of which is naturally implanted in us, as we can see in regard to first principles. But as Damascene says (*De Fid. Orth.* i. I, 3), *the knowledge of God is naturally implanted in all.* Therefore the existence of God is self-evident.

Obj. 2. Further, those things are said to be self-evident which are known as soon as the terms are known, which the Philosopher (I *Poster.* iii.) says is true of the first principles of demonstration. Thus, when the nature of a whole and of a part is known, it is at once recognized that every whole is greater than its part. But as soon as the signification of the word 'God' is understood, it is at once seen that God exists. For by this word is signified that thing than which nothing greater can be conceived. But that which exists actually and mentally is greater than that which exists only mentally. Therefore, since as soon as the word 'God' is understood it exists mentally, it also follows that it exists actually. Therefore the proposition 'God exists' is self-evident.

Obj. 3. Further, the existence of truth is self-evident. For whoever denies the existence of truth grants that truth does not exist: and, if truth does not exist, then the proposition 'Truth does not exist' is true: and if there is anything true, there must be truth. But God is truth itself: *I am the way, the truth, and the life* (John xiv. 6). Therefore 'God exists' is self-evident.

On the contrary, No one can mentally admit the opposite of what is self-evident, as the Philosopher (*Metaph.* iv., lect. vi.) states concerning the first principles of demonstration. But the opposite of the proposition 'God is' can be mentally admitted: *The fool said in his heart, There is no God* (Ps. lii. I). Therefore, that God exists is not self-evident.

I answer that, A thing can be self-evident in either of two ways: on the one hand, self-evident in itself, though not to us; on the other, self-evident in itself, and to us. A proposition is self-evident because the predicate is included in the essence of the subject, as 'Man is an animal,' for animal is contained in the essence of man. If, therefore, the essence of the predicate and subject be known to all, the proposition will be self-evident to all; as is clear with regard to the first principles of demonstration, the terms of which are common things that no one is ignorant of, such as being and non-being, whole and part, and suchlike. If, however, there are some to whom the essence of the predicate and subject is unknown, the proposition will be self-evident in itself, but not to those who do not know the meaning of the predicate and subject of the proposition. Therefore, it happens, as Boethius says (*Hebdom., the title of which is 'Whether all that is, is good'*), 'that there are some mental concepts self-evident only to the learned, as that incorporeal substances are not in space.' Therefore I say that this proposition, 'God exists,' of itself is self-evident, for the predicate is the same as the subject; because God is His own existence as will be hereafter shown (Q. III., A. 4). Now because we do not know the essence of God, the proposition is not self-evident to us; but needs to be demonstrated by things that are more known to us, though less known in their nature—namely, by effects.

Reply Obj. 1. To know that God exists in a general and confused way is implanted in us by nature, inasmuch as God is man's beatitude. For man naturally desires happiness, and what is naturally desired by man must be naturally known to him. This, however, is not to know absolutely that God exists; just as to know that someone is approaching is not the same as to know that Peter is approaching, even though it is Peter who is approaching; for many there are who imagine that man's perfect good which is happiness, consists in riches, and others in pleasures, and others in something else.

Reply Obj. 2. Perhaps not everyone who hears this word 'God' understands it to signify something than which nothing greater can be thought, seeing that some have believed God to be a body. Yet, granted that everyone understands that by this word 'God' is signified something than which nothing greater can be thought, nevertheless, it does not therefore follow that he understands that what the word signifies exists actually, but only that it exists mentally. Nor can it be argued that it actually exists, unless it be admitted that there actually exists something than which nothing greater can be thought; and this precisely is not admitted by those who hold that God does not exist.

Reply Obj. 3. The existence of truth in general is self-evident but the existence of a Primal Truth is not self-evident to us.

THIRD ARTICLE
WHETHER GOD EXISTS?

We proceed thus to the Third Article:—

Objection 1. It seems that God does not exist; because if one of two contraries be infinite, the other would be altogether destroyed. But the word 'God' means that He is infinite goodness. If, therefore, God existed, there would be no evil discoverable; but there is evil in the world. Therefore God does not exist.

Obj. 2. Further, it is superfluous to suppose that what can be accounted for by a few principles has been produced by many. But it seems that everything we see in the world can be accounted for by other principles, supposing God did not exist. For all natural things can be reduced to one principle, which is nature; and all voluntary things can be reduced to one principle, which is human reason, or will. Therefore there is no need to suppose God's existence.

On the contrary, It is said in the person of God: *I am Who am* (Exod. iii. 14).

I answer that, The existence of God can be proved in five ways.

The first and more manifest way is the argument from motion. It is certain, and evident to our senses, that in the world some things are in motion. Now whatever is in motion is put in motion by another, for nothing can be in motion except it is in potentiality to that towards which it is in motion; whereas a thing moves inasmuch as it is in act. For motion is nothing else than the reduction of something from potentiality to actuality. But nothing can be reduced from potentiality to actuality, except by something in a state of actuality. Thus that which is actually hot, as fire, makes wood, which is potentially hot, to be actually hot, and thereby moves and changes it. Now it is not possible that the same thing should be at once in actuality and potentiality in the same respect, but only in different respects. For what is actually hot cannot simultaneously be potentially hot; but it is simultaneously potentially cold. It is therefore impossible that in the same respect and in the same way a thing should be both mover and moved, *i.e.,* that it should move itself. Therefore, whatever is in motion must be put in motion by another. If that by which it is put in motion be itself put in motion, then this also must needs be put in motion by another, and that by another again. But this cannot go on to infinity, because then there would be no first mover, and, consequently, no other mover; seeing that subsequent movers move only inasmuch as they are put in motion by the first mover; as the staff moves only because it is put in motion by the hand. Therefore it is necessary to arrive at a first mover, put in motion by no other; and this everyone understands to be God.

The second way is from the nature of efficient cause. In the world of sense we find there is an order of efficient causes. There is no case known (neither is it, indeed, possible) in which a thing is found to be the efficient cause of itself; for so it would be prior to itself, which is impossible. Now in efficient causes it is not possible to go on to infinity, because in all efficient causes following in order, the first is the cause of the intermediate cause, and the intermediate is the cause of the ultimate cause, whether the intermediate cause be several, or one only. Now to take away the cause is to take away the effect. Therefore, if there be no first cause among efficient causes, there will be no ultimate, nor any intermediate cause. But if in efficient causes it is possible to go on to infinity, there will be no first efficient cause, neither will there be an ultimate effect, nor any intermediate efficient causes; all of which is plainly false. Therefore it is necessary to admit a first efficient cause, to which everyone gives the name of God.

The third way is taken from possibility and necessity, and runs thus. We find in nature things that are possible to be and not to be, since they are found to be generated, and to corrupt, and consequently, they are possible to be and not to be. But it is impossible for these always to exist, for that which is possible not to be at some time is not. Therefore, if everything is possible not to be, then at one time there could have been nothing in existence. Now if this were true, even now there would be nothing in existence, because that which does not exist only begins to exist by something already existing. Therefore, if at one time nothing was in existence, it would have been impossible for anything to have begun to exist; and thus even now nothing would be in existence—which is absurd. Therefore, not all beings are merely possible, but there must exist something the existence of which is necessary. But every necessary thing either has its necessity caused by another, or not. Now it is impossible to go on to infinity in necessary things which have their necessity caused by another, as has been already proved in regard to efficient causes. Therefore we cannot but postulate the existence of some being having of itself its own necessity, and not receiving it from another, but rather causing in others their necessity. This all men speak of as God.

The fourth way is taken from the gradation to be found in things. Among beings there are some more and some less good, true, noble, and the like. But 'more' and 'less' are predicated of different things, according as they resemble in their different ways something which is the maximum, as a thing is said to be hotter according as it more nearly resembles that which is hottest; so that there is something which is truest, something best; something noblest, and, consequently, something which is uttermost being, for those things that are greatest in truth are greatest in being, as it is written in *Metaph.* ii. Now the maximum in any genus is the cause of all in that genus; as fire, which is the maximum of heat, is the cause of all hot things. Therefore there must also be something which is to all beings the cause of their being, goodness, and every other perfection; and this we call God.

The fifth way is taken from the governance of the world. We see that things which lack intelligence, such as natural bodies, act for an end, and this is evident from their acting always, or nearly always, in the same way, so as to obtain the best result. Hence it is plain that not fortuitously, but designedly, do they achieve their end. Now whatever lacks intelligence cannot move towards an end, unless it be directed by some being endowed with knowledge and intelligence; as the arrow is shot to its mark by the archer. Therefore some intelligent being exists by whom all natural things are directed to their end; and this being we call God.

Reply Obj. 1. As Augustine says (*Enchir.* xi.): *Since God is the highest good, He would not allow any evil to exist in His works, unless His omnipotence and goodness were such as to bring good even out of evil.* This is part of the infinite goodness of God, that He should allow evil to exist, and out of it produce good.

Reply Obj. 2. Since nature works for a determinate end under the direction of a higher agent, whatever is done by nature must needs be traced back to God, as to its first cause. So also whatever is done voluntarily must also be traced back to some higher cause other than human reason or will, since these can change and fail; for all things that are changeable and capable of defect must be traced back to an immovable and self-necessary first principle, as was shown in the body of the *Article.*

(All readings from the *Summa theologiae* translated by members of the English Dominican Province)

On the Soul

(from *Summa theologiae*, Part I)

QUESTION LXXV
ON MAN WHO IS COMPOSED OF A SPIRITUAL
AND A CORPOREAL SUBSTANCE

FIRST ARTICLE
WHETHER THE SOUL IS A BODY?

We proceed thus to the First Article:—

Objection 1. It would seem that the soul is a body. For the soul is the moving principle of the body. Nor does it move unless moved. First, because seemingly nothing can move unless it is itself moved, since nothing gives what it has not; for instance, what is not hot does not give heat. Secondly, because if there be anything that moves and is not moved, it must be the cause of eternal, unchanging movement, as we find proved *Phys.* viii. 6; and this does not appear to be the case in the movement of an animal, which is caused by the soul. Therefore the soul is a mover moved. But every mover moved is a body. Therefore the soul is a body.

Obj. 2. Further, all knowledge is caused by means of a likeness. But there can be no likeness of a body to an incorporeal thing. If, therefore, the soul were not a body, it could not have knowledge of corporeal things.

Obj. 3. Further, between the mover and the moved there must be contact. But contact is only between bodies. Since, therefore, the soul moves the body, it seems that the soul must be a body.

On the contrary, Augustine says (*De Trin.* vi. 6) that the soul is *simple in comparison with the body, inasmuch as it does not occupy space by its bulk.*

I answer that, To seek the nature of the soul, we must premise that the soul is defined as the first principle of life in those things which live; for we call living things *animate,* and those things which have no life, *inanimate.* Now life is shown principally by two actions, knowledge and movement. The philosophers of old, not being able to rise above their imagination, supposed that the principle of these actions was something corporeal: for they asserted that only bodies were real things; and that what is not corporeal is nothing: hence they maintained that the soul is something corporeal. This opinion can be proved to be false in many ways; but we shall make use of only one proof, based on universal and certain principles, which shows clearly that the soul is not a body.

It is manifest that not every principle of vital action is a soul, for then the eye would be a soul, as it is a principle of vision; and the same might be applied to the other instruments of the soul: but it is the *first* principle of life, which we call the soul. Now, though a body may be a principle of life, as the heart is a principle of life in an animal, yet nothing corporeal can be the first principle of life. For it is clear that to be a principle of life, or to be a living thing, does not belong to a body as such; since, if that were the case, every body would be a living thing or a principle of life. Therefore a body is competent to be a living thing or even a principle of life, as *such* a body. Now that it is actually such a body, it owes to some principle which is called its act. Therefore the soul, which is the first principle of life, is not a body, but the act of a body; thus heat, which is the principle of calefaction, is not a body, but an act of a body.

Reply Obj. 1. As everything which is in motion must be moved by something else, a process which cannot be prolonged indefinitely, we must allow that not every mover is moved. For, since to be moved is to pass from potentiality to actuality, the mover gives what it has to the thing moved, inasmuch as it causes it to be in act. But, as is shown in *Phys.* viii. 6, there is a mover which is altogether immovable, and not moved either essentially, or accidentally; and such a mover can cause an invariable movement. There is, however, another kind of mover, which, though not moved essentially, is moved accidentally; and for this reason it does not cause an invariable movement; such a mover is the soul. There is, again, another mover, which is moved essentially—namely, the body. And because the philosophers of old believed that nothing existed but bodies, they maintained that every mover is moved; and that the soul is moved directly, and is a body.

Reply Obj. 2. The likeness of the thing known is not of necessity actually in the nature of the knower; but given a thing which knows potentially, and afterwards knows actually, the likeness of the thing known must be in the nature of the knower, not actually, but only potentially; thus colour is not actually in the pupil of the eye, but only potentially. Hence it is necessary, not that the likeness of corporeal things should be actually in the nature of the soul, but that there be a potentiality in the soul for such a likeness. But the ancient philosophers omitted to distinguish between actuality and potentiality; and so they held that the soul must be a body in order to have knowledge of a body; and that it must be composed of the principles of which all bodies are formed in order to know all bodies.

Reply Obj. 3. There are two kinds of contact; of *quantity,* and of *power.* By the former a body can be touched only by a body; by the latter a body can be touched by an incorporeal thing, which moves that body.

SECOND ARTICLE
WHETHER THE HUMAN SOUL IS SOMETHING SUBSISTENT?

We proceed thus to the Second Article:—

Objection 1. It would seem that the human soul is not something subsistent. For that which subsists is said to be *this particular thing.* Now *this particular thing* is said not of the soul, but of that which is composed of soul and body. Therefore the soul is not something subsistent.

Obj. 2. Further, everything subsistent operates. But the soul does not operate; for, as the Philosopher says (*De Anima* i. 4), *to say that the soul feels or understands is like saying that the soul weaves or builds.* Therefore the soul is not subsistent.

Obj. 3. Further, if the soul were subsistent, it would have some operation apart from the body. But it has no operation apart from the body, not even that of understanding: for the act of understanding does not take place without a phantasm, which cannot exist apart from the body. Therefore the human soul is not something subsistent.

On the contrary, Augustine says (*De Trin.* x. 7): *Whoever understands that the nature of the soul is that of a substance and not that of a body, will see that those who maintain the corporeal nature of the soul, are led astray through associating with the soul those things without which they are unable to think of any nature—i.e., imaginary pictures of corporeal things.* Therefore the nature of the human intellect is not only incorporeal, but it is also a substance, that is, something subsistent.

I answer that, It must necessarily be allowed that the principle of intellectual operation which we call the soul, is a principle of both incorporeal and subsistent. For it is clear that by means of the intellect man can have knowledge of all corporeal things. Now whatever knows certain things cannot have any of them in its own nature; because that which is in it naturally would impede the knowledge of anything else. Thus we observe that a sick man's tongue being vitiated by a feverish and bitter humour, is insensible to anything sweet, and everything seems bitter to it. Therefore, if the intellectual principle contained the nature of a body it would be unable to know all bodies. Now every body has its own determinate nature. Therefore it is impossible for the intellectual principle to be a body. It is likewise impossible for it to understand by means of a bodily organ; since the determinate nature of that organ would impede knowledge of all bodies; as when a certain determinate colour is not only in the pupil of the eye, but also in a glass vase, the liquid in the vase seems to be of that same colour.

Therefore the intellectual principle which we call the mind or the intellect has an operation *per se* apart from the body. Now only that which subsists can have an operation *per se*. For nothing can operate but what is actual: wherefore a thing operates according as it is; for which reason we do not say that heat imparts heat, but that what is hot gives heat. We must conclude, therefore, that the human soul, which is called the intellect or the mind, is something incorporeal and subsistent.

Reply Obj. 1. *This particular thing* can be taken in two senses. Firstly, for anything subsistent; secondly, for that which subsists, and is complete in a specific nature. The former sense excludes the inherence of an accident or of a material form; the latter excludes also the imperfection of the part, so that a hand can be called *this particular thing* in the first sense, but not in the second. Therefore, as the human soul is a part of human nature, it can indeed be called *this particular thing,* in the first sense, as being something subsistent; but not in the second, for in this sense, what is composed of body and soul is said to be *this particular thing.*

Reply Obj. 2. Aristotle wrote those words as expressing not his own opinion, but the opinion of those who said that to understand is to be moved, as is clear from the context. Or we may reply that to operate *per se* belongs to what exists *per se.* But for a thing to exist *per se,* it suffices sometimes that it be not inherent, as an accident or a material form; even though it be part of something. Nevertheless, that is rightly said to subsist *per se,* which is neither inherent in the above sense, nor part of anything else. In this sense, the eye or the hand cannot be said to subsist *per se;* nor can it for the reason be said to operate *per se.* Hence the operation of the parts is through each part attributed to the whole. For we say that man sees with the eye, and feels with the hand, and not in the same sense as when we say that what is hot gives heat by its heat; for heat, strictly speaking, does not give heat. We may therefore say that the soul understands, as the eye sees; but it is more correct to say that man understands through the soul.

Reply Obj. 3. The body is necessary for the action of the intellect, not as its organ of action, but on the part of the object; for the phantasm is to the intellect what colour is to the sight. Neither does such a dependence on the body prove the intellect to be non-subsistent; otherwise it would follow that an animal is non-subsistent, since it requires external objects of the sense in order to perform its act of perception.

THIRD ARTICLE
WHETHER THE SOULS OF BRUTE ANIMALS ARE SUBSISTENT?

We proceed thus to the Third Article:—

Objection 1. It would seem that the souls of brute animals are subsistent. For man is of the same *genus* as other animals; and, as we have just shown (A. 2), the soul of man is subsistent. Therefore the souls of other animals are subsistent.

Obj. 2. Further, the relation of the sensitive faculty to sensible objects is like the relation of the intellectual faculty to intelligible objects. But the intellect, apart from the body, apprehends intelligible objects. Therefore the sensitive faculty, apart from the body, perceives sensible objects. Therefore, since the souls of brute animals are sensitive, it follows that they are subsistent; just as the human intellectual soul is subsistent.

Obj. 3. Further, the soul of brute animals moves the body. But the body is not a mover, but is moved. Therefore the soul of brute animals has an operation apart from the body.

On the contrary, Is what is written in the Book *De Eccl. Dogm.* (xvi., xvii.): *Man alone we believe to have a subsistent soul: whereas the souls of animals are not subsistent.*

I answer that, The ancient philosophers made no distinction between sense and intellect, and referred both to a corporeal principle, as has been said (A. I). Plato, however, drew a distinction between intellect and sense; yet he referred both to an incorporeal principle, maintaining that sensing, just as understanding, belongs to the soul as such. From this it follows that even the souls of brute animals are subsistent. But Aristotle held that of the operations of the soul, understanding alone is performed without a corporeal organ. On the other hand, sensation and the consequent operations of the sensitive soul are evidently accompanied with change in the body; thus in the act of vision, the pupil of the eye is affected by a reflection of colour: and so with the other senses. Hence it is clear that the sensitive soul has no *per se* operation of its own, and that every operation of the sensitive soul belongs to the composite. Wherefore we conclude that as the souls of brute animals have no *per se* operations they are not subsistent. For the operation of anything follows the mode of its being.

Reply Obj. 1. Although man is of the same *genus* as other animals, he is of a different *species*. Specific difference is derived from the difference of form; nor does every difference of form necessarily imply a diversity of *genus*.

Reply Obj. 2. The relation of the sensitive faculty to the sensible object is in one way the same as that of the intellectual faculty to the intelligible object, in so far as each is in potentiality to its object. But in another way their relations differ, inasmuch as the impression of the object on the sense is accompanied with change in the body; so that excessive strenght of the sensible corrupts sense; a thing that never occurs in the case of the intellect. For an intellect that understands the highest of intelligible objects is more able afterwards to understand those that are lower.—If, however, in the process of intellectual operation the body is weary, this result is accidental, inasmuch as the intellect requires the operation of the sensitive powers in the production of the phantasms.

Reply Obj. 3. Motive power is of two kinds. One, the appetitive power, commands motion. The operation of this power in the sensitive soul is not apart from the body; for anger, joy and passions of a like nature are accompanied by change in the body. The other motive power is that which executes motion in adapting the members for obeying the appetite; and the act of this power does not consist in moving, but in being moved. Whence it is clear that to move is not an act of the sensitive soul without the body.

SIXTH ARTICLE
WHETHER THE HUMAN SOUL IS INCORRUPTIBLE?

We proceed thus to the Sixth Article:—

Objection 1. It would seem that the human soul is corruptible. For those things that have a like beginning and process seemingly have a like end. But the beginning, by generation, of men is like that of animals, for they are made from the earth. And the process of life is alike in both; because *all things breathe alike, and man hath nothing more than the beast,* as it is written (Eccles. iii. 19). Therefore, as the same text concludes, *the death of man and beast is one, and the condition of both is equal.* But the souls of brute animals are corruptible. Therefore, also, the human soul is corruptible.

Obj. 2. Further, whatever is out of nothing can return to nothingness; because the end should correspond to the beginning. But as it is written (Wisd. ii. 2), *We are born of nothing;* which is true, not only of the body, but also of the soul. Therefore, as is concluded in the same passage, *After this we shall be as if we had not been,* even as to our soul.

Obj. 3. Further, nothing is without its own proper operation. But the operation proper to the soul, which is to understand through a phantasm, cannot be without the body. For the soul understands nothing without a phantasm; and there is no phantasm without the body as the Philosopher says (*De Anima* i. 1). Therefore the soul cannot survive the dissolution of the body.

On the contrary, Dionysius says (*Div. Nom.* iv.) that human souls owe to Divine goodness that they are *intellectual,* and that they have an *incorruptible substantial life.*

I answer that, We must assert that the intellectual principle which we call the human soul is incorruptible. For a thing may be corrupted in two ways—*per se,* and accidentally. Now it is impossible for any substance to be generated or corrupted accidentally, that is, by the generation or corruption of something else. For generation and corruption belong to a thing, just as existence belongs to it, which is acquired by generation and lost by corruption. Therefore, whatever has existence *per se* cannot be generated or corrupted except *per se;* while things which do not subsist, such as accidents and material forms, acquire existence or lose it through the generation or corruption of composites things. Now it was shown above (AA. 2, 3) that the souls of brutes are not self-subsistent, whereas the human soul is; so that the souls of brutes are corrupted, when their bodies are corrupted; while the human soul could not be corrupted unless it were corrupted *per se.* This, indeed, is impossible, not only as regards the human soul, but also as regards anything subsistent that is a form alone. For it is clear that what belongs to a thing by virtue of itself is inseparable from it; but existence belongs to a form, which is an act, by virtue of itself. Wherefore matter acquires actual existence as it acquires the form; while it is corrupted so far as the form is separated from it. But it is impossible for a form to be separated from itself; and therefore it is impossible for a subsistent form to cease to exist.

Granted even that the soul is composed of matter and form, as some pretend, we should nevertheless have to maintain that it is incorruptible. For corruption is found only where there is contrariety; since generation and corruption are from contraries and into contraries. Wherefore the heavenly bodies, since they have no matter subject to contrariety, are incorruptible. Now there can be no contrariety in the intellectual soul; for it receives according to the manner of its existence, and those things which it receives are without contrariety; for the notions even of contraries are not themselves contrary, since contraries belong to the same knowledge. Therefore it is impossible for the intellectual soul to be corruptible. Moreover we may take a sign of this from the fact that everything naturally aspires to existence after its own manner. Now, in things that have knowledge, desire ensues upon knowledge. The senses indeed do not know existence, except under the conditions of *here* and *now,* whereas the intellect apprehends existence absolutely, and for all time; so that everything that has an intellect naturally desires always to exist. But a natural desire cannot be in vain. Therefore every intellectual substance is incorruptible.

Reply Obj. 1. Solomon reasons thus in the person of the foolish, as expressed in the words of Wisd. ii. Therefore the saying that man and animals have a like beginning in generation is true of the body; for all animals alike are made of earth. But it is not true of the soul. For the souls of brutes are produced by some power of the body; whereas the human soul is produced by God. To signify this, it is written of other animals: *Let the earth bring forth the living soul* (Gen. i. 24): while of man it is written (*Ibid.* ii. 7) that *He breathed into his face the breath of life.* And so in the last chapter of Ecclesiastes (xii. 7) it is concluded: (*Before*) *the dust returns into its earth from whence it was; and the spirit return to God Who gave it.* Again the process of life is alike as to the body, concerning which it is written (Eccles. iii. 19): *All things breathe alike,* and (Wisd. ii. 2), *The breath of our nostrils is smoke.* But the process is not alike of the soul; for man is intelligent, whereas animals are not. Hence it is false to say: *Man has nothing more than beasts.* Thus death comes to both alike as to the body, but not as to the soul.

Reply Obj. 2. As a thing can be created by reason, not of a passive potentiality, but only of the active potentiality of the Creator, Who can produce something out of nothing, so when we say that a thing can be reduced to nothing, we do not imply in the creature a potentiality to non-existence, but in the Creator the power of ceasing to sustain existence. But a thing is said to be corruptible because there is in it a potentiality to non-existence.

Reply Obj. 3. To understand through a phantasm is the proper operation of the soul by virtue of its union with the body. After separation from the body it will have another mode of understanding, similar to other substances separated from bodies, as will appear later on (Q. LXXXIX., A. I).

The Unity of Man

(from *Summa theologiae*, Part I)

QUESTION LXXVI
OF THE UNION OF BODY AND SOUL

FIRST ARTICLE
WHETHER THE INTELLECTUAL PRINCIPLE IS UNITED TO THE BODY AS ITS FORM?

We proceed thus to the First Article:—

Objection 1. It seems that the intellectual principle is not united to the body as its form. For the Philosopher says (*De Anima* iii. 4) that the intellect is *separate,* and that it is not the act of any body. Therefore it is not united to the body as its form.

Obj. 2. Further, every form is determined according to the nature of the matter of which it is the form; otherwise no proportion would be required between matter and form. Therefore if the intellect were united to the body as its form, since every body has a determinate nature, it would follow that the intellect has a determinate nature; and thus, it would not be capable of knowing all things, as is clear form what has been said (Q. LXXV., A. 2); which is contrary to the nature of the intellect. Therefore the intellect is not united to the body as its form.

Obj. 3. Further, whatever receptive power is an act of a body, receives a form materially and individually; for what is received must be received according to the condition of the receiver. But the form of the thing understood is not received into the intellect materially and individually, but rather immaterially and universally: otherwise, the intellect would not be capable of the knowledge of immaterial and universal objects, but only of individuals, like the senses. Therefore the intellect is not united to the body as its form.

Obj. 4. Further, power and action have the same subject; for the same subject is what can, and does, act. But the intellectual action is not the action of a body, as appears from the above (Q. LXXV., A. 2). Therefore neither is the intellectual faculty a power of the body. But virtue or power cannot be more abstract or more simple than the essence from which the virtue or power is derived. Therefore, neither is the substance of the intellect the form of a body.

Obj. 5. Further, whatever has *per se* existence is not united to the body as its form; because a form is that by which a thing exists: so that the very existence of a form does not belong to the form by itself. But the intellectual principle has *per se* existence and is subsistent, as was said above (Q. LXXV., A. 2). Therefore it is not united to the body as its form.

Obj. 6. Further, whatever exists in a thing by reason of its nature exists in it always. But to be united to matter belongs to the form by reason of its nature; because form is the act of matter, not by any accidental quality, but by its own essence; otherwise matter and form would not make a thing substantially one, but only accidentally one. Therefore, a form cannot be without its own proper matter. But the intellectual principle, since it is incorruptible, as was shown above

(Q. LXXV., A. 6), remains separate from the body, after the dissolution of the body. Therefore the intellectual principle is not united to the body as its form.

On the contrary, According to the Philosopher, *Metaph.* viii. (Did. vii. 2), difference is derived from the form. But the difference which constitutes man is *rational,* which is applied to man on account of his intellectual principle. Therefore the intellectual principle is the form of man.

I answer that, We must assert that the intellect which is the principle of intellectual operation is the form of the human body. For that whereby primarily anything acts is a form of the thing to which the act is to be attributed: for instance, that whereby a body is primarily healed is health, and that whereby the soul knows primarily is knowledge; hence health is a form of the body, and knowledge is a form of the soul. The reason is because nothing acts except so far as it is in act; wherefore a thing acts by that whereby it is in act. Now it is clear that the first thing by which the body lives is the soul. And as life appears through various operations in different degrees of living things, that whereby we primarily perform each of all these vital actions is the soul. For the soul is the primary principle of our nourishment, sensation, and local movement; and likewise of our understanding. Therefore this principle by which we primarily understand, whether it be called the intellect or the intellectual soul, is the form of the body. This is the demonstration used by Aristotle (*De Anima* ii. 2).

But if anyone say that the intellectual soul is not the form of the body he must first explain how it is that this action of understanding is the action of this particular man; for each one is conscious that it is himself who understands. Now an action may be attributed to anyone in three ways, as is clear from the Philosopher (*Phys.* v. I); for a thing is said to move or act, either by virtue of its whole self, for instance, as a physician heals; or by virtue of a part, as a man sees by his eye; or through an accidental quality, as when we say that something that is white builds, because it is accidental to the builder to be white. So when we say that Socrates or Plato understands, it is clear that this is not attributed to him accidentally; since it is ascribed to him as man, which is predicated of him essentially. We must therefore say either that Socrates understands by virtue of his whole self, as Plato maintained, holding that man is an intellectual soul; or that intellect is a part of Socrates. The first cannot stand, as was shown above (Q. LXXV., A. 4), for this reason, that it is one and the same man who is conscious both that he understands, and that he senses. But one cannot sense without a body: therefore the body must be some part of man. It follows therefore that the intellect by which Socrates understands is a part of Socrates, so that in some way it is united to the body of Socrates.

The Commentator held that this union is through the intelligible species, as having a double subject, in the possible intellect, and in the phantasms which are in the corporeal organs. Thus, through the intelligible species the possible intellect is linked to the body of this or that particular man. But this link or union does not sufficiently explain the fact, that the act of the intellect is the act of Socrates. This can be clearly seen from comparison with the sensitive faculty, from which Aristotle proceeds to consider things relating to the intellect. For the relation of phantasms to the intellect is like the relation of colours to the sense of sight, as he says *De Anima* iii. 5, 7. Therefore, as the species of colours are in the sight, so are the species of phantasms are in the possible intellect. Now it is clear that because the colours, the images of which are in the sight, are on a wall, the action of see-ing is not attributed to the wall: for we do not say that the wall sees, but rather that it is seen. Therefore, from the fact that the species of phantasms are in the possible intellect, it does not follow that Socrates, in whom are the phantasms, understands, but that he or his phantasms are understood.

Some, however, tried to maintain that the intellect is united to the body as its motor; and hence that the intellect and body form one thing so that the act of the intellect could be attributed to the whole. This is, however, absurd for many reasons. First, because the intellect does not move the body except through the appetite, the movement of which presupposes the operation of the intellect. The reason therefore why Socrates understands is not because he is moved by his intellect, but rather, contrariwise, he is moved by his intellect because he understands. Secondly, because, since Socrates is an individual in a nature of one essence composed of matter and form, if the intellect be not the form, it follows that it must be outside the essence, and then the intellect is to the whole Socrates as a motor to the thing moved. Whereas the act of intellect remains in the agent, and does not pass into something else, as does the action of heating. Therefore the action of understanding cannot be attributed to Socrates for the reason that he is moved by his intellect. Thirdly, because the action of a motor is never attributed to the thing moved, except as to an instru-ment; as the action of a carpenter to a saw. Therefore, if understanding is attrib-uted to Socrates, as the action of what moves him, it follows that it is attributed to him as to an instrument. This is contrary to the teaching of the Philosopher, who holds that understanding is not possible through a corporeal instrument (*De Anima* iii. 4). Fourthly, because, although the action of a part be attributed to the whole, as the action of the eye is attributed to a man; yet it is never attrib-uted to another part, except perhaps indirectly; for we do not say that the hand sees because the eye sees. Therefore if the intellect and Socrates are united in the above manner, the action of the intellect cannot be attributed to Socrates. If, however, Socrates be a whole composed of a union of the intellect with whatever else belongs to Socrates, and still the intellect be united to those other things only as a motor, it follows that Socrates is not one absolutely, and consequently neither a being absolutely, for a thing is a being according as it is one.

There remains, therefore, no other explanation than that given by Aristotle—namely, that this particular man understands, because the intellectual principle is his form. Thus from the very operation of the intellect it is made clear that the intellectual principle is united to the body as its form.

The same can be clearly shown from the nature of the human species. For the nature of each thing is shown by its operation. Now the proper operation of man as man is to understand; because he thereby surpasses all other animals. Whence Aristotle concludes (*Ethic.* x. 7) that the ultimate happiness of man must consist in this operation as properly belonging to him. Man must therefore derive his species from that which is the principle of this operation. But the species of anything is derived from its form. It follows therefore that the intellectual principle is the proper form of man.

But we must observe that the nobler a form is, the more it rises above corporeal matter, the less it is merged in matter, and the more it excels matter by its power and its operation; hence we find that the form of a mixed body has another operation not caused by its elemental qualities. And the higher we advance in the nobility of forms, the more we find that the power of the form excels the elementary matter; as the vegetative soul excels the form of the metal, and the sensitive soul excels the vegetative soul. Now the human soul is the highest and noblest of forms. Wherefore it excels corporeal matter in its power by the fact that it has an operation and a power in which corporeal matter has no share whatever. This power is called the intellect.

It is well to remark that if anyone holds that the soul is composed of matter and form, it would follow that in no way could the soul be the form of the body. For since the form is an act, and matter is only in potentiality, that which is composed of matter and form cannot be the form of another by virtue of itself as a whole. But if it is a form by virtue of some part of itself, then that part which is the form we call the soul, and that of which it is the form we call the *primary animate,* as was said above (Q. LXXV., A. 5).

Reply Obj. 1. As the Philosopher says (*Phys.* ii. 2), the ultimate natural form to which the consideration of the natural philosopher is directed is indeed separate; yet it exists in matter. He proves this from the fact that *man and the sun generate man from matter.* It is separate indeed according to its intellectual power, because the intellectual power does not belong to a corporeal organ, as the power of seeing is the act of the eye; for understanding is an act which cannot be performed by a corporeal organ, like the act of seeing. But it exists in matter so far as the soul itself, to which this power belongs, is the form of the body, and the term of human generation. And so the Philosopher says (*De Anima* iii.) that the intellect is separate, because it is not the faculty of a corporeal organ.

From this it is clear how to answer the Second and Third objections: since, in order that man may be able to understand all things by means of his intellect, and that his intellect may understand immaterial things and universals, it is sufficient that the intellectual power be not the act of the body.

Reply Obj. 4. The human soul, by reason of its perfection, is not a form merged in matter, or entirely embraced by matter. Therefore there is nothing to prevent some power thereof not being the act of the body, although the soul is essentially the form of the body.

Reply Obj. 5. The soul communicates that existence in which it subsists to the corporeal matter, out of which and the intellectual soul there results unity of existence; so that the existence of the whole composite is also the existence of the soul. This is not the case with other non-subsistent forms. For this reason the human soul retains its own existence after the dissolution of the body; whereas it is not so with other forms.

Reply Obj. 6. To be united to the body belongs to the soul by reason of itself, as it belongs to a light body by reason of itself to be raised up. And as a light body remains light, when removed from its proper place, retaining meanwhile an aptitude and an inclination for its proper place; so the human soul retains its proper existence when separated from the body, having an aptitude and a natural inclination to be united to the body.

On the Various Kinds of Law
(from *Summa theologiae*, Parts I–II)

QUESTION XCI
FIRST ARTICLE
WHETHER THERE IS AN ETERNAL LAW?

We proceed thus to the First Article:—

Objection 1. It seems that there is no eternal law. Because every law is imposed on someone. But there was not someone from eternity on whom a law could be imposed: since God alone was from eternity. Therefore no law is eternal.

Obj. 2. Further, promulgation is essential to law. But promulgation could not be from eternity: because there was no one to whom it could be promulgated from eternity. Therefore no law can be eternal.

Obj. 3. Further, a law implies order to an end. But nothing ordained to an end is eternal: for the last end alone is eternal. Therefore no law is eternal.

On the contrary, Augustine says (*De Lib. Arb.* i.): *That Law which is the Supreme Reason cannot be understood to be otherwise than unchangeable and eternal.*

I answer that, As stated above (Q. XC., A. 1 *ad* 2; AA. 3, 4), a law is nothing else but a dictate of practical reason emanating from the ruler who governs a perfect community. Now it is evident, granted that the world is ruled by Divine providence, as was stated in the First Part (Q. XXII., AA. I, 2), that the whole community of the universe is governed by Divine Reason. Wherefore the very Idea of the government of things in God the Ruler of the universe, has the nature of a law. And since the Divine Reason's conception of things is not subject to time but is eternal, according to Prov. viii. 23, therefore it is that this kind of law must be called eternal.

Reply Obj. 1. Those things that are not in themselves, exist with God, inasmuch as they are foreknown and preordained by Him, according to Rom. iv. 17: *Who calls those things that are not, as those that are.* Accordingly, the eternal concept of the Divine law bears the character of an eternal law, in so far as it is ordained by God to the government of things foreknown by Him.

Reply Obj. 2. Promulgation is made by word of mouth or in writing; and in both ways the eternal law is promulgated: because both the Divine Word and the writing of the Book of Life are eternal. But the promulgation cannot be from eternity on the part of the creature that hears or reads.

Reply Obj. 3. The law implies order to the end actively, in so far as it directs certain things to the end; but not passively,—that is to say, the law itself is not ordained to the end,—except accidentally, in a governor whose end is extrinsic to him, and to which end his law must needs be ordained. But the end of the Divine government is God Himself, and His law is not distinct from Himself. Wherefore the eternal law is not ordained to another end.

SECOND ARTICLE
WHETHER THERE IS IN US A NATURAL LAW?

We proceed thus to the Second Article:—

Objection 1. It seems that there is no natural law in us. Because man is governed sufficiently by the eternal law: for Augustine says (*De Lib. Arb.* i.) that *the eternal law is that by which it is right that all things should be most orderly.* But nature does not abound in superfluities as neither does she fail in necessaries. Therefore no law is natural to man.

Obj. 2. Further, by the law man is directed, in his acts, to the end, as stated above (Q. XC., A. 2). But the directing of human acts to their end is not a function of nature, as is the case in irrational creatures, which act for an end solely by their natural appetite; whereas man acts for an end by his reason and will. Therefore no law is natural to man.

Obj. 3. Further, the more a man is free, the less is he under the law. But man is freer than all the animals, on account of his free-will, with which he is endowed above all other animals. Since therefore other animals are not subject to a natural law, neither is man subject to a natural law.

On the contrary, The gloss on Rom. ii. 14: *When the Gentiles, who have not the law, do by nature those things that are of the law,* comments as follows: *Although they have no written law, yet they have the natural law, whereby each one knows, and is conscious of, what is good and what is evil.*

I answer that, As stated above (Q. XC., A. I *ad* I), law, being a rule and measure, can be in a person in two ways: in one way, as in him that rules and measures; in another way, as in that which is ruled and measured, since a thing is ruled and measured, in so far as it partakes of the rule or measure. Wherefore, since all things subject to Divine Providence are ruled and measured by the eternal law, as was stated above (A. I); it is evident that all things partake somewhat of the eternal law, in so far as, namely, from its being imprinted on them, they derive their respective inclinations to their proper acts and ends. Now among all others, the rational creature is subject to Divine providence in the most excellent way, in so far as it partakes of a share of providence, by being provident both for itself and for others. Wherefore it has a share of the Eternal Reason, whereby it has a natural inclination to its proper act and end: and this participation of the eternal law in the rational creature is called the natural law. Hence the Psalmist after saying (Ps. iv. 6): *Offer up the sacrifice of justice,* as though someone asked what the works of justice are, adds: *Many say, Who showeth us good things?* in answer to which question he says: *The light of Thy countenance, O Lord, is signed upon us:* thus implying that the light of natural reason, whereby we discern what is good and what is evil, which is the function of the natural law, is nothing else than an imprint on us of the Divine light. It is therefore evident that the natural law is nothing else than the rational creature's participation of the eternal law.

Reply Obj. 1. This argument would hold, if the natural law were something different from the eternal law: whereas it is nothing but a participation thereof, as stated above.

Reply Obj. 2. Every act of reason and will in us is based on that which is according to nature, as stated above (Q. X., A. I): for every act of reasoning is based on principles that are known naturally, and every act of appetite in respect of the means is derived from the natural appetite in respect of the last end. Accordingly the first direction of our acts to their end must needs be in virtue of the natural law.

Reply Obj. 3. Even irrational animals partake in their own way of the Eternal Reason, just as the rational creature does. But because the rational creature partakes thereof in an intellectual and rational manner, therefore the participation of the eternal law in the rational creature is properly called a law, since a law is something pertaining to reason, as stated above (Q. XC., A. I). Irrational creatures, however, do not partake thereof in a rational manner, wherefore there is no participation of the eternal law in them, except by way of similitude.

THIRD ARTICLE
WHETHER THERE IS A HUMAN LAW?

We proceed thus to the Third Article:—

Objection 1. It seems that there is not a human law. For the natural law is a participation of the eternal law, as stated above (A. 2). Now through the eternal law *all things are most orderly,* as Augustine states (*De Lib. Arb.* i.). Therefore the natural law suffices for the ordering of all human affairs. Consequently there is no need for a human law.

Obj. 2. Further, a law bears the character of a measure, as stated above (Q. XC., A. I). But human reason is not a measure of things, but vice versa (*cf. Metaph.* x.). Therefore no law can emanate from human reason.

Obj. 3. Further, a measure should be most certain, as stated in *Metaph.* x. But the dictates of human reason in matters of conduct are uncertain, according to *Wis.* ix. 14: *The thoughts of mortal men are fearful, and our counsels uncertain.* Therefore no law can emanate from human reason.

On the contrary, Augustine (*De Lib. Arb.* i.) distinguishes two kinds of law, the one eternal, the other temporal, which he calls human.

I answer that, As stated above (Q. XC., A. I, *ad* 2), a law is a dictate of the practical reason. Now it is to be observed that the same procedure takes place in the practical and in the speculative reason: for each proceeds from principles to conclusions, as stated above (*ibid.*). Accordingly we conclude that just as, in the speculative reason, from naturally known indemonstrable principles, we draw the conclusions of the various sciences, the knowledge of which is not imparted to us by nature, but acquired by the efforts of reason, so too it is from the precepts of the natural law, as from general and indemonstrable principles, the the human reason needs to proceed to the more particular determination of certain matters. These particular determinations, devised by human reason, are called human laws, provided the other essential conditions of law be observed, as stated above (Q. XC., AA. 2, 3, 4). Wherefore Tully says in his *Rhetoric* (*De Invent. Rhet.* ii.) that *justice has its source in nature; thence certain things came into custom by reason of their utility; afterwards these things which emanated from nature and were approved by custom, were sanctioned by fear and reverence for the law.*

Reply Obj. 1. The human reason cannot have a full participation of the dictate of the Divine Reason, but according to its own mode, and imperfectly. Consequently, as on the part of the speculative reason, by a natural participation of Divine Wisdom, there is in us the knowledge of certain general principles, but not proper knowledge of each single truth, such as that contained ins the Divine Wisdom; so too, on the part of the practical reason, man has a natural participation of the eternal law, according to certain general principles, but not as regards the particular determinations of individual cases, which are, however, contained in the eternal law. Hence the need for human reason to proceed further to sanction them by law.

Reply Obj. 2. Human reason is not, of itself, the rule of things: but the principles impressed on it by nature, are general rules and measures of all things relating to human conduct, whereof the natural reason is the rule and measure, although it is not the measure of things that are from nature.

Reply Obj. 3. The practical reason is concerned with practical matters, which are singular and contingent: but not with necessary things, with which the speculative reason is concerned. Wherefore human laws cannot have that inerrancy that belongs to the demonstrated conclusions of sciences. Nor is it necessary for every measure to be altogether unerring and certain, but according as it is possible in its own particular genus.

Love and Happiness
On Love (from *Summa theologiae and contra Gentes*, I-II)

The name *love* is given to the principle of movement towards the end loved . . . and this principle is the subject's connaturalness with the thing it tends to; it may be called *natural love*: thus the connaturalness of a heavy body for the center, because of its weight, may be called its natural love. Likewise the fittingness of the sensitive tendency towards some good is called *sensitive love*, and of the intellectual tendency, the will, is called *intellectual love*: sensitive love is in the sensitive appetite, and intellectual love is in the intellectual appetite. 26, 1, c (tr. abh)

The union of lover and beloved is two-fold: *real union*, when lover and beloved are actually together with each other, and *union of affection*, which binds them together whether they are actually with each other or not. Union of affection is had either by love of *desire* or love of *friendship*, each following on the apprehension of a unique oneness between lover and beloved. When we love a thing by desiring it, it's because we see it as required by our well-being. When we love a person in friendship, we wish good to that person just as we wish it for ourselves: we think of our friend as our other self. Hence, Aristotle calls a friend one's "other self", and Augustine says, "Well did one say to his friend, 'Thou half of my soul'" (tr. abh)

The first of these unions is caused *effectively* by love; because love moves man to desire and seek the presence of the beloved, as of something suitable and belonging to him. The second union is caused *formally* by love; because love itself is this union or bond. In this sense Augustine says (*De Trin.* viii. 10) that *love is a vital principle uniting, or seeking to unite two together, the lover, to wit, and the beloved.* For in describing it as *uniting* he refers to the union of affection, without which there is no love: and in saying that *it seeks to unite,* he refers to real union. 28, 1, c.

Mutual indwelling may be understood as referring both to the apprehensive and to the appetitive power. Because, as to the apprehensive power, the beloved is said to be in the lover, inasmuch as the beloved abides in the apprehension of the lover, according to Phil. i. 7, *For that I have you in my heart:* while the lover is said to be in the beloved, according to apprehension, inasmuch as the lover is not satisfied wth a superficial apprehension of the beloved, but strives to gain an intimate knowledge of everything pertaining to the beloved, so as to penetrate into his very soul. Thus it is written concerning the Holy Ghost, Who is God's Love, that He *searcheth all things, yea the deep things of God* (I Cor. ii. 1o).

As to the appetitive power, the object loved is said to be in the lover, inasmuch as it is in his affections, by a kind of complacency: causing him either to take pleasure in it, or in its good, when present; or, in the absence of the object loved, by his longing, to tend towards it with the love of desire towards the good that he wills to the beloved, with the love of friendship: not indeed from any extrinsic cause (as when we desire one thing on account of another, or wish good to another on account of something else), but because the complacency in the beloved is rooted in the lover's heart. For this reason we speak of love as being *intimate;* and of *the deep yearning of charity.* On the other hand, the lover is in the beloved, by the love of desire and by the love of friendship, but not in the same way. For the love of desire is not satisfied with any external or superficial possession or enjoyment of the beloved; but seeks to possess the beloved perfectly, by penetrating into his heart, as it were. Whereas, in the love of friendship, the lover is in the beloved, inasmuch as he reckons what is good or evil to his friend, as being so to himself; and his friend's will as his own, so that it seems as though he felt the good or suffered the evil in the person of his friend. Hence it is proper to friends *to desire the same things, and to grieve and rejoice at the same,* as the Philosopher says (*Ethic.* ix. 3 and *Rhet.* ii. 4). Consequently in so far as he reckons what affects his friend as affecting himself, the lover seems to be in the beloved, as though he were become one with him: but in so far as, on the other hand, he wills and acts for his friend's sake as for his own sake, looking on his friend as identified with himself, thus the beloved is in the lover.

In yet a third way, mutual indwelling in the love of friendship can be understood in regard to reciprocal love: inasmuch as friends return love for love, and both desire and do good things for one another. 28, 2, c.

On Ultimate Happiness (from *Summa contra Gentes*, Book III)

CHAPTER XXXVII
THAT MAN'S ULTIMATE HAPPINESS
CONSISTS IN CONTEMPLATING GOD

If then the final happiness of man does not consist in those exterior advantages which are called goods of fortune, nor in goods of the body, nor in goods of the soul in its sentient part, nor in the intellectual part in respect of the moral virtues, nor in the virtues of the practical intellect, called art and prudence, it remains that the final happiness of man consists in the contemplation of truth. This act alone in man is proper to him, and is in no way shared by any other being in this world. This is sought for its own sake, and is directed to no other end beyond itself. By this act man is united in likeness with pure spirits, and even comes to know them in a certain way. For this act also man is more self-sufficient, having less need of external things. Likewise to this act all other human activities seem to be directed as to their end. For to the perfection of contemplation there is requisite health of body; and all artificial necessaries of life are means to health. Another requisite is rest from the disturbing forces of passion: that is attained by means of the moral virtues and prudence. Likewise rest from exterior troubles, which is the whole aim of civil life and government. Thus, if we look at things rightly, we may see that all human occupations seem to be ministerial to the service of the contemplators of truth.

Now it is impossible for human happiness to consist in that contemplation which is by intuition of first principles,—a very imperfect study of things, as being the most general, and not amounting to more than a potential knowledge: it is in fact not the end but the beginning of human study: it is supplied to us by nature, and not by any close investigation of truth. Nor can happiness consist in the sciences, the object-matter of which is the meanest things, whereas happiness should be an activity of intellect dealing with the noblest objects of intelligence. Therefore the conclusion remains that the final happiness of man consists in contemplation guided by wisdom to the study of the things of God. Thus we have reached by way of induction the same conclusion that was formerly established by deductive reasoning, that the final happiness of man does not consist in anything short of the contemplation of God.

CHAPTER XLVIII
THAT MAN'S ULTIMATE HAPPINESS
IS NOT IN THIS LIFE

If then human happiness does not consist in the knowledge of God, whereby He is commonly known by all or most men according to some vague estimate, nor again in the knowledge of God whereby He is known demonstratively in speculative science, nor in the knowledge of God whereby He is known by faith, as has been shown above; if again it is impossible in this life to arrive at a higher knowledge of God so as to know Him in His essence, or to understand other pure spirits, and thereby attain to a nearer knowledge of God; and still final happiness must be placed in some knowledge of God; it follows that it is impossible for the final happiness of man to be in this life.

2. The last end of man bounds his natural desire, so that, when that is reached, nothing further is sought: for if there is still a tendency to something else, the end of rest is not yet gained. But that cannot be in this life: for the more one understands, the more is the desire of understanding, natural to all men, increased.

3. When one gains happiness, he gains also stability and rest. All have this idea of happiness, that it involves stability as a necessary condition: hence the philosopher says that we do not take man for a chameleon. But in this life there is no stability: for however happy a man be called, sicknesses and misfortunes may always happen to debar him from that activity, whatever it is, wherein happiness consists.

4. It seems unfitting and irrational that the period of development should be great and the period of duration small: for it would follow that nature for the greater part of its time went without its final perfection. Hence we see that animals that live for a short time take a short time in arriving at maturity. But if human happiness consists in perfect activity according to perfect virtue, whether intellectual or moral, such happiness cannot accrue to man till after a long lapse of time; and this is especially apparent in speculative activity, in which the happiness of man is ultimately placed. For scarcely in extreme age can a man arrive a perfect view of scientific truth; and then for the most part there is little of human life left.

5. That is the perfect good of happiness, which is absolutely free from admixture of evil, as that is perfect whiteness, which is absolutely unmingled with black. But it is impossible for man in the state of this life to be altogether free from evils,—not to say bodily evils, as hunger, thirst, cold and heat, but even from evils of the soul. There is no man living who is not at times disturbed by inordinate passions, who does not at times overstep the mean in which virtue consists, or fall short of it, who is not in some things deceived, or ignorant of what he wishes to know, or driven to weak surmises on points where he would like absolute certainty.

6. Man naturally shrinks from death, and is sad at the thought of it. Yet man must die, and therefore cannot be perfectly happy while here he lives.

7. Happiness consists, not in habit, but in activity: for habits are for the sake of acts. But it is impossible in this life to do any act continually.

8. The more a thing is desired and loved, the greater grief and sadness does its loss bring. But if final happiness be in this world, it will certainly be lost, at least by death; and it is uncertain whether it will last till death, since to any man there may possibly happen in this life diseases totally debarring him from any virtuous activity, such as insanity. Such happiness therefore must always have a natural pendent of sadness.

But it may be replied that whereas happiness is the good of an intelligent nature, true and perfect happiness belongs to those in whom intelligent nature is found in its perfection, that is, in pure spirits; but in man it is found imperfectly by way of a limited participation. And this seems to have been the mind of Aristotle: hence, enquiring whether misfortunes take away happiness, after showing that happiness lies in virtuous activities, which are the most permanent things in this life, he concludes that they who enjoy such perfection in this life are "happy for men," meaning that they do not absolutely attain happiness, but only in a human way.

Now it is demonstrable that the aforesaid answer is not to the undoing of the arguments above alleged. For (*a*) though man is inferior in the order of nature to pure spirits, yet he is superior to irrational creatures; and therefore he must gain his final end in a more perfect way than they. But they gain their final end so perfectly as to seek nothing further. Thus the natural desire of dumb animals is at rest in the enjoyment of sensual delights. Much more must the natural desire of man be put to rest by his arrival at his last end. But that is impossible in this life: therefore it must be attained after this life.

(*b*) It is impossible for a natural desire to be empty and vain: for nature does nothing in vain. But the desire of nature (for happiness) would be empty and vain, if it never possibly could be fulfilled. Therefore this natural desire of man is fulfillable. But not in this life. Therefore it must be fulfilled after this life.

Alexander and Averroes laid it down that the final happiness of man is not in such knowledge as is possible to man through the speculative sciences, but in a knowledge gained by conjunction with a separately subsistent intelligence, which conjunction they conceived to be possible to man in this life. But because Aristotle saw that there was no other knowledge for man in this life than that which is through the speculative sciences, he supposed man not to gain perfect happiness, but a limited measure of happiness suited to his state. In all which investigation it sufficiently appears how hard pressed on this side and on that these fine geniuses (*praeclara ingenia*) were. From this stress of difficulty we shall find escape in positing, according to the proofs already given, that man can arrive at true happiness after this life, the soul of man being immortal. In this disembodied state the soul will understand in the way in which pure spirits understand. The final happiness of man then will be in the knowledge of God, which the human soul has after this life according to the manner in which pure spirits know Him.

Therefore the Lord promises us *reward in heaven* (Matt. v, 12), and says that the saints shall be *as the angels* (Matt. xxii, 30), who *see the face of God in heaven* (Matt. xviii, 10).

(Tr. Joseph Rickaby)

REVIEW QUESTIONS

1. Show the importance of the rediscovery of Aristotle for Western thought.
2. How does the epistemology of St. Thomas lead to the conclusion, contrary to Plato's view, that body and soul form one being in man?
3. In what way is Thomas' philosophy existential?
4. What is St. Thomas' position on the norm for judging right from wrong?
5. How does St. Thomas demonstrate the existence of God?
6. Discuss St. Thomas' view on the presence of evil in the world.
7. What is St. Thomas' view on happiness and how a person achieves it?
8. Discuss the meaning of eternal law and natural law in St. Thomas.

Suggestions for Further Reading

Clarke, W. N. *The One and the Many: A Contemporary Thomistic Metaphysics.* Southbend, Notre Dame University Press, 2001.

Davies, Brian, *The Thought of Thomas Aquinas.* New York, Oxford University Press, 1993.

Gilson, E. *The Christian Philosophy of St. Thomas Aquinas.* Tr. Shook, L. New York, Random House, 1956.

Kenny, A. *Aquinas.* New York, Hill and Wang, 1980.

McDermott, T. ed. *St. Thomas Aquinas, Selected Philosophical Writing.* New York, Oxford University Press, 1993.

10

William of Ockham
(c. 1280–1349)

Toward the Late Middle Ages

The intellectual life of theology, which began in earnest in the early thirteenth century, continued unabated into the early fourteenth; it was expressed in academic centers throughout Europe in a busy program of study, lectures, public defense of theses, and public disputations that involved masters and students alike in the ongoing excitement of divine science. Besides the theological factiousness that sometimes arose, there were legitimate preferences in theology that one might have embraced as more fitting articulations of a faith all theologians held in common. Such preferences were coming to be recognized in the theological undertakings of the Dominicans and Franciscans, young religious orders which, within a dozen years of each other, established chairs of theology at the University of Paris, the most prestigious school of theology in Christendom. Toward the end of the century, the Dominicans counted Albert the Great and Thomas Aquinas among their most respected theologians, and the Franciscans did the same with Alexander of Hales and Bonaventure. Though it would be unhistorical to talk of different types of theology clashing with each other in the early part of the thirteenth century, the rediscovered Aristotle had to compete successfully against a series of prohibitions laid down by churchmen fearful of the faith's being contaminated by a "pagan" philosophy.

But the lively fourteenth-century discussion of theology between masters and students "in the schools" (hence the term *scholasticism*) led to the development of different traditions and put to rest any temptation to think that a common faith necessarily generates a common philosophy. Christian thinkers, though expressing a commonality of belief, held widely divergent philosophies, divergent not only as to style in St. Augustine, let us say, and in St. Thomas, but also as to the reach of the human mind in matters like the proof-value of arguments for the existence of God and the immortality of the soul, the epistemological import of universal ideas, the meaning of natural law, the relative importance of intellect and will, the unity of body and soul, or the precedence of essence over existence. Yet in the philosophical experience of any period, current ideas are the progenitors of the next generation, and often there is a family resemblance, as mentioned earlier, among divergent philosophies. The thirteenth, fourteenth, and fifteenth centuries formed such a period, and the fourteenth century, the century of theologians like Duns Scotus and William of Ockham, was the natural offspring of the thirteenth.

Given a family resemblance, a philosopher of the thirteenth century would have recognized the kind of problem his fifteenth-century counterpart was dealing with and would have recognized that the questions arising in his time had multiplied themselves in the succeeding two centuries. St. Thomas would have seen his concerns in the philosophy of Scotus, and Scotus his concerns in the philosophy of Ockham, but both Scotus and Ockham proceeded along radically different paths from their progenitors.

Duns Scotus: God and the Creaturely World

Interestingly, St. Augustine was the patrimony of all medieval theologians so that, even after the towering authority of Aristotle was re-introduced in the West, the philosophical makeup of a thinker like Aquinas was that of an Augustinian Aristotelianism. But among the theologians of the next generation, no doubt feeling the impact of the famous prohibitions of 1277 purporting to safeguard the faith by condemning certain theses of "Aristotelianism," was Duns Scotus, whose philosophical makeup was that of an Aristotelian Augustinianism, thus restoring the great Latin Father to pride of place without losing the benefit of the Stagirite's mighty contributions. Scotus and Ockham were both early fourteenth-century figures, both born in the British Isles, both Franciscans, and both schooled at Oxford University. Ockham is more representative of the century because all the currents of the time ran through him, but we can begin with some reflections on Scotus to get an idea of the trajectory that philosophy started to take after St. Thomas.

Though he died young and left most of his writings unfinished, Duns Scotus c. 1265–1308 exercised a profound influence for several centuries, gaining a reputation for the subtlety of his distinctions. It was this very propensity and his lack of literary grace that disenchanted the literary humanists of the Renaissance, who mocked him and the "Duns-men" as hair splitters and sophists, thus causing the word *dunce* to enter pejoratively into present-day language. Yet this same Duns Scotus was hailed by the American philosopher C. S. Peirce as one of the profoundest metaphysicians who ever lived and was spoken of as reality's "rarest veinéd unraveller" by the poet Gerard Manley Hopkins out of gratitude for deepening his insight into the inwardness of being, called *inscape* by the poet.

As one who studies the science of God, the theologian must be prepared to give his reasons for saying that God exists, and his reasons have to fall into one of two categories: either we *know* that God exists or we *hold* that God exists on nonrational grounds. Scotus definitely belongs to the first category, and though his proof is complicated in itself, it has historical complications as well. He rejects any form of argumentation that can be called physical, such as Aristotle's argument for the Prime Mover, because it cannot go beyond the physical things with which it begins. Yet the existence of God "is demonstrable by a demonstration of fact from creatures." Contrary to some Arabian commentators on Aristotle who saw necessity in whatever God does outside Himself, and wanting to maintain God's freedom at all costs, Scotus shifted the emphasis from the fact of a contingent thing's *existence* to the fact of its being *possible,* it being true, of course, that a conclusion of a thing's possibility can be made from its actuality: Whatever is actual was possible, though whatever is possible is not therefore actual. Now Scotus felt on safer ground because he was able to show that God both exists and is free at the same time; if there are possibles, it is only because a being necessarily exists that can freely produce them as possible, and so he argues: something is possible; since its possibility does not come from within itself, it must come from something else as its cause; but an infinite series of causes to account for possibility is impossible; therefore, something necessarily and actually exists that freely causes possibles, and is itself uncaused.

It's clear that Scotus is working from a concept of metaphysics radically different from that of St. Thomas. This concept, perhaps oversimplified, is that *essence is prior to existence.* The first thing the intellect knows, and therefore the primary "intelligible," is not that a thing *is,* but *what* it is, so that "being" refers first and foremost to "essence." In other words, existence is a "modality" of essence, and not the other way around. One cannot speak of essence without speaking of some corresponding degree of existence, and when a thing actually exists, it is because God has willed to "complete" the existential capabilities of that essence in its individual determination. It is not as though existence must be added to essence, as in the metaphysics of Aquinas, for it is already present in the texture of essence, simply awaiting a further determination on God's part.

The indeterminateness of essence can be garnered from the fact that the response to the question "what?" when asked of Socrates is exactly the same as when asked of Peter, Paul, Mary, James, and so on; that response is "man"; man can be predicated of one or many, it is both singular and universal. What makes the *singular* referent an individual is the *thisness* (*haecceitas* in Latin) it possesses, which makes it unique and unshared by anything else. So, for example, there must be something in Socrates that makes him Socrates and no one else; his color, his shape, his size, and so on are only external signs of his individuality. The thisness of Socrates is the very "form," Scotus says, that functions as the determining element previously discussed.

We are now in a better position to understand Scotus' view on the relationship of creatures to God. By a special act, God produces an individually existing thing separate from Himself: "Now what is primarily the term of a creative act as such is formally an individual or a 'this.'" Yet, every created thing, before it is created, is "creatable," which means that somehow it is present in the very being of God and pertains to the very essence of God. But not everything that pertains to the very essence of God is for that reason creatable, for creatibility itself is a matter of divine option; otherwise Scotus would, he felt, fall into the trap of putting God under necessity and creatures under fatalism. God's designations, then, are possibles; they are essences that, in God and by God, have a direct reference to existence subject to a further and ultimate determination (form) as this or that individual created thing. Existence, then, is not a determination that comes from without, as already indicated; it comes from within the texture of essence. This is the heart of the difference between Scotus' and Thomas' existentialism.

Another feature of Scotist metaphysics—that being can be predicated "univocally" of God and creatures—enters at this point. Recall the huge problem faced by St. Thomas and in fact by any philosopher who is concerned with the relationship between God and creatures: If you call a creature a being and then call God a being, are you therefore saying they are the same, as when you say that Socrates is a man and Paul is a man? If being means exactly the same, then it is *univocal;* if there is no similarity of meaning, it is *equivocal.* If the first were true, God and creatures are one; if the second, there is no way of talking about God at all. So Thomas developed the third way of *analogy,* a way allowing being to be said of God in a radically different way from the way it is said of creatures, and yet with some similarity. Thomas could do this because his metaphysics of existence allows an analogy between the way God is proportioned to His existence and the way creatures are proportioned to their existence. But Scotus's metaphysics of essence would not permit this interpretation of analogy, for he insisted that being expresses a commonness between God and creatures; being is univocal, at least in one sense of the word: "It is clear that 'being' has a primacy of commonness in regard to the primary intelligibles, that is, to the quidditative concepts of the genera, species, individuals, and all their essential parts, and to the Uncreated Being."

But being, for Scotus, is not a genus or a class, like "man" or "animal"; it transcends them; it is a "transcendental," like "wise" and "good." So the difference between God and creatures, of whom being is truly said, is in the way the transcendental applies, that is, either as infinite or finite: "Whatever [predicates] are common to God and creatures are of such kind [i.e., transcendental], pertaining as they do to being in its indifference to what is infinite and finite. For in so far as they pertain to God they are infinite, whereas in so far as they belong to creatures they are finite."

In Scotus' creaturely world, as with theologians generally, it is the creature man, endowed with the special grace of intellect and will, who can relate to God knowingly and lovingly. If one asks which is the higher faculty, he will find, according to Scotus, that it is the will, for it is by the will, a "rational will" to be sure, that man achieves what he exists for—the love of God. We saw how much Scotus wants to protect the freedom of God against all necessity, so that His will is the pervasive force of creation, and the highest expression of His will toward man is His love. In return, the highest expression of man's free will is in loving God. In a sense, the love of God for man and the love of man for God is a mutual union of freedoms. Man's actions, then, are considered good if they are done in accordance with the love of God; the love of God becomes the norm of morality, which is acknowledged by man in the right use of his reason.

The completion of man's love for God is attained in life beyond death. As a Christian theologian, Scotus believes that man is immortal, but, hard as he tries to say that immortality can be proved by reason, he rejects all rational arguments that purport to prove it; the most these arguments show is that immortality is probable. He considers all the arguments he finds in Aristotle, Aquinas, and even Augustine, and yet his summary opinion is:"It can be stated that although there are probable reasons for this second proposition [i.e., that the intellective soul is immortal] these are not demonstrative, nor for that matter are they even necessary reasons." Nevertheless, immortality is a certainty, and we can readily understand how this fact creates for Scotus a further opportunity to rejoice in the certainty of faith as a gift of God.

William of Ockham: Forerunner of Things Modern

As hinted at earlier, much of William of Ockham's writings were forged out of his experiences in having been personally drawn into the ecclesiastical and secular turbulence of the fourteenth century, especially his works on church and state. He was probably born at Ockham, near London, around the year 1280. As a young man he went to Oxford to study theology and stayed there to lecture on the Bible and the *Sentences* of Peter Lombard. He was a baccalaureate and, though he had completed all the requirements, save for holding a formal professorship, he was never officially a Master of Theology, but only a "beginning" professor, an *inceptor,* whence the title later on of Venerable Inceptor. In all probability he was blocked from an appointment as professor by the former chancellor of Oxford, an ardent Thomist, who denounced him for heresy to Pope John XXII at Avignon in southern France, the pope's residence in exile. Ockham went to Avignon in 1324 to defend himself, but the affair dragged on for several years and was never satisfactorily concluded.

A dispute had long been developing among the Franciscans as to whether or not, in imitation of Christ, the Franciscan friars ought to possess property; this debate became known as the controversy on Franciscan poverty. When the pope tried to settle it by declaring it heretical to deny that Christ or the Apostles possessed property, the Franciscans were split on accepting this decision as final, Ockham being among those who rejected it. After a long study of the question, he publicly stated his position and, when he realized that in all likelihood he would incur papal denunciation, he sought refuge with the Emperor Ludwig of Bavaria who, with his own goals in mind, had just returned from Rome where he installed an antipope and in return was crowned Holy Roman Emperor. Ockham asked for protection and offered in exchange to defend Ludwig's imperial prerogatives against the pope; legend has it that he proclaimed to Ludwig, "O Emperor, defend me with your sword, and I will defend you with my pen." Despite the dubiousness of the remark, from 1328 on Ockham lived in Munich under the emperor's protection and went on to write works on the relative authority of church and state which became hugely influential. In the end he maintained what was a fairly balanced view on authority in a century troubled by the sorting out of levels of power.

After Ludwig died in 1347, William of Ockham initiated the process of reconciling himself with the pope and his own order, but before that was accomplished he fell victim to the Black Death in 1349. Among his many works the following should be mentioned: *On Logic, Commentary on the Sentences, Quodlibetal Questions, Commentary on Aristotle's "Physics,"* and his political writings, especially *The Treatise on Papal* and *Imperial Power.*

Voluntarism and Empiricism

As with all the other theologian-philosophers of the Middle Ages, Ockham's philosophy centered on God, the fulcrum around which everything else moves. All such philosophies hold that God is supreme in every respect—in knowledge, in being, in goodness, in power; yet in how these attributes are to be understood there can be significant differences. All hold, for example, that God's will is supreme; yet there is a vast difference in the way Ockham fashions his understanding of the divine will. It is not only that things exist because God wills them to exist but also that they are the way they are because God wills them to be that way; in other words, a thing is the kind of thing it is not according to the nature of reality, but according to God's *will.* The name attached to this view of God's will is *voluntarism* (from the Latin *voluntas,* meaning will). At bottom, voluntarism means that there is no necessity for a thing to be what it is before God wills it; for that would be putting God under a necessity and contrary to His absolutely free will. It does not follow that a thing could be different from what it is, or that I, if God so chose, could have been someone else; that would be meaningless. It is simply that God willed this *to be this,* period; all things then are possible to God, except what is clearly contradictory, though to know what is contradictory is an extremely narrow option for man.

The same voluntarism extends to the realm of ethics, for it is God's will here too that determines the morality of an action. If God wills an action to be designated as good, it is good; bad if he designates it so. As Ockham writes in his *Commentary on the Sentences,* "God cannot be obliged to any act whatsoever; by that fact alone, whatever God wills is right." The ultimate norm of morality then is God's will and though practically speaking there may be little or no difference between Ockham and, let us say, Thomas Aquinas in judging the morality of individual actions, there is a profound theoretical difference. For Aquinas there is, as we will recall, an eternal law that is one with the divine being, and as participated by human beings it is called *natural law;* so we may say of an immoral action, it is bad, that is why God forbids it; not, as with Ockham, God forbids it, that is why it is bad. Inasmuch as the moral law of Ockham is not in place by the nature of reality, but "put in place," or "posited," by God, it is often referred to as *positivistic.*

Whatever exists that is not God exists because God has willed it; it is the result of His creative act; there is no necessity for any creature to exist, so the only way we have of knowing what God has willed is by experience: since things need not be the way they are, and are what they are only by divine will, then the only way we know the things God has willed is to know them by experience, and perhaps Ockham's voluntarism, sponsoring his empirical cast of mind, foreshadowed the empirical tradition of his fellow Britons in time to come.

Cause and Effect

This amalgam of voluntarism and empiricism was a powerful force in Ockham's understanding of causality. Led by experience, the only relationship we can affirm between the termini called cause and effect is that of observed sequences, clearly anticipating David Hume. We are in no way privy to the influence one thing has over another; so in no way can we say the effect is necessarily in the cause. This is not true of God, of course, because God is the primary and universal cause, and if creatures are causes it is only by divine dispensation and properly called secondary causes. As expected of the empiricist, lest the metaphysically freed universe tend to fly apart for lack of causal cohesion, Ockham was obliged to hold to a causal sequence: But we must remind ourselves that "to hold" a causal sequence is not "to know" it. "To hold" is a radically different assent of the mind from "to know." One implication of this position on secondary causes leads to the following analysis: If God is the primary and universal cause, it is clear that He can do directly what secondary causes can do; they can, on occasion, be dispensed with. Now by experience, in the substance-accident context, we know only accidents (qualities); if then God causes accidents to exist through substance, He can occasionally cause them to exist without substance. This, Ockham maintains, is what God does in the case of the Eucharist, for He directly supports the qualities of bread and wine without employing the substance as their support.

Fitting in systematically with this view of the divine surveillance of the world is the principle that has become known as *Ockham's razor*. It is the principle by which Ockham tries to avoid multiplying explanations of things where they are not absolutely necessary; that is, we ought to try to understand reality with as few causes, explanations, or entities as possible. The form in which this principle is stated is usually given as "entities are not to be multiplied without necessity." Thought not the first to employ such a principle of parsimony, Ockham gave it prominence, tied in as it was, with his teaching on voluntarism. Inasmuch as God's will is what determines whether entities exist, we do not know which of them are necessary except as made evident by experience, strict reasoning, or divine revelation.

Question: Man is, God is; Are They Therefore the Same?

Among the things made evident to us by experience is that individuals exist. That only individuals can exist is a matter of clearly seeing the contradiction involved in a thing supposedly individual and universal at the same time. This position, for Ockham, directly entails two other problems: the notion of being as univocal and the meaning of universals. The unique question for the philosophical theist is how the being of God stands to the being of creatures. When we say "God is a being" and "I am a being," does it follow from the use of the same predicate that God and I are the same insofar as "being" is concerned, just as when I say "Fido is a dog" and "Lassie is a dog" that both are the same insofar as "dog" is concerned? Parmenides foreshadowed the problem when he denied any differentiation between the "being" of one thing as against the "being" of another. As regards God and creatures, St. Thomas put the dilemma clearly: If "being" is used in the same way (univocally) of God and creatures, then they are the same; if not used in the same way at all (equivocally), then there is nothing common between them and therefore there is no way whatsoever of talking about God; to avoid both extremes he then devised the "analogy" of being in which there is a sameness, or commonality, in the way each stands to existence. Ockham however, with Scotus, felt that there is a way of using "being" univocally without compromising radical distinction. Actually a concept can be used of radically different things: Fido and Lassie are, as individuals, radically different beings, and this radical dissimilarity is not lost when we say "dog" of each one; the *way we know* is not necessarily the *way things are,* any more than the concept "two" means there is an actually existing number outside the mind. So, for Ockham, when "being" is used of God and creatures, it is used in the same way (univocally), but as a concept, not as a metaphysical statement. Philosophical agnosticism is not at all the consequence of this position, for Ockham argues that indeed our beginning knowledge of God comes from creatures since it is from them we first learn of the meaning of being.

Nominalism and Its Implicit Problems

This aspect of Ockham's exploration of how the mind stands to reality is of a piece with his view on the meaning of "universals," that is, universal knowledge. Again, reminding ourselves that historically universals have been referred to variously as essences, ideas, natures, or forms, Plato's extreme realist position requires things to be outside the mind exactly as known inside the mind. Aristotle, and the main line of epistemological realists, maintained the real existence of things we know, but not necessarily as we know them; the universal-in-the-mind is founded on a thing-in-reality but not in literal correspondence with it. Scotus held that a common nature really existed in things which was distinct but somehow contained in the individual. Ockham rejected all these positions in favor of what he thought was eminent common sense: Only individual things exist, therefore each individual thing has, or is, its own nature; there is then no commonality among things, only similarity. But the problem of universals is not only a metaphysical one; it is also a problem of logic and how signs, or terms, are used. On this basis, Ockham is sometimes referred to as a "nominalist," for whom only names are common, thus linking him up with the long-standing medieval controversy on universals reaching back to the twelfth century and forward to the revival of nominalism among the disciples of Ockham in the ensuing years.

Ockham's ability to shuttle back and forth so readily from the logical to the metaphysical parts of a problem stemmed from his abiding interest in logic. Leading up to the fourteenth century were any number of outstanding logicians, beginning with Peter Abelard several hundred years before. By Ockham's time a prodigious contribution, readily identifiable as "medieval logic," has been generated. The basic structure of logic was, of course, laid down by Aristotle, and his elaborations on the role of word, proposition, and syllogism had become its classic foundation; but even Aristotle knew that his discoveries were only a beginning. For his part, Ockham conceived logic broadly as a science of language, particularly in its function as a vehicle for what the mind is thinking about, for mental discourse. He therefore gave prime attention to what words, or terms, signify and the mode of their signification.

Ockham and Luther

It is not to our purpose here to proceed through all the definitions and distinctions Ockham makes in his studies in logic, but there is one that has a bearing on the strained relationship between theology and philosophy that developed in the centuries immediately following. The distinction between a *real* and *nominal* definition is not new with Ockham; it even goes back as far as Aristotle, though not explained in the same way. A real definition answers the question, What is this thing?; it is an expression telling us what the actual reality is like; it is on the metaphysical side. A nominal definition answers the question, What is the meaning of this term?; it is an expression telling us of the elements or contents found in the term; it is on the logical side. When this distinction is applied to the attributes of God, as when we say "good," "infinite," "all-knowing," we could never be saying what God is like in reality because we do not know; "good," "infinite," and "all-knowing" must therefore pertain to the nominal definition inasmuch as they tell us what is in the term *God*. That being so, knowledge of God becomes further estranged from our intellectual competence and points to a growing antirational and antimetaphysical mind with the consequence that natural theology becomes impotent in favor of faith.

It can even be argued that Ockham's view of divine power led the way to eventual skepticism, for, if God acts according to an absolute will, and His actions are in that sense arbitrary, then we could never *know* for certain how He, at this very moment, is governing the world. In trying to lift God above every trace of constraint, even that of being known by a creaturely intellect, Ockham in effect began driving an intellectual wedge between God and human reason, thus making Him inaccessible to natural, human knowledge; the only remedy therefore for the natural incapacity of our intellect, call it skepticism, was to invoke the supernatural gift of faith. This is clearly seen in Martin Luther, two centuries later, for whom the glory of faith lay in the fact that it is a gift from on high and transcends the capabilities of the human intellect which, on its own, cannot rise to a sure knowledge of God; it is no wonder that Luther could refer to Ockham as "my dear master." These are unmistakable indicators that Ockham marks the end of a distinct period in the history of philosophy and looks toward a new one. As the eminent medievalist, Etienne Gilson, writes," . . . the doctrine of Ockham marked a turning point in the history of philosophy as well as of theology. In theology his doctrine was paving the way to the 'positive theology' of the moderns. In philosophy, it was paving the way to modern empiricism. In both cases it really was a *via moderna:* a modern way."

Readings

On the Problem of Universals
(from *Logic, I,* 14)

Since it is not sufficient for the logician to have a general knowledge of terms, it is necessary for him to know terms in detail and, having treated the general divisions of terms, we must continue with the consideration of certain points under several headings of this division.

First we must deal with terms of second intention; secondly with terms of the first intention. It is said that terms of the second intention are terms like 'universal,' 'genus,' 'species,' etc. But before we say anything about the five kinds of universals, we ought to say something about that aspect of 'universal' which is predicated of every universal and which opposes it to the term 'singular'.

The first thing we must know is that 'singular' is taken in two senses. In one sense the name 'singular' signifies that a thing is one and not many. Taken in this sense, those who hold that a universal is a certain quality of the mind predicable of many things and that it stands for those things and not for itself, have also to say that every universal is truly and really singular: because every word, even if it is regarded as common, is truly and really singular and numerically one: it is one thing in itself and not many. Though the intention of the mind signifies many things outside itself, it remains truly and really singular and numerically one: it is one and not many, although it signifies many things.

In the second sense, the name 'singular' is taken for that which is one thing and not many, and is not destined to be a sign of many things. Whence, if you call universal that which is not numerically one, which a good number of logicians do, then I say that nothing is a universal, unless perhaps you would want to abuse the word by comparing it to a word like 'people' which you then proceed to call a universal because it is not one, but many; that would indeed be childish.

It must be said therefore that every universal is one singular thing, and is not universal except in its signification, that is, as a sign of many things. And this is what Avicenna has to say in the fifth book of his *Metaphysics:* "one form in the intellect refers to a multitude, and in this respect it is a universal, for it is an intention in the intellect whose relationship with individuals is universal, is nevertheless individual in relationship to the singular mind in which it is impressed." What he is saying is that the universal is one particular intention of the mind and it is its nature to be predicated of many things; it is called universal, not for itself, but for the many of which it is predicated; but because of the fact that it is one form really existing in the intellect, it is called a singular. Thus, singular in the first sense is predicated of the universal, but not singular in the second sense, the sense in which we say that the sun is a universal cause and yet it is truly a particular and singular thing, consequently a singular and particular cause. For the sun is called "universal cause" in that it is the cause of many things,—of all things on earth that can be generated or corrupted; moreover, it is called a "particular cause" inasmuch as it is one cause and not several. Thus the intention of the mind is called "universal" because it is a sign predicable of many; yet it is called "singular" because it is one thing and not many.

We must, however, be aware that there are two kinds of universal. One kind is naturally universal because it can by nature be predicated in a proportionate way of many things, much as smoke naturally signifies fire, or a groan the pain of a sick person, or laughter inner happiness; such a universal is nothing more than the intention of the mind, such that there is no universal outside the mind, whether substance or accident. I shall subsequently speak of this kind of universal. The other kind of universal is conventional; that is, an uttered word, which is truly a single quality, is universal because by convention it signifies many. Whence, just as the word is said to be common, it can also be said to be universal, not by the nature of the thing but only by the agreement of those using it.

A Universal Is Not a Thing Outside the Mind
(from *Logic, I,* 15)

Because it is not enough merely to state these things without some clear proof, I shall adduce some reasons for them.

That a universal is not a substance existing outside the mind can clearly be demonstrated:

First, no universal is a substance both singular and numerically one. If that were true, it would follow that Socrates is a universal, because there is no greater reason for one universal to be a singular substance than another; no singular substance therefore is a universal, for every substance is numerically one and singular: everything is either one thing and not many, or it is many things. If it is one and not many, it is numerically one: and all call it such. However, if any substance is many things, it is either many singular things or many universal things. If it is the first of these options, then any substance would be many singular substances and, following the same reasoning, there would be some substance that would be several men; thus, although a universal would be distinguished from a particular in one instance, it would not be distinguished from particulars in general. If, however, a substance were many universal things, I take one as an example and ask, is this one thing and not many?, or is it many things? if the answer to the first question is 'yes,' then of course it is singular; if it is the second, then a follow-up question must be asked; is it many singular or many universal things? Thus, either this process will go on *ad infinitum,* or it stands that no substance is universal without being singular. And so it rests, that no substance is universal.

Furthermore, if any universal were one substance existing in singular things and distinct from them, it would follow that it could exist without them, for every thing naturally prior to another can exist without it by divine power; which consequence is absurd.

Furthermore, if that opinion were true, no individual could be created because something of the individual would have pre-existed, for it would not have gotten its whole being from nothing if the universal in it existed before in another individual. It would follow that God could not annihilate one individual of a substance without destroying the other individuals, inasmuch as in annihilating one individual, He would destroy all that pertained to the essence of the individual and consequently the universal which is in it and in the others; it would follow too that the other individuals would not remain, because they could not remain without a part of themselves which the universal is held to be.

Furthermore, a universal so described could not be entirely extrinsic to the essence of the individual and, being of the essence of the individual, it would follow that the individual is composed of universals and thus there would be no more singular than universal . . .

A Universal Is Indistinct Knowledge of Many
(from *Commentary on Aristotle's 'On Interpretation'*)

Another opinion is possible in that the activity of the mind is itself the act of knowing. And because this option seems to me to be more probable than any other opinion which holds that these activities of the mind are in the soul as its true qualities, I shall explain it in its more usual form . . .

I say that anyone wishing to hold this opinion may suppose that the intellect elicits from within itself knowledge of this singular thing only, which knowledge is an act of the mind naturally standing for that singular thing. The spoken word "Socrates", by convention, stands for one thing it signifies; no listener misunderstands it as referring to the word "Socrates" as running, but rather to the signified Socrates as running. The spoken word, by convention, stands for a thing; the act of the intellect, by nature, stands for a thing.

Now beyond the knowledge of singular things, the intellect forms for itself another kind of knowledge which does not refer to one thing more than another.

It is by such indistinct knowledge that singular things outside the mind are known. When we say we have indistinct knowledge of man, we do not recognize one man more than another, but we are able to distinguish man from donkey . . .

And so it can be said that such knowledge obtains for an infinite number of singulars without being knowledge proper to any one of them, and this is because there is some specific likeness found among them and not others.

(Tr. P. Boehnet)

On the Notion of Being
(from *Logic*, I, 38)

The first thing we must know about 'being' is that it can be taken in two senses: in the first, the term 'being' corresponds with a concept that is universal and can therefore be predicated of all things . . . but in the second sense, not withstanding its universality, the term 'being' is also equivocal and therefore cannot be predicated of all subjects in the same way, for then they are being taken as things signified. . . .

Further, it is known that, as the Philosopher shows in the fourth book of *Metaphysics*, 'being' is used to apply to what *is*, whether intrinsically or incidentally . . . The distinction between 'intrinsic' and 'incidental' indicates that 'being' is not used intrinsically only. This is exemplified in Aristotle's saying a musician is 'just', by which he means to refer to the musician as *being* just incidentally. He is simply speaking to the different ways we predicate one thing of another. tr. ABH

(For Ockham, even though universals do not refer to real extra-mental objects, they can still be used as terms in propositions. Whence, when he raises the question whether there is anything common between God and creatures, he can answer both "yes" and "no"; for example, can we use 'being' of God and creatures?—"yes", propositionally, as terms in a proposition; "no", metaphysically, as though 'being' were really the same in both. ABH)

REVIEW QUESTIONS

1. What is the importance of William of Ockham in the history of fourteenth-century Europe?
2. Explain the meaning of voluntarism. How does it tie in with ethics?
3. What is meant by the phrase "Ockham's razor"?
4. What is Ockham's position on the problem of individuals and universals?
5. How could Ockham's view of divine power lead to skepticism?

SUGGESTIONS FOR FURTHER READING

Boehner, P., ed. *Ockham: Philosophical Writings A Selection.* Indianapolis, Hackett, 1990.

Leff, Gordon. *William of Ockham.* Manchester, England, University of Manchester Press, 1975.

McCord, Marilyn. *William Ockham,* 2 vols. South Bend, IN, University of Notre Dame Press, 1989.

PART THREE

THE MODERN PERIOD

The Spirit of Modern Philosophy: Philosophy and the Rise of Science

The seventeenth century marked a turning point in the intellectual history of Europe in which the turmoils and agonies of previous times began to achieve a recognizable direction and a clear identity; it deserves to be called the beginning of a new age. It was one of those rare centuries that bristled with fresh ideas, new paths, and rich possibilities, and with a spirit uplifted by the opening up of unexpected horizons in human self-understanding. All areas of intellectual activity were ventilated by its creative breath: literature, art, theology, political science; philosophy and science alone boasted of such geniuses as Galileo, Descartes, Spinoza, Leibniz, Pascal, Bacon, Locke, Harvey, Huyghens, Kepler, and Newton. Indeed, Alfred North Whitehead proclaimed the seventeenth-century formulation of the laws of gravity and the three laws of motion the "greatest single intellectual success which mankind has achieved."

The period covering the two and a half centuries or so prior to the seventeenth saw the Middle Ages come to an end. It was a theocentric age for most of Europe, an age of common faith, religious practice, Church, and a society shaped by them that lasted for hundreds of years. But a unified Christianity was not destined to last, and long before the Reformation took place, many forces were at work wearing unity away. For a whole range of reasons, the Church was looked on as having abandoned the simplicity of its founder, of having lost the sense of the sacred in its mission and ministers, and of having, in the name of God, abused its power in public and private life. The longer internal reform was delayed, the more dissatisfaction grew and the more the forces at work coalesced. Among them was the ongoing struggle between Church and state, each trying to define and enlarge its sphere of jurisdiction against the other. The struggle was epitomized in the quarrel between Pope Boniface VIII and King Philip IV (the Fair) of France, for when the pope laid claim to supremacy in France as part of his universal dominion, the king took violent measures against him and finally had him clapped in jail.

Similarly, the unity between theology and philosophy that had prevailed in the High Middle Ages was beginning to dissolve. The general rubric of "faith seeking understanding," indicative of the willingness of theology to use other areas of knowledge in its service, had been mainly true of philosophy; we have already seen, for example, the role played by the two great Greek traditions, Platonic and Aristotelian, in transferring insights from philosophy to theology. But this relationship, which had proven so fruitful, was now becoming suspect, and theology and philosophy were under pressure to assert their independence. As we have seen, this is clearly demonstrated in the powerful figure of William of Ockham, whose teaching that the transcendence of God places Him so much beyond rational grasp as to make Him unknowable except by faith began to weaken metaphysics as the foundation of philosophy, a view destined to hold for centuries. Ockham's political views were just as divisive and aligned him with the swelling antipapal sentiment; he was compelled to flee to the protection of Emperor Ludwig IV of Bavaria.

The forces that tended to erode the medieval world continued into the Renaissance that followed—broadly speaking, from the late fourteenth century to the middle of the sixteenth. Church and state were still at odds with each other, the state still trying to organize itself into a center of life for its citizens and the Church still trying to maintain its internal unity against powerful centrifugal forces. The situation of each cannot be better personified than in two notable figures, *Niccolo Machiavelli* (1469-1527) and *Martin Luther* (1483-1546). Machiavelli, after many years as a civil servant in Florence, came to the conclusion that, no Christian order being possible, the hope for an orderly existence rests with the state, and that the order and unity of the state can be defended against enemies within and without only by a strong monarch who displays absolute rule. His "prince" had to be both a lion and a fox, endowed with cunning and power, dedicated to the belief that when the safety of the country is at stake, "no consideration of what is just or unjust, merciful or cruel, praiseworthy or shameful, must intervene." Though not as influential in Italy as in other parts of Europe, Machiavelli's work is the first effort of its kind in modern political theory.

The collective energy of all the reformers before him, crying for renovation of the Church, finally exploded in Luther, an Augustinian monk, with such power that it sent shock waves throughout Europe that are still felt today. As a brilliant professor and theologian—a new St. Paul, they called him—he was an Ockhamist regarding God's total Otherness and His absolute will, and emphasized the powerlessness of human reason compared with faith. In his intensely religious soul, so many pressures were growing from his sense of creatureliness and unworthiness that he despaired of his own salvation unless he rejected the pretensions of reason, so-called good works, ecclesiastical authority, the fearfulness of sin, and his own will; he had only to believe firmly in the Lord Jesus. Despite his enigmatic traits, he was the right person at the right time to release the pent-up frustration of the people with Church and authority, thus bringing to a definitive end the unity of medieval religion and inaugurating a new age of religion in Europe.

There were so many cross-currents during the age of Machiavelli and Luther that the intellectual history of the time is not a straight line; it resembles less the neat track of an arrow in flight than the surface of a boiling cauldron whose ingredients keep pushing to the top. It was the time when learned books were being written in the vernacular; Machiavelli wrote in Italian, and Luther in German. The advent of movable type and the printing press, made books far more available than manuscripts ever had been. Art and architecture peaked in artists such as da Vinci, Raphael, Titian, and Michelangelo. It was an age in which the Counter-Reformation was initiated by Pope Paul III shortly before Luther died. And it was an age, with the Copernican revolutionary doctrine of a heliocentric universe, in which modern science began in earnest.

In regard to our immediate concern, the dominant position of theology as "queen of the sciences" slowly receded, accompanied by the separation of philosophy from theology; this allowed a greater effort to explain things to the satisfaction of reason without first invoking divine causality for the successful workings of nature. In finding new grounds for certitude, it meant that the individual was free to follow his own intellectual direction. In some cases, this resulted in *classical humanism,* a renewed interest in the pre-Christian classics, both Greek and Latin, hoping to find there a sure basis for man's self-understanding. In other cases, it resulted in the hope of discovering the meaning of man on his own terms, a kind of philosophical humanism: Now that reason had been separated from revelation, the proper study of mankind was man. Although there was, however short-lived, a revival in Platonic studies, particularly in the Florentine Academy of Marsilio Ficino, who tried to show the compatibility of Platonic ideals with Christianity, the fortunes of philosophy during the Renaissance were the fortunes of Aristotelianism tied, as it was, to the great theological systems of the late thirteenth and early fourteenth centuries. Aristotelianism was beginning to fall out of favor as its philosophy or its science came to be viewed as confining, dogmatic, or simply wrong.

This turn of events could only terminate, in some instances, in a feeling of despair of finding any real certitude, especially the kind required for the conduct of life. Such was the attitude of the eminent essayist *Michel de Montaigne* (1533–1592), who found any system building offensive and, to that extent, was anti-scholastic if not antirational. If his motto was "I don't know," reminiscent of the skepticism of later Greek philosophy, it was because philosophy had no sure response to the important question for one who is concerned about the values of life. Some philosophers, Montaigne said, persuasively demonstrate that the soul is immortal; others that it is not, or that we have none to worry about. Philosophy thus cancels itself out and offers no solutions for human perplexities. Better turn to nature, or revelation, or history, or social conventions, not because there is absolute truth in them but because as "truths of fact" they offer the best chance for equanimity.

Though *Francis Bacon* (1561–1626) agreed with the antischolastic stand of Montaigne, he did not agree with his view that the human mind is incapable of certitude. In this Bacon represents the new spirit straining for recognition, the spirit of science, the spirit of experiment, and the spirit of induction which would provide, in his view, the opportunity to achieve certitude that the human mind had never enjoyed before. Though not a scientist himself, but a civil servant for years, Bacon had a high regard for the experimental method as the way to know the world, and believed that knowing the world is the precondition for improving it. His project for the Great Instauration, or Renewal, was human control of the universe for the betterment of man. Since "not much can be known in nature by the way which is now in use," the way has to be cleared up first. The obstacles in the way, he wrote in *Novum Organum,* are the false opinions and errors, called *idols,* accumulated from the past. Of the four groups of idols—of the tribe, the cave, the marketplace, and the theater—it is the last that is devoted to philosophy. Here Bacon sweepingly rejects all past philosophies because they systematically departed from the real world to create unreal worlds of their own: "These I call Idols of the Theater; because in my judgment all the received systems are but so many stage-plays, representing worlds of their own creation after an unreal and scenic fashion." Even the so-called empirical school of philosophy is to be rejected because of the "narrowness" of its experiments and its hurry to draw conclusions far more sweeping than those warranted by its findings. Bacon sees the fruitfulness of the scientific method in carefully monitored experimentation and in directing its conclusions to the advancement of man.

The man who best exemplifies, after Bacon's paradigm, the passing of the old worldview and the advent of the new is *Galileo Galilei* (1564–1642), the scientist who mocked the Aristotelians while he wrested secrets from nature using the new method of experimentation and reflection. In him, the medieval worldview, mainly because of its religious entwinements, battled with the new scientific spirit in one of the most dramatic moments in intellectual history. Though a professor at the University of Padua, Galileo pitied the academics who had eyes only for books and not for the real world, and were therefore unfit for the investigation of nature. For centuries the Aristotelian world picture had put the earth at the center of the universe, with the planets and the sun revolving around it. The earth, and not the sun, was the center for two reasons: The sun could be "observed" turning about the earth, and the earth was where man dwelled. For the Christian believer, there was an additional reason for holding the same view: Sacred Scripture gave countless examples of the "fact" that the sun moves and not the earth, and Sacred Scripture, as God's word, cannot be wrong. Some time before Galileo, Copernicus, the Polish canon and astronomer, began to theorize that something was amiss with the received system because it did not square with his observations and mathematical calculations. However, the mere switch of the sun's position with that of the earth would generally set the universe aright. This view came to be supported by other astronomers, like Johannes Kepler, but it was Galileo who was able, with the aid of the newly invented telescope, to strengthen the conviction that Copernicus was right.

Because of this tension between religion and science, Church authorities, fearful of yet another shock to ecclesiastical stability and the truth of faith, and concerned about the ordinary person's belief, put Copernicus' book *On Revolutions* on the Index of Prohibited Books in 1616, and in 1633 tried and condemned Galileo. Kneeling before the eminent cardinals and inquisitors, the seventy-year-old Galileo had to recant his "errors" that the sun is the center of the world and does not move, and that the earth is not the center of the world and that it moves. A sympathetic story has it that as the old man got up, he shook his head and said, "Still, it moves!" The dismay this event caused in the intellectual world cannot be calculated, but as an indication, Descartes pulled back his book *Traité du monde* because it accepted the Copernican view; it was published only after he died.

It is clear, then, that the new picture of the planetary system was more than just another event in the history of astronomy; it was, in actuality, a *revolution.* It was a revolution in our understanding of nature, for a cosmology two thousand years old was not to be overturned lightly. It was a revolution in the role of authority, for now the authority of neither Aristotle nor the Bible could be offered in evidence. It was, overall, a revolution in man's understanding of himself, for man could not achieve a radically new view of nature, of authority, and of the Bible without envisioning a whole new tissue of relationships in which he identified himself.

Such was the intellectual atmosphere at the beginning of the new age. In the ensuing chapters, the seventeenth-century philosophers Descartes, Spinoza, Leibniz on the continent, and Hobbes and Locke in England will be presented as the immediate heirs of this experience, and the problems they focus on derive directly from it. Later, Berkeley, Hume, and Kant still deal with questions originating in the early seventeenth century but give special attention to the question of human knowledge. Finally, Hegel and Mill represent the last phase of modern philosophy before an entirely new direction occurs leading to the contemporary period.

SUGGESTIONS FOR FURTHER READING

Burtt, E. O. *The English Philosophers from Bacon to Mill.* New York, Modern Library, 1939.
Kuhn, T. S. *The Copernican Revolution.* Cambridge, Harvard University Press, 1957.
Scruton, Roger. *Modern Philosophy.* New York, Penguin, 1997.
Willey, B. *Seventeenth Century Background.* Garden City, Doubleday Anchor, 1953.

11

René Descartes
(1596–1650)

Skepticism of the kind personified by Montaigne was completely unacceptable to Descartes because it was a skepticism of the intellect. Considering it intolerable for the highest human faculty to be unsure of itself, his ardent desire was to discover a path to certitude, certitude no one could question, in short, an "unshakable certitude," a *quid inconcussum*. His response had to emerge from the new scientific spirit, and it fell to him to employ the method of mathematics as the key to certitude and the weapon against skepticism.

René Descartes was born in 1596 near Tours in France and died in 1650. He was educated at the Jesuit College of La Fléche, which had long enjoyed a reputation for excellence in mathematics. For several years he saw military service in Germany and other places in central Europe; he lived in Paris for a few years, but requiring a quieter life, he went in 1628 to Holland, where he expected to find more leisure and a freer intellectual atmosphere. In 1649 he went to Sweden at the invitation of Queen Christina, who wanted to be tutored in the new philosophy by the great man himself. He was there for only a few months during the winter, which proved so uncongenial to his health that he succumbed to tuberculosis early in 1650. His major works in philosophy include *Discourse on Method* (1637), *Meditations on First Philosophy* (1641), *Principles of Philosophy* (1644), and *The Passions of the Soul* (1649); published post-humously were *Rules for the Direction of the Mind* and *Traité du monde,* which, as previously noted, was written fairly early but withheld when Galileo was condemned.

Universal Mathematics: The Goal
of the Cartesian Method

The education of Descartes in mathematics was no accident, for interest in mathematics was the mark of the times. It dominated the seventeenth century to such an extent that any intellectual, whatever his concerns, was enormously interested in mathematics as well. As we saw in discussing Pythagoras, mathematics has a fascination all its own. It is the language of the sciences and, in many cases, controls their progress; it is a powerfully unifying force; and, above all, it is *certain,* for one step does not follow another without being inevitable. Small wonder that, for Descartes and for many like him, mathematics was the paradigm for all knowledge.

As he pondered the question of certitude, the young Descartes saw that if mathematics is certain, all other areas of knowledge can be seen as certain too if they can be shown to be mathematical in some way; to show them to be mathematical is the primary objective of his method. In the second part of the *Discourse on Method,* Descartes recounts an incident from his early years. While he was in Germany on military service and musing during a winter night in a "stove-heated room" on the problem of the unity of the sciences, it suddenly occurred to him that harmony among disparate things is always the achievement of one agent: diverse parts of the universe harmonized by one divine law; the grace of a building wrought by one workman; the beauty of a city laid out by one master designer. In a variation on the last example, a master designer, instead of razing all the old buildings, razes only some; the others he saves by putting them in "brackets," later to reincorporate them into the new plan if they are seen to fit. Such, at any rate, was Descartes' hope, and the attempt to mathematicize all knowledge is appropriately called *universal mathematics.*

Mathematics is deductive; that is, from a prior truth, other truths are drawn out or deduced; what is enfolded is unfolded; what is implicit is made explicit. But the process must have a beginning, which is variously called *quantity* or *extension,* the characteristic that allows things to be thought of as spatial. The concept of quantity does not require one to know what a thing is composed of, as long as it has dimensionality. And so begins the interplay of plane figures, lines, solids, and numbers, which leads to the beguiling array of relationships known as mathematics.

Descartes' plan, despite its inherent difficulties, had the appearance of simplicity and the spark to make it attractive to those who longed to replace the old scholasticism. If quantity is the initial truth of mathematics, and from it all other mathematical truths are deduced, all that has to be done is to discover what is parallel to quantity in other sciences and from it to deduce or intuit the body of truths proper to those sciences. The deductive method, for Descartes, is valid not only for mathematics but also for medicine, ethics, philosophy, and all other areas of knowledge.

To proceed in an orderly fashion, Descartes devised four rules to be followed as part of his *method:* (1) to accept nothing as true that is not known to be true, and to use in making a judgment only what is presented to the mind so clearly and distinctly that it cannot be doubted; (2) to divide each problem into its essential parts; (3) to begin with those things that are easiest to know and proceed to the more complex; (4) to make sure that nothing is omitted. In the first rule, we see that "clear and distinct" characteristics are required by Descartes for making a true judgment; they are invoked by him at every turn in working out his basic philosophy. Further, he distinguishes three classes of ideas: adventitious, invented (factitious), and *clear and distinct;* it is the last class that is the most important for Descartes from an epistemological point of view, for it is their very clarity and distinctness that make these ideas undoubtable and therefore the basis for certitude. And if he were asked, "How do clear and distinct ideas get into our minds?" Descartes, to avoid a further series of questions that could go on indefinitely and therefore supply no answer, would respond that they do not "get" there, they "are" there—they are *innate.* Questions about the existence and nature of innate ideas have caused a great deal of controversy, but without doubt such ideas were attractive to a mathematical-deductive mind. Following a line, then, that seems to express Descartes' view, innate ideas are not to be thought of as fully formed objects in the mind waiting for recognition; rather, they are produced by the natural tendency of the mind to think in a given way when the occasion occurs. This belief is somewhat reminiscent of Socrates' view of learning as a drawing out of what is already in the mind.

One of these ideas serves as the basis of a judgment that, as true, is destined to become the initial principle in Descartes' philosophy. To discover what that idea-judgment is, constitutes part of the Cartesian method and is referred to as the *method of doubt,* therefore, *methodic doubt:* the process of calling into question any judgment or proposition, regardless of how true it may seem to be, in order to get to one that cannot be doubted or that, perhaps, in the very act of being doubted, is affirmed. This does not mean that all other judgments, like old buildings, are permanently rejected; rather, they are temporarily stored away to be reconsidered later. We can call into doubt, for example, judgments based on sensations because they sometimes appear contradictory or because, as far as we know, they may be caused by an evil demon; in short, "I could feign that I had no body, that there was no world, nor any place in which I might be."

I Think Therefore I Am

But, Descartes continues, "I could not feign that I was not," and so the proposition *I think, therefore I am* (cogito ergo sum) is beyond doubt, or is affirmed while doubting, and is therefore true and certain. For Descartes, then, this truth is known immediately, that is, without any other medium or means; it is an idea directly grasped, an *intuition* of the self as a thinking being. Even though the famous phrase looks like an abbreviated syllogism—as though from the fact that I think I conclude that I exist—Descartes meant it to be taken as one intuition but with two moments: The first moment is of the self as *thinking,* the second moment is of the self as *being.* For Descartes, I *know* this; it is true, it is unshakable, it is the *quid inconcussum.*

Three Major Truths: Man, God and the World

With such a starting point, Descartes could safely proceed to the explication of the major truths of his philosophical system: the nature of man, the existence of God, and the existence of the external world.

That man exists, there is no doubt, as we have seen in the statement *I think, therefore I am.* Yet in the clarity and distinctness of this truth there is *nothing but* thought, that is, I am a *thinking* being, and my nature is the nature of my thinking. The nature of man is spirit and only spirit. To anticipate a bit—since we do not yet know whether the external world exists—what Descartes is saying is that the idea of thought does not contain within itself the idea of matter, so that matter, or body, cannot be part of the definition of man and does not belong to his nature. We will shortly discuss the huge problem of the mind–body relationship in Descartes and the meaning of Cartesian dualism as it follows from the understanding of man as thought only.

The second truth, the existence of God, is made possible by the presence in our minds of the idea of an all-perfect being, and there are two approaches to this idea. The first is in line with traditional approaches: the idea of an all-perfect being, inasmuch as it is all-perfect, cannot be of our making because we are imperfect beings; therefore it must be caused in us by a being that is all-perfect. The second approach, however, though reminiscent of the ontological argument of St. Anselm, is thoroughly Cartesian. The idea of the all-perfect being possesses in itself the idea of every perfection possible: the idea of being supreme, eternal, infinite, all-knowing, all-good, and so on. More than that, the idea of the all-perfect *necessarily* contains within itself the idea of existence; therefore, the all-perfect exists. The all-perfect, God, does not have a mental, or ideal, existence only, but an existence *outside* the mind; God really exists. There is no argument against the fact that a triangle necessarily implies three interior angles equaling 180 degrees, so there is no argument against the fact that the *existence* of God is necessarily implied in the idea of God. When some persons opposed this view with the objection that from the idea of a golden mountain you cannot infer its existence, Descartes responded, "of course not," because the idea of its existence is not necessarily implied in the idea of the golden mountain. The *only* idea in which the idea of existence is necessarily implied is the idea of the all-perfect.

By the end of the seventeenth century, the ontological argument had gained many adherents, including Spinoza and Leibniz; but other philosophers, not possessing the Cartesian mind, maintained that the only way to conclude that God exists is to *begin* with the *existence* of something you can experience; otherwise if your route begins *in the mind,* it stays there.

The third major truth, the existence of the external world, also begins with clear and distinct ideas. Descartes announces his project economically with the words, "There now remains only the inquiry as to whether material things exist," and he proceeds by examining the ideas of them insofar as they "are in my thought, and to determine which of them are distinct and which confused." Upon examination, then, we discern the idea of matter in its pure, geometrical form, namely, *quantity,* or *extension* "in length, breadth and depth"; it is clear and distinct, but the idea of existence is not necessarily included in it, unlike the second deduction, in which the idea of existence is necessarily included in the idea of the all-perfect. Along with our awareness of the idea of extension, we are aware of ideas of *sensation,* that is, of "ideas received by way of the senses." They come to us at various times, often uncontrolled and even unwanted, yet they exist. They, therefore, do not come from the mind itself, and the only possible conclusion is that they come from another substance called *body,* with which the mind experiences some kind of union, and in virtue of which it becomes related epistemologically to all other bodies. There is then an *external world,* a world outside mind, that is different in substance from mind.

A critic of Descartes could anticipate a sense of triumph in objecting that sensations offer no guarantee whatsoever of the existence of bodily things because we cannot rule out the possibility that sensations deceive us into making a false conclusion. But Descartes then played his trump card asking, how can you possibly speak of deception where God is involved? If I am deceived regarding my sensations, then God is thereby charged with deceiving me! But God is all-truthful and would not, could not, deceive me or allow me to be deceived; therefore, the conclusion that bodily things exist is both certain and true.

The Mind–Body Problem

Philosophers can and do lean in one direction or another in considering the problem of knowledge, and in a sense one's epistemological orientation is the key to one's philosophical makeup. The question is, how does the mind get to know in the first place? Historically, this question has two answers: The mind is already endowed with something like innate ideas, or the mind starts out as a blank and somehow acquires knowledge. In classical modern philosophy these opposing views were taken up by Descartes and his younger English contemporary, John Locke. For Descartes, as we have seen, ideas are innate, already present in the mind, so that the question of how they get there in the first place is superfluous: When mind is given, so are innate ideas. This position was required of Descartes in view of his basic philosophy of man, namely, that man is mind only, and in the consequent separation of mind and body, sensation becomes the activity of body only; so the question of how sensation could lead to intellectual knowledge becomes problematical. But Locke's view was that we have no innate ideas, for it is obvious, from our experience, that we come to know things for the first time as we sense them; so the mind, to begin with, is a clear slate, a *tabula rasa,* a tablet on which nothing has yet been written; writing appears as sensation takes place; nothing is in the intellect unless it is first in the sense—a belief that has been accepted by a host of philosophers from Aristotle on down.

Descartes must have felt that there was something untidy about his epistemology, perhaps because he sensed that somehow he was flying in the face of experience; this would explain why he required body and mind to be in the closest relationship without essentially being united, as in the Aristotelian doctrine.

Locke, on the other hand, felt that he was indeed relying on experience, and that is why he looked to sensation as the origin of all knowledge; but in this view he went so far as to hold that, for all we know, it might be possible, in God's power, for matter to be endowed with the ability to think. What Descartes held was that knowledge originated in the intellect itself, without the partnership of sense. What Locke held was that the origin of knowledge was in the sense, to the possible exclusion of intellect as partner, a position taken to its logical extreme in the next century by David Hume.

We now have a better vantage point from which to explain some other aspects of the mind–body relationship. It is clear that Descartes' real world admits two substances, body (quantity, extension, matter) and mind (spirit, thought); his position is often referred to as *Cartesian dualism.* His toughest problem is the relationship of mind to body, for having determined that man is by nature mind, the question becomes: How closely is mind related to body without forming one being? The traditional Aristotelian view is that man is *one* being composed of two principles, body and soul; body and soul are dual principles of one being. In the living organism they are not separated, for the soul is the life-giving principle to the body and is, therefore, one with it. This view Descartes eschewed and, while speaking in the context of mind and body, avoided the use of the word *soul* because it denoted an essential ordering to the body. Nevertheless, while not speaking of them as forming one being, Descartes spoke of body and mind as intimately related, as two independent substances acting together, close but separate.

What then is the *living* body for Descartes? Having come thus far, there is only one possible answer: The body is an aggregate of physical parts operating on physical principles only; it is a *machine* or an automaton. But it is a machine so exquisite, so finely honed to its task, that only God could fashion it. The body is not really a living thing; it has no need of a soul; it is not enlivened. And if a living thing has no need of a soul, then its activities are similar to those of any material thing: *All* material things operate on the basis of physical principles only. So, in a broader sense, movement in the universe is not all due to the activity of spirit, as held centuries before, but to matter's own inherent powers, and it was on this fact, as Descartes saw it, that he based his hopes for man's control of the universe for man's benefit.

Descartes' influence was vast; it dominated philosophical thought in continental Europe for the next century and a half. He satisfied himself and all those in tune with his rationalist approach that he had found a way to combat skepticism compatible with the mathematical model, and he compelled subsequent philosophers to rethink basic problems such as knowledge and certitude, mind and body, experience and deduction. That is why the metaphysical problems he dealt with—man, God, world—keep coming back in modern philosophy. Some interesting conclusions, however, were reached by a number of philosophers who were won over by the attractiveness of Descartes' method but could not follow him all the way; they moved on to extreme positions already latent in the Cartesian scheme. Bishop Berkeley, as we shall see, had to part company with Descartes on his way of getting to the material world, and concluded that the only reality is spirit and that sensations were nothing more than "states of mind."

At the other extreme, La Mettrie maintained that Descartes never convincingly demonstrated the need for spirit and concluded that man is only a machine.

Descartes was the first of three outstanding seventeenth-century philosophers on the continent usually referred to as *rationalists*. This name is applied because it signifies a tendency, in the matter of knowledge, to move from the mind outward to things, a tendency often found in the mathematical mind. In the following pages, we will consider the other two rationalists, Spinoza and Leibniz.

READINGS

Discourse on Method

PART II

I was then in Germany, to which country I had been attracted by the wars which are not yet at an end. And as I was returning from the coronation of the Emperor to join the army, the setting in of winter detained me in a quarter where, since I found no society to divert me, while fortunately I had also no cares or passions to trouble me, I remained the whole day shut up alone in a stove-heated room, where I had complete leisure to occupy myself with my own thoughts. One of the first of the considerations that occurred to me was that there is very often less perfection in works composed of several portions, and carried out by the hands of various masters, than in those on which one individual alone has worked. Thus we see that buildings planned and carried out by one architect alone are usually more beautiful and better proportioned than those which many have tried to put in order and improve, making use of old walls which were built with other ends in view. In the same way also, those ancient cities which, originally mere villages, have become in the process of time great towns, are usually badly constructed in comparison with those which are regularly laid out on a plain by a surveyor who is free to follow his own ideas. Even though, considering their buildings each one apart, there is often as much or more display of skill in the one case than in the other, the former have large buildings and small buildings indiscriminately placed together, thus rendering the streets crooked and irregular, so that it might be said that it was chance rather than the will of men guided by reason that led to such an arrangement. . . .

It is true that we do not find that all the houses in a town are rased to the ground for the sole reason that the town is to be rebuilt in another fashion, with streets made more beautiful; but at the same time we see that many people cause their own houses to be knocked down in order to rebuild them, and that sometimes they are forced so to do where there is danger of the houses falling of themselves, and when the foundations are not secure. From such examples I argued to myself that there was no plausibility in the claim of any private individual to reform a state by altering everything, and by overturning it throughout, in order to set it right again. Nor is it likewise probable that the whole body of the

Sciences, or the order of teaching established by the Schools should be reformed. But as regards all the opinions which up to this time I had embraced, I thought I could not do better than endeavour once for all to sweep them completely away, so that they might later on be replaced, either by others which were better, or by the same, when I had made them conform to the uniformity of a rational scheme. And I firmly believed that by this mean I should succeed in directing my life much better than if I had only built on old foundations, and relied on principles of which I allowed myself to be in youth persuaded without having inquired into their truth....

But like one who walks alone and in the twilight I resolved to go so slowly, and to use so much circumspection in all things, that if my advance was but very small, at least I guarded myself well from falling. I did not wish to set about the final rejection of any single opinion which might formerly have crept into my beliefs without having been introduced there by means of Reason, until I had first of all employed sufficient time in planning out the task which I had undertaken, and in seeking the true Method of arriving at a knowledge of all the things of which my mind was capable.

Among the different branches of Philosophy, I had in my younger days to a certain extent studied Logic; and in those of Mathematics, Geometrical Analysis and Algebra—three arts or sciences which seemed as though they ought to contribute something to the design I had in view. But in examining them I observed in respect to Logic that the syllogisms and the greater part of the other teaching served better in explaining to others those things that one knows (or like the art of Lully, in enabling one to speak without judgment of those things of which one is ignorant) than in learning what is new. And although in reality Logic contains many precepts which are very true and very good, there are at the same time mingled with them so many others which are hurtful or superfluous, that it is almost as difficult to separate the two as to draw a Diana or a Minerva out of a block of marble which is not yet roughly hewn. And as to the Analysis of the ancients and the Algebra of the moderns, besides the fact that they embrace only matters the most abstract, such as appear to have no actual use, the former is always so restricted to the consideration of symbols that it cannot exercise the Understanding without greatly fatiguing the Imagination; and in the latter one is so subjected to certain rules and formulas that the result is the construction of an art which is confused and obscure, and which embarrasses the mind, instead of a science which contributes to its cultivation. This made me feel that some other Method must be found, which, comprising the advantages of the three, is yet exempt from their faults. And as a multiplicity of laws often furnishes excuses for evil-doing, and as a State is hence much better ruled when, having but very few laws, these are most strictly observed; so, instead of the great number of precepts of which Logic is composed, I believed that I should find the four which I shall state quite sufficient, provided that I adhered to a firm and constant resolve never on any single occasion to fail in their observance.

The first of these was to accept nothing as true which I did not clearly recognize to be so: that is to say, carefully to avoid precipitation and prejudice in judgments, and to accept in them nothing more than what was presented to my mind so clearly and distinctly that I could have no occasion to doubt it.

The second was to divide up each of the difficulties which I examined into as many parts as possible, and as seemed requisite in order that it might be resolved in the best manner possible.

The third was to carry on my reflections in due order, commencing with objects that were the most simple and easy to understand, in order to rise little by little, or by degrees, to knowledge of the most complex, assuming an order, even if a fictitious one, among those which do not follow a natural sequence relatively to one another.

The last was in all cases to make enumerations so complete and reviews so general that I should be certain of having omitted nothing.

Those long chains of reasoning, simple and easy as they are, of which geometricians make use in order to arrive at the most difficult demonstrations, had caused me to imagine that all those things which fall under the cognizance of man might very likely be mutually related in the same fashion; and that, provided only that we abstain from receiving anything as true which is not so, and always retain the order which is necessary in order to deduce the one conclusion from the other, there can be nothing so remote that we cannot reach to it, nor so recondite that we cannot discover it. And I had not much trouble in discovering which objects it was necessary to begin with, for I already knew that it was with the most simple and those most easy to apprehend. Considering also that of all those who have hitherto sought for the truth in the Sciences, it has been the mathematicians alone who have been able to succeed in making any demonstrations, that is to say producing reasons which are evident and certain, I did not doubt that it had been by means of a similar kind that they carried on their investigations. . . .

As a matter of fact, I can venture to say that the exact observation of the few precepts which I had chosen gave me so much facility in sifting out all the questions embraced in these two sciences, that in the two or three months which I employed in examining them—commencing with the most simple and general, and making each truth that I discovered a rule for helping me to find others—not only did I arrive at the solution of many questions which I had hitherto regarded as most difficult, but, towards the end, it seemed to me that I was able to determine in the case of those of which I was still ignorant, by what means, and in how far, it was possible to solve them. In this I might perhaps appear to you to be very vain if you did not remember that having but one truth to discover in respect to each matter, whoever succeeds in finding it knows in its regard as much as can be known. It is the same as with a child, for instance, who has been instructed in Arithmetic and has made an addition according to the rule prescribed; he may be sure of having found as regards the sum of figures given to him all that the human mind can know. For, in conclusion, the Method which teaches us to follow the true order and enumerate exactly every term in the matter under investigation contains everything which gives certainty to the rules of Arithmetic.

But what pleased me most in this Method was that I was certain by its means of exercising my reason in all things, if not perfectly, at least as well as was in my power. And besides this, I felt in making use of it that my mind gradually accustomed itself to conceive of its objects more accurately and distinctly; and not having restricted this Method to any particular matter, I promised myself to apply it as usefully to the difficulties of other sciences as I had done to those of Algebra. Not that on this account I dared undertake to examine just at once all those that might present themselves; for that would itself have been contrary to the order which the Method prescribes. But having noticed that the knowledge of these difficulties must be dependent on principles derived from Philosophy in which I yet found nothing to be certain, I thought that it was requisite above all to try to establish certainty in it. I considered also that since this endeavour is the most important in all the world, and that in which precipitation and prejudice were most to be feared, I should not try to grapple with it till I had attained to a much riper age than that of three and twenty, which was the age I had reached. I thought, too, that I should first of all employ much time in preparing myself for the work by eradicating from my mind all the wrong opinions which I had up to this time accepted, and accumulating a variety of experiences fitted later on to afford matter for my reasonings, and by ever exercising myself in the Method which I had prescribed, in order more and more to fortify myself in the power of using it.

Meditations on First Philosophy

TO THE MOST WISE AND ILLUSTRIOUS DEAN
AND DOCTORS OF THE SACRED FACULTY
OF THEOLOGY IN PARIS

The motive which induces me to present to you this Treatise is so excellent, and, when you become acquainted with its design, I am convinced that you will also have so excellent a motive for taking it under your protection, that I feel that I cannot do better, in order to render it in some sort acceptable to you, than in a few words to state what I have set myself to do.

I have always considered that the two questions respecting God and the Soul were the chief of those that ought to be demonstrated by philosophical rather than theological argument. For although it is quite enough for us faithful ones to accept by means of faith the fact that the human soul does not perish with the body, and that God exists, it certainly does not seem possible ever to persuade infidels of any religion, indeed, we may almost say, of any moral virtue, unless, to begin with, we prove these two facts by means of the natural reason. And inasmuch as often in this life greater rewards are offered for vice than for virtue, few people would prefer the right to the useful, were they restrained neither by the fear of God nor the expectation of another life; and although it is absolutely true that we must believe that there is a God, because we are so taught in the Holy Scriptures, and, on the other hand, that we must believe the Holy Scriptures because they come from God (the reason of this is, that, faith being a gift of God, He who gives the grace to cause us to believe other things can likewise give it to cause us to believe that He exists), we nevertheless could not place this argument before infidels, who might accuse us of reasoning in a circle. And, in truth, I have noticed that you, along with all the theologians, did not only affirm that the existence of God may be proved by the natural reason, but also that it may be inferred from the Holy Scriptures, that knowledge about Him is much clearer than that which we have of many created things, and, as a matter of fact, is so easy to acquire, that those who have it not are culpable in their ignorance. This indeed appears from the Wisdom of Solomon, chapter xiii., where it is said *'Howbeit they are not to be excused; for if their understanding was so great that they could discern the world and the creatures, why did they not rather find out the Lord thereof?'* and in Romans, chapter i., it is said that they are *'without excuse';* and again in the same place, by these words *'that which may be known of God is manifest in them,'* it seems as though we were shown that all that which can be known of God may be made manifest by means which are not derived from anywhere but from ourselves, and from the simple consideration of the nature of our minds. Hence I thought it not beside my purpose to inquire how this is so, and how God may be more easily and certainly known than the things of the world.

And as regards the soul, although many have considered that it is not easy to know its nature, and some have even dared to say that human reasons have convinced us that it would perish with the body, and that faith alone could believe the contrary, nevertheless, inasmuch as the Lateran Council held under Leo X (in the eighth session) condemns these tenets, and as Leo expressly ordains Christian philosophers to refute their arguments and to employ all their powers in making known the truth, I have ventured in this treatise to undertake the same task.

More than that, I am aware that the principal reason which causes many impious persons not to desire to believe that there is a God, and that the human soul is distinct from the body, is that they declare that hitherto no one has been able to demonstrate these two facts; and although I am not of their opinion but, on the contrary, hold that the greater part of the reasons which have been brought forward concerning these two questions by so many great men are, when they are rightly understood, equal to so many demonstrations, and that it is almost impossible to invent new ones, it is yet in my opinion the case that nothing more useful can be accomplished in philosophy than once for all to seek with care for the best of these reasons, and to set them forth in so clear and exact a manner, that it will henceforth be evident to everybody that they are veritable demonstrations. And, finally, inasmuch as it was desired that I should undertake this task by many who were aware that I had cultivated a certain Method for the resolution of difficulties of every kind in the Sciences—a method which it is true is not novel, since there is nothing more ancient than the truth, but of which they were aware that I had made use successfully enough in the matters of difficulty—I have thought that it was my duty also to make trial of it in the present matter. . . .

SYNOPSIS OF THE SIX FOLLOWING MEDITATIONS

In the First Meditation I expound the grounds on which we may doubt in general of all things, and especially of material objects, so long, at least, as we have no other foundations for the sciences than those we have hitherto possessed. Now, although the utility of a doubt so general may not be manifest at first sight, it is nevertheless of the greatest, since it delivers us from all prejudice, and affords the easiest pathway by which the mind may withdraw itself from the senses; and, finally, makes it impossible for us to doubt wherever we afterwards discover truth.

In the Second, the mind which, in the exercise of the freedom peculiar to itself, supposes that no object is, of the existence of which it has even the slightest doubt, finds that, meanwhile, it must itself exist. And this point is likewise of the highest moment, for the mind is thus enabled easily to distinguish what pertains to itself, that is, to the intellectual nature, from what is to be referred to the body. But since some, perhaps, will expect, at this stage of our progress, a statement of the reasons which establish the doctrine of the immortality of the soul, I think it proper here to make such aware, that it was my aim to write nothing of which I could not give exact demonstration, and that I therefore felt myself obliged to adopt an order similar to that in use among the geometers, viz., to premise all upon which the proposition in question depends, before coming to any conclusion respecting it. Now, the first and chief pre-requisite for the knowledge of the immortality of the soul is our being able to form the clearest possible conception (*conceptus—*concept) of the soul itself, and such as shall be absolutely distinct from all our notions of body; and how this is to be accomplished is there shown. There is required, besides this, the assurance that all objects which we clearly and distinctly think are true (really exist) in that very mode in which we think them: and this could not be established previously to the Fourth Meditation. Further, it is necessary, for the same purpose, that we possess a distinct conception of corporeal nature, which is given partly in the Second and partly in the Fifth and Sixth Meditations. And, finally, on these grounds, we are necessitated to conclude, that all those objects which are clearly and distinctly conceived to be diverse substances, as mind and body, are substances really reciprocally distinct; and this inference is made in the Sixth Meditation. The absolute distinction of mind and body is, besides, confirmed in this Second Meditation, by showing that we cannot conceive body unless as divisible; while, on the other hand, mind cannot be conceived unless as indivisible. For we are not able to conceive the half of a mind, as we can of any body, however small, so that the natures of these two substances are to be held, not only as diverse, but even in some measure as contraries. I have not, however, pursued this discussion further in the present treatise, as well for the reason that these considerations are sufficient to show that the destruction of the mind does not follow from the corruption of the body, and thus to afford to men the hope of a future life, as also because the premises from which it is competent for us to infer the immortality of the soul, involve an explication of the whole principles of physics: in order to establish, in the first place, that generally all substances, that is, all things which can exist only in consequence of having been created by God, are in their own nature incorruptible, and can never cease to be, unless God himself, by refusing his concurrence to them, reduce them to nothing; and, in the second place, that body, taken generally, is a substance, and therefore can never perish, but that the human body, in as far as it differs from other bodies, is constituted only by a certain configuration of members, and by other accidents of this sort, while the human mind is not made up of accidents, but is a pure substance. For although all the accidents of the mind be changed—although, for example, it think certain things, will others, and perceive others, the mind itself does not vary with these changes; while, on the contrary, the human body is no longer the same if a change take place in the form of any of its parts: from which it follows that the body may, indeed, without difficulty perish, but that the mind is in its own nature immortal.

In the Third Meditation, I have unfolded at sufficient length, as appears to me, my chief argument for the existence of God. But yet, since I was there desirous to avoid the use of comparisons taken from material objects, that I might withdraw, as far as possible, the minds of my readers from the senses, numerous obscurities perhaps remain, which, however, will, I trust, be afterwards entirely removed in the replies to the objections: thus, among other things, it may be difficult to understand how the idea of a being absolutely perfect, which is found in our minds, possesses so much objective reality [*i.e.,* participates by representation in so many degrees of being and perfection] that it must be held to arise from a course absolutely perfect. This is illustrated in the replies by the comparison of a highly perfect machine, the idea of which exists in the mind of some workmen; for as the objective (*i.e.,* representative) perfection of this idea must have some cause, viz., either the science of the workman, or of some other person from whom he has received the idea, in the same way the idea of God, which is found in us, demands God himself for its cause.

In the Fourth, it is shown that all which we clearly and distinctly perceive (apprehend) is true; and, at the same time, is explained wherein consists the nature of error; points that require to be known as well for confirming the preceding truths, as for the better understanding of those that are to follow. But, meanwhile, it must be observed, that I do not at all there treat of Sin, that is, of error committed in the pursuit of good and evil, but of that sort alone which arises in the determination of the true and the false. Nor do I refer to matters of faith, or to the conduct of life, but only to what regards speculative truths, and such as are known by means of the natural light alone.

In the Fifth, besides the illustration of corporeal nature, taken generally, a new demonstration is given of the existence of God, not free, perhaps, any more than the former, from certain difficulties, but of these the solution will be found in the replies to the objections. I further show in what sense it is true that the certitude of geometrical demonstrations themselves is dependent on the knowledge of God.

Finally, in the Sixth, the act of the understanding *(intellectio)* is distinguished from that of the imagination *(imaginatio);* the marks of this distinction are described; the human mind is shown to be really distinct from the body, and, nevertheless, to be so closely conjoined therewith, as together to form, as it were, a unity. The whole of the errors which arise from the senses are brought under review, while the means of avoiding them are pointed out; and, finally, all the grounds are adduced from which the existence of material objects may be inferred; not, however, because I deemed them of great utility in establishing what they prove, viz., that there is in reality a world, that men are possessed of bodies, and the like, the truth of which no one of sound mind ever seriously doubted; but because, from a close consideration of them, it is perceived that they are neither so strong nor clear as the reasonings which conduct us to the knowledge of our mind and of God; so that the latter are, of all which come under human knowledge, the most certain and manifest—a conclusion which it was my single aim in these Meditations to establish; on which account I here omit mention of the various other questions which, in the course of the discussion, I had occasion likewise to consider.

Meditations on the First Philosophy in which the Existence of God and the Distinction Between Mind and Body Are Demonstrated

MEDITATION V
OF THE ESSENCE OF MATERIAL THINGS,
AND, AGAIN, OF GOD THAT HE EXISTS

Many other matters respecting the attributes of God and my own nature or mind remain for consideration; but I shall possibly on another occasion resume the investigation of these. Now (after first noting what must be done or avoided, in order to arrive at a knowledge of the truth) my principal task is to endeavor to emerge from the state of doubt into which I have these last days fallen, and to see whether nothing certain can be known regarding material things.

But before examining whether any such objects as I conceive exist outside of me, I must consider the ideas of them in so far as they are in my thought, and see which of them are distinct and which confused.

In the first place, I am able distinctly to imagine that quantity which philosophers commonly call continuous, or the extension in length, breadth, or depth, that is in this quantity, or rather in the object to which it is attributed. Further, I can number in it many different parts, and attribute to each of its parts many sorts of size, figure, situation and local movement, and, finally, I can assign to each of these movements all degrees of duration.

And not only do I know these things with distinctness when I consider them in general, but, likewise [however little I apply my attention to the matter], I discover an infinitude of particulars respecting numbers, figures, movements, and other such things, whose truth is so manifest, and so well accords with my nature, that when I begin to discover them, it seems to me that I learn nothing new, or recollect what I formerly knew—that is to say, that I for the first time perceive things which were already present to my mind, although I had not as yet applied my mind to them.

And what I here find to be most important is that I discover in myself an infinitude of ideas of certain things which cannot be esteemed as pure negations, although they may possibly have no existence outside of my thought, and which are not framed by me, although it is within my power either to think or not to think them, but which possess natures which are true and immutable. For example, when I imagine a triangle, although there may nowhere in the world be such a figure outside my thought, or ever have been, there is nevertheless in this figure a certain determinate nature, form, or essence, which is immutable and eternal, which I have not invented, and which in no wise depends on my mind, as appears from the fact that diverse properties of that triangle can be demonstrated, viz. that its three angles are equal to two right angles, that the greatest side is subtended by the greatest angle, and the like, which now, whether I wish it or do not wish it, I recognise very clearly as pertaining to it, although I never thought of the matter at all when I imagined a triangle for the first time, and which therefore cannot be said to have been invented by me.

Nor does the objection hold good that possibly this idea of a triangle has reached my mind through the medium of my senses, since I have sometimes seen bodies triangular in shape; because I can form in my mind an infinitude of other figures regarding which we cannot have the least conception of their ever having been objects of sense, and I can nevertheless demonstrate various properties pertaining to their nature as well as to that of the triangle, and these must certainly all be true since I conceive them clearly. Hence they are something, and not pure negation; for it is perfectly clear that all that is true is something, and I have already fully demonstrated that all that I know clearly is true. And even although I had not demonstrated this, the nature of my mind is such that I could not prevent myself from holding them to be true so long as I conceived them clearly; and I recollect that even when I was still strongly attached to the objects of sense, I counted as the most certain those truths which I conceived clearly as regards figures, numbers, and the other matters which pertain to arithmetic and geometry, and, in general, to pure and abstract mathematics.

But now, if just because I can draw the idea of something from my thought, it follows that all which I know clearly and distinctly as pertaining to this object does really belong to it, may I not drive from this an argument demonstrating the existence of God? It is certain that I no less find the idea of God, that is to say, the idea of a supremely perfect Being, in me, than that of any figure or number whatever it is; and I do not know any less clearly and distinctly that an [actual and] eternal existence pertains to this nature than I know that all that which I am able to demonstrate of some figure or number truly pertains to the nature of this figure or number, and therefore, although all that I concluded in the preceding Meditations were found to be false, the existence of God would pass with me as at least as certain as I have ever held the truths of mathematics (which concern only numbers and figures) to be.

This indeed is not at first manifest, since it would seem to present some appearance of being a sophism. For being accustomed in all other things to make a distinction between existence and essence, I easily persuade myself that the existence can be separated from the essence of God, and that we can thus conceive God as not actually existing. But, nevertheless, when I think of it with more attention, I clearly see that existence can no more be separated from the essence of God than can its having its three angles equal to two right angles as separated from the essence of a [rectilinear] triangle, or the idea of a mountain from the idea of a valley; and so there is not any less repugnance to our conceiving a God (that is, a Being supremely perfect) to whom existence is lacking (that is to say, to whom a certain perfection is lacking), than to conceive of a mountain which has no valley.

But although I cannot really conceive of a God without existence any more than a mountain without a valley, still from the fact that I conceive of a mountain with a valley, it does not follow that there is such a mountain in the world; similarly although I conceive of God as possessing existence, it would seem that it does not follow that there is a God which exists; for my thought does not impose any necessity upon things, and just as I may imagine a winged horse, although no horse with wings exists, so I could perhaps attribute existence to God, although no God existed.

But a sophism is concealed in this objection; for from the fact that I cannot conceive a mountain with a valley, it does not follow that there is any mountain or any valley in existence, but only that the mountain and the valley, whether they exist or do not exist, cannot in any way be separated one from the other. While from the fact that I cannot conceive God without existence, it follows that existence is inseparable from Him, and hence that He really exists; not that my thought can bring this to pass, or impose any necessity on things, but, on the contrary, because the necessity which lies in the thing itself, i.e. the necessity of the existence of God determines me to think in this way. For it is not within my power to think of God without existence (that is of a supremely perfect Being devoid of a supreme perfection) though it is in my power to imagine a horse either with wings or without wings.

And we must not here object that it is in truth necessary for me to assert that God exists after having presupposed that He possesses every sort of perfection, since existence is one of these, but that as a matter of fact my original supposition was not necessary, just as it is not necessary to consider that all quadrilateral figures can be inscribed in the circle; for supposing I thought this, I should be constrained to admit that the rhombus might be inscribed in the circle since it is a quadrilateral figure, which, however, is manifestly false. [We must not, I say, make any such allegations because] although it is not necessary that I should at any time entertain the notion of God, nevertheless whenever it happens that I think of a first and a sovereign Being, and, so to speak, derive the idea of Him from the storehouse of my mind, it is necessary that I should attribute to Him every sort of perfection, although I do not get so far as to enumerate them all, or to apply my mind to each one in particular. And this necessity suffices to make me conclude (after having recognised that existence is a perfection) that this first and sovereign Being really exists; just as though it is not necessary for me ever to imagine any triangle, yet, whenever I wish to consider a rectilinear figure composed only of three angles, it is absolutely essential that I should attribute to it all those properties which serve to bring about the conclusion that its three angles are not greater than two right angles, even although I may not then be considering this point in particular. But when I consider which figures are capable of being inscribed in the circle, it is in no wise necessary that I should think that all quadrilateral figures are of this number; on the contrary, I cannot even pretend that this is the case, so long as I do not desire to accept anything which I cannot conceive clearly and distinctly. And in consequence there is a great difference between the false suppositions such as this, and the true ideas born within me, the first and principal of which is that of God. For really I discern in many ways that this idea is not something factitious, and depending solely on my thought, but that it is the image of true and immutable nature; first of all, because I cannot conceive anything but God himself to whose essence existence [necessarily] pertains; in the second place because it is not possible for me to conceive two or more Gods in this same position; and, granted that there is one such God who now exists, I see clearly that it is necessary that He should have existed from all eternity, and that He must exist eternally; and finally, because I know an infinitude of other properties in God, none of which I can either diminish or change.

For the rest, whatever proof or argument I avail myself of, we must always return to the point that it is only those things which we conceive clearly and distinctly that have the power of persuading me entirely. And although amongst the matters which I conceive of in this way, some indeed are manifestly obvious to all, while others only manifest themselves to those who consider them closely and examine them attentively; still, after they have once been discovered, the latter are not esteemed as any less certain than the former. For example, in the case of every right-angled triangle, although it does not so manifestly appear that the square of the base is equal to the squares of the two other sides as that this base is opposite to the greatest angle; still, when this has once been apprehended, we are just as certain of its truth as of the truth of the other. And as regards God, if my mind were not pre-occupied with prejudices, and if my thought did not find itself on all hands diverted by the continual pressure of sensible things, there would be nothing which I could know more immediately and more easily than Him. For is there anything more manifest than that there is a God, that is to say, a Supreme Being, to whose essence alone existence pertains?

And although for a firm grasp of this truth I have need of a strenuous application of mind, at present I not only feel myself to be as assured of it as of all that I hold as most certain, but I also remark that the certainty of all other things depends on it so absolutely, that without this knowledge it is impossible ever to know anything perfectly.

For although I am of such a nature that as long as I understand anything very clearly and distinctly, I am naturally impelled to believe it to be true, yet because I am also of such a nature that I cannot have my mind constantly fixed on the same object in order to perceive it clearly, and as I often recollect having formed a past judgment without at the same time properly recollecting the reasons that led me to make it, it may happen meanwhile that other reasons present themselves to me, which would easily cause me to change my opinion, if I were ignorant of the facts of the existence of God, and thus I should have no true and certain knowledge, but only vague and vacillating opinions. Thus, for example, when I consider the nature of a [rectilinear] triangle, I who have some little knowledge of the principles of geometry recognise quite clearly that the three angles are equal to two right angles, and it is not possible for me not to believe this so long as I apply my mind to its demonstration; but so soon as I abstain from attending to the proof, although I still recollect having clearly comprehended it, it may easily occur that I come to doubt its truth, if I am ignorant of there being a

God. For I can persuade myself of having been so constituted by nature that I can easily deceive myself even in those matters which I believe myself to apprehend with the greatest evidence and certainty, especially when I recollect that I have frequently judged matters to be true and certain which other reasons have afterwards impelled me to judge to be altogether false.

But after I have recognised that there is a God—because at the same time I have also recognised that all things depend upon Him, and that He is not a deceiver, and from that have inferred that what I perceive clearly and distinctly cannot fail to be true—although I no longer pay attention to the reasons for which I have judged this to be true, provided that I recollect having clearly and distinctly perceived it no contrary reason can be brought forward which could ever cause me to doubt of its truth; and thus I have a true and certain knowledge of it. And this same knowledge extends likewise to all other things which I recollect having formerly demonstrated, such as the truths of geometry and the like; for what can be alleged against them to cause me to place them in doubt? Will it be said that my nature is such as to cause me to be frequently deceived? But I already know that I cannot be deceived in the judgment whose grounds I know clearly. Will it be said that I formerly held many things to be true and certain which I have afterwards recognised to be false? But I had not had any clear and distinct knowledge of these things, and not as yet knowing the rule whereby I assure myself of the truth, I had been impelled to give my assent from reasons which I have since recognised to be less strong than I had at the time imagined them to be. What further objection can then be raised? That possibly I am dreaming (an objection I myself made a little while ago), or that all the thoughts which I now have are no more true than the phantasies of my dreams? But even though I slept the case would be the same, for all that is clearly present to my mind is absolutely true.

And so I very clearly recognise that the certainty and truth of all knowledge depends alone on the knowledge of the true God, in so much that, before I knew Him, I could not have a perfect knowledge of any other thing. And now that I know Him I have the means of acquiring a perfect knowledge of an infinitude of things, not only of those which relate to God Himself and other intellectual matters, but also of those which pertain to corporeal nature in so far as it is the object pure mathematics [which have no concern with whether it exists or not].

MEDITATION VI
OF THE EXISTENCE OF MATERIAL THINGS, AND OF THE REAL DISTINCTION BETWEEN THE SOUL AND BODY OF MAN

Nothing further now remains but to inquire whether material things exist. And certainly I at least know that these may exist in so far as they are considered as the objects of pure mathematics, since in this aspect I perceive them clearly and distinctly. For there is no doubt that God possesses the power to produce everything that I am capable of perceiving with distinctness, and I have never deemed that anything was impossible for Him, unless I found a contradiction in attempting to conceive it clearly. Further, the faculty of imagination which I possess, and of which, experience tells me, I make use when I apply myself to the consideration of material things, is capable of persuading me of their existence; for when I attentively consider what imagination is, I find that it is nothing but a certain application of the faculty of knowledge to the body which is immediately present to it, and which therefore exists.

And to render this quite clear, I remark in the first place the difference that exists between the imagination and pure intellection [or conception]. For example, when I imagine a triangle, I do not conceive it only as a figure comprehended by three lines, but I also apprehend these three lines as present by the power and inward vision of my mind, and this is what I call imagining. But if I desire to think of a chiliagon, I certainly conceive truly that it is a figure composed of a thousand sides, just as easily as I conceive of a triangle that it is a figure of three sides only; but I cannot in any way imagine the thousand sides of a chiliagon [as I do the three sides of a triangle], nor do I, so to speak, regard them as present [with the eyes of my mind]. And although in accordance with the habit I have formed of always employing the aid of my imagination when I think of corporeal things, it may happen that in imagining a chiliagon I confusedly represent to myself some figure, yet it is very evident that this figure is not a chiliagon, since it in no way differs from that which I represent to myself when I think of a myriagon or any other many-sided figure; nor does it serve my purpose in discovering the properties which go to form the distinction between a chiliagon and other polygons. But if the question turns upon a pentagon, it is quite true that I can conceive its figure as well as that of a chiliagon without the help of my imagination; but I can also imagine it by applying the attention of my mind to each of its five sides, and at the same time to the space which they enclose. And thus I clearly recognise that I have need of a particular effort of mind in order to effect the act of imagination, such as I do not require in order to understand, and this particular effort of mind clearly manifests the difference which exists, between imagination and pure intellection.

I remark besides that this power of imagination which is in one, inasmuch as it differs from the power of understanding, is in no wise a necessary element in my nature, or in [my essence, that is to say, in] the essence of my mind; for although I did not possess it I should doubtless ever remain the same as I now am, from which it appears that we might conclude that it depends on something which differs from me. And I easily conceive that if some body exists with which my mind is conjoined and united in such a way that it can apply itself to consider it when it pleases, it may be that by this means it can imagine corporeal objects; so that this mode of thinking differs from pure intellection only inasmuch as mind in its intellectual activity in some manner turns on itself, and considers some of the ideas which it possesses in itself; while in imagining it turns towards the body, and there beholds in it something conformable to the idea which it has either conceived of itself or perceived by the senses. I easily understand, I say, that the imagination could be thus constituted if it is true that body exists; and because I can discover no other convenient mode of explaining it, I conjecture with probability that body does exist; but this is only with probability, and although I examine all things with care, I nevertheless do not find that from this distinct idea of corporeal nature, which I have in my imagination, I can derive any argument from which there will necessarily be deduced the existence of body.

But I am in the habit of imagining many other things besides this corporeal nature which is the object of pure mathematics, to wit, the colours, sounds, scents, pain, and other such things, although less distinctly. And inasmuch as I perceive these things much better through the senses, by the medium of which, and by the memory, they seem to have reached my imagination, I believe that, in order to examine them more conveniently, it is right that I should at the same time investigate the nature of sense perception, and that I should see if from the ideas which I apprehend by this mode of thought, which I call feeling, I cannot derive some certain proof of the existence of corporeal objects.

And first of all I shall recall to my memory those matters which I hitherto held to be true, as having perceived them through the senses, and the foundations on which my belief has rested; in the next place I shall examine the reasons which have since obliged me to place them in doubt; in the last place I shall consider which of them I must now believe.

First of all, then, I perceived that I had a head, hands, feet, and all other members of which this body—which I considered as a part, or possibly even as the whole, of myself—is composed. Further I was sensible that this body was placed amidst many others, from which it was capable of being affected in many different ways, beneficial and hurtful, and I remarked that a certain feeling of pleasure accompanied those that were beneficial, and pain those which were harmful. And in addition to this pleasure and pain, I also experienced hunger, thirst, and other similar appetites, as also certain corporeal inclinations towards joy, sadness, anger, and other similar passions. And outside myself, in addition to extension, figure, and motions of bodies, I remarked in them hardness, heat, and all other tactile qualities, and, further, light and colour, and scents and sounds, the variety of which gave me the means of distinguishing the sky, the earth, the sea, and generally all the other bodies, one from the other. And certainly, considering the ideas of all these qualities which presented themselves to my mind, and which alone I perceived properly or immediately, it was not without reason that I believed myself to perceive objects quite different from my thought, to wit, bodies from which those ideas proceeded; for I found by experience that these ideas presented themselves to me without my consent being requisite, so that I could not perceive any object, however desirous I might be, unless it were present to the organs of sense; and it was not in my power not to perceive it, when it was present. And because the ideas which I received through the senses were much more lively, more clear, and even, in their own way, more distinct than any of those which I could of myself frame in meditation, or than those I found impressed on my memory, it appeared as though they could not have proceeded from my mind, so that they must necessarily have been produced in me by some other things. And having no knowledge of those objects excepting the knowledge which the ideas themselves gave me, nothing was more likely to occur to my mind than that the objects were similar to the ideas which were caused. And because I likewise remembered that I had formerly made use of my senses rather than my reason, and recognised that the ideas which I formed of myself were not so distinct as those which I perceived through the senses, and that they were most frequently even composed of portions of these last, I persuaded myself easily that I had no idea in my mind which had not formerly come to me through the senses. Nor was it without some reason that I believed that this body (which by a certain special right I call my own) belonged to me more properly and more strictly than any other; for in fact I could never be separated from it as from other bodies; I experienced in it and on account of it all my appetites and affections, and finally I was touched by the feeling of pain and the titillation of pleasure in its parts, and not in the parts of other bodies which were separated from it. But when I inquired, why, **from some**, I know not what, painful sensation, there follows sadness of mind, and **from the** pleasurable sensation there arises joy, or why this mysterious pinching **of the** stomach which I call hunger causes me to desire to eat, and dryness of throat causes a desire to drink, and so on, I could give no reason excepting that nature taught me so; for there is certainly no affinity (that I at least can understand) between the craving of the stomach and the desire to eat, any more than between the perception of whatever causes pain and the thought of sadness which arises from this perception. And in the same way it appeared to me that I had learned from nature all the other judgments which I formed regarding the objects of my senses, since I remarked that these judgments were formed in me before I had the leisure to weigh and consider any reasons which might oblige me to make them.

But afterwards many experiences little by little destroyed all the faith which I had rested in my senses; for I from time to time observed that those towers which from afar appeared to me to be round, more closely observed seemed square, and that colossal statues raised on the summit of these towers, appeared as quite tiny statues when viewed from the bottom; and so in an infinitude of other cases I found error in judgments founded on the external senses. And not only in those founded on the external senses, but even in those founded on the internal as well; for is there anything more intimate or more internal than pain? And yet I have learned from some persons whose arms or legs have been cut off, that they sometimes seemed to feel pain in the part which had been amputated, which made me think that I could not be quite certain that it was a certain member which pained me, even although I felt pain in it. And to those grounds of doubt I have lately added two others, which are very general; the first is that I never have believed myself to feel anything in waking moments which I cannot also sometimes believe myself to feel when I sleep, and as I do not think that these things which I seem to feel in sleep, proceed from objects outside of me, I do not see any reason why I should have this belief regarding objects which I seem to perceive while awake. The other was that being still ignorant, or rather supposing myself to be ignorant, of the author of my being, I saw nothing to prevent me from having been so constituted by nature that I might be deceived even in matters which seemed to me to be most certain. And as to the grounds on which I was formerly persuaded of the truth of sensible objects, I had not much trouble in replying to them. For since nature seemed to cause me to lean towards many things from which reason repelled me, I did not believe that I should trust much to the teachings of nature. And although the ideas which I receive by the senses do not depend on my will, I did not think that one should for that reason conclude that they proceeded from things different from myself, since possibly some faculty might be discovered in me—though hitherto unknown to me—which produced them.

But now that I begin to know myself better, and to discover more clearly the author of my being, I do not in truth think that I should rashly admit all the matters which the senses seem to teach us, but, on the other hand, I do not think that I should doubt them all universally.

And first of all, because I know that all things which I apprehend clearly and distinctly can be created by God as I apprehend them, it suffices that I am able to apprehend one thing apart from another clearly and distinctly in order to be certain that the one is different from the other, since they may be made to exist in separation at least by the omnipotence of God; and it does not signify by what power this separation is made in order to compel me to judge them to be different: and, therefore, just because I know certainly that I exist, and that meanwhile I do not remark that any other thing necessarily pertains to my nature or essence, excepting that I am a thinking thing, I rightly concluded that my essence consists solely in the fact that I am a thinking thing [or a substance whose whole essence or nature is to think]. And although possibly (or rather certainly, as I shall say in a moment) I possess a body with which I am very intimately conjoined, yet because, on the one side, I have a clear and distinct idea of myself inasmuch as I am only a thinking and unextended thing, and as, on the other, I possess a distinct idea of body, inasmuch as it is only an extended and unthinking thing, it is certain that this I [that is to say, my soul by which I am what I am], is entirely and absolutely distinct from my body, and can exist without it.

I further find in myself faculties employing modes of thinking peculiar to themselves, to wit, the faculties of imagination and feeling, without which I can easily conceive myself clearly and distinctly as a complete being; while, on the other hand, they cannot be so conceived apart from me, that is without an intelligent substance in which they reside, for [in the notion we have of these faculties, or, to use the language of the Schools] in their formal concept, some kind of intellection is comprised, from which I infer that they are distinct from me as its modes are from a thing. I observe also in me some other faculties such as that of change of position, the assumption of different figures and such like, which cannot be conceived, any more than can the preceding, apart from some substance to which they are attached, and consequently cannot exist without it; but it is very clear that these faculties, if it be true that they exist, must be attached to some corporeal or extended substance, and not to an intelligent substance, since in the clear and distinct conception of these there is some sort of extension found to be present, but no intellection at all. There is certainly further in me a certain passive faculty of perception, that is, of receiving and recognising the ideas of sensible things, but this would be useless to me [and I could in no way avail myself of it], if there were not either in me or in some other thing another active faculty capable of forming and producing these ideas. But this active faculty cannot exist in me [inasmuch as I am a thing that thinks] seeing that it does not presuppose thought, and also that those ideas are often produced in me without my contributing in any way to the same, and often even against my will; it is thus necessarily the case that the faculty resides in some substance different from me in which all the reality which is objectively in the ideas that are produced by this faculty is formally or eminently contained, as I remarked before. And this substance is either a body, that is, a corporeal nature in which there is contained formerly [and really] all that which is objectively [and by representation] in those ideas, or it is God Himself, or some other creature more noble than body in which that same is contained eminently. But, since God is no deceiver, it is very manifest that he does not communicate to me these ideas immediately and by Himself, nor yet by the intervention of some creature in which their reality is not formally, but only eminently, contained. For since He has given me no faculty to recognise that this is the case, but, on the other hand, a very great inclination to believe [that they are sent to me or] that they are conveyed to me by corporeal objects, I do not see how He could be defended from the accusation of deceit if these ideas were produced by causes other than corporeal objects. Hence we must allow that corporeal things exist. However, they are perhaps not exactly what we perceive by the senses, since this comprehension by the senses is in many instances very obscure and confused; but we must at least admit that all things which I conceive in them clearly and distinctly, that is to say, all things which, speaking generally, are comprehended in the object of pure mathematics, are truly to be recognised as external objects.

As to other things, however, which are either particular only, as, for example, that the sun is of such and such a figure, etc., or which are less clearly and distinctly conceived, such as light, sound, pain and the like, it is certain that although they are very dubious and uncertain, yet on the sole ground that God is not a deceiver, and that consequently He has not permitted any falsity to exist in my opinion which He has not likewise given me the faculty of correcting, I may assuredly hope to conclude that I have within me the means of arriving at the truth even here. And first of all there is no doubt that in all things which nature teaches me there is some truth contained; for my nature; considered in general, I now understand no other thing than either God Himself or else the order and disposition which God has established in created things; and by my nature in particular I understand no other thing than the complexus of all the things which God has given me.

But there is nothing which this nature teaches me more expressly [nor more sensibly] than that I have a body which is adversely affected when I feel pain, which has need of food or drink when I experience the feelings of hunger and thirst, and so on; nor can I doubt there being some truth in all this.

Nature also teaches me by these sensations of pain, hunger, thirst, etc., that I am not only lodged in my body as a pilot in a vessel, but that I am very closely united to it, and so to speak so intermingled with it that I seem to compose with it one whole. For if that were not the case, when my body is hurt, I, who am merely a thinking thing, should not feel pain, for I should perceive this wound by the understanding only, just as the sailor perceives by sight when something is damaged in his vessel; and when my body has need of drink or food, I should clearly understand the fact without being warned of it by confused feelings of hunger and thirst. For all these sensations of hunger, thirst, pain, etc. are in truth none other than certain confused modes of thought which are produced by the union and apparent intermingling of mind and body.

Moreover, nature teaches me that many other bodies exist around mine, of which some are to be avoided, and others sought after. And certainly from the fact that I am sensible of different sorts of colours, sounds, scents, tastes, heat, hardness, etc., I very easily conclude that there are in the bodies from which all these diverse sense-perceptions proceed certain variations which answer to them, although possibly these are not really at all similar to them. And also from the fact that amongst these different sense-perceptions some are very agreeable to me and others disagreeable, it is quite certain that my body (or rather myself in my entirety, inasmuch as I am formed of body and soul) may receive different impressions agreeable and disagreeable from the other bodies which surround it.

But there are many other things which nature seems to have taught me, but which at the same time I have never really received from her, but which have been brought about in my mind by a certain habit which I have of forming inconsiderate judgments on things; and thus it may easily happen that these judgments contain some error. Take, for example, the opinion which I hold that all space in which there is nothing that affects [or makes an impression on] my senses is void; that in a body which is warm there is something entirely similar to the idea of heat which is in me; that in a white or green body there is the same whiteness or greenness that I perceive; that in a bitter or sweet body there is the same taste, and so on in other instances; that the stars, the towers, and all other distant bodies are of the same figure and size as they appear from far off to our eyes, etc. But in order that in this there should be nothing which I do not conceive distinctly, I should define exactly what I really understand when I say that I am taught somewhat by nature. For here I take nature in a more limited signification than when I term it the sum of all things given me by God, since in this sum many things are comprehended which only pertain to mind (and to these I do not refer in speaking of nature) such as the notion which I have of the fact that what has once been done cannot ever be undone and an infinitude of such things which I know by the light of nature [without the help of the body]; and seeing that it comprehends many other matters besides which only pertain to body, and are no longer here contained under the name of nature, such as the quality of weight which it possesses and the like, with which I also do not deal; for in talking of nature I only treat of those things given by God to me as a being composed of mind and body. But the nature here described truly teaches me to flee from things which cause the sensation of pain, and seek after the things which communicate to me the sentiment of pleasure and so forth; but I do not see that beyond this it teaches me that from those diverse sense-perceptions we should ever form any conclusion regarding things outside of us, without having [carefully and maturely] mentally examined them beforehand. For it seems to me that it is mind alone, and not mind and body in conjunction, that is requisite to a knowledge of the truth in regard to such things. Thus, although a star makes no larger an impression on my eye than the flame of a little candle there is yet in me no real or positive propensity impelling me to believe that it is not greater than that flame; but I have judged it to be so from my earliest years, without any rational foundation. And although in approaching fire I feel heat, and in approaching it a little too near I even feel pain, there is at the same time no reason in this which could persuade me that there is in the fire something resembling this heat any more than there is in it something resembling the pain; all that I have any reason to believe from this is, that there is something in it, whatever it may be, which excites in me these sensations of heat or of pain. So also, although there are spaces in which I find nothing which excites my senses, I must not from that conclude that these spaces contain no body; for I see in this, as in other similar things, that I have been in the habit of perverting the order of nature, because these perceptions of sense having been placed within me by nature merely for the purpose of signifying to my mind what things are beneficial or hurtful to the composite whole of which it forms a part, and being up to that point sufficiently clear and distinct, I yet avail myself of them as though they were absolute rules by which I might immediately determine the essence of the bodies which are outside me, as to which, in fact, they can teach me nothing but what is most obscure and confused.

But I have already sufficiently considered how, notwithstanding the supreme goodness of God, falsity enters into the judgments I make. Only here a new difficulty is presented—one respecting those things the pursuit or avoidance of which is taught me by nature, and also respecting the internal sensations which I possess, and in which I seem to have sometimes detected error [and thus to be directly deceived by my own nature]. To take an example, the agreeable taste of some food in which poison has been intermingled may induce me to partake of the poison, and thus deceive me. It is true, at the same time, that in this case nature may be excused, for it only induces me to desire food in which I find a pleasant taste, and not to desire the poison which is unknown to it; and thus I can infer nothing from this fact, except that my nature is not omniscient, at which there is certainly no reason to be astonished, since man, being finite in nature, can only have knowledge the perfectness of which is limited.

But we not unfrequently deceive ourselves even in those things to which we are directly impelled by nature, as happens with those who when they are sick desire to drink or eat things hurtful to them. It will perhaps be said here that the cause of their deceptiveness is that their nature is corrupt, but that does not remove the difficulty, because a sick man is none the less truly God's creature than he who is in health; and it is therefore as repugnant to God's goodness for the one to have a deceitful nature as it is for the other. And as a clock composed of wheels and counter-weights no less exactly observes the laws of nature when it is badly made, and does not show the time properly, than when it entirely satisfies the wishes of its maker, and as, if I consider the body of a man as being a sort of machine so built up and composed of nerves, muscles, veins, blood and skin, that though there were no mind in it at all, it would not cease to have the same motions as to present, exception being made of these movements which are due to the direction of the will, and in consequence depend upon the mind [as opposed to those which operate by the disposition of its organs], I easily recognise that it would be as natural to this body, supposing it to be, for example, dropsical, to suffer the parchedness of the throat which usually signifies to the mind the feeling of thirst, and to be disposed by this parched feeling to move the nerves and other parts in the way requisite for drinking, and thus to augment its malady and do harm to itself, as it is natural to it, when it has no indisposition, to be impelled to drink for its good by a similar cause. And although, considering the use to which the clock has been destined by its maker, I may say that it deflects from the order of its nature when it does not indicate the hours correctly; and as, in the same way, considering the machine of the human body as having been formed by God in order to have in itself all the movements usually manifested there, I have reason for thinking that it does not follow the order of nature when, if the throat is dry, drinking does harm to the conservation of health, nevertheless I recognise at the same time that this last mode of explaining nature is very different from the other. For this is but a purely verbal characterisation depending entirely on my thought, which compares a sick man and a badly constructed clock with the idea which I have of a healthy man and a well made clock, and it is hence extrinsic to the things to which it is applied; but according to the other interpretation of the term nature I understand something which is truly found in things and which is therefore not without some truth.

But certainly although in regard to the dropsical body it is only so to speak to apply an extrinsic term when we say that its nature is corrupted, inasmuch as apart from the need to drink, the throat is parched; yet in regard to the composite whole, that is to say, to the mind or soul united to this body, it is not a purely verbal predicate, but a real error of nature, for it to have thirst when drinking would be hurtful to it. And thus it still remains to inquire how the goodness of God does not prevent the nature of man so regarded from being fallacious.

In order to begin this examination, then, I here say, in the first place, that there is a great difference between mind and body, inasmuch as body is by nature always divisible, and the mind is entirely indivisible. For, as a matter of fact, when I consider the mind, that is to say, myself inasmuch as I am only a thinking thing, I cannot distinguish in myself any parts, but apprehend myself to be clearly one and entire; and although the whole mind seems to be united to the whole body, yet if a foot, or an arm, or some other part, is separated from my body, I am aware that nothing has been taken away from my mind. And the faculties of willing, feeling, conceiving, etc. cannot be properly speaking said to be its parts, for it is one and the same mind which employs itself in willing and in feeling and understanding. But it is quite otherwise with corporeal or extended objects, for there is not one of these imaginable by me which my mind cannot easily divide into parts, and which consequently I do not recognise as being divisible; this would be sufficient to teach me that the mind or soul of man is entirely different from the body, if I had not already learned it from other sources.

I further notice that the mind does not receive the impressions from all parts of the body immediately, but only from the brain, or perhaps even from one of its smallest parts, to wit, from that in which the common sense is said to reside, which, whenever it is disposed in the same particular way, conveys the same thing to the mind, although meanwhile the other portions of the body may be differently disposed, as is testified by innumerable experiments which it is unnecessary here to recount.

I notice, also, that the nature of body is such that none of its parts can be moved by another part a little way off which cannot also be moved in the same way by each one of the parts which are between the two, although this more remote part does not act at all. As, for example, in the cord ABCD [which is in tension] if we pull the last part D, the first part A will not be moved in any way differently from what would be the case if one of the intervening parts B or C were pulled, and the last part D were to remain unmoved. And in the same way, when I feel pain in my foot, my knowledge of physics teaches me that this sensation is communicated by means of nerves dispersed through the foot, which, being extended like cords from there to the brain, when they are contracted in the foot, at the same time contract the inmost portions of the brain which is their extremity and place of origin, and then excite a certain movement which nature has established in order to cause the mind to be affected by a sensation of pain represented as existing in the foot. But because these nerves must pass through the tibia, the thigh, the loins, the back and the neck, in order to reach from the leg to the brain, it may happen that although their extremities which are in the foot are not affected, but only certain ones of their intervening parts [which pass by the loins or the neck], this action will excite the same movement in the brain that might have been excited there by a hurt received in the foot, in consequence of which the mind will necessarily feel in the foot the same pain as if it had received a hurt. And the same holds good of all the other perceptions of our senses.

I notice finally that since each of the movements which are in the portion of the brain by which the mind is immediately affected brings about one particular sensation only, we cannot under the circumstances imagine anything more likely than that this movement, amongst all the sensations which it is capable of impressing on it, causes mind to be affected by that one which is best fitted and most generally useful for the conservation of the human body when it is in health. But experience makes us aware that all the feelings with which nature inspires us are such as I have just spoken of; and there is therefore nothing in them which does not give testimony to the power and goodness of the God [who has produced them]. Thus, for example, when the nerves which are in the feet are violently or more than usually moved, their movement, passing through the medulla of the spine to the inmost parts of the brain, gives a sign to the mind which makes it feel somewhat, to wit, pain, as though in the foot, by which the mind is excited to do its utmost to remove the cause of the evil as dangerous and hurtful to the foot. It is true that God could have constituted the nature of man in such a way that this same movement in the brain would have conveyed something quite different to the mind; for example, it might have produced consciousness of itself either in so far as it is in the brain, or as it is in the foot, or as it is in some other place between the foot and the brain, or it might finally have produced consciousness of anything else whatsoever; but none of all this would have contributed so well to the conservation of the body. Similarly, when we desire to drink, a certain dryness of the throat is produced which moves its nerves, and by their means the internal portions of the brain; and this movement causes in the mind the sensation of thirst, because in this case there is nothing more useful to us than to become aware that we have need to drink for the conservation of our health; and the same holds good in other instances.

From this it is quite clear that, notwithstanding the supreme goodness of God, the nature of man, inasmuch as it is composed of mind and body, cannot be otherwise than sometimes a source of deception. For if there is any cause which excites, not in the foot but in some part of the nerves which are extended between the foot and the brain, or even in the brain itself, the same movement which usually is produced when the foot is detrimentally affected, pain will be experienced as though it were in the foot, and the sense will thus naturally be deceived; for since the same movement in the brain is capable of causing but one sensation in the mind, and this sensation is much more frequently excited by a cause which hurts the foot than by another existing in some other quarter, it is reasonable that it should convey to the mind pain in the foot rather than in any other part of the body. And although the parchedness of the throat does not always proceed, as it usually does, from the fact that drinking is necessary for the health of the body, but sometimes comes from quite a different cause, as is the case with dropsical patients, it is yet much better than it should mislead on this occasion than if, on the other hand, it were always to deceive us when the body is in good health; and so on in similar cases.

And certainly this consideration is of great service to me, not only in enabling me to recognise all the errors to which my nature is subject, but also in enabling me to avoid them or to correct them more easily. For knowing that all my senses more frequently indicate to me truth than falsehood respecting the things which concern that which is beneficial to the body, and being able almost always to avail myself of many of them in order to examine one particular thing, and, besides that, being able to make use of my memory in order to connect the present with the past, and of my understanding which already has discovered all the causes of my errors, I ought no longer to fear that falsity may be found in matters every day presented to me by my senses. And I ought to set aside all the doubts of these past days as hyperbolical and ridiculous, particularly that very common uncertainty respecting sleep, which I could not distinguish from the waking state; for at present I find a very notable difference between the two, inasmuch as our memory can never connect our dreams one with the other, or with the whole course of our lives, as it unites events which happen to us while we are awake. And, as a matter of fact, if someone, while I was awake, quite suddenly appeared to me and disappeared as fast as do the images which I see in sleep, so that I could not know from whence the form came nor whither it went, it would not be without reason that I should deem it a spectre or a phantom formed by my brain [and similar to those which I form in sleep], rather than a real man. But when I perceive things as to which I know distinctly both the place from which they proceed, and that in which they are, and the time at which they appeared to me; and when, without any interruption, I can connect the perceptions which I have of them with the whole course of my life, I am perfectly assured that these perceptions occur while I am waking and not during the sleep. And I ought in no wise to doubt the truth of such matters, if, after having called up all my senses, my memory, and my understanding, to examine them, nothing is brought to evidence by any one of them which is repugnant to what is set forth by the others. For because God is in no wise a deceiver, it follows that I am not deceived in this. But because the exigencies of action often oblige us to make up our minds before having leisure to examine matters carefully, we must confess that the life of man is very frequently subject to error in respect to individual objects, and we must in the end acknowledge the infirmity of our nature.

(From *The Philosophical Works of Descartes,* trans. by E. S. Haldane and G. R. T. Ross. New York: Dover Publications, Inc., 1911.)

REVIEW QUESTIONS

1. Describe the philosophical skepticism of the seventeenth century to which Descartes reacted.
2. Discuss the role of *cogito ergo sum* (I think, therefore I am) in the philosophy of Descartes.
3. What is the meaning of deduction? What is its role in mathematics?
4. Is there any difference between *deduction* and *rationalism?*
5. Explain Descartes' philosophical method.
6. What is the meaning of *universal mathematics?* Compare Descartes with Pythagoras.
7. Explain how Descartes arrives at the conclusion that man consists of spirit only. How does this generate the mind–body problem?
8. Discuss the following: the mind–body problem as originated in modern times by Descartes stemmed from his failure to be consistently faithful to experience.
9. Compare the ontological argument of Descartes with that of St. Anselm.
10. What do you think of Descartes' demonstration of the existence of the external world?
11. In what way can Cartesian philosophy be considered as paving the way for a mechanistic interpretation of the world?

SUGGESTIONS FOR FURTHER READING

Anscombe, G. E. M., Geach, P. T., and Koyre, A. ed. *Descartes' Philosophical Writings.* Indianapolis, Bobbs-Merrill, 1971.

Kenny, A. *Descartes, A Study of His Philosophy.* New York, Random House, 1968.

The Philosophical Works of Descartes, 2 vols. Tr. Haldane, E. S. and Ross, G. T. R. New York, Dover, 1955.

Williams, Bernard. *Descartes: The Project of Pure Enquiry.* New York, Penguin, 1986.

12

Baruch Spinoza
(1632–1677)

The seventeenth century is the only century in which a book entitled *Ethics, Demonstrated in a Geometrical Manner* could have been written. It was a tribute by Baruch (Benedict) Spinoza to the mathematical method, to the demand for rigorous fidelity to clear and distinct ideas, and to the certitude attending the deductive method. Spinoza (1632–1677) was of Jewish–Portuguese ancestry; his family emigrated to Amsterdam so that they could practice their faith freely. The young Spinoza was an intense student, a linguist, a scholar of Jewish sacred writings and of the Kabbala, an amalgam of Jewish and neo-Platonic writings. As he began to develop his own thought, he became less able to accept the orthodox Judaism of his family and was at length excommunicated from the synagogue at the age of twenty-four. He earned his livelihood as a lens maker, which was, in a sense, the practical aspect of his theoretical knowledge of optics. Though he led a retired life, he was the center of active philosophical discussion; he enjoyed a wide reputation in intellectual circles, not because of the publication of his works, which for the most part appeared posthumously, but because of privately circulated papers. He was even offered a professorship in philosophy at the University of Heidelberg but rejected it, feeling that he could better maintain his intellectual freedom unattached to academe.

Self-understanding in the Context of Pantheistic Monism

The title of Spinoza's major work is a declaration of his main interest: the conduct of human life. What, he asked, can we finally count on as happiness for man, as blessedness, as salvation? To achieve this objective, Spinoza had to develop an entire metaphysics that embraced all reality; only then could reality's constituents, like human conduct, be meaningfully considered. If a part is not seen in its totality, it is not seen at all. Spinoza's effort to see totality first has been likened to seeing reality as a pyramid from the top down rather than from the base up. His philosophical vision is of all reality as a whole, as one; if *one* reality is given, only *one* substance is given, which Spinoza variously calls *substance, nature,* or *God.* If there is only one substance, everything is one with substance or one with nature or one with God. Spinoza's system is *monistic,* and because there is a complete identification of reality with God, his metaphysics has often been called *pantheistic monism.* Further, striking a chord reminiscent of Greek philosophy, Spinoza held that, because whatever is, *is,* there is a necessity pervading reality and things are necessarily what they are.

Spinoza's notion of God goes completely against the traditional doctrine, in which God is transcendent, personal, and infinitely free; He is the Creator who chooses to create *freely,* not out of necessity. Of all reality, God is the only necessary being; all other beings, though they truly are, are beings whose existence is not necessary. Bearing in mind that one's theist is someone else's atheist, it is not surprising that Spinoza was an atheist to many of his contemporaries; in comparison to the romantic writers of the following century, he was a man who was drunk with God.

Let us follow the course Spinoza takes to make his system cohere. In the *Ethics,* which looks like a manual of mathematics, with definitions, axioms, theorems, and Q.E.D.s, the definition of substance is given as "that which is in itself, and is conceived through itself . . . that of which a conception can be formed independently of any other conception." As we analyze this definition, a number of concepts emerge. Typical of the rationalist cast of mind, the movement is from idea to things, and the *conception* of realty is what reality *is.* There is a perfect correspondence between the logical order (within the mind) and the ontological order (outside the mind). Further, what can the definition of substance refer to, except reality taken as a whole? It cannot refer to any part of reality, for any part, by its nature, cannot be conceived of except in reference to the whole; therefore, it cannot be "conceived through itself." Again, substance has to be *infinite,* for anything less than infinite would mean that it could not be "formed independently of any other conception."

Spinoza's use of the word *substance* differs greatly, therefore, from the traditional use where it is generally correlative with *accident.* An accident is a quality like white, square, or smiling; it is clear that these qualities do not exist on their own, for *something* has to be white or square or smiling (except the smile of the Cheshire cat!). The something that is white or square or smiling is called *substance,* and, in a relative sense, it exists on its own: The accidents exist in and through the substance, but the substance does not exist in and through the accidents. Spinoza, then, in his use of the word *substance,* intensified the meaning of independence and made it apply uniquely to reality taken as a whole.

Even though Spinoza considers everything as one with substance, we still have to ask, how does he understand individual things *as individual?* His answer is that individuals exist as modes or modifications of substance; this requires some explanation. Substance is infinite and possesses an infinite number of constituents called *attributes.* An attribute is defined as that which the intellect perceives as constituting the essence of substance. That is, attributes are not conceivable in and through anything other than themselves; therefore we can only perceive them as constituting the essence of substance. However, only two such attributes are known to us: *extension* and *thought.* Extension (body, matter, quantity) refers to all extended things taken together as one, and thought (mind, understanding, spirit) refers to all minds taken together as one. Now, all particular things of our experience—this person, this pencil, this act, this mental activity—come under either the attribute of thought or the attribute of extension. They are called by Spinoza *modes:* A mode is a modification of substance, or that which exists in and is conceived through something other than itself. This scheme of substance-attribute-mode is Spinoza's response to a problem as old as philosophy itself: How is reality as one related to reality as many? Regarding an individual pencil, a full statement of Spinoza's view would be as follows: This pencil is a mode-of-substance-under-the-attribute-of-body; that is, all individuals (particulars) are one-with-substance without losing their own individuality (particularity).

Spinoza's reaction to Cartesian dualism can be appreciated at this juncture. For Descartes, "John" is identifiable as a man because mind and body are *two* substances joined so that they may act together. For Spinoza, however, "John" is identifiable as man because mind and body are two attributes of *one* substance; these two attributes do not have to be brought together, as in Descartes' view, because they are already together. Without trying to discuss the merits of either scheme, it is quite clear that Descartes' solution to the mind–body problem was unsatisfactory to Spinoza because there was no way, once their unity was disturbed, to reunite them. Spinoza's scheme ensures that there is no separation to start with.

Intuitive Knowledge

All philosophers, in one way or another, hold to a hierarchy of knowledge; that is, there are degrees of knowledge, one of higher value than another. Spinoza speaks of three types of knowledge, the first of which is knowledge that is *confused and inadequate,* inasmuch as it pertains to ideas of sensation; the second which is *scientific* knowledge is knowledge that is adequate and clear, manifesting some consistency and logical relationship among ideas. The third degree is the one Spinoza has been pursuing all along, namely, *intuitive* knowledge—the intuition of things as they are in the whole of reality, the vision of things in nature; it is the grasp of unity, or the intellectual contemplation of the real as one with God. Intellectual contemplation of God is, we will recall, the final stage of man's ascent to God in the Western tradition and is the chief characteristic of man's happiness, inchoate here but complete hereafter. It signifies the utmost clarity in our understanding of who God is and our relationship with Him. Because we see Him as He is, we love Him as He is, as the all-good and loving God who created us by a free act of His loving creation. But for Spinoza, intellectual contemplation is the seeing of things in their eternal *necessity*. Things are what they are because they have to be that way; in God all things are necessary. Pleasure and pain, good and evil, take on a new appearance once necessity is grasped. Evil, for example, is evil only from man's viewpoint, not God's; when seen from God's viewpoint, evil is understood to be natural and part of nature's necessity. Human freedom, which, for Spinoza, is philosophy's ultimate goal, is not the prerogative of spontaneous choice but the highest intellectual grasp of necessity, the intuition of the eternal God. It is the third kind of knowledge, from which arises, necessarily, the intellectual love of God. Freedom, happiness, blessedness, and salvation are synonyms and consist in "the constant and eternal love towards God, or is God's love towards men." The one who understands this is the wise man, described by Spinoza as the person who is conscious of himself, of God, and of things, and, guided by eternal necessity, always possesses true acquiescence of his spirit. Such an understanding is found in very few people but, indeed, "all things excellent are as difficult as they are rare."

The fact that, for Spinoza, every single thing must be thought of in concert with others has special relevance for his philosophy of community. Insofar as human beings associate with one another naturally, the consideration of society is found in the *Ethics;* but his ideas on the political shaping of society are found in the political works, *Theologico-Political Treatise* and *A Political Treatise.*

All things act according to the powers assigned to them by nature, and inasmuch as this principle applies to men in a unique way, men lead their lives by power, even to the extent that they achieve, sometimes by force and cunning, what they can for themselves: "By the right and ordinance of nature, I merely mean those natural laws wherewith we conceive every individual to be conditioned by nature, so as to live and act in a given way . . . the rights of an individual extend to the utmost limits of his power as it has been conditioned. Now it is the sovereign law and right of nature that each individual should endeavor to preserve itself as it is, without regard to anything but itself." The phrase used here, *natural law*, has nothing to do with the traditional scholastic use of the phrase, in which it is defined as moral law; for Spinoza it is simply a statement of fact regarding the place man occupies in nature's pyramid. Left to themselves, in the state of nature, human beings would be a sorry lot indeed, for "men are naturally enemies."

Live According to Reason

These raw characteristics of man's nature are compensated for by *reason*. Human life is to be a life of reason, for by it man is able to hold his emotions, especially anger and hatred, in control, and it is precisely this which is made possible by human beings living together with each other: "to man there is nothing more useful than man—nothing." Everyone wants to live without fear, putting at a distance enmity, hatred, anger, and deceit: "when all is said, they will find that men can provide for their wants much more easily by mutual help, and that only by unifying their forces can they escape from the dangers that on every side beset them." So man, by the use of his reason, is able to achieve a higher view of his relationship to other men and to understand that his nature demands society; man is social by nature.

But unless there is some sort of agreement to live together, there will be no living together at all: "men must necessarily come to an agreement to live together as securely and well as possible." This agreement, or *compact,* makes it possible to give man's social nature an organized, specific shape called the *state;* men, by this general compact, yield to the ruling or sovereign power those individual rights that will enable the state to flourish within the sphere of reason. Thus, the good that redounds to man by ceding these rights for the common weal far surpasses what he could lay claim to alone. The laws of the sovereign, directed as they are to the common good, must be obeyed by all, and so firm is Spinoza on this point that he identifies sin with disobedience: "Sin, then, is nothing else but disobedience, which is therefore punished by the right of the State only." Peace, freedom, religious tolerance, justice, harmony, and security all follow a government founded on reason. And of all the various types of civil states, the one having the best promise of reasonableness is *democracy,* defined as "a society which wields all its power as a whole." Further, democracy is, of all forms of government, "the most natural, and the most consonant with individual liberty."

During his lifetime, though he had acquired a reputation for rigorous and innovative thinking, Spinoza was roundly criticized and condemned by both philosophers and theologians. A century or so later, he was rediscovered and reevaluated principally by the German romantics, who saw in his writings a kinship with their own feeling of a closeness with nature. Even so great a writer as Goethe said that his chief concern, in accordance with the teachings of Spinoza, was to gain eternity for his spirit.

READINGS

Definitions and Axioms
(from *Ethics*, Part I)

DEFINITIONS

I. By that which is *self-caused,* I mean that of which the essence involves existence, or that of which the nature is only conceivable as existent.

II. A thing is called *finite after its kind,* when it can be limited by another thing of the same nature; for instance, a body is called finite because we always conceive another greater body. So, also, a thought is limited by another thought, but a body is not limited by thought, nor a thought by body.

III. By *substance,* I mean that which is in itself, and is conceived through itself: in other words, that of which a conception can be formed independently of any other conception. → God/Nature/Universe

IV. By *attribute,* I mean that which the intellect perceives as constituting the essence of substance. → Everything else; us, furniture, etc.

diff? {

V. By *mode,* I mean the modifications of substance, or that which exists in, and is conceived through, something other than itself.

VI. By *God,* I mean a being absolutely infinite—that is, a substance consisting in infinite attributes, of which each expresses eternal and infinite essentiality.

Explanation.—I say absolutely infinite, not infinite after its kind: for, of a thing infinite only after its kind, infinite attributes may be denied; but that which is absolutely infinite, contains in its essence whatever expresses reality, and involves no negation.

VII. That thing is called free, which exists solely by the necessity of its own nature, and of which the action is determined by itself alone. On the other hand, that thing is necessary, or rather constrained, which is determined by something external to itself to a fixed and definite method of existence or action.

VIII. By *eternity,* I mean existence itself, in so far as it is conceived necessarily to follow solely from the definition of that which is eternal.

Explanation.—Existence of this kind is conceived as an eternal truth, like the essence of a thing, and, therefore, cannot be explained by means of continuance or time, though continuance may be conceived without a beginning or end.

AXIOMS

I. Everything which exists, exists either in itself or in something else.

II. That which cannot be conceived through anything else must be conceived through itself.

III. From a given definite cause an effect necessarily follows; and, on the other hand, if no definite cause be granted, it is impossible that an effect can follow.

IV. The knowledge of an effect depends on and involves the knowledge of a cause.

V. Things which have nothing in common cannot be understood, the one by means of the other; the conception of one does not involve the conception of the other.

VI. A true idea must correspond with its ideate or object.

VII. If a thing can be conceived as non-existing, its essence does not involve existence.

Seven Propositions on Substance

(from *Ethics*, Part I)

PROPOSITIONS

PROP. I. *Substance is by nature prior to its modifications.*

Proof.—This is clear from Deff. iii. and v.

PROP. II. *Two substances, whose attributes are different, have nothing in common.*

Proof.—Also evident from Deff. iii. For each must exist in itself, and be conceived through itself; in other words, the conception of one does not imply the conception of the other.

PROP. III. *Things which have nothing in common cannot be one the cause of the other.*

Proof.—If they have nothing in common, it follows that one cannot be apprehended by means of the other (Ax. v.), and, therefore, one cannot be the cause of the other (Ax. iv.). *Q.E.D.*

PROP. IV. *Two or more distinct things are distinguished one from the other, either by the difference of the attributes of the substances, or by the difference of their modifications.*

Proof.—Everything which exists, exists either in itself or in something else (Ax. i.),—that is (by Deff. iii. and v.), nothing is granted in addition to the understanding, except substance and its modifications. Nothing is, therefore, given besides the understanding, by which several things may be distinguished one from the other, except the substances, or, in other words (see Ax. iv.), their attributes and modifications. *Q.E.D.*

PROP. V. *There cannot exist in the universe two or more substances having the same nature or attribute.*

Proof.—If several distinct substances be granted, they must be distinguished one from the other, either by the difference of their attributes, or by the difference of their modifications (Prop. iv.). If only by the difference of their attributes, it will be granted that there cannot be more than one with an identical attribute. If by the difference of their modifications—as substance is naturally prior to its modifications (Prop. i.),—it follows that setting the modifications aside, and considering substance in itself, that is truly (Deff. iii. and v.), there cannot be conceived one substance different from another—that is (by Prop. iv.), there cannot be granted several substances, but one substance only. *Q.E.D.*

PROP. VI. *One substance cannot be produced by another substance.*

Proof.—It is impossible that there should be in the universe two substances with an identical attribute, i.e. which have anything common to them both (Prop. ii.), and, therefore (Prop. iii.), one cannot be the cause of another, neither can one be produced by the other. *Q.E.D.*

Corollary.—Hence it follows that a substance cannot be produced by anything external to itself. For in the universe nothing is granted, save substances and their modifications (as appears from Ax. i. and Deff. iii. and v.). Now (by the last Prop.) substance cannot be produced by another substance, therefore it cannot be produced by anything external to itself. *Q.E.D.* This is shown still more readily by the absurdity of the contradictory. For, if substance be produced by an external cause, the knowledge of it would depend on the knowledge of its cause (Ax. iv.), and (by Def. iii.) it would itself not be substance.

PROP. VII. *Existence belongs to the nature of substance.*

Proof.—Substance cannot be produced by anything external (Corollary, Prop. vi.), it must, therefore, be its own cause—that is, its essence necessarily involves existence, or existence belongs to its nature.

The Third Degree of Knowledge and the Love of God
(from *Ethics*, Part V)

. . . From all that has been said above it is clear, that we, in many cases, perceive and form our general notions:—(1.) From particular things represented to our intellect fragmentarily, confusedly, and without order through our senses (II. xxix. Coroll.); I have settled to call such perceptions by the name of knowledge from the mere suggestions of experience. (2.) From symbols, e.g., from the fact of having read or heard certain words we remember things and form certain ideas concerning them, similar to those through which we imagine things (II. xviii. note). I shall call both these ways of regarding things *knowledge of the first kind, opinion, or imagination.* (3.) From the fact that we have notions common to all men, and adequate ideas of the properties of things (II. xxxviii. Coroll., xxxix. and Coroll. and xl.); this I call *reason* and *knowledge of the second kind.* Besides these two kinds of knowledge, there is, as I will hereafter show, a third kind of knowledge, which we will call intuition. This kind of knowledge proceeds from an adequate idea of the absolute essence of certain attributes of God to the adequate knowledge of the essence of things.

PROP. XXV. *The highest endeavour of the mind, and the highest virtue is to understand things by the third kind of knowledge.*

Proof.—The third kind of knowledge proceeds from an adequate idea of certain attributes of God to an adequate knowledge of the essence of things (see its definition II. xl. note ii.); and, in proportion as we understand things more in this way, we better understand God (by the last Prop.); therefore (IV. xxviii.) the highest virtue of the mind, that is (IV. Def. viii.) the power, or nature, or (III. vii.) highest endeavour of the mind, is to understand things by the third kind of knowledge. *Q.E.D.*

PROP. XXVI. *In proportion as the mind is more capable of understanding things by the third kind of knowledge, it desires more to understand things by that kind.*

Proof.—This is evident. For, in so far as we conceive the mind to be capable of conceiving things by this kind of knowledge, we, to that extent, conceive it as determined thus to conceive things; and consequently (Def. of the Emotions, i.), the mind desires so to do, in proportion as it is more capable thereof. *Q.E.D.*

PROP. XXVII. *From this third kind of knowledge arises the highest possible mental acquiescence.*

Proof.—The highest virtue of the mind is to know God (IV. xxviii.), or to understand things by the third kind of knowledge (V. xxv.), and this virtue is greater in proportion as the mind knows things more by the said kind of knowledge (V. xxiv.): consequently, he who knows things by this kind of knowledge passes to the summit of human perfection, and is therefore (Def. of the Emotions, ii.) affected by the highest pleasure, such pleasure being accompanied by the idea of himself and his own virtue; thus (Def. of the Emotions, xxv.), from this kind of knowledge arises the highest possible acquiescence. *Q.E.D.*

PROP. XXVIII. *The endeavour or desire to know things by the third kind of knowledge cannot arise from the first, but from the second kind of knowledge.*

Proof.—This proposition is self-evident. For whatsoever we understand clearly and distinctly, we understand either through itself, or through that which is conceived through itself; that is, ideas which are clear and distinct in us, or which are referred to the third kind of knowledge (II. xl. note ii.) cannot follow from ideas that are fragmentary and confused, and are referred to knowledge of the first kind, but must follow from adequate ideas, or ideas of the second and third kind of knowledge; therefore (Def. of the Emotions, i.), the desire of knowing things by the third kind of knowledge cannot arise from the first, but from the second kind. *Q.E.D.*

PROP. XXIX. *Whatsoever the mind understands under the form of eternity, it does not understand by virtue of conceiving the present actual existence of the body, but by virtue of conceiving the essence of the body under the form of eternity.*

Proof.—In so far as the mind conceives the present existence of its body, it to that extent conceives duration which can be determined by time, and to that extent only has it the power of conceiving things in relation to time (V. xxi. II. xxvi.). But eternity cannot be explained in terms of duration (I. Def. viii. and explanation). Therefore to this extent the mind has not the power of conceiving things under the form of eternity, but it possesses such power, because it is of the nature of reason to conceive things under the form of eternity (II. xliv. Coroll. ii.), and also because it is of the nature of the mind to conceive the essence of the body under the form of eternity (V. xxiii.), for besides these two there is nothing which belongs to the essence of mind (II. xiii.). Therefore this power of conceiving things under the form of eternity only belongs to the mind in virtue of the mind's conceiving the essence of the body under the form of eternity. *Q.E.D.*

Note.—Things are conceived by us as actual in two ways; either as existing in relation to a given time and place, or as contained in God and following from the necessity of the divine nature. Whatsoever we conceive in this second way as true or real, we conceive under the form of eternity, and their ideas involve the eternal and infinite essence of God, as we showed in II. xlv. and note, which see.

PROP. XXX. *Our mind, in so far as it knows itself and the body under the form of eternity, has to that extent necessarily a knowledge of God, and knows that it is in God, and is conceived through God.*

Proof.—Eternity is the very essence of God, in so far as this involves necessary existence (I. Def. viii.). Therefore to conceive things under the form of eternity, is to conceive things in so far as they are conceived through the essence of God as real entities, or in so far as they involve existence through the essence of God; wherefore our mind, in so far as it conceives itself and the body under the form of eternity, has to that extent necessarily a knowledge of God, and knows, &c. *Q.E.D.*

PROP. XXXI. *The third kind of knowledge depends on the mind, as its formal cause, in so far as the mind itself is eternal.*

Proof.—The mind does not conceive anything under the form of eternity, except in so far as it conceives its own body under the form of eternity (V xxix.); that is, except in so far as it is eternal (V. xxi. xxiii.); therefore (by the last Prop.), in so far as it is eternal, it possesses the knowledge of God, which knowledge is necessarily adequate (II. xlvi.); hence the mind, in so far as it is eternal, is capable of knowing everything which can follow from this given knowledge of God (II. xl.), in other words, of knowing things by the third kind of knowledge (see Def. in II. xl. note ii.), whereof accordingly the mind (III. Def. i.), in so far as it is eternal, is the adequate or formal cause of such knowledge. *Q.E.D.*

Note.—In proportion, therefore, as a man is more potent in this kind of knowledge, he will be more completely conscious of himself and of God; in other words, he will be more perfect and blessed, as will appear more clearly in the sequel. But we must here observe that, although we are already certain that the mind is eternal, in so far as it conceives things under the form of eternity, yet, in order that what we wish to show may be more readily explained and better understood, we will consider the mind itself, as though it had just begun to exist and to understand things under the form of eternity, as indeed we have done hitherto; this we may do without any danger of error, so long as we are careful not to draw any conclusion, unless our premises are plain.

PROP. XXXII. *Whatsoever we understand by the third kind of knowledge, we take delight in and our delight is accompanied by the idea of God as cause.*

Proof.—From this kind of knowledge arises the highest possible mental acquiescence, that is (Def. of the Emotions, xxv.), pleasure, and this acquiescence is accompanied by the idea of the mind itself (V. xxvii.), and consequently (V. xxx.) the idea also of God as cause. *Q.E.D.*

Corollary.—From the third kind of knowledge necessarily arises the intellectual love of God. From this kind of knowledge arises pleasure accompanied by the idea of God as cause, that is (Def. of the Emotions, vi.), the love of God; not in so far as we imagine him as present (V. xxix.), but in so far as we understand him to be eternal; this is what I call the intellectual love of God.

PROP. XXXIII. *The intellectual love of God, which arises from the third kind of knowledge, is eternal.*

Proof.—The third kind of knowledge is eternal (V. xxxi. I. Ax. iii.); therefore (by the same Axiom) the love which arises therefrom is also necessarily eternal. *Q.E.D.*

Note. Although this love towards God has (by the foregoing Prop.) no beginning, it yet possesses all the perfections of love, just as though it had arisen as we feigned in the Coroll. of the last Prop. Nor is there here any difference, except that the mind possesses as eternal those same perfections which we feigned to accrue to it, and they are accompanied by the idea of God as eternal cause. If pleasure consists in the transition to a greater perfection, assuredly blessedness must consist in the mind being endowed with perfection itself.

PROP. XXXVI. *The intellectual love of the mind towards God is that very love of God whereby God loves himself, not in so far as he is infinite, but in so far as he can be explained through the essence of the human mind regarded under the form of eternity; in other words, the intellectual love of the mind towards God is part of the infinite love wherewith God loves himself.*

Proof.—This love of the mind must be referred to the activities of the mind (V. xxxii. Coroll. an III. iii.); it is itself, indeed, an activity whereby the mind regards itself accompanied by the idea of God as cause (V. xxxii. and Coroll.); that is (I. xxv. Coroll. and II. xi. Coroll.), an activity whereby God, in so far as he can be explained through the human mind, regards himself accompanied by the idea of himself; therefore (by the last Prop.), this love of the mind is part of the infinite love wherewith God loves himself. *Q.E.D.*

Corollary.—Hence it follows that God, in so far as he loves himself, loves man, and, consequently, that the love of God towards men, and the intellectual love of the mind toward God are identical.

Note.—From what has been said we clearly understand, wherein our salvation, or blessedness, or freedom, consists: namely, in the constant and eternal love towards God, or in God's love towards men. This love or blessedness is, in the Bible, called Glory, and not undeservedly. For whether this love be referred to God or to the mind, it may rightly be called acquiescence of spirit, which (Def. of the Emotions, xxv.xxx.) is not really distinguished from glory. In so far as it is referred to God, it is (V. xxxv.) pleasure, if we may still use that term, accompanied by the idea of itself, and, in so far as it is referred to the mind, it is the same (V. xxvii.).

Again, since the essence of our mind consists solely in knowledge, whereof the beginning and the foundation is God (I. xv. and II. xlvii. note), it becomes clear to us, in what manner and way our mind, as to its essence and existence, follows from the divine nature and constantly depends on God. I have thought it worth while here to call attention to this, in order to show by this example how the knowledge of particular things, which I have called intuitive or of the third kind (II. xl. note ii.), is potent, and more powerful than the universal knowledge, which I have styled knowledge of the second kind. For, although in Part I. I showed in general terms, that all things (and consequently, also, the human mind) depend as to their essence and existence on God, yet that demonstration, though legitimate and placed beyond the chances of doubt, does not affect our mind so much, as when the same conclusion is derived from the actual essence of some particular thing, which we say depends on God.

PROP. XLI. *Even if we did not know that our mind is eternal, we should still consider as of primary importance piety and religion, and generally all things which, in Part IV., we showed to be attributable to courage and highmindedness.*

Proof.—The first and only foundation of virtue, or the rule of right living is (IV. xxii. Coroll. and xxiv.) seeking one's own true interest. Now, while we determined what reason prescribes as useful, we took no account of the mind's eternity, which has only become known to us in this Fifth Part. Although we were ignorant at that time that the mind is eternal, we nevertheless stated that the qualities attributable to courage and high-mindedness are of primary importance. Therefore, even if we were still ignorant of this doctrine, we should yet put the aforesaid precepts of reason in the first place. *Q.E.D.*

Note.—The general belief of the multitude seems to be different. Most people seem to believe that they are free, in so far as they may obey their lusts, and that they cede their rights, in so far as they are bound to live according to the commandments of the divine law. They therefore believe that piety, religion, and, generally, all things attributable to firmness of mind, are burdens, which, after death, they hope to lay aside, and to receive the reward for their bondage, that is, for their piety and religion; it is not only by this hope, but also, and chiefly, by the fear of being horribly punished after death, that they are induced to live according to the divine commandments, so far as their feeble and infirm spirit will carry them.

If men had not this hope and this fear, but believed that the mind perishes with the body, and that no hope of prolonged life remains for the wretches who are broken down with the burden of piety, they would return to their own inclinations, controlling everything in accordance with their lusts, and desiring to obey fortune rather than themselves. Such a course appears to me not less absurd than if a man, because he does not believe that he can by wholesome food sustain his body for ever, should wish to cram himself with poisons and deadly fare; or if, because he sees that the mind is not eternal or immortal, he should prefer to be out of his mind altogether, and to live without the use of reason; these ideas are so absurd as to be scarcely worth refuting.

PROP. XLII. *Blessedness is not the reward of virtue, but virtue itself; neither do we rejoice therein, because we control our lusts, but, contrariwise, because we rejoice therein, we are able to control our lusts.*

Proof.—Blessedness consists in love towards God (V. xxxvi. and note), which love springs from the third kind of knowledge (V. xxxii. Coroll.); therefore this love (III. iii. lix.) must be referred to the mind, in so far as the latter is active; therefore (IV. Def. viii.) it is virtue itself. This was our first point. Again, in proportion as the mind rejoices more in this divine love or blessedness, so does it the more understand (V. xxxii.); that is (V. iii. Coroll.), so much the more power has it over the emotions, and (V. xxxviii.) so much the less is it subject to those emotions which are evil; therefore, in proportion as the mind rejoices in this divine love or blessedness, so has it the power of controlling lusts. And, since human power in controlling the emotions consists solely in the understanding, it follows that no one rejoices in blessedness, because he has controlled his lusts, but, contrariwise, his power of controlling his lusts arises from this blessedness itself. *Q.E.D.*

Note.—I have thus completed all I wished to set forth touching the mind's power over the emotions and the mind's freedom. Whence it appears, how potent is the wise man, and how much he surpasses the ignorant man, who is driven only by his lusts. For the ignorant man is not only distracted in various ways by external causes without ever gaining the true acquiescence of his spirit, but moreover lives, as it were unwitting of himself, and of God, and of things, and as soon as he ceases to suffer, ceases also to be.

Whereas the wise man, in so far as he is regarded as such, is scarcely at all disturbed in spirit, but, being conscious of himself, and of God, and of things, by a certain eternal necessity, never ceases to be, but always possesses true acquiescence of his spirit.

If the way which I have pointed out as leading to this result seems exceedingly hard, it may nevertheless be discovered. Needs must it be hard, since it is so seldom found. How would it be possible, if salvation were ready to our hand, and could without great labour be found, that it should be by almost all men neglected? But all things excellent are as difficult as they are rare.

(Trans. R. H. M. Elwes)

REVIEW QUESTIONS

1. Spinoza's view of reality has been described as looking from the top of a pyramid down. Is this a suitable description?
2. Explain why Spinoza rejects any kind of pluralism, such as Cartesian dualism, in favor of monism. Does his monism lead to pantheism?
3. Spinoza admits differences in the universe; how does he do this and yet hold to absolute unity?
4. What is the meaning of necessity in Spinoza's thought?
5. For Spinoza, how do necessity and freedom relate to each other?
6. How does Spinoza equate the highest degree of knowledge with blessedness?
7. Why is there, in Spinoza's view, a need for human beings to establish a civil society?
8. How does Spinoza's view of substance compare with Aristotle's?

SUGGESTIONS FOR FURTHER READING

Curley, E., ed. and tr. *Spinoza Reader.* Princeton, Princeton University Press, 1994.
Hampshire, S. *Spinoza.* Baltimore, Penguin, 1988.
Scruton, R. *Spinoza, A Very Short Introduction.* New York, Oxford University Press, 2002.
Wolfson, H. A. *The Philosophy of Spinoza.* New York, Meridian, 1934.

13

Gottfried Wilhelm Leibniz (1646–1716)

The third continental rationalist philosopher is Gottfried Wilhelm Leibniz. He was born in Leipzig in 1646 and entered the university there at the age of fifteen. As a student he was an avid reader, delving into the works of philosophers like Aristotle, the Schoolmen, and Descartes, as well as those of scientists like Kepler and Galileo. Later he took up studies in mathematics and law, and was awarded a doctorate of laws at the age of twenty-one. For some time he served on diplomatic missions, and his travels in that capacity gave him the opportunity to meet many of the great persons of the day. On one such occasion he met Spinoza, eager to learn at firsthand something of his curious doctrines but Spinoza's drastic departure from the God of tradition made Leibniz a permanent critic of his philosophy. He looked upon Spinoza's "atheism" as a logical outcome of Cartesianism, to which he had maintained a long-standing opposition because of its interpretation of the physical world. An inventive mathematician, he discovered the calculus, or perhaps, due to several chronological ambiguities, he should be thought of as codiscovering it with the celebrated Sir Isaac Newton; he invented the first calculating machine. He had a profound devotion to science, and to advance its cause he founded an academy of sciences in Berlin that became highly esteemed. In another direction entirely, he expended a great effort in trying to bring about a reunion of the Christian churches—an ecumenist far ahead of his time. Time, however, was not kind to Leibniz in his declining years; his public service diminished, his influence waned, and when he died in 1716 he was generally a forgotten man—his death not even acknowledged by the academy he established.

Preestablished Harmony

If there is any one theme that serves as a key to Leibniz's philosophy, it is the theme of harmony—of *universal harmony* in which the world is seen as a harmoniously functioning whole because it is an ordered system founded by God. The image of the clock is a favorite with Leibniz, as with other authors of the same period, who marveled at the ingenuity of the clockmaker in being able to assemble the gears and springs and countless other moving parts to tell the precise time. The universe is "God's clock," and its wonderful functioning, in all its cunning detail, causes us to wonder at the ingenuity of the One who made it. Carrying this imagery still further, Leibniz refers to universal ordering as *preestablished harmony* because, in the very first moment of establishing the universe, God built an order into it that works itself out in the course of time. With particular reference to Cartesian dualism, Leibniz felt that Descartes' solution to the mind–body problem was unsatisfactory, so he suggested that the two substances might be thought of as two clocks, a soul clock and a body clock, and when a body event took place, a corresponding soul event took place at the same moment, not because the body event caused the soul event but because both events were caused simultaneously by God. On the religious level, Leibniz's interest in ecumenism was an attempt at ecclesiastical harmony, and his *Theodicy* was a mighty effort to reconcile evil in the world with God's goodness. All of these ideas were foreshadowed in the young Leibniz's essay *The Art of Combining Things,* in which he held that, given the consistent ordering of things, the universe lends itself to discovery by deductive reasoning.

It is to this question of harmony that Leibniz's most popularly known work, *The Monadology,* is addressed. By now we have come to appreciate the perennial nature of the problem of the one and the many, the problem of reconciling plurality and unity. To develop a solution, Leibniz devised an entirely new scheme, a scheme based on the existence of substances that he calls *monads* (from the Greek *monos,* meaning one). Anything of our experience is an aggregate, or is composed, but if we divide anything composed, the components themselves, being physical will always have the characteristics of being composed. Since endless division is theoretically if not physically possible, we must conclude that an aggregate is ultimately composed of *indivisible* things that, in consequence, have no parts, no extension, no figure; they are "simple" substances, called *monads,* and because they lie beyond the physical, they are *metaphysical.* They are not like atoms in the classical sense because the classical atom was the ultimate *physical* thing, not metaphysical.

In order to bring an infinite number of monads together in an overarching unity, Leibniz concludes, as did Spinoza, that the whole universe is in every part, and every part is in the whole universe, or, in terms of monads, the whole universe is in every monad, and every monad is in the whole universe. Leibniz ingeniously models his explanation of unity on the activity of knowledge. He holds that every monad is a *perceiving* entity; that is, is endowed with *perception,* however rudimentary, whereby the universe is registered, or mirrored, within it. Further, monads themselves are *windowless,* which means that they are not open to influence by other monads, which might cause them to have this perception, but are open only to God, who, as the supreme cause and orderer, brings the relationship among monads into perfect harmony. In understanding what Leibniz is after, it is helpful to recall Aristotle's dictum that the mind is one with what it knows. When the mind knows the tree, on the *level of knowledge,* the tree and the mind become one; the mind is one-with-the-tree, and the tree is one-with-the-mind. Likewise, for Leibniz, in every perception the perceiver and the object perceived become one, and inasmuch as any one monad is open to all others, the monad is one-with-the-universe and the universe is one-with-the-monad. The universe, therefore, and the part are one-with-each-other: plurality and unity—the many and the one—are expressions of a continuous whole.

With his system of monads Leibniz feels he has safeguarded God's supreme causality, ascertained the inner core of preestablished harmony, and maintained the individuality of things along with the unity of the universe.

God and the Existence of Evil

That God exists, for Leibniz, is as incontestable as the air we breathe. He finds convincing the arguments offered by various philosophers of the past, such as the ontological argument of St. Anselm and Descartes, the argument from eternal truths of St. Augustine, and the arguments from casuality developed by the Schoolmen. With regard to the last, however, Leibniz adds his own terminological refinement by using the phrase *sufficient reason.* The *principle of sufficient reason* means, in this context, that any contingent being, from the mere fact that it does not have to be, and yet is, must have a sufficient reason for its existence which, however, is not found in the contingent being itself; therefore, the sufficient reason for its existence must be found in a being whose existence is necessary (that is, sufficient reason unto itself), which must be, which cannot not be—namely, God.

It was not so much the existence of God that puzzled Leibniz but another problem: Granted that God is all perfect and all good, how is it possible for evil to exist in a world that the good God has made? Leibniz did not shirk this problem but tried to face it head on with one of his lengthier works, *Theodicy,* whose subtitle is *Essays on the Goodness of God, the Freedom of Man and the Origin of Evil.* In the preface, Leibniz refers to "the great question of the Free and the Necessary . . . in the production and origin of Evil" as one of the "great labyrinths where our reason very often goes astray." Every human being is touched by the problem; every human being can draw up a sad catalog of sufferings, and every human being must respond in some way. And every philosopher as well, from Socrates to Sartre, who claims a sensitivity to the moral climate of the universe, has had to search for some answer to evil in the pattern of the real.

As an ardent advocate of harmony in the universe, Leibniz could never have opted for a two-God system, as devised in some religions, wherein the God of Good presides over good in the world and the God of Evil over evil, the two locked in enduring combat. For Leibniz, this would be skirting the problem; common sense and philosophical consistency require him to aver that there is but one problem—which turns, however, on an internal polarity between God and evil. Out of fidelity to one's own intellect, the demand for a coherent view of the universe includes the existence of God, who, among His other attributes, is good; on the other hand, out of fidelity to one's own experience, the ravages of evil cannot be denied. So Leibniz's precise problem is to *reconcile* the goodness of God with the presence of evil in the world, a problem often referred to as *theodicy.*

In one sense, for Leibniz, evil has to be present in anything that is not perfect; only God is perfect; therefore, anything less than God has to be limited, and insofar as it is limited, imperfect, or evil: "where shall we find the source of evil? . . . there is an *original imperfection in the creature* before sin, because the creature is limited in its essence." To this kind of evil Leibniz assigns the term *metaphysical evil.* It is found in the very nature of created being and is therefore to be found in any world God might choose to create. But even though this given world is imperfect, it is the *best possible* world God could have created, for anything less than the best would be an insult to His goodness: "Now this supreme wisdom, united to a goodness that is no less infinite, cannot but have chosen the best." Leibniz did not feel that God's omnipotence was being compromised at all by saying that this is the best possible world, for a "better" world would be a contradiction. The caricature of Leibniz's position written by Voltaire in his *Candide,* witty as it is, hardly does justice to the huge problem the philosopher is trying to face.

In order to produce a world containing the greatest amount of good, God creates one in which there will be, and God knows there will be, evil. In that sense, God permits the evil so that He can produce the good; He does not cause or choose the evil. In an analogy, Leibniz observes that the downstream motion of a river carries the boats along with it, but the more heavily laden ones proceed more slowly; so, the river is the cause of the motion, not the retardation. Just so, "God is the cause of perfection in the nature and the actions of the creature, but the limitation of the receptivity of the creature is the cause of the defects there are in its action." Leibniz aligns himself with "the Platonists, St. Augustine and the Schoolmen" who say that God is not the cause of the "formal element" of evil, defined as "privation," or lack of perfection; God is not the cause of a being's lack of perfection, because such lack belongs to its very nature; but inasmuch as He is the cause of the being, He is only the cause of the good.

Physical evil consists in sufferings, sorrows, and miseries, which are brought about by man's evil will or by the "monstrosities of nature." Once again, the larger framework must be invoked, for small disorders are to be expected for the sake of the great order, and Leibniz quotes approvingly the adage of St. Bernard, "It belongs to the great order that there should be some small disorders." Upheavals of nature, whether eruptions, conflagration, or floods, are indeed evil; but considering the vast timescale involved and the fact that this earth is to be cultivated by man, even these evils redound to greater good.

Moral evil is sin, that is, an imperfection in the human act; it lacks the moral perfection that should be present in such an act. Once again, Leibniz links this concept to the basic notion of metaphysical evil in that God does not will such an evil to take place, but He does will the goodness of the created *free* nature, knowing that it will sometimes lapse; but even this is permitted, not willed, for the production of greater good in the world. In creating man as free, God has to allow that freedom to stand.

Whether or not Leibniz was successful in solving the problem of evil, his effort is an outstanding example of the philosopher bending his genius to a condition that "perplexes almost all the human race."

Mathematics and Logic

We saw that Leibniz was convinced of the supreme orderliness of the universe, and this, in turn, was the primary requisite for a mind steeped in mathematics looking for a mathematical opening to new discoveries in the universe. Like Descartes, who had high expectations for his universal mathematics, Leibniz tried to develop a new logic that would go beyond the traditional forms. This new logic, called *universal characteristic,* would include only a few principles, and these would be *symbolized* in such a way as to make the logic a supple instrument for discovering new truths in any area of knowledge such as physics, mathematics, medicine, or theology, or for inventing new machines of all descriptions that would be useful in practical life: "Once the characteristic numbers are established for most concepts, mankind will possess a new instrument which will enhance the capabilities of the mind to a far greater extent than optical instruments strengthen the eyes, and will supersede the microscope and telescope to the same extent that reason is superior to eyesight." When he was only twenty-five years old, he had already created an imposing number of successful machines made possible by the use of symbolic logic: an arithmetic machine, a "living geometer," optical tubes, an instrument for locating ships, and a submarine.

Though much of Leibniz's philosophy met with a sympathetic response, support from his contemporaries for his new logic was never forthcoming. The events of later centuries proved that he was indeed far ahead of his time, for much work in this area was done by mathematicians and logicians like Boole, Whitehead, and Russell; still later, in our time, the insights of Leibniz have come to fruition in the dazzling versatility of computer technology.

Descartes, Spinoza, and Leibniz were the three outstanding figures in seventeenth-century philosophy in continental Europe, and though they espoused different philosophies, they shared many common interests: the quest for certitude in knowledge; metaphysical questions concerning God, man, and the world; and the problem of unity and plurality. But the reason they are often referred to as *rationalists* is, as we have seen, their confidence in the method of deduction and their high expectations from the analysis of ideas. Their counterparts in Britain, though, felt that with such emphasis being placed on the deductive method, there was a danger of losing the empirical, an ardent champion of which was Francis Bacon. However, it was John Locke more than anyone else who staked out the claim for the empirical in the context of an even-tempered philosophy. But before we learn how he did this, we should first see Thomas Hobbes at work, for Hobbes himself was enthusiastic about the prospects of the deductive method.

READINGS

From *The Monadology*

1. The monad of which we shall here speak is merely a simple substance, which enters into composites; simple, that is to say, without parts.

2. And there must be simple substances, since there are composites; for the composite is only a collection or aggregatum of simple substances.

3. Now where there are no parts, neither extension, nor figure, nor divisibility is possible. And these monads are the true atoms of nature, and, in a word, the elements of all things.

4. Their dissolution also is not at all to be feared, and there is no conceivable way in which a simple substance can perish naturally.

5. For the same reason there is no conceivable way in which a simple substance can begin naturally, since it cannot be formed by composition.

6. Thus it may be said that the monads can only begin or end all at once, that is to say, they can only begin by creation and end by annihilation; whereas that which is composite begins or ends by parts.

7. There is also no way of explaining how a monad can be altered or changed in its inner being by any other creature, for nothing can be transposed within it, nor can there be conceived in it any internal movement which can be excited, directed, augmented or diminished within it, as can be done in composites, where there is change among the parts. The monads have no windows through which anything can enter or depart. The accidents cannot detach themselves nor go about outside of substances, as did formerly the sensible species of the Schoolmen. Thus neither substance nor accident can enter a monad from outside.

8. Nevertheless, the monads must have some qualities, otherwise they would not even be entities. And if simple substances did not differ at all in their qualities there would be no way of perceiving any change in things, since what is in the compound can only come from the simple ingredients, and the monads, if they had no qualities, would be indistinguishable from one another, seeing also they do not differ in quantity. Consequently, a plenum being supposed, each place would always receive, in any motion, only the equivalent of what it had had before, and one state of things would be indistinguishable from another.

9. It is necessary, indeed, that each monad be different from every other. For there are never in nature two beings which are exactly alike and in which it is not possible to find an internal difference, or one founded upon an intrinsic quality (*dénomination*).

10. I take it also for granted that every created being, and consequently the created monad also, is subject to change, and even that this change is continuous in each.

11. It follows from what has just been said, that the natural changes of the monads proceeds from an *internal principle,* since an external cause could not influence their inner being.

12. But, besides the principle of change, there must be an individuating *detail of changes,* which forms, so to speak, the specification and variety of the simple substances.

13. This detail must involve a multitude in the unity or in that which is simple. For since every natural change takes place by degrees, something changes and something remains; and consequently, there must be in the simple substance a plurality of affections and of relations, although it has no parts.

14. The passing state, which involves and represents a multitude in unity or in the simple substance, is nothing else than what is called *perception,* which must be distinguished from apperception or consciousness, as will appear in what follows. . . .

15. The action of the internal principle which causes the change or the passage from one perception to another, may be called *appetition;* it is true that desire cannot always completely attain to the whole perception to which it ends, but it always attains something of it and reaches new perceptions.

16. We experience in ourselves a multiplicity in a simple substance, when we find that the most trifling thought of which we are conscious involves a variety in the object. Thus all those who admit that the soul is a simple substance ought to admit this multiplicity in the monad. . . .

18. The name of *entelechies* might be given to all simple substances or created monads, for they have within themselves a certain perfection. . . .

19. If we choose to give the name *soul* to everything that has *perceptions* and *desires* in the general sense which I have just explained, all simple substances or created monads may be called souls, but as feeling is something more than a simple perception. I am willing that the general name of monads or entelechies shall suffice for those simple substances which have only perception, and that those substances only shall be called *souls* whose perception is more distinct and is accompanied by memory. . . .

29. But the knowledge of necessary and eternal truths is what distinguishes us from mere animals and furnishes us with *reason* and the sciences, raising us to a knowledge of ourselves and of God. This is what we call the rational soul or *spirit* in us.

30. It is also by the knowledge of necessary truths, and by their abstractions, that we rise to *acts of reflection,* which make us think of that which calls itself "*I*", and to observe that this or that is within *us:* and it is thus that, in thinking of ourselves, we think of being, of substance, simple or composite, of the immaterial and of God himself, conceiving that what is limited in us is in him without limits. And these reflective acts furnish the principal objects of our reasonings.

31. Our reasonings are founded on *two great principles, that of contradiction,* in virtue of which we judge that to be *false* which involves contradiction, and that *true,* which is opposed or contradictory to the false.

32. And *that of sufficient reason,* in virtue of which we hold that no fact can be real or existent, no statement true, unless there be a sufficient reason why it is so and not otherwise, although most often these reasons cannot be known to us.

33. There are also two kinds of *truths,* those of *reasoning* and those of *fact.* Truths of reasoning are necessary and their opposite is impossible, and those of *fact* are contingent and their opposite is possible. When a truth is necessary its reason can be found by analysis, resolving it into more simple ideas and truths until we reach those which are primitive.

34. It is thus that mathematicians by analysis reduce speculative *theorems* and practical *canons* to *definitions, axioms* and *postulates.*

35. And there are finally simple ideas, definitions of which cannot be given; there are also axioms and postulates, in a word, *primary principles,* which cannot be proved, and indeed need no proof; and these are *identical propositions,* whose opposite involves an express contradiction.

36. But there must also be a *sufficient reason* for *contingent truths* or those of *fact,*—that is, for the sequence of things diffused through the universe of created objects—where the resolution into particular reasons might run into a detail without limits, on account of the immense variety of the things in nature and the division of bodies *ad infinitum.* There is an infinity of figures and of movements, present and past, which enter into the efficient cause of my present writing, and there is an infinity of slight inclinations and dispositions, past and present, of my soul, which enter into the final cause.

37. And as all this *detail* only involves other contingents, anterior or more detailed, each one of which needs a like analysis for its explanation, we make no advance: and the sufficient or final reason must be outside of the sequence or *series* of this detail of contingencies, however infinite it may be.

38. And thus it is that the final reason of things must be found in a necessary substance, in which the detail of changes exists only eminently, as in their source; and this is what we call God.

39. Now this substance, being a sufficient reason of all this detail, which also is linked together throughout, *there is but one God, and this God is sufficient.*

40. We may also conclude that this supreme substance, which is unique, universal and necessary, having nothing outside of itself which is independent of it, and being a pure consequence of possible being, must be incapable of limitations and must contain as much of reality as is possible.

41. Whence it follows that God is absolutely perfect, *perfection* being only the magnitude of positive reality taken in its strictest meaning, setting aside the limits or bounds in things which have them. And where there are no limits, that is, in God, perfection is absolutely infinite.

42. It follows also that the creatures have their perfections from the influence of God, but that their imperfections arise from their own nature, incapable of existing without limits. For it is by this that they are distinguished from God.

43. It is also true that in God is the source not only of existences but also of essences, so far as they are real, or of that which is real in the possible. This is because the understanding of God is the region of eternal truths, or of the ideas

on which they depend, and because, without him, there would be nothing real in the possibilities, and not only nothing existing but also nothing possible.

44. For, if there is a reality in essences or possibilities or indeed in the eternal truths, this reality must be founded in something existing and actual, and consequently in the existence of the necessary being, in whom essence involves existence, or with whom it is sufficient to be possible in order to be actual.

45. Hence God alone (or the necessary being) has this prerogative, that he must exist if he is possible. And since nothing can hinder the possibility of that which possesses no limitations, no negation, and, consequently, no contradiction, this alone is sufficient to establish the existence of God *a priori.* We have also proved it by the reality of the eternal truths. But we have a little while ago [§§36–39] proved it also *a posteriori,* since contingent beings exist, which can only have their final or sufficient reason in a necessary being who has the reason of his existence in himself.

46. Yet we must not imagine, as some do, that the eternal truths, being dependent upon God, are arbitrary and depend upon his will, as Descartes seems to have held, and afterwards M. Poiret. This is true only of contingent truths, the principle of which is *fitness* or the choice of the *best,* whereas necessary truths depend solely on his understanding and are its internal object.

47. Thus God alone is the primitive unity or the original simple substance; of which all created or derived monads are the products, and are generated, so to speak, by continual fulgurations of the Divinity, from moment to moment, limited by the receptivity of the creature, to whom limitation is essential. . . .

51. But in simple substances the influence of one monad upon another is purely *ideal* and it can have its effect only through the intervention of God, inasmuch as in the ideas of God a monad may demand with reason that God in regulating the others from the commencement of things, have regard to it. For since a created monad can have no physical influence upon the inner being of another, it is only in this way that one can be dependent upon another. . . .

53. Now, as there is an infinity of possible universes in the ideas of God, and as only one of them can exist, there must be a sufficient reason for the choice of God, which determines him to select one rather than another.

54. And this reason can only be found in the *fitness,* or in the degrees of perfection, which these worlds contain, each possible world having a right to claim existence according to the measure of perfection which it possesses.

55. And this is the cause of the existence of the Best; namely, that his wisdom makes it known to God, his goodness makes him choose it, and his power makes him produce it.

56. Now this *connection,* or this adaptation, of all created things to each and of each to all, brings it about that each simple substance has relations which express all the others, and that, consequently, it is a perpetual living mirror of the universe. . . .

60. Besides, we can see, in what I have just said, the *a priori* reasons why things could not be otherwise than they are. Because God, in regulating all, has had regard to each part, and particularly to each monad, whose nature being representative, nothing can limit it to representing only a part of things; although it may be

true that this representation is but confused as regards the detail of the whole universe, and can be distinct only in the case of a small part of things, that is to say, in the case of those which are nearest or greatest in relation to each of the monads; otherwise each monad would be a divinity. It is not as regards the object but only as regards the modification of the knowledge of the object, that monads are limited. They all tend confusedly toward the infinite, toward the whole; but they are limited and differentiated by the degrees of their distinct perceptions.

61. And composite substances are analogous in this respect with simple substances. For since the world is a *plenum,* rendering all matter connected, and since in a plenum every motion has some effect on distant bodies in proportion to their distance, so that each body is affected not only by those in contact with it, and feels in some way all that happens to them, but also by their means is affected by those which are in contact with the former, with which it itself is in immediate contact, it follows that this intercommunication extends to any distance whatever. And consequently, each body feels all that happens in the universe, so that he who sees all, might read in each that which happens everywhere, and even that which has been or shall be, discovering in the present that which is removed in time as well as in space. . . .

62. Thus, although each created monad represents the entire universe, it represents more distinctly the body which is particularly attached to it, and of which it forms the entelechy; and as this body expresses the whole universe through the connection of all matter in a plenum, the soul also represents the whole universe in representing this body, which belongs to it in a particular way.

63. The body belonging to a monad, which is its entelechy or soul, constitutes together with the entelechy what may be called a *living being,* and together with the soul what may be called an *animal.* . . .

64. Thus each organic body of a living being is a kind of divine machine or natural automaton, which infinitely surpasses all artificial automata. Because a machine which is made by man's art is not a machine in each one of its parts; for example, the teeth of a brass wheel have parts or fragments which to us are no longer artificial and have nothing in themselves to show the special use to which the wheel was intended in the machine. But nature's machines, that is, living bodies, are machines even in their smallest parts *ad infinitum.* Herein lies the difference between nature and art, that is, between the divine art and ours. . . .

66. Whence we see that there is a world of creatures, of living beings, of animals, of entelechies, of souls, in the smallest particle of matter.

67. Each portion of matter may be conceived of as a garden full of plants, and as a pond full of fishes. But each branch of the plant, each member of the animal, each drop of its humors is also such a garden or such a pond. . . .

69. Therefore there is nothing fallow, nothing sterile, nothing dead in the universe, no chaos, no confusion except in appearance; somewhat as a pond would appear from a distance, in which we might see the confused movement and swarming, so to speak, of the fishes in the pond, without discerning the fish themselves.

70. We see thus that each living body has a ruling entelechy, which in the animals is the soul; but the members of this living body are full of other living beings, plants, animals, each of which has also its entelechy or governing soul.

71. But it must not be imagined, as has been done by some people who have misunderstood my thought, that each soul has a mass or portion of matter belonging to it or attached to it forever, and that consequently it possesses other inferior living beings, destined to its service forever. For all bodies are, like rivers, in a perpetual flux, and parts are entering into them and departing from them continually.

72. Thus the soul changes its body only gradually and by degrees, so that it is never deprived of all its organs at once. There is often a metamorphosis in animals, but never metempsychosis nor transmigration of souls. There are also no entirely *separate* souls, nor *genii* without bodies. God alone is wholly without body. . . .

78. These principles have given me the means of explaining naturally the union or rather the conformity of the soul and the organic body. The soul follows its own peculiar laws and the body also follows its own laws, and they agree in virtue of the *pre-established harmony* between all substances, since they are all representations of one and the same universe.

79. Souls act according to the laws of final causes, by appetitions, ends and means. Bodies act in accordance with the laws of efficient causes or of motion. And the two realms, that of efficient causes and that of final causes, are in harmony with each other. . . .

83. Among other differences which exist between ordinary souls and minds (*esprits*), some of which I have already mentioned, there is also, this, that souls in general are the living mirrors or images of the universe of creatures, but minds or spirits are in addition images of the Divinity itself, or of the author of nature, able to know the system of the universe and to imitate something of it by architectonic samples, each mind being like a little divinity in its own department.

84. Hence it is that spirits are capable of entering into a sort of society with God, and that he is, in relation to them, not only what an inventor is to his machine (as God is in relation to the other creatures), but also what a prince is to his subjects, and even a father to his children.

85. Whence it is easy to conclude that the assembly of all spirits (*esprits*) must compose the City of God, that is, the most perfect state which is possible, under the most perfect of monarchs.

86. This City of God, this truly universal monarchy, is a moral world within the natural world, and the highest and most divine of the works of God; it is in this that the glory of God truly consists, for he would have none if this greatness and goodness were not known and admired by spirits. It is, too, in relation to this divine city that he properly has goodness; whereas his wisdom and his power are everywhere manifest.

87. As we have above established a perfect harmony between two natural kingdoms, the one of efficient, the other of final causes, we should also notice here another harmony between the physical kingdom of nature and the moral kingdom of grace; that is, between God considered as the architect of the mechanism of the universe and God considered as monarch of the divine city of spirits.

88. This harmony makes things progress toward grace by natural means. This globe, for example, must be destroyed and repaired by natural means, at such

times as the government of spirits may demand it, for the punishment of some and the reward of others.

89. It may be said, farther, that God as architect satisfies in every respect God as legislator, and that therefore sins, by the order of nature and perforce even of the mechanical structure of things, must carry their punishment with them; and that in the same way, good actions will obtain their rewards by mechanical ways through their relations to bodies, although this cannot and ought not always happen immediately.

90. Finally, under this perfect government, there will be no good action unrewarded, no bad action unpunished; and everything must result in the well-being of the good, that is, of those who are not disaffected in this great State, who, after having done their duty, trust in providence, and who love and imitate, as is meet, the author of all good, finding pleasure in the contemplation of his perfections, according to the nature of truly *pure love,* which takes pleasure in the happiness of the beloved. This is what causes wise and virtuous persons to work for all which seems in harmony with the divine will, presumptive or antecedent, and nevertheless to content themselves with that which God in reality brings to pass by his secret, consequent and decisive will, recognizing that if we could sufficiently understand the order of the universe, we should find that it surpasses all the wishes of the wisest, and that it is impossible to render it better than it is, not only for all in general, but also for ourselves in particular, if we are attached, as we should be, to the author of all, not only as to the architect and efficient cause of our being, but also as to our master and final cause, who ought to be the whole aim of our will, and who, alone, can make our happiness.

(Trans. by Robert Latta)

Evil as Privation
(from *Theodicy,* #20)

But it is necessary also to meet the more speculative and metaphysical difficulties which have been mentioned, and which concern the cause of evil. The question is asked first of all, whence does evil come? *Si Deus est, unde malum? Si non est, unde bonum?* The ancients attributed the cause of evil to *matter,* which they believed uncreate and independent of God: but we, who derive all being from God, where shall we find the source of evil? The answer is, that it must be sought in the ideal nature of the creature, in so far as this nature is contained in the eternal verities which are in the understanding of God, independently of his will. For we must consider that there is *an original imperfection in the creature* before sin, because the creature is limited in its essence; whence ensues that it cannot know all, and that it can deceive itself and commit other errors. Plato said in *Timaeus* that the world originated in Understanding united to Necessity. Others have united God and Nature. This can be given a reasonable meaning. God will be the Understanding; and the Necessity, that is, the essential nature of things, will be the object of the understanding, in so far as this object consists in the eternal verities. But his object is inward and abides in the divine understanding. And therein is found not only the primitive form of good, but also the origin of evil: the Region of the Eternal Verities must be substituted for matter when we are concerned with seeking out the source of things.

This region is the ideal cause of evil (as it were) as well as of good: but, properly speaking, the formal character of evil has no *efficient* cause, for it consists in privation, as we shall see, namely, in that which the efficient cause does not bring about. That is why the Schoolmen are wont to call the cause of evil *deficient.*

The Analogy of the Boat
(from *Theodicy,* #30–1)

Let us suppose that the current of one and the same river carried along with it various boats, which differ among themselves only in the cargo, some being laden with wood, others with stone, and some more, the others less. That being so, it will come about that the boats most heavily laden will go more slowly than the others, provided it be assumed that the wind or the oar, or some other similar means, assist them not at all. It is not, properly speaking, weight which is the cause of this retardation, since the boats are going down and not upwards; but it is the same cause which also increases the weight in bodies that have greater density, which are, that is to say, less porous and more charged with matter that is proper to them: for the matter which passes through the pores, not receiving the same movement, must not be taken into account. It is therefore matter itself which originally is inclined to slowness or privation of speed; not indeed of itself to lessen this speed, having once received it, since that would be action, but to moderate by its receptivity the effect of the impression when it is to receive it. Consequently, since more matter is moved by the same force of the current when the boat is more laden, it is necessary that it go more slowly; and experiments on the impact of bodies, as well as reason, show that twice as much force must be employed to give equal speed to a body of the same matter but of twice the size. But that indeed would not be necessary if the matter were absolutely indifferent to repose and to movement, and if it had not this natural inertia whereof we have just spoken to give it a kind of repugnance to being moved. Let us now compare the force which the current exercises on boats, and communicates to them, with the action of God, who produces and conserves whatever is positive in creatures, and gives them perfection, being and force: let us compare, I say, the inertia of matter with the natural imperfection of creatures, and the slowness of the laden boat with the defects to be found in the qualities and the action of the creature; and we shall find that there is nothing so just as this comparison. The current is the cause of the boat's movement but not of its retardation; God is the cause of perfection in the nature and the actions of the creature, but the limitation of the receptivity of the creature is the cause of the defects there are in its action.

Thus the Platonists, St. Augustine and the Schoolmen were right to say that God is the cause of the material element of evil which lies in the positive, and not of the formal element, which lies in privation. Even so one may say that the current is the cause of the material element of the retardation, but not of the formal; that is, it is the cause of the boat's speed without being the cause of the limits to this speed. And God is no more the cause of sin than the river's current is the cause of the retardation of the boat.

There is, then, a wholly similar relation between such and such an action of God, and such and such a passion or reception of the creature, which in the ordinary course of things is perfected only in proportion to its 'receptivity,' such is the term used. And when it is said that the creature depends upon God in so far as it exists and in so far as it acts, and even that conservation is a continual creation, this is true in that God gives ever to the creature and produces continually all that in it is positive, good and perfect, every perfect gift coming from the Father of lights. The imperfections, on the other hand, and the defects in operations spring from the original limitation that the creature could not but receive with the first beginning of its being, through the ideal reasons which restrict it. For God could not give the creature all without making of it a God; therefore there must needs be different degrees in the perfection of things, and limitations also of every kind.

No Better World Possible
(from *Theodicy,* #193–5)

Up to now I have shown that the Will of God is not independent of the rules of Wisdom, although indeed it is a matter for surprise that one should have been constrained to argue about it, and to do battle for a truth so great and so well established. But it is hardly less surprising that there should be people who believe that God only half observes these rules, and does not choose the best, although his wisdom causes him to recognize it; and, in a word, that there should be writers who hold that God could have done better....

Yet philosophers and theologians dare to support dogmatically such a belief; and I have many times wondered that gifted and pious persons should have been capable of setting bounds to the goodness and the perfection of God. For to assert that he knows what is best, that he can do it and that he does it not, is to avow that it rested with his will only to make the world better than it is; but that is what one calls lacking goodness. It is acting against that axiom already quoted: *Minus bonum habet rationem mali.* If some adduce experience to prove that God could have done better, they set themselves up as ridiculous critics of his works. To such will be given the answer given to all those who criticize God's course of action, and who from this same assumption, that is, the alleged defects of the world, would infer that there is an evil God, or at least a God neutral between good and evil. And if we hold the same opinion ... we shall, I say, receive this answer: You have known the world only since the day before yesterday, you see scarce farther than your nose, and you carp at the world. Wait until you know more of the world and consider therein especially the parts which present a complete whole (as do organic bodies); and you will find there a contrivance and a beauty transcending all imagination. Let us thence draw conclusions as to the wisdom and the goodness of the author of things, even in things that we know not. We find in the universe some things which are not pleasing to us; but let us be aware that it is not made for us alone. It is nevertheless made for us if we are wise: it will serve us if we use it for our service; we shall be happy in it if we wish to be.

Someone will say that it is impossible to produce the best, because there is no perfect creature, and that it is always possible to produce one which would be more perfect. I answer that what can be said of a creature or of a particular substance, which can always be surpassed by another, is not to be applied to the universe, which, since it must extend through all future eternity, is an infinity. Moreover, there is an infinite number of creatures in the smallest particle of matter, because of the actual division of the *continuum* to infinity. And infinity, that is to say, the accumulation of an infinite number of substances, is, properly speaking, not a whole any more than the infinite number itself, whereof one cannot say whether it is even or uneven. That is just what serves to confute those who make of the world a God, or who think of God as the Soul of the world; for the world or the universe cannot be regarded as an animal or as a substance.

(Tr. c. Huggard)

Review Questions

1. Why did Leibniz reject Spinoza's conception of God?
2. Discuss the notion of *harmony* as the key to Leibniz's philosophy.
3. What were the basic reasons for Leibniz's development of the system of monadology?
4. Compare Leibniz's view of substance with that of Spinoza.
5. How does Leibniz defend God from the charge of being the author of evil?

Suggestions for Further Reading

Broad, C. D. *Leibniz: An Introduction.* New York, Cambridge University Press, 1975.
Mates, B. *The Philosophy of Leibniz.* New York, Oxford University Press, 1986.
Parkinson, G., ed. *Philosophical Writings* (everyman). Boston, Tuttle, 1995.
Savile, A., *Leibniz.* New York, Routledge, 2000.

14

Thomas Hobbes (1588–1679)

Between the Deductive and the Empiric

On the whole, seventeenth-century European philosophy was uncongenial to the medieval scholastic tradition. As a reaction on the continent, as we have seen, philosophy took the form of rationalism, but in Britain, philosophy, uncongenial to both rationalism and scholasticism, was beginning to move in the direction of empiricism. Although Francis Bacon's *Novum Organum* was a frontal attack on Aristotelianism and a tour de force for the experimental method, it did not mean the collapse of the deductive method in England. Thomas Hobbes, sympathetic to continental thought as a result of several visits to France and Italy, chose to base his system of politics on the deductive method, taking as his inspiration the geometry of Euclid and the experiments of Galileo; from these he produced the unique political treatise for which he is best known, the *Leviathan*.

Thomas Hobbes was born in Malmesbury in 1588. Well-tutored in the classics, he entered Oxford University where his education was based on the scholastic tradition to which he developed an aversion, especially in the form of Aristotelianism, for which he later coined the pejorative term *Aristotelity*. Under influential patronage, a wider world of prominent people, rich libraries, and travel abroad opened up to him as he began to foster an interest in politics by his translating Thucydides' *History of the Peloponnesian Wars*.

Hobbes might well have thought that Thucydides' *History* would serve as a beacon for his fellow Englishmen, who were in a state of political turmoil, with years of civil war between the supporters of the monarchy and those who opposed it, between the royalists and the parliamentarians. The violence produced by both sides, exemplified in the eventual beheading of King Charles I in 1649, brought Hobbes to the conclusion that civil war was among the greatest evils that could befall mankind. Thus, without surrendering his love of the classics, he was drawn bit by bit to political philosophy and devoted his middle years to developing a paradigm for political stability.

Though his trips abroad were occasioned by tutorship, at least one was not, for Hobbes' political views, especially those espoused in his first philosophical work, *The Elements of Law,* were beginning to gain some recognition and because they were taken to be supportive of the king, when the parliamentarians got into power he thought it best for his health to leave England; he did so in 1641, referring to himself, later on, as the "first of all that fled." His intellectual life abroad was not less fashioned and nourished than at home, and though his intellectual experiences and excitements can be considered on their own, they all evolved together in the direction of the political philosophy culminating in *Leviathan,* published in 1651. In a sense, the origin of this work goes back to one of his earlier trips to the continent when he happened upon Euclid's book *The Elements of Geometry;* in it he read a proposition that he felt could not have been arrived at by demonstration, but as he read further he saw how Euclid actually did demonstrate a complex conclusion by proceeding step by step, from very simple mathematical propositions, and, in the charming words of his contemporary biographer, "by G—, said he . . . *this is impossible!*" It was not as though Hobbes never knew anything before about the deductive method, but as so often happens, the realization of it came suddenly, and the path became clear to him for deducing the principles of politics from the initial starting point of human behavior, which would be evident to all.

A subsequent visit to the continent brought him into contact with Descartes, from whom he learned firsthand of his attempt to mathematicize philosophy, and Galileo, from whose brilliant scientific discoveries he became fascinated with the idea that motion, not rest as in Aristotle, was the natural state of physical things. In the eleven-year period following his flight from London, and despite being under siege from many quarters, Hobbes finally returned to London in 1651. From then on he led a retired but active life dedicated to writing on mathematical and philosophical topics and by rendering his beloved classics, the *Odyssey* and the *Iliad,* into English. He died in 1679.

Anyone breaking new ground faces enormous difficulties in establishing the uniqueness of his position while trying to relate it to cognate ideas of the past. This is certainly true of Hobbes, who, though not always prompt to acknowledge the influence of past philosophers, did actually produce, in the view of some commentators, the masterpiece of political philosophy written in English and one of the most comprehensive systems of political philosophy in the classical modern period. In recent years there has been a renewed interest in his work, and even though there has never been a completely settled interpretation of his philosophy, contemporary studies have reevaluated his analysis of language and have compelled a second look at notions like morality, the role of God in his system, his immersion in scriptural concerns, the charge of atheism, and whether his theory of society was actually an early apology for a bourgeois society. There are further questions pertaining to nominalism and skepticism, and to what extent these are operative principles of his philosophy. Yet none of these questions prevents a presentation of the main line of his doctrine that all can agree with, as it is given in the *Leviathan* and extended on some points in his other works.

Hobbes begins by laying down strict parameters: The scope of philosophy is limited to the corporeal world. Body is his interest, and he means by it what Descartes and other philosopher-scientists of the seventeenth century meant by it—quantity, extension, tridimensionality, space-occupying. And inasmuch as *substance* is another word for *body,* and discourse touching on God or anything else as *incorporeal substance* is contradictory: "And according to this acceptation of the word, Substance and Body, signify the same thing; and therefore Substance incorporeal are words, which when they are joined together, destroy one another, as if a man should say, an Incorporeal Body." One reason for Hobbes' insistence on this idea springs from his view that the notions of God, infinite, eternal, incorporeal, and so on, are incomprehensible and therefore are not the object of reason, but of faith. We may know *that* God is, but not *what* He is; so, even if we grant the existence of these notions, they are beyond rationality, though not beyond actuality.

But another reason for Hobbes' insistence on the corporeal is the deductive certitude with which reality as mechanical can be treated. That is why the chief property of body for Hobbes is *motion,* the discovery of which so excited him in his visit to Galileo and which paved the way for a mechanistic philosophy of the universe, Cartesian in approach, and amenable to the making of a system in which only motion is understandable. The cause-and-effect relationship, or the knowledge of *consequences,* holds throughout, supplying Hobbes with the intellectual instrument for understanding the unity already present in the universe, or the unity he wants to introduce, whence is derived Hobbes' definition of philosophy: "The Knowledge acquired by Reasoning, from the Manner of the Generation of any thing, to the Properties; or from the Properties, to some possible Way of Generation of the same; to the end be able to produce, as far as matter, and human force permit, such Effects, as human life requires." Note that a constitutive part— and as far as politics is concerned, the most important part—of philosophy is its orientation to the practical good of mankind. Philosophy is divided into two main parts, one pertaining to natural bodies and their consequences and the other to political bodies and their consequences; it is on this second part that Hobbes brings his philosophical method to bear.

Hobbes really wanted his system to be a *system*. It is debatable whether his system actually does or does not hold together, but logical consistency has to be seen as yielding to his desire for the end to be achieved. That is why he wanted everything to be held together by some kind of necessity, and the necessity he focused on was the necessity of matter in motion, from which other truths of his system could be *deduced:* "From seeing life is but a motion of Limbs, the beginning whereof is some principal part within; why may we not say, that all *Automata* (Engines that move themselves by springs and wheels as doth a watch) have an artificial life? For what is the Heart, but *Spring;* and the *Nerves,* but so many *Wheels,* giving motion to the whole Body . . . ?" And if man is made this way by the art of nature, man can, in turn, by his nature-imitating art, create society as an *artificial animal:* "For by Art is created that great *Leviathan* called a *Common-wealth,* or *State* (in Latin, *Civitas*) which is but an Artificial Man," in which sovereign, subjects, magistrates, rewards, punishment, business and so on are all likened to parts of the natural body. With this is mind, Hobbes proceeds to create a state of affairs that would be the best human art could devise for man's "commodious living." But deduction, indispensable as it is for system building, relies on prior knowledge to begin with, and for Hobbes this comes from experiencing what men actually do, by observing their actual conduct—a matter evident to all. From man's actual conduct, Hobbes would "resolve" where it comes from and "compose" where it ought to go.

The Nature of Man and the Role of Reason

What, then, is man really like? Basically, man is distrustful of his fellowman. If anyone doubts this, Hobbes avers, let him confirm it by his own experience: "Let him therefore consider with himself, when taking a journey, he arms himself, and seeks to go well accompanied; when going to sleep, he locks his doors; when even in his house he locks his chest; and this when he knows there be Laws, and public Officers, armed to revenge all injuries shall be done him; what opinion has he of his fellow subjects, when he rides armed; of his fellow Citizens when he locks his doors; and of his children, and servants, when he locks his chests. Does he not there as much accuse mankind by his actions, as I do by my words?"

With this experience, Hobbes probes a little deeper to uncover what man is originally, or primitively, or, to use his words, what man is *by nature.* Thus, Hobbes concludes that there is a *natural state of man,* a "state of nature" that is not to be taken as a historical fact, yet not as a mere abstraction either, for it is that condition to which man would be reduced were it not for the civilizing effects of organized society. The state of nature is not a pretty one, and it is tellingly described in a famous paragraph: "In such condition, there is no place for industry: because the fruit thereof is uncertain; and consequently no Culture of the Earth; no Navigation, nor use of the commodities that may be imported by Sea; no commodious Building; no Instruments of moving, and removing such things as require much force; no Knowledge of the face of the Earth; no account of Time; no Arts; no Letters; no Society; and which is worst of all, continual fear, and danger of violent death; And the life of man, solitary, poor, nasty, brutish, and short." For Hobbes, the natural state of man is nothing short of a state of war. Regarding the use of the phrase "state of nature," Hobbes is the first writer to use it in this way; with a far different meaning, in a theological context, it is as old as Christianity, in which it signifies the natural state of man before the advent of divine grace, which raises the "natural" state of man to a "supernatural" one, although the natural never really existed.

But man can emerge from this sorry state that "mere Nature" has placed him in by attending to other aspects of his nature, namely, his passions and his reason.

Among man's passions, the most fundamental one—the one that moves him to action—is *self-preservation,* or, as Hobbes also puts it, the *fear of death,* especially violent death, which he abhorred during the English civil wars. That is why he designates the *liberty* man has to preserve his life as the lodestar of his political theory and calls it *the* "Right of Nature": On it all other rights and laws depend, and from it they can be deduced. In a word, the fear of death "inclines" man to its opposite, *peace;* peace is the only antidote to war. If man's passion for self-preservation inclines him to peace, it is *reason* that "discovers" the way. Reason, for Hobbes, though endowed with many functions, is a guide to conduct and is the ultimate arbiter of the morality of man's actions. From the way he uses the word *reason* and the phrase "right reason"—reminiscent of St. Thomas' use of it—we can reasonably ask, despite his thumping of Aristotle and the Schoolmen, whether he is not actually in their tradition in this matter. Reason, then, becomes Hobbes' vehicle for deducing the moral-political structure of the institution whose sole purpose is to ensure peace, namely, the *Commonwealth.* In the title of his masterpiece, Hobbes calls the Commonwealth the *Leviathan,* a reference to the biblical sea giant that rules as "king over all the children of pride."

Deduction of the Laws of Society: The "Commonwealth"

Hobbes then proceeds by reason to deduce the *laws of nature,* that is, the rules by which man advances the cause of peace and protects himself against the destruction of his life. There are nineteen such laws and, though they are general, they implicitly contain all the particularities that comprise the bulk of Hobbes' work. Of the nineteen, which he sets forth in the fourteenth and fifteenth chapters of *Leviathan,* the first three are the operative heart of his doctrine.

The *first* law, the fundamental law of nature, is: "That every man ought to endeavour Peace, as far as he has hope of obtaining it; and when he cannot obtain it, that he may seek and use all helps and advantages of War." The purpose of this effort is "to seek Peace, and follow it."

To endeavor peace is the purpose of the *second* law: "That a man be willing, when others are so too, as far forth as for peace and defense of himself he shall think it necessary, to lay down this right to all things; and be contented with so much liberty against other men, as he would allow other men against himself." In the state of nature, men, acting individually, have the right to "all things" as would preserve their lives, and it is this right that becomes the object of concern if man is going to seek peace, not as an individual, but collectively with others; a mutual agreement among men would allow the enlargement of life for all. Such a mutual agreement is called by Hobbes a *Contract,* that is, a mutual transfer of rights by which all parties hope to achieve some higher good, and insofar as a contract may not involve the immediate delivery of what is contracted for but does involve the trust of another for future delivery, it is called a *pact,* or *covenant.*

This gives rise to the *third* law: "That men perform their Covenants made." Here is the entire matter of mutual trust, the violation of which causes injustice and injury and the undoing of the contract trustfully made.

Following the internal logic of the Laws of Nature—to ensure the endeavor toward peace, the reasonable laying down of rights, and the making and keeping of contracts—brings Hobbes to the only possible conclusion: that some kind of Common Power must be established to make the agreement of men "constant and lasting," and "thereby to secure them in such sort, as that by their own authority, and by the fruits of the Earth, they may nourish themselves and live contentedly." The common power envisioned by Hobbes is "one Man or an Assembly of men," called *Sovereign,* upon whom men can confer their power and strength, and who would act in any way whatsoever to guarantee the peace and safety of his subjects. Hobbes takes pains to point out that no one is giving up his person, which is inalienable, but that individuals contract with each other to give up their right of self-governance to the Sovereign so that all, united together, are themselves the author of the actions taken by the Sovereign. "This done, the Multitude so united in one Person, is called a *Commonwealth."* And thus is the "artificial man," which Hobbes set out to create, created.

Hobbes elaborates in detail the rights of the Sovereign, such as his power of appointing public ministers, controlling trade, meting out punishment, governing religious matters, and supervising education, to indicate that the Sovereign's power is *absolute* and that his subjects have the obligation to obey. Yet, to use current phraseology, the Sovereign is authoritarian but not totalitarian, for subjects have rights that are nontransferable, or inalienable, such as integrity of life and limb, use of food and medicine necessary to maintain life and health, freedom from self-incrimination, buying and selling, and choice of residence; these and other similar rights the Sovereign must respect and in no way contravene.

Unity is the key to the commonwealth; the full title of Hobbes' work, *Leviathan, or the Matter, Form, and Power of a Commonwealth Ecclesiastical and Civil,* informs us that he is not writing of *two* commonwealths, one ecclesiastical and one civil, but of *one* commonwealth in which both ecclesiastical and civil governance are to be found. That this is the case is shown by the care he takes in explaining that what we know about God *naturally* (that is, through the natural dictates of right reason) is not at variance with what we know about God *prophetically* (that is, knowing the laws He gave through His chosen people). It is only reasonable for Hobbes to conclude that the prophetical is subsumed in the natural, because the natural is *eo ipso* prior, and this subsumption in no way destroys the features of the prophetical. The vast canvassing of Sacred Scripture that occupies almost half of the *Leviathan* is a painstaking, and clearly devotional, analysis of God's word in which Hobbes tries ingeniously to show that the Kingdom of God as described in the Bible is nothing less than the very commonwealth he discovered in the nature of man. So, the subsumption of the ecclesiastical into the civil has the authority of God's word to support it. Because the civil predominates, and because we know God's rule through the dictates of reason, the commonwealth is valid for "infidel" Sovereigns with non-Christian subjects, as it is for Christian Sovereigns with Christian subjects.

Motivated by the notion that philosophy is worthy of the name only when it deals with the benefit of mankind, perhaps Hobbes was all too conscious of making a truly original contribution to political philosophy. Certainly with the notions of the state of nature, the social contact, and the structure of the commonwealth, he felt that his vision of a new era of political stability was logical and unimpeachable, and therefore ought to enlist the support of the universities. On the one hand, he wrote in a tradition they were comfortable with, for to the extent that Socrates, Plato, and Aristotle held for a state that would best suit its citizens, Hobbes was in full agreement. On the other hand, ideals are far from making a state work, and Hobbes knew he was going beyond these philosophers in founding a *practical* political philosophy. He differed from them on a major theoretical point as well, for the great Greek thinkers maintained that man was social by nature, whereas Hobbes maintained that man was individual and even asocial by nature, so that if a society is formed, it is for the sake of the individual, anxious to preserve himself in peace and security—in the view of some commentators, a kind of political hedonism. Yet, given the time in which he lived, Hobbes sought a genuine balance between society and the individual; this is reflected in his attempt to steer a middle course between the king and the people by denying that the king had direct authority by divine right to rule over a society that awaited him, as opposed to a Sovereign established by the several wills of all those who authorized his power, the momentous idea being that the people were able to empower the Sovereign. Hobbes thought of his doctrine as being universal, and if it is true that the universal can be achieved only through the particular, the particular set of circumstances prompting his mind and heart to work for universal peace was the English civil war, and so he concludes his treatise on the commonwealth of peace by reminding his readers, ruefully and hopefully, that it was "occasioned by the disorders of the present time."

READING

From Leviathan, or the Matter, Form, and Power of a Commonwealth Ecclesiastical and Civil

CHAPTER XIII
OF THE NATURAL CONDITION OF MANKIND AS CONCERNING THEIR FELICITY, AND MISERY

Nature hath made men so equal, in the faculties of the body and mind; as that, though there be found one man sometimes manifestly stronger in body or of quicker mind than another, yet when all is reckoned together, the difference between man and man is not so considerable, as that one man can thereupon claim to himself any benefit, to which another may not pretend as well as he. For as to the strength of body, the weakest has strength enough to kill the strongest, either by secret machination or by confederacy with others that are in the same danger with himself.

And as to the faculties of the mind—setting aside the arts grounded upon words, and especially that skill of proceeding upon general and infallible rules, called science; which very few have, and but in few things; as being not a native faculty, born with us; nor attained, as prudence, while we took after somewhat else—I find yet a greater equality amongst men, than that of strength. For prudence is but experience which equal time equally bestows on all men, in those things they equally apply themselves unto. That which may perhaps make such equality incredible, is but a vain conceit of one's own wisdom, which almost all men think they have in a greater degree than the vulgar; that is, than all men but themselves, and a few others, whom by fame, or for concurring with themselves, they approve. For such is the nature of men, that howsoever they may acknowledge many others to be more witty, or more eloquent, or more learned, yet they will hardly believe there be many so wise as themselves; for they see their own wit at hand, and other men's at a distance. But this proveth rather that men are in that point equal, than unequal. For there is not ordinarily a greater sign of the equal distribution of anything, than that every man is contented with his share.

From this equality of ability, ariseth equality of hope in the attaining of our ends. And therefore if any two men desire the same thing, which nevertheless they cannot both enjoy, they become enemies; and in the way to their end, which is principally their own conservation, and sometimes their delectation only, endeavor to destroy, or subdue one another. And from hence it comes to pass that where an invader hath no more to fear than another man's single power; if one plant, sow, build, or possess a convenient seat, others may probably be expected to come prepared with forces united, to dispossess and deprive him, not only of the fruit of his labor, but also for his life or liberty. And the invader again is in the like danger of another.

And from this difference of one another, there is no way for any man to secure himself so reasonable as anticipation; that is, by force or wiles to master the persons of all men he can, so long, till he see no other power great enough to endanger him: and this is no more than his own conservation requireth, and is generally allowed. Also because there be some, that taking pleasure in contemplating their own power in the acts of conquest, which they pursue farther than their security requires; if others, that otherwise would be glad to be at ease within modest bounds, should not by invasion increase their power, they would not be able long time, by standing only on their defense, to subsist. And by consequence, such augmentation of dominion over men being necessary to a man's conservation, it ought to be allowed him.

Again, men have no pleasure, but on the contrary a great deal of grief, in keeping company, where there is no power able to overawe them all. For every man looketh that his companion should value him at the same rate he sets upon himself; and upon all signs of contempt, or undervaluing, naturally endeavors, as far as he dares (which amongst them that have no common power to keep them in quiet, is far enough to make them destroy each other), to extort a greater value from his contemners by damage, and from others by the example.

So that in the nature of man, we find three principal causes of quarrel. First, competition; second, difference; thirdly, glory.

The first maketh men invade for gain; the second, for safety; and the third, for reputation. The first use violence to make themselves masters of other men's persons, wives, children, and cattle; the second, to defend them; the third, for trifles, as a word, a smile, a different opinion, and any other sign of undervalue, either direct in their persons, or by reflection in their kindred, their friends, their nation, their profession, or their name.

Hereby it is manifest that during the time men live without a common power to keep them all in awe, they are in that condition which is called war: and such a war as is of every man against every man. For war consisteth not in battle only, or the act of fighting, but in a tract of time wherein the will to contend by battle is sufficiently known, and therefore the notion of time is to be considered in the nature of war, as it is in the nature of weather. For as the nature of foul weather lieth not in a shower or two of rain, but in an inclination thereto of many days together; so the nature of war consisteth not in actual fighting, but in the known disposition thereto, during all the time there is no assurance to the contrary. All other time is peace.

Whatsoever therefore is consequent to a time of war, where every man is enemy to every man; the same is consequent to the time, wherein men live without other security than what their own strength and their own invention shall furnish them withal. In such condition there is no place for industry, because the fruit thereof is uncertain: and consequently no culture of the earth: no navigation, nor use of the commodities that may be imported by sea; no commodious building; no instruments of moving, and removing, such things as require much force; no knowledge of the face of the earth; no account of time; no arts; no letters; no society; and which is worst of all, continual fear, and danger of violent death; and the life of man, solitary, poor, nasty, brutish, and short.

It may seem strange to some man that has not well weighed these things, that nature should thus dissociate, and render men apt to invade and destroy one another; and he may therefore, not trusting to this inference, made from the passions, desire perhaps to have the same confirmed by experience. Let him therefore consider with himself, when taking a journey, he arms himself and seeks to go well accompanied; when going to sleep, he locks his doors; when even in his house he locks his chests; and this when he knows there be laws, and public officers, armed, to revenge all injuries shall be done him; what opinion he has of his fellow-subjects, when he rides armed; of his fellow-citizens, when he locks his doors; and of his children, and servants, when he locks his chests. Does he not there as much accuse mankind by his actions, as I do by my words? But neither of us accuse man's nature in it. The desires, and other passions of man, are in themselves no sin. No more are the actions that proceed from those passions, till they know a law that forbids them; which till laws be made they cannot know; nor can any law be made, till they have agreed upon the person that shall make it.

It may peradventure be thought, there was never such a time nor condition of war as this; and I believe it was never generally so, over all the world; but there are many places where they live so now. For the savage people in many places of America, except the government of small families, the concord whereof dependeth on natural lust, have no government at all; and live at this day in that brutish manner, as I said before. Howsoever, it may be perceived what manner of life there would be, where there were no common power to fear; by the manner of life which men that have formerly lived under a peaceful government, use to degenerate into a civil war.

But though there had never been any time wherein particular men were in a condition of war one against another; yet in all times, kings, and persons of sovereign authority, because of their independency, are in continual jealousies, and in the state and posture of gladiators; having their weapons pointing, and their eyes fixed on one another; that is, their forts, garrisons, and guns upon the frontiers of their kingdoms; and continual spies upon their neighbors; which is a posture of war. But because they uphold thereby the industry of their subjects, there does not follow from it that misery which accompanies the liberty of particular men.

To this war of every man against every man, this also is consequent: *that nothing can be unjust.* The notions of right and wrong, justice and injustice, have there no place. Where there is no common power, there is no law; where no law, no justice. Force and fraud are in war the two cardinal virtues. Justice and injustice are none of the faculties neither of the body nor mind. If they were, they might be in a man that were alone in the world, as well as his senses and passions. They are qualities that relate to men in society, not in solitude. It is consequent also to the same condition, that there be no propriety, no dominion, no *mine* and *thine* distinct; but only that to be every man's, that he can get; and for so long as he can keep it. And thus much for the ill condition which man by mere nature is actually placed in; though with a possibility to come out of it, consisting partly in the passions, partly in his reason.

The passions that incline men to peace are fear of death, desire of such things as are necessary to commodious living, and a hope by their industry to obtain them. And reason suggesteth convenient articles of peace, upon which men may be drawn to agreement. These articles are they which otherwise are called the Laws of Nature whereof I shall speak more particularly in the two following chapters.

CHAPTER XIV
OF THE FIRST AND SECOND NATURAL LAWS, AND OF CONTRACTS

The right of nature, which writers commonly call *jus naturale,* is the liberty each man hath to use his own power, as he will himself, for the preservation of his own nature; that is to say, of his own life; and consequently, of doing anything, which in his own judgment and reason, he shall conceive to be the aptest means thereunto.

By *liberty,* is understood, according to the proper signification of the word, the absence of external impediments: which impediments, may oft take away part of a man's power to do what he would; but cannot hinder him from using the power left him, according as his judgment and reason shall dictate to him.

A *law of nature, lex naturalis,* is a precept or general rule, found out by reason, by which a man is forbidden to do that which is destructive of his life, or taketh away the means of preserving the same; and to omit that by which he thinketh it may be best preserved. For though they that speak of this subject use to confound *jus* and *lex, right* and *law;* yet they ought to be distinguished; because *right* consisteth in liberty to do or to forbear, whereas *law* determineth and bindeth to one of them; so that law and right differ as much as obligation and liberty; which in one and the same matter are inconsistent.

And because the condition of man, as hath been declared in the precedent chapter, is a condition of war of everyone against everyone; in which case everyone is governed by his own reason, and there is nothing he can make use of that may not be a help unto him in preserving his life against his enemies; it followeth, that in such a condition every man has a right to everything; even to one another's body. And therefore, as long as this natural right of every man to everything endureth, there can be no security to any man, how strong or wise soever he be, of living out the time which nature ordinarily alloweth men to live. And consequently it is a precept, or general rule of reason, *that every man ought to endeavor peace, as far as he has hope of obtaining it; and when he cannot obtain it, that he may seek and use all helps and advantages of war.* The first branch of which rule containeth the first and fundamental law of nature; which is, *to seek peace and follow it.* The second, the sum of the right of nature; which is, *by all means we can, to defend ourselves.*

From this fundamental law of nature, by which men are commanded to endeavor peace, is derived this second law: *that a man be willing, when others are so too, as far forth as for peace and defense of himself he shall think it necessary, to lay down this right to all things; and be contented with so much liberty against other men, as he would allow other men against himself.* For as long as every man holdeth this right, of doing anything he liketh, so long are all men in the condition of war. But if other men will not lay down their right, as well as he, then there is no reason for anyone to divest himself of his; for that were to expose himself to prey, which no man is bound to, rather than to dispose himself to peace. This is that law of the Gospel: *whatsoever you require that others should do to you, that do ye to them.* And that law of all men, *quod tibi fieri non vis, alteri ne feceris.*

To *lay down* a man's *right* to anything, is to *divest* himself of the *liberty,* of hindering another of the benefit of his own right to the same. For he that renounceth or passeth away his right, giveth not to any other man a right which he had not before; because there is nothing to which every man had not right by nature; but only standeth out of his way, that he may enjoy his own original right, without hindrance from him, not without hindrance from another. So that the effect which redoundeth to one man, by another man's defect of right, is but so much diminution of impediments to the use of his own right original.

Right is laid aside, either by simply renouncing it, or by transferring it to another. By *simply renouncing,* when he cares not to whom the benefit thereof redoundeth. By *transferring,* when he intendeth the benefit thereof to some certain person or persons. And when a man hath in either manner abandoned or granted away his right; then is he said to be *obliged,* or bound, not to hinder those to whom such right is granted or abandoned, from the benefit of it; and that he *ought,* and it is his *duty,* not to make void that voluntary act of his own; and that such hindrance is *injustice,* an *injury,* as being *sine jure;* the right being before renounced, or transferred. So that injury, or injustice, in the controversies of the world, is somewhat like to that, which in the disputations of scholars is called *absurdity.* For as it is there called an absurdity to contradict what one maintained in the beginning; so in the world, it is called injustice, and injury, voluntarily to undo that which from the beginning he had voluntarily done. The way by which a man either simply renounceth, or transferreth his right, is a declaration, or signification, by some voluntary and sufficient sign or signs, that he doth so renounce or transfer, or hath so renounced or transferred the same, to him that accepteth it. And these signs are either words only, or actions only, or, as it happeneth most often, both words and actions. And the same are the bonds, by which men are bound and obliged—bonds that have their strength, not from their own nature, for nothing is more easily broken than a man's word, but from fear of some evil consequence upon the rupture.

Whensoever a man transferreth his right, or renounceth it; it is either in consideration of some right reciprocally transferred to himself, or for some other good he hopeth for thereby. For it is a voluntary act; and of the voluntary acts of every man, the object is some *good to himself.* And therefor there be some rights which no man can be understood by any words, or other signs, to have abandoned or transferred. As first a man cannot lay down the right of resisting them that assault him by force, to take away his life; because he cannot be understood to aim thereby, at any good to himself. The same may be said of wounds, and chains, and imprisonment; both because there is no benefit consequent to such patience, as there is to the patience of suffering another to be wounded or imprisoned; as also because a man cannot tell, when he seeth men proceed against him by violence, whether they intend his death or not. And lastly the motive, an end for which this renouncing and transferring of right is introduced, is nothing else but the security of a man's person, in his life, and in the means of so preserving life as not to be weary of it. And therefore if a man by words, or other signs, seem to despoil himself of the end for which those signs were intended, he is not to be understood as if he meant it, or that it was his will, but that he was ignorant of how such words and actions were to be interpreted.

The mutual transferring of right, is that which men call *contract.*

There is difference between transferring of right to the thing, and transferring, or tradition—that is delivery—of the thing itself. For the thing may be delivered together with the translation of the right, as in buying and selling with ready money, or exchange of goods, or lands; and it may be delivered sometime after.

Again, one of the contractors may deliver the thing contracted for on his part, and leave the other to perform his part at some determinate time after, and in the meantime be trusted; and then the contract on his part is called *pact,* or *covenant:* or both parts may contract now to perform hereafter; in which cases, he that is to perform in time to come, being trusted, his performance is called *keeping of promise,* or faith; and the failing of performance, if it be voluntary, *violation of faith.*

CHAPTER XV
OF OTHER LAWS OF NATURE

From that law of nature by which we are obliged to transfer to another such rights as, being retained, hinder the peace of mankind, there followeth a third; which is this, *that men perform their covenants made;* without which, covenants are in vain, and but empty words; and the right of all men to all things remaining, we are still in the condition of war.

And in this law of nature, consisteth the fountain and original of *justice.* For where no covenant hath preceded, there hath no right been transferred, and every man has right to everything; and consequently, no action can be unjust. But when a covenant is made, then to break it is *unjust* and the definition of *injustice* is no other than *the not performance of covenant.* And whatsoever is not unjust, is *just.*

But because covenants of mutual trust, where there is a fear of not performance on either part, as hath been said in the former chapter, are invalid; though the original of justice be the making of covenants; yet injustice actually there can be none, till the cause of such fear be taken away; which while men are in the natural condition of war, cannot be done. Therefore before the names of just and unjust can have place, there must be some coercive power, to compel men equally to the performance of their covenants, by the terror of some punishment greater than the benefit they expect by the breach of their covenant; and to make good that propriety which by mutual contract men acquire, in recompense of the universal right they abandon; and such power there is none before the erection of a commonwealth. And this is also to be gathered out of the ordinary definition of justice in the Schools; for they say, that *justice is the constant will of giving to every man his own.* And therefore where there is no own, that is no propriety, there is no injustice; and where is no coercive power erected, that is, where there is no commonwealth, there is no propriety; all men having right to all things; therefore where there is no commonwealth, there nothing is unjust. So that the nature of justice consisteth in keeping of valid covenants; but the validity of covenants begins not but with the constitution of a civil power sufficient to compel men to keep them, and then it is also that propriety begins....

CHAPTER XVII
OF THE CAUSES, GENERATIONS, AND DEFINITION
OF A COMMONWEALTH

The only way to erect such a common power, as may be able to defend them from the invasion of foreigners and the injuries of one another, and thereby to secure them in such sort as that, by their own industry, and by the fruits of the earth, they may nourish themselves and live contentedly; is, to confer all their power and strength upon one man, or upon one assembly of men, that may reduce all their wills, by plurality of voices, unto one will; which is as much as to say, to appoint one man, or assembly of men, to bear their person; and everyone to own and acknowledge himself to be author of whatsoever he that so beareth their person, shall act or cause to be acted in those things which concern the common peace and safety; and therein to submit their wills, everyone to his will, and their judgments, to his judgment. This is more than consent, or concord; it is a real unity of them all, in one and the same person, made by covenant of every man with every man, in such manner as if every man should say to every man, "*I authorize and give up my right of governing myself to this man, or to this assembly of men, on this condition, that thou give up thy right to him, and authorize all his actions in like manner.*" This done, the multitude so united in one person is called a commonwealth, in Latin *civitas.* This is the generation of that great *LEVIATHAN,* or rather, to speak more reverently, of that mortal god, to which we owe under the immortal God, our peace and defense. For by this authority, given him by every particular man in the commonwealth, he hath the use of so much power and strength conferred on him, that by terror thereof he is enabled to perform the wills of them all, to peace at home and mutual aid against their enemies abroad. And in him consisteth the essence of the commonwealth; which, to define it, is *one person, of whose acts a great multitude, by mutual covenants one with another, have made themselves every one the author, to the end he may use the strength and means of them all, as he shall think expedient, for their peace and common defense.*

And he that carrieth this person, is called *sovereign,* and said to have sovereign power; and everyone besides, his *subject.*

The attaining to this sovereign power is by two ways. One, by natural force; as when a man maketh his children to submit themselves and their children to his government, as being able to destroy them if they refuse; or by war subdueth his enemies to his will, giving them their lives on that condition. The other, is when men agree amongst themselves to submit to some man, or assembly of men, voluntarily, on confidence to be protected by him against all others. This latter, may be called a political commonwealth, or commonwealth by *institution;* and the former, a commonwealth by *acquisition.* And first, I shall speak of a commonwealth by institution.

CHAPTER XVIII
OF THE RIGHTS OF SOVEREIGNS BY INSTITUTION

A Commonwealth is said to be *instituted,* when a multitude of men do agree and covenant, everyone with everyone, that to whatsoever man, or assembly of men, shall be given by the major part the right to present the person of them all, that is to say, to be their *representative;* everyone, as well he that voted for it as he that voted against it, shall authorize all the actions and judgments of that man, or assembly of men, in the same manner as if they were his own, to the end to live peaceably amongst themselves and be protected against other men.

From this institution of a commonwealth are derived all the *rights* and *faculties* of him, or them, on whom sovereign power is conferred by the consent of the people assembled.

First, because they covenant, it is to be understood they are not obliged by former covenant to anything repugnant hereunto. And consequently they that have already instituted a commonwealth, being thereby bound by covenant to own the actions and judgments of one, cannot lawfully make a new covenant amongst themselves, to be obedient to any other, in anything whatsoever, without his permission. And therefore, they that are subject to a monarch, cannot without his leave cast off monarchy, and return to the confusion of a disunited multitude; nor transfer their person from him that beareth it, to another man, or other assembly of men; for they are bound, every man to every man, to own, and be reputed author of all, that he that already is their sovereign shall do and judge fit to be done; so that any one man dissenting, all the rest should break their covenant made to that man, which is injustice; and they have also every man given the sovereignty to him that beareth their person; and therefore if they depose him, they take from him that which is his own, and so again it is injustice. . . .

Secondly, because the right of bearing the person of them all, is given to him they make sovereign, by covenant only of one to another, and not of him to any of them; there can happen no breach of covenant on the part of the sovereign; and consequently none of his subjects, by any pretense of forfeiture, can be freed from his subjection. That he which is made sovereign maketh no covenant with his subjects beforehand, is manifest; because either he must make it with the whole multitude, as one party to the covenant, or he must make a several covenant with every man. With the whole, as one party, it is impossible, because as yet they are not one person; and if he make so many several covenants as there be men, those covenants after he hath the sovereignty are void; because what act soever can be pretended by any one of them for breach thereof, is the act both of himself and of all the rest, because done in the person, and by the right of every one of them in particular.

Thirdly, because the major part hath by consenting voices declared a sovereign, he that dissented must now consent with the rest; that is, be contented to avow all the actions he shall do, or else justly be destroyed by the rest. For if he voluntarily entered into the congregation of them that were assembled, he sufficiently declared thereby his will, and therefore tacitly covenanted to stand to what the major part should ordain; and therefore if he refuse to stand thereto, or make protestation against any of their decrees, he does contrary to his covenant, and therefore unjustly. And whether he be of the congregation or not, and whether his consent be asked or not, he must either submit to their decrees, or be left in the condition of war he was in before; wherein he might without injustice be destroyed by any man whatsoever.

Fourthly, because every subject is by this institution author of all the actions and judgments of the sovereign instituted; it follows that whatsoever he doth, it can be no injury to any of his subjects, nor ought he to be by any of them accused of injustice. For he that doth anything by authority from another, doth therein no injury to him by whose authority he acteth; but by this institution of a commonwealth, every particular man is author of all the sovereign doth; and consequently he that complaineth of injury from his sovereign, complaineth of that whereof he himself is author; and therefore ought not to accuse any man but himself; no nor himself of injury, because to do injury to one's self, is impossible. It is true that they that have sovereign power may commit iniquity, but not injustice, or injury, in the proper signification.

Fifthly, and consequently to that which was said last, no man that hath sovereign power can justly be put to death, or otherwise in any manner by his subjects punished. For seeing every subject is author of the actions of his sovereign, he punisheth another for the actions committed by himself.

And because the end of this institution, is the peace and defense of them all, and whosoever has right to the end has right to the means; it belongeth of right, to whatsoever man or assembly that hath the sovereignty, to be judge both of the means of peace and defense, and also of the hindrances and disturbances of the same; and to do whatsoever he shall think necessary to be done, both beforehand, for the preserving of peace and security, by prevention of discord at home and hostility from abroad, and, when peace and security are lost, for the recovery of the same. And therefore,

Sixthly, it is annexed to the sovereignty, to be judge of what opinions and doctrines are averse, and what conducing to peace; and consequently, on what occasions, how far, and what men are to be trusted withal, in speaking to multitudes of people; and who shall examine the doctrines of all books before they be published. . . .

Seventhly, is annexed to the sovereignty, the whole power of prescribing the rules, whereby every man may know what goods he may enjoy, and what actions he may do, without being molested by any of his fellow-subjects; and this is it men call *propriety.* For before constitution of sovereign power, as hath already been shown, all men had right to all things; which necessarily causeth war; and therefore his propriety, being necessary to peace, and depending on sovereign power, is the act of that power, in order to the public peace. . . .

Eighthly, is annexed to the sovereignty, the right of judicature; that is to say, of hearing and deciding all controversies which may arise concerning law, either civil or natural, or concerning fact. For without the decision of controversies, there is no protection of one subject against the injuries of another. . . .

Ninthly, is annexed to the sovereignty, the right of making war and peace with other nations and commonwealths; that is to say, of judging when it is for the public good, and how great forces are to be assembled, armed, and paid for that end; and to levy money upon the subjects, to defray the expenses thereof. . . .

Tenthly, is annexed to the sovereignty, the choosing of all counsellors, ministers, magistrates, and offices, both in peace and war. For seeing the sovereign is charged with the end, which is the common peace and defense, he is understood to have power to use such means as he shall think most fit for his discharge.

Eleventhly, to the sovereign is committed the power of rewarding with riches, or honor, and of punishing with corporal or pecuniary punishment, or with ignominy, every subject according to the law he hath formerly made; or if there be no law made, according as he shall judge most to conduce to the encouraging of men to serve the commonwealth, or deterring of them from doing disservice to the same.

Lastly, considering what value men are naturally apt to set upon themselves, what respect they look for from others, and how little they value other men; from whence continually arise amongst them, emulation, quarrels, factions, and at last war, to the destroying of one another and diminution of their strength against a common enemy; it is necessary that there be laws of honor, and a public rate of the worth of such men as have deserved or are able to deserve well of the commonwealth; and that there be force in the hands of some or other, to put those laws in execution. . . .

These are the rights which make the essence of sovereignty, and which are the marks whereby a man may discern in what man, or assembly of men, the sovereign power is placed and resideth. For these are incommunicable and inseparable. . . .

CHAPTER XIX
OF THE SEVERAL KINDS OF COMMONWEALTH BY INSTITUTION, AND OF SUCCESSION TO THE SOVEREIGN POWER

The difference of commonwealths consisteth in the difference of the sovereign, or the person representative of all and every one of the multitude. And because the sovereignty is either in one man, or in an assembly of more than one; and into that assembly either every man hath right to enter, or not everyone, but certain men distinguished from the rest; it is manifest, there can be but three kinds of commonwealth. For the representative must needs be one man, or more; and if more, then it is the assembly of all, or but of a part. When the representative is one man, then is the commonwealth a *monarchy;* when an assembly of all that will come together, then it is a *democracy,* or popular commonwealth; when an assembly of a part only, then it is called an *aristocracy.* Other kind of commonwealth there can be none; for either one, or more, or all, must have the sovereign power, which I have shown to be indivisible, entire. . . .

CHAPTER XXI
OF THE LIBERTY OF SUBJECTS

Liberty, or freedom, signifieth, properly, the absence of opposition; by opposition, I mean external impediments of motion; and may be applied no less to irrational and inanimate creatures, than to rational. For whatsoever is so tied, or environed, as it cannot move but within a certain space, which space is determined by the opposition of some external body, we say it hath not liberty to go further. And so of all living creatures, whilst they are imprisoned or restrained, with walls or chains, and of the water whilst it is kept in by banks or vessels, that otherwise would spread itself into a larger space, we use to say, they are not at liberty to move in such manner, as without those external impediments they would. But when the impediment of motion is in the constitution of the thing itself, we use not to say it wants the liberty, but the power to move; as when a stone lieth still, or a man is fastened to his bed by sickness.

And according to this proper and generally received meaning of the word, *a 'freeman' is he that in those things which by his strength and wit he*

is able to do, is not hindered to do what he has a will to. But when the words
'free' and 'liberty' are applied to anything but bodies, they are abused; for that
which is not subject to motion is not subject to impediment; and therefore,
when it is said, for example, the way is free, no liberty of the way is signified,
but of those that walk in it without stop. And when we say a gift is free, there
is not meant any liberty of the gift, but of the giver, that was not bound by law
or covenant to give it. So when we speak 'freely,' it is not the liberty of voice or
pronunciation, but of the man, whom no law hath obliged to speak otherwise
than he did. Lastly, from the use of the word *free-will,* no liberty can be
inferred of the will, desire, or inclination, but the liberty of the man; which consisteth in this, that he finds no stop, in doing what he has the will, desire, or
inclination to do.

But as men, for the attaining of peace and conservation of themselves thereby, have made an artificial man, which we call a commonwealth; so also have they
made artificial chains, called *civil laws,* which they themselves, by mutual
covenants, have fastened, at one end, to the lips of that man or assembly to whom
they have given the sovereign power, and at the other end to their own ears.
These bonds, in their own nature but weak, may nevertheless be made to hold, by
the danger, though not by the difficulty, of breaking them.

Fear and liberty are consistent; as when a man throweth his goods into the
sea for *fear* the ship should sink, he doth it nevertheless very willingly, and may
refuse to do it if he will; it is therefore the action of one that was *free;* so a man
sometimes pays his debt, only for fear of imprisonment, which because nobody
hindered him from detaining, was the action of a man at *liberty.* And generally all
actions which men do in commonwealths, for fear of the law, are actions which
the doers had liberty to omit.

Liberty and necessity are consistent; as in the water, that hath not only
liberty, but a *necessity* of descending by the channel; so likewise in the actions
which men voluntarily do; which, because they proceed from their will, proceed from *liberty;* and yet, because every act of man's will, and every desire,
and inclination proceedeth from some cause, and that from another cause, in a
continual chain, whose first link is in the hand of God the first of all causes,
proceed from *necessity.* So that to him that could see the connection of those
causes, the necessity of all men's voluntary actions, would appear manifest.
And therefore God, that seeth and disposeth all things, seeth also that the liberty of man in doing what he will, is accompanied with the necessity of doing
that which God will, and no more nor less. For though men may do many
things which God does not command, nor is therefore author of them; yet they
can have no passion nor appetite to anything of which appetite God's will is
not the cause. And did not His will assure the *necessity* of man's will, and consequently of all that on man's will dependeth, the *liberty* of men would be a
contradiction, and impediment to the omnipotence and liberty of God. And
this shall suffice, as to the matter in hand, of that natural liberty, which only is
properly called liberty.

In relation to these bonds only it is, that I am to speak now of the *liberty
of subjects.* For seeing there is no commonwealth in the world wherein there

be rules enough set down, for the regulating of all the actions and words of men; as being a thing impossible; it followeth necessarily that in all kinds of actions by the laws pretermitted, men have the liberty of doing what their own reasons shall suggest, for the most profitable to themselves. For if we take liberty in the proper sense for corporal liberty; that is to say, freedom from chains and prison; it were very absurd for men to clamor as they do, for the liberty they so manifestly enjoy. Again, if we take liberty for an exemption from laws, it is no less absurd for men to demand as they do, that liberty by which all other men may be masters of their lives. And yet, as absurd as it is, this is it they demand; not knowing that the laws are of no power to protect them, without a sword in the hands of a man, or men, to cause those laws to be put in execution. The liberty of a subject lieth therefore only in those things which in regulating their actions, the sovereign hath pretermitted; such as is the liberty to buy, and sell, and otherwise contract with one another; to choose their own abode, their own diet, their own trade of life, and institute their children as they themselves think fit; and the like.

Nevertheless we are not to understand that by such liberty, the sovereign power of life and death is either abolished or limited. For it has been already shown that nothing the sovereign representative can do to a subject, on what pretense soever, can properly be called injustice, or injury; because every subject is author of every act the sovereign doth; so that he never wanteth right to anything, otherwise than as he himself is the subject of God, and bound thereby to observe the laws of nature. . . .

The liberty whereof there is so frequent and honorable mention in the histories and philosophy of the ancient Greeks and Romans, and in the writings and discourse of those that from them have received all their learning in the politics, is not the liberty of particular men, but the liberty of the commonwealth; which is the same with that which every man then should have, if there were no civil laws nor commonwealth at all. And the effects of it also be the same. For as amongst masterless men, there is perpetual war of every man against his neighbor; no inheritance, to transmit to the son, nor to expect from the father; no propriety of goods or lands; no security; but a full and absolute liberty in every particular man; so in states, and commonwealths not dependent on one another, every commonwealth, not every man, has an absolute liberty, to do what it shall judge—that is to say, what that man, or assembly that representeth it, shall judge—most conducting to their benefit. But withal, they live in the condition of a perpetual war, and upon the confines of battle, with their frontiers armed, and cannons planted against their neighbors round about. The Athenians and Romans were free; that is, free commonwealths; not that any particular men had the liberty to resist their own representative, but that their representative had the liberty to resist or invade other people. There is written on the turrets of the city of Lucca in great characters at this day, the word *libertas;* yet no man can thence infer that a particular man has more liberty or immunity from the service of the commonwealth here than in Constantinople. Whether a commonwealth be monarchical or popular, the freedom is still the same. . . .

Review Questions

1. Discuss Hobbes' intention to deduce a philosophical system beginning with motion or, more precisely, matter-in-motion.
2. Describe the natural state of man according to Hobbes.
3. For Hobbes, what reasons do human beings have to seek society?
4. What, for Hobbes, is the nature of the Contract prerequisite to society?
5. In Hobbes' view, why is there a need for a Commonwealth, or State?
6. As Hobbes describes it, do individuals have rights in a Commonwealth? Do sovereigns?
7. Why is Hobbes so concerned with squaring his views on the State with the Bible?

Suggestions for Further Reading

Gaskin, J. C., ed. *Leviathan.* New York, Oxford University Press, 1996.
Richards, P. *Hobbes.* Baltimore, Penguin, 1956.
Tuck, R. *Hobbes.* New York, Oxford University Press, 1989.

15

John Locke (1632–1704)

Empiricism

The word *empiricism* or the adjectival forms *empiric* and *empirical* come from the Greek word *empeirikos,* which refers to an experiment or trial. Today it generally means "based on direct observation or experimentation," such as in the statement "the natural sciences are empirical" or "one of the branches of psychology is empirical psychology." When used in philosophy, it still bears the idea of directness inasmuch as it refers to knowledge gained directly from *experience,* but it refers mainly to *sense* experience. Pure positions, however, are seldom, if ever, held in philosophy because they represent such extremes that they become untenable; if, therefore, rationalism and empiricism are opposed to each other, it does not follow that the rationalist is so committed to the deductive method that he discounts sense experience entirely, or that the empiricist is so committed to sense experience that he rejects the deductive method entirely. The difference between them is rather a question of emphasis: The more the sense aspect is stressed to the exclusion of the deductive, the more empirical the position is; the more the deductive aspect is stressed to the exclusion of the sense, the more rationalist the position is. The position taken, therefore, is considered extreme or moderate depending on the degree of emphasis.

John Locke

The ascending priority of experience in England at this time can be seen in John Locke's rejection of innate ideas, his reliance on sensation as the beginning of all knowledge, and his hesitancy regarding the metaphysical tendency of the human mind. All of these clearly move him away from continental rationalism and indicate his role in shaping modern empiricism.

He was born in 1632 near Bristol, England. Educated early in classical studies, he entered Oxford where, on top of his dislike for Aristotle and scholastic philosophy as taught there, he grew enthusiastic over the new scientific spirit. Though at one time he evinced an interest in becoming a clergyman, he never did, but he never lost his fondness for theology and was never anything but a devout Christian.

Under the patronage of the Earl of Shaftesbury, Locke was able to pursue his intellectual interests, one of which was the reading of Descartes, whose clarity and logic fascinated him and, though he reacted against some basic tenets of Cartesianism, such as innate ideas, he subscribed to others, and it may well be that his consequent interest in knowledge, which culminated in his masterwork on human understanding, began with his study of Descartes.

Probably for health reasons, as well as the uncertain future of his patron, Locke went for several years to Montpellier, France, where, among other activities, his chief philosophical occupation was to continue working on his *Essay*, which he had begun years before. He then returned to England and renewed his relationship with Shaftesbury, but when his patron's political star began falling, Locke wisely made off to Holland as a voluntary exile, remaining there until after the accession of King William in 1688. Naturally Locke fell under suspicion too and, when King Charles II stripped him of his studentship at Christ Church, he was even obliged to go into hiding. Meanwhile he was developing his thoughts on government, political liberty, and religious tolerance, for which he was achieving public recognition, so that upon his return to London in 1689, he was acknowledged and esteemed as a defender of William's ascendancy.

After his return, for the sake of the peace and quiet his health required, he accepted the invitation of Sir Francis and Lady Masham to retire to their family home at Oates, about twenty miles outside London, where he lived from 1691. He never stopped working. He edited the unfinished manuscript of his long-time friend Robert Boyle under the title *General History of the Air*. He gave more attention to theological questions, which he had always enjoyed but which was given impetus by his friendship in Holland with the liberal theologian Philip von Limborch; finally, he became involved in a now famous controversy with Bishop Edward Stillingfleet over his philosophical-theological views.

Locke died in 1704. His epitaph, which he himself had written, reads in part: "Stay, Traveller. Nearby lies John Locke. If you ask what kind of man he was, he answers that he lived contentedly in his modest way. He gave himself to learning for one purpose only, to pursue the truth. This you may learn from his writings, which will tell you about him more faithfully than the suspect praise of an epitaph." Locke's more important works are *Two Treatises of Civil Government* (1689), *An Essay Concerning Human Understanding* (1690), *Letters on Toleration* (1689–93), and *The Reasonableness of Christianity* (1695).

The Philosophy of Knowledge

The questions of *what* we know and *how* we know are focal points of entire philosophies from pre-Socratic times, through the Middle Ages, and down to the seventeenth century. At this point the consideration of knowledge again achieves primary importance, and Descartes' preoccupation with certitude becomes the point at which modern philosophy's steady exploration of epistemological problems begins to take hold. In this exploration, Locke's attention was given to the kind of inquiry that later became known as *criticism*. Certainly Locke saw the problem inherent in the Cartesian position of how, given mind and body as the two constituents of reality, mind comes to know things outside itself, and Locke had enough common sense to avoid the same pitfall. He began his study of knowledge in an informal way. In one of his many discussions with friends, the subject of knowledge came up and led to some perplexities that, as Locke tells his readers, made it "necessary to examine our abilities, and see what *objects* our understandings were, or were not, fitted to deal with." He thought that all he would have to say on the subject could be contained in one sheet of paper, but "new discoveries led me still on, and so it grew insensibly to the bulk it now appears in." The "bulk" is, of course, *An Essay Concerning Human Understanding,* on which the author spent twenty years of his life. Though he himself was aware that it was overwritten and not at every point thought through, it is a monument in the history of epistemology, and, in the end, a testimony to the mystery of human knowledge. Locke was convinced that the human mind could arrive at an understanding of things sufficient for man to be human: The "candle" in us, he says, "shines light enough for all our purposes." And if we lack certitude in some respects, we have sufficient probability "to govern all our concernments."

Locke's goal is stated succinctly in the opening line of the introduction: "Since it is the *understanding* that sets men above the rest of sensible beings, and gives them all the advantage and dominion which he has over them, it is certainly a subject, even for its nobleness, worth our labour to inquire into." The plan of the *Essay,* spelled out in four books, centers on three main considerations: the origin of ideas, the use of language, and the different kinds of assent given by the mind. The first of these considerations is handled negatively in Book I, inasmuch as innate ideas must be rejected; therefore, a method is laid out in Book II to discover how our ideas originate. Book III is committed to language, the analysis of words, terms, and names that "the mind makes use of for the understanding of things, or conveying its knowledge to others." The assent of the mind is founded on evidence, so that the first half of Book IV is devoted to the basis and limits of knowledge that warrant certitude; the second half considers other warrants for assent, namely, faith and opinion.

Locke uses the term *idea* in its broadest possible sense to stand for whatever the mind thinks about; it is the term that "serves best to stand for whatsoever is the *object* of the understanding when a man thinks"; Locke therefore uses it "to express whatever is meant by *phantasm, notion, species,* or *whatever it is which the mind can be employed about in thinking.*" He later hesitatingly refers to ideas as "instruments, or materials of our knowledge."

Mind: No Innate Ideas but an "Empty Cabinet"

In holding that these "objects" *cannot be innate,* Locke comes down strongly on the side of the empiricist against the widely received doctrine of Descartes; knowledge simply does not originate in ideas already possessed by man *before* experience. If any truths were innate, they would be universal. But speculative truths are not universal: Children do not know them, nor people of unsound mind, nor the uneducated; this fact alone would disavow innate knowledge. Even more dramatic is the situation of moral principles, for there are individuals who show very little moral sense, and indeed, there are whole nations whose moral posture is, in some matters, completely reprehensible to the Western mind; these opposing positions cannot both be right: "Whatever practical principle is innate, cannot but be known to every one to be just and good. It is therefore little less than a contradiction to suppose, that whole nations of men should, both in their professions and practice, unanimously and universally give the lie to what, by the most invincible evidence, every one of them knew to be true, right, and good."

The mind, as Locke goes on to describe in Book II, comes into the world as an "empty cabinet" waiting to be filled, or a "white paper" (in other terminology, a *tabula rasa,* a clean slate) to be written upon: "Whence has [the mind] all the *materials* of reason and knowledge? To this I answer, in one word, from *experience.*" Experience is had by way of sensation and reflection, the two "fountains of knowledge." The senses convey to the mind whatever it requires to produce perceptions of sensible qualities like yellow, heat, soft, and bitter: "This great source of most of the ideas we have, depending wholly upon our senses, and derived by them to the understanding, I call *sensation.*" Inward operations such as perception, thinking, doubting, believing, reasoning, knowing and willing the mind is aware of itself as having, and is aware that they are different from, though follow upon, ideas of sensation: "I call this *reflection,* the ideas it affords being such only as the mind gets by reflecting on its own operations within itself."

Kinds of Ideas Based on Sensation and Reflection

Locke's analysis of the kinds of ideas we have is extensive and leads to many distinctions and divisions, but the chief division is into *simple* and *complex* ideas. Simple ideas are those that are "passively received," that is, ideas the mind receives, or is passive in—*passive* meaning involuntary or spontaneous: "In this part the understanding is merely passive; and whether or no it will have these beginnings, and as it were materials of knowledge, is not in its own power." Simple ideas are "unmixed" or "uncompounded," each being but "one uniform appearance, or conception in the mind." Such ideas are supplied either by sensation or reflection and are characterized by the unmistakable impressions their objects make upon us. If supplied by sensation, they can come through one sense only, "ideas of one sense," such as white, sour, solid, and so on; or through two senses, namely, sight and touch, such as space, figure, rest, and motion. If supplied by reflection, the simple ideas are those of perception or thinking (understanding) and volition or willing (will), such as remembrance, discerning, reasoning, knowledge, and faith. Lastly, simple ideas can originate from sensation and reflection together, as in pleasure or delight, pain or uneasiness, power, existence, and unity. Simple ideas, taken all in all, are original and unanalyzable and are therefore the basic materials from which *all other knowledge* the mind has "is made." No wonder Locke referred to sensation and reflection, the sources of simple ideas, as the two fountains of knowledge.

Complex ideas enter as ideas that are made, for the mind, contrary to its passive posture in receiving simple ideas, is active in producing them. The mind produces them out of simple ideas and does so in one of three ways: by combining several simple ideas, by separating them from other ideas accompanying them in their real existence (abstraction), or by placing them, as it were, side by side (relationship). Although there is an infinite variety of complex ideas, they can be classified into ideas of modes, substances, or relations—for example, beauty, gratitude, number, infinity, cause and effect, identity and diversity, and moral relations. It is clear that Locke's account of the origin of our ideas is painstaking and thorough, though there are some aspects of his analysis that will be subject to further discussion later inasmuch as they have a special bearing on empiricism.

Any philosopher who talks about ideas must talk about words as well. As he moves to Book III, Locke tells us "that there is so close a connection between ideas and words . . . that it is impossible to speak clearly and distinctly of our knowledge, which all consists in propositions, without considering, first, the nature, use, and signification of Language." When Locke later evaluates the importance of signs, he ascribes the major role to words that "the mind makes use of for the understanding of things."

As *signs,* words may well stand for things, but their first signification is of ideas; if ideas are "invisible," words are "sensible" and are referred to as *marks:* Words are "sensible marks of ideas; and the ideas they stand for are their proper and immediate signification." Inasmuch as ideas represent things, or may represent them, so do words. Things, however, exist "in particular," not "in general," and so if we were to use, for ourselves or for others when we try to communicate, different words for each thing that exists, we would speak only with great difficulty or not at all. To get around this problem beyond using particular words, the mind uses *general* words, like *horse,* by collecting individual things into "bundles" according to their similarities and not according to anything *real* represented by them; the mind simply makes "for the easier and readier improvement, and communication" of knowledge. These considerations not only show the ingenuity of language, along with its imperfections and abuse, but also, for Locke, how much more work had to be done on the doctrine of signs, including both ideas and words, which would perhaps "afford us another sort of logic and critic, than what we have been hitherto acquainted with."

Threefold Knowledge of Existence

The first half of Book IV takes up at last the question of *knowledge,* which, of course, is directly tied in with ideas and which Locke defines as "the perception of the connexion of and agreement, or disagreement and repugnancy of any of our ideas." Though there are several kinds of agreement and disagreement, there are only three *degrees of knowledge:* intuitive, demonstrative, and sensitive. *Intuitive* knowledge is the perception of the "agreement of two ideas *immediately by themselves,* without the intervention of any other"; thus, we know that three is greater than two and that a circle is not a triangle. This degree of knowledge is basic; the certainty of all knowledge depends on it. *Demonstrative* knowledge is achieved when the agreement or disagreement is not immediately apparent but requires the intervention of other ideas, such as the idea that three angles of a triangle are equal to two right angles. Demonstrative knowledge is certain, but its certainty is not as readily available as that of intuitive knowledge. *Sensitive* knowledge offers a special problem to Locke to which we shall return. It is the perception of "the particular existence of finite being" outside us; that is, we are certain that the idea we receive from an external object is in our minds, and to that extent sensitive knowledge shares the intuitive; but that is the end of our certainty here, for we do not know what they are. When the dimension of real existence is added, Locke wants to extend "certain knowledge" (agreement of ideas among themselves) to "*real* and certain knowledge" when there is an agreement between ideas and reality.

Other philosophers might stop here in saying that what we know is true, but Locke makes another distinction in holding that *truth* lies in the propositions that express agreement or disagreement; and when we perceive the relationship, it is knowledge of the truth. Here again, the idea of animal and the idea of the mythical centaur agree with one another, and the proposition "centaur is animal" is *not really* true, only verbally so. Real truth exists only where there is an agreement between the ideas in proposition and existence in nature.

Whatever falls short of knowledge, and yet is embraced by us with assurance, is called *faith* or *opinion.* At work is probability, not proof, and the more probable the grounds are, the more persuasive they are for our assent; probability supplies the defect of our knowledge. If the probability is solidly grounded on our experience or the experience of others, our confidence is produced and our assent is warranted, but in no case can faith and reason be applied to each other, and in every case faith must be reasonable. To that extent, to believe in the word of God is reasonable.

It was previously indicated that more ought to be said about certain points of Locke's epistemology, one of which turns on the question of the *objectivity* of the simple ideas of sensation, that is, those ideas we gain through one or more of our senses, like color, taste, figure, and rest. As described in Chapter Eight, Book II, Locke distinguishes between ideas and *qualities:* Qualities in bodies have the power to produce ideas of themselves in us. When these qualities are inseparable from the body they are found in, they are called *primary* qualities, and the corresponding ideas of solidity, extension, figure, motion, and number they cause in us are "ideas of primary qualities"; regardless of the changes a body undergoes, it will still have solidity, extension, and so on. These qualities *really* reside in the object, and our ideas are faithful resemblances of them. But *secondary* qualities are vastly different, for though they produce sensations (color, taste, etc.) in us, they are *not really* found in the objects that cause them, and therefore do not resemble them.

The distinction between primary and secondary qualities was not original with Locke, but others who had used it, like Galileo and Boyle, did so in a scientific sense, and no particular problem occurred. When, however, Locke defines idea as "the immediate object of perception, thought or understanding," the question naturally arises, how do we know what connection ideas have with things in order to make a valid distinction between primary and secondary qualities, or even whether there is a connection *at all* between ideas and things? Two reactions to this question are possible: either to move in the direction of idealism, as Berkeley did, or to advance a relentless brand of empiricism, as Hume did. In either case, the response is precisely to a soft spot in Locke's epistemology as to how sense experience causes the mind to achieve a satisfactory relationship with real existence.

Locke's further distinction between simple and complex ideas was, as we have seen, necessary to his philosophy of knowledge. In assigning a basic role to sensation, he joined many other philosophers of the past, but he went beyond them in letting it preside over a domain hitherto reserved to metaphysics. He maintained, we should recall, that ideas contain *real truth* when they agree with something *existing in nature,* and when he proceeded to speak of "our threefold knowledge of existence," he was speaking of our knowledge of man, God, and "other things": "I say, then, that we have knowledge of our *own* existence by intuition; of the existence of *God* by demonstration; and of *other things* by sensation." My own existence is so clear that it needs no proof and is established even in doubting. With regard to God, the fact that there is at least one actual being that had a beginning is evidence of an eternal Being. Knowledge of other things is obtained by sensation. Note that the order of discovering the entities man, God, and other things is exactly that of Descartes.

But it is precisely here that an important part of Locke's empiricism is located. The knowledge of ourselves by intuition and of God by demonstration is not peculiar to Locke, but the knowledge of other things by sensation is. Take *substance,* for example; Locke writes extensively on its meaning, showing that where there is "white" there must be "something white," even though we do not sense it. Locke *knows* that God exists and that man exists; however, he does not *know* that substance exists because it is not an object of sensation—it simply cannot be one of those "other things." Yet there is reason to *suppose* substance to be real. In a now famous hypothesis, Locke tries to show the limitations of our knowledge by offering the possibility that *matter* can *think:* "it is not harder to conceive how thinking should exist without matter, than how matter should think." Later on, in talking of

God's power, Locke writes, "We have the ideas of *matter* and *thinking,* but possibly shall never be able to know whether any mere material being thinks or no," and then says that God, in His omnipotence, may be able to bring it about. The human mind, then, cannot move with certainty to the conclusion that the existence of substance is required by the existence of qualities, a conclusion that lies at the heart of metaphysics. Locke did not push this line of reasoning to its ultimate, as David Hume later did; but it is clear that he is already paving the way for the disenfranchisement of metaphysics, which, through Hume, culminates in the antimetaphysical stance of Immanuel Kant and generations of philosophers after him.

So, for Locke, the scope of knowledge is to be seen in the high, though not absolute, priority given to sensation, which causes the mind, already in sure possession of the knowledge of God's existence and its own, to be unknowing before those things whose existence it may suppose but that sense experience does not support.

By comparing rationalism and empiricism in general terms, the meaning of Locke's commitment to sensation becomes clearer. Epistemologically, rationalism and empiricism can be differentiated by the *direction of movement* in the process of knowing. When we come to know something, there is a movement involved, a process whereby we go from one state to another, from not knowing to knowing. Rationalism sees this movement as flowing from the mind to things; that is, the mind tells us, prior to experience, what things are. But for empiricism, the movement flows in the reverse direction, from things to mind; that is, in our experience, things tell us what they are. The rationalist tends to construct reality, to favor the deductive method, to think more speculatively, to sponsor ideals, to build utopias, to generate an idealistic ethics, and to suspect the body in its performance. The empiricist, on the other hand, tends to accept reality as it is given in sense experience, to favor induction, to think more pragmatically, to foster politics, to see ethics as utilitarian or behaviorist, and to hold the intellect's claims at bay. We have seen how Descartes, the exemplar of all rationalists, turned to the mind first and followed its movement mathematically to the nature of man, the existence of God, and the external world, employing thereby an epistemology that alienated sense knowledge. However faithful Descartes thought he was to the claims of his rational side, he rejected the immediate claims of his sensitive side and could never, therefore, develop a vehicle to prove the validity of knowledge as a whole. With Locke, the pendulum started to swing the other way and completed its arc in the next generation with Hume; thus, as we have seen, the claims of metaphysics were firmly held to be without merit.

Philosophy of Government

John Locke's influence on the philosophy of government is no less profound than his wide-ranging influence on the philosophy of knowledge. Even though his *Two Treatises of Civil Government* were issued in part to justify the ascendancy of King William after the Glorious Revolution of 1688, they stand on their own among the great documents of modern times, supporting the notion that there is no power to govern without the consent of the governed, a concept that was politically alive for some years before Locke and given earlier expression by Thomas Hobbes. Just as the political situation in England a generation before Hobbes prompted him to publish *Leviathan,* so the political situation at the time of Locke prompted him to publish the *Treatises* in 1689, stating in the preface his desire to "establish the throne of our great restorer, our present King William; to make good his title in consent of the people . . . and to justify to the world the people of England, whose love of their just and natural rights, with their resolution to preserve them, saved the nation, when it was on the very brink of slavery and ruin."

Locke's political genius lay in organizing ideas currently abroad and honing them, according to his own insights, into a persuasive essay on government *by choice* on the part of the people. Though there is much to be found in the first of the *Two Treatises,* it resembles more closely a tract for the times, and so it is the *Second Treatise* one turns to as the main source of his political philosophy. If people arrive, by consent, at a new state of affairs for themselves, Locke first wants to clarify the prior state, and so he begins, like Hobbes, with a discussion of the *state of nature.* The state of nature is a state of perfect freedom in which men may do as they are wont, "within the bounds of the law of nature," independent of other men. All men are equal by nature, no one having more power or jurisdiction than any other, unless, Locke adds, by some clearly defined divine appointment; this equality of men is the absolute foundation of mutual love from which all maxims of justice and charity are derived.

Yet the state of nature as the state of freedom is not a state of license, of "uncontrollable liberty," for all of our actions are governed by the law of nature, which is *reason* itself: "and reason, which is that law, teaches all mankind who will but consult it, that, being all equal and independent, no one ought to harm another in his life, health, liberty or possessions." What is reasonable is in accordance with the law; what is unreasonable is not. Under this rubric anyone may mete out punishment and reparation against a criminal, whose crime is to act contrary to the law of nature by invading the life of the other.

So described, Locke, who has Hobbes clearly in mind without naming him, does not share his predecessor's pessimism regarding the natural state of man and refuses to liken the state of nature to the state of war. Yet, the state of nature, not being paradise, requires a political society to uplift it: "civil government is the proper remedy for the inconveniences of the state of nature"; the word *inconveniences* is a disingenuous understatement, for, as Locke shows later on, a political society of some kind is necessary if only to restrain the willfulness of men in trying to overreach each other.

In extending his remarks to the family, Locke affirms, again contrary to Hobbes, that society is natural to man. Even though the family requires a "voluntary compact" between a man and a woman to begin with, it is a society given by nature and one into which a person is born. Man in society is part of man's experience, and, for Locke, so much so that he opens his discussions on civil society by remarking, "God having made man such a creature, that in his own judgment it was not good for him to be alone, put him under strong obligations of necessity, convenience, and inclination to drive him into society, as well as fitted him with understanding and language to continue and enjoy it."

When it comes to a civil society, because by nature all men are free, equal, and independent, there can be no subjection to a political power except by consent, by the *common consent* of all those who agree, not so much to surrender their individual liberty of the state of nature as to carry it over into a new state. If Locke looks to an "original compact," it is not to be taken in a chronological sense but rather in a conceptual sense, for he is trying to establish a rational basis for empowering a government. The power so consented to is not absolute, for absolute power can wreak incalculable harm, but just so much as allows men "the mutual preservation of their lives, liberties, and estates, which I call by the general name, property." Consent is a contract between person and person, not between person and king; between person and king is the relationship of *trust,* that is, the community entrusts the government with the duty to work for the good of the community; the government is the trustee of the community: "To this end it is that men give up all their natural power to the society which they enter into, and the community put the legislative power into such hands as they think fit, with this trust, that they shall be governed by declared laws, or else their peace, quiet, and property will still be at the same uncertainty as it was in the state of nature."

There are many points of government that Locke does not consider, such as the rights of minorities, or does not satisfactorily cover, such as how successive generations of people give their consent, but all the ideas just discussed, together with further ideas on majority rule, the separation of powers, the right to change governments, the right to depose a government bent on enslavement, and separation of church and state, became part of common political thinking in the eighteenth century and created a rich legacy for those who would establish constitutional governments, especially the Founding Fathers of the United States.

READINGS

From Essay Concerning Human Understanding

INTRODUCTION

1. Since it is the *understanding* that sets man above the rest of sensible beings, and gives him all the advantage and dominion which he has over them; it is certainly a subject, even for its nobleness, worth our labour to inquire into. The understanding, like the eye, whilst it makes us see and perceive all other things, takes no notice of itself; and it requires art and pains to set it at a distance and make it its own object. But whatever be the difficulties that lie in the way of this inquiry; whatever it be that keeps us so much in the dark to ourselves; sure I am that all the light we can let in upon our minds, all the acquaintance we can make with our own understandings, will not only be very pleasant, but bring us great advantage, in directing our thoughts in the search of other things.

2. This, therefore, being my purpose—to inquire into the original, certainty, and extent of *human knowledge,* together with the grounds and degrees of *belief, opinion, and assent;*—I shall not at present meddle with the physical consideration of the mind; or trouble myself to examine wherein its essence consists; or by what motions of our spirits or alterations of our bodies we come to have any *sensation* by our organs, or any *ideas* in our understandings; and whether those ideas do in their formation, any or all of them, depend on matter or not. These are speculations which, however curious and entertaining, I shall decline, as lying out of my way in the design I am now upon. It shall suffice to my present purpose, to consider the discerning faculties of a man, as they are employed about the objects which they have to do with. And I shall imagine I have not wholly misemployed myself in the thoughts I shall have on this occasion, if, in this historical, plain method, I can give any account of the ways whereby our understandings come to attain those notions of things we have; and can set down any measures of the certainty of our knowledge; or the grounds of those persuasions which are to be found amongst men, so various, different, and wholly contradictory; and yet asserted somewhere or other with such assurance and confidence, that he that shall take a view of the opinions of mankind, observe their opposition, and at the same time consider the fondness and devotion wherewith they are embraced, the resolution and eagerness wherewith they are maintained, may perhaps have reason to suspect, that either there is no such thing as truth at all, or that mankind hath no sufficient means to attain a certain knowledge of it.

3. It is therefore worth while to search out the bounds between opinion and knowledge; and examine by what measures, in things whereof we have no certain knowledge, we ought to regulate our assent and moderate our persuasion. In order whereunto I shall pursue this following method:—

First, I shall inquire into the original of those *ideas,* notions, or whatever else you please to call them, which a man observes, and is conscious to himself he has in his mind; and the ways whereby the understanding comes to be furnished with them.

Secondly, I shall endeavour to show what *knowledge* the understanding hath by those ideas; and the certainty, evidence, and extent of it.

Thirdly, I shall make some inquiry into the nature and grounds of *faith or opinion:* whereby I mean that assent which we give to any proposition as true, of whose truth yet we have no certain knowledge. And here we shall have occasion to examine the reasons and degrees of *assent.*

BOOK I

Chapter I
No Innate Speculative Principles

1. It is an established opinion amongst some men, that there are in the understanding certain innate principles; some primary notions, κοιναι ∈ υυοιαι, characters, as it were stamped upon the mind of man; which the soul receives in its very first being, and brings into the world with it. It would be sufficient to convince unprejudiced

readers of the falseness of this supposition, if I should only show (as I hope I shall in the following parts of this Discourse) how men, barely by the use of their natural faculties, may attain to all the knowledge they have, without the help of any innate impressions; and may arrive at certainty, without any such original notions or principles. For I imagine any one will easily grant that it would be impertinent to suppose the ideas of colours innate in a creature to whom God hath given sight, and a power to receive them by the eyes from external objects: and no less unreasonable would it be to attribute several truths to the impressions of nature, and innate characters, when we may observe in ourselves faculties fit to attain as easy and certain knowledge of them as if they were originally imprinted on the mind.

But because a man is not permitted without censure to follow his own thoughts in the search of truth, when they lead him ever so little out of the common road. I shall set down the reasons that made me doubt of the truth of that opinion, as an excuse for my mistake, if I be in one; which I leave to be considered by those who, with me, dispose themselves to embrace truth wherever they find it.

2. There is nothing more commonly taken for granted than that there are certain *principles,* both *speculative* and *practical,* (for they speak of both), universally agreed upon by all mankind: which therefore, they argue, must needs be the constant impressions which the souls of men receive in their first beings, and which they bring into the world with them, as necessarily and really as they do any of their inherent faculties.

3. This argument, drawn from universal consent, has this misfortune in it, that if it were true in matter of fact, that there were certain truths wherein all mankind agreed, it would not prove them innate, if there can be any other way shown how men may come to that universal agreement, in the things they do consent in, which I presume may be done.

4. But, which is worse, this argument of universal consent, which is made use of to prove innate principles, seems to me a demonstration that there are none such: because there are none to which all mankind give an universal assent. I shall begin with the speculative, and instance in those magnified principles of demonstration, 'Whatsoever is, is,' and 'It is impossible for the same thing to be and not to be'; which, of all others, I think have the most allowed title to innate. These have so settled a reputation of maxims universally received, that it will no doubt be thought strange if any one should seem to question it. But yet I take liberty to say, that these propositions are so far from having an universal assent, that there are a great part of mankind to whom they are not so much as known.

5. For, first, it is evident, that all children and idiots have not the least apprehension or thought of them. And the want of that is enough to destroy that universal assent which needs be the necessary concomitant of all innate truths: it seeming to me near a contradiction to say, that there are truths imprinted on the soul, which it perceives or understands not: imprinting, if it signify anything, being nothing else but the making certain truths to be perceived. For to imprint anything on the mind without the mind's perceiving it, seems to me hardly intelligible. If therefore children and idiots have souls, have minds, with those impressions upon them, *they* must unavoidably perceive them, and necessarily know and assent to these truths; which since they do not, it is evident that there are no such impressions. For if they

are not notions naturally imprinted, how can they be innate? and if they are notions imprinted, how can they be unknown? To say a notion is imprinted on the mind, and yet at the same time to say, that the mind is ignorant of it, and never yet took notice of it, is to make this impression nothing. No proposition can be said to be in the mind which it never yet knew, which it was never yet conscious of. For if any one may, then, by the same reason, all propositions that are true, and the mind is capable ever of assenting to, may be said to be in the mind, and to be imprinted: since, if any one can be said to be in the mind, which it never yet knew, it must be only because it is capable of knowing it; and so the mind is of all truths it ever shall know. Ney, thus truths may be imprinted on the mind which it never did, nor ever shall know; for a man may live long, and die at last in ignorance of many truths which his mind was capable of knowing, and that with certainty. . . .

Chapter II
No Innate Practical Principles

2. Whether there be any such moral principles, wherein all men do agree, I appeal to any who have been but moderately conversant in the history of mankind, and looked abroad beyond the smoke of their own chimneys. Where is that practical truth that is universally received, without doubt or question, as it must be if innate? *Justice,* and keeping of contracts, is that which most men seem to agree in. This is a principle which is thought to extend itself to the dens of thieves, and the confederacies of the greatest villains; and they who have gone furthest towards the putting off of humanity itself, keep faith and rules of justice one with another. I grant that outlaws themselves do this one amongst another: but it is without receiving these as the innate laws of nature. They practise them as rules of convenience within their own communities: but it is impossible to conceive that he embraces justice as a practical principle, who acts fairly with his fellow-highwayman, and at the same time plunders or kills the next honest man he meets with. Justice and truth are the common ties of society; and therefore even outlaws and robbers, who break with all the world besides, must keep faith and rules of equity amongst themselves; or else they cannot hold together. But will any one say, that those that live by fraud or rapine have innate principles of truth and justice which they allow and assent to?

BOOK II

Chapter I
Of Ideas in General and Their Original

1. Every man being conscious to himself that he thinks; and that which his mind is applied about whilst thinking being the ideas that are there, it is past doubt that men have in their minds several ideas,—such as are those expressed by the words *whiteness, hardness, sweetness, thinking, motion, man, elephant, army, drunkenness,* and others: it is in the first place then to be inquired, *How he comes by them?*

2. Let us then suppose the mind to be, as we say, white paper, void of all characters, without any ideas:—How comes it to be furnished? Whence comes it

by that vast store which the busy and boundless fancy of man has painted on it with an almost endless variety? Whence has it all the *materials* of reason and knowledge? To this I answer, in one word, from EXPERIENCE. In that all our knowledge if founded; and from that it ultimately derives itself. Our observation employed either, about external sensible objects, or about the internal operations of our minds perceived and reflected on by ourselves, is that which supplies our understandings with all the *materials* of thinking. These two are the fountains of knowledge, from whence all the ideas we have, or can naturally have, do spring.

3. First, our Senses, conversant about particular sensible objects, do convey into the mind several distinct perceptions of things, according to those various ways wherein those objects do affect them. And thus we come by those *ideas* we have of *yellow, white, heat, cold, soft, hard, bitter, sweet,* and all those which we call sensible qualities; which when I say the senses convey into the mind, I mean, they from external objects convey into the mind what produces there those perceptions. This great source of most of the ideas we have, depending wholly upon our senses, and derived by them to the understanding, I call SENSATION.

4. Secondly, the other fountain from which experience furnisheth the understanding with ideas is,—the perception of the operations of our own mind within us, as it is employed about the ideas it has got;—which operations, when the soul comes to reflect on and consider, do furnish the understanding with another set of ideas, which could not be had from things without. And such are *perception, thinking, doubting, believing, reasoning, knowing, willing,* and all the different actings of our minds;—which we being conscious of, and observing in ourselves, do from these receive into our understandings as distinct ideas as we do from bodies affecting our senses. This source of ideas every man has wholly in himself; and though it be not sense, as having nothing to do with external objects, yet it is very like it, and might properly enough be called internal sense. But as I call the other Sensation, so I call this REFLECTION, the ideas it affords being such only as the mind gets by reflecting on its own operations within itself. By reflection then, in the following part of this discourse, I would be understood to mean, that notice which the mind takes of its own operations, and the manner of them, by reason whereof there come to be ideas of these operations in the understanding. These two, I say, viz. external material things, as the objects of SENSATION, and the operations of our own minds within, as the objects of REFLECTION, are to me the only originals from whence all our ideas take their beginnings. The term *operations* here I use in a large sense, as comprehending not barely the actions of the mind about its ideas, but some sort of passions arising sometimes from them, such as is the satisfaction or uneasiness arising from any thought.

Chapter II
Of Simple Ideas

1. The better to understand the nature, manner, and extent of our knowledge, one thing is carefully to be observed concerning the ideas we have; and that is, that some of them are *simple* and some *complex.*

Though the qualities that affect our senses are, in the things themselves, so united and blended, that there is no separation, no distance between them; yet it is plain, the ideas they produce in the mind enter by the senses simple and unmixed. For, though the sight and touch often take in from the same object, at the same time, different ideas;—as a man sees at once motion and colour; the hand feels softness and warmth in the same piece of wax: yet the simple ideas thus united in the same subject, are as perfectly distinct as those that come in by different senses. The coldness and hardness which a man feels in a piece of ice being as distinct ideas in the mind as the smell and whiteness of a lily; or as the taste of sugar, and smell of a rose. And there is nothing can be plainer to a man than the clear and distinct perception he has of those simple ideas; which, being each in itself uncompounded, contains in it nothing but *one uniform appearance, or conception in the mind,* and is not distinguishable into different ideas.

2. These simple ideas, the materials of all our knowledge, are suggested and furnished to the mind only by those two ways above mentioned, Viz. sensation and reflection.

Chapter III
Of Simple Ideas of Sense

1. The better to conceive the ideas we receive from sensation, it may not be amiss for us to consider them, in reference to the different ways whereby they make their approaches to our minds, and make themselves perceivable by us.

First, then. There are some which come into our minds *by one sense only.*

Secondly. There are others that convey themselves into the mind *by more senses than one.*

Thirdly. Others that are had from *reflection only.*

Fourthly. There are some that make themselves way, and are suggested to the mind *by all the ways of sensation and reflection.*

We shall consider them apart under these several heads.

There are some ideas which have admittance only through one sense, which is peculiarly adapted to receive them. Thus light and colours, as white, red, yellow, blue; with their several degrees or shades and mixtures, as green, scarlet, purple, sea-green, and the rest, come in only by the eyes. All kinds of noises, sounds, and tones, only by the ears. The several tastes and smells, by the nose and palate. And if these organs, or the nerves which are the conduits to convey them from without to their audience in the brain,—the mind's presence-room (as I may so call it)—are any of them so disordered as not to perform their functions, they have no postern to be admitted by; no other way to bring themselves into view, and be perceived by the understanding.

The most considerable of those belonging to the touch, are heat and cold, and solidity: all the rest, consisting almost wholly in the sensible configuration, as smooth and rough; or else, more or less firm adhesion of the parts, as hard and soft, tough and brittle, are obvious enough.

Chapter V
Of Simple Ideas of Divers Senses

The ideas we get by more than one sense are, of *space* or *extension, figure, rest, and motion.* For these make perceivable impression, both on the eyes and touch;

and we can receive and convey into our minds the ideas of the extension, figure, motion, and rest of bodies, both by seeing and feeling. But having occasion to speak more at large of these in another place, I here only enumerate them.

Chapter VI
Of Simple Ideas of Reflection

The mind receiving the ideas mentioned in the foregoing chapters from without, when it turns its view inward upon itself, and observes its own actions about those ideas it has, takes from thence other ideas, which are as capable to be the objects of its contemplation as any of those it received from foreign things.

The two great and principle actions of the mind, which are most frequently considered, and which are so frequent that every one that pleases may take notice of them in himself, are these two:—

Perception, or *Thinking;* and *Volition,* or *Willing.*

[The power of thinking is called the *Understanding,* and the power of volition is called the *Will;* and these two powers or abilities in the mind are denominated faculties.]

Of some of the *modes* of these simple ideas of reflection, such as are *remembrance, discerning, reasoning, judging, knowledge, faith, &c.,* I shall have occasion to speak hereafter.

Chapter VII
Of Simple Ideas of Both Sensation and Reflection

1. There be other simple ideas which convey themselves into the mind by all the ways of sensation and reflection, viz. *pleasure* or *delight,* and its opposite, *pain, or uneasiness; power; existence; unity.*

2. Delight or uneasiness, one or other of them, join themselves to almost all our ideas both of sensation and reflection: and there is scarce any affection of our senses from without, any retired thought of our mind within, which is not able to produce in us pleasure or pain. By pleasure and pain, I would be understood to signify, whatsoever delights or molests us; whether it arises from the thoughts of our minds, or anything operating on our bodies. For, whether we call it satisfaction, delight, pleasure, happiness, &c., on the one side, or uneasiness, trouble, pain, torment, anguish, misery, &c., on the other, they are still but different degrees of the same thing, and belong to the ideas of pleasure and pain, delight or uneasiness; which are the names I shall most commonly use for those two sorts of ideas.

Chapter VIII
Some Further Considerations Concerning
Our Simple Ideas of Sensation

7. To discover the nature of our ideas the better, and to discourse of them intelligibly, it will be convenient to distinguish them *as they are ideas or perceptions in our minds;* and *as they are modifications of matter in the bodies that cause such perceptions in us:* that so we may not think (as perhaps usually is done) that they are exactly the images and resemblances of something inherent in the subject; most of those of sensation being in the mind no more the likeness of something

existing without us, than the names that stand for them are the likeness of our ideas, which yet upon hearing they are apt to excite in us.

8. Whatsoever the mind perceives *in itself,* or is the immediate object of perception, thought, or understanding, that I call *idea;* and the power to produce any idea in our mind. I call *quality* of the subject wherein that power is. Thus a snowball having the power to produce in us the ideas of white, cold, and round,—the power to produce those ideas in us, as they are in the snowball, I call qualities; and as they are sensations or perceptions in our understandings, I call them ideas; which *ideas,* if I speak of sometimes as in the things themselves, I would be understood to mean those qualities in the objects which produce them in us.

9. Qualities thus considered in bodies are.

First, such as are utterly inseparable from the body, in what state soever it be; and such as in all the alterations and changes it suffers, all the force can be used upon it, it constantly keeps; and such as sense constantly finds in every particle of matter which has bulk enough to be perceived; and the mind finds inseparable from every particle of matter, though less than to make itself singly be perceived by our senses: v.g. Take a grain of wheat, divide it into two parts; each part has still solidity, extension, figure, and mobility: divide it again, and it retains still the same qualities; and so divide it on, till the parts become insensible; they must retain still each of them all those qualities. For division (which is all that a mill, or pestle, or any other body, does upon another, in reducing it to insensible parts) can never take away either solidity, extension, figure, or mobility from any body, but only makes two or more distinct separate masses of matter, of that which was but one before; all which distinct masses, reckoned as so many distinct bodies, after division, make a certain number.

These I call *original* or *primary qualities* of body, which I think we may observe to produce simple ideas in us, viz. solidity, extension, figure, motion or rest, and number.

10. *Secondly,* such qualities which in truth are nothing in the objects themselves but powers to produce various sensations in us by their primary qualities, i.e. by the bulk, figure, texture, and motion of their insensible parts, as colours, sounds, tastes, &c. These I call *secondary qualities.* . . .

15. From whence I think it easy to draw this observation,—that the ideas of primary qualities of bodies are resemblances of them, and their patterns do really exist in the bodies themselves, but the ideas produced in us by these secondary qualities have no resemblance of them at all. There is nothing like our ideas, existing in the bodies themselves. They are, in the bodies we denominate from them, only a power to produce those sensations in us: and what is sweet, blue, or warm in idea, is but the certain bulk, figure, and motion of the insensible parts, in the bodies themselves, which we call so.

16. Flame is denominated hot and light; snow, white and cold; and manna, white and sweet, from the ideas they produce in us. Which qualities are commonly thought to be the same in those bodies that those ideas are in us, the one the perfect resemblance of the other, as they are in a mirror, and it would by most men be judged very extravagant if one should say otherwise. And yet he that will consider

that the same fire that, at one distance produces in us the sensation of warmth, does, at a nearer approach, produce in us the far different sensation of pain, ought to bethink himself what reason he has to say—that this idea of warmth, which was produced in him by the fire, is *actually in the fire;* and his idea of pain, which the same fire produced in him the same way, is *not* in the fire. Why are whiteness and coldness in snow, and pain not, when it produces the one and the other idea in us; and can do neither, but by the bulk, figure, number, and motion of its solid parts?

17. The particular bulk, number, figure, and motion of the parts of fire or snow are really in them,—whether any one's senses perceive them or no: and therefore they may be called real qualities, because they really exist in those bodies. But light, heat, whiteness, or coldness, are no more really in them than sickness or pain is in manna. Take away the sensation of them; let not the eyes see light or colours, nor the ears hear sounds; let the palate not taste, nor the nose smell, and all colours, tastes, odours, and sounds, *as they are such particular ideas,* vanish and cease, and are reduced to their causes, i.e. bulk, figure, and motion of parts.

Chapter XII
Of Complex Ideas

1. We have hitherto considered those ideas, in the reception whereof the mind is only passive, which are those simple ones received from sensation and reflection before mentioned, whereof the mind cannot make one to itself, nor have any idea which does not wholly consist of them. But as the mind is wholly passive in the reception of all its simple ideas, so it exerts several acts of its own, whereby out of its simple ideas, as the materials and foundations of the rest, the others are framed. The acts of the mind, wherein it exerts its power over its simple ideas, are chiefly these three: (1) Combining several simple ideas into one compound one; and thus all *complex ideas* are made, (2) The second is bringing two ideas, whether simple or complex, together, and setting them by one another, so as to take a view of them at once, without uniting them into one; by which way it gets all its *ideas of relations,* (3) The third is separating them from all other ideas that accompany them in their real existence; this is called abstraction; and thus all its *general ideas* are made. This shows man's power, and its ways of operation, to be much the same in the material and intellectual world. For the materials in both being such as he has no power over, either to make or destroy, all that man can do is either to unite them together, or to set them by one another, or wholly separate them. I shall here begin with the first of these in the consideration of complex ideas, and come to the other two in their due places. As simple ideas are observed to exist in several combinations united together, so the mind has a power to consider several of them united together as one idea; and that not only as they are united in external objects, but as itself has joined them together. Ideas thus made up of several simple ones put together, I call *complex;*—such as are beauty, gratitude, a man, an army, the universe; which, though complicated of various simple ideas, or complex ideas made up of simple ones, yet are, when the mind pleases, considered each by itself, as one entire thing, and signified by one name.

2. In this faculty of repeating and rejoining together its ideas, the mind has great power in varying and multiplying the objects of its thoughts, infinitely beyond what sensation or reflection furnished it with: but all this still confined to those simple ideas which it received from those two sources, and which are the ultimate materials of all its compositions. For simple ideas are all from things themselves, and of these the mind *can* have no more, nor other than what are suggested to it. It can have no other ideas of sensible qualities than what come from without by the senses; nor any ideas of other kind of operations of a thinking substance, than what it finds in itself. But when it has once got these simple ideas, it is not confined barely to observation, and what offers itself from without; it can, by its own power, put together those ideas it has, and make new complex ones, which it never received so united.

3. *Complex ideas,* however compounded and decompounded, though their number be infinite, and the variety endless, wherewith they fill and entertain the thoughts of men; yet I think they may be all reduced under these three heads:—

1. Modes.
2. Substances.
3. Relations.

4. First. *Modes* I call such complex ideas which, however compounded, contain not in them the supposition of subsisting by themselves, but are considered as dependences on, or affections of substances:—such as are the ideas signified by the words triangle, gratitude, murder, &c. And if in this I use the word mode in somewhat a different sense from its ordinary signification. I beg pardon; it being unavoidable in discourses, differing from the ordinary received notions, either to make new words, or to use old words in somewhat a new signification; the latter whereof, in our present case, is perhaps the more tolerable of the two.

5. Of these *modes,* there are two sorts which deserve distinct consideration:—

First, there are some which are only variations, or different combinations of the same simple idea, without the mixture of any other;—as a dozen, or score; which are nothing but the ideas of so many distinct units added together, and these I call *simple modes* as being contained within the bounds of one simple idea.

Secondly, there are others compounded of simple ideas of several kinds, put together to make one complex one;—v.g. beauty, consisting of a certain composition of colour and figure, causing delight to the beholder; theft, which being the concealed change of the possession of anything, without the consent of the proprietor, contains, as is visible, a combination of several ideas of several kinds; and these I call *mixed modes.*

6. Secondly, the ideas of *substances* are such combinations of simple ideas as are taken to represent distinct *particular* things subsisting by themselves; in which the supposed or confused idea of substance, such as it is, is always the first and chief. Thus if to substance be joined the simple idea of a certain dull whitish

colour, with certain degrees of weight, hardness, ductility, and fusibility, we have the idea of lead; and a combination of the ideas of a certain sort of figure, with the powers of motion, thought and reasoning, joined to substance, make the ordinary idea of a man. Now of substances also, there are two sorts of ideas:—one of single substances, as they exist separately, as of a man or a sheep; the other of several of those put together, as an army of men, or flock of sheep—which collective ideas of several substances thus put together are as much each of them one single idea as that of a man or an unit.

7. Thirdly, the last sort of complex ideas is that we call *relation,* which consists in the consideration and comparing one idea with another.

Of these several kinds we shall treat in their order.

8. If we trace the progress of our minds, and with attention observe how it repeats, adds together, and unites its simple ideas received from sensation or reflection, it will lead us further than at first perhaps we should have imagined. And, I believe, we shall find, if we warily observe the originals of our notions, that *even the most abstruse ideas,* how remote soever they may seem from sense, or from any operations of our own minds, are yet only such as the understanding frames to itself, by repeating and joining together ideas that it had either from objects of sense, or from its own operations about them: so that those even large and abstract ideas are derived from sensation or reflection, being no other than what the mind, by the ordinary use of its own faculties, employed about ideas received from objects of sense, or from the operations it observes in itself about them, may, and does, attain unto.

This I shall endeavour to show in the ideas we have of space, time, and infinity, and some few others that seem the most remote, from those originals.

Chapter XXIII
Of Our Complex Ideas of Substances

1. The mind being, as I have declared, furnished with a great number of the simple ideas, conveyed in by the senses as they are found in exterior things, or by reflection on its own operations, takes notice also that a certain number of these simple ideas go constantly together; which being presumed to belong to one thing, and words being suited to common apprehensions, and made use of for quick dispatch, are called, so united in one subject, by one name; which, by inadvertency, we are apt afterward to talk of and consider as one simple idea, which indeed is a complication of many ideas together: because, as I have said, not imagining how these simple ideas *can* subsist by themselves, we accustom ourselves to suppose some *substratum* wherein they do subsist, and from which they do result, which therefore we call *substance.*

2. So that if any one will examine himself concerning his notion of pure substance in general, he will find he has no other idea of it at all, but only a supposition of he knows not what *support* of such qualities which are capable of producing simple ideas in us; which qualities are commonly called accidents. If any one should be asked, what is the subject wherein colour or weight inheres, he would have nothing to say, but the solid extended parts. . . . The idea then we have, to which we give the *general* name substance, being nothing but the

supposed, but unknown, support of those qualities we find existing, which we imagine cannot subsist *sine re substante,* without something to support them, we call that support *substantia;* which, according to the true import of the word, is, in plain English, standing under or upholding.

3. An obscure and relative idea of *substance in general* being thus made we come to have the ideas of *particular sorts of substances,* by collecting *such* combinations of simple ideas as are, by experience and observation of men's senses, taken notice of to exist together, and are therefore supposed to flow from the particular internal constitution, or unknown essence of the substance. Thus we come to have the ideas of a man, horse, gold, water, &c.; of which substances, whether any one has any other *clear* idea, further than of certain simple ideas co-existent together, I appeal to every one's own experience. It is the ordinary qualities observable in iron, or a diamond, put together, that make the true complex idea of those substances, which a smith or a jeweller commonly knows better than a philosopher; who, whatever *substantial forms* he may talk of, has no other idea of those substances, than what is framed by a collection of those simple ideas which are to be bound in them: only we must take notice, that our complex ideas of substances, besides all those simple ideas they are made up of, have always the confused idea of something to which they belong, and in which they subsist: and therefore when we speak of any sort of substance, we say it is a thing having such or such qualities; as body is a thing that is extended, figured, and capable of motion; spirit, a thing capable of thinking; and so hardness, friability, and power to draw iron, we say, are qualities to be found in a loadstone. These, and the like fashions of speaking, intimate that the substance is supposed always *something besides* the extension, figure, solidity, motion, thinking, or other observable ideas, though we know not what it is.

4. Hence, when we talk or think of any particular sort of corporeal substances, as horse, stone, &c., though the idea we have of either of them be but the complication or collection of those several simple ideas of sensible qualities, which we used to find united in the thing called horse or stone; yet, *because we cannot conceive how they should subsist alone, nor one in another,* we suppose them existing in and supported by some common subject; which support we denote by the name substance, though it be certain we have no clear or distinct idea of what that thing we suppose a support.

5. The same thing happens concerning the operations of the mind, viz. thinking, reasoning, fearing, &c., which we concluding not to subsist of themselves, nor apprehending how they can belong to body, or be produced by it, we are apt to think these the actions of some other *substance,* which we call *spirit;* whereby yet it is evident that, having no other idea or notion of matter, but something wherein those many sensible qualities which affect our senses do subsist; by supposing a substance wherein thinking, knowing, doubting, and a power of moving, &c., do subsist, we have as clear a notion of the substance of spirit, as we have of body; the one being supposed to be (without knowing what it is) the *substratum* to those simple ideas we have from without; and the other supposed (with a like ignorance of what it is) to be the *substratum* to those operations we experiment in ourselves within. . . .

29. To conclude. Sensation convinces us that there are solid extended substances; and reflection, that there are thinking ones: experience assures us of the existence of such beings, and that the one hath a power to move body by impulse, the other by thought; this we cannot doubt of. Experience, I say, every moment furnishes us with the clear ideas both of the one and the other. But beyond these ideas, as received from their proper sources, our faculties will not reach. If we would inquire further into their nature, causes, and manner, we perceive not the nature of extension clearer than we do of thinking. If we would explain them any further, one is as easy as the other; and there is no more difficulty to conceive how *a substance we know not* should, by thought, set body into motion, than how *a substance we know not* should, by impulse, set body into motion. So that we are no more able to discover wherein the ideas belonging to body consist, than those belonging to spirit. From whence it seems probable to me, that the simple ideas we receive from sensation and reflection are the boundaries of our thoughts; beyond which the mind, whatever efforts it would make, is not able to advance one jot; nor can it make any discoveries, when it would pry into the nature and hidden causes of these ideas.

BOOK IV

Chapter I
Of Knowledge in General

1. Since the mind, in all its thoughts and reasonings, hath no other immediate object but its own ideas, which it alone does or can contemplate, it is evident that our knowledge is only conversant about them.

2. *Knowledge* then seems to me to be nothing but *the perception of the connexion of and agreement, or disagreement and repugnancy of any of our ideas.* In this alone it consists. Where this perception is, there is knowledge, and where it is not, there, though we may fancy, guess, or believe, yet we always come short of knowledge. For when we know that white is not black, what do we else but perceive, that these two ideas do not agree? When we possess ourselves with the utmost security of the demonstration, that the three angles of a triangle are equal to two right ones, what do we more but perceive, that equality to two right ones does necessarily agree to, and is inseparable from the three angles of a triangle?

3. But to understand a little more distinctly wherein this agreement or disagreement consists, I think we may reduce it all to these four sorts:

I. *Identity, or diversity.*
II. *Relation.*
III. *Co-existence, or necessary connexion.*
IV. *Real existence.*

4. *First.* As to the first sort of agreement or disagreement, viz. *identity or diversity.* It is the first act of the mind, when it has any sentiments or ideas at all, to perceive its ideas; and so far as it perceives them, to know each what it is, and

thereby also to perceive their difference, and that one is not another. This is so absolutely necessary, that without it there could be no knowledge, no reasoning, no imagination, no distinct thoughts at all. By this the mind clearly and infallibly perceives each idea to agree with itself, and to be what it is; and all distinct ideas to disagree, i.e. the one not to be the other: and this it does without pains, labour, or deduction; but at first view, by its natural power of perception and distinction. And though men of art have reduced this into those general rules, *What is, is* and *It is impossible for the same thing to be and not to be,* for ready application in all cases, wherein there may be occasion to reflect on it: yet it is certain that the first exercise of this faculty is about particular ideas. A man infallibly knows, as soon as ever he has them in his mind, that the ideas he calls *white* and *round* are the very ideas they are; and that they are not other ideas which he calls *red* or *square.* Nor can any maxim or proposition in the world make him know it clearer or surer than he did before, and without any such general rule. This then is the first agreement or disagreement which the mind perceives in its ideas; which it always perceives at first sight: and if there ever happen any doubt about it, it will always be found to be about the names, and not the ideas themselves, whose identity and diversity will always be perceived, as soon and clearly as the ideas themselves are; nor can it possibly be otherwise.

5. *Secondly,* the next sort of agreement or disagreement the mind perceives in any of its ideas may, I think, be called *relative,* and is nothing but the perception of the *relation* between any two ideas, of what kind soever, whether substances, modes, or any other. For, since all distinct ideas must eternally be known not to be the same, and so be universally and constantly denied one of another, there could be no room for any positive knowledge at all, if we could not perceive any relation between our ideas, and find out the agreement or disagreement they have one with another, in several ways the mind takes of comparing them.

6. *Thirdly.* The third sort of agreement or disagreement to be found in our ideas, which the perception of the mind is employed about, is *co-existence* or *non-co-existence* in the *same subject;* and this belongs particularly to substances. Thus when we pronounce concerning gold, that it is fixed, our knowledge of this truth amounts to no more but this, that fixedness, or a power to remain in the fire unconsumed, is an idea that always accompanies and is joined with that particular sort of yellowness, weight, fusibility, malleableness, and solubility in *aqua regia,* which make our complex idea signified by the word gold.

7. *Fourthly.* The fourth and last sort is that of *actual real existence* agreeing to any idea.

Within these four sorts of agreement or disagreement is, I suppose, contained all the knowledge we have, or are capable of. For all the inquiries we can make concerning any of our ideas, all that we know or can affirm concerning any of them, is. That it is, or is not, the same with some other; that it does or does not always co-exist with some other idea in the same subject; that it has this or that relation with some other idea; or that is has a real existence without the mind. Thus, 'blue is not yellow,' is of identity. 'Two triangles upon equal bases between two parallels are equal,' is of relation. 'Iron is susceptible of magnetical impressions,' is of co-existence. 'God is,' is of real existence. Though identity and co-existence are truly nothing but relations, yet they are such peculiar ways of agreement or disagreement of our ideas, that they deserve well to be considered as distinct heads, and not under relation in general; since they are so different grounds of affirmation and negation, as will easily appear to any one, who will but reflect on what is said in several places of this *Essay.*

I should now proceed to examine the several degrees of our knowledge, but that it is necessary first, to consider the different acceptations of the word *knowledge.*

Chapter II
Of the Degrees of Our Knowledge

1. All our knowledge consisting, as I have said, in the view the mind has of its own ideas, which is the utmost light and greatest certainty we, with our faculties, and in our way of knowledge, are capable of, it may not be amiss to consider a little the degree of its evidence. The different clearness of our knowledge seems to me to lie in the different way of perception the mind has of the agreement or disagreement of any of its ideas. For if we will reflect on our own ways of thinking, we will find, that sometimes the mind perceives the agreement or disagreement of two ideas *immediately by themselves,* without the intervention of any other; and this I think we may call *intuitive knowledge.* For in this the mind is at no pains of proving or examining, but perceives the truth as the eye doth light, only by being directed towards it. Thus the mind perceived that *white* is not *black,* that a *circle* is not a *triangle,* that *three* are more than *two* and equal to *one and two.* Such kinds of truths the mind perceives at the first sight of the ideas together, by bare intuition; without the intervention of any other idea: and this kind of knowledge is the clearest and most certain that human frailty is capable of. This part of knowledge is irresistible, and, like bright sunshine, forces itself immediately to be perceived, as soon as ever the mind turns its view that way; and leaves no room for hesitation, doubt, or examination, but the mind is presently filled with the clear light of it. *It is on this intuition that depends all the certainty and evidence of all our knowledge;* which certainty every one finds to be so great, that he cannot imagine, and therefore not require a greater: for a man cannot conceive himself capable of a greater certainty than to know that any idea in his mind is such as he perceives it to be; and that two ideas, wherein he perceives a difference, are different and not precisely the same. He that demands a greater certainty than this, demands he knows not what, and shows only that he has a mind to be a sceptic, without being able to be so. Certainty depends so wholly on this intuition, that, in the next degree of knowledge which I call demonstrative, this intuition is necessary in all the connexions of the intermediate ideas, without which we cannot attain knowledge and certainty.

2. The next degree of knowledge is, where the mind perceives the agreement or disagreement of any ideas, but not immediately. Though wherever the mind perceives the agreement or disagreement of any of its ideas, there be certain knowledge; yet it does not always happen, that the mind sees that agreement or disagreement, which there is between them, even where it is discoverable; and in that case remains in ignorance, and at most gets no further than a probable

conjecture. The reason why the mind cannot always perceive presently the agreement or disagreement of two ideas, is, because those ideas, concerning whose agreement or disagreement the inquiry is made, cannot by the mind be so put together as to show it. In this case then, when the mind cannot so bring its ideas together as by their immediate comparison, and as it were juxta-position or application one to another, to perceive their agreement or disagreement, it is fain, *by the intervention of other ideas* (one or more, as it happens) to discover the agreement or disagreement which it searches; and this is that which we call *reasoning*. Thus, the mind being willing to know the agreement or disagreement in bigness between the three angles of a triangle and two right ones, cannot by an immediate view and comparing them do so because the three angles of a triangle cannot be brought at once, and be compared with any other one, or two, angles; and so of this the mind has no immediate, no intuitive knowledge. In this case the mind is fain to find out some other angles, to which the three angles of a triangle have an equality; and, finding those equal to two right ones, comes to know their equality to two right ones.

3. Those intervening ideas, which serve to show the agreement of any two others, are called *proofs;* and where the agreement and disagreement is by this means plainly and clearly perceived, it is called *demonstration;* it being *shown* to the understanding, and the mind made to see that it is so. A quickness in the mind to find out these intermediate ideas, (that shall discover the agreement or disagreement of any other,) and to apply them right, is, I suppose, that which is called *sagacity.*

4. This knowledge, by intervening proofs, though it be certain, yet the evidence of it is not altogether clear and bright, nor the assent so ready, as in intuitive knowledge. For, though in demonstration the mind does at last perceive the agreement or disagreement of the ideas it considers; yet it is not without pains and attention: there must be more than one transient view to find it. A steady application and pursuit are required to this discovery: and there must be a progression by steps and degrees, before the mind can in this way arrive at certainty, and come to perceive the agreement or repugnancy between two ideas that need proofs and the use of reason to show it. . . .

14. These two, viz. intuition and demonstration, are the degrees of our *knowledge;* whatever comes short of one of these, with what assurance soever embraces, is but *faith* or *opinion,* but not knowledge, at least in all general truths. There is, indeed, another perception of the mind, employed about *the particular existence of finite beings without us,* which, going beyond bare probability, and yet not reaching perfectly to either of the foregoing degrees of certainty, passes under the name *knowledge.* There can be nothing more certain than that the idea we receive from an external object is in our minds: this is intuitive knowledge. But whether there be anything more than barely that idea in our minds; whether we can thence certainly infer the existence of anything without us, which corresponds to that idea, is that whereof some men think there may be a question made; because men may have such ideas in their minds, when no such thing exists, no such object affects their senses. But yet here I think we are provided with an evidence that puts us past doubting. For I ask any one. Whether he be not invincibly conscious to himself of a different perception, when he looks on the sun by

day, and thinks on it by night; when he actually tastes wormwood, or smells a rose, or only thinks on that savour or odour? We as plainly find the difference there is between any idea revived in our minds by our own memory, and actually coming into our minds by our senses, as we do between any two distinct ideas. If any one say, a dream may do the same thing, and all these ideas may be produced in us without any external objects; he may please to dream that I make him this answer:—1. That it is no great matter, whether I remove his scruple or no: where all is but a dream, reasoning and arguments are of no use, truth and knowledge nothing. 2. That I believe he will allow a very manifest difference between dreaming of being in the fire, and being actually in it. But yet if he be resolved to appear so skeptical as to maintain, that what I call being actually in the fire is nothing but a dream; and that we cannot thereby certainly know, that any such thing as fire actually exists without us: I answer. That we certainly finding that pleasure or pain follows upon the application of certain objects to us, whose existence we perceive, or dream that we perceive, by our senses; this certainty is as great as our happiness or misery, beyond which we have no concernment to know or to be. So that, I think, we may add to the two former sorts of knowledge this also, of the existence of particular external objects, by that perception and consciousness we have of the actual entrance of ideas from them, and allow these three degrees of knowledge, viz. *intuitive, demonstrative,* and *sensitive:* in each of which there are different degrees and ways of evidence and certainty.

Chapter III
Of the Extent of Human Knowledge

1. Knowledge, as has been said, lying in the perception of the agreement or disagreement of any of our ideas, it follows from hence. That,

First, we can have knowledge no further than we have *ideas.*

2. Secondly, That we can have no knowledge further than we can have *perception* of that agreement or disagreement. Which perception being: 1. Either by *intuition,* or the immediate comparing any two ideas; or, 2. By *reason,* examining the agreement or disagreement of two ideas, by the intervention of some others; or, 3. By *sensation,* perceiving the existence of particular things: hence it also follows:

3. Thirdly, That we cannot have an *intuitive knowledge* that shall extend itself to all our ideas, and all that we would know about them, because we cannot examine and perceive all the relations they have one to another, by juxta-position, or an immediate comparison one with another. Thus, having the ideas of an obtuse and an acute angled triangle, both drawn from equal bases, and between parallels, I can, by intuitive knowledge, perceive the one not to be the other, but cannot that way know whether they be equal or no; because their agreement or disagreement in equality can never be perceived by an immediate comparing them: the difference of figure makes their parts incapable of an exact immediate application; and therefore there is need of some intervening qualities to measure them by, which is demonstration, or rational knowledge.

4. Fourthly, It follows, also, from what is above observed, that our *rational knowledge* cannot reach to the whole extent of our ideas: because between two

different ideas we would examine, we cannot always find such mediums as we can connect one to another with an intuitive knowledge in all the parts of the deduction; and wherever that fails, we come short of knowledge and demonstration.

5. Fifthly, *Sensitive knowledge* reaching no further than the existence of things actually present to our senses, is yet much narrower than either of the former.

6. Sixthly, From all which it is evident, that the *extent of our knowledge* comes not only short of the reality of things, but even of the extent of our own ideas. Though our knowledge be limited to our ideas, and cannot exceed them either in extent or perfection; and though these be very narrow bounds, in respect of the extent of All-being, and far short of what we may justly imagine to be in some even created understandings, not tied down to the dull and narrow information that is to be received from some few, and not very acute, ways of perception, such as are our senses; yet it would be well with us if our knowledge were but as large as our ideas, and there were not many doubts and inquiries *concerning the ideas we have,* whereof we are not, nor I believe ever shall be in this world resolved. Nevertheless, I do not question but that human knowledge, under the present circumstances of our beings and constitutions, may be carried much further than it has hitherto been, if men would sincerely, and with freedom of mind, employ all that industry and labour of thought, in improving the means of discovering truth, which they do for the colouring or support of falsehood, to maintain a system, interest, or party they are once engaged in. But yet after all, I think I may, without injury to human perfection, be confident, that our knowledge would never reach to all we might desire to know concerning those ideas we have; nor be able to surmount all the difficulties, and resolve all the questions that might arise concerning any of them. We have the ideas of a *square,* a *circle,* and *equality;* and yet, perhaps, shall never be able to find a circle equal to a square, and certainly know that it is so. We have the ideas of *matter* and *thinking,* but possibly shall never be able to know whether [any mere material being] thinks or no; it being impossible for us, by the contemplation of our own ideas, without revelation, to discover whether Omnipotency has not given to some systems of matter, fitly disposed, a power to perceive and think, or else joined and fixed to matter, so disposed, a thinking immaterial substance: it being, in respect of our notions, not much more remote from our comprehension to conceive that GOD can, if he pleases, superadd to a *faculty of thinking,* than that he should superadd to it *another substance with a faculty of thinking;* since we know not wherein thinking consists, nor to what sort of substances the Almighty has been pleased to give that power, which cannot be in any created being, but merely by the good pleasure and bounty of the Creator.

Chapter IX
Of Our Threefold Knowledge of Existence

1. Hitherto we have only considered the essences of things; which being only abstract ideas, and thereby removed in our thoughts from particular existence (that being the proper operation of the mind, in abstraction, to consider an idea under no other existence but what it has in the understanding) gives us no knowledge of

real existence at all. Where, by the way, we may take notice, that universal propositions of whose truth or falsehood we can have certain knowledge concern not existence: and further, that all particular affirmations or negations that would not be certain if they were made general, are only concerning existence; they declaring only the accidental union or separation of ideas in things existing, which, in their abstract natures, have no known necessary union or repugnancy.

2. But, leaving the nature of propositions, and different ways of predication to be considered more at large in another place, let us proceed now to inquire concerning our knowledge of the *existence of things,* and how we come by it. I say, then, that we have the knowledge of *our own* existence by intuition; of the existence of *God* by demonstration; and of *other things* by sensation.

3. As for our *own existence,* we perceive it so plainly and so certainly, that it neither needs nor is capable of any proof. For nothing can be more evident to us than our own existence. I think, I reason, I feel pleasure and pain: can any of these be more evident to me than my own existence? If I doubt of all other things, that very doubt makes me perceive my own existence, and will not suffer me to doubt of that. For if I know I feel pain, it is evident I have as certain perception of my own existence, as of the existence of the pain I feel: or if I know I doubt, I have as certain perception of the existence of the thing doubting, as of that thought which I *call doubt.* Experience then convinces us, that we have an *intuitive knowledge* of our own existence, and an internal infallible perception that we are. In every act of sensation, reasoning, or thinking, we are conscious to ourselves of our own being; and, in this matter, come not short of the highest degree of certainty.

Chapter X
Of Our Knowledge of the Existence of God

1. Though God has given us no innate ideas of himself; though he has stamped no original characters on our minds, wherein we may read his being; yet having furnished us with those faculties our minds are endowed with, he hath not left himself without witness: since we have sense, perception, and reason, and cannot want a clear proof of him, as long as we carry *ourselves* about us. Nor can we justly complain of our ignorance in this great point; since he has so plentifully provided us with the means to discover and know him; so far as is necessary to the end of our being, and the great concernment of our happiness. But, though this be the most obvious truth that reason discovers, and though its evidence be (if I mistake not) equal to mathematical certainty: yet it requires thought and attention; and the mind must apply itself to a regular deduction of it from some part of our intuitive knowledge, or else we shall be as uncertain and ignorant of this as of other propositions, which are in themselves capable of clear demonstration. To show, therefore, that we are capable of *knowing,* i.e. *being certain* that there is a God, and *how we may come by* this certainty, I think we need go no further than ourselves, and that undoubted knowledge we have of our own existence.

2. I think it is beyond question, that man has a clear idea of his own being; he knows certainly he exists, and that he is something. He that can doubt whether he be anything or no, I speak not to; no more than I would argue with pure nothing, or endeavour to convince nonentity that it were something. If any

one pretends to be so sceptical as to deny his own existence (for really to doubt of it is manifestly impossible) let him for me enjoy his beloved happiness of being nothing, until hunger or some other pain convince him of the contrary. This, then, I think I may take for a truth, which every one's certain knowledge assures him of, beyond the liberty of doubting, viz. that he is *something that actually exists.*

3. In the next place, man knows, by an intuitive certainty, that bare *nothing can no more produce any real being, than it can be equal to two right angles.* If a man knows not that nonentity, or the absence of all being, cannot be equal to two right angles, it is impossible he should know any demonstration in Euclid. If, therefore, we know there is some real being, and that nonentity cannot produce any real being, it is an evident demonstration, that *from eternity there has been something;* since what was not from eternity has a beginning; and what had a beginning must be produced by something else. . . .

From what has been said, it is plain to me we have a more certain knowledge of the existence of a God, than of anything our senses have not immediately discovered to us. Nay, I presume I may say, that we more certainly know that there is a God, than that there is anything else without us. When I say we *know,* I mean there is such a knowledge within our reach which we cannot miss, if we will but apply our minds to that, as we do to several other inquiries. . . .

Chapter XI
Of Our Knowledge of the Existence of Other Things

1. The knowledge of our own being we have by intuition. The existence of a God, reason clearly makes known to us, as has been shown.

The knowledge of the existence of *any other thing* we can have only by *sensation:* for there being no necessary connexion of real existence with any *idea* a man hath in his memory; nor of any other existence but that of God with the existence of any particular man: no particular man can know the existence of any other being, but only when, by actual operating upon him, it makes itself perceived by him. For, the having the idea of anything in our mind, no more proves the existence of that thing, than the picture of a man evidences his being in the world, or the visions of a dream make thereby a true history.

2. It is therefore the *actual receiving* of ideas from without that gives us notice of the existence of other things, and makes us know, that something doth exist at that time without us, which causes that idea in us; though perhaps we neither know nor consider how it does it. For it takes not from the certainty of our senses, and the ideas we receive by them, that we know not the manner wherein they are produced: v.g. whilst I write this, I have, by the paper affecting my eyes, that idea produced in my mind, which, whatever object causes, I call *white;* by which I know that the quality or accident (i.e. whose appearance before my eyes always causes that idea) doth really exist, and hath a being without me. And of this, the greatest assurance I can possibly have, and to which my faculties can attain, is the testimony of my eyes, which are the proper and sole judges of this thing; whose testimony I have reason to rely on as so certain, that I can no more doubt, whilst I write this, that I see white and black, and that something really

exists that causes that sensation in me, than that I write or move my hand; which is a certainty as great as human nature is capable of, concerning the existence of anything, but a man's self alone, and of God.

From The Second Treatise of Civil Government

Chapter I
The Introduction

3. Political power, then I take to be a right of making laws with penalties of death, and consequently all less penalties, for the regulating and preserving of property, and of employing the force of the community in the execution of such laws, and in the defense of the commonwealth from foreign injury, and all this only for the public good.

Chapter II
Of the State of Nature

4. To understand political power aright, and derive it from its original, we must consider what state all men are naturally in, and that is a state of perfect freedom to order their actions and dispose of their possessions and persons as they think fit, within the bounds of the law of nature, without asking leave, or depending upon the will of any other man.

A state also of equality, wherein all the power and jurisdiction is reciprocal, no one having more than another; there being nothing more evident than that creatures of the same species and rank, promiscuously born to all the same advantages of nature, and the use of the same faculties, should also be equal one amongst another without subordination or subjection, unless the Lord and Master of them all should by any manifest declaration of His will set one above another, and confer on him by an evident and clear appointment an undoubted right to dominion and sovereignty.

6. But though this be a state of liberty, yet it is not a state of license; though man in that state have an uncontrollable liberty to dispose of his person or possession, yet he has not liberty to destroy himself, or so much as any creature in his possession, but where some nobler use than its bare preservation calls for it. The state of nature has a law of nature to govern it, which obliges everyone; and reason, which is that law, teaches all mankind who will but consult it, that, being all equal and independent, no one ought to harm another in his life, health, liberty, or possessions. For men being all the workmanship of one omnipotent and infinitely wise Maker—all the servants of one sovereign Master, sent into the world by His order, and about His business—they are His property, whose workmanship they are, made to last during His, not one another's pleasure; and being furnished with like faculties, sharing all in one community of nature, there cannot be supposed any such subordination among us, that may authorize us to destroy one another, as if we were made for one another's uses, as the inferior

ranks of creatures are for ours. Everyone, as he is bound to preserve himself, and not to quit his station willfully, so, by the like reason, when his own preservation comes not in competition, ought he, as much as he can, to preserve the rest of mankind, and not, unless it be to do justice on an offender, take away or impair the life, or what tends to the preservation of the life, the liberty, health, limb, or goods of another.

7. And that all men may be restrained from invading others' rights, and from doing hurt to one another, and the law of nature be observed, which willeth the peace and preservation of all mankind, the execution of the law of nature is in that state put into every man's hand, whereby everyone has a right to punish the transgressors of that law to such a degree as may hinder its violation. For the law of nature would, as all other laws that concern men in this world, be in vain if there were nobody that, in the state of nature, had a power to execute that law, and thereby preserve the innocent and restrain offenders. And if anyone in the state of nature may punish another for any evil he has done, everyone may do so. For in that state of perfect equality, where naturally there is no superiority or jurisdiction of one over another, what any may do in prosecution of that law, everyone must needs have a right to do.

Chapter VII
Of Political or Civil Society

77. God having made man such a creature, that in his own judgment it was not good for him to be alone, put him under strong obligations of necessity, convenience, and inclination to drive him into society, as well as fitted him with understanding and language to continue and enjoy it. The first society was between man and wife, which gave beginning to that between parents and children; to which, in time, that between master and servant came to be added; and though all these might, and commonly did meet together, and make up but one family, wherein the master or mistress of it had some sort of rule proper to a family; each of these, or all together, came short of political society, as we shall see, if we consider the different ends, ties, and bounds of each of these.

78. Conjugal society is made by a voluntary compact between man and woman, and though it consists chiefly in such a communion and right in one another's bodies as is necessary to its chief end, procreation, yet it draws with it mutual support and assistance, and a communion of interests too, as necessary not only to unite their care and affection, but also necessary to their common offspring, who have a right to be nourished and maintained by them till they are able to provide for themselves. . . .

84. The society betwixt parents and children, and the distinct rights and powers belonging respectively to them, I have treated of so largely in the foregoing chapter that I shall not here need to say anything of it; and I think it is plain that it is far different from a politic society. . . .

89. Wherever, therefore, any number of men so unite into one society, as to quit everyone his executive power of the law of nature, and to resign it to the public, there, and there only, is a political, or civil society. And this is done wherever any number of men, in the state of nature, enter into society to make one people, one

body politic, under one supreme government, or else when anyone joins himself to, and incorporates with, any government already made. For hereby he authorises the society, or, which is all one, the legislative thereof, to make laws for him, as the public good of the society shall require, to the execution whereof his own assistance (as to his own decrees) is due. And this puts men out of a state of nature into that of a commonwealth, by setting up a judge on earth with authority to determine all the controversies and redress the injuries that may happen to any member of the commonwealth; which judge is the legislative, or magistrates appointed by it. And wherever there are any number of men, however associated, that have no such decisive power to appeal to, there they are still in the state of nature.

Chapter XIX
Of the Dissolution of Government

221. There is therefore secondly another way whereby governments are dissolved, and that is when the legislative or the prince, either of them, act contrary to their trust.

First, The legislative acts against the trust reposed in them when they endeavor to invade the property of the subject, and to make themselves or any part of the community masters or arbitrary disposers of the lives, liberties, or fortunes of the people.

222. The reason why men enter into society is the preservation of their property; and the end why they choose and authorize a legislative is that there may be laws made, and rules set, as guards and fences to the properties of all the members of the society to limit the power and moderate the dominion of every part and member of the society. For since it can never be supposed to be the will of the society that the legislative should have a power to destroy that which everyone designs secure by entering into society, and for which the people submitted themselves to legislators of their own making, whenever the legislators endeavor to take away and destroy the property of the people, or to reduce them to slavery under arbitrary power, they put themselves into a state of war with the people, who are thereupon absolved from any further obedience, and are left to the common refuge which God hath provided for all men against force and violence. Whensoever, therefore, the legislative shall transgress this fundamental rule of society, and either by ambition, fear, folly, or corruption, endeavor to grasp themselves or put into the hands of any other an absolute power over the lives, liberties, and estates of the people, by this breach of trust they forfeit the power the people had put into their hands, for quite contrary ends, and it devolves to the people, who have a right to resume their original liberty, and by the establishment of the new legislative (such as they shall think fit) provide for their own safety and security, which is the end for which they are in society. What I have said here concerning the legislative in general, holds true also concerning the supreme executor, who having a double trust put in him, both to have a part in the legislative and the supreme execution of the law, acts against both when he goes about to set up his own arbitrary will as the law of the society. He acts also contrary to his trust when he either employs the force, treasure, and offices of the society, to corrupt the representatives, and gain them to his purposes; or openly pre-engages the electors,

and prescribes to their choice such whom he has by solicitations, threats, promises, or otherwise won to his designs, and employs them to bring in such, who have promised beforehand what to vote and what to enact. Thus to regulate candidates and electors, and new-model the ways of election, what is it but to cut up the government by the roots, and poison the very fountain of public security? For the people having reserved to themselves the choice of their representatives as the fence to their properties, could do it for no other end but that they might always be freely chosen, and, so chosen, freely act and advise as the necessity of the commonwealth and the public good should upon examination and mature debate be judged to require. This those who give their votes before they hear the debate, and have weighed the reason on all sides, are not capable of doing. To prepare such an assembly as this, and endeavor to set up the declared abettors of his own will for the true representatives of the people and the law-makers of the society, is certainly as great a breach of trust and as perfect a declaration of a design to subvert the government as is possible to be met with. To which if one shall add rewards and punishments visibly employed to the same end and all the arts of perverted law made use of to take off and destroy all that stand in the way of such a design, and will not comply and consent to betray the liberties of their country, it will be past doubt what is doing. What power they ought to have in the society who thus employ it contrary to the trust that went along with it in its first institution is easy to determine; and one cannot but see that he who has once attempted any such thing as this cannot any longer be trusted.

223. To this perhaps it will be said that, the people being ignorant and always discontented, to lay the foundation of government in the unsteady opinion and uncertain humor of the people is to expose it to certain ruin; and no government will be able long to subsist if the people may set up a new legislative whenever they take offense at the old one. To this I answer: Quite the contrary. People are not so easily got out of their old forms as some are apt to suggest. They are hardly to be prevailed with to amend the acknowledged faults in the frame they have been accustomed to. And if there be any original defects, or adventitious ones introduced by time or corruption, it is not an easy thing to get them changed, even when all the world sees there is an opportunity for it. This slowness and aversion in the people to quit their old constitutions has, in the many revolutions which have been seen in this kingdom, in this and former ages still kept us to, or after some interval of fruitless attempts still brought us back again to, our old legislative of Kings, Lords, and Commons. And whatever provocations have made the crown be taken from some of our princes' heads, they never carried the people so far as to place it in another line.

224. But it will be said, this hypothesis lays a ferment for frequent rebellion. To which I answer:

First, no more than any other hypothesis. For when the people are made miserable, and find themselves exposed to the ill-usage of arbitrary power, cry up their governors as much as you will for sons of Jupiter, let them be sacred and divine, descended, or authorized from heaven, give them out for whom or what you please, the same will happen. The people generally ill-treated, and contrary to right, will be ready upon any occasion to ease themselves of a burden that sits heavy upon them. They will wish and seek for the opportunity, which in the change, weakness, and accidents of human affairs seldom delays long to offer itself. He must have lived but a little while in the world who has not seen examples of this in his time, and he must have read very little who cannot produce examples of it in all sorts of governments in the world.

225. Secondly, I answer, such revolutions happen not upon every little mismanagement in public affairs. Great mistakes in the ruling part, many wrong and inconvenient laws, and all the slips of human frailty will be borne by the people without mutiny or murmur. But if a long train of abuses, prevarications and artifices, all tending the same way, make the design visible to the people—and they cannot but feel what they lie under, and see whither they are going—it is not to be wondered that they should then rouse themselves and endeavor to put the rule into such hands which may secure to them the needs for which government was at first erected, and without which ancient names and specious forms are so far from being better that they are much worse than the state of nature or pure anarchy; the inconveniences being all as great and as near, but the remedy farther off and more difficult.

226. Thirdly, I answer that this power in the people of providing for their safety anew by a new legislative when their legislators have acted contrary to their trust by invading their property, is the best fence against rebellion, and the probablest means to hinder it. For rebellion being an opposition, not to persons, but authority, which is founded only in the constitutions and laws of the government, those whoever they be who by force break through, and by force justify their violation of them, are truly and properly rebels. For when men by entering into society and civil government have excluded force, and introduced laws for the preservation of property, peace, and unity amongst themselves, those who set up force again in opposition to the laws do *rebellare*—that is, bring back again the state of war—and are properly rebels; which they who are in power (by the pretense they have to authority, the temptation of force they have in their hands, and the flattery of those about them) being likeliest to do, the properest way to prevent the evil is to show them the danger and injustice of it who are under the greatest temptation to run into it.

Review Questions

1. What is Locke's role in the history of British empiricism?
2. What goals did Locke have in mind in his exploration of human knowledge? Are they the same as Descartes'?
3. If, for Locke, ideas are not innate, how do they originate?
4. Differentiate Locke's three kinds of knowledge: intuitive, demonstrative, and sensitive.
5. What problem does Locke have with the idea of substance?
6. Distinguish between rationalism and empiricism.
7. Compare the views of Locke and Hobbes on the state of nature.
8. Discuss Locke's view that common consent in civil society is based on trust.

SUGGESTIONS FOR FURTHER READING

Ayers, M. *Locke.* New York, Routledge, 1993.

Chappell, Vere. *Locke.* New York, Oxford University Press, 1998.

Fraser, A. C., ed. *An Essay Concerning Human Understanding,* 2 vols. New York, Dover, 1959.

O'Connor, D. J. *John Locke.* Baltimore, Penguin, 1952.

16

George Berkeley
(1685–1753)

Immaterialist/Empiricist

In the previous chapter, mention was made of the idealism of Berkeley as one of the possible consequences of Locke's view of the relationship of ideas to material things, yet Berkeley can also be seen as a link between the moderate empiricism of Locke and the extreme empiricism of Hume. Thus we have an interesting characterization of Berkeley as an idealist and an empiricist at the same time. A plausible way to understand this is by attending to Berkeley's reference to himself as an *immaterialist* rather than an idealist, which means that he thought of himself as a realist inasmuch as things perceived are real even though they do not attach to material things outside the mind. The very being of sense objects is their *being perceived,* and if in the past there were philosophers who insisted on a substance called *matter* to which our ideas refer, it was the result of an errant metaphysics. Berkeley's philosophy of immaterialism, summarized in the phrase "to be is to be perceived" (*esse est percipi*), is a gauntlet thrown down in the face of common sense and is an event in the history of philosophy that commands our examination.

George Berkeley was born in 1685 in Kilkenny, Ireland, and, though of an English family and in contrast to others of similar birth, he thought of himself as Irish. At Trinity College, Dublin, he steeped himself in the classics and read programmatically in philosophy; in 1707 he was made a fellow of the college and then was ordained a priest, as required by the college's statutes.

Berkeley's first visit to London in 1713 was the beginning of an eight-year period that, at various stages, took him to France and Italy as chaplain and tutor. When in London, he was made welcome at the royal court and in literary circles, where he was befriended by such well-known figures as Addison, Steele, Pope, and Swift, among whom he achieved a reputation as a man of charm and character, as well as learning. During a visit to Paris in 1715, he went to see Malebranche, who was sick and confined to his bed. As the story goes—if it's not true, it's still fun to pass on—they got into a heated argument which brought on such a "violent increase of his disorder" that the old man died a few days later, perhaps the first recorded case of death by metaphysics!

On his return to Dublin in 1721, Berkeley lectured in divinity at Trinity and tried to give some realistic shape to a project in the New World, a college in Bermuda to educate the "savages" for the ministry. After his appointment as dean of Derry, he was able to travel to the colonies where his advice on college education was eagerly sought and he became a benefactor of Harvard and Yale. Many years later, as a remembrance of his interest in early college education in America, California's Berkeley was named after him, a fitting complement to the verse he wrote on his hopes for education in America: "Westward the Course of Empire takes its way."

Back in Ireland, Berkeley was installed as the Bishop of Cloyne in 1734, a post he held for the next two decades. He was a beloved churchman, filled with concern for the welfare of his people; he kept on writing, but none of his major works were done at this time. However, because of the inadequacy of medical services in his diocese, he wrote a widely read book entitled *Siris,* in which he encouraged the use of a liquid he learned of in America known as *tar-water,* a mixture of water and pine resin; he referred to it as a "medicine that cures or relieves all different species of distempers." The book, whose subtitle is "Philosophical Reflexions and Inquiries concerning the Virtues of Tar Water," is an enthusiastic, curious work in which the author, seriously committed to both medicine and religion, attempts to link the health properties of tar-water, through the great chain of being, with the triune God. In this work, as in his others, the learned bishop desired to see God as the end of all his labors. He died in Oxford in 1753.

His chief works are *An Essay towards a New Theory of Vision* (1709), *A Treatise Concerning the Principles of Human Knowledge* (1710), and *Three Dialogues between Hylas and Philonous* (1713).

Skepticism and Language

If there is any guiding principle that runs through all of Berkeley's works, it is the presence of God to the universe, but especially to man, who therefore, out of duty and love, must find ways to reaffirm His existence, put down skepticism, and rout the free thinkers. The *Principles,* for example, begins in God's name: "What I here make public has, after a long and scrupulous inquiry, seemed to me evidently true, and not unuseful to be known, particularly to those who are tainted with scepticism, or want a demonstration of the existence and immateriality of God, or the natural immortality of the soul." It also ends in God's name: "For after all, what serves the first place in our studies is the consideration of *God,* and our *duty;* which to promote, as it was the main drift and design of my labours, so shall I esteem them altogether useless and ineffectual, if by what I have said I cannot inspire my readers with a pious sense of the presence of God."

But if God has equipped man for a human journey through life, man's mind must be suitable to the task, so it is not the mind's incapacity that has led to confusion and difficulties in assenting to the divine; it is only when man uses his mind incorrectly that absurdities of all kinds begin to arise. So Berkeley's purpose, he tells us, is to remove all absurdities that philosophy has become encrusted with and, like so many philosophers before him, to sweep clean, uproot the confusion, and start anew.

Berkeley's first contention, then, is that confusion abounds because of the abuse of language, words being so carelessly used as to be assigned meaning when they have none—the same fear that Hobbes and Locke had before him. The main culprit in the abuse of language is *abstraction,* a power some falsely believe we possess to "frame abstract ideas," which then leads to a use of words matching these abstract ideas and endowing them with meaning they do not have. Berkeley arrives at this conclusion by beginning with "qualities" that traditionally belong, in one way or another, to the thing they are qualities of, such as "white" paper. But qualities of things never exist on their own, apart from other qualities with which they are "mixed," so, for example, "white" and "extended" are found together in the paper; we are told by some philosophers, complains Berkeley, that the mind is able to consider each quality apart from the others, and so to "abstract." Then the power of abstraction is enlarged to include triangles and triangularity, animal and animality, man and humanity, and so on, separating something common to all instances of triangle, animal, and man from all the particular features with which these objects are found in reality. Berkeley will allow the separation of particular parts from other particular parts of the same object, but that is as far as he will go; to separate by abstraction what is "general" can in no way refer to what is "particular." Regarding the "doctrine" of abstraction, Berkeley is at a loss to understand what it is "that inclines the men of speculation to embrace an opinion so remote from common sense as that seems to be." If anyone says that abstract ideas really refer to things, that is bad enough, but it is worse if he assigns words to these ideas and pretends that the assigned words have meaning in referring to real things. That, for Berkeley, is the abuse of words.

Yet there is an obvious "universal" content implied when we use the same word or notion of many things, as "man" of Peter, James, and John. This is accounted for not because there is a common nature among the particulars, which is impossible, but because our imagination enables us to hold together the similarities among things and so to use a word "universally," knowing full well that only particulars exist. Because it would be impossible to assign a word or name to every particular thing that exists, Berkeley suggests that universal words or names are a convenient way to refer to particulars, but they do so "indifferently" by not taking into account the differences that make things particular. David Hume, who succeeds Berkeley in the English empirical tradition, praised him on this point when he wrote, "A great philosopher has disputed the received opinion . . . and has asserted that all general ideas are nothing but particular ones. . . . As I look upon this to be one of the greatest and most valuable discoveries that has been made of late years in the republic of letters, I shall here endeavour to confirm it by some arguments, which I hope will put it beyond all doubt and controversy."

Berkeley's foray against abstraction is total: Qualities, whether primary or secondary, are not abstracted; there is no externally existing nature common to particular things; there is no substance "out there" to act as a support for qualities, and he even reprimands Locke for wavering on the question. He declared that we simply do not know if there is such an entity as material substance or not.

"To be is to be Perceived"

Further, it is clear for Berkeley that it is a *mind* (spirit, soul, my self) that works at various objects of knowledge which, if they are "ideas imprinted on the sense," are sensory objects, and which, if they are ideas coming from within the mind itself, are mental objects. In either case, it is the *perceiving* mind at work. Relying on this fundamental distinction, Berkeley gets to the heart of the thesis for which he is remembered in the history of philosophy: *Sensible objects have a mental existence only.* No one ever had any problem with the fact that sensing is in the sensing subject, but Berkeley was the first to hold that the very things sensed are *in* the subject: The mind's sense objects are in the mind itself; sense *is* the sensing mind. To show the absolute correlation between the *existence* of sensed things and the *perception* of them, Berkeley invites us to attend to "what is meant by the term *exist* when applied to sensible things." To take his example, when I say that the table is in my study, I *mean* that by sight, touch, or smell, I *perceive* it; the *existence* of the table means nothing more than my *perception* of it: *To be is to be perceived (esse est percipi).* It is a mistake, brought about by abstraction, to think that sensible objects have an existence beyond being perceived; sensible objects, or ideas, are what they are and cannot be taken as signs of anything else.

An immediate corollary to the doctrine that "to be is to be perceived" as it applies to material things is that *no* "unthinking thing" exists outside the mind; the only thing that exists is the thinking thing, the "perceiver." The world is a spiritual world, for only spirits exist. In Berkeley's view, the demonstration that only the spiritual world exists is the trump card against materialism, for, with matter gone, the prejudices of the materialists are gone too. Berkeley's effort was a bit more philosophical than the storied demonstration of Dr. Samuel Johnson who said, "I refute Berkeley thus" as he kicked a stone with his foot. Historically, Berkeley represents one extreme of the mind–body duality created by Descartes: All mind, no body; others represent the other extreme: all body, no mind. The irony here is that Berkeley arrived at this extreme on the strength of a position that ranks him among the bold empiricists of modern philosophy.

The Existence of God

Having come thus far with Berkeley in his firm emphasis on ideas, spirit, and mind, one might think that his affirmation of God would take on the coloration of the Cartesian argument, moving from the idea of the all-perfect to the existence of the all-perfect. But this is never advanced by him, and in *Alciphron,* a beautifully written Christian apologetic against the free-thinking "minute philosophers" personified by Alciphron, when the ontological argument is mentioned. Berkeley's sentiment appears to be against it. Rather, he hews to the causal argument by pointing out that the ideas in us must be caused: "yet it is evident to everyone, that those things which are called the works of Nature, that is, the far greater part of the ideas or sensations perceived by us, are not produced by, or dependent on the wills of men. There is therefore some other spirit that causes them, since it is repugnant that they should subsist by themselves." For Berkeley, the argument is clear, evident, and immediate: "Hence it is evident, that God is known as certainly and immediately as any other mind or spirit whatsoever, distinct from ourselves." His argument is consistent with his philosophy of immaterialism.

Both in answering the objections that might be raised against immaterialism and in refuting the arguments against God's existence, benignity, or providence made by the skeptics, Berkeley unhesitatingly maintains the primacy of his new principles of knowledge, or "the great advantages that arise from the belief of immaterialism." One is able to see the advantages of physics and mathematics, now that phenomena are nothing more than ideas and are free from endless disputes concerning gravity, extension, divisibility, and so on; in metaphysics, questions like abstraction and substance are put to rest; and above all, in morality, for now the mind is immediately present to God and not through the mediation of unthinking second causes. However, the goal of understanding the immediate presence of God is not itself given immediately, for it takes the unyielding steadiness of the pilgrim to get there. In the last lines of his last work, we see that Berkeley thought of himself as just such a pilgrim: "The eye by long use comes to see even in the darkest cavern: and there is no subject so obscure but we may discern some glimpse of truth by long poring on it. Truth is the cry of all, but the game of few. . . . He that would make a real progress in knowledge must dedicate his age as well as youth, the later growth as well as first fruits, at the alter of Truth."

From A Treatise Concerning the Principles of Human Knowledge

PREFACE

What I have here make public has, after a long and scrupulous inquiry, seemed to me evidently true, and not unuseful to be known, particularly to those who are tainted with scepticism, or want a demonstration of the existence and immateriality of God, or the natural immortality of the soul. Whether it be so or no, I am content the reader should impartially examine; since I do not think myself any further concerned for the success of what I have written than as it is agreeable to truth. But to the end this may not suffer, I make it my request that the reader suspend his judgment till he has once, at least, read the whole through with that degree of attention and thought which the subject matter shall seem to deserve. For as there are some passages that, taken by themselves, are very liable (nor could it be remedied) to gross misinterpretation, and to be charged with most absurd consequences, which, nevertheless, upon an entire perusal will appear not to follow from them: so likewise, though the whole should be read over, yet if this be done transiently, it is very probable my sense may be mistaken; but to a thinking reader, I flatter myself, it will be throughout clear and obvious. As for the characters of novelty and singularity, which some of the following notions may seem to bear, it is, I hope, needless to make any apology on that account. He must surely be either very weak, or very little acquainted with the sciences, who shall reject a truth that is capable of demonstration, for no other reason but because it is newly known and contrary to the prejudices of mankind. Thus much I thought fit to premise, in order to prevent, if possible, the hasty censures of a sort of men, who are too apt to condemn an opinion before they right comprehend it.

INTRODUCTION

Philosophy being nothing else but the study of wisdom and truth, it may with reason be expected that those who have spent most time and pains in it should enjoy a greater calm and serenity of mind, a greater clearness and evidence of knowledge, and be less disturbed with doubts and difficulties than other men. Yet so it is, we see the illiterate bulk of mankind that walk the highroad of plain common sense, and are governed by the dictates of nature, for the most part easy and undisturbed. To them nothing that is familiar appears unaccountable or difficult to comprehend. They complain not of any want of evidence in their sense, and are out of all danger of becoming sceptics. But no sooner do we depart from sense and instinct to follow the light of a superior principle, to reason, mediate, and reflect on the nature of things, but a thousand scruples spring up in our minds concerning those things which before we seemed fully to comprehend. Prejudices and errors of sense do from all parts discover themselves to our view; and, endeavoring to correct these by reason, we are insensibly drawn into uncouth paradoxes, difficulties, and inconsistencies, which multiply and grow upon us as we advance in speculation, till at length, having wandered through many intricate mazes, we find ourselves just where we were, or, which is worse, sit down in a forlorn scepticism.

2. The cause of this is thought to be the obscurity of things, or the natural weakness and imperfection of our understandings. It is said the faculties we have are few, and those designed by nature for the support and comfort of life, and not to penetrate into the inward essence and constitution of things. Besides, the mind of man being finite, when it treats of things which partake of infinity it is not to be wondered at if it run into absurdities and contradictions, out of which it is impossible it should ever extricate itself, it being of the nature of infinite not to be comprehended by that which is finite.

3. But perhaps we may be too partial to ourselves in placing the fault originally in our faculties, and not rather in the wrong use we make of them. It is a hard thing to suppose that right deductions from true principles should ever end in consequences which cannot be maintained or made consistent. We should believe that God has dealt more bountifully with the sons of men than to give them a strong desire for that knowledge which he had placed quite out of their reach. This were not agreeable to the wonted indulgent methods of Providence, which whatever appetites it may have implanted in the creatures, doth usually furnish them with such means as, if rightly made use of, will not fail to satisfy them. Upon the whole, I am inclined to think that the far greater part, if not all, of those difficulties which have hitherto amused philosophers, and blocked up the way to knowledge, are entirely owing to ourselves—that we have first raised a dust and then complain we cannot see. . . .

6. In order to prepare the mind of the reader for the easier conceiving what follows, it is proper to premise somewhat, by way of introduction, concerning the nature and abuse of language. But the unraveling this matter leads me in some measure to anticipate my design, by taking notice of what seems to have had a chief part in rendering speculation intricate and perplexed, and to have occasioned innumerable errors and difficulties in almost all parts of knowledge. And that is the opinion that the mind hath a power of framing *abstract ideas* or notions of things. He who is not a perfect stranger to the writings and disputes of philosophers must needs acknowledge that no small part of them are spent about abstract ideas. These are in a more especial manner thought to be the object of those sciences which go by the name of *logic* and *metaphysics,* and of all that which passes under the notion of the most abstracted and sublime learning, in all which one shall scarce find any question handled in such a manner as does not suppose their existence in the mind, and that it is well acquainted with them. . . .

9. And as the mind frames to itself abstract ideas of qualities or modes, so does it, by the same precision or mental separation, attain abstract ideas of the more compounded beings, which include several coexistent qualities. For

example, the mind having observed that Peter, James, and John, resemble each other, in certain common agreements of shape and other qualities, leaves out of the complex or compounded idea it has of Peter, James, and any other particular man, that which is peculiar to each, retaining only what is common to all; and so makes an abstract idea wherein all the particulars equally partake, abstracting entirely from and cutting off all those circumstances and differences which might determine it to any particular existence. And after this manner it is said we come by the abstract idea of man or, if you please, humanity or human nature; wherein it is true, there is included colour, because there is no man but has some colour, but then it can be neither white, nor black, nor any particular colour; because there is no one particular colour wherein all men partake. So likewise there is included stature, but then it is neither tall stature nor low stature, nor yet middle stature, but something abstracted from all these. And so of the rest. Moreover, there being a great variety of other creatures that partake in some parts, but not all, of the complex idea of *man,* the mind leaving out those parts which are peculiar to men, and retaining those only which are common to all the living creatures, frameth the idea of *animal,* which abstracts not only from all particular men, but also all birds, beasts, fishes, and insects. The constituent parts of the abstract idea of animal are body, life, sense and spontaneous motion. By *body* is meant, body without any particular shape or figure, there being no one shape or figure common to all animals, without covering, either of hair or feathers, or scales etc. nor yet naked: hair, feathers, scales, and nakedness being the distinguishing properties of particular animals, and for that reason left out of the *abstract idea.* Upon the same account the spontaneous motion must be neither walking, nor flying, nor creeping, it is nevertheless a motion; but what that motion is, it is not easy to conceive.

10. Whether others have this wonderful faculty of *abstracting their ideas,* they best can tell: for myself I find indeed I have a faculty of imagining, or representing to myself the ideas of those particular things I have perceived and of variously compounding and dividing them. I can imagine a man with two heads or the upper parts of a man joined to the body of a horse. I can consider the hand, the eye, the nose, each by itself abstracted or separated from the rest of the body. But then whatever hand or eye I imagine, it must have some particular shape and colour. Likewise the idea of man that I frame to myself, must be either of a white, or a black, or a tawny, a straight, or a crooked, a tall, or a low, or a middle-sized man. I cannot by any effort of thought conceive the abstract idea above described.

PART ONE

1. It is evident to anyone who takes a survey of the objects of human knowledge, that they are either ideas actually imprinted on the senses, or else such as are perceived by attending to the passions and operations of the mind, or lastly ideas formed by help of memory and imagination, either compounding, dividing, or barely representing those originally perceived in the aforesaid ways. By sight I have the ideas of light and colours with their several degrees

and variations. By touch I perceive, for example, hard and soft, heat and cold, motion and resistance, and of all these more and less either as to quantity or degree. Smelling furnishes me with odours, the palate with tastes, and hearing conveys sounds to the mind in all their variety of tone and composition. And as several of these are observed to accompany each other, they come to be marked by one name, and so to be reputed as one thing. Thus, for example, a certain colour, taste, smell, figure and consistence having been observed to go together, are accounted one distinct thing, signified by the name *apple.* Other collections of ideas constitute a stone, a tree, a book, and the like sensible things; which, as they are pleasing or disagreeable, excite the passions of love, hatred, joy, grief, and so forth.

2. But besides all that endless variety of ideas or objects of knowledge, there is likewise something which knows or perceives them, and exercises divers operations, as willing, imagining, remembering about them. This perceiving, active being is what I call *mind, spirit, soul* or *my self.* By which words I do not denote any one of my ideas, but a thing entirely distinct from them, wherein they exist, or, which is the same thing, whereby they are perceived; for the existence of an idea consists in being perceived.

3. That neither our thoughts, nor passions, nor ideas formed by the imagination, exist without the mind, is what everybody will allow. And it seems no less evident that the various sensations or ideas imprinted on the sense, however blended or combined together (that is, whatever objects they compose) cannot exist otherwise than in a mind perceiving them. I think an intuitive knowledge may be obtained of this by anyone that shall attend to what is meant by the term *exist* when applied to sensible things. The table I write on, I say, exists, that is, I see and feel it; and if I were out of my study I should say it existed, meaning thereby that if I was in my study I might perceive it, or that some other spirit actually does perceive it. There was an odour, that is, it was smelled; there was a sound, that is to say, it was heard; a colour or figure, and it was perceived by sight or touch. This is all that I can understand by these and the like expressions. For as to what is said of the absolute existence of unthinking things without any relation to their being perceived, that seems perfectly unintelligible. Their *esse* is *percipi,* nor is it possible they should have any existence out of the minds or thinking things which perceive them.

4. It is indeed an opinion strangely prevailing amongst men, that houses, mountains, rivers, and in a word all sensible objects, have an existence natural or real, distinct from their being perceived by the understanding. But with how great an assurance and acquiescence soever this principle may be entertained in the world; yet whoever shall find in his heart to call it in question may, if I mistake not, perceive it to involve a manifest contradiction. For what are the forementioned objects but the things we perceive by sense, and what do we perceive besides our own ideas or sensations; and is it not plainly repugnant that any one of these or any combination of them should exist unperceived?

5. If we thoroughly examine this tenet, it will, perhaps, be found at bottom to depend on the doctrine of *abstract ideas.* For can there be a nicer

strain of abstraction than to distinguish the existence of sensible objects from their being perceived, so as to conceive them existing unperceived? Light and colours, heat and cold, extension and figures, in a word the things we see and feel, what are they but so many sensations, notions, ideas or impressions on the sense; and is it possible to separate, even in thought, any of these from perception? . . .

Hence as it is impossible for me to see or feel anything without an actual sensation of that thing, so is it impossible for me to conceive in my thoughts any sensible thing or object distinct from the sensation or perception of it. . . .

7. From what has been said, it follows, there is not any other substance than spirit, or that which perceives. But for the fuller proof of this point, let it be considered, the sensible qualities are colour, figure, motion, smell, taste, and such like, that is, the ideas perceived by sense. Now for an idea to exist in an unperceiving thing is a manifest contradiction; for to have an idea is all one as to perceive: that therefore wherein colour, figure, and the like qualities exist, must perceive them; hence it is clear there can be no unthinking substance or *substratum* of those ideas.

8. But, say you, though the ideas themselves do not exist without the mind, yet there may be things like them whereof they are copies or resemblances, which things exist without the mind, in an unthinking substance. I answer, an idea can be like nothing but an idea; a colour or figure can be like nothing but another colour or figure. If we look but ever so little into our thoughts, we shall find it impossible for us to conceive a likeness except only between our ideas. Again, I ask whether those supposed originals or external things, of which our ideas are the pictures or representations, be themselves perceivable or no? If they are, then they are ideas, and we have gained our point; but if you say they are not, I appeal to anyone whether it be sense to assert a colour is like something which is invisible; hard or soft, like something which is intangible; and so of the rest.

9. Some there are who make a distinction betwixt *primary* and *secondary* qualities: by the former, they mean extension, figure, motion, rest, solidity or impenetrability, and number: by the latter they denote all other sensible qualities, as colours, sounds, tastes, and so forth. The ideas we have of these they acknowledge not to be the resemblances of any thing existing without the mind or unperceived; but they will have our ideas of the primary qualities to be patterns or images of things which exist without the mind, in an unthinking substance which they call *matter.* By matter therefore we are to understand an inert, senseless substance, in which extension, figure, and motion do actually subsist. But it is evident from what we have already shown, that extension, figure and motion are only ideas existing in the mind, and that an idea can be like nothing but another idea, and that consequently neither they nor their archetypes can exist in an unperceiving substance. Hence it is plain that the very notion of what is called *matter* or *corporeal substance* involves a contradiction in it. . . .

16. But let us examine a little the received opinion. It is said extension is a mode or accident of matter, and that matter is the *substratum* that supports it.

Now I desire that you would explain what is meant by matter's *supporting* extension: say you, I have no idea of matter, and therefore cannot explain it. I answer, though you have no positive, yet if you have any meaning at all, you must at least have a relative idea of matter; though you know not what it is, yet you must be supposed to know what relation it bears to accidents, and what is meant by its supporting them. It is evident *support* cannot here to taken in its usual or literal sense, as when we say that pillars support a building: in what sense therefore must it be taken?

17. If we inquire into what the most accurate philosophers declare themselves to mean by *material substance,* we shall find them acknowledge, they have no other meaning annexed to those sounds, but the idea of being in general, together with the relative notion of its supporting accidents. The general idea of being appeareth to me the most abstract and incomprehensible of all other; and as for its supporting accidents, this, as we have just now observed, cannot be understood in the common sense of those words; it must therefore be taken in some other sense, but what that is they do not explain. So that when I consider the two parts or branches which make the signification of the words *material substance* I am convinced there is no distinct meaning annexed to them. But why should we trouble ourselves any farther, in discussing this material *substratum* or support of figure and motion, and other sensible qualities? Does it not suppose they have an existence without the mind? And is not this a direct repugnancy, and altogether inconceivable? . . .

23. But say you, surely there is nothing easier than to imagine trees, for instance, in a park, or books existing in a closet, and nobody by to perceive them. I answer, you may so, there is no difficulty in it: but what is all this, I beseech you, more than framing in your mind certain ideas which you call books and trees, and at the same time omitting to frame the idea of anyone that may perceive them? But do not you yourself perceive or think of them all the while? This therefore is nothing to the purpose: it only shows you have the power of imagining or forming ideas in your mind; but it doth not show that you can conceive it possible the objects of your thought may exist without the mind: to make out this, it is necessary that you conceive them existing unconceived or unthought of, which is a manifest repugnancy.

24. It is very obvious, upon the least inquiry into our own thoughts, to know whether it be possible for us to understand what is meant by the *absolute existence of sensible objects in themselves, or without the mind.* To me it is evident those words mark out either a direct contradiction, or else nothing at all. And to convince others of this, I know no readier or fairer way than to entreat they would calmly attend to their own thoughts: and if by this attention, the emptiness or repugnancy of those expressions does appear, surely nothing more is requisite for their conviction. It is on this therefore that I insist, to wit, that the absolute existence of unthinking things are words without a meaning, or which include a contradiction. This is what I repeat and inculcate, and earnestly recommend to the attentive thoughts of the reader. . . .

29. But whatever power I may have over my own thoughts, I find the ideas actually perceived by sense have not a like dependence on my will. When in

broad daylight I open my eyes, it is not in my power to choose whether I shall see or no, or to determine what particular objects shall present themselves to my view; and so likewise as to the hearing and other senses, the ideas imprinted on them are not creatures of my will. There is therefore some other will or spirit that produces them.

30. The ideas of sense are more strong, lively, and distinct than those of the imagination; they have likewise a steadiness, order, and coherence, and are not excited at random, as those which are the effects of human wills often are, but in a regular train or series, the admirable connexion whereof sufficiently testifies the wisdom and benevolence of its Author. Now the set rules or established methods, wherein the mind we depend on excites in us the ideas of sense, are called the *Laws of Nature:* and these we learn by experience, which teaches us that such and such ideas are attended with such and such other ideas, in the ordinary course of things. . . .

33. The ideas imprinted on the senses by the Author of Nature are called *real things:* and those excited in the imagination, being less regular, vivid and constant, are more properly termed *ideas,* or *images of things,* which they copy and represent. But then our sensations, be they never so vivid and distinct, are nevertheless *ideas,* that is, they exist in the mind, or are perceived by it, as truly as the ideas of its own framing. The ideas of sense are allowed to have more reality in them, that is, to be more strong, orderly, and coherent than the creatures of the mind; but this is no argument that they exist without the mind. They are also less dependent on the spirit or thinking substance which perceives them, in that they are excited by the will of another and more powerful spirit: yet still they are *ideas,* and certainly no *idea,* whether faint or strong, can exist otherwise than in a mind perceiving it.

REVIEW QUESTIONS

1. Discuss Berkeley's treatment of abstract ideas.
2. What link is there between Locke's view of substance and Berkeley's?
3. Only individual things exist, and yet we use one name, such as *tree,* for many things; what justifies such common usage for Berkeley?
4. Regarding sense knowledge, what is the meaning of Berkeley's statement that "to be is to be perceived"?
5. Why does Berkeley refer to his philosophy as *immaterialism?*
6. How does Berkeley assume that his epistemology will rout the "freethinkers"?

SUGGESTIONS FOR FURTHER READING

Jessop, T. E., ed. *Berkeley, Philosophical Writings.* London, Nelson, 1952.
Jessop, T. E. *George Berkeley.* London, Longmans, 1959.
Urmson, J. O. *Berkeley.* New York, Oxford University Press, 1982.

17

David Hume (1711–1776)

Hume's Influence in British Empiricism

In decisively capitalizing on the empirical openings supplied by John Locke and George Berkeley, David Hume occupies a critical place in the development of British empiricism and in the emergence of the antimetaphysical character of subsequent modern European philosophy.

Hume was born in Edinburgh in 1711. As a young man he undertook, at his family's behest, the study of law, but soon abandoned it for a program of private study in literature and philosophy. To relieve himself of the depression brought on by intense study, he moved to France for several years, settling down for a time in La Flèche, a place he learned to love as suited to quiet reflection; he enjoyed conversation with the learned and hospitable Jesuits there, and must have often been reminded of Descartes, who was educated by them a century and a quarter before. La Flèche was also the place where Hume completed *A Treatise of Human Nature,* published in London in 1739–1740. Though he had high expectations for its success, the *Treatise* received very little recognition, and Hume himself later referred to it as having fallen "deadborn from the press." However, this did not prevent him from revising several parts of this "juvenile work" in the years ahead.

Thoroughly committed to writing, Hume did achieve success with the appearance of *Essays Moral and Political* in 1742. With a growing reputation, and with the help of some good friends, he made a bid for the chair of philosophy at the University of Edinburgh, but because he was now beginning to be known as a person with ideas that ran contrary to the moral and religious views prevailing in Scotland, he failed. Sometime later, however, he was appointed librarian to the Faculty of Advocates, a post that, though it provided practically no income, gave him the opportunity to begin his *History of England;* he soon resigned his librarianship.

After spending some time as a military attaché, Hume took up residence in Edinburgh, and with the publication of additional volumes of his history of England and various essays, he was acknowledged as a distinguished man of letters, proclaimed by some as the most polished contemporary writer in the English language. From 1763 to 1765 he was secretary to the British embassy in Paris, and his stay there was marked by a gracious welcome in intellectual circles, where he was known not only as a respected writer and philosopher but also as a charming and witty gentleman. He was esteemed by *les philosophes* Voltaire, Diderot, D'Alembert, and d'Holbach. Later he was introduced to Jean-Jacques Rousseau, whom he befriended and invited to return with him to Edinburgh; but even though Hume was acknowledged to have had an affable and sociable personality, an unhappy turn of events brought the friendship to an end. He spent his last years in Edinburgh, where he died in 1776. In addition to the works published during his lifetime, several others were published posthumously, including *Dialogues concerning Natural Religion* and his autobiography, edited by his friend Adam Smith.

A "Science" of Man: Sensation as the Parameter of Knowledge

Isaac Newton's huge success with the scientific method had a profound influence on the empirical Hume. If Newton startled the world by arguing, as he put it, from phenomena "without feigning hypotheses," and thus effectively uniting the work of his predecessors, then perhaps a substantial dose of empiricism in philosophy would have the same salutary results. Certainly this was Hume's intention as he tried to make his study of man as empirical as possible, and so labeled his "philosophy" of man a "science" of man; the subtitle of his main work announces it as an "attempt to introduce the experimental method" into the study of human nature.

Because Hume's approach follows that of Locke and Berkeley, the basic ingredients of his epistemology seem familiar. Experience provides the first access to knowledge for man, and whatever man knows by experience is called *perception* by Hume. Perceptions are divided into *impressions* and *ideas,* which are distinguished by the degree of *vividness* (vivacity) with which they are given to us. Impressions are the immediate data of experience; they are lively, direct, and forceful, so that they make an "impression" on us. They include not only sensations but also passions and emotions. Ideas are "copies" or "faint images" of our impressions in thinking and reasoning. Ideas, in turn, are subject to two divisions. The first division is into *ideas of memory,* which are recollections of events, as well as the order in which they took place; and *ideas of imagination,* which are free associations of perceptions with one another. The second division is into *simple* and *complex*. Simple ideas are those that permit no distinction or separation, such as particular colors or tastes; complex ideas are those that do permit distinction or separation, such as relations, modes, and substances.

The importance of these distinctions is that impressions provide our chief access to knowledge, and the more closely our ideas correspond to our impressions, the more reliable they are. "Every simple idea has a simple impression, which resembles it," which is not the case with complex ideas, many of which have no impressions that correspond to them. In other words, if impressions are the direct consequence of our experience, they are the main vehicle for our knowledge of objects, and it is precisely here that Hume must draw up his defenses against causality and substance, the two considerations, as we saw in Locke, that lie at the heart of metaphysics.

Classical Metaphysics Re-visited

The classical formulation of causality states that whatever comes into being requires a cause, that new existences do not explain themselves and are necessarily effects; it is a self-evident truth. But for Hume, the idea of cause and effect does not come from our experience, is not a fact of sensation, and is therefore not found among our impressions. It is only a *supposed necessity* that whatever comes into existence must have a cause. He suggests that there is no difficulty in separating the idea of cause from that of a new existence: "The separation, therefore, of the idea of a cause from that of a beginning of existence, is plainly possible for the imagination; and consequently the actual separation of these objects is so far possible, that it implies no contradiction nor absurdity."

The most Hume admits, based on his principle of the association of ideas, is that we constantly associate in our minds those objects that are constantly associated outside them: there is, for example, a *constant conjunction* between flame and heat, and so our minds associate one with the other as cause and effect: "Thus we remember to have seen that species of object we call *flame*, and to have felt that species of sensation we call *heat*. We likewise call to mind their constant conjunction in all past instances. Without further ceremony, we call the one *cause* and the other *effect*, and infer the existence of the one from that of the other." The relationship between cause and effect is only mental, not real, and where there is no constant conjunction, we cannot say anything; for example, we cannot say that the next falling of a pebble will not extinguish the sun.

Having denied the knowability of causal influence, Hume still has to explain why the human mind is prone to associate two events as though they were cause and effect. To do this, he invokes what he calls *belief*. In a sense, though we do not *know* causality, we *believe* it. Again, Hume uses liveliness, or vividness, to explain belief. Characteristic of the way we react in some instances is the *feeling* we have about a relationship, such as the strong feeling I have in associating flame with heat. It is the *manner* in which we conceive a thing: "So that as belief does nothing but vary the manner, in which we conceive any object, it can only bestow on our ideas an additional force and vivacity. An opinion, therefore, or belief may be most accurately defined, *a lively idea related to or associated with a present impression.*"

The treatment Hume gives to causality is similarly given to *substance,* and here too Hume exploits the opening made by Locke. In comparison with traditional metaphysics, which holds to the existence of substance as a reality we must conclude to, given the existence of qualities, substance has no further meaning than that of a mere "collection of particular qualities, nor have we any other meaning when we either talk or reason concerning it." *Substance* is simply the name used to signify that collection. Every quality has its own existence and may exist apart from every other quality and, indeed, "from that unintelligible chimera of a substance."

What is true of substance in general is true of one substance in particular, namely, the *soul.* In his tract on the soul, Hume states that there is no way of knowing that there is such a thing as immaterial substance, and he argues to the inconclusiveness of the so-called metaphysical demonstrations. Because we have no impression of a soul, Hume is prompted to ask those philosophers "who pretend that we have an idea of the substance of our minds, to point out the impression that produces it, and tell distinctly after what manner that impression operates, and from what object it is derived." That is, if we don't know it empirically through sensation, we don't know it.

As we saw earlier, the denial of the intellect's ability to get to substance and causality is a denial of metaphysics. Though the mind, even for Hume, requires sense reports to be unified in some way, this is still not sufficient to say that it *is* so; it is a mental requirement, not an existential one. Separate sense reports remain separate; separate reports, for example, of "red," "sweet," and "round" remain that way even when we call them collectively "apple"—the mind, that is, endows them with a unity they *really* do not have. Similarly, the causal influence is not sensed, though in classical metaphysics it is *understood,* and therefore real. But for Hume, our belief in causal influence does not warrant our saying that it *is* so.

These Humean positions have a remarkable corollary when it comes to the question of self-identification. What, for Hume, is the *self?* Do we have anything like *personal identity?* With Hume's insistence that distinct perceptions mean distinct existences, the mind does not perceive any real connection between them. A multiplicity of experiences, yes, but no single experience in which unity of self is perceived: "When I turn my reflection on *myself,* I never can perceive this *self* without some one or more perceptions; nor can I ever perceive any thing but the perceptions. 'Tis the composition of these, therefore, which forms the self."

Having previously rejected the soul as anything knowable, which would have grounded the unity of man, Hume is quite consistent in rejecting self and personal identity as anything knowable either, except perhaps as a succession of related objects that sometimes leads us to believe erroneously that they are one thing. The atom-like independence of our perceptions requires a vision of man as "nothing but a bundle or collection of different perceptions, which succeed each other with an inconceivable rapidity, and are in perpetual flux and movement."

Or, a few lines later, "The mind is a kind of theatre, where several perceptions successively make their appearance; pass, re-pass, glide away, and mingle in an infinite variety of postures and situations." Hume never really decides what it is that *endures* throughout all this succession.

The same attitude prevails with regard to God. We have no impression of Him; we can construct no valid argument for His existence; we cannot get to know whether He exists; but we must allow some probability, on the strength of order in the world, of an existence resembling human intelligence that is the principle of order. Toward the end of *Dialogues concerning Natural Religion,* in the opinion expressed by one of the members of the dialogue, Hume seems to be setting forth his own view; "If the whole of Natural Theology, as some people seem to maintain, resolves itself into one simple, though somewhat ambiguous, at least undefined proposition, *That the cause or causes of order in the universe probably bear some remote analogy to human intelligence,*" then "what can the most inquisitive, contemplative, and religious man do more than give a plain, philosophical assent to the proposition, as often as it occurs; and believe that the arguments, on which it is established, exceed the objections, which lie against it?" It is difficult to reconcile this view of God with the rest of Hume's philosophy, but perhaps what he was trying to do was to free any belief in God from an absolute "dogmatism," that is, acceptance without justification.

In the moral sphere the empirical method still obtains, for whatever is true in the physical sphere regarding the basic propositions on cause and effect is also true of the moral sphere. The morality of an action is not the result of a will that causes the action, or of the reason that understands and judges the quality of the action; virtue and vice are the objects of *feeling.* Take vice, for example; it is not reason but feeling that reveals it: "You never can find it, till you turn your reflection into your own breast, and find a sentiment of disapprobation, which arises in you, towards this action. Here is a matter of fact; but 'tis the object of feeling, not of reason." If the terminology of traditional moral value is to be kept, *virtue* becomes a feeling of agreeableness, pleasure, and easiness, whereas *vice* becomes a feeling of disagreeableness, pain, and uneasiness: "Nothing can be more real, or concern us more, than our own sentiments of pleasure and uneasiness; and if these be favourable to virtue, and unfavourable to vice, no more can be requisite to the regulation of our conduct and behavior." Hume's philosophy is a good example of how empiricism in matters of knowledge is linked with its counterpart in matters of morality, an affiliation that runs deep in the British tradition.

Hume's views on the operation of the senses and the work of reason seem to be summed up in a phrase he uses in an appendix to the *Treatise:* the "privilege of a skeptic." Skepticism attaches to Hume just as much as it did to Montaigne, but the analysis of our knowing powers was not a project for Montaigne, as it was for Hume. After sifting through so many problems concerned with the sense and the objects of sense, and after accounting for the various activities of the mind, "knowledge," concludes Hume, "resolves itself into probability," and it is this probability, as the basis of belief, that becomes the only requirement for living humanly. If dogmatism is acceptance without justification, a healthy skepticism is its cure: "A true skeptic," he writes, "will be diffident of his philosophical doubts, as well as of his philosophical convictions," and as a consequence, "will never refuse any innocent satisfaction, which offers itself, upon account of either of them."

The human side of David Hume the philosopher is captured in the honesty and charm of the following confession: "I dine, I play a game of back-gammon, I converse, and am merry with my friends; and when after three or four hours' amusement, I wou'd return to these speculations, they appear so cold, and strain'd, and ridiculous, that I cannot find in my heart to enter into them any farther. . . . I am ready to throw all my books and papers into the fire, and resolve never more to renounce the pleasures of life for the sake of reasoning and philosophy." That this is but a temptation is seen in his oft-quoted words: "Be a philosopher; but amidst all your philosophy, be still a man."

READINGS

Impressions and Ideas

(from *An Enquiry Concerning Human Understanding*, Section II)

11. Every one will readily allow, that there is a considerable difference between the perceptions of the mind, when a man feels the pain of excessive heat, or the pleasure of moderate warmth, and when he afterwards recalls to his memory this sensation, or anticipates it by his imagination. These faculties may mimic or copy the perceptions of the senses; but they never can entirely reach the force and vivacity of the original sentiment. The utmost we say of them, even when they operate with greatest vigour, is, that they represent their object in so lively a manner, that we could almost say we feel or see it: But, except the mind be disordered by disease or madness, they never can arrive at such a pitch of vivacity, as to render these perceptions altogether undistinguishable. All the colours of poetry, however splendid, can never paint natural objects in such a manner as to make the description be taken for a real landskip. The most lively though is still inferior to the dullest sensation.

We may observe a like distinction to run through all the other perceptions of the mind. A man in a fit of anger, is actuated in a very different manner from one who only thinks of that emotion. If you tell me, that any person is in love, I easily understand your meaning, and form a just conception of his situation; but never can mistake that conception for the real disorders and agitations of the passion. When we reflect on our past sentiments and affections, our thought is faithful mirror, and copies its objects truly; but the colours which it employs are faint and dull, in comparison of those in which our original perceptions were clothed. It requires no nice discernment or metaphysical head to mark the distinction between them.

12. Here therefore we may divide all the perceptions of the mind into two classes or species, which are distinguished by their different degrees of force and vivacity. The less forcible and lively are commonly denominated *Thoughts* or *Ideas*.

The other species want a name in our language, and in most others; I suppose, because it was not requisite for any, but philosophical purposes, to rank them under a general term or appellation. Let us, therefore, use a little freedom, and call them *Impressions;* employing that word in a sense somewhat different from the usual. By the term *impression,* then, I mean all our more lively perceptions, when we hear, or see, or feel, or love, or hate, or desire, or will. And impressions are distinguished from ideas, which are the less lively perceptions, of which we are conscious, when we reflect on any of those sensations or movements above mentioned.

13. Nothing, at first view, may seem more unbounded than the thought of man, which not only escapes all human power and authority, but is not even retrained within the limits of nature and reality. To form monsters, and join incongruous shapes and appearances, costs the imagination no more trouble than to conceive the most natural and familiar objects. And while the body is confined to one planet, along which it creeps with pain and difficulty; the thought can in an instant transport us into the most distant regions of the universe; or even beyond the universe, into the unbounded chaos, where nature is supposed to lie in total confusion. What never was seen, or heard of, may yet be conceived; nor is any thing beyond the power of thought, except what implies an absolute contradiction.

But though our thought seems to possess this unbounded liberty, we shall find, upon a nearer examination, that it is really confined within very narrow limits, and that all this creative power of the mind amounts to no more than the faculty of compounding, transposing, augmenting, or diminishing the materials afforded us by the senses and experience. When we think of a golden mountain, we only join two consistent ideas, *gold,* and *mountain,* with which we were formerly acquainted. A virtuous horse we can conceive; because, from our own feeling, we can conceive virtue; and this we may unite to the figure and shape of a horse, which is an animal familiar to us. In short, all the materials of thinking are derived either from our outward or inward sentiment: the mixture and composition of these belongs alone to the mind and will. Or, to express myself in philosophical language, all our ideas or more feeble perceptions are copies of our impressions or more lively ones.

Doubts Concerning the Understanding:
The Cause-and-Effect Relationship
(from *An Enquiry Concerning Human Understanding,* Section IV)

PART I

20. All the objects of human reason or enquiry may naturally be divided into two kinds, to wit, *Relations of Ideas,* and *Matters of Fact.* Of the first kind are the sciences of Geometry, Algebra, and Arithmetic; and in short, every affirmation which is either intuitively or demonstratively certain. *That the square of the hypothenuse is equal to the square of the two sides,* is a proposition which expresses a relation

between these figures. *That three times five is equal to the half of thirty,* expresses a relation between these numbers. Propositions of this kind are discoverable by the mere operation of thought, without dependence on what is anywhere existent in the universe. Though there never were a circle of triangle in nature, the truths demonstrated by Euclid would for ever retain their certainty and evidence.

21. Matters of fact, which are the second objects of human reason, are not ascertained in the same manner; nor is our evidence of their truth, however great, of a like nature with the foregoing. The contrary of every matter of fact is still possible; because it can never imply a contradiction, and is conceived by the mind with the same facility and distinctness, as if ever so conformable to reality. *That the sun will not rise tomorrow* is no less intelligible a proposition, and implies no more contradiction than the affirmation, *that it will rise.* We should in vain, therefore, attempt to demonstrate its falsehood. Were it demonstratively false, it would imply a contradiction, and could never be distinctly conceived by the mind.

It may, therefore, be a subject worthy of curiosity, to enquire what is the nature of that evidence which assures us of any real existence and matter of fact, beyond the present testimony of our sense, or the records of our memory.

22. All reasonings concerning matter of fact seem to be founded on the relation of *Cause and Effect.* By means of that relation alone we can go beyond the evidence of our memory and senses. If you were to ask a man, why he believes any matter of fact, which is absent; for instance, that his friend is in the country, or in France; he would give you a reason; and this reason would be some other fact; as a letter received from him, or the knowledge of his former resolutions and promises. A man finding a watch or any other machine in a desert island, would conclude that there had once been men in that island. All our reasonings concerning fact are of the same nature. And here it is constantly supposed that there is a connexion between the present fact and that which is inferred from it. Were there nothing to bind them together, the inference would be entirely precarious. The hearing of an articulate voice and rational discourse in the dark assures us of the presence of some person: Why? because these are the effects of the human make and fabric, and closely connected with it. If we anatomize all the other reasonings of this nature, we shall find that they are founded on the relation of cause and effect, and that this relation is either near or remote, direct or collateral. Heat and light are collateral effects of fire, and the one effect may justly be inferred from the other.

23. If we would satisfy ourselves, therefore, concerning the nature of that evidence, which assures us of matters of fact, we must enquire how we arrive at the knowledge of cause and effect.

I shall venture to affirm, as a general proposition, which admits no exception, that the knowledge of this relation is not, in any instance, attained by reasonings *a priori;* but arises entirely from experience, when we find that any particular objects are constantly conjoined with each other. Let an object be presented to a man of ever so strong natural reason and abilities; if that object be entirely new to him, he will not be able, by the most accurate examination of its sensible qualities, to discover any of its causes or effects. Adam, though his rational faculties be supposed, at the very first, entirely perfect, could not have inferred from the fluidity and transparency of water that it would suffocate him, or from the light and warmth of fire that it would consume him. No object ever discovers, by the qualities which appear to the senses, either the causes which produced it, or the effects which will arise from it; nor can our reason, unassisted by experience, ever draw any inference concerning real existence and matter of fact.

24. This proposition, *that causes and effects are discoverable, not by reason but by experience,* will readily be admitted with regard to such objects, as we remember to have once been altogether unknown to us; since we must be conscious of the utter inability, which we then lay under, of foretelling what would arise from them. Present two smooth pieces of marble to a man who has no tincture of natural philosophy; he will never discover that they will adhere together in such a manner as to require great force to separate them in a direct line, while they make so small a resistance to a lateral pressure. Such events, as bear little analogy to the common course of nature, are also readily confessed to be known only by experience; nor does any man imagine that the explosion of gunpowder, or the attraction of a loadstone, could even be discovered by arguments *a priori*. In like manner, when an effect is supposed to depend upon an intricate machinery or secret structure of parts, we make no difficulty in attributing all our knowledge of it to experience. Who will assert that he can give the ultimate reason, why milk or bread is proper nourishment for a man, not for a lion or a tiger?

But the same truth may not appear, at first sight, to have the same evidence with regard to events, which have become familiar to us from our first appearance in the world, which bear a close analogy to the whole course of nature, and which are supposed to depend on the simple qualities of objects, without any secret structure of parts. We are apt to imagine that we could discover these effects by the mere operation of our reason, without experience. We fancy, that were we brought on a sudden into this world, we could at first have inferred that one Billiard-ball would communicate motion to another upon impulse; and that we needed not to have waited for the event, in order to pronounce with certainty concerning it. Such is the influence of custom, that, where it is strongest, it not only covers our natural ignorance, but even conceals itself, and seems not to take place, merely because it is found in the highest degree.

25. But to convince us that all the laws of nature, and all the operations of bodies without exception, are known only by experience, the following reflections may, perhaps, suffice. Were any object presented to us, and were we required to pronounce concerning the effect, which will result from it, without consulting past observation; after what manner, I beseech you, must the mind proceed in this operation? It must invent or imagine some event, which it ascribes to the object as its effect; and it is plain that this invention must be entirely arbitrary. The mind can never possibly find the effect in the supposed cause, by the most accurate scrutiny and examination. For the effect is totally different from the cause, and consequently can never be discovered in it. Motion in the second Billiard-ball is a quite distinct event from motion in the first; nor is there anything in the one to suggest the smallest hint of the other. A stone or piece of metal raised into the air, and left without any support, immediately falls; but to consider the matter *a priori,* is there anything we discover in

this situation which can beget the idea of a downward, rather than an upward, or any other motion, in the stone or metal?

And as the first imagination or invention of a particular effect, in all natural operations, is arbitrary, where we consult not experience; so must we also esteem the supposed tie or connexion between the cause and effect, which binds them together, and renders it impossible that any other effect could result from the operation of that cause. When I see, for instance, a Billiard-ball moving in a straight line towards another; even suppose motion in the second ball should by accident be suggested to me, as the result of their contact or impulse; may I not conceive, that a hundred different events might as well follow from that cause? May not both these balls remain at absolute rest? May not the first ball return in a straight line, or leap off from the second in any line or direction? All these suppositions are consistent and conceivable. Why then should we give the preference to one, which is no more consistent or conceivable than the rest? All our reasonings *a priori* will never be able to show us any foundation for this preference.

In a word, then, every effect is a distinct event from its cause. It could not, therefore, be discovered in the cause, and the first invention or conception of it, *a priori,* must be entirely arbitrary. And even after it is suggested, the conjunction of it with the cause must appear equally arbitrary; since there are always many other effects, which, to reason, must seem fully as consistent and natural. In vain, therefore, should we pretend to determine any single event, or infer any cause or effect, without the assistance of observation and experience.

26. Hence we may discover the reason why no philosopher, who is rational and modest, has ever pretended to assign the ultimate cause of any natural operation, or to show distinctly the action of that power, which produces any single effect in the universe. It is confessed, that the utmost effort of human reason is to reduce the principles, productive of natural phenomena, to a greater simplicity, and to resolve the many particular effects into a few general causes, by means of reasonings from analogy, experience, and observation. But as to the causes of these general causes, we should in vain attempt their discovery; nor shall we ever be able to satisfy ourselves, by any particular explication of them. These ultimate springs and principles are totally shut up from human curiosity and enquiry. Elasticity, gravity, cohesion of parts, communication of motion by impulse; these are probably the ultimate causes and principles which we shall ever discover in nature; and we may esteem ourselves sufficiently happy, if, by accurate enquiry and reasoning, we can trace up the particular phenomena to, or near to, these general principles. The most perfect philosophy of the natural kind only staves off our ignorance a little longer: as perhaps the most perfect philosophy of the moral or metaphysical kind serves only to discover larger portions of it. Thus the observation of human blindness and weakness is the result of all philosophy, and meets us at every turn, in spite of our endeavours to elude or avoid it.

27. Nor is geometry, when taken into the assistance of natural philosophy, ever able to remedy this defect, or lead us into the knowledge of ultimate causes, by all that accuracy of reasoning for which it is so justly celebrated. Every part of mixed mathematics proceeds upon the supposition that certain laws are established by nature in her operations; and abstract reasonings are employed, either to

assist experience in the discovery of these laws, or to determine their influence in particular instances, where it depends upon any precise degree of distance and quantity. Thus, it is a law of motion, discovered by experience, that the moment or force of any body in motion is in the compound ratio or proportion of its solid contents and its velocity; and consequently, that a small force may remove the greatest obstacle or raise the greatest weight, if, by any contrivance or machinery, we can increase the velocity of that force, so as to make it an overmatch for its antagonist. Geometry assists us in the application of this law, by giving us the just dimensions of all the parts and figures which can enter into any species of machine; but still the discovery of the law itself is owing merely to experience, and all the abstract reasonings in the world could never lead us one step towards the knowledge to it. When we reason *a priori,* and consider merely any object or cause, as it appears to the mind, independent of all observation, it never could suggest to us the notion of any distinct object, such as its effect; much less, show us the inseparable and inviolable connexion between them. A man must be very sagacious who could discover by reasoning that crystal is the effect of heat, and ice of cold, without being previously acquainted with the operation of these qualities.

PART II

28. But we have not yet attained any tolerable satisfaction with regard to the question first proposed. Each solution still gives rise to a new question as difficult as the foregoing, and leads us on to farther enquiries. When it is asked, *What is the nature of all our reasonings concerning matter of fact?* the proper answer seems to be, that they are founded on the relation of cause and effect. When again it is asked, *What is the foundation of all our reasonings and conclusions concerning that relation?* it may be replied in one word, Experience. But if we still carry on our sifting humour, and ask, *What is the foundation of all conclusions from experience?* this implies a new question, which may be of more difficult solution and explication. Philosophers, that give themselves airs of superior wisdom and sufficiency, have a hard task when they encounter persons of inquisitive dispositions, who push them from every corner to which they retreat, and who are sure at last to bring them to some dangerous dilemma. The best expedient to prevent this confusion, is to be modest in our pretensions; and even to discover the difficulty ourselves before it is objected to us. By this means, we may make a kind of merit of our very ignorance.

I shall content myself, in this section, with an easy task, and shall pretend only to give a negative answer to the question here proposed. I say then, that, even after we have experience of the operations of cause and effect, our conclusions from that experience are *not* founded on reasoning, or any process of the understanding. This answer we must endeavour both to explain and to defend.

29. It must certainly be allowed, that nature has kept us at a great distance from all her secrets, and has afforded us only the knowledge of a few superficial qualities of objects; while she conceals from us those powers and principles on which the influence of those objects entirely depends. Our senses inform us of the colour, weight, and consistence of bread; but neither sense nor reason can

ever inform us of those qualities which fit it for the nourishment and support of a human body. Sight or feeling conveys an idea of the actual motion of bodies; but as to that wonderful force or power, which would carry on a moving body for ever in a continued change of place, and which bodies never lose but by communicating it to others; of this we cannot form the most distant conception. But notwithstanding this ignorance of natural powers and principles, we always presume, when we see like sensible qualities, that they have like secret powers, and expect that effects, similar to those which we have experienced, will follow from them. If a body of like colour and consistence with that bread, which we have formerly eat, be presented to us, we make no scruple of repeating the experiment, and foresee, with certainty, like nourishment and support. Now this is a process of the mind or thought, of which I would willingly know the foundation. It is allowed on all hands that there is no known connexion between the sensible qualities and the secret powers; and consequently, that the mind is not led to form such a conclusion concerning their constant and regular conjunction, by anything which it knows of their nature. As to past *Experience,* it can be allowed to give *direct* and *certain* information of those precise objects only, and that precise period of time, which fell under its cognizance: but why this experience should be extended to future times, and to other objects, which for aught we know, may be only in appearance similar; this is the main question on which I would insist. The bread, which I formerly eat, nourished me; that is, a body of such sensible qualities was, at that time, endued with such secret powers: but does it follow, that other bread must also nourish me at another time, and that like sensible qualities must always be attended with like secret powers? The consequence seems nowise necessary. At least, it must be acknowledged that there is here a consequence drawn by the mind; that there is a certain step taken; a process of thought, and an inference, which wants to be explained. These two propositions are far from being the same, *I have found that such an object has always been attended with such an effect,* and *I foresee, that other objects, which are, in appearance, similar, will be attended with similar effects.* I shall allow, if you please, that the one proposition may justly be inferred from the other: I know, in fact, that it always is inferred. But if you insist that the inference is made by a chain of reasoning, I desire you to produce that reasoning. The connexion between these propositions is not intuitive. There is required a medium, which may enable the mind to draw such an inference, if indeed it be drawn by reasoning and argument. What that medium is, I must confess, passes my comprehension; and it is incumbent on those to produce it, who assert that it really exists, and is the origin of all our conclusions concerning matter of fact.

30. This negative argument must certainly, in process of time, become altogether convincing, if many penetrating and able philosophers shall turn their enquiries this way and no one be ever able to discover any connecting proposition or intermediate step, which supports the understanding in this conclusion. But as the question is yet new, every reader may not trust so far to his own penetration, as to conclude, because an argument escapes his enquiry, that therefore it does not really exist. For this reason it may be requisite to venture upon a more difficult

task; and enumerating all the branches of human knowledge, endeavour to show that none of them can afford such an argument.

All reasonings may be divided into two kinds, namely, demonstrative reasoning, or that concerning relations of ideas, and moral reasoning, or that concerning matters of fact and existence. That there are no demonstrative arguments in the case seems evident; since it implies no contradiction that the course of nature may change, and that an object, seemingly like those which we have experienced, may be attended with different or contrary effects. May I not clearly and distinctly conceive that a body, falling from the clouds, and which, in all other respects, resembles snow, has yet the taste of salt or feeling of fire? Is there any more intelligible proposition than to affirm, that all the trees will flourish in December and January, and decay in May and June? Now whatever is intelligible, and can be distinctly conceived, implies no contradiction, and can never be proved false by any demonstrative argument or abstract reasoning *a priori.*

If we be, therefore, engaged by arguments to put trust in past experience, and make it the standard of our future judgement, these arguments must be probable only, or such as regard matter of fact and real existence, according to the division above mentioned. But that there is no argument of this kind, must appear, if our explication of the species of reasoning be admitted as solid and satisfactory. We have said that all arguments concerning existence are founded on the relation of cause and effect; that our knowledge of that relation is derived entirely from experience; and that all our experimental conclusions proceed upon the supposition that the future will be conformable to the past. To endeavour, therefore, the proof of this last supposition by probable arguments, or arguments regarding existence, must be evidently going in a circle, and taking that for granted, which is the very point in question.

31. In reality, all arguments from experience are founded on the similarity which we discover among natural objects, and by which we are induced to expect effects similar to those which we have found to follow from such objects. And though none but a fool or madman will even pretend to dispute the authority of experience, or to reject that great guide of human life, it may surely be allowed a philosopher to have so much curiosity at least as to examine the principle of human nature, which gives this mighty authority to experience, and makes us draw advantage from the similarity which nature has placed among different objects. From causes which appear *similar* we expect similar effects. This is the sum of all our experimental conclusions. Now it seems evident that, if this conclusion were formed by reason, it would be as perfect at first, and upon one instance, as after ever so long a course of experience. But the case is far otherwise. Nothing so like as eggs; yet no one, on account of this appearing similarity, expects the same taste and relish in all of them. It is only after a long course of uniform experiments in any kind, that we attain a firm reliance and security with regard to a particular event. Now where is that process of reasoning which, from one instance, draws a conclusion, so different from that which it *infers* from a hundred instances that are nowise different from that single one? This question I propose as much for the sake of information, as with an intention of raising difficulties. I cannot find, I cannot imagine any such reasoning. But I keep my mind still open to instruction, if any one will vouchsafe to bestow it on me.

32. Should it be said that, from a number of uniform experiments, we infer a connexion between the sensible qualities and the secret powers; this, I must confess, seems the same difficulty, couched in different terms. The question still recurs, on what process of argument this inference is founded? Where is the medium, the interposing ideas, which join propositions so very wide of each other? It is confessed that the colour, consistence, and other sensible qualities of bread appear not, of themselves, to have any connexion with the secret powers of nourishment and support. For otherwise we could infer these secret powers from the first appearance of these sensible qualities, without the aid of experience; contrary to the sentiment of all philosophers, and contrary to plain matter of fact. Here, then, is our natural state of ignorance with regard to the powers and influence of all objects. How is this remedied by experience? It only shows us a number of uniform effects, resulting from certain objects, and teaches us that those particular objects, at that particular time, were endowed with such powers and forces. When a new object, endowed with similar sensible qualities, is produced, we expect similar powers and forces, and look for a like effect. From a body of like colour and consistence with bread we expect like nourishment and support. But this surely is a step or progress of the mind, which wants to be explained. When a man says, *I have found, in all past instances, such sensible qualities conjoined with such secret powers:* And when he says, *Similar sensible qualities will always be conjoined with similar secret powers,* he is not guilty of a tautology, nor are these propositions in any respect the same. You say that the one proposition is an inference from the other. But you must confess that the inference is not intuitive; neither is it demonstrative: Of what nature is it, then? To say it is experimental, is begging the question. For all inferences from experience suppose, as their foundation, that the future will resemble the past, and that similar powers will be conjoined with similar sensible qualities. If there be any suspicion that the course of nature may change, and that the past may be no rule for the future, all experience becomes useless, and can give rise to no inference or conclusion. It is impossible, therefore, that any arguments from experience can prove this resemblance of the past to the future; since all these arguments are founded on the supposition of that resemblance. Let the course of things be allowed hitherto ever so regular; that alone, without some new argument or inference, proves not that, for the future, it will continue so. In vain do you pretend to have learned the nature of bodies from your past experience. Their secret nature, and consequently all their effects and influence, may change, without any change in their sensible qualities. This happens sometimes, and with regard to some objects: Why may it not happen always, and with regard to all objects? What logic, what process of argument secures you against this supposition? My practice, you say, refutes my doubts. But you mistake the purport of my question. As an agent, I am quite satisfied in the point; but as a philosopher, who has some share of curiosity, I will not say scepticism, I want to learn the foundation of this inference. No reading, no enquiry has yet been able to remove my difficulty, or give me satisfaction in a matter of such importance. Can I do better than propose the difficulty to the public, even though, perhaps, I have small hopes of obtaining a solution? We shall at least, by this means, be sensible of our ignorance, if we do not argument our knowledge.

33. I must confess that a man is guilty of unpardonable arrogance who concludes, because an argument has escaped his own investigation, that therefore it does not really exist. I must also confess that, though all the learned, for several ages, should have employed themselves in fruitless search upon any subject, it may still, perhaps, be rash to conclude positively that the subject must, therefore, pass all human comprehension. Even though we examine all the sources of our knowledge, and conclude them unfit for such a subject, there may still remain a suspicion, that the enumeration is not complete, or the examination not accurate. But with regard to the present subject, there are some considerations which seem to remove all this accusation of arrogance or suspicion of mistake.

It is certain that the most ignorant and stupid peasants—nay infants, nay even brute beasts—improve by experience, and learn the qualities of natural objects, by observing the effects which result from them. When a child has felt the sensation of pain from touching the flame of a candle, he will be careful not to put his hand near any candle; but will expect a similar effect from a cause which is similar in its sensible qualities and appearance. If you assert, therefore, that the understanding of the child is led into this conclusion by any process of argument or ratiocination, I may justly require you to produce that argument; nor have you any pretence to refuse so equitable a demand. You cannot say that the argument is abstruse, and may possibly escape your enquiry; since you confess that it is obvious to the capacity of a mere infant. If you hesitate, therefore, a moment, or if, after reflection, you produce any intricate or profound argument, you, in a manner, give up the question, and confess that it is not reasoning which engages us to suppose the past resembling the future, and to expect similar effects from causes which are, to appearance, similar. This is the proposition which I intended to enforce in the present section. If I be right, I pretend not to have made any mighty discovery. And if I be wrong, I must acknowledge myself to be indeed a very backward scholar; since I cannot now discover an argument which, it seems, was perfectly familiar to me long before I was out of my cradle.

The Advantages of Scepticism

(from *An Enquiry Concerning Human Understanding*, Section XII, Part III)

129. There is, indeed, a more *mitigated* scepticism or *academical* philosophy, which may be both durable and useful, and which may, in part, be the result of this Pyrrhonism, or *excessive* scepticism, when its undistinguished doubts are, in some measure, corrected by common sense and reflection. The greater part of mankind are naturally apt to be affirmative and dogmatical in their opinions; and while they see objects only on one side, and have no idea of any counterpoising argument, they throw themselves precipitately into the principles, to which they are inclined; nor have they any indulgence for those who entertain opposite sentiments. To hesitate or balance perplexes their understanding, checks their passion, and suspends their action. They are, therefore, impatient till they escape from a state, which to them is

so uneasy; and they think, that they could never remove themselves far enough from it, by the violence of their affirmations and obstinacy of their belief. But could such dogmatical reasoners become sensible of the strange infirmities of human understanding, even in its most perfect state, and when most accurate and cautious in its determinations; such a reflection would naturally inspire them with more modesty and reserve, and diminish their fond opinion of themselves, and their prejudice against antagonists. The illiterate may reflect on the disposition of the learned, who, amidst all the advantages of study and reflection, are commonly still diffident in their determinations; and if any of the learned be inclined, from their natural temper, to haughtiness and obstinacy, a small tincture of Pyrrhonism might abate their pride, by showing them, that the few advantages, which they may have attained over their fellows, are but inconsiderable, if compared with the universal perplexity and confusion, which is inherent in human nature. In general, there is a degree of doubt, and caution, and modesty, which, in all kinds of scrutiny and decision, ought for ever to accompany a just reasoner.

130. Another species of *mitigated* scepticism which may be of advantage to mankind, and which may be the natural result of the Pyrrhonian doubts and scruples, is the limitation of our enquiries to such subjects as are best adapted to the narrow capacity of human understanding. The imagination of man is naturally sublime, delighted with whatever is remote and extraordinary, and running, without control, into the most distant parts of space and time in order to avoid the objects, which custom has rendered too familiar to it. A correct *Judgement* observes a contrary method, and avoiding all distant and high enquiries, confines itself to common life, and to such subjects as fall under daily practice and experience; leaving the more sublime topics to the embellishment of poets and orators, or to the arts of priests and politicians. To bring us to so salutary a determination, nothing can be more serviceable, than to be once thoroughly convinced of the force of the Pyrrhonian doubt, and of the impossibility, that anything, but the strong power of natural instinct, could free us from it. Those who have a propensity to philosophy, will still continue their researches; because they reflect, that, besides the immediate pleasure, attending such an occupation, philosophical decisions are nothing but the reflections of common life, methodized and corrected. But they will never be tempted to go beyond common life, so long as they consider the imperfection of those faculties which they employ, their narrow reach, and their inaccurate operations. While we cannot give a satisfactory reason, why we believe, after a thousand experiments, that a stone will fall, or fire burn; can we ever satisfy ourselves concerning any determination, which we may form, with regard to the origin of worlds, and the situation of nature, from, and to eternity?

This narrow limitation, indeed, of our inquiries, is, in every respect, so reasonable, that it suffices to make the slightest examination into the natural powers of the human mind and to compare them with their objects, in order to recommend it to us. We shall then find what are the proper subjects of science and enquiry.

131. It seems to me, that the only objects of the abstract science or of demonstration are quantity and number, and that all attempts to extend this more perfect species of knowledge beyond these bounds are mere sophistry and illusion. As the component parts of quantity and number are entirely similar, their relations become

intricate and involved; and nothing can be more curious, as well as useful, then to trace, by a variety of mediums, their equality or inequality, through their different appearances. But as all other ideas are clearly distinct and different from each other, we can never advance farther, by our utmost scrutiny, than to observe this diversity, and, by an obvious reflection, pronounce one thing not to be another. Or if there be any difficulty in these decisions, it proceeds entirely from the undeterminate meaning of words, which is corrected by juster definitions. That *the square of the hypothenuse is equal to the squares of the other two sides,* cannot be known, let the terms be ever so exactly defined, without a train of reasoning and enquiry. But to convince us of this proposition, that *where there is no property, there can be no injustice,* it is only necessary to define the terms, and explain injustice to be a violation of property. This proposition is, indeed, nothing but a more imperfect definition. It is the same case with all those pretended syllogistical reasonings, which may be found in every other branch of learning, except the sciences of quantity and number; and these may safely, I think, be pronounced the only proper objects of knowledge and demonstration.

132. All other enquiries of men regard only matter of fact and existence; and these are evidently incapable of demonstration. Whatever *is* may *not be.* No negation of a fact can involve a contradiction. The nonexistence of any being, without exception, is as clear and distinct an idea as its existence. The proposition, which affirms it not to be, however false, is no less conceivable and intelligible, than that which affirms it to be. The case is different with the sciences, properly so called. Every proposition, which is not true, is there confused and unintelligible. That the cube root of 64 is equal to be the half of 10, is a false proposition, and can never be distinctly conceived. But that Caesar, or the angel Gabriel, or any being never existed, may be a false proposition, but still is perfectly conceivable and implies no contradiction.

The existence, therefore, of any being can only be proved by arguments from its cause or its effect; and these arguments are founded entirely on experience. If we reason *a priori,* anything may appear able to produce anything. The falling of a pebble may, for aught we know, extinguish the sun; or the wish of a man control the planets in their orbits. It is only experience, which teaches us the nature and bounds of cause and effect, and enables us to infer the existence of one object from that of another. Such is the foundation of moral reasoning, which forms the greater part of human knowledge, and is the source of all human action and behaviour.

Moral reasonings are either concerning particular or general facts. All deliberations in life regard the former; as also all disquisitions in history, chronology, geography, and astronomy.

The sciences, which treat of general facts, are politics, natural philosophy, physic, chemistry, &c, where the qualities, causes and effects of a whole species of objects are enquired into.

Divinity or Theology, as it proves the existence of a Deity, and the immortality of souls, is composed partly of reasonings concerning particular, partly concerning general facts. It has a foundation in reason, so far as it is supported by experience. But its best and most solid foundation is *faith* and divine revelation.

Morals and criticism are not so properly objects of the understanding as of taste and sentiment. Beauty, whether moral or natural, is felt, more properly than perceived. Or if we reason concerning it, and endeavour to fix its standard, we regard a new fact, to wit, the general tastes of mankind, so some such fact, which may be the object of reasoning and enquiry.

When we run over libraries, persuaded of these principles, what havoc must we make? If we take in our hand any volume; of divinity or school metaphysics, for instance, let us ask, *Does it contain any abstract reasoning concerning quantity or number?* No. *Does it contain any experimental reasoning concerning matter of fact and existence?* No. Commit it then to the flames: for it can contain nothing but sophistry and illusion.

Dialogues Concerning Natural Religion

II

I must own, Cleanthes, said Demea, that nothing can more surprise me, than the light, in which you have, all along, put this argument. By the whole tenor of your discourse, one would imagine that you were maintaining the being of a God, against the cavils of atheists and infidels; and were necessitated to become a champion for that fundamental principle of all religion. But this, I hope, is not by any means a question among us. No man; no man, at least, of common sense, I am persuaded, ever entertained a serious doubt with regard to a truth, so certain and self-evident. The question is not concerning the *being,* but the *nature* of God. This, I affirm, from the infirmities of human understanding, to be altogether incomprehensible and unknown to us. The essence of that supreme mind, his attributes, the manner of his existence, the very nature of his duration; these and every particular, which regards so divine a being, are mysterious to men. Finite, weak, and blind creatures, we ought to humble ourselves in his august presence, and, conscious of our frailties, adore in silence his infinite perfections, which eye hath not seen, ear hath not heard, neither hath it entered into the heart of man to conceive them. They are covered in a deep cloud from human curiosity: it is profaneness to attempt penetrating through these sacred obscurities; and next to the impiety of denying his existence, is the temerity of prying into his nature and essence, decrees and attributes.

But lest you should think, that my *piety* has here got the better of my *philosophy,* I shall support my opinion, if it needs any support, by a very great authority. I might cite all the divines almost, from the foundation of Christianity, who have ever treated of this or any other theological subject: but I shall confine myself, at present, to one equally celebrated for piety and philosophy. It is Father Malebranche, who, I remember, thus expresses himself. 'One ought not so much (says he) to call God a spirit, in order to express positively what he is, as in order to signify that he is not matter. He is a Being infinitely perfect; of this we cannot doubt. But in the same manner as we ought not to imagine, even supposing him corporeal, that he is clothed with a human body, as the Anthropomorphites asserted, under color that that figure was the most perfect of any; so neither ought we to imagine, that the spirit of God has human ideas, or bears any resemblance to our spirit; under colour that we know nothing more perfect than a human mind. We ought rather to believe, that as he comprehends the perfections of matter without being material . . . he comprehends also the perfections of created spirits, without being spirit, in the manner we conceive spirit: that his true name is, *He that is,* or, in other words, Being without restriction, All Being, the Being infinite and universal.'

After so great an authority, Demea, replied Philo, as that which you have produced, and a thousand more, which you might produce, it would appear ridiculous in me to add my sentiment, or express my approbation of your doctrine. But surely, where reasonable men treat these subjects the question can never be concerning the being, but only the nature of the Deity. The former truth, as you well observe, is unquestionable and self-evident. Nothing exists without a cause; and the original cause of this universe (whatever it be) we call God; and piously ascribe to him every species of perfection. Whoever scruples this fundamental truth, deserves every punishment, which can be inflicted among philosophers, to wit, the greatest ridicule, contempt and disapprobation. But as all perfection is entirely relative, we ought never to imagine, that we comprehend the attributes of this divine Being, or to suppose, that his perfections have any analogy or likeness to the perfections of a human creature. Wisdom, thought, design, knowledge; these we justly ascribe to him; because these words are honorable among men, and we have no other language or other conceptions, by which we can express our adoration of him. But let us beware, lest we think, that our ideas any wise correspond to his perfections, or that his attributes have any resemblance to these qualities among men. He is infinitely superior to our limited view and comprehension; and is more the object of worship in the temple, than of disputation in the schools.

In reality, Cleanthes, continued he, there is no need of having recourse to that affected scepticism, so displeasing to you, in order to come at this determination. Our ideas reach no farther than our experience; we have no experience of divine attributes and operations: I need not conclude my syllogism; you can draw the inference yourself. And it is a pleasure to me (and I hope to you too) that just reasoning and sound piety here concur in the same conclusion, and both of them establish the adorably mysterious and incomprehensible nature of the Supreme Being.

Not to lose any time in circumlocutions, said Cleanthes, addressing himself to Demea, much less in replying to the pious declamations of Philo; I shall briefly explain how I conceive this matter. Look round the world; contemplate the whole and every part of it: you will find it to be nothing but one great machine, subdivided into an infinite number of lesser machines, which again admit of subdivisions, to a degree beyond what human senses and faculties can trace and explain. All these various machines, and even their most minute parts, are adjusted to each other with an accuracy, which ravishes into admiration all men, who have ever contemplated them. The curious adapting of means to ends, throughout all nature, resembles exactly, though it much exceeds, the productions of human contrivance; of human design, thought, wisdom, and intelligence. Since therefore the effects resemble each other, we are led to infer, by all the rules of analogy, that the causes also resemble; and that the Author of Nature is somewhat similar to the mind of men; though possessed of much larger faculties, proportioned to the grandeur of the work, which he has executed. By this argument *a posteriori,* and by this argument alone, do we prove at once the existence of a Deity, and his similarity to human mind and intelligence.

I shall be so free, Cleanthes, said Demea, as to tell you, that from the beginning, I could not approve of your conclusion concerning the similarity of the Deity to men; still less can I approve of the mediums, by which you endeavor to establish it. What! No demonstration of the being of a God! No abstract arguments! No proofs *a priori!* Are which have hitherto been so much insisted on by philosophers, all fallacy, all sophism? Can we reach no farther in this subject than experience and probability? I will not say, that this is betraying the cause of a deity: but surely, by this affected candor, you give advantage of atheists, which they never could obtain, by the mere dint of argument and reasoning.

What I chiefly scruple in this subject, said Philo, is not so much, that all religious arguments are by Cleanthes reduced to experience, as that they appear not to be even the most certain and irrefragable of that inferior kind. That a stone will fall, that fire will burn, that the earth has solidity, we have observed a thousand and a thousand times; and when any new instance of this nature is presented, we draw without hesitation the accustomed inference. The exact similarity of the cases gives us a perfect assurance of a similar event; and a stronger evidence is never desired nor sought after. But wherever you depart, in the least, from the similarity of the cases, you diminish proportionably the evidence; and may at last bring it to a very weak *analogy,* which is confessedly liable to error and uncertainty. After having experienced the circulation of the blood in human creatures, we make no doubt that it takes place in Titius and Maevius: but from its circulation in frogs and fishes, it is only a presumption, though a strong one, from analogy, that it takes place in men and other animals. The analogical reasoning is much weaker, when we infer the circulation of the sap in vegetables from our experience, that the blood circulates in animals; and those, who hastily followed that imperfect analogy, are found, by more accurate experiments, to have been mistaken.

If we see a house, Cleanthes, we conclude, with the greatest certainty, that it had an architect or builder; because this is precisely that species of effect, which we have experienced to proceed from that species of cause. But surely you will not affirm, that the universe bears such a resemblance to a house, that we can with the same certainty infer a similar cause, or that the analogy is here entire and perfect. The dissimilitude is so striking, that the utmost you can here pretend to is a guess, a conjecture, a presumption concerning a similar cause; and how that pretension will be received in the world. I leave you to consider.

It would surely be very ill received, replied Cleanthes; and I should be deservedly blamed and detested, did I allow, that the proofs of a Deity amounted to no more than a guess or conjecture. But is the whole adjustment of means to ends in a house and in the universe so slight a resemblance? The economy of final causes?

The order, proportion, and arrangement of every part? Steps of a stair are plainly contrived that human legs may use them in mounting; and this inference is certain and infallible. Human legs are also contrived for walking and mounting; and this inference, I allow, is not altogether so certain, because of the dissimilarity which you remark; but does it, therefore, deserve the name only of presumption or conjecture?

Good God! cried Demea, interrupting him, where are we? Zealous defenders of religion allow, that the proofs of a Deity fall short of perfect evidence! and you, Philo, on whose assistance I depended, in proving the adorable mysteriousness of the Divine Nature, do you assent to all these extravagant opinions of Cleanthes? For what other name can I give them? Or why spare my censure, when such principles are advanced, supported by such an authority, before so young a man as Pamphilus?

You seem not to apprehend, replied Philo, that I argue with Cleanthes in his own way; and by showing him the dangerous consequences of his tenets, hope at last to reduce him to our opinion. But what sticks most with you, I observe, is the representation which Cleanthes has made of the argument *a posteriori;* and finding, that that argument is likely to escape your hold and vanish into air, you think it so disguised, that you can scarcely believe it to be set in its true light. Now, however much I may dissent, in other respects, from the dangerous principles of Cleanthes, I must allow, that he has fairly represented that argument; and I shall endeavour so to state the matter to you, that you will entertain no farther scruples with regard to it.

Were a man to abstract from everything which he knows or has seen, he would be altogether incapable, merely from his own ideas, to determine what kind of scene the universe must be, or to give the preference to one state or situation of things above another. For as nothing which he clearly conceives, could be esteemed impossible or implying a contradiction, every chimera of his fancy would be upon an equal footing; nor could he assign any just reason, why he adheres to one idea or system, and rejects the others, which are equally possible.

Again; after he opens his eyes, and contemplates the world, as it really is, it would be impossible for him, at first, to assign the cause of any one event; much less, of the whole of things or of the universe. He might set his fancy a rambling; and she might bring him in an infinite variety of reports and representations. These would all be possible; but being all equally possible, he would never, of himself, give a satisfactory account for his preferring one of them to the rest. Experience alone can point out to him the true cause of any phenomenon.

Now, according to this method of reasoning, Demea, it follows (and is, indeed, tacitly allowed by Cleanthes himself) that order, arrangement, or the adjustment of final causes is not, of itself, any proof of design; but only so far as it has been experienced to proceed from that principle. For aught we can know *a priori,* matter may contain the source or spring of order originally, within itself, as well as mind does; and there is no more difficulty in conceiving, that the several elements, from an internal unknown cause, may fall into the most exquisite arrangement, than to conceive that their ideas, in the great, universal mind, from a like internal, unknown cause, fall into that arrangement. The equal possibility of both these suppositions is allowed. But by experience we find (according to Cleanthes), that there is a difference between them. Throw several pieces of steel together, without shape or form; they will never arrange themselves so as to compose a watch: stone, and mortar, and wood, without an architect, never erect a house. But the ideas in a human mind, we see, by an unknown, inexplicable economy, arrange themselves so as to form the plan of a watch or house. Experience, therefore, proves, that there is an original principle of order in mind, not in matter. From similar effects we infer similar causes. The adjustment of means to ends is alike in the universe, as in a machine of human contrivance. The causes, therefore, must be resembling.

I was from the beginning scandalized, I must own, with this resemblance, which is asserted, between the Deity and human creatures; and must conceive it to imply such a degradation of the Supreme Being as no sound theist could endure. With your assistance, therefore, Demea, I shall endeavor to defend what you justly called the adorable mysteriousness of the Divine Nature, and shall refute this reasoning of Cleanthes, provided he allows, that I have made a fair representation of it.

When Cleanthes had assented, Philo, after a short pause, proceeded in the following manner.

That all inferences, Cleanthes, concerning fact, are founded on experience, and that all experimental reasonings are founded on the supposition, that similar causes prove similar effects, and similar effects similar causes; I shall not, at present, much dispute with you. But observe, I entreat you, with what extreme caution all just reasoners proceed in the transferring of experiments to similar cases. Unless the cases be exactly similar, they repose no perfect confidence in applying their past observation to any particular phenomenon. Every alternation of circumstances occasions a doubt concerning the event; and it requires new experiments to prove certainly, that the new circumstances are of no moment or importance. A change in bulk, situation, arrangement, age, disposition of the air, or surrounding bodies; any of these particulars may be attended with the most unexpected consequences; and unless the objects be quite familiar to us, it is the highest temerity to expect with assurance, after any of these changes, an event similar to that which before fell under our observation. The slow and deliberate steps of philosophers, here, if anywhere, are distinguished from the precipitate march of the vulgar, who, hurried on by the smallest similitudes, are incapable of all discernment or consideration.

But can you think, Cleanthes, that your usual phlegm and philosophy have been preserved in so wide a step as you have taken, when you compared to the universe, houses, ships, furniture, machines; and from their similarity in some circumstances inferred a similarity in their causes? Thought, design, intelligence, such as we discover in man and other animals, is no more than one of the springs and principles of the universe, as well as heat or cold, attraction or repulsion, and a hundred others, which fall under daily observation. It is an active cause, by which some particular parts of nature, we find, produce alterations on other parts. But can a conclusion, with any propriety, be transferred from parts to the whole? Does not the great disproportion bar all comparison and inference? From observing the growth of a hair, can we learn anything concerning the generation of a man? Would the manner of a leaf's blowing, even though perfectly known, afford us any instruction concerning the vegetation of a tree?

But allowing that we were to take the *operations* of one part of nature upon another for the foundation of our judgment concerning the *origin* of the whole (which never can be admitted), yet why select so minute, so weak, so bounded a principle as the reason and design of animals is found to be upon this planet? What peculiar privilege has this little agitation of the brain which we call *thought,* that we must thus make it the model of the whole universe? Our partiality in our own favor does indeed present it on all occasions; but sound philosophy ought carefully to guard against so natural an illusion.

So far from admitting, continued Philo, that the operations of a part can afford us any just conclusion concerning the origin of the whole. I will not allow any one part to form a rule for another part, if the latter be very remote from the former. Is there any reasonable ground to conclude, that the inhabitants of other planets possess thought, intelligence, reason, or anything similar to these faculties in men? When Nature has so extremely diversified her manner of operation in this small globe; can we imagine, that she incessantly copies herself throughout so immense a universe? And if thought, as we may well suppose, be confined merely to this narrow corner, and has even there so limited a sphere of action; with what propriety can we assign it for the original cause of all things? The narrow views of a peasant, who makes his domestic economy the rule for the government of kingdoms, is in comparison a pardonable sophism.

But were we ever so much assured, that a thought and reason, resembling the human, were to be found throughout the whole universe, and were its activity elsewhere vastly greater and more commanding than it appears in this globe; yet I cannot see, why the operations of a world, constituted, arranged, adjusted, can with any propriety be extended to a world, which is in its embryo state, and is advancing towards that constitution and arrangement. By observation, we know somewhat of the economy, action, and nourishment of a finished animal; but we must transfer with great caution that observation to the growth of a fetus in the womb, and still more, to the formation of an animalcule in the loins of its male parent. Nature, we find, even from our limited experience, possesses an infinite number of springs and principles, which incessantly discover themselves on every change of her position and situation. And what new and unknown principles would actuate her in so new and unknown a situation as that of the formation of a universe, we cannot, without the utmost temerity, pretend to determine.

A very small part of this great system, during a very short time, is very imperfectly discovered to us; and do we thence pronounce decisively concerning the origin of the whole?

Admirable conclusion! Stone, wood, brick, iron, brass, have not, at this time, in this minute globe of earth, an order or arrangement without human art and contrivance; therefore the universe could not originally attain its order and arrangement, without something similar to human art. But is a part of nature a rule for another part very wide of the former? Is it a rule for the whole? Is a very small part a rule for the universe? Is nature in one situation, a certain rule for nature in another situation, vastly different from the former?

And can you blame me, Cleanthes, if I here imitate the prudent reserve of Simonides, who, according to the noted story, being asked by Hiero, *What God was?* desired a day to think of it, and then two days more; and after that manner continually prolonged the term, without ever bringing in his definition or description? Could you even blame me, if I had answered at first *that I did not know* and was sensible that this subject lay vastly beyond the reach of my faculties? You might cry out sceptic and raillier as much as you pleased; but having found, in so many other subjects, much more familiar, the imperfections and even contradictions of human reason, I never should expect any success from its feeble conjectures, in a subject, so sublime, and so remote from the sphere of our observation. When two species of objects have always been observed to be conjoined together, I can infer, by custom, the existence of one wherever I see the existence of the other; and this I call an argument from experience. But how this argument can have place, where the objects, as in the present case, are single, individual, without parallel, or specific resemblance, may be difficult to explain. And will any man tell me with a serious countenance, that an orderly universe must arise from some thought and art, like the human; because we have experience of it? To ascertain this reasoning, it were requisite, that we had experience of the origin of worlds; and it is not sufficient surely, that we have seen ships and cities arise from human art and contrivance. . . .

Philo was proceeding in this vehement manner, somewhat between jest and earnest, as it appeared to me; when he observed some signs of impatience in Cleanthes, and then immediately stopped short. What I had to suggest, said Cleanthes, is only that you would not abuse terms, or make use of popular expressions to subvert philosophical reasonings. You know, that the vulgar often distinguish reason from experience, even where the question relates only to matter of fact and existence; though it is found, where that reason is properly analyzed, that it is nothing but a species of experience. To prove by experience the origin of the universe from mind is not more contrary to common speech than to prove the motion of the earth from the same principle. And a caviler might raise all the same objections to the Copernican system, which you have urged against my reasonings. Have you other earths, might he say, which you have seen to move? Here. . . .

Yes! cried Philo, interrupting him, we have other earths. Is not the moon another earth, which we see to turn round its center? Is not Venus another earth, where we observe the same phenomenon? Are not the revolutions of the sun also a confirmation, from analogy, of the same theory? All the planets, are they not earths, which revolve about the sun? Are not the satellites moons, which move round Jupiter and Saturn, and along with these primary planets, round the sun? These analogies and resemblances, with others, which I have not mentioned, are the sole proofs of the Copernican system; and to you it belongs to consider, whether you have any analogies of the same kind to support your theory.

In reality, Cleanthes, continued he, the modern system of astronomy is now so much received by all inquirers, and has become so essential a part even of our earliest education, that we are not commonly very scrupulous in examining the reasons upon which it is founded. It is now become a matter of mere curiosity to study the first writers on that subject, who had the full force of prejudice to encounter, and were obliged to turn their arguments on every side, in order to render them popular and convincing. But if we peruse Galileo's famous Dialogues concerning the system of the world, we shall find, that that great genius, one of the sublimest that ever existed, first bent all his endeavors to prove, that there was no foundation for the distinction commonly made between elementary and celestial substances. The schools, proceeding from the illusions of sense, had carried this distinction very far; and had established the latter substances to be ingenerable, incorruptible, unalterable, impassable; and had assigned all the opposite qualities to the former. But Galileo, beginning with the moon, proved its similarity in every particular to the earth; its convex figure, its natural darkness when not illuminated, its density, its distinction into solid and liquid, the variations of its phases, the mutual illuminations of the earth and moon, their mutual eclipses, the inequalities of the lunar surface, etc. After many instances of this kind, with regard to all the planets, men plainly saw, that these bodies became proper objects of experience; and that the similarity of their nature enabled us to extend the same arguments and phenomena from one to the other.

In this cautious proceeding of the astronomers, you may read your own condemnation. Cleanthes; or rather may see, that the subject in which you are engaged exceeds all human reason and inquiry. Can you pretend to show any such similarity between the fabric of a house, and the generation of a universe? Have you ever seen nature in any such situation as resembles the first arrangement of the elements? Have worlds ever been formed under your eye? and have you had leisure to observe the whole progress of the phenomenon, from the first appearance of order to its final consummation? If you have, then cite your experience, and deliver your theory.

REVIEW QUESTIONS

1. Explain how Hume's empiricism derives from Locke through Berkeley.
2. In what sense is Hume a skeptic?
3. Discuss the fate of metaphysics as a science in Hume's philosophy.
4. What is the meaning of constant conjunction in Hume's analysis of causality?
5. Show the relationship of substance in Hume to that in Locke and Berkeley.
6. Why is personal identity a problem in Hume's philosophy?
7. Discuss Hume's general approach to the problem of moral right and wrong.

SUGGESTIONS FOR FURTHER READING

Selby-Bigge, L. A., ed. *Enquiries Concerning Human Understanding and Concerning the Principles of Morals,* 3rd ed., with notes by P. N. Nidditch. New York, Oxford University Press, 1975.

Kemp Smith, N. *The Philosophy of David Hume.* London, Macmillan, 1949.

Mossner, E. C. *The Life of David Hume.* Oxford, Clarendon Press, 1980.

18

Immanuel Kant
(1724–1804)

The skeptical soundings of human knowledge taken by Hume had a far-reaching effect on Immanuel Kant, who credited Hume with arousing him from his "dogmatic slumber"; generations of modern philosophers have shared Kant's feeling. He was born in 1724 in the small Prussian town of Königsberg in northeast Germany. His parents were religious people and, though Kant always retained a genuine regard for religion and a deep moral sense, he rejected the puritanical pietism that prevailed in his family. His life was undramatic and hardly filled with the traveling spirit of many of his predecessors; as a matter of sober fact, he never got beyond thirty miles of his native town. His schooling was all done locally, including his years at the University of Königsberg, which shared the quiet anonymity of the town. He was much influenced there by a young professor of philosophy, Martin Knutsen, who introduced him to the rationalist tradition of Leibniz and Christian Wolff, as well as to the world of Newtonian physics. For several years he was a family tutor, and then a lecturer with the title of *Privatdozent* at the university, in which capacities he broadened his intellectual interests by the number of subjects he was called upon to teach, ranging from logic to geology. In 1770 he received an appointment as professor of philosophy. Though perhaps it is not readily recognizable in his works, he is reported to have been an excellent lecturer, full of wit and good humor. His first important book was not published until he was fifty-seven years old, and then his works appeared in profusion. The three works on which his reputation chiefly rests are the *Critique of Pure Reason* (1781), *Critique of Practical Reason* (1790), and *Critique of the Faculty of Judgment* (1793).

In his famous daily routine, Kant is a perfect example of German orderliness, rising each day at the same time and performing the day's activities, whether drinking coffee, preparing class, or taking lunch, all at a fixed hour. The poet Heine wrote: "Neighbors knew that it was exactly half past three when Immanuel Kant in his grey coat, with his bamboo cane in his hand, left his house door and went to the Lime tree avenue, which is still called, in memory of him, the 'Philosopher's Walk.'" He almost always took his midday meal at a nearby inn with a friend, but even this was subject to routine; on one occasion, when the friend was late, Kant proceeded to leave just as his friend was arriving. Kant simply doffed his hat and kept going on his way!

A *"Copernican Revolution"* in *Epistemology*

Descartes' search for certitude as a reaction to skepticism was buoyed by his hopes for a universal mathematics, but his hopes inaugurated an entire cycle that ironically began against the skepticism of Montaigne and ended in the skepticism of Hume. Kant confronted a similar problem. He appreciated immensely what Hume was trying to do, but at the same time, he took his own path: "I openly confess my recollection of David Hume was the very thing which many years ago first interrupted my dogmatic slumber and gave my investigation in the field of speculative philosophy a quite new direction." But no progress could be made until philosophy, especially metaphysics, saw the need to reevaluate itself, to become self-critical, as the sciences had become. The sciences had indeed made progress, but only after they successfully restructured themselves in terms of method.

Hitherto, according to Kant, in the knowledge–object relationship, the *object* of knowledge was the first consideration for philosophers; with him, however, it was the *manner of knowing* the object that came first. All attempts to advance knowledge ended in failure when it was assumed that knowledge must conform to objects; therefore, "We must make trial whether we may not have more success in the tasks of metaphysics, if we suppose that objects must conform to our knowledge." For Kant, this was so drastic a change from the past that he likened it to the revolution in astronomy brought about by Copernicus. Questions like What are our knowing faculties capable of?, What is their internal structure?, What are the conditions of knowledge?, and What are the boundaries of knowledge? become the focal questions in Kantian *criticism* and explain the presence of the word *Critique* in the titles of his chief works. The derivative terms *critical problem* and *critical philosophy,* insofar as they pertain to the exploration of our knowing faculties, stem from the legacy left by Kant.

How is this conformity of the object with the mind to be brought about? Holding fast to the belief that "all our knowledge begins with experience," and referring to experiential knowledge as *a posteriori,* Kant also holds that knowledge is in some fashion *a priori,* that is, "altogether independent of experience, and even of all sensuous expressions." Kant does not mean that we have innate ideas, as with Descartes, but that the knowing faculty possesses within itself, therefore *a priori,* the elements required for knowledge before experience takes place. It is the *a priori* nature of this knowledge that allows certain of our judgments to be necessary and universal, which Hume could not allow, because necessity and universality are not to be found in sense experience. Accordingly Kant distinguishes between judgments that are analytic and those that are synthetic. An *analytic judgment* is one whose predicate is already contained in the subject; it adds nothing new to the subject, it only "explicates" what is there. For example, in the judgment "all bodies are extended," the concept "body" necessarily contains "extensions," so that to deny it would be a contradiction. A *synthetic judgment,* on the other hand, is one whose predicate is not contained in the subject, and therefore adds something new to it; it "augments" it. For example, in the judgment "all bodies are heavy," the concept "heavy" is not contained in the concept "body." This distinction would appear to be sufficient, but Kant further distinguishes synthetic judgments into synthetic *a posteriori,* in which we know the predicate as belonging to the subject only by experience; judgments of this kind offer no special problem. But *synthetic a priori* offer a problem, though Kant is quite comfortable with it. In the proposition "Everything that happens has a cause," from experience I know "something that happens," but I do not know "has a cause" from experience; therefore the necessity and universality attaching to the proposition must be given *a priori.* Many subsequent philosophers have found great difficulty in supporting the notion of synthetic *a priori,* which seems to have something contradictory about it; in consequence, it has become the center of controversy. For our purposes, however, we have noted that Kant himself was comfortable with the distinction.

Sensibility, Understanding, and (Pure) Reason

To continue, the mind has many faculties, three of which are described in the *Critique of Pure Reason:* sensibility, understanding, and (pure) reason. Relying on the experience of sense, called *a posteriori,* the mind receives impressions of whatever exists, but it receives them on its own terms; that is, the mind imposes itself on the sensible, and its manner of imposing itself is the manner in which it knows impressions; in Kant's terms, we have knowledge of objects *a priori,* that is, we are able to "determine something in regard to them prior to their being given." If a housewife is making a batch of cookies, she "imposes" a cookie cutter on the formless dough in order to achieve the shape she wants. As far as knowledge is concerned, the sense objects to be known are formless until the mind imposes its forms on them, and the very forms it imposes are the way things *appear* to the mind, and are therefore called *appearances,* or *phenomena.* Kant was convinced of the truth of Newton's view that the two chief characteristics of the physical world, space and time, are *absolutes;* that is, their existence is independent of the human mind; Kant adapted this view so that space and time became absolutes in the very structure of the mind, coming into play in the act of sensation. Sensibility grasps the world of phenomena in two forms, space and time; because they are built-in ways of knowing and are present before sense experience takes place, they are called by Kant *a priori* forms.

Whatever is given to the mind in sensibility is subject to conceptual rendering by the *understanding;* that is, whatever is *given* in sensibility is *thought* in understanding: "If the *receptivity* of our mind, its power of receiving representations in so far as it is in any wise affected, is to be entitled sensibility, then the mind's power of producing representations from itself, the *spontaneity* of knowledge, should be called the understanding. . . . Without sensibility no object would be given to us, without understanding no object would be thought." The understanding organizes the phenomena, synthesizes them, makes judgments; just as sensibility functions through *a priori* forms, the understanding functions through *a priori* concepts, whence they are called *categories* by Kant. There are twelve such categories: unity, plurality, totality; reality, negation, limitation; substance, cause, community; possibility, existence, necessity. It is under these headings that all judging or thinking takes place. Kant's view, then, is that *knowledge* is limited to the combined role of sensibility and understanding, both of which are concerned with sense experience, though in different ways.

The third of the mind's faculties, reason, has several functions, and is called *pure reason* in its functioning with objects of thought that have no connection with the sensible realm, namely, the soul, the world, and God. The word Kant uses to express these objects is *noumena,* to oppose them to phenomena. Phenomena pertain to the sensible world, noumena to the suprasensible. Phenomena are appearances because they are given in the sense; noumena are not appearances because they are not given in the sense. Phenomena are objects of experience; noumena are not objects of experience, they are transcendent. Because they are objects of experience, phenomena can be known; because they are not objects of experience, noumena cannot be known. Pure reason, by its very nature, seeks to transcend the objects of experience it; *must* think the ideas of soul, world, and God. At the same time it criticizes itself, which is the "critique" of pure reason, and realizes the limitation of its own activity because the ideas it has *cannot be known* as corresponding to objects outside the mind: "all illusion consists in holding the subjective ground of our judgments to be objective." Thus metaphysics is necessary but illusory.

But do such significant ideas as soul, world, and God, unknowable in the context of pure reason, have to be dismissed? Indeed not, for their very presence in the reason indicates that they must have a role to play. That role is one of unification, the bringing together of the disparate parts of our knowledge: The sensibility endows the sense manifold with the unity of space and time; the understanding endows the phenomena with the unity of its concepts; and finally, the reason endows the concepts with the unity of its transcendental ideas. Kant calls this function of reason a "peculiar vocation"; "The transcendental Ideas therefore express the peculiar vocation of reason as a principle of systematic unity in the use of understanding." The caution here is not to be misled into thinking that real objects correspond to the ideas. Their function is to "regulate"; as *regulative* ideas they are principles of unity, unifying under the rubric of "as if": as if the soul existed, as if the world existed, as if God existed. The regulative ideas of the soul give us the unity of a continuing self, or ego; the idea of the world gives us a sense of total oneness in the physical manifold; and the idea of God, in Kant's words, "directs us to look upon all connection in the world *as if* it originated from an all-sufficient necessary cause." However, the full meaning of soul, world, and God requires the consideration of the *Critique of Practical Reason* and Kant's other moral works.

The Structure of Morality

Though it would be misleading to say that the *Critique of Practical Reason* takes up where the *Critique of Pure Reason* leaves off, because for Kant each of these faculties is self-contained, there is certainly a continuity between the two in terms of his intention to explore the full range of experience, which is the basis, though not the extent, of all we hold to be true. Moral experience is a new kind of experience and is totally different from the sense experience with which pure reason begins. Just as Kant analyzes one function of the reason to arrive at the critique of pure reason (more precisely, pure theoretical reason), he analyzes a second function of the reason to arrive at the critique of practical reason (more precisely, pure practical reason).

This analysis begins with a feeling of *duty,* a sense of obligation, an experience of oughtness that we recognize in ourselves in the face of certain kinds of actions we are called upon to perform. Kant considers this sense of oughtness as a given; we do not demonstrate its existence; we neither deduce it nor induce it; we have no need to prove it. Because it is a datum, and therefore does not derive from anything else, it must be understood in terms of nothing but itself. As the first step in this understanding, Kant clearly sees that oughtness entails *freedom.* That is, we must be free to do what we ought; otherwise, we risk a stark contradiction in saying that we ought to do what we cannot do. If the rest of nature is governed by necessity, the will is not. Kant's insistence on freedom is behind all of his writings on practical reason and morality; he supports it even while being unsure about how to reconcile it with the necessity of nature: "Yet for *practical purposes* the narrow footpath of freedom is the only one on which it is possible to make use of reason in our conduct; hence it is just as impossible for the subtlest philosophy as for the commonest reason of men to argue away freedom. Philosophy must then assume that no real contradiction will be found between freedom and physical necessity of the same human actions, for it cannot give up the conception of nature any more than that of freedom." No determinist view of morality can possibly make allowance for freedom, and therefore no genuine expression of what ought to be can enter the determinist's lexicon. Freedom is the basic ingredient of a human act; without it there can be no "ought."

Though the acknowledgment of duty comes from within me as an individual, it is just as clear and unmistakable, for Kant, that what is imposed on me is imposed on all, and so the binding aspect of duty is one with the binding aspect of *law,* in virtue of which it binds all; that is, duty is given to me as a law inasmuch as it binds me together with all others. The words *categorical* and *imperative* reinforce each other in emphasizing the obligatory character of law, whence the term *categorical imperative* is used by Kant to express a course of moral action whose intrinsic morality is grasped. Though Kant produces several formulations of the categorical imperative, the first one directly announces the aspect of universality: "Act only on a maxim through which you can at the same time will that it should become a universal law."

As is true of all law, the more general its scope, the less a particular action is envisioned; the law has to be applied to the individual case. There is an analogy here with the *a priori* form of space that does not apply to any particular thing until the phenomenon is given, and only then is the phenomenon "spatialized"; so the law does not become particular until an individual action is to be placed. For example, in the case of a man beset by a series of misfortunes, Kant asks "whether it would not be contrary to his duty to himself to take his own life." Kant answers this by pointing out the contradiction involved in a system of nature whose special feature is the improvement of life to allow it to be destroyed. Suicide cannot be universalized; therefore, it is morally wrong.

Holiness and Happiness

At this point, several ideas flow together. Observance of the law, reflected in a person's acting out of fidelity to his will, is the basic path man has to follow to achieve the highest good, the *summum bonum*, which brings about man's happiness. Perfect accordance of the will with the moral law is a demand of a rational being, and yet perfect accordance is not possible in this life; as Kant puts it, "Perfect accordance of the will with the moral law is *holiness*, a perfection of which no rational being of the sensible world is capable at any moment of his existence." Progress toward the perfect will is endless, and only based on the supposition of the soul's endless duration, called *immortality*, can such progress be asserted. In addition, the possibility of the *summum bonum* could not be realized at all without involving the existence of a cause, connecting happiness with morality, namely, God: "it is morally necessary to assume the existence of God."

The immortality of the soul and the existence of God are, for Kant, *postulates*, a term borrowed from mathematics, which means that although a proposition cannot be proven to be true, it must be accepted as true. That parallel lines never meet is a postulate, held to be true without being subject to proof. God and the soul must be accepted as true for the sake of maintaining the integrity of the moral order; should either one not be taken as true, the moral order would crumble, and this would be the final infidelity to our original moral experience.

Once again, it is extremely illuminating, and perhaps indicative of the unyielding claim of truth to be permanent, that Kant's movement against skepticism, which terminates in the philosophical need for the soul, God, and the world, is remarkably akin to Descartes' movement against skepticism, which terminated in the same need.

Though philosophers have many problems with Kant, his constant view of "the starry heavens above and the moral law within" has permeated modern philosophy and make him, for many fellow philosophers, the "absolutely indispensible philosopher."

READINGS

Introduction

(from *Critique of Pure Reason*)

I. OF THE DIFFERENCE BETWEEN PURE AND EMPIRICAL KNOWLEDGE

That all our knowledge begins with experience there can be no doubt. For how is it possible that the faculty of cognition should be awakened into exercise otherwise than by means of objects which affect our sense, and partly of themselves produce representations, partly rouse our powers of understanding into activity, to compare, to connect, or to separate these, and so to convert the raw material of our sensuous impressions into a knowledge of objects, which is called experience? In respect of time, therefore, no knowledge of ours is antecedent to experience, but begins with it.

But, though all our knowledge begins with experience, it by no means follows, that all arises out of experience. For, on the contrary, it is quite possible that our empirical knowledge is a compound of that which we receive through impressions, and that which the faculty of cognition supplies from itself (sensuous impressions giving merely the *occasion*), an addition which we cannot distinguish from the original element given by sense, till long practice has made us attentive to, and skilful in separating it. It is, therefore, a question which requires close investigation, and is not to be answered at first sight—whether there exists a knowledge altogether independent of experience, and even of all sensuous impressions? Knowledge of this kind is called *a priori,* in contra-distinction to empirical knowledge, which has its sources *a posteriori,* that is, in experience.

But the expression, '*a priori,*' is not as yet definite enough, adequately to indicate the whole meaning of the question above started. For, in speaking of knowledge which has its sources in experience, we are wont to say, that this or that may be known *a priori,* because we do not derive this knowledge immediately from experience, but from a general rule, which, however, we have itself borrowed from experience. Thus, if a man undermined his house, we say, 'he might know *a priori* that it would have fallen;' that is, he needed not to have waited for the experience that it did actually fall. But still, *a priori,* he could not know even this much. For, that bodies are heavy, and, consequently, that they fall when their supports are taken away, must have been known to him previously, by means of experience.

By the term 'knowledge *a priori,*' therefore, we shall in the sequel understand, not such as is independent of this or that kind of experience, but such as is absolutely so of all experience. Opposed to this is empirical knowledge, or that which is possible only *a posteriori,* that is, through experience. Knowledge *a priori* is either pure or impure. Pure knowledge *a priori* is that with which no empirical element is mixed up. For example, the proposition, 'Every change has a cause,' is a proposition *a priori,* but impure, because change is a conception which can only be derived from experience.

II. THE HUMAN INTELLECT, EVEN IN AN
UNPHILOSOPHICAL STATE, IS IN POSSESSION
OF CERTAIN COGNITIONS 'A PRIORI'

The question now is as to a *criterion,* by which we may securely distinguish a pure from an empirical cognition. Experience no doubt teaches us that this or that object is constituted in such and such a manner, but not that it could not possibly exist otherwise. Now, in the first place, if we have a proposition which contains the idea of necessity in its very conception, it is a judgment *a priori;* if, moreover, it is not derived from any other proposition, unless from one equally involving the idea of necessity, it is absolutely *a priori.* Secondly, an empirical judgment never exhibits strict and absolute, but only assumed and comparative universality (by induction); therefore, the most we can say is—so far as we have hitherto observed, there is no exception to this or that rule. If, on the other hand, a judgment carries with it strict and absolute universality, that is, admits of no possible exception, it is not derived from experience, but is valid absolutely *a priori.*

Empirical universality is, therefore, only an arbitrary extension of validity, from that which may be predicated of a proposition valid in most cases, to that which is asserted of a proposition which holds good in all; as, for example, in the affirmation, 'All bodies are heavy.' When, on the contrary, strict universality characterizes a judgment, it necessarily indicates another peculiar source of knowledge, namely, a faculty of cognition *a priori.* Necessity and strict universality, therefore, are infallible tests for distinguishing pure from empirical knowledge, and are inseparably connected with each other. But as in the use of these criteria the empirical limitation is sometimes more easily detected than the contingency of the judgment, or the unlimited universality which we attach to a judgment is often a more convincing proof than its necessity, it may be advisable to use the criteria separately, each by itself infallible.

Now, that in the sphere of human cognition we have judgments which are necessary, and in the strictest sense universal, consequently pure *a priori,* it will be an easy matter to show. If we desire an example from the sciences, we need only take any proposition in mathematics. If we cast our eyes upon the commonest operations of the understanding, the proposition, 'Every change must have a cause,' will amply serve our purpose. In the latter case, indeed, the conception of a cause so plainly involves the conception of a necessity of connection with an effect, and of a strict universality of the law, that the very notion of a cause would entirely disappear, were we to derive it, like Hume, from a frequent association of what happens with that which precedes, and the habit thence originating of connecting representations—the necessity inherent in the judgment being therefore merely subjective. Besides, without seeking for such examples of principles existing *a priori* in cognition, we might easily show that such principles are the indispensable basis of the possibility of experience itself, and consequently prove their existence *a priori.* For whence could our experience itself acquire certainty, if all the rules on which it depends were themselves empirical, and consequently fortuitous? No one, therefore, can admit the validity of the use of such rules as first principles. But, for the present, we may content ourselves with having established the fact, that we do possess and exercise a faculty of pure *a priori* cognition; and, secondly, with having pointed out the proper tests of such cognition, namely, universality and necessity.

Not only in judgments, however, but even in conceptions, is an *a priori* origin manifest. For example, if we take away by degrees from our conceptions of a body all that can be referred to mere sensuous experience—colour, hardness or softness, weight, even impenetrability—the body will then vanish; but the space which it occupied still remains, and this it is utterly impossible to annihilate in thought. Again, if we take away, in like manner, from our empirical conception of any object, corporeal or incorporeal, all properties which mere experience has taught us to connect with it, still we cannot think away those through which we cogitate it as substance, or adhering to substance, although our conception of substance is more determined than that of an object. Compelled, therefore, by that necessity with which the conception of substance forces itself upon us, we must confess that it has its seat in our faculty of cognition *a priori.*

III. PHILOSOPHY STANDS IN NEED OF A SCIENCE WHICH SHALL DETERMINE THE POSSIBILITY, PRINCIPLES, AND EXTENT OF HUMAN KNOWLEDGE 'A PRIORI'

Of far more importance than all that has been above said, is the consideration that certain of our cognitions rise completely above the sphere of all possible experience, and by means of conceptions, to which there exists in the whole extent of experience no corresponding object, seem to extend the range of our judgments beyond its bounds. And just in this transcendental or supersensible sphere, where experience affords us neither instruction nor guidance, lie the investigations of *Reason,* which, on account of their importance, we consider far preferable to, and as having a far more elevated aim than, all that the understanding can achieve within the sphere of sensuous phenomena. So high a value do we set upon these investigations, that even at the risk of error, we persist in following them out, and permit neither doubt nor disregard nor indifference to restrain us from the pursuit. These unavoidable problems of mere pure reason are GOD, FREEDOM (of will), and IMMORTALITY. The science which, with all its preliminaries, has for its especial object the solution of these problems is named metaphysics—a science which is at the very outset dogmatical, that is, it confidently takes upon itself the execution of this task without any previous investigation of the ability or inability of reason for such an undertaking.

Now the safe ground of experience being thus abandoned, it seems nevertheless natural that we should hesitate to erect a building with the cognitions we possess, without knowing whence they come, and on the strength of principles, the origin of which is undiscovered. Instead of thus trying to build without a foundation, it is rather to be expected that we should long ago have put the question, how the understanding can arrive at these *a priori* cognitions and what is the extent, validity, and worth which they may possess? We say, this is natural enough, meaning by the word natural, that which is consistent with a just and reasonable way of thinking; but if we understand by the term, that which usually happens, nothing indeed could be more natural and more comprehensible than that this investigation should be left long unattempted. For one part of pure knowledge, the science of mathematics, has been long firmly established, and thus leads us to form flattering expectations with regard to others, though these may be of quite a different nature. Besides, when we get beyond the bounds of experience, we are of course safe from opposition in that quarter; and the charm of widening the range of our knowledge is so great, that unless we are brought to a standstill by some evident contradiction, we hurry on undoubtingly in our course. This, however, may be avoided, if we are sufficiently cautious in the construction of our fictions, which are not the less fictions on that account.

Mathematical science affords us a brilliant example, how far, independently of all experience, we may carry our *a priori* knowledge. Is it true that the mathematician occupies himself with objects and cognitions only in so far as they can be represented by means of intuition. But this circumstance is easily overlooked, because the said intuition can itself be given *a priori,* and therefore is hardly to be distinguished from a mere pure conception. Deceived by such a proof of the power of reason, we can perceive no limits to the extension of our knowledge. The light dove cleaving in free flight the thin air, whose resistance it feels, might imagine that her movements would be far more free and rapid in airless space. Just in the same way did Plato, abandoning the world of sense because of the narrow limits it sets to the understanding, venture upon the wings of ideas beyond it, into the void space of pure intellect. He did not reflect that he made no real progress by all his efforts; for he met with no resistance which might serve him for a support, as it were, whereon to rest, and on which he might apply his powers, in order to let the intellect acquire momentum for its progress. It is, indeed, the common fate of human reason in speculation, to finish the imposing edifice of thought as rapidly as possible, and then for the first time to begin to examine whether the foundation is a solid one or no. Arrived at this point, all sorts of excuses are sought after, in order to console us for its want of stability, or rather, indeed, to enable us to dispense altogether with so late and dangerous an investigation. But what frees us during the process of building from all apprehension or suspicion, and flatters us into the belief of its solidity, is this. A great part, perhaps the greatest part, of the business of our reason consists in the analysation of the conceptions which we already possess of objects. By this means we gain a multitude of cognitions, which although really nothing more than elucidations or explanations of that which (though in a confused manner) was already thought in our conceptions, are, at least in respect of their form, prized as new introspections; whilst, so far as regards their matter or content, we have really made no addition to our conceptions, but only disinvolved them. But as this process does furnish real *a priori* knowledge, which has a sure progress and useful results, reason, deceived by this, slips in, without being itself aware of it, assertions of a quite different kind; in which, to given conceptions it adds others, *a priori* indeed, but entirely foreign to them, without our knowing how it arrives at these, and, indeed, without such a question ever suggesting itself. I shall therefore at once proceed to examine the difference between these two modes of knowledge.

IV. OF THE DIFFERENCE BETWEEN ANALYTICAL AND SYNTHETICAL JUDGMENTS

In all judgments wherein the relation of a subject to the predicate is cogitated (I mention affirmative judgments only here; the application to negative will be very easy), this relation is possible in two different ways. Either the predicate B belongs to the subject A, as somewhat which is contained (though covertly) in the conception A; or the predicate B lies completely out of the conception A, although it stands in connection with it. In the first instance, I term the judgment analytical, in the second, synthetical. Analytical judgments (affirmative) are therefore those in which the connection of the predicate with the subject is cogitated through identity; those in which this connection is cogitated without identity, are called synthetical judgments. The former may be called *explicative,* the latter *augmentative* judgments; because the former add in the predicate nothing to the conception of the subject, but only analyse it into its constituent conceptions, which were thought already in the subject, although in a confused manner; the latter add to our conceptions of the subject a predicate which was not contained in it, and which no analysis could ever have discovered therein. For example, when I say, 'All bodies are extended,' this is an analytical judgment. For I need not go beyond the conception of *body* in order to find extension connected with it, but merely analyse the conception, that is, become conscious of the manifold properties which I think in that conception, in order to discover this predicate in it: it is therefore an analytical judgment. On the other hand, when I say, 'All bodies are heavy,' the predicate is something totally different from that which I think in the mere conception of a body. By the addition of such a predicate, therefore, it becomes a synthetical judgment.

Judgments of experience, as such, are always synthetical. For it would be absurd to think of grounding an analytical judgment on experience, because in forming such a judgment I need not go out of the sphere of my conceptions, and therefore recourse to the testimony of experience is quite unnecessary. That 'bodies are extended' is not an empirical judgment, but a proposition which stands firm *a priori.* For before addressing myself to experience, I already have in my conception all the requisite conditions for the judgment, and I have only to extract the predicate from the conception, according to the principle of contradiction, and thereby at the same time become conscious of the necessity of the judgment, a necessity which I could never learn from experience. On the other hand, though at first I do not at all include the predicate of weight in my conception of body in general, that conception still indicates an object of experience, a part of the totality of experience, to which I can still add other parts; and this I do when I recognize by observation that bodies are heavy. I can cognize beforehand by analysis the conception of body through the characteristics of extension, impenetrability, shape, etc., all which are cogitated in this conception. But now I extend my knowledge, and looking back on experience from which I had derived this conception of body, I find weight at all times connected with the above characteristics, and therefore I synthetically add to my conceptions this as a predicate, and say, 'All bodies are heavy.' Thus it is experience upon which rests the possibility of the synthesis of the predicate of weight with the conception of body, because both conceptions, although the one is not contained in the other, still belong to one another (only contingently, however), as parts of a whole, namely, of experience, which is itself a synthesis of intuitions.

But to synthetical judgments *a priori,* such aid is entirely wanting. If I go out of and beyond the conception A, in order to recognize another B as connected with it, what foundation have I to rest on, whereby to render the synthesis possible? I have here no longer the advantage of looking out in the sphere of experience for what I want. Let us take, for example, the proposition, 'Everything that happens has a cause.' In the conception of *something that happens,* I indeed think an existence which a certain time antecedes, and from this I can derive analytical judgments. But the conception of a cause lies quite out of the above conception, and indicates something entirely different from 'that which happens,' and is consequently not contained in that conception. How then am I able to assert concerning the general conception—'that which happens'—something entirely different from that conception, and to recognize the conception of cause although not contained in it, yet as belonging to it, and even necessarily? what is here the unknown = X, upon which the understanding rests when it believes it has found, out of the conception A a foreign predicate B, which it nevertheless considers to be connected with it? It cannot be experience, because the principle adduced annexes the two representations, cause and effect, to the representation existence, not only with universality, which experience cannot give, but also with the expression of necessity, therefore completely *a priori* and from pure conceptions. Upon such synthetical, that is augmentative propositions, depends the whole aim of our speculative knowledge *a priori;* for although analytical judgments are indeed highly important and necessary, they are so, only to arrive at that clearness of conceptions which is requisite for a sure and extended synthesis, and this alone is a real acquisition.

Transcendental Illusion
(from *Critique of Pure Reason*)

We termed Dialectic in general a logic of appearance. This does not signify a doctrine of *probability;* for probability is truth, only cognized upon insufficient grounds, and though the information it gives us is imperfect, it is not therefore deceitful. Hence it must not be separated from the analytical part of logic. Still less must *phenomenon* and *appearance* be held to be identical. For truth or illusory appearance does not reside in the object, in so far as it is intuited, but in the judgment upon the object, in so far as it is thought. It is therefore quite correct to say that the senses do not err, not because they always judge correctly, but because *they do not* judge at all. Hence truth and error, consequently also, illusory appearance as the cause of error, are only to be found in judgment, that is, in the relation of an object to our understanding. In a cognition, which completely harmonizes with the laws of the understanding, no error can exist. In a representation of the senses—as not containing any judgment—there is also no error. But no power of nature can of itself deviate from its own laws. Hence neither the understanding *per se* (without the influence of another cause), nor the senses *per se,* would fall into error; the former could not, because, if it acts only according to its own laws, the effect (the judgment) must necessarily accord with these laws. But in accordance with the laws of the understanding consists the formal element in all truth. In the senses there is no judgment—neither a true nor a false one. But, as we have no source of cognition besides these two, it follows that error is caused solely by the unobserved influence of the sensibility upon the understanding. And thus it happens that the subjective grounds of a judgment blend and are confounded with the objective, and cause them to deviate from their proper determination, just as a body in motion would always of itself proceed in a straight line, but if another impetus gives to it a different direction, it will then start off into a curvilinear line of motion. To distinguish the peculiar action of the understanding from the power which mingles with it, it is necessary to consider an erroneous judgment as the diagonal between two forces, that determine the judgment in two different directions, which, as it were, form an angle, and to resolve this composite operation into the simple ones of the understanding and the sensibility. In pure *a priori* judgments this must be done by means of transcendental reflection, whereby, as has been already shown, each representation has its place appointed in the corresponding faculty of cognition, and consequently the influence of the one faculty upon the other is made apparent.

It is not at present our business to treat of empirical illusory appearance (for example, optical illusion), which occurs in the empirical application of otherwise correct rules of the understanding, and in which the judgment is misled by the influence of imagination. Our purpose is to speak of *transcendental illusory appearance,* which influences principles—that are not even applied to experience, for in this case we should possess a sure test of their correctness— but which leads us, in disregard to all the warnings of criticism, completely beyond the empirical employment of the categories, and deludes us with the chimera of an extension of the sphere of the *pure understanding.* We shall term those principles, the application of which is confined entirely within the limits of possible experience, *immanent;* those, on the other hand, which transgress these limits, we shall call *transcendent* principles. But by these latter I do not understand principles of the *transcendental* use or misuse of the categories, which is in reality a mere fault of the judgment when not under due restraint from criticism, and therefore not paying sufficient attention to the limits of the sphere in which the pure understanding is allowed to exercise its functions; but real principles which exhort us to break down all those barriers, and to lay claim to a perfectly new field of cognition, which recognizes no line of demarcation. Thus *transcendental* and *transcendent* are not identical terms. The principles of the pure understanding, which we have already propounded, ought to be of empirical and not of transcendental use, that is, they are not applicable to any object beyond the sphere of experience. A principle which removes these limits, nay, which authorizes us to overstep them, is called *transcendent.* If our criticism can succeed in exposing the illusion in these pretended principles, those which are limited in their employment to the sphere of experience, may be called, in opposition to the others, *immanent* principles of the pure understanding.

Logical illusion, which consists merely in the imitation of the form of reason (the illusion in sophistical syllogism), arises entirely from a want of due attention to logical rules. So soon as the attention is awakened to the case before us, this illusion totally disappears. Transcendental illusion, on the contrary, does not cease to exist, even after it has been exposed, and its nothingness clearly perceived by means of transcendental criticism. Take, for example, the illusion in the proposition: 'The world must have a beginning in time.' The cause of this is as follows. In our reason, subjectively considered as a faculty of human cognition, there exist fundamental rules and maxims of its exercise, which have completely the appearance of objective principles. Now from this cause it happens, that the subjective necessity of a certain connection of our conceptions, is regarded as an objective necessity of the determination of things in themselves. This illusion it is impossible to avoid, just as we cannot avoid perceiving that the sea appears to be higher at a distance than it is near the shore, because we see the former by means of higher rays than the latter, or, which is a still stronger case, as even the astronomer cannot prevent himself from seeing the moon larger at its rising than some time afterwards, although he is not deceived by this illusion.

Transcendental dialectic will therefore content itself with exposing the illusory appearance in transcendental judgments, and guarding us against it; but to make it, as in the case of logical illusion, entirely disappear and cease to be illusion, is utterly beyond its power. For we have here to do with a natural and unavoidable illusion, which rests upon subjective principles, and imposes these upon us as objective, while logical dialectic, in the detection of sophisms, has to do merely with an error in the logical consequence of the propositions, or with an artificially constructed illusion, in imitation of the natural error. There is, therefore, a natural and unavoidable dialectic of pure reason—not that in which the bungler, from want of the requisite knowledge, involves himself, nor that which the sophist devises for the purpose of misleading, but that which is an inseparable adjunct of human reason, and which, even after its illusions have been exposed, does not cease to deceive, and continually to lead reason into momentary errors, which it becomes necessary continually to remove.

The Three Regulative Ideas of Pure Reason
(from *Critique of Pure Reason*)

And now we can clearly perceive the result of our transcendental dialectic, and the proper aim of the ideas of pure reason—which become dialectical solely from misunderstanding and inconsiderateness. Pure reason is, in fact, occupied with itself, and not with any object. Objects are not presented to it to be embraced in the unity of an empirical conception; it is only the cognitions of the understanding that are presented to it, for the purpose of receiving the unity of a rational conception, that is, of being connected according to a principle. The unity of reason is the unity of system; and this systematic unity is not an objective principle, extending its dominion over objects, but a subjective maxim, extending its authority over the empirical cognition of objects. The systematic connection which reason gives to the empirical employment of the understanding, not only advances the extension of that employment, but ensures its correctness, and thus the principle of a systematic unity of this nature is also objective, although only in an indefinite respect *(principium vagum).* It is not, however, a constitutive principle, determining an object to which it directly relates; it is merely a regulative principle or maxim, advancing and strengthening the empirical exercise of reason, by the opening up of new paths of which the understanding is ignorant, while it never conflicts with the laws of its exercise in the sphere of experience.

But reason cannot cogitate this systematic unity, without at the same time cogitating an object of the idea—an object that cannot be presented in any experience, which contains no concrete example of a complete systematic unity. This being *(ens rationis ratiocinatae)* is therefore a mere idea, and is not assumed to be a thing which is real absolutely and in itself. On the contrary, it forms merely the problematical foundation of the connection which the mind introduces among the phenomena of the sensuous world. We look upon this connection, in the light of the above-mentioned idea, as if it drew its origin from the supposed being which corresponds to the idea. And yet all we aim at is the possession of this idea as a secure foundation for the systematic unity of experience—a unity indispensable to reason, advantageous to the understanding, and promotive of the interests of empirical cognition.

We mistake the true meaning of this idea, when we regard it as an enouncement, or even as a hypothetical declaration of the existence of a real thing, which we are to regard as the origin or ground of a systematic constitution of the universe. On the contrary, it is left completely undetermined what the nature or properties of this so-called ground may be. The idea is merely to be adopted as a point of view, from which this unity, so essential to reason and so beneficial to the understanding, may be regarded as radiating. In one word, this transcendental thing is merely the schema of a regulative principle, by means of which Reason, so far as in her lies, extends the dominion of systematic unity over the whole sphere of experience.

The first object of an idea of this kind is the Ego, considered merely as a thinking nature or soul. If I wish to investigate the properties of a thinking being, I must interrogate experience. But I find that I can apply none of the categories to this object, the schema of these categories, which is the condition of their application, being given only in sensuous intuition. But I cannot thus attain to the cognition of a systematic unity of all the phenomena of the internal sense. Instead, therefore, of an empirical conception of what the soul really is, reason takes the conception of the empirical unity of all thought, and, by cogitating this unity as unconditioned and primitive, constructs the rational conception or idea of a simple substance which is in itself unchangeable, possessing personal identity, and in connection with other real things external to it; in one word, it constructs the idea of a simple self-subsistent intelligence. But the real aim of reason in this procedure is the attainment of principles of systematic unity for the explanation of the phenomena of the soul. That is, reason desires to be able to represent all the determinations of the internal sense, as existing in one subject, all powers as deduced from one fundamental power, all changes as mere varieties in the condition of being which is permanent and always the same, and all *phenomena* in space as entirely different in their nature from the procedure of thought. Essential simplicity (with the other attributes predicated of the Ego) is regarded as the mere schema of this regulative principle; it is not assumed that it is the actual ground of the properties of the soul. For these properties may rest upon quite different grounds, of which we are completely ignorant; just as the above predicates could not give us any knowledge of the soul as it is in itself, even if we regarded them as valid in respect of it, inasmuch as they constitute a mere idea, which cannot be represented *in concreto*. Nothing but good can result from a psychological idea of this kind, if we only take proper care not to consider it as more than an idea; that is, if we regard it as valid merely in relation to the employment of reason, in the sphere of the phenomena of the soul. Under the guidance of this idea, or principle, no empirical laws of corporeal phenomena are called in to explain that which is a phenomenon of the *internal sense* alone; no windy hypotheses of the generation, annihilation, and palingenesis of souls are admitted. Thus the consideration of this object of the internal sense is kept pure, and unmixed with heterogeneous elements; while the investigation of reason aims at reducing all the grounds of explanation employed in this sphere of knowledge to a single principle. All this is best effected, nay, cannot be effected otherwise than by means of such a schema, which requires us to regard this ideal thing as an actual existence. The psychological idea is therefore meaningless and inapplicable, except as the schema of a regulative conception. For, if I ask whether the soul is not really of a spiritual nature—it is a question which has no meaning. From such a conception has been abstracted, not merely all corporeal nature, but all nature, that is, all the predicates of a possible experience; and consequently, all the conditions which enable us to cogitate an object to this conception have disappeared. But, if these conditions are absent, it is evident that the conception is meaningless.

The second regulative idea of speculative reason is the conception of the universe. For nature is properly the only object presented to us, in regard to which reason requires regulative principles. Nature is twofold—thinking and corporeal nature. To cogitate the latter in regard to its internal possibility, that is, to determine the application of the categories to it, no idea is required—no representation which transcends experience. In this sphere, therefore, an idea is impossible, sensuous intuition being our only guide; while, in the sphere of psychology, we require the fundamental idea (I), which contains *a priori* a certain form of thought, namely, the unity of the Ego. Pure reason has therefore nothing left but nature in general, and the completeness of conditions in nature in accordance with some principle. The absolute totality of the series of these conditions is an idea, which can never be fully realized in the empirical exercise of reason, while it is serviceable as a rule for the procedure of reason in relation to that totality. It requires us, in the explanation of given phenomena (in the regress or ascent in the series), to proceed as if the series were infinite in itself, that is, were prolonged *in indefinitum;* while, on the other hand, where reason is regarded as itself the determining cause (in the region of freedom), we are required to proceed as if we had not before us an object of sense, but of the pure understanding. In this latter case, the conditions do not exist in the series of phenomena, but may be placed quite out of and beyond it, and the series of conditions may be regarded as if it had an absolute beginning from an intelligible cause. All this proves that the cosmological ideas are nothing but regulative principles, and not constitutive; and that their aim is not to realize an actual totality in such series. The full discussion of this discussion of this subject will be found in its proper place in the chapter on the antinomy of pure reason.

The third idea of pure reason, containing the hypothesis of a being which is valid merely as a relative hypothesis, is that of the one and all-sufficient cause of all cosmological series, in other words, the idea of God. We have not the slightest ground absolutely to admit the existence of an object corresponding to this idea; for what can empower or authorize us to affirm the existence of a being of the highest perfection—a being whose existence is absolutely necessary, merely because we possess the conception of such a being? The answer is—it is the existence of the world which renders this hypothesis necessary. But this answer makes it perfectly evident, that the idea of this being, like all other speculative ideas, is essentially nothing more than a demand upon reason that it shall regulate the connection which it and its subordinate faculties introduce into the phenomena of the world by principles of systematic unity, and consequently, that it shall regard all phenomena as originating from one all embracing being, as the supreme and all-sufficient cause. From this it is plain that the only aim of reason in this procedure is the establishment of its own formal rule for the extension of its dominion in the world of experience; that it does not aim at an extension of its cognition *beyond the limits of experience;* and that, consequently, this idea does not contain any constitutive principle.

The highest formal unity, which is based upon ideas alone, is the unity of all things—a unity in accordance with an aim or purpose; and the speculative interest of reason renders it necessary to regard all order in the world as if it originated from the intention and design of a supreme reason. This principle unfolds to the view of reason in the sphere of experience new and enlarged prospects, and invites it to connect the phenomena of the world according to teleological laws, and in this way to attain to the highest possible degree of systematic unity. The hypothesis of a supreme intelligence, as the sole cause of the universe—an intelligence which has for us no more than an ideal existence, is accordingly always of the greatest service to reason. Thus, if we presuppose, in relation to the figure of the earth (which is round, but somewhat flattened at the poles), or that of mountains or seas, wise designs on the part of an author of the universe, we cannot fail to make, by the light of this supposition, a great number of interesting discoveries. If we keep to this hypothesis, as a principle which is purely regulative, even error cannot be very detrimental. For, in this case, error can have no more serious consequences than that, where we expected to discover a teleological connection *(nexus finalis),* only a mechanical or physical connection appears. In such a case, we merely fail to find the additional form of unity we expected, but we do not lose the rational unity which the mind requires in its procedure in experience. But even a miscarriage of this sort cannot affect the law in its general and teleological relations. For although we may convict an anatomist of an error, when he connects the limb of some animal with a certain purpose; it is quite impossible to *prove* in a single case, that any arrangement of nature, be it what it may, is entirely without aim or design. And thus medical physiology, by the aid of a principle presented to it by pure reason, extends its very limited empirical knowledge of the purposes of the different parts of an organized body so far, that it may be asserted with the utmost confidence, and with the approbation of all reflecting men, that every organ or bodily part of an animal has its use and answers a certain design. Now, this is a supposition, which, if regarded as of a constitutive character, goes much farther than any experience or observation of ours can justify. Hence it is evident that it is nothing more than a regulative principle of reason, which aims at the highest degree of systematic unity, by the aid of the idea of a causality according to design in a supreme cause—a cause which it regards as the highest intelligence.

(Trans. J. M. D. Meiklejohn)

The Categorical Imperative
(from *Foundations of the Metaphysics of Morals*)

Everything in nature works according to laws. Only a rational being has the capacity of acting according to the conception of laws, i.e., according to principles. This capacity is will. Since reason is required for the derivation of actions from laws, will is nothing else than practical reason. If reason infallibly determines the will, the actions which such a being recognizes as objectively necessary are also subjectively necessary. That is, the will is a faculty of choosing only that which reason, independently of inclination, recognizes as practically necessary, i.e., as good. But if reason of itself does not sufficiently determine the will, and if the will is subjugated to the subjective conditions (certain incentives) which do not always agree with objective conditions; in a word, if the will is not of itself in complete accord with reason (the actual case of men), then the actions which are recognized as objectively necessary are subjectively contingent, and the determination of such a will according to objective laws is constraint. That is, the relation of objective laws to a will which is not completely good is conceived as the determination of the will of a rational being by principles of reason to which this will is not by nature necessarily obedient.

The conception of an objective principle, so far as it constrains a will, is a command (of reason), and the formula of this command is called an *imperative*.

All imperatives are expressed by an "ought" and thereby indicate the relation of an objective law of reason to a will which is not in its subject constitution necessarily determined by this law. This relation is that of constraint. Imperatives say that it would be good to do or to refrain from doing something, but they say it to a will which does not always do something simply because it is presented to it as a good thing to do. Practical good is what determines the will by means of the conception of reason and hence not by subjective causes but, rather, objectively, i.e., on grounds which are valid for every rational being as such. It is distinguished from the pleasant, as that which has an influence on the will only by means of a sensation from merely subjective causes, which hold only for the senses of this or that person and not as a principle of reason which holds for everyone.

A perfectly good will, therefore, would be equally subject to objective laws (of the good), but it could not be conceived as constrained by them to act in accord with them, because, according to its own subjective constitution, it can be determined to act only through the conception of the good. Thus no imperatives hold for the divine will or, more generally, for a holy will. The "ought" is here out of place, for the volition of itself is necessarily in unison with the law. Therefore imperatives are only formulas expressing the relation of objective laws of volition in general to the subjective imperfection of the will of this or that rational being, e.g., the human will.

All imperatives command either hypothetically or categorically. The former present the practical necessity of a possible action as a means to achieving something else which one desires (or which one may possibly desire). The categorical imperative would be one which presented an action as of itself objectively necessary, without regard to any other end.

If I think of a hypothetical imperative as such, I do not know what it will contain until the condition is stated [under which it is an imperative]. But if I think of a categorical imperative, I know immediately what it contains. For since the imperative contains besides the law only the necessity of the maxim of acting in accordance with this law, while the law contains no condition to which it is restricted, there is nothing remaining in it except the universality of law as such to which the maxim of the action should conform; and in effect this conformity alone is represented as necessary by the imperative.

There is, therefore, only one categorical imperative. It is: Act only according to that maxim by which you can at the same time will that it should become a universal law.

Now if all imperatives of duty can be derived from this one imperative as a principle, we can at least show what we understand by the concept of duty and what it means, even though it remain undecided whether that which is called duty is an empty concept or not.

The universality of law according to which effects are produced constitutes what is properly called nature in the most general sense (as to form), i.e., the existence of things so far as it is determined by universal laws. [By analogy], then, the universal imperative of duty can be expressed as follows: Act as though the maxim of your action were by your will to become a universal law of nature.

We shall now enumerate some duties, adopting the usual division of them into duties to ourselves and to others and into perfect and imperfect duties.

1. A man who is reduced to despair by a series of evils feels a weariness with life but is still in possession of his reason sufficiently to ask whether it would not be contrary to his duty to himself to take his own life. Now he asks whether the maxim of his action could become a universal law of nature. His maxim, however, is: For love of myself, I make it my principle to shorten my life when by a longer duration it threatens more evil than satisfaction. But it is questionable whether this principle of self-love could become a universal law of nature. One immediately sees a contradiction in a system of nature, whose law would be to destroy life by the feeling whose special office is to impel the improvement of life. In this case it would not exist as nature; hence that maxim cannot obtain as a law of nature, and thus it wholly contradicts the supreme principle of all duty.

2. Another man finds himself forced by need to borrow money. He well knows that he will not be able to repay it, but he also sees that nothing will be loaned him if he does not firmly promise to repay it at a certain time. He desires to make such a promise, but he has enough conscience to ask himself whether it is not improper and opposed to duty to relieve his distress in such a way. Now, assuming he does decide to do so, the maxim of his action would be as follows: When I believe myself to be in need of money, I will borrow money and promise to repay it, although I know I shall never do so. Now this principle of self-love or of his own benefit may very well be compatible with his whole future welfare, but the question is whether it is right. He changes the pretension of self-love into a universal law and then puts the question: How would it be if my maxim became a universal law? He immediately sees that it could never hold as a universal law of nature and be consistent with itself; rather it must necessarily contradict itself. For the universality of a law which says that anyone who believes himself to be in need could promise what he pleased with the intention of not fulfilling it would make the promise itself and the end to be accomplished by it impossible; no one would believe what was promised to him but would only laugh at any such assertion as vain pretense.

3. A third finds in himself a talent which could, by means of some cultivation, make him in many respects a useful man. But he finds himself in comfortable circumstances and prefers indulgence in pleasure to troubling himself with broadening and improving his fortunate natural gifts. Now, however, let him ask whether his maxim of neglecting his gifts, besides agreeing with his propensity to idle amusement, agrees also with what is called duty. He sees that a system of nature could indeed exist in accordance with such a law, even though man (like the inhabitants of the South Sea Islands) should let his talents rust and resolve to devote his life merely to idleness, indulgence, and propagation—in a word, to pleasure. But he cannot possibly will that this should become a universal law of nature or that it should be implanted in us by a natural instinct. For, as a rational being, he necessarily wills that all his faculties should be developed, inasmuch as they are given to him for all sorts of possible purposes.

4. A fourth man, for whom things are going well, sees that others (whom he could help) have to struggle with great hardships, and he asks, "What concern

of mine is it? Let each one be as happy as heaven wills, or as he can make himself; I will not take anything from him or even envy him; but to his welfare or to his assistance in time of need I have no desire to contribute." If such a way of thinking were a universal law of nature, certainly the human race could exist, and without doubt even better than in a state where everyone talks of sympathy and good will or even exerts himself occasionally to practice them while, on the other hand, he cheats when he can and betrays or otherwise violates the rights of man. Now although it is possible that a universal law of nature according to that maxim could exist, it is nevertheless impossible to will that such a principle should hold everywhere as a law of nature. For a will which resolved this would conflict with itself, since instances can often arise in which he would need the love and sympathy of others, and in which he would have robbed himself, by such a law of nature springing from his own will, of all hope of the aid he desires.

(Tr. Lewis White Beck)

Postulates of Pure Practical Reason
(from *Critique of Practical Reason*)

IV. THE IMMORTALITY OF THE SOUL AS A POSTULATE
OF PURE PRACTICAL REASON

The achievement of the highest good in the world is the necessary object of a will determinable by the moral law. In such a will, however, the complete fitness of intentions to the moral law is the supreme condition of the highest good. This aptness, therefore, must be just as possible as its object, because it is contained in the command that requires us to promote the latter. But complete fitness of the will to the moral law is holiness, which is a perfection of which no rational being in the world of sense is at any time capable. But since it is required as practically necessary, it can be found only in an endless progress to that complete fitness; on principles of pure practical reason, it is necessary to assume such a practical progress as the real object of our will.

This infinite progress is possible, however, only under the presupposition of an infinitely enduring existence and personality of the same rational being; this is called the immortality of the soul. Thus the highest good is practically possible only on the supposition of the immortality of the soul, and the latter, as inseparably bound to the moral law, is a postulate of pure practical reason. By a postulate of pure practical reason I understand a theoretical proposition which is not as such demonstrable, but which is an inseparable corollary of an *a priori* unconditionally valid practical law.

The thesis of the moral destiny of our nature, viz., that it is able only in an infinite progress to attain complete fitness to the moral law, is of great use, not merely for the present purpose of supplementing the impotence of speculative reason, but also with respect to religion. Without it, either the moral law is completely degraded from its holiness, by being made out as lenient (indulgent) and thus compliant to our convenience, or our notions of our vocation and our expectation are strained to an unattainable destination, i.e., a hoped-for complete attainment of holiness of will, thus losing themselves in fanatical theolosophical dreams which completely contradict our knowledge of ourselves. In either case, we are only hindered in the unceasing striving toward and precise and persistent obedience to a command of reason which is stern, unindulgent, truly commanding, really and not just ideally possible. Only endless progress from lower to higher stages of moral perfection is possible to a rational but finite being. The Infinite Being, to whom the temporal condition is nothing, sees in this series, which is for us without end, a whole conformable to the moral law; holiness, which His law inexorably commands in order to be true to His justice in the share He assigns to each in the highest good, is to be found in a single intellectual intuition of the existence of rational beings. All that can be granted to a creature with respect to hope for this share is consciousness of his tried character. And on the basis of his previous progress from the worse to the morally better, and of the immutability of intention which thus becomes known to him, he may hope for a further uninterrupted continuation of this progress, however long his existence may last, even beyond his life. But he cannot hope here or at any foreseeable point of his future existence to be fully adequate to God's will, without indulgence or remission which would not harmonize with justice. This he can do only in the infinity of his duration which God alone can survey.

V. THE EXISTENCE OF GOD AS A POSTULATE OF PURE PRACTICAL REASON

The moral law led, in the foregoing analysis, to a practical problem which is assigned solely by pure reason and without any concurrence of sensuous incentives. It is the problem of the completeness of the first and principal part of the highest good, viz., morality; since this problem can be solved only in eternity, it led to the postulate of immortality. The same law must also lead us to affirm the possibility of the second element of the highest good, i.e., happiness proportional to that morality; it must do so just as disinterestedly as heretofore, by a purely impartial reason. This it can do on the supposition of the existence of God as necessarily belonging to the possibility of the highest good (the object of our will which is necessarily connected with the moral legislation of pure reason). We proceed to exhibit this connection in a convincing manner.

Happiness is the condition of a rational being in the world, in whose whole existence everything goes according to wish and will. It thus rests on the harmony of nature with his entire end and with the essential determining ground of his will. But the moral law commands, as a law of freedom, by grounds of determination which are wholly independent of nature and its harmony with our faculty of desire (as incentives). Still, the acting rational being in the world is not at the same time the cause of the world and of nature itself. Hence there is not the slightest ground in the moral law for a necessary connection between the morality and proportionate happiness of a being which belongs to the world as one of its parts and as thus dependent on it. Not being nature's cause, his will cannot by its own strength bring nature, as it touches on his happiness, into complete harmony with his practical principles. Nevertheless, in the practical task of pure reason, i.e., in the necessary endeavor after the highest good, such a connection is postulated as necessary: we should seek to further the highest good (which therefore must be at least possible). Therefore also the existence is postulated of a cause of the whole of nature, itself distinct from nature, which contains the ground of the exact coincidence of happiness with morality. This supreme cause, however, must contain the ground of the agreement of nature not merely with a law of the will of rational beings but with the idea of this law so far as they make it the supreme ground of determination of the will. Thus it contains the ground of the agreement of nature not merely with actions moral in their form but also with their morality as the motive to such actions, i.e., with their moral intention. Therefore, the highest good is possible in the world only on the supposition of a supreme cause of nature which has a causality corresponding to the moral intention. Now a being which is capable of actions by the idea of laws is an intelligence (a rational being), and the causality of such a being according to this idea of laws is his will. Therefore, the supreme cause of nature, in so far as it must be presupposed for the highest good, is a being which is the cause (and consequently the author) of nature through understanding and will, i.e., God. As a consequence, the postulate of the possibility of a highest derived good (the best world) is at the same time the postulate of the reality of a highest original good, namely, the existence of God. Now it was our duty to promote the highest good; and it is not merely our privilege but a necessity connected with duty as a requisite to presuppose the possibility of this highest good. Thus presupposition is made only under the condition of the existence of God, and this condition inseparably connects this supposition with duty. Therefore, it is morally necessary to assume the existence of God.

(Trans. Thomas Abbott)

REVIEW QUESTIONS

1. Kant's "criticism" of knowledge occupies an important place in modern philosophy. What does it mean, and how does it tie in with the work of his predecessors like Descartes, Locke, Berkeley, and Hume?
2. Would you say that Kant's several *Critiques* are an attempt to refute skepticism?
3. Describe the genesis of sense knowledge for Kant; in what way is it *a priori?* In what way *a posteriori?*
4. Why does Kant call *pure reason* pure? *practical reason* practical?
5. Relate the fate of metaphysics in modern philosophy to Kant and Hume.
6. According to Kant, must the metaphysical entities unknown to reason be rejected in every sense?
7. According to Kant, how do we arrive at moral judgments?
8. How does Kant relate moral law to holiness?

Suggestions for Further Reading

Cassirer, E. *Kant's Life and Thought.* New Haven, Yale University Press, 1981.
Critique of Pure Reason. Tr. Kemp Smith, N. New York, St. Martin's Press, 1969.
Critique of Practical Reason. Tr. Beck, L. W. Indianapolis, Bobbs-Merrill, 1956.
Höffe, Ottfried, *Immanuel Kant.* Albany, SUNY, 1994.
Körner, S. *Kant.* New Haven, Yale University Press, 1982.

19

Georg Wilhelm Friedrich Hegel (1770–1831)

Georg Wilhelm Friedrich Hegel was one of the philosophers of the next generation who, while acknowledging Kant as an indispensable philosopher, was bound by his own vision of absolute unity to reject the dichotomy introduced by Kant in separating the practical from the speculative order and sensibility from reason. As a consequence, Hegel launched a gigantic effort to establish unity and reconciliation at the heart of reality.

He was born in Stuttgart in 1770 and died in Berlin in 1831. He was a student in theology at the University of Tübingen, together with Schelling the philosopher and Hölderlin the poet. He was not a brilliant student, and his leaving certificate indicated that his knowledge of philosophy was inadequate—a much needed source of comfort for all students of philosophy! Upon leaving the university he became a tutor for several families, first in Bern and later in Frankfurt. In 1801 he received an appointment at the University of Jena as *Privatdozent* and a few years later as professor. His first great work, and the one that sets forth the prevailing lines of his thought despite the haste with which it was brought to completion—on the eve of the Battle of Jena between the French and Prussian troops—was *The Phenomenology of Mind* in 1807. Because of the battle the University was closed, and Hegel, in order to make a living, removed first to Bamberg to edit a paper and later to Nürnberg, where he was appointed director of the gymnasium. He married in 1811. He left Nürnberg to accept a post at the University of Heidelberg for a year, after which he went to the University of Berlin, where he remained until his death. At Berlin he was hailed as a brilliant lecturer, and his lectures became the basis of his works on history, art, nature, and religion. Besides the *Phenomenology*, Hegel's other chief works include *The Science of Logic* (1816), *The Encyclopedia of the Philosophical Sciences* (1817), and *Outlines of the Philosophy of Right* (1821).

Unity: Against Mind–Body Dualism

Unity in reality is a constant theme in philosophy, but at certain times the need to articulate it is more pressing than at others, and thus the systems of thinkers like Pythagoras, Plotinus, Nicholas of Cusa, Spinoza, Leibniz, and now Hegel arise. Though there are many problems attaching to the question of unity, there is one in modern philosophy which we have already seen: the mind–body problem. We will recall that Descartes' reaction to skepticism involved an elaboration of a new philosophical method, powerful enough to overcome the haunting lack of certitude that some attributed to the human mind. Methodic doubt led to the discovery of the *cogito* as the first truth in the Cartesian scheme, which, by a deductive process inspired by mathematics, led to the definition of man as spirit only. The body, never *essentially* united with the spirit, enjoyed its own separate existence as a substance, and thus the Cartesian picture of reality presented two substances, entirely separate from each other.

What Descartes accepted as certain became, in turn, a problem for succeeding philosophers who were unhappy with the tenuous relationship he delineated between mind and body. Leibniz, maintaining that his monads were separate substances, accounted for their unity by a marvelous harmony established by God among them and their mind and body components. Spinoza rejected any separability whatsoever, holding to a one-substance reality of which mind and body were attributes.

In a manner of speaking, Descartes, Spinoza, and Leibniz faced the mind–body problem *ontologically;* that is, inasmuch as they were concerned with the knowability of extramental (objective) reality, the question of the unity of substance, vis-à-vis mind and body, was real (objective). Locke, Hume, and Kant, however, faced the same problem *epistemologically;* that is, inasmuch as they were concerned with *how* we know, the question of unity was more subjective (mental) than real (objective, extramental).

We have, then, in Descartes and Kant, two widely divergent reactions to skepticism, each of which, following its own inner logic, terminated in a sundered view of reality. Descartes' reaction led to a reality whose two component substances were divorced from each other, whereas Kant's led to a cleavage between sensibility and reason—a division no less significant than Descartes', but on the subject side.

The Whole of Reality: The Absolute, Idea, Nature, Spirit, Mind, God

A divided reality was a scandal to Hegel; his fundamental purpose, therefore, was to overcome division, separateness, opposition, and even contradiction by seeing reality *as a whole* and by following the implications of wholeness down to the smallest detail. The whole of reality, in its very totality, is called the *Absolute* by Hegel; other names are variously used depending on the context: *Idea, Nature,*

Spirit, Mind, God. Inasmuch as movement, for Hegel, is constitutive of reality, the Absolute cannot be considered simply as being *there,* as though static and immobile, one of the difficulties with Spinoza's concept of the Absolute. No, the Absolute is being on the move, pushing forward, dynamic, with an activity reminiscent of the constant flux of Heraclitus. This dynamism is not the motion of blind, unconscious forces, for consciousness is the very life of the Absolute; yet the notion of consciousness, if modeled after Aristotle's designation of God as Self-thinking Thought, is not enough, for it remains entirely subjective. In order to account for objects in the world, the nature of Spirit has to account for both subject and object at the same time and in the same activity; the self-consciousness of Spirit looks both ways, to subjectivity and objectivity, and its *objectifying* is the *process* whereby Spirit becomes more fully itself while creating objects. To the notion of *Self-thinking* Thought, the notion of *externalizing* has to be added; the realm of objects is the emergence of appearances as the "making known" of the Mind, whence the phrase *phenomenology of the Mind.*

For Hegel, the difficulty with Kant was the cul-de-sac in knowledge caused by so overloading the subject side of the subject–object relationship that there was no obvious vehicle for reaching the object. To overcome this problem, Hegel looked upon the process of objectification from the epistemological point of view, holding that the Spirit, conscious of the emergence of objects from within itself, knows itself in an act of self-consciousness, so that the one activity, as previously indicated, accounts for both subject and object in the knowledge equation: In one activity Spirit knows subjectively what it produces objectively. Subject and object are two sides of the same coin, both essential to Spirit in the process of unfolding.

Identity in Difference

A further look at this process discloses the *necessary opposition,* or *contradiction,* from which the unfolding takes place; Being has to be itself, while opposed to itself; to be identical with itself, while different from itself; its "very self-identity is internal distinction." The Absolute's difference in its own identity, its *identity in difference,* is an affirmation of its being and not-being at the same time and is the reason why becoming is possible at all within the Absolute. The processive movement, a "self-producing course of activity, maintaining its advance by returning back into itself," is called the *dialectical movement,* or simply the *dialectic* (from the Greek, meaning back and forth, as in conversation).

Though the terminology of *thesis, antithesis,* and *synthesis* is not that of Hegel, it has often been used to explain the concept of dialectic, particularly as it has taken a permanent place in the Marxist tradition of modern philosophy. Hegel often speaks of things in threes, in triads, so that an interaction between the first two will produce the third. In the highest triad, the Absolute, as it is actually posited—that is, in its positive affirmation of being—is called *thesis;* its contradiction, the element of non-being, is called *antithesis;* the interaction between these two is the dialectical movement of becoming, the issue of which is called *synthesis*. Recalling that Idea is also a word used by Hegel for the totality, the process is often referred to as *dialectical idealism,* to be compared later with Marx's use of the dialectic, for which he employed the term *dialectical materialism.*

But expressions of the Spirit can vary insofar as they bear a remote or close similarity to it. The realm of nature, because it is matter, is of the first type; it is the realm of mechanics, physics, and organics, where particularity holds sway and a lack of freedom is the common denominator. Because matter stands in opposition to idea, deduction is impossible and things have to be known *empirically,* a grudging admission on Hegel's part that natural sciences have a legitimate role and their own method, for he had gone so far as to deny that Newton's physics was a *true* physics. Still, the world of matter somehow belongs to the life of the Spirit and shares the dialectical process, and it is interesting to see to what lengths Hegel is willing to go to make them fit. For example, an acid and a base are so called only in relation to each other, and the fact that they enter into a process whereby they neutralize each other "makes their existence lie in being cancelled and superseded, or makes it into a universal; and acid and base possess truth merely *qua* universal."

Individual/Social

It is, however, in the realm of *ethical action* that the Spirit finds itself more sympathetically expressed and, following the rule of process, even this expression is subject to increasing levels of kinship with pure Spirit. The individual at first feeds his own individuality with every kind of self-satisfaction, without taking into account the universal aspect of his action. This aspect begins to assert itself among many individuals who, while trying to act together, still act as individuals—a kind of herd of animals. Stark individuality gradually gives way to the recognition that true individuality has meaning only in *social* life, and with this recognition individuals enter the sphere of spiritual existence. The life of the Spirit in the socialized individual ranges in degree from the simplest society of the family to the complex society of state government.

With social life, there immediately arises a course of action called *law,* which reason perceives as the fulcrum balancing individuality with universality so that one is not achieved without the other. The individual, thus seeing himself endowed with universality through the laws of the social order, sees himself as possessing a whole spectrum of rights that constitute him as a *person.* This progression is not any easy one, for the Spirit as individual in working its way to the Spirit as universal is conscious of this *estrangement* and must overcome the struggles imposed by various cultures and civilizations, even though the highest levels of finite life are found in society.

Human life, as finite Spirit, reaches its highest level in morality, for here, with Hegel following the lead of Kant, society mediates universal law for the individual, in virtue of which the moral will is the one that is conscious of, and does, its Duty; this is what constitutes freedom. Conscience, then, is the self-legislating individual will, conscious of the universality flowing into it from society; and this activity of the will is the supreme achievement of the finite Spirit.

But the finite Spirit is the Spirit conscious of itself in finite modes only, not yet having achieved the consciousness of itself as Infinite. This last consciousness requires two more stages. The first stage is Religion, conceived by Hegel as a kind of gathering up of all previous modes of the finite into a single totality and expressed in a variety of art forms and religious terms. In the final stage, however, all "forms" and "terms" and every other type of *representation* are put aside because they are finite, and the Spirit comes to know itself *through itself,* in the perfect act of what Hegel calls *Absolute Knowledge.*

Hegel's system of metaphysical idealism, in all its minute abstraction, stands as one of the greatest efforts philosophers have made to reach the interconnections of all reality and to grasp being, finite and infinite, as a seamless garment. The observation that there are today few formal Hegelians does not do justice to the towering influence Hegel once had. In Germany, Britain, Italy, and the United States in the nineteenth and early twentieth centuries, there were many philosophers who considered themselves followers and interpreters of the master. And in non-philosophical fields, there is no way of measuring the influence of the man who offered a fresh scheme to theologians for the reinterpretation of Christianity, a primer of subjective analysis for phenomenologists, a basic terminology for psychologists, and a dialectical framework for Marxian philosophy, to say nothing of his influence on the study of history, sociology, and law.

READINGS

The Absolute as Process of Self-Becoming
(from *Phenomenology of Mind,* Preface)

In my view—a view which the developed exposition of the system itself can alone justify—everything depends on grasping and expressing the ultimate truth not as Substance but as Subject as well. At the same time we must note that concrete substantiality implicates and involves the universal or the immediacy of knowledge itself, as well as that immediacy which is being, or immediacy *qua* object *for* knowledge. If the generation which heard God spoken of as the One Substance was shocked and revolted by such a characterization of his nature, the reason lay partly in the instinctive feeling that in such a conception self-consciousness was simply submerged, and not preserved. But partly, again, the opposite position, which maintains thinking to be merely subjective thinking, abstract universality as such, is exactly the same bare uniformity, is undifferentiated, unmoved substantiality. And even if, in the third place, thought combines with itself the being of substance, and conceives immediacy or intuition

(*Anschauung*) as thinking, it is still a question whether this intellectual intuition does not fall back into that inert, abstract simplicity, and exhibit and expound reality itself in an unreal manner.

The living substance, further, is that being which is truly subject, or, what is the same thing, is truly realized and actual (*wirklich*) solely in the process of positing itself, or in mediating with its own self its transitions from one state or position to the opposite. As subject it is pure and simple negativity, and just on that account a process of splitting up what is simple and undifferentiated, a process of duplicating and setting factors in opposition, which [process] in turn is the negation of this indifferent diversity and of the opposition of factors it entails. True reality is merely this process of reinstating self-identity, of reflecting into its own self in and from its other, and is not an original and primal unity as such, not an immediate unity as such. It is the process of its own becoming, the circle which presupposes its end as its purpose, and has its end for its beginning; it becomes concrete and actual only by being carried out, and by the end it involves.

The life of God and divine intelligence, then, can, if we like, be spoken of as love disporting with itself; but this idea falls into edification, and even sinks into insipidity, if it lacks the seriousness, the suffering, the patience, and the labour of the negative. *Per se* the divine life is no doubt undisturbed identity and oneness with itself, which finds no serious obstacle in otherness and estrangement, and none in the surmounting of this estrangement. But this "per se" is abstract generality, where we abstract from its real nature, which consists in its being objective to itself, conscious of itself on its own account (*für sich zu sein*); and where consequently we neglect altogether the self-movement which is the formal character of its activity. If the form is declared to correspond to the essence, it is just for that reason a misunderstanding to suppose that knowledge can be content with the "per se", the essence, but can do without the form, that the absolute principle, or absolute intuition, makes the carrying out of the former, or the development of the latter, needless. Precisely because the form is as necessary to the essence as the essence to itself, absolute reality must not be conceived of and expressed as essence alone, i.e. as immediate substance, or as pure self-intuition of the Divine, but as form also, and with the entire wealth of the developed form. Only then is it grasped and expressed as really actual.

The truth is the whole. The whole, however, is merely the essential nature reaching its completeness through the process of its own development. Of the Absolute it must be said that it is essentially a result, that only at the end is it what it is in very truth; and just in that consists its nature, which is to be actual, subject, or self-becoming, self-development. Should it appear contradictory to say that the Absolute has to be conceived essentially as a result, a little consideration will set this appearance of contradiction in its true light. The beginning, the principle, or the Absolute, as at first or immediately expressed, is merely the universal. If we say "all animals", that does not pass for zoology; for the same reason we see at once that the words absolute, divine, eternal, and so on do not express what is implied in them; and only mere words like these, in point of fact, express intuition as the immediate. Whatever is more than a word like that, even the mere transition to a proposition, is a form of mediation, contains a process towards another state from which we must return once more. It is this process of mediation, however, that is rejected with horror, as if absolute knowledge were being surrendered when more is made of mediation than merely the assertion that it is nothing absolute, and does not exist in the Absolute.

This horrified rejection of mediation, however, arises as a fact from want of acquaintance with its nature, and with the nature of absolute knowledge itself. For mediating is nothing but self-identity working itself out through an active self-directed process; or, in other words, it is reflection into self, the aspect in which the ego is for itself, objective to itself. It is pure negativity, or, reduced to its utmost abstraction, the process of bare and simple becoming. The ego, or becoming in general, this process of mediating, is, because of its being simple, just immediacy coming to be, and is immediacy itself. We misconceive therefore the nature of reason if we exclude reflection or mediation from ultimate truth, and do not take it to be a positive moment of the Absolute. It is reflection which constitutes truth the final result, and yet at the same time does away with the contrast between result and the process of arriving at it. For this process is likewise simple, and therefore not distinct from the form of truth, which consists in appearing as simple in the result; it is indeed just this restoration and return to simplicity. While the embryo is certainly, in itself, implicitly a human being, it is not so explicitly, it is not by itself a human being (*für sich*); man is explicitly man only in the form of developed and cultivated reason, which has made itself to be what it is implicitly. Its actual reality is first found here. But this result arrived at is itself simple immediacy; for it is self-conscious freedom, which is at one with itself, and has not set aside the opposition it involves and left it there, but has made its account with it and become reconciled to it.

What has been said may also be expressed by saying that reason is purposive activity. The exaltation of so-called nature at the expense of thought misconceived, and more especially the rejection of external purposiveness, have brought the idea of purpose in general into disrepute. All the same, in the sense in which Aristotle, too, characterizes nature as purposive activity, purpose is the immediate, the undisturbed, the unmoved which is self-moving; as such it is subject. Its power of moving, taken abstractly, is its existence for itself, or pure negativity. The result is the same as the beginning solely because the beginning is purpose. Stated otherwise, what is actual and concrete is the same as its inner principle or notion simply because the immediate *qua* purpose contains within it the self or pure actuality. The realized purpose, or concrete actuality, is movement and development unfolded. But this very unrest is the self; and it is one and the same with that immediacy and simplicity characteristic of the beginning just for the reason that it is the result, and has returned upon itself—while this latter again is just the self, and the self is self-referring and self-relating identity and simplicity.

The need to think of the Absolute as subject, has led men to make use of statements like "God is the eternal", the "moral order of the world", or "love", etc. In such propositions the truth is just barely stated to be Subject, but not set forth as the process of reflectively mediating itself with itself. In a proposition of that kind we begin with the word God. By itself this is a meaningless sound, a mere name; the predicate says afterwards *what* it is, gives it content and meaning: the empty beginning becomes real knowledge only when we thus get to the end of the statement. So far as that goes, why not speak alone of the eternal, of the moral order of the world, etc., or, like the ancients, of pure conceptions such as being, the one, etc., i.e. of what gives the meaning without adding the meaningless sound at all? But this word just indicates that it is not a being or essence or universal in general that is put forward, but something reflected into self, a subject. Yet at the same time this acceptance of the Absolute as Subject is merely anticipated, not really affirmed. The subject is taken to be a fixed point, and to it as their support the predicates are attached, by a process falling within the individual knowing about it, but not looked upon as belonging to the point of attachment itself; only by such a process, however, could the content be presented as subject. Constituted as it is, this process cannot belong to the subject; but when that point of support is fixed to start with, this process cannot be otherwise constituted, it can only be external. The anticipation that the Absolute is subject is therefore not merely not the realization of this conception; it even makes realization impossible. For it makes out the notion to be a static point, while its actual reality is self-movement, self-activity.

Among the many consequences that follow from what has been said, it is of importance to emphasize this, that knowledge is only real and can only be set forth fully in the form of science, in the form of system; and further, that a so-called fundamental proposition or first principle of philosophy, even if it is true, is yet none the less false just because and in so far as it is merely a fundamental proposition, merely a first principle. It is for that reason easily refuted. The refutation consists in bringing out its defective character; and it *is* defective because it is merely the universal, merely a principle, the beginning. If the refutation is complete and thorough, it is derived and developed from the nature of the principle itself, and not accomplished by bringing in from elsewhere other counter assurances and chance fancies. It would be strictly the development of the principle, and thus the completion of its deficiency, were it not that it misunderstands its own purport by taking account solely of the negative aspect of what it seeks to do, and is not conscious of the positive character of its process and result. The really positive working out of the beginning is at the same time just as much the very reverse, it is a negative attitude towards the principle we start from, negative, that is to say, of its one-sided form, which consists in being primarily immediate, a mere purpose. It may therefore be regarded as a refutation of what constitutes the basis of the system; but more correctly it should be looked at as a demonstration that the *basis* or principle of the system is in point of fact merely its *beginning.*

That the truth is only realized in the form of system, that substance is essentially subject, is expressed in the idea which represents the Absolute as Spirit (*Geist*)—the grandest conception of all, and one which is due to modern times and its religion. Spirit is alone Reality. It is the inner being of the world, that which essentially is, and is *per se;* it assumes objective, determinate form, and enters into relations with itself—it is externality (otherness), and exists for self; yet, in this determination, and in its otherness, it is still one with itself—it is self-contained and self-complete, in itself and for itself at once. This self-containedness, however, is first something known by us, it is implicit in its nature (*an sich*); it is Substance spiritual. It has to become self-contained *for itself,* on its own account; it must be knowledge of spirit, and must be consciousness of itself as spirit. This means, it must be presented to itself as an object, but at the same time straightway annual and transcend this objective form; it must be its own object in which it finds itself reflected. So far as its spiritual content is produced by its own activity, it is only *we* [the thinkers] who know spirit to be for itself, to be objective to itself; but in so far as spirit knows itself to be for itself, then this self-production, the pure notion, is the sphere and element in which its objectification takes effect, and where it gets its existential form. In this way it is in its existence aware of itself as an object in which its own self is reflected. Mind, which, when thus developed, knows itself to be mind, is science. Science is its realization, and the kingdom it sets up for itself in its own native element.

Consciousness and the Dialectical Process
(from *Phenomenology of Mind,* Introduction)

As the foregoing has been stated, provisionally and in general, concerning the manner and the necessity of the process of the inquiry, it may also be of further service to make some observations regarding the method of carrying this out. This exposition, viewed as a process of relating science to phenomenal knowledge, and as an inquiry and critical examination into the reality of knowing, does not seem able to be effected without some presupposition which is laid down as an ultimate criterion. For an examination consists in applying an accepted standard, and, on the final agreement or disagreement therewith of what is tested, deciding whether the latter is right or wrong; and the standard in general, and so science, were this the criterion, is thereby accepted as the essence or inherently real (*Ansich*). But, here, where science first appears on the scene, neither science nor any sort of standard has justified itself as the essence or ultimate reality; and without this no examination seems able to be instituted.

This contradiction and the removal of it will become more definite if, to begin with, we call to mind the abstract determinations of knowledge and of truth as they are found in consciousness. Consciousness, we find, *distinguishes* from itself something, to which at the same time it *relates* itself; or, to use the current expression, there is something *for* consciousness; and the determinate form of this process of relating, or of there being something for a consciousness, is knowledge. But from this being for another we distinguish being in itself or *per se;* what is related to knowledge is likewise distinguished from it, and posited as also existing outside this relation; the aspect of being *per se* or in itself is called Truth. What really lies in these determinations does not further concern us here; for since the object of our inquiry is phenomenal knowledge, its determinations are also taken up, in the first instance, as they are immediately offered to us. And they are offered to us very much in the way we have just stated.

If now our inquiry deals with the truth of knowledge, it appears that we are inquiring what knowledge is in itself. But in this inquiry knowledge is *our* object, it is *for us;* and the essential nature (*Ansich*) of knowledge, were this to come to light, would be rather its being *for us:* what we should assert to be its essence would rather be, not the truth of knowledge, but only our knowledge of it. The essence or the criterion would lie in us; and that which was to be compared with this standard, and on which a decision was to be passed as a result of this comparison, would not necessarily have to recognize that criterion.

But the nature of the object which we are examining surmounts this separation, or semblance of separation, and presupposition. Consciousness furnishes its own criterion in itself, and the inquiry will thereby be a comparison of itself with its own self; for the distinction, just made, falls inside itself. In consciousness there is one element *for* an other, or, in general, consciousness implicates the specific character of the moment of knowledge. At the same time this "other" is to consciousness not merely *for it,* but also outside this relation, or has a being in itself, i.e. there is the moment of truth. Thus in what consciousness inside itself declares to be the essence or truth we have the standard which itself sets up, and by which we are to measure its knowledge. Suppose we call knowledge the notion, and the essence or truth "being" or the object, then the examination consists in seeing whether the notion corresponds with the object. But if we call the inner nature of the object, or what it is in itself, the notion, and, on the other side, understand by object the notion *qua* object, i.e. the way the notion is *for* an other, then the examination consists in our seeing whether the object corresponds to its own notion. It is clear, of course, that both of these processes are the same. The essential fact, however, to be borne in mind throughout the whole inquiry is that both these moments, notion and object, "being for another" and "being in itself", themselves fall within that knowledge which we are examining. Consequently we do not require to bring standards with us, nor to apply *our* fancies and thoughts in the inquiry; and just by our leaving these aside we are enabled to treat and discuss the subject as it actually is in itself and for itself, as it is in its complete reality.

But not only in this respect, that notion and object, the criterion and what is to be tested, are ready to hand in consciousness itself, is any addition of ours superfluous, but we are also spared the trouble of comparing these two and of making an examination in the strict sense of the term; so that in this respect, too, since consciousness tests and examines itself, all we are left to do is simply and solely to look on. For consciousness is, on the one hand, consciousness of the object, on the other, consciousness of itself; consciousness of what to it is true, and consciousness of its knowledge of that truth. Since both are for the same consciousness, it is itself their comparison; it is the same consciousness that decides and knows whether its knowledge of the object corresponds with this object or not. The object, it is true, appears only to be in such wise for consciousness as consciousness knows it. Consciousness does not seem able to get, so to say, behind it as it is, not for consciousness, but in itself, and consequently seems also unable to test knowledge by it. But just because consciousness has, in general, knowledge of an object, there is already present the distinction that the inherent nature, what the object is in itself, is one thing to consciousness, while knowledge, or the being of the object *for* consciousness, is another moment. Upon this distinction, which is present as a fact, the examination turns. Should both, when thus compared, not correspond, consciousness seems bound to alter its knowledge, in order to make it fit the object. But in the alteration of the knowledge, the object itself also, in point of fact, is altered; for the knowledge which existed was essentially a knowledge of the object; with change in the knowledge, the object also becomes different, since it belonged essentially to this knowledge. Hence consciousness comes to find that what formerly to it was the essence is not what is *per se,* or what was *per se* was only *per se for consciousness.* Since, then, in the case of its object consciousness finds its knowledge not corresponding with this object, the object likewise fails to hold out; or the standard for examining is altered when that, whose criterion this standard was to be, does not hold its ground in the course of the examination; and the examination is not only an examination of knowledge, but also of the criterion used in the process.

This dialectic process which consciousness executes on itself—on its knowledge as well as on its object—in the sense that out of it the new and true object arises, is precisely what is termed Experience. In this connection, there is a moment in the process just mentioned which should be brought into more decided prominence, and by which a new light is cast on the scientific aspect of the following exposition. Consciousness knows something; this something is the essence or what is *per se.* This object, however, is also the *per se,* the inherent reality, *for consciousness.* Hence comes ambiguity of this truth. Consciousness, as we see, has now two objects; one is the first *per se,* the second is the existence *for consciousness* of this *per se.* The last object appears at first sight to be merely the reflection of consciousness into itself, i.e. an idea not of an object, but solely of its knowledge of that first object. But, as was already indicated, by that very process the first object is altered; it ceases to be what is *per se,* and becomes consciously something which is *per se* only *for consciousness.* Consequently, then, what this real *per se* is for consciousness is truth: which, however, means that this is the essential reality, or the object which consciousness has. This new object contains the nothingness of the first; the new object is the *experience* concerning that first object.

In this treatment of the course of experience, there is an element in virtue of which it does not seem to be in agreement with what is ordinarily understood by experience. The transition from the first object and the knowledge of it to the other object, in regard to which we say we have had experience, was so stated that the knowledge of the first object, the existence *for consciousness* of the first *ens per se,* is itself to be the second object. But it usually seems that we learn by experience the untruth of our first notion by appealing to some other object which we may happen to find casually and externally; so that, in general, what we have is merely the bare and simple apprehension of what is in and for itself. On the view above given, however, the new object is seen to have come about by a transformation or conversion of consciousness itself. This way of looking at the matter is *our* doing, what *we* contribute; by its means the series of experiences through which consciousness passes is lifted into a scientifically constituted sequence, but this does not exist for the consciousness we contemplate and consider. We have here, however, the same sort of circumstance, again, of which we spoke a short time ago when dealing with the relation of this exposition to scepticism, viz. that the result which at any time comes about in the case of an untrue mode of knowledge cannot possibly collapse into an empty nothing, but must necessarily be taken as the negation of that of which it is a result—a result which contains what truth the preceding mode of knowledge has in it. In the present instance the position takes this form: since what at first appeared as object is reduced, when it passes into consciousness, to what knowledge takes it to be, and the implicit nature, the real in itself, becomes what this entity *per se* is *for consciousness;* this latter is the new object, whereupon there appears also a new mode or embodiment of consciousness, of which the essence is something other than that of the preceding mode. It is this circumstance which carries forward the whole succession of the modes or attitudes of consciousness in their own necessity. It is only this necessity, this origination of the new object—which offers itself to consciousness without consciousness knowing how it comes by it—that to us, who watch the process, is to be seen going on, so to say, behind its back. Thereby there enters into its process a moment of being *per se* or of being for us, which is not expressly presented to that consciousness which is in the grip of experience itself. The *content*, however, of what we see arising, exists for it, and we lay hold of and comprehend merely its formal character, i.e. its *bare* origination; *for it*, what has thus arisen has merely the character of object, while, *for us*, it appears at the same time as a process and coming into being.

In virtue of that necessity this pathway to science is itself *eo ipso* science, and is, moreover, as regards its content, Science of the Experience of Consciousness.

The experience which consciousness has concerning itself can, by its essential principle, embrace nothing less than the entire system of consciousness, the whole realm of the truth of mind, and in such wise that the moments of truth are set forth in the specific and peculiar character they here possess—i.e. not as abstract pure moments, but as they are for consciousness, or as consciousness itself appears in its relation to them, and in virtue of which they are moments of the whole, are embodiments or modes of consciousness. In pressing forward to its true form of existence, consciousness will come to a point at which it lays aside its semblance of being hampered with what is foreign to it, with what is only for it and exists as an other; it will reach a position where appearance becomes identified with essence, where, in consequence, its exposition coincides with just this very point, this very stage of the science proper of mind. And, finally, when it grasps this its own essence, it will connote the nature of absolute knowledge itself.

(Trans. J. M. Baillie, N.Y. Dover Publications, 2004)

REVIEW QUESTIONS

1. Explain how Hegel attempts to overcome all separation and division in reality.
2. Compare Hegel's view of reality-as-a-whole with that of Spinoza.
3. How does Hegel tackle the problem of Spirit as absolute being, yet becoming at the same time?
4. Explain what Hegel means by the dialectical movement.
5. How does the individual maintain his individuality in Hegel's view of reality-as-one-Substance?

SUGGESTIONS FOR FURTHER READING

Mure, G. R. G. *An Introduction to Hegel.* New York, Oxford University Press, 1940.
Phenomenology of Mind. Tr. Baillie, J. B. London, Macmillan, 1931.
Singer, P. *Hegel.* New York, Oxford University Press, 2002.

20

John Stuart Mill
(1806–1873)

In his timely, sensitive, and clearheaded analyses of moral and political life, John Stuart Mill bridges the contemporary and classical modern periods. He can be seen as a contemporary philosopher inasmuch as he championed personal value in his advocacy of individuality, sought for some way to ground humanity in view of a declining Christianity, and tried to improve the conditions of the working class of England. But perhaps he can be seen more clearly as working in the empirical tradition of Locke, Berkeley, and Hume: His view of man was sympathetic to that tradition; he elaborated its moral implications anew as utilitarianism; and his thoughts on government reach back to Locke.

He was born in London in 1806, the oldest child of James and Harriet Mill. His father was a Scotsman who, in pursuing an intellectual career in London, became a respected author and a devoted follower of the utilitarian philosopher Jeremy Bentham. In the opening pages of his *Autobiography,* the younger Mill describes how his father became the principal shaper of his early life by putting him through one of the most exacting programs of home education ever recorded. As a child he learned Greek at age three and read Greek authors in their own language before he was seven (Plato at age eight); he did arithmetic as well and commenced the study of Latin. He read extensively, and each morning he had to give an account of his previous day's reading to his father. Such an intense intellectual regime, coupled with his father's inability to show any "signs of feeling," took its toll on the child's development, for the normal playfulness, feelings, and friendships of childhood were not his: "I never was a boy," he wrote. His education was completely areligious, which was surprising only in that his father, who embraced a humanistic religion, had once studied for the ministry. On the eve of his son's visit to France at age thirteen, James Mill thought it was wise to advise his intellectually superior offspring that he was not like other young men of his own age. From the beginning, John Stuart Mill was destined for a life of the mind.

The Shaping of Mill's Philosophy

Though Mill was well schooled in Bentham's philosophy, it was only after reading a treatise on his teaching by a Swiss disciple that the full force of the "greatest happiness" doctrine struck him. In "one of the turning points in [his] mental history," he saw the futility of past speculation on morality, and in its place he "had a grand conception" laid before him "of changes to be effected in the condition of mankind through that doctrine." In the next few years this ardent apostle began writing on his own, contributing, as a reformer and radical, articles to the newly founded *Westminster Review.*

Mill was never an academician, but did his studying and writing in conjunction with his work as a civil servant in the East India Company. Though the job itself was not demanding, young Mill's self-imposed regimen was a heavy one and led to a mental overload that ended in a breakdown and a depression lasting for several months. He had thought that, with a Benthamite outlook, he had a satisfying object in life, and his conception of his own happiness "was entirely identified with this object." The depression did not abate until he was able to allow sentiments earlier denied him grow into a larger and warmer sense of humanity than he had previously possessed; this was occasioned by the reading of Wordsworth's poetry. He did not cease believing in Benthamism, whose principles he clung to permanently, but he was now able to see them less formalistically and more humanly, and to realize that there were more levels of happiness than Bentham was ready to admit; this vision henceforth supported him. The vision was given an additional and unexpected personal dimension when he formed a lasting friendship with Harriet Taylor, who became his wife when her husband died. Her inspiration was such, according to Mill's account, that she must be credited as co-author of several of his most important works. During those years he completed *A System of Logic* (1843), *The Principles of Political Economy* (1848), and *On Liberty* (1859). A few years after his wife's death, he published *Considerations on Representative Government* (1861) and edited some earlier essays under the title of *Utilitarianism* (1863).

Surprised by an invitation to run for Parliament, and after weighing the pros and cons of the active political life versus the theoretical, Mill agreed to run and was elected in 1865. During his few years as a member of Parliament, he fought for the exploited Negroes in Jamaica, for reform to enfranchise the working class in England, and for the redistribution of land in Ireland. His last original work was *An Examination of Sir William Hamilton's Philosophy* (1865). His *Autobiography* and *Three Essays on Religion* were published posthumously. At his death in 1873, looking back on a life devoted to the cause of human happiness and the alleviation of human misery, he said to his stepdaughter, "You know that I have done my work."

Utilitarianism

We have already seen what constituted Mill's work, for, from his early years on, he addressed himself to the "condition of mankind" by applying the principles of utilitarianism. For the maturing Mill, however, Bentham's utilitarian formulation became far too narrow, although it was never as ludicrously gross as its opponents often made it out to be. Mill argued the fundamental soundness of Bentham's insight but tried to depart from a too quantitative analysis of pleasure and pain. Toward the beginning of *Utilitarianism* he states:"The creed which accepts as the foundation of morals, Utility, or the Greatest Happiness Principle, holds that actions are right in proportion as they tend to promote happiness, wrong as they tend to promote the reverse of happiness. By happiness is intended pleasure, and the absence of pain; by unhappiness, pain, and the privation of pleasure." Mill immediately amplifies the meaning of pleasure and happiness by insisting that "some *kinds* of pleasure are more desirable and more valuable than others"—quality too must enter into one's judgment. Once one understands the level of dignity that attaches to the human being over other beings, and understands that there are different levels of value in the human being itself, one understands, as Mill puts it, that "It is better to be a human being dissatisfied than a pig satisfied; better to be Socrates dissatisfied than a fool satisfied."

Simple as this statement sounds, Mill knew it was complex, particularly regarding the need to make a moral judgment. Is there moral rightness to begin with? How do we estimate right and wrong? By intuition, deduction, reason, trial and error, our feelings? On these questions Mill brings his empiricism to bear. We do not have direct knowledge of the moral or ethical value of an act; there is no place for intuition in morality, no special faculty of immediate moral apprehension. Yet Mill did not want to deny the role of moral feelings, for even early in his career he expostulated against those who denied their existence. Feelings are not innate; they are acquired, brought about by education and experience and subject to rational control:"the moral faculty, if not part of our nature, is a natural outgrowth from it; capable . . . in a small degree, of springing up spontaneously; and susceptible of being brought by cultivation to a high degree of development."

Morality: Freedom and Determinism

As Mill asserts in *A System of Logic,* the study of moral sciences which include ethics, politics, character analysis, psychology, and sociology, has not achieved the scientific exactness of the physical sciences and it will be a long time before it does. "Bad generalizations" (empiricism in Mill's use of the word) regarding human behavior are totally unacceptable, but that does not mean that human behavior is not subject to the *law of causation,* as everything in nature is; it is simply that we do not know enough about the causes at work. Though in some respects more detailed in Mill, the law of causation is pure Hume and means that "every consequent has an invariable antecedent," or, more exactly, "the cause of a phenomenon" is defined "to be the antecedent, or the concurrence of antecedents, on which it is invariably and *unconditionally* consequent." Mill's view is that the uniformity prevailing in nature, and embodied in its laws, prevails in man too, but those causes for the most part remain to be discovered. He had hopes for the positivist enterprise of Auguste Comte in his discovery of the laws of man's social development, and for the associationist psychology of David Hartley in which particular experiences associated with pleasure and pain lead to moral conclusions. If we were able to know *all* the antecedents of a given action, on the basis of the law of causation, we could predict it, but the human being is so complex that our present state of science disallows prediction.

But this belief completely negates free will, and thus Mill finds himself in the classical nutcracker between freedom and determinism; how this "Philosophical Necessity" weighed on his mind like an incubus is movingly told in the *Autobiography:* If one is free, the whole law of causation collapses; if one is determined, one becomes "the helpless slave of antecedent circumstances." Is there any way of saying that we have real control over our character formation and still are subject to the law of causation? Mill believed that he had finally made a breakthrough by admitting, on the one hand, that "our character is formed by circumstances" and, on the other, that "our own desires can do much to shape those circumstances." Thus there is a midway point between determinism–fatalism and the doctrine propounding free will as a special undetermined causal agency in man. Laying aside any question as to the objective satisfactoriness of Mill's treatment, it did settle matters for him; he indicated in the chapter's concluding words that his resolution was "sufficiently established for the purposes of this treatise."

Inductive Logic

The last book of the *Logic* is entitled "On the Logic of the Moral Sciences," and inasmuch as the consideration of moral science is not necessary for the study of logic proper, it may not unreasonably be asked whether, over a ten-year period, Mill wrote his principal opus for the sake of the last book. The principles of induction he painstakingly elaborates in the *Logic* are precisely the ones he uses to substantiate most of his writing on the moral sciences. But long before the last chapter is reached, Mill's monumental logic unfolds. It was his set purpose to do for inductive reasoning what Aristotle did for deductive reasoning, and in the opinion of many he succeeded. The syllogism, proper to deduction, is valid but, for Mill, does not give very much, if any, new knowledge; new knowledge is the domain of induction. In reality, all inference is from particulars to particulars: from a number of particular instances, I draw a general truth or proposition that, relying on the uniformity of nature, I apply to any future instance of the same. I do not, therefore, deduce that "the Duke of Wellington is mortal" from the proposition "All men are mortal," as though it were a given major proposition; rather, I deduce it only in the sense that "a general truth is but an aggregate of particular truths," and so it is really from the particular instances of the death of John and Thomas and others that I infer the generalization (make the conclusion) that "All men are mortal," in which the particular man, the Duke of Wellington, is included. It is on this basis that the law of causation, Mill's golden thread, rests and becomes applicable to the activities of the universe as a whole and those of man in particular.

Social Questions

The moral sciences are theoretical and practical at the same time, so a philosopher like John Stuart Mill, in turning his attention to social problems, does so in the best tradition of the speculative-cum-practical. Social problems, always connected with some kind of injustice, require a social philosophy, and a social philosophy, in turn, requires a philosophy of political economy, hence the subtitle of Mill's *Principles of Political Economy* is "With Some of Their Applications to Social Philosophy." It appeared in 1848, the same year as the *Communist Manifesto,* although there is scant evidence that Mill knew of the writings of Karl Marx laboring in the British Museum. Mill, at home with economics since childhood, often reflected on the link between wealth and freedom; this theme was brought to a head with the Irish potato famine of 1846-1847, "when the stern necessities of the time seemed to afford a chance of gaining attention for what appeared to me the only mode of combining relief to immediate destitution with permanent improvement of the social and economical condition of the Irish people." He had already been working on his huge *Political Economy,* culling raw material from hundreds of examples the world over, not least from the impoverished working class in England, but it was the Irish problem that prompted him to finish it in less than two years so that it could be published as soon as possible. And since an overall philosophy was necessary to have political economy make any sense at all, it was, of course, the utilitarian philosophy of greatest happiness that he once again put to work.

The inductive pattern discussed above covers the whole range in political economy from the production of wealth to its distribution, though the laws governing each are significantly different. On the production side Mill analyzes the relationship of capital and labor, and on the distribution side the roles of wages, property, slavery, profits, and rent, along with the options of communism and socialism; the flows of money, trade, taxes, debts, and government functions are considered as part of the production–distribution cycle. All this is done with the ultimate goal of improving the condition of mankind by first changing modes of thought: "I am now convinced, that no great improvements in the lot of mankind are possible, until a great change takes place in the fundamental constitution of their modes of thought."

A further contribution to this work is Mill's espousal of human freedom as stated in his essay *On Liberty,* a work published in 1859 and that he predicted had a better chance of survival than anything else he had written; his prediction has been amply supported. The subject of this work, as stated in its opening sentence, is "Civil, or Social Liberty: the nature and limits of the power which can be legitimately exercised by society over the individual." Society will always have its defenders and its champions, but not the individual; so, *On Liberty* is a ringing proclamation of individual freedom, which historically has been buffeted by two forces, the state and "prevailing opinion"; it is therefore indispensable to find the limit of legitimate interference between state and collective opinion on one side and individual independence on the other. There is one very simple principle, Mill asserts, that governs the dealings of society with the individual in terms of the use of power: "That principle is, that the sole end for which mankind are warranted, individually or collectively, in interfering with the liberty of action of any of their number, is self-protection. That the only purpose for which power can be rightfully exercised over any member of a civilised community, against his will, is to prevent harm to others."

This general principle safeguards the individual in his pursuit of good as he sees it, his "inward domain of consciousness," his liberty to unite with others for any reason not involving harm to others, and his freedom of thought and discussion. If anyone wishes to look for historical personifications of these ideals, let him consider Socrates and Jesus, both of whom were put down by state and public opinion, and the Roman emperor Marcus Aurelius, who, despite his tragic persecution of the Christians, was still a man of "unblemished justice" and "tenderest heart."

Mill delicately tries to delineate the boundaries between the individual and the state, and he sees the state's obligation in restraining an individual if his actions are injurious to others. He formulates two maxims, two principles, which he says form the entire doctrine of *On Liberty:* "The maxims are, first, that the individual is not accountable to society for his actions, in so far as these concern the interests of no person but himself. Advice, instruction, persuasion, and avoidance by other people if thought necessary by them for their own good, are the only measures by which society can justifiably express its dislike or disapprobation of his conduct. Secondly, that for such actions as are prejudicial to the interests of others, the individual is accountable, and may be subjected either to social or to legal punishment, if society is of opinion that the one or the other is requisite for its protection." Mill's application of the greatest happiness doctrine, this time in his concern for the individual and for minorities, is evidenced again, and the liberty of which he speaks bids the state to exert itself in fostering it, for anything else will result in a state that dwarfs its men, and "with small men no great thing can really be accomplished."

Role of Religion

We have stated that one of Mill's goals in philosophy was to find ground for humanity in view of a declining Christianity. This statement was not meant to imply a conscious goal on Mill's part, for it must be recognized, as Mill did, that he never shed religious beliefs because he never had any. Rather, this statement was

meant to indicate the situation of a philosopher straining after the human dimension, and doing so without any palpable support of religion. Yet, *Three Essays on
Religion* was published posthumously by his stepdaughter not "on account of
reluctance to encounter whatever odium might result from the free expression of
his opinions on religion"; rather, it "was in accord with the Author's habit in regard
to the public utterance of his religious opinions." Be that as it may, these essays
indicate Mill's willingness to accept at least the argument from the design of
Nature toward the probability of the world's being created but not by an omnipotent intelligence, and perhaps a pragmatic defense of believing in God inasmuch as
such belief is conducive to good. On the other hand, religion as "supernatural"
must be eschewed in the present stage of man's development, regardless of how
necessary its services were in the early stages; immortality is "utterly opposed to
every presumption that can be deduced from the light of Nature"; and the supernatural origin of the "received maxims of morality" entails a "very real evil" because
it consecrates them and puts them beyond discussion or criticism. In sum, religion
has its utility, but whatever recommendation is found in supernatural religion is
found eminently in the "Religion of Humanity," for it is able to direct the emotions
and desires toward an ideal object and to fulfill the functions of religion by a sense
of unity with mankind and a deep feeling for the general good. The Religion of
Humanity "is not only capable of fulfilling these functions, but would fulfill them
better than any form whatever of supernaturalism . . . it is a better religion than
any of those which are ordinarily called by that title."

In this grand conception of the Religion of Humanity, the figure of Christ has
a preeminent place; consider the following passage written by Mill shortly before
he died: "But about the life and sayings of Jesus there is a stamp of personal originality combined with profundity of insight, which if we abandon the idle expectation of finding scientific precision where something very different was aimed at,
must place the Prophet of Nazareth, even in the estimation of those who have no
belief in his inspiration, in the very first rank of the men of sublime genius of whom
our species can boast . . . it remains a possibility that Christ actually was what he
supposed himself to be—not God, for he never made the smallest pretense to that
character . . . —but a man charged with a special, express and unique commission
from God to lead mankind to truth and virtue."

READINGS

What Utilitarianism Is

(from *Utilitarianism*)

A passing remark is all that needs to be given to the ignorant blunder of supposing
that those who stand up for utility as the test of right and wrong, use the term in
that restricted and merely colloquial sense in which utility is opposed to pleasure.
An apology is due to the philosophical opponents of utilitarianism, for even the

momentary appearance of confounding them with anyone capable of so absurd a misconception; which is the more extraordinary, inasmuch as the contrary accusation, of referring everything to pleasure, and that too in its grossest form, is another of the common charges against utilitarianism: and, as has been pointedly remarked by an able writer, the same sort of persons, and often the very same persons, denounce the theory "as impracticably dry when the word utility precedes the word pleasure, and as too practically voluptuous when the word pleasure precedes the word utility." Those who know anything about the matter are aware that every writer, from Epicurus to Bentham, who maintained the theory of utility, meant by it, not something to be contradistinguished from pleasure, but pleasure itself, together with exemption from pain; and instead of opposing the useful to the agreeable or the ornamental, have always declared that the useful means these, among other things. Yet the common herd, including the herd of writers, not only in newspapers, and periodicals, but in books of weight and pretension, are perpetually falling into this shallow mistake. Having caught up the word 'utilitarian,' while knowing nothing whatever about it but its sound, they habitually express by it the rejection, or the neglect, of pleasure in some of its forms: of beauty, of ornament, or of amusement. Nor is the term thus ignorantly misapplied solely in disparagement, but occasionally in compliment: as though it implied superiority to frivolity and the mere pleasures of the moment. And this perverted use is the only one in which the word is popularly known, and the one from which the new generation are acquiring their sole notion of its meaning. Those who introduced the word, but who had for many years discontinued it as a distinctive appellation, may well feel themselves called upon to resume it, if by doing so they can hope to contribute anything towards rescuing it from this utter degradation.

The creed which accepts as the foundation of morals *utility*, or the *greatest happiness principle*, holds that actions are right in proportion as they tend to promote happiness, wrong as they tend to produce the reverse of happiness. By 'happiness' is intended pleasure, and the absence of pain; by 'unhappiness,' pain, and the privation of pleasure. To give a clear view of the moral standard set up by the theory, much more requires to be said; in particular, what things it includes in the ideas of pain and pleasure; and to what extent this is left an open question. But these supplementary explanations do not affect the theory of life on which this theory of morality is grounded—namely, that pleasure, and freedom from pain, are the only things desirable as ends; and that all desirable things (which are as numerous in the utilitarian as in any other scheme) are desirable either for the pleasure inherent in themselves, or as means to the promotion of pleasure and the prevention of pain.

Now such a theory of life excites in many minds, and among them in some of the most estimable in feeling and purpose, inveterate dislike. To suppose that life has (as they express it) no higher end than pleasure—no better and nobler object of desire and pursuit—they designate as utterly mean and groveling; as a doctrine worthy only of swine, to whom the followers of Epicurus were, at a very early period, contemptuously likened; and modern holders of the doctrine are occasionally made the subject of equally polite comparisons by its German, French, and English assailants.

When thus attacked, the Epicureans have always answered that it is not they but their accusers who represent human nature in a degrading light; since the accusation supposes human beings to be capable of no pleasures except those of which swine are capable. If this supposition were true, the charge could not be gainsaid, but would then be no longer an imputation; for if the sources of pleasure were precisely the same to human beings and to swine, the rule of life which is good enough for the one would be good enough for the other. The comparison of the Epicurean life to that of beasts is felt as degrading, precisely because a beast's pleasures do not satisfy a human being's conceptions of happiness. Human beings have faculties more elevated than the animal appetites, and when once made conscious of them, do not regard anything as happiness which does not include their gratification. I do not, indeed, consider the Epicureans to have been by any means faultless in drawing out their scheme of consequences from the utilitarian principle. To do this in any sufficient manner, many Stoic, as well as Christian elements require to be included. But there is no known Epicurean theory of life which does not assign to the pleasures of the intellect, of the feelings and imagination, and of the moral sentiments, a much higher value as pleasures than to those of mere sensation. It must be admitted, however, that utilitarian writers in general have placed the superiority of mental over bodily pleasures chiefly in the greater permanency, safety, uncostliness, etc., of the former—that is, in their circumstantial advantages rather than in their intrinsic nature. And on all these points utilitarians have fully proved their case; but they might have taken the other, and, as it may be called, higher ground, with entire consistency. It is quite compatible with the principle of utility to recognize the fact, that some *kinds* of pleasure are more desirable and more valuable than others. It would be absurd that while, in estimating all other things, quality is considered as well as quantity, the estimation of pleasures should be supposed to depend on quantity alone.

If I am asked what I mean by difference of quality in pleasures, or what makes one pleasure more valuable than another merely as a pleasure, except its being greater in amount, there is but one possible answer. Of two pleasures, if there be one to which all or almost all who have experience of both give a decided preference, irrespective of any feeling of moral obligation to prefer it, that is the more desirable pleasure. If one of the two is, by those who are competently acquainted with both, placed so far above the other that they prefer it, even though knowing it to be attended with a greater amount of discontent, and would not resign it for any quantity of the other pleasure which their nature is capable of, we are justified in ascribing to the preferred enjoyment a superiority in quality, so far outweighing quantity as to render it, in comparison, of small account.

Now it is an unquestionable fact that those who are equally acquainted with, and equally capable of appreciating and enjoying, both, do give a most marked preference to the manner of existence which employs their higher faculties. Few human creatures would consent to be changed into any of the lower animals, for a promise of the fullest allowance of a beast's pleasures; no intelligent human being would consent to be a fool, no instructed person would be an ignoramus, no person of feeling and conscience would be selfish and base, even though they should be persuaded that the fool, the dunce, or the rascal is better satisfied with his lot than they are with theirs. They would not resign what they possess more than he for the most complete satisfaction of all the desires which they have in common with him. If they ever fancy they would, it is only in cases of unhappiness so extreme, that to escape from it they would exchange their lot for almost any other, however undesirable in their own eyes. A being of higher faculties requires more to make him happy, is capable probably of more acute suffering, and certainly accessible to it at more points, than one of an inferior type; but in spite of these liabilities, he can never really wish to sink into what he feels to be a lower grade of existence. We may give what explanation we please of this unwillingness: we may attribute it to pride, a name which is given indiscriminately to some of the most and to some of the least estimable feelings of which mankind are capable; we may refer it to the love of liberty and personal independence, an appeal to which was with the Stoics one of the most effective means for the inculcation of it; to the love of power, or to the love of excitement, both of which do really enter into and contribute to it: but its most appropriate appellation is a sense of dignity, which all human beings possess in one form or other, and in some, though by no means in exact, proportion to their higher faculties, and which is so essential a part of the happiness of those in whom it is strong, that nothing which con-flicts with it could be, otherwise than momentarily, an object of desire to them. Whoever supposes that this preference takes place at a sacrifice of happiness—that the superior being, in anything like equal circumstances, is not happier than the inferior—confounds the two very different ideas, of *happiness* and *content.* It is indisputable that the being whose capacities of enjoyment are low, has the greatest chance of having them fully satisfied; and a highly endowed being will always feel that any happiness which he can look for, as the world is constituted, is imperfect. But he can learn to bear its imperfections, if they are at all bearable; and they will not make him envy the being who is indeed unconscious of the imperfections, but only because he feels not at all the good which those imperfections qualify. It is better to be a human being dis-satisfied than a pig satisfied; better to be Socrates dissatisfied than a fool satis-fied. And if the fool, or the pig, are of a different opinion, it is because they only know their own side of the question. The other party to the comparison knows both sides.

Of the Law of Universal Causation
(from *A System of Logic*)

1. [*The universal law of successive phenomena is the Law of Causation*] The phenomena of nature exist in two distinct relations to one another; that of simultaneity, and that of succession. Every phenomenon is related, in an uniform manner, to some phenomena that coexist with it, and to some that have preceded and will follow it.

Of the uniformities which exist among synchronous phenomena, the most important, on every account, are the laws of number; and next to them those of space, or, in other words, of extension and figure. The laws of number are common to synchronous and successive phenomena. That two and two make four, is equally true whether the second two follow the first two or accompany them. It is as true of days and years as of feet and inches. The laws of extension and figure (in other words, the theorems of geometry, from its lowest to its highest branches) are, on the contrary, laws of simultaneous phenomena only. The various parts of space, and of the objects which are said to fill space, coexist; and the unvarying laws which are the subject of the science of geometry, are an expression of the mode of their coexistence.

This is a class of laws, or in other words, of uniformities, for the comprehension and proof of which it is not necessary to suppose any lapse of time, any variety of facts or events succeeding one another. The propositions of geometry are independent of the succession of events. All things which possess extension, or, in other words, which fill space, are subject to geometrical laws. Possessing extension, they possess figure; possessing figure, they must possess some figure in particular, and have all the properties which geometry assigns to that figure. If one body be a sphere and another a cylinder, of equal height and diameter, the one will be exactly two-thirds of the other, let the nature and quality of the material be what it will. Again, each body, and each point of a body, must occupy some place or position among other bodies; and the position of two bodies relatively to each other, of whatever nature the bodies be, may be unerringly inferred from the position of each of them relatively to any third body.

In the laws of number, then, and in those of space, we recognise in the most unqualified manner, the rigorous universality of which we are in quest. Those laws have been in all ages the type of certainty, the standard of comparison for all inferior degrees of evidence. Their invariability is so perfect, that it renders us unable even to conceive any exception to them; and philosophers have been led, though (as I have endeavoured to show) erroneously, to consider their evidence as lying not in experience, but in the original constitution of the intellect. If, therefore, from the laws of space and number, we were able to deduce uniformities of any other description, this would be conclusive evidence to us that those other uniformities possessed the same rigorous certainty. But this we cannot do. From laws of space and number alone, nothing can be deduced but laws of space and number.

Of all truths relating to phenomena, the most valuable to us are those which relate to the order of their succession. On a knowledge of these is founded every reasonable anticipation of future facts, and whatever power we possess of influencing those facts to our advantage. Even the laws of geometry are chiefly of practical importance to us as being a portion of the premises from which the order of the succession of phenomena may be inferred. Inasmuch as the motion of the bodies, the action of forces, and the propagation of influences of all sorts, take place in certain lines and over definite spaces, the properties of those lines and spaces are an important part of the laws to which those phenomena are themselves subject. Again, motions, forces, or other influences, and times, are numerable quantities; and the properties of number are applicable to them as to all other things. But though the laws of number and space are important elements in the ascertainment of uniformities of succession, they can do nothing towards it when taken by themselves. They can only be made instrumental to that purpose when we combine with them additional premises, expressive of uniformities of succession already known. By taking, for instance, as premises these propositions, that bodies acted upon by an instantaneous force move with uniform velocity in straight lines; that bodies acted upon by a continuous force move with accelerated velocity in straight lines; and that bodies acted upon by two forces in different directions move in the diagonal of a parallelogram, whose sides represent the direction and quantity of those forces; we may by combining these truths with propositions relating to the properties of straight lines and of parallelograms (as that a triangle is half a parallelogram of the same base and altitude) deduce another important uniformity of succession, viz., that a body moving round a centre of force describes areas proportional to the times. But unless there had been laws of succession in our premises, there could have been no truths of succession in our conclusions. A similar remark might be extended to every other class of phenomena really peculiar; and, had it been attended to, would have prevented many chimerical attempts at demonstrations of the indemonstrable, and explanations which do not explain.

It is not, therefore, enough for us that the laws of space, which are only laws of simultaneous phenomena, and the laws of number, which though true of successive phenomena do not relate to their succession, possess the rigorous certainly and universality of which we are in search. We must endeavour to find some law of succession which has those same attributes, and is therefore fit to be made the foundation of processes for discovering, and of a test for verifying, all other uniformities of succession. This fundamental law must resemble the truths of geometry in their most remarkable peculiarity, that of never being, in any instance whatever, defeated or suspended by any change of circumstances.

Now among all those uniformities in the succession of phenomena, which common observation is sufficient to bring to light, there are very few which have any, even apparent, pretension to this rigorous indefeasibility: and of those few, one only has been found capable of completely sustaining it. In that one, however, we recognize a law which is universal also in another sense; it is coextensive with the entire field of successive phenomena, all instances whatever of succession being examples of it. This law is the Law of Causation. The truth that every fact which has a beginning has a cause, is coextensive with human experience.

This generalization may appear to some minds not to amount to much, since after all it asserts only this: "it is a law, that every event depends on some law:" "it is a law, that there is a law for everything." We must not, however, conclude that the generality of the principle is merely verbal; it will be found on inspection to be no vague or unmeaning assertion, but a most important and really fundamental truth.

6. [*The cause is not the invariable antecedent, but the* unconditional *invariable antecedent*] It now remains to advert to a distinction which is of first-rate importance both for clearing up the notion of cause, and for obviating a very specious objection often made against the view which we have taken of the subject.

When we define the cause of anything (in the only sense in which the present inquiry has any concern with causes) to be "the antecedent which it invariably follows," we do not use this phrase as exactly synonymous with "the antecedent which it invariably *has* followed in our past experience." Such a mode of conceiving causation would be liable to the objection very plausibly urged by Dr. Reid, namely, that according to this doctrine night must be the cause of day, and day the cause of night; since these phenomena have invariably succeeded one another from the beginning of the world. But it is necessary to our using the word cause, that we should believe not only that the antecedent always *has* been followed by the consequent, but that, as long as the present constitution of things endures, it always *will* be so. And this would not be true of day and night. We do not believe that night will be followed by day under all imaginable circumstances, but only that it will be so *provided* the sun rises above the horizon. If the sun ceased to rise, which, for aught we know, may be perfectly compatible with the general laws of matter, night would be, or might be, eternal. On the other hand, if the sun is above the horizon, his light not extinct, and no opaque body between us and him, we believe firmly that unless a change takes place in the properties of matter, this combination of antecedents will be followed by the consequent, day; that if the combination of antecedents could be indefinitely prolonged, it would be always day; and that if the same combination had always existed, it would always have been day, quite independently of night as a previous condition, of day. The existence of the sun (or some such luminous body), and there being no opaque medium in a straight line between that body and the part of the earth where we are situated, are the sole conditions; and the union of these, without the addition of any superfluous circumstance, constitutes the cause. This is what writers mean when they say that the notion of cause involves the idea of necessity. If there be any meaning which confessedly belongs to the term necessity, it is *unconditionalness.* That which is necessary, that which *must* be, means that which will be, whatever supposition we may make in regard to all other things. The succession of day and night evidently is not necessary in this sense. It is conditional on the occurrence of other antecedents. That which will be followed by a given consequent when, and only when, some third circumstance also exists, is not the cause, even though no case should ever have occurred in which the phenomenon took place without it.

Invariable sequence, therefore, is not synonymous with causation, unless the sequence, besides being invariable, is unconditional. There are sequences, as uniform in past experience as any others whatever, which yet we do not regard as cases of causation, but as conjunctions in some sort accidental. Such, to an accurate thinker, is that of day and night. The one might have existed for any length of time, and the other not have followed the sooner for its existence; it follows only if certain other antecedents exist; and where those antecedents existed, it would follow in any case. No one, probably, ever called night the cause of day; mankind must so soon have arrived at the very obvious generalization, that the state of general illumination which we call day would follow from the presence of a sufficiently luminous body, whether darkness had preceded or not.

We may define, therefore, the cause of a phenomenon, to be the antecedent, or the concurrence of antecedents, on which it is invariably and *unconditionally* consequent. Or if we adopt the convenient modification of the meaning of the word cause, which confines it to the assemblage of positive conditions without the negative, then instead of "unconditionally," we must say, "subject to no other than negative conditions."

To some it may appear, that the sequence between night and day being invariable in our experience, we have as much ground in this case as experience can give in any case, for recognising the two phenomena as cause and effect; and that to say that more is necessary—to require a belief that the succession is unconditional, or in other words that it would be invariable under all changes of circumstances, is to acknowledge in causation an element of belief not derived from experience. The answer to this is, that it is experience itself which teaches us that one uniformity of sequence is conditional and another unconditional. When we judge that the succession of night and day is a derivative sequence, depending on something else, we proceed on grounds of experience. It is the evidence of experience which convinces us that day could equally exist without being followed by night, and that night could equally exist without being followed by day. To say that these beliefs are "not generated by our mere observation of sequence," is to forget that twice in every twenty-four hours, when the sky is clear, we have an *experimentum crucis* that the cause of day is the sun. We have an experimental knowledge of the sun which justifies us on experimental grounds in concluding, that if the sun were always above the horizon there would be day, though there had been no night, though there had been no day. We thus know from experience that the succession of night and day is not unconditional. Let me add, that the antecedent which is only conditionally invariable, is not the invariable antecedent. Though a fact may, in experience, have always been followed by another fact, yet if the remainder of our experience teaches us that it might not always be so followed, or if the experience itself is such as leaves room for a possibility that the known cases may not correctly represent all possible cases, the hitherto invariable antecedent is not accounted the cause; but why? Because we are not sure that it *is* the invariable antecedent. . . .

On the Probable Futurity of the Labouring Classes
(from *Principles of Political Economy*)

1. [*The theory of dependence and protection is no longer applicable to the condition of modern society*] The observations in the preceding chapter had for their principal object to deprecate a false ideal of human society. Their applicability to the practical purposes of present times, consists in moderating the inordinate importance attached to the mere increase of production, and fixing attention upon

improved distribution, and a large remuneration of labour, as the two desiderata. Whether the aggregate produce increases absolutely or not, is a thing in which, after a certain amount has been obtained, neither the legislator nor the philanthropist need feel any strong interest: but, that it should increase relatively to the number of those who share in it, is of the utmost possible importance; and this, (whether the wealth of mankind be stationary, or increasing at the most rapid rate ever known in an old country) must depend on the opinions and habits of the most numerous class, the class of manual labourers.

When I speak, either in this place or elsewhere, of "the labouring classes," or of labourers as a "class," I use those phrases in compliance with custom, and as descriptive of an existing, but by no means a necessary or permanent state of social relations. I do not recognise as either just or salutary, a state of society in which there is any "class" which is not labouring; any human beings, exempt from bearing their share of the necessary labours of human life, except those unable to labour, or who have fairly earned rest by previous toil. So long, however, as the great social evil exists of a non-labouring class, labourers also constitute a class, and may be spoken of, though only provisionally, in that character.

Considered in its moral and social aspect, the state of the labouring people has latterly been a subject of much more speculation and discussion than formerly; and the opinion that it is not now what it ought to be, has become very general. The suggestions which have been promulgated, and the controversies which have been excited, on detached points rather than on the foundations of the subject, have put in evidence the existence of two conflicting theories, respecting the social position desirable for manual labourers. The one may be called the theory of dependence and protection, the other that of self-dependence.

According to the former theory, the lot of the poor, in all things which affect them collectively, should be regulated *for* them, not *by* them. They should not be required or encouraged to think for themselves, or give to their own reflection or forecast an influential voice in the determination of their destiny. . . .

I do not affirm that what has always been must always be, or that human improvement has no tendency to correct the intensely selfish feelings engendered by power; but though the evil may be lessened, it cannot be eradicated, until the power itself is withdrawn. This, at least, seems to me undeniable, that long before the superior classes could be sufficiently improved to govern in the tutelary manner supposed, the inferior classes would be too much improved to be so governed.

Of the working men, at least in the more advanced countries of Europe, it may be pronounced certain, that the patriarchal or paternal system of government is one to which they will not again be subject. That question was decided, when they were taught to read, and allowed access to newspapers and political tracts; when dissenting preachers were suffered to go among them, and appeal to their faculties and feelings in opposition to the creeds professed and countenanced by their superiors; when they were brought together in numbers, to work socially under the same roof; when railways enabled them to shift from place to place, and change their patrons and employers as easily as their coats; when they were encouraged to seek a share in the government, by means of the electoral franchise. The working classes have taken their interests into their own hands, and are perpetually showing that they think the interests of their employers not identical with their own, but opposite to them. Some among the higher classes flatter themselves that these tendencies may be counteracted by moral and religious education: but they have let the time go by for giving an education which can serve their purpose. The principles of the Reformation have reached as low down in society as reading and writing, and the poor will not much longer accept morals and religion of other people's prescribing. I speak more particularly of this country, especially the town population, and the districts of the most scientific agriculture or the highest wages, Scotland and the north of England. Among the more inert and less modernized agricultural population of the southern counties, it might be possible for the gentry to retain, for some time longer, something of the ancient deference and submission of the poor, by bribing them with high wages and constant employment; by insuring them support, and never requiring them to do anything which they do not like. But these are two conditions which never have been combined, and never can be, for long together. A guarantee of subsistence can only be practically kept up, when work is enforced and superfluous multiplication restrained by at least a moral compulsion. It is then, that the would-be revivers of old times which they do not understand, would feel practically in how hopeless a task they were engaged. The whole fabric of patriarchal or seignorial influence, attempted to be raised on the foundation of caressing the poor, would be shattered against the necessity of enforcing a stringent Poor-law.

3. [*Probable effects of improved intelligence in causing a better adjustment of population—Would be promoted by the social independence of women*] It appears to me impossible but that the increase of intelligence, of education, and of the love of independence among the working classes, must be attended with a corresponding growth of the good sense which manifests itself in provident habits of conduct, and that population, therefore, will bear a gradually diminishing ratio to capital and employment. This most desirable result would be much accelerated by another change, which lies in the direct line of the best tendencies of the time; the opening of industrial occupations freely to both sexes. The same reasons which make it no longer necessary that the poor should depend on the rich, make it equally unnecessary that women should depend on men; and the least which justice requires is that law and custom should not enforce dependence (when the correlative protection has become superfluous) by ordaining that a woman, who does not happen to have a provision by inheritance, shall have scarcely any means open to her of gaining a livelihood, except as a wife and mother. Let women who prefer that occupation, adopt it; but that there should be no option, no other *carrière* possible for the great majority of women, except in the humbler departments of life, is a flagrant social injustice. The ideas and institutions by which the accident of sex is made the groundwork of an inequality of legal rights, and a forced dissimilarity of social functions, must ere long be recognized as the greatest hindrance to moral, social, and even intellectual improvement. On the present occasion I shall only indicate, among the probable consequences of the industrial and social independence of women, a great diminution of the evil of over-population. It is by devoting one-half of the human species to that

exclusive function, by making it fill the entire life of one sex, and interweave itself with almost all the objects of the other, that the animal instinct in question is nursed into the disproportionate preponderance which it has hitherto exercised in human life.

Liberty
(from *On Liberty*)

CHAPTER 1
INTRODUCTORY

The subject of this essay is not the so-called liberty of the will, so unfortunately opposed to the misnamed doctrine of philosophical necessity; but civil, or social liberty: the nature and limits of the power which can be legitimately exercised by society over the individual. A question seldom stated and hardly ever discussed in general terms, but which profoundly influences the practical controversies of the age by its latent presence, and is likely soon to make itself recognized as the vital question of the future. It is so far from being new, that, in a certain sense, it has divided mankind almost from the remotest age; but in the stage of progress into which the more civilized portions of the species have now entered, it presents itself under new conditions, and requires a different and more fundamental treatment. . . .

But in political and philosophical theories, as well as in persons, success discloses faults and infirmities which failure might have concealed from observation. The notion that the people have no need to limit their power over themselves, might seem axiomatic when popular government was a thing only dreamed about, or read of as having existed at some distant period of the past. Neither was that notion necessarily disturbed by such temporary aberrations as those of the French Revolution, the worst of which were the work of a usurping few, and which, in any case, belonged not to the permanent working of popular institutions, but to a sudden and convulsive outbreak against monarchical and aristocratic despotism. In time, however, a democratic republic came to occupy a large portion of the earth's surface, and made itself felt as one of the most powerful members of the community of nations; and elective and responsible government became subject to the observations and criticisms which wait upon a great existing fact. It was now perceived that such phrases as 'self-government,' and 'the power of the people over themselves,' do not express the true state of the case. The 'people' who exercise the power are not always the same people with those over whom it is exercised; and the 'self-government' spoken of is not the government of each by himself, but of each by all the rest. The will of the people, moreover, practically means the will of the most numerous or the most active *part* of the people; the majority, or those who succeed in making themselves accepted as the majority: the people, consequently *may* desire to oppress a part of their number, and precautions are as much needed against this as against any other abuse of power. The limitation, therefore, of the power of government over individuals loses none of its importance when the holders of power are regularly accountable to the community, that is, to the strongest party therein. This view of things, recommending itself equally to the intelligence of thinkers and to the inclination of those important classes in European society to whose real or supposed interests democracy is adverse, has had no difficulty in establishing itself; and in political speculations 'the tyranny of the majority' is now generally included among the evils against which society requires to be on its guard.

Like other tyrannies, the tyranny of the majority was at first, and is still vulgarly, held in dread chiefly as operating through the acts of the public authorities. But reflecting persons perceived that when society is itself the tyrant—society collectively over the separate individuals who compose it—its means of tyrannizing are not restricted to the acts which it may do by the hands of its political functionaries. Society can and does execute its own mandates; and if it issues wrong mandates instead of right, or any mandates at all in thing with which it ought not to meddle, it practices a social tyranny more formidable than many kinds of political oppression, since, though not usually upheld by such extreme penalties, it leaves fewer means of escape, penetrating much more deeply into the details of life, and enslaving the soul itself. Protection, therefore, against the tyranny of the magistrate is not enough: there needs protection also against the tyranny of the prevailing opinion and feeling; against the tendency of society to impose, by other means than civil penalties, its own ideas and practices as rules of conduct on those who dissent from them; to fetter the development, and, if possible, prevent the formation, of any individuality not in harmony with its ways, and compels all characters to fashion themselves upon the model of its own. There is a limit to the legitimate interference of collective opinion with individual independence; and to find that limit, and maintain it against encroachment, is as indispensable to a good condition of human affairs, as protection against political despotism.

But though this proposition is not likely to be contested in general terms, the practical question, where to place the limit—how to make the fitting adjustment between individual independence and social control—is a subject on which nearly everything remains to be done. All that makes existence valuable to anyone, depends on the enforcement of restraints upon the actions of other people. Some rules of conduct, therefore, must be imposed, by law in the first place, and by opinion on many things which are not fit subjects for the operation of law. What these rules should be is the principal question in human affairs; but if we except a few of the most obvious cases, it is one of those which least progress has been made in resolving. No two ages, and scarcely any two countries, have decided it alike; and the decision of one age or country is a wonder to another. Yet the people of any given age and country no more suspect any difficulty in it, than if it were a subject on which mankind had always been agreed. The rules which obtain among themselves appear to them self-evident and self-justifying. This all but universal illusion is one of the examples of the magical influence of custom, which is not only, as the proverb says, a second nature, but is continually mistaken for the first.

The effect of custom, in preventing any misgiving respecting the rules of conduct which mankind impose on one another, is all the more complete because the subject is one on which it is not generally considered necessary that reasons should be given, either by one person to others or by each to himself. . . . Wherever there is an ascendant class, a larger portion of the morality of the country emanates from its class interests, and its feelings of class superiority. The morality between Spartans and Helots, between planters and Negroes, between princes and subjects, between nobles and roturiers, between men and women, has been for the most part the creation of these class interests and feelings; and the sentiments thus generated react in turn upon the moral feelings of the members of the ascendant class, in their relations among themselves. Where, on the other hand, a class, formerly ascendant, has lost its ascendancy, or where its ascendancy is unpopular, the prevailing moral sentiments frequently bear the impress of an impatient dislike of superiority. Another grand determining principle of the rules of conduct, both in act and forbearance, which have been enforced by law or opinion, has been the servility of mankind towards the supposed preferences or aversions of their temporal masters or of their gods. This servility, though essentially selfish, is not hypocrisy; it gives rise to perfectly genuine sentiments of abhorrence; it made men burn magicians and heretics. Among so many baser influences, the general and obvious interests of society have of course had a share, and a large one, in the direction of the moral sentiments; less, however, as a matter of reason, and on their own account, than as a consequence of the sympathies and antipathies which grew out of them; and sympathies and antipathies which had little or nothing to do with the interests of society, have made themselves felt in the establishment of moralities with quite as great force.

The object of this essay is to assert one very simple principle, as entitled to govern absolutely the dealings of society with the individual in the way of compulsion and control, whether the means used be physical force in the form of legal penalties, or the moral coercion of public opinion. That principle is, that the sole end for which mankind are warranted, individually or collectively, in interfering with the liberty of action of any of their number, is self-protection. That the only purpose for which power can be rightfully exercised over any member of a civilized community, against his will, is to prevent harm to others. His own good, either physical or moral, is not a sufficient warrant. He cannot rightfully be compelled to do or forbear because it will be better for him to do so, because it will make him happier, because, in the opinions of others, to do so would be wise, or even right. These are good reasons for remonstrating with him, or reasoning with him, or persuading him, or entreating him, but not for compelling him, or visiting him with any evil in case he do otherwise. To justify that, the conduct from which it is desired to deter him must be calculated to produce evil to someone else. The only part of the conduct of anyone, for which he is amenable to society, is that which concerns others. In the part which merely concerns himself, his independence is, of right, absolute. Over himself, over his own body and mind, the individual is sovereign.

It is perhaps hardly necessary to say that this doctrine is meant to apply only to human beings in the maturity of their faculties. We are not speaking of children, or of young persons below the age which the law may fix as that of manhood or woman-hood.Those who are still in a state to require being taken care of by others, must be protected against their own actions as well as against external injury. For the same reason, we may leave out of consideration those backward states of society in which the race itself may be considered as in its nonage.The early difficulties in the way of spontaneous progress are so great, and there is seldom any choice of means for over-coming them; and a ruler full of the spirit of improvement is warranted in the use of any expedients that will attain an end, perhaps otherwise unattainable. Despotism is a legitimate mode of government in dealing with barbarians, provided the end be their improvement, and the means justified by actually effecting that end. Liberty, as a principle, has no application to any state of things anterior to the time when mankind have become capable of being improved by free and equal discus-sion. Until then, there is nothing for them but implicit obedience to an Akbar or a Charlemagne, if they are so fortunate as to find one. But as soon as mankind have attained the capacity of being guided to their own improvement by conviction or persuasion (a period long since reached in all nations with whom we need here con-cern ourselves), compulsion, either in the direct form or in that of pains and penal-ties for non-compliance, is no longer admissible as a means to their own good, and justifiable only for the security of others.

But there is a sphere of action in which society, as distinguished from the individual, has, if any, only an indirect interest; comprehending all that portion of a person's life and conduct which affects only himself, or if it also affects others, only with their free, voluntary, and undeceived consent and participation. When I say only himself, I mean directly, and in the first instance; for whatever affects himself, may affect others through himself; and the objection which may be grounded on this contingency, will receive consideration in the sequel. This, then, is the appropriate region of human liberty. It comprises, *first,* the inward domain of consciousness; demanding liberty of conscience in the most comprehensive sense; liberty of thought and feeling; absolute freedom of opinion and sentiment on all subjects, practical or speculative, scientific, moral, or theological.The liberty of expressing and publishing opinions may seem to fall under a different principle, since it belongs to that part of the conduct of an individual which concerns other people; but, being almost of as much importance as the liberty of thought itself, and resting in great part on the same reasons, is practically insepa-rable from it. *Secondly,* the principle requires liberty of tastes and pursuits; of framing the plan of our life to suit our own character; of doing as we like, subject to such consequences as may follow: without impediment from our fellow-creatures, so long as what we do does not harm them, even though they should think our conduct foolish, perverse, or wrong. *Thirdly,* from this liberty of each individual, follows the liberty, within the same limits, of combination among individuals; freedom to unite, for any purpose not involving harm to others: the persons combining being supposed to be of full age, and not forced or deceived.

No society in which these liberties are not, on the whole, respected, is free, whatever may be its form of government; and none is completely free in which they do not exist absolute and unqualified.The only freedom which deserves the name, is that of pursuing our own good in our own way, so long as we do not attempt to deprive others of theirs, or impede their efforts to obtain it. Each is the proper guardian of his own health, whether bodily, or mental and spiritual. Mankind are greater gainers by suffering each other to live as seems good to themselves, than by compelling each to live as seems good to the rest. . . .

REVIEW QUESTIONS

1. What is the basic idea of Mill's utilitarianism?
2. Explain the meaning of the law of causation in Mill; does it differ from Hume's? How does it apply to living in society? How is it reconciled to freedom?
3. Describe Mill's defense of the individual and the minority in the face of a capitalist economy.
4. Describe Mill's view of the individual's claim to liberty while still a member of society.
5. The true religion is the Religion of Humanity; explain what Mill means.

SUGGESTIONS FOR FURTHER READING

Autobiography. New York, Viking Press, 1990.
Cipaldi, Nicholas, *John Stuart Mill.* New York, Cambridge Univeersity Press, 2005.
Ryan, Alan. *J. S. Mill.* London, Routledge and Kegan Paul, 1974.
Thomas, W. *J. S. Mill.* New York, Oxford University Press, 1985.

PART FOUR

THE CONTEMPORARY PERIOD

The Spirit of Contemporary Philosophy: The Ascendancy of the Person

Continuity with the past allows the time of any given age to be fixed differently by different authors. Thus, the "contemporary period" can be set at an earlier or later time depending on the author's purpose. So if, among the many features of contemporary philosophy, concern for the *human person* is seen as giving it its unique coloring, then the three mid-nineteenth-century philosophers Kierkegaard, Nietzsche, and Marx are the ones to begin with, and the philosophical humanism they espoused must be seen as part of the historical context in which they appeared.

The "Revolution" of 1848: Re-assertion of Humanity

The year 1848, as a prism of the political and cultural forces at work, is the most significant year of the nineteenth century in Europe. This was the year in which the dissatisfaction of the masses, smoldering for decades, erupted all over Europe with such power that it is often referred to as the Revolution of 1848. Except

449

for some concessions to liberalism in England, France, and Belgium, most of mid-nineteenth-century Europe lived under political repression. The hope for freedom generated by the French Revolution was dashed by the personal goals and final defeat of Napoleon and sealed at the Congress of Vienna in 1815 when the monarchical claims of the Old Regime were reasserted in central Europe. But the masses still longed for change: They wanted social reform, economic improvement, and a role in determining how they were to be governed; many ethnic groups yearned for their rights as independent bodies. Longings that could not find expression in politics were embodied in the activity of young university students, writers, artists, and musicians—Chopin composing one polonaise after another out of compassion for his suffering, Poland and Byron fighting for Greek independence from Turkey—"romantics" all because they yearned for the unfulfilled. Throughout 1848, beginning in Paris, there were demonstrations, uprisings, and insurrections across the continent, massive efforts to proclaim a variety of rights and freedoms. For a short time, these movements appeared to be on the verge of success, but within three years the Old Regime prevailed and the longing for human dignity went unfulfilled.

The invention of new machines to speed production and transportation took a horrible toll on humanity during the Industrial Revolution, when the absence of social conscience drove thousands of workers into a subhuman existence and robbed children of their childhood. Poverty and crisis, the lot of too many in the years immediately preceding 1848, were symbolized in the great bread riots of 1847 that broke out in several European cities. That the *Communist Manifesto* of Marx and Engels should have appeared in 1848 was no coincidence.

Rise of Humanist Interest

Science, begun so enthusiastically in the seventeenth century, continued to make a steady stream of contributions in the nineteenth. The laboratory of Justus Liebig was world famous; Faraday's name became one with electricity; organic chemistry was discovered and the way paved for the creation of synthetic substances; Louis Pasteur made medical history; and toward the turn of the century the names of Roentgen, Curie, Einstein, and Planck gained a permanent place in the history of physics. But it was the science of biology, which up to then had been mainly the classification of types, that revealed the transcendent nature of the living body, for Gregor Mendel's experiments revealed the laws of heredity whereby characteristics are transmitted from one generation to another, and Charles Darwin's discovery of natural selection established the theory of the evolution of living beings, including man. Evolution corroborated the conclusion of geologists that the age of the earth far exceeded the biblical 4,004 years—once again, as in the seventeenth century, causing religious believers to readjust their interpretation of the Bible.

Toward the end of the nineteenth century, another revolution took place that extended well into the twentieth: the revolution in psychology led by Sigmund

Freud. In his discovery of the subconscious, and of how the subconscious becomes the unknown source of human activity, Freud was searching for the key to restore wholeness in those persons in whom it had been shattered. In the context of the nineteenth century, an individual so in need of help was seen as another example of the struggle for human personhood; the forces of suppression were viewed as never really overcome but only temporarily driven into the subconscious, to resurface later with the same power to destroy; such an individual is still struggling for freedom, for dignity, and for personhood.

Clearly then, the overarching concern of the contemporary period, especially in its initial phases, was the human person, and thinkers and activists in general were bent on either probing or expressing the concepts of human value and dignity. But the main philosophical problem was how to ground human value: Is human dignity self-contained? Is human value a value unto itself? Is there anything "higher," in virtue of which the person is to be understood? The responses to these questions were clearly divided into a humanism that was God centered or not—a theistic humanism or an atheistic humanism. But the responses were not the result of academic argumentation for the existence or nonexistence of God; they were the result of reactions to the God of tradition, and in this struggle the opponents of institutionalized religion, particularly Christianity, carried the day. The areligious humanist saw the church, Protestant or Catholic, as concerned with institutions and empty formulas, not the humanness of its members. And precisely because the church professed to stand for the ultimate good of man, it was to be ultimately blamed for man's sorry plight.

The Lived Existence of the Human Being

This is the background to the distinctive change that took place in philosophy, heralding a new age and called by some a "Copernican revolution." The course of philosophy in the hundred years preceding the mid-nineteenth century was focused on the object: with *objective* questions asked about what we know and how we know it; if man was considered a proper object of philosophy, it was precisely as an object rather than as a human being, with personhood in danger of being lost in the abstractions of transcendentalism. As we previously cautioned ourselves in regard to the emergence of new ideas, it is not as though, up to this time, no attention at all had been given to the individual as a human being; now, however, there is a definite change in the texture of inquiry: The human being in his *lived existence* becomes the focus of concern. Existence is not abstract; it pertains to the *concrete* individual, whose very condition of existence is the experience with which a philosopher should begin.

Man thus became the subject of philosophy and, though Kierkegaard, Nietzsche, and Marx approached man from different viewpoints, their hope was to rediscover human values and human dignity. The point of contact with human existence for Kierkegaard was the *religious* man, for Nietzsche the *cultural* man, and for Marx the *laboring* man; although their paths led through different terrains, the unmistakable common horizon was humanity. This was the key to the Copernican revolution.

The importance of humanist themes continued unabated, and in the next generation, Bergson and James, following their lifelong interest in biology and psychology, felt humanity was under an imperative to perfect itself in holiness. In the immediate past, Husserl had a profound humanist tendency, but was committed to fashioning a new philosophical method called phenomenology, which method in turn came to be the method employed by Heidegger in his metaphysical quest with profound humanist implications, and by Sartre in his elaboration of existentialism.

Alongside this development is the emergence of the philosophy of mathematical logic and language analysis, whose key contributors are Russell, Wittgenstein, and Quine.

This section is rounded out by considering some other current dimensions: the phenomenal rise of women in philosophy, represented by Susanne Langer; the foreordained impact of computer technology on the age-old mind–body problem, as seen by John Searle; a fresh look at political philosophy in the theory of justice of John Rawls; and the aggressive review of the value of life as propounded by Peter Singer; and the question of deconstruction inaugurated by Jacques Derrida.

Suggestions for Further Reading

Ayer, A. J. *Philosophy in the Twentieth Century.* New York, Random House, 1982.

Calhoone, L. ed., *From Modernism to Postmodernism, An Anthology.* New York, Blackwell, 2003.

Passmore, J. A. *Recent Philosophers.* Peru, IL., Open Court, 1985.

Skorupski, John. *English-Language Philosophy 1750-1945.* New York, Oxford Press, 1993.

Whitehead, A. N. *Science and the Modern World.* New York, New American Library, 1949.

21

Søren Kierkegaard (1813–1855)

As a philosopher totally responding to the personal dimension of life, Søren Kierkegaard understandably reacted against the abstractions of Hegel, which he saw as hardly touching the real world—without place for the being whose meaning is our only real concern, the individual person. He spent his brief life trying to rectify this neglect.

Philosophical Mission: The Primacy of the Individual

Kierkegaard was born in Copenhagen, Denmark, in 1813 into a rigidly pietistic family. His father was a good man but endowed with a somber sense of God as a severe demander of righteous behavior, with misbehavior likely to be punished by a proportionate displeasure. He was a successful businessman and an influential figure, though he had a moody and melancholy disposition. The personality traits of his father contributed heavily to the psychological burden, the already introspective young man had to carry, and he did the only thing he could to free himself, revolting against religion and, indeed, life in general. He enrolled at the University of Copenhagen in theology, though his main interests were always philosophy and literature; he read enthusiastically the works of Plato, Shakespeare, and the romantic authors. He led a rather free-spirited life as a student, and gradually his earlier cynicism wore off as he came to see the importance of personal commitment to ethical and religious values. He wrote of a moment of "indescribable joy" in May 1838, "a joy which cools and refreshes us like a breath of wind, a wave of air, from the trade wind which blows from the plains of Mamre to the everlasting habitations." So strong did this feeling of commitment become that he broke his engagement to a girl he loved because he felt that the requirements of married life would detract from his self-appointed mission, which was to establish the individual as the centerpiece of philosophy. One of the elements of this mission was a profound distrust of institutions, which, by their own inner logic, tend to manipulate, if not absorb, the individual. This is why Kierkegaard, though he fervently held that one's authentic individuality is measured by how one stands before God, declaimed against the Danish state church, and every institutionalized religion, as inimical to the true interests of the individual. He died in 1855. Though he died young, he had written voluminously and passionately. His chief works are *Fear and Trembling* (1843), *Either/Or* (1843), *Philosophical Fragments* (1844), and *Concluding Scientific Postscript to the Philosophical Fragments* (1846).

Kierkegaard is an intensely personal philosopher because, for him, philosophy is nothing more than a personal reflection on one's lived experience. Life is too precious and mysterious to be entrusted to a system of abstract logic, which is why, while not oblivious to Hegel's undoubted merits, Kierkegaard rejected his idealism as the vehicle capable of destroying the individual. The human being must be fully aware of his individuality; it is his prized possession and unshared by any other creature. But the temptation to lose oneself is all too great, particularly among the masses of people whom the individual must live with; the *crowd*, by its very nature, is a destroyer of the individual: "a crowd in its very concept is the untruth, by reason of the fact that it renders the individual completely impenitent and irresponsible."

Personhood Achieved in Relationship with God

If the individual person is primary in Kierkegaard's thought, and if authentic personhood resides in one's relationship with God, then the first question to be asked is, how does one, for Kierkegaard, come to know God? His personalism precludes a systematic, reasoned approach to God's existence, for this would narrow down the infinite God to the very argument used to prove His existence and would make it impossible for God to be thought of as being any different from the categories used to know Him. I therefore do not *prove* that God exists; yet, it must be acknowledged that, whatever method reason uses to increase its understanding, it comes up against what is unknown, and it is this very fact that compels me to recognize His existence *as* the Unknown. I am, according to Kierkegaard, driven by a troubled kind of certainty to assent to this Unknown, to the very God who blesses the *leap* I have made toward Him. In Kierkegaard's own words: "So also with the proof for God's existence. As long as I keep my hold on the proof, i.e., continue to demonstrate, the existence does not come out, if for no other reason than that I am engaged in proving it; but when I let the proof go, the existence is there." He goes on: "Must not this also be taken into account, this little moment, brief as it may be—it need not be long, for it is a *leap*." So, the intellectual commitment I make to the existence of God is profoundly personal and touches the mystery of the person-to-person relationship that, though reasonable, is not a matter of reason: Because God is in every sense believable and welcoming, I, by my personal choice, believe in Him; I make, in Kierkegaard's unusual expression, a leap toward Him, confident that the very meaning of my personhood requires it.

Kierkegaard's description of his awareness of God's existence and his response to that awareness is the immediate background of his notion of *self-actualization,* which, of all notions, is the one that summarizes his thought. *Crowd* existence, previously mentioned, violates self-identity, personhood, and human dignity, whereas the goal of self-actualization is the affirmation of the individual as an individual, the making actual of the true self within. Self-actualization is a summons, not only to my rational life, for man is much more than reason, but to my affective and emotional life as well. The individual, in the process of realizing himself, becomes a measure of himself, of society, and of mankind; he even measures God in the sense that a God–*man* relationship has no meaning for *me,* but a God–*me* relationship has. The relationship I have with God is the *ultimate* form of self-actualization because it represents the deepest level of *commitment to the truth* I can discover in myself. Truth is not impersonal, for it is what draws me to commit myself to it. I am not personally committed, let us say, to a mathematical truth, but I am committed to those conditions, circumstances, ideas, things, actions, and individuals that touch the living me. In Kierkegaard's own words, written as early as 1835, he said, "What I really need is to get clear about *what I must do,* not what I must know, except insofar as knowledge must precede every act. What matters is to find a purpose, to see what it really is that God wills that *I* shall do; the crucial thing is to find a truth which is truth *for me,* to find *the idea for which I am willing to live and die.* Of what use would it be to me to discover a so-called objective truth, to work through the philosophical systems so that I could, if asked, make critical judgments about them, could point out the fallacies in each system; of what use would it be to me to be able to develop a theory of the state, getting details from various sources and combining them into a whole, and constructing a world I did not live in but merely held up for others to see; of what use would it be to me to be able to formulate the meaning of Christianity, to be able to explain many specific points—if it had no deeper meaning *for me and for my life?*"

Self-actualization

Throughout many of his works, Kierkegaard presents us with a description of self-actualization as a movement through several stages or levels in which the self is progressively realized. It is a growth, or even a dialectical development of sorts, in which the person mounts to the highest level of existence possible to him. He describes three such stages: the esthetic, the ethical, and the religious. Recalling that the word *esthetic* means "pertaining to the sense," the first stage is marked by its saturation with sense experience; the individual acts not out of any moral standard or firm religious faith, but out of pleasure or impulse or emotion, without care for accountability. Because life is seemingly without restraints, the esthetic man equates his carefree ways with freedom. However, this kind of life cannot continue without grave consequences because, like a stone skimming over the water and suddenly going down beneath the surface, the esthetic man sees the dispersion of his unanchored life amid an empty feeling of selflessness and *despair,* a category that Kierkegaard acutely and poignantly analyzes. Such despair signifies the moment when a person recognizes that his emptiness is in fact a beckoning to a higher level of life; it is a "despair in truth," the boundary between the esthetic stage and the ethical. This is also the moment of choice; the esthetic man must choose to ascend to the ethical stage or to stay in the esthetic: either-or. Kierkegaard selects literary or real-life figures to typify these stages; the examplar of the esthetic man is Don Juan, the legendary lover. Here is a man who refuses to make the choice to go higher. As depicted in Mozart's opera, Don Giovanni is a lover of wine, women, and song, and as he sings of the carefree life he has led and refuses to give up, he is consumed in the flames of the burning palace, symbolic of the fires of hell.

The second, or ethical, stage is characterized by the effort to conquer the dispersion of life by the primacy of duty. A person accepts *morality* as the response of one's own inwardness and a further step in the actualization of the self. Though moral standards are universal and pertain to all men, they oblige me personally to choose a life of consistency and seriousness that were absent in the first stage. A person lays aside the "freedom" of the first stage and accepts his new state with all of its obligations; he lays aside, for example, the sexual carelessness of the esthetic life and, in taking a wife, accepts marriage in its full consequences. Socrates represented this kind of seriousness in his attitude toward universal obligation inasmuch as the firm stand he took before his accusers led to the surrender of his life; he is, in Kierkegaard's eyes, a "tragic hero" who renounced his life to "express the universal."

Yet, even if it is true that the universal pertains to me as an individual—for "the ethical quality is jealous for its own integrity"—it may fail to provide me, as an individual, with support in certain exceptional instances. So, it is possible, in those instances, for the universal to be transcended, and this possibility leads to the next stage.

The transition to the third stage is not an easy one. A person has to see himself "before God," to see himself as he really is, with a chasm between himself and God because of the sins he has committed and the fear he has of opening himself to the ultimate Goodness. This point, for Kierkegaard, is a higher point than the acceptance of the moral law because it marks the highest personal transformation whereby the self can become fully actualized in its relationship with God. It is the highest of *either-or* choices, for it requires the highest commitment a person can make; and because no human can measure the demands of God, the choice, for all of its sureness, is blind; this is the *leap* a person may be called upon to make, a leap from time to eternity, from the finite to the infinite, from human to divine—a movement of *faith* accompanied by all the passion befitting a critical juncture in one's life. As the paragon of faith, Kierkegaard chooses the Old Testament patriarch Abraham, singled out in the Bible as the "father of all those who believe." Heeding God's command, addressed to him as an individual, Abraham, with all the reluctance a human being can experience at surrendering his greatest love, was willing to sacrifice his son Isaac, until his hand was stayed by the admonition of an angel. The example of Abraham, Kierkegaard tells us, offers two salient points of instruction. The first is that the leap of faith is *absurd:* On the one side, a person is sure that he must believe; on the other side is the vast uncertainty of what faith leads him to. To that extent the leap of faith is absurd, reminiscent of the paradox of faith as stated by the ancient Christian, Tertullian: "I believe because it is absurd." The second point of instruction is that Abraham's stance before God is the stance of an *individual,* answering to no one but God, and inasmuch as Abraham is not following the universal standard of morality, he is *breaking through the universal:* "The paradox of faith," writes Kierkegaard, "is this, that the individual is higher than the universal."

This third stage, the religious, is the final stage of self-actualization. It is a freedom, a freedom first of all from the *dread* that haunts a person who takes life seriously but who feels life's meaning to be so elusive, so inconsistent, so absurd as to bring him to the verge of annihilation. Dread is the companion of death, which is itself a universal phenomenon. It is the point at which the human being must ask whether life is an enduring value or, when all the votes are counted, nothing more than a dance on the edge of nothingness. We saw, with Socrates, that the response we make to the problem of death is the key to the meaning of life: Death is not primarily a biological problem, but a value problem. For Kierkegaard, it is in the context of a life-giving faith that the fear of death is met and dread, which gnaws away at the substance of life at every level, is overcome. This is especially true of the person who experiences a profound sense of guilt at the prospect and actuality of sin. Dread, however, recedes at the coming of faith; guilt is assuaged with the saving love of God: "Here is the reason for joy: at every moment both present and future it is eternally certain that nothing invented by the most morbid imagination and translated into fact, which can shake the belief that God is love."

Kierkegaard, as a committed but noninstitutionalized Christian, sees complete freedom and complete selfhood as realizable in Christ; it is He, by His incarnation, who entered the "zone of the existential," thus creating the hoped-for bridge between time and eternity. For Kierkegaard, love of Christ is translated into the fundamental understanding of reality: "Christ says: I will manifest myself to him who loves me . . . and the lover . . . himself is transformed into the likeness of the thing beloved, and to become what one loves is the only fundamental way of understanding." Having possessed a "troubled truth," the man of faith now possesses the assurance that all absurdity dissolves when he says, "*I* believe."

Kierkegaard's philosophy places him in the forefront of the personalist tradition. Eschewing the academic because it would restrict him to its categories, he delves into the unlit regions to discover the wellsprings of the human person. This aspect of this thought has worked its way into contemporary appreciation of personhood and left an indelible impression on existentialism; it has given fresh insights to the psychologist and the theologian, as well as to the philosopher.

The Search for Personal Meaning
(from *Journals*)

What I really need is to get clear about what I must do, not what I must know, except insofar as knowledge must precede every act. What matters is to find a purpose, to see what it really is that God wills that I shall do; the crucial thing is to find a truth which is truth for me, to find the idea for which I am wiling to live and die. Of what use would it be to me to discover a so-called objective truth, to work through the philosophical systems so that I could, if asked, make critical judgments about them, could point out the fallacies in each system; of what use would it be to me to be able to develop a theory of the state, getting details from various sources and combining them into a whole, and constructing a world I did not live in but merely held up for others to see; of what use would it be to me to be able to formulate the meaning of Christianity, to be able to explain many specific points—if it had no deeper meaning for me and for my life? And the better I was at it, the more I saw others appropriate the creations of my mind, the more tragic my situation would be, not unlike that of parents who in their poverty are forced to send their children out into the world and turn them over to the care of others. Of what use would it be to me for truth to stand before me, cold and naked, not caring whether or not I acknowledged it, making me uneasy rather than trustingly receptive. I certainly do not deny that I still accept an imperative of knowledge and that through it men may be influenced, but then it must come alive in me, and this is what I now recognize as the most important of all. This is what my soul thirsts for as the African deserts thirst for water. This is what is lacking, and this is why I am like a man who has collected furniture, rented an apartment, but as yet has not found the beloved to share life's ups and downs with him. But in order to find that idea—or, to put it more correctly—to find myself, it does no good to plunge still farther into the world. That was just what I did before. The reason I thought it would be good to throw myself into law was that I believed I could develop my keenness of mind in the many muddles and messes of life. Here, too, was offered a whole mass of details in which I could lose myself; here, perhaps, with the given facts, I could construct a totality, an organic view of criminal life, pursue it in all its dark aspects (here, too, a certain fraternity of spirit is very evident). I also wanted to become a lawyer so that by putting myself in another's role I could, so to speak, find a substitute for my own life and by means of this external change find some diversion.

This is what I needed to lead a *completely human life* and not merely one of *knowledge,* so that I could base the development of my thought not on—yes, not on something called objective—something which in any case is not my own, but upon something which is bound up with the deepest roots of my existence *[Existents],* through which I am, so to speak, grafted into the divine, to which I cling fast even though the whole world may collapse. *This is what I need, and this is what I strive for.* I find joy and refreshment in contemplating the great men who have found that precious stone for which they sell all, even their lives, whether I see them becoming vigorously engaged in life, confidently proceeding on their chosen course without vacillating, or discover them off the beaten path, absorbed in themselves and in working toward their high goal. I even honor and respect the by-path which lies so close by. It is this inward action of man, this God-side of man, which is decisive, not a mass of data, for the latter will no doubt follow and will not then appear as accidental aggregates or as a succession of details, one after the other, without a system, without a focal point. I, too, have certainly looked for this focal point. I have vainly sought an anchor in the boundless sea of pleasure as well as in the depths of knowledge. I have felt the almost irresistible power with which one pleasure reaches a hand to the next; I have also felt the counterfeit enthusiasm it is capable of producing. I have also felt the boredom, the shattering, which follows on its heels. I have tasted the fruits of the tree of knowledge and time and again have delighted in their savoriness. But this joy was only in the moment of cognition and did not leave a deeper mark on me. It seems to me that I have not drunk from the cup of wisdom but have fallen into it. I have sought to find the principle for my life through resignation *[Resignation],* by supposing that since everything proceeds according to inscrutable laws it could not be otherwise, by blunting my ambitions and the antennae of my vanity. Because I could not get everything to suit me, I abdicated with a consciousness of my own competence, somewhat the way decrepit clergymen resign with pension. What did I find? Not my self *[Jeg],* which is what I did seek to find in that way (I imagined my soul, if I may say so, as shut up in a box with a spring lock, which external surroundings would release by pressing the spring).—Consequently the seeking and finding of the Kingdom of Heaven was the first thing to be resolved. But it is just as useless for a man to want first of all to decide the externals and after that the fundamentals as it is for a cosmic body, thinking to form itself, first of all to decide the nature of its surface, to what bodies it should turn its light, to which its dark side, without first letting the harmony of centrifugal and centripetal forces realize *[realisere]* its existence *[Existents]* and letting the rest come of itself. One must first learn to know himself before knowing anything else (γνωθι σέ αυτον). Not until a man has inwardly understood himself and then sees the course he is to take does his life gain peace and meaning; only then is he free of that irksome, sinister traveling companion—that irony of life which manifests itself in the sphere of knowledge and invites true knowing to begin with a not-knowing (Socrates), just as God created the world from nothing. But in the waters of morality it is especially at home to those who still have not entered the tradewinds of virtue. Here it tumbles a person about in a horrible way, for a time lets him feel happy and content in his resolve to go ahead along the right path, then hurls him into the abyss of despair. Often it lulls a man to sleep with the thought, "After all, things cannot be otherwise," only to awaken him suddenly to a rigorous interrogation. Frequently it seems to let a veil of forgetfulness fall over the past, only to make every single trifle appear in a strong light again. When he struggles along the right path, rejoicing in having overcome temptation's power, there may come at almost the same time, right on the heels of perfect victory, an apparently insignificant external circumstance which pushes him down, like Sisyphus, from the height of the crag. Often when a person has concentrated on something, a minor external circumstance arises which destroys everything. (As in the case of a man who, weary of life, is about to throw himself into the Thames and at the crucial moment is halted by the sting of a mosquito.) Frequently a person feels his very best when the illness is the worst, as in tuberculosis. In vain he tries to resist it but he has not sufficient strength, and it is no help to him that he has gone through the same thing many times; the kind of practice acquired in this way does not apply here. Just as no one who has been taught a great deal about swimming is able to keep afloat in a storm, but only the man who is intensely convinced and has experiences that he is actually lighter than water, so a person who lacks this inward point of poise is unable to keep afloat in life's storms.—Only when a man has understood himself in this way is he able to maintain an independent existence and thus avoid surrendering his own I. How often we see (in a period when we extol that Greek historian because he knows how to appropriate an unfamiliar style so delusively like the original author's, instead of censuring him, since the first prize always goes to an author for having his own style—that is, a mode of expression and presentation qualified by his own individuality)—how often we see people who either out of mental-spiritual laziness live on the crumbs that fall from another's table or for more egotistical reasons seek to identify themselves with others, until eventually they believe it all, just like the liar through frequent repetition of his stories. Although I am still far from this kind of interior understanding of myself, with profound respect for its significance I have sought to preserve my individuality—worshipped the unknown God. With a premature anxiety I have tried to avoid coming in close contact with those things whose force of attraction might be too powerful for me. I have sought to appropriate much from them, studied their distinctive characteristics and meaning in human life, but at the same time guarded against coming, like the moth, too close to the flame. I have had little to win or to lose in association with the ordinary run of men, partly because what they do—so-called practical life—does not interest me much, partly because their coldness and indifference to the spiritual and deeper currents in man alienate me even more from them. With few exceptions my companions have had no special influence upon me. A life that has not arrived at clarity about itself must necessarily exhibit an uneven side-surface; confronted by certain facts *[Facta]* and their apparent disharmony, they simply halted there, for, as I see it, they did not have sufficient interest to seek a resolution in a higher harmony or to recognize the necessity of it. Their opinion of me was always one-sided, and I have vacillated between putting too much or too little weight on what they said. I have now withdrawn from their influence and the potential variations of my life's compass resulting from it. Thus I am again standing at the point where I must begin again in another way. I shall now calmly attempt to look at myself and begin to initiate inner action; for only thus will I be able, like a child calling itself "I" in its first consciously undertaken act, be able to call myself "I" in a profounder sense.

But that takes stamina, and it is not possible to harvest immediately what one has sown. I will remember that philosopher's method of having his disciples keep silent for three years; then I dare say it will come. Just as one does not begin a feast at sunrise but at sundown, just so in the spiritual world one must first work forward for some time before the sun really shines for us and rises in all its glory; for although it is true as it says that God lets his sun shine upon the good and the evil and lets the rain fall on the just and the unjust, it is not so in the spiritual world. So let the die be cast—I am crossing the Rubicon! No doubt this road takes me into battle, but I will not renounce it. I will not lament the past—why lament? I will work energetically and not waste time in regrets, like the person stuck in a bog and first calculating how far he has sunk without recognizing that during the time he spends on that he is sinking still deeper. I will hurry along the path I have found and shout to everyone I meet: Do not look back as Lot's wife did, but remember that we are struggling up a hill.

(From *Søren Kierkegaard's Journals and Papers,* Vol. 5, ed. by Howard V. Hong and Edna H. Hong. Bloomington: Indiana University Press, 1978. Reprinted by permission of Indiana University Press.)

Abraham and "Breaking Through the Universal"
(from *Fear and Trembling*)

It was early in the morning when Abraham arose: he embraced Sarah, the bride of his old age, and Sarah kissed Isaac, who took away her disgrace, Isaac her pride, her hope for all the generations to come. They rode along the road in silence, and Abraham stared continuously and fixedly at the ground until the fourth day, when he looked up and saw Mount Moriah far away, but once again he turned his eyes toward the ground. Silently he arranged the firewood and bound Isaac; silently he drew the knife—then he saw the ram that God had selected. This he sacrificed and went home. —From that day henceforth, Abraham was old; he could not forget that God had ordered him to do this. Isaac flourished as before, but Abraham's eyes were darkened, and he saw joy no more. . . .

The ethical as such is the universal, and as the universal it applies to everyone, which from another angle means that it applies at all times. It rests immanent in itself, has nothing outside itself that is its τέλος [end, purpose] but it is itself the τέλος for everything outside itself, and when the ethical has absorbed this into itself, it goes not further. The single individual, sensately and psychically qualified in immediacy, is the individual who has his τέλοζ in the universal, and it is his ethical task continually to express himself in this, to annul his singularity in order to become the universal. As soon as the single individual asserts himself in his singularity before the universal, he sins, and only by acknowledging this can he be reconciled again with the universal. Every time the single individual, after having entered the universal, feels an impulse to assert himself as the single individual, he is in a spiritual trial *[Anfaegtelse],* from which he can work himself only by repentently surrendering as the single individual in the universal. If this is the highest that can be said of man and his existence, then the ethical is of the same nature as a person's eternal salvation, which is his τέλοζ forevermore and at all times, since it would be a contradiction for this to be capable of being surrendered (that is, teleologically suspended), because as soon as this is suspended it is relinquished, whereas that which is suspended is not relinquished but is preserved in the higher, which is its τέλοζ . . .

Faith is precisely the paradox that the single individual as the single individual is higher than the universal, is justified before it, not as inferior to it but as superior—yet in such a way, please note, that it is the single individual who, after being subordinate as the single individual to the universal, now by means of the universal becomes the single individual who as the single individual is superior, that the single individual as the single individual stands in an absolute relation to the absolute. This position cannot be mediated, for all mediation takes place only by virtue of the universal; it is and remains for all eternity a paradox, impervious to thought. And yet faith is this paradox, or else (and I ask the reader to bear these consequences in mente [in mind] even though it would be too prolix for me to write them all down) or else faith has never existed simply because it has always existed, or else Abraham is lost.

It is certainly true that the single individual can easily confuse this paradox with spiritual trial, but it ought not to be concealed for that reason. It is certainly true that many persons may be so constituted that they are repulsed by it, but faith ought not therefore to be made into something else to enable one to have it, but one ought rather to admit not having it, while those who have faith ought to be prepared to set forth some characteristics whereby the paradox can be distinguished from a spiritual trial.

The story of Abraham contains just such a teleological suspension of the ethical. There is no dearth of keen minds and careful scholars who have found analogies to it. What their wisdom amounts to is the beautiful proposition that basically everything is the same. If one looks more closely, I doubt very much that anyone in the whole wide world will find one single analogy, except for a later one, which proves nothing if it is certain that Abraham represents faith and that it is manifested normatively in him, whose life not only is the most paradoxical that can be thought but is also so paradoxical that it simply cannot be thought. He acts by virtue of the absurd, for it is precisely the absurd that he as the single individual is higher than the universal. This paradox cannot be mediated, for as soon as Abraham begins to do so, he has to confess that he was in a spiritual trial, and if that is the case, he will never sacrifice Isaac, or if he did sacrifice Isaac, then in repentance he must come back to the universal. He gets Isaac back again by virtue of the absurd. Therefore, Abraham is at no time a tragic hero but is something entirely different, either a murderer or a man of faith. Abraham does not have the middle term that saves the tragic hero. This is why I can understand a tragic hero but cannot understand Abraham, even though in a certain demented sense I admire him more than all others.

In ethical terms, Abraham's relation to Isaac is quite simply this: the father shall love the son more than himself. But within its own confines the ethical has various gradations. We shall see whether this story contains any higher expression for the ethical that can ethically explain his behavior, can ethically justify his suspending the ethical obligation to the son, but without moving beyond the teleology of the ethical. . . .

The paradox of faith, then, is this: that the single individual is higher than the universal, that the single individual—to recall a distinction in dogmatics rather rare these days—determines his relation to the universal by his relation to the absolute, not his relation to the absolute by his relation to the universal. The paradox may also be expressed in this way: that there is an absolute duty to God, for in this relationship of duty the individual relates himself as the single individual absolutely to the absolute. In this connection, to say that it is a duty to love God means something different from the above, for if this duty is absolute, then the ethical is reduced to the relative. From this it does not follow that the ethical should be invalidated; rather, the ethical receives a completely different expression, a paradoxical expression, such as, for example, that love to God may bring the knight of faith to give his love to the neighbor—an expression opposite to that which, ethically speaking, is duty.

If this is not the case, then faith has no place in existence, then faith is a spiritual trial and Abraham is lost, inasmuch as he gave in to it. . . .

Now we are face to face with the paradox. Either the single individual as the single individual can stand in an absolute relation to the absolute, and consequently the ethical is not the highest, or Abraham is lost: he is neither a tragic hero nor an esthetic hero.

Here again it may seem that the paradox is the simplest and easiest of all. May I repeat, however, that anyone who remains convinced of this is not a knight of faith, for distress and anxiety are the only justification conceivable, even if it is not conceivable in general, for then the paradox is canceled.

Abraham remains silent—*but he cannot speak.* Therein lies the distress and anxiety. Even though I go on talking night and day without interruption, if I cannot make myself understood when I speak, then I am not speaking. This is the case with Abraham. He can say everything, but one thing he cannot say, and if he cannot say that—that is, say it in such a way that the other understands it— then he is not speaking. The relief provided by speaking is that it translates me into the universal. Now, Abraham can describe his love for Isaac in the most beautiful words to be found in any language. But this is not what is on his mind; it is something deeper, that he is going to sacrifice him because it is an ordeal. No one can understand the latter, and thus everyone can only misunderstand the former.

Socrates can be used as an example. He was an intellectual tragic hero. His death sentence is announced to him. At that moment he dies, for anyone who does not understand that it takes the whole power of the spirit to die and that the hero always dies before he dies will not advance very far in his view of life. As a hero Socrates is now required to be calm and collected, but as an intellectual tragic hero he is required to have enough spiritual strength in the final moment to consummate himself. He cannot, as does the ordinary tragic hero, concentrate on self-control in the presence of death, but he must make this movement as quickly as possible so that he is instantly and consciously beyond this struggle and affirms himself. Thus, if Socrates had been silent in the crisis of death, he would have diminished the effect of his life and aroused a suspicion that the elasticity of irony in him was not a world power but a game, the resilience of which had to be used on an inverted scale in order to sustain him in pathos at the crucial moment.

These brief suggestions are indeed not applicable to Abraham if one expects to be able to find by means of some analogy an appropriate final word for Abraham, but they do apply if one perceives the necessity for Abraham to consummate himself in the final moment, not to draw the knife silently but to have a word to say, since as the father of faith he has absolute significance oriented to spirit. . . .

And what was the contemporary age's verdict on the tragic hero? That he was great and that it admired him. And that honorable assembly of noble-minded men, the jury that every generation sets up to judge the past generation—it gave the same verdict. But there was no one who could understand Abraham. And yet what did he achieve? He remained true to his love. But anyone who loves God needs no tears, no admiration; he forgets the suffering in the love. Indeed, so completely has he forgotten it that there would not be the slightest trace of his suffering left if God himself did not remember it, for he sees in secret and recognizes distress and counts the tears and forgets nothing.

Thus, either there is a paradox, that the single individual as the single individual stands in an absolute relation to the absolute, or Abraham is lost.

(From *Fear and Trembling*. Trans. by Howard V. Hong and Edna H. Hong. In: *Fear and Trembling/Repetition*. Princeton: Princeton University Press, 1983.)

The Subjective Truth, Inwardness; Truth Is Subjectivity
(from *Concluding Unscientific Postscript*)

The objective accent falls on WHAT is said, the subjective accent on HOW it is said. . . . Objectively the interest is focussed merely on the thought-content, subjectively on the inwardness. At its maximum this inward "how" is the passion of the infinite, and the passion of the infinite is the truth. But the passion of the infinite is precisely subjectivity, and thus subjectivity becomes the truth. Objectively there is no infinite decisiveness, and hence it is objectively in order to annul the difference between good and evil, together with the principle of contradiction, and therewith also the infinite difference between the true and the false. Only in subjectivity is there decisiveness, to seek objectivity is to be in error. It is the passion of the infinite that is the decisive factor and not its content, for its content is precisely itself. In this manner subjectivity and the subjective "how" constitute the truth.

But the "how" which is thus subjectively accentuated precisely because the subject is an existing individual, is also subject to a dialectic with respect to time. In the passionate moment of decision, where the road swings away from objective knowledge, it seems as if the infinite decision were thereby realized. But in the same moment the existing individual finds himself in the temporal order, and the subjective "how" is transformed into a striving, a striving which receives indeed its impulse and a repeated renewal from the decisive passion of the infinite, but is nevertheless a striving.

When subjectivity is the truth, the conceptual determination of the truth must include an expression for the antithesis to objectivity, a memento of the fork in the road where the way swings off; this expression will at the same time serve as an indication of the tension of the subjective inwardness. Here is such a definition of truth: *An objective uncertainty held fast in an appropriation-process of the most passionate inwardness is the truth,* the highest truth attainable for an *existing* individual. At the point where the way swings off (and where this is cannot be specified objectively, since it is a matter of subjectivity), there objective knowledge is placed in abeyance. Thus the subject merely has, objectively, the uncertainty; but it is this which precisely increases the tension of that infinite passion which constitutes his inwardness. The truth is precisely the venture which chooses an objective uncertainty with the passion of the infinite. I contemplate the order of nature in the hope of finding God, and I see omnipotence and wisdom; but I also see much else that disturbs my mind and excites anxiety. The sum of all this is an objective uncertainty. But it is for this very reason that the inwardness becomes as intense as it is, for it embraces this objective uncertainty with the entire passion of the infinite. In the case of a mathematical proposition the objectivity is given, but for this reason the truth of such a proposition is also an indifferent truth.

But the above definition of truth is an equivalent expression for faith. Without risk there is no faith. Faith is precisely the contradiction between the infinite passion of the individual's inwardness and the objective uncertainty. If I am capable of grasping God objectively, I do not believe, but precisely because I cannot do this I must believe. If I wish to preserve myself in faith I must constantly be intent upon holding fast the objective uncertainty, so as to remain out upon the deep, over seventy thousand fathoms of water, still preserving my faith.

In the principle that subjectivity, inwardness, is the truth, there is comprehended the Socratic wisdom, whose everlasting merit it was to have become aware of the essential significance of existence, of the fact that the knower is an existing individual. For this reason Socrates was in the truth by virtue of his ignorance, in the highest sense in which this was possible within paganism. . . .

When subjectivity, inwardness, is the truth, the truth becomes objectively a paradox; and the fact that the truth is objectively a paradox shows in its turn that subjectivity is the truth. For the objective situation is repellent; and the expression for the objective repulsion constitutes the tension and the measure of the corresponding inwardness. The paradoxical character of the truth is its objective uncertainty; this uncertainty is an expression for the passionate inwardness, and this passion is precisely the truth. So far the Socratic principle. The eternal and essential truth, the truth which has an essential relationship to an existing individual because it pertains essentially to existence (all other knowledge being from the Socratic point of view accidental, its scope and degree a matter of indifference), is a paradox. But the eternal essential truth is by no means in itself a paradox; but it becomes paradoxical by virtue of its relationship to an existing individual. The Socratic ignorance gives expression to the objective uncertainty attaching to the truth, while his inwardness in existing is the truth. To anticipate here what will be developed later, let me make the following remark. The Socratic ignorance is an analogue to the category of the absurd, only that there is still less of objective certainty in the absurd, and in the repellent effect that the absurd exercises. It is certain only that it is absurd, and precisely on that account it incites to an infinitely greater tension in the corresponding inwardness. The Socratic inwardness in existing is an analogue to faith; only that the inwardness of faith, corresponding as it does, not to the repulsion of the Socratic ignorance, but to the repulsion exerted by the absurd, is infinitely more profound. . . .

The infinite merit of the Socratic position was precisely to accentuate the fact that the knower is an existing individual, and that the task of existing is his essential task. Making an advance upon Socrates by failing to understand this, is quite a mediocre achievement. This Socratic principle we must therefore bear in mind, and then inquire whether the formula may not be so altered as really to make an advance beyond the Socratic position.

Subjectivity, inwardness, has been posited as the truth; can any expression for the truth be found which has a still higher degree of inwardness? Aye, there is such an expression, provided the principle that subjectivity or inwardness is the truth begins by positing the opposite principle: that subjectivity is untruth. Let us not at this point succumb to such haste as to fail in making the necessary distinctions. Speculative philosophy also says that subjectivity is untruth, but says it in order to stimulate a movement in precisely the opposite direction, namely, in the direction of the principle that objectivity is the truth. Speculative philosophy determines subjectivity negatively as tending toward objectivity. This second determination of ours, however, places a hindrance in its own way while proposing to begin, which has the effect of making the inwardness far more intensive. Socratically speaking, subjectivity is untruth if it refuses to understand that subjectivity is truth, but, for example, desires to become objective. Here, on the other hand, subjectivity in beginning upon the task of becoming the truth through a subjectifying process, is in the difficulty that it is already untruth. Thus, the labor of the task is thrust backward, backward, that is, in inwardness. So far is it from being the case that the way tends in the direction of objectivity, that the beginning merely lies still deeper in subjectivity. . . .

The paradox emerges when the eternal truth and existence are placed in juxtaposition with one another; each time the stamp of existence is brought to bear, the paradox becomes more clearly evident. Viewed Socratically the knower was simply an existing individual, but now the existing individual bears the stamp of having been essentially altered by existence.

Let us now call the untruth of the individual Sin. Viewed eternally he cannot be sin, nor can he be eternally presupposed as having been in sin. By coming into existence therefore (for the beginning was that subjectivity is untruth), he becomes a sinner. He is not born as a sinner in the sense that he is presupposed as being a sinner before he is born, but he is born in sin and as a sinner. This we might call Original Sin. But if existence has in this manner acquired a power over him, he is prevented from taking himself back into the eternal by way of recollection. If it was paradoxical to posit the eternal truth in relationship to an existing individual, it is now absolutely paradoxical to posit it in relationship to such an individual as we have here defined. But the more difficult it is made for him to take himself out of existence by way of recollection, the more profound is the inwardness that his existence may have in existence; and when it is made impossible for him, when he is held so fast in existence that the back door of recollection is forever closed to him, then his inwardness will be the most profound possible. But let us never forget that the Socratic merit was to stress the fact that the knower is an existing individual; for the more difficult the matter becomes, the greater the temptation to hasten along the easy road of speculation, away from fearful dangers and crucial decisions, to the winning of renown and honors and property, and so forth. If even Socrates understood the dubiety of taking himself speculatively out of existence back into the eternal, although no other difficulty confronted the existing individual except that he existed, and that existing was his essential task, now it is impossible. Forward he must, backward he cannot go.

Subjectivity is the truth. By virtue of the relationship subsisting between the eternal truth and the existing individual, the paradox came into being. Let us now go further, let us suppose that the eternal essential truth is itself a paradox. How does the paradox come into being? By putting the eternal essential truth into juxtaposition with existence. Hence when we posit such a conjunction within the truth itself, the truth becomes a paradox. The eternal truth has come into being in time: this is the paradox. If in accordance with the determinations just posited, the subject is prevented by sin from taking himself back into the eternal, now he need not trouble himself about this; for now the eternal essential truth is not behind him but in front of him, through its being in existence or having existed, so that if the individual does not existentially and in existence lay hold of the truth, he will never lay hold of it. . . .

When Socrates believed that there was a God, he held fast to the objective uncertainty with the whole passion of his inwardness, and it is precisely in this contradiction and in this risk, that faith is rooted. Now it is otherwise. Instead of the objective uncertainty, there is here a certainty, namely, that objectively it is absurd; and this absurdity, held fast in the passion of inwardness, is faith. The Socratic ignorance is as a witty jest in comparison with the earnestness of facing the absurd; and the Socratic existential inwardness is as Greek lightmindedness in comparison with the grave strenuosity of faith.

What now is the absurd? The absurd is—that the eternal truth has come into being in time, that God has come into being, has been born, has grown up, and so forth, precisely like any other individual human being, quite indistinguishable from other individuals. . . . The absurd is precisely by its objective repulsion the measure of the intensity of faith in inwardness. Suppose a man who wishes to acquire faith; let the comedy begin. He wishes to have faith, but he wishes also to safeguard himself by means of an objective inquiry and its approximation-process. What happens? With the help of the approximation-process the absurd becomes something different; it becomes probable, it becomes increasingly probable, it becomes extremely and emphatically probable. Now he is ready to believe it, and he ventures to claim for himself that he does not believe as shoemakers and tailors and simple folk believe, but only after long deliberation. Now he is ready to believe it; and lo, now it has become precisely impossible to believe it. Anything that is almost probable, or probable, or extremely and emphatically probable, is something he can almost know, or as good as know, or extremely and emphatically almost *know*—but it is impossible to *believe*. For the absurd is the object of faith, and the only object that can be believed. . . .

If speculative philosophy wishes to take cognizance of this, and say as always, that there is no paradox when the matter is viewed eternally, divinely, theocentrically—then I admit that I am not in a position to determine whether the speculative philosopher is right, for I am only a poor existing human being, not competent to contemplate the eternal either eternally or divinely or theocentrically, but compelled to content myself with existing. So much is certain, however, that speculative philosophy carries everything back, back past the Socratic position, which at least comprehended that for an existing individual existence is essential; to say nothing of the failure of speculative philosophy to take time to grasp what it means to be so critically situated in existence as the existing individual in the experiment. . . .

Christianity has declared itself to be the eternal essential truth which has come into being in time. It has proclaimed itself as the Paradox, and it has required of the individual the inwardness of faith in relation to that which stamps itself as an offense to the Jews and a folly to the Greeks—and an absurdity to the understanding. It is impossible more strongly to express the fact that subjectivity is truth, and that the objectivity is repellent, repellent even by virtue of its absurdity. And indeed it would seem very strange that Christianity should have come into the world merely to receive an explanation; as if it had been somewhat bewildered about itself, and hence entered the world to consult that wise man, the speculative philosopher, who can come to its assistance by furnishing the explanation. It is impossible to express with more intensive inwardness the principle that subjectivity is truth, than when subjectivity is in the first instance untruth, and yet subjectivity is the truth. . . .

If the speculative philosopher explains the paradox so as to remove it, and now in his knowledge knows that it is removed, that the paradox is not the essential relationship that the eternal essential truth bears to an existing individual in the extremity of his existence, but only an accidental relative-relationship to those of limited intelligence: in that case there is established an essential difference between the speculative philosopher and the plain man, which confounds existence from the foundations. God is affronted by getting a group of hangers-on, an intermediary staff of clever brains; and humanity is affronted because the relationship to God is not identical for all men. The godly formula set up above for the difference between the plain man's knowledge of the simple, and the simple wise man's knowledge of the same, that the difference consists in the insignificant trifle that the wise man knows that he knows, or knows that he does not know, what the plain man knows—this formula is by no means respected by speculative philosophy, nor does it respect the likeness involved in this distinction between the plain man and the wise man, namely, that both know the same thing. For the speculative philosopher and the plain man do not by any means know the same thing, when the plain man believes the paradox, and the speculative philosopher knows it to be abrogated. According to the above-mentioned formula, however, which honors God and loves men, the difference is that the wise man also knows that it must be a paradox, this paradox that he himself believes. Hence they both know essentially the same thing; the wise man does not know everything else about the paradox, but knows that he knows this about the paradox. The simple wise man will thus seek to apprehend the paradox more and more profoundly as a paradox, and will not engage in the business of explaining the paradox by understanding that there is none. . . .

Faith has in fact two tasks: to take care in every moment to discover the improbable, the paradox; and then to hold it fast with the passion of inwardness. The common conception is that the improbable, the paradoxical, is something to which faith is related only passively; it must provisionally be content with this relationship, but little by little things will become better, as indeed seems probable. O miraculous creation of confusions in speaking about faith! One is to begin believing, in reliance upon the probability that things will soon become better. In this way probability is after all smuggled in, and one is prevented from believing; so that it is easy to understand that the fruit of having been for a long time a believer is, that one no longer believes, instead of, as one might think, that the fruit is a more intensive inwardness in faith. No, faith is self-active in its relation to the improbable and the paradoxical, self-active in the discovery, and self-active in every moment holding it fast—in order to believe. Merely to lay hold of the improbable requires all the passion of the infinite and its concentration in itself; for the improbable and the paradoxical are not to be reached by the understanding's quantitative calculation of the more and more difficult. Where the understanding despairs, faith is already

present in order to make the despair properly decisive, in order that the movement of faith may not become a mere exchange within the bargaining sphere
of the understanding. But to believe against the understanding is martyrdom;
to begin to get the understanding a little in one's favor, is temptation and ret-
rogression. This martyrdom is something that the speculative philosopher is
free from. That he must pursue his studies, and especially that he must read
many modern books, I admit is burdensome; but the martyrdom of faith is not
the same thing. What I therefore fear and shrink from, more than I fear to die
and to lose my sweetheart, is to say about Christianity that it is to a certain
degree true. If I lived to be seventy years old, if I shortened the night's sleep
and increased the day's work from year to year, inquiring into Christianity—
how insignificant such a little period of study, viewed as entitling me to judge
in so lofty a fashion about Christianity! For to be so embittered against Christianity after a casual acquaintance with it, that I declared it to be false: that
would be far more pardonable, far more human. But this lordly superiority
seems to me the true corruption, making every saving relationship impossible—and it may possibly be the case, that Christianity is the truth. . . .

My principal thought was that in our age, because of the great increase of
knowledge, we had forgotten what it means to *exist,* and what *inwardness* signifies,
and that the misunderstanding between speculative philosophy and Christianity
was explicable on that ground. I now resolved to go back as far as possible, in order
not to reach the religious mode of existence too soon, to say nothing of the specifically Christian mode of religious existence, in order not to leave difficulties unex-
plored behind me. If men had forgotten what it means to exist religiously, they had
doubtless also forgotten what it means to exist as human beings; this must therefore
be set forth. But above all it must not be done in a dogmatizing manner, for then the
misunderstanding would instantly take the explanatory effort to itself in a new misunderstanding, as if existing consisted in getting to know something about this or
that. If communicated in the form of knowledge, the recipient is led to adopt the
misunderstanding that it is knowledge he is to receive, and then we are again in the
sphere of knowledge.

(From Søren Kierkegaard, *Concluding Unscientific Postscript.* Trans. David F. Swenson and Walter Lowrie.
Copyright 1941, © 1969 renewed by Princeton University Press. Excerpts reprinted by permission
by Princeton University Press.)

REVIEW QUESTIONS

1. In what way does Kierkegaard mark a turning point in nineteenth-century
   philosophy?
2. Can Kierkegaard's philosophy be seen as a reaction to the impersonalism
   of Hegel's philosophy?
3. Can the leap, which is beyond reason, be called reasonable?
4. Discuss the individual versus the crowd.

5. Explain Kierkegaardian self-actualization.
6. Compare the personal dimension of truth in Kierkegaard with that of St. Augustine.
7. Discuss the story of Abraham and explain why it is, for Kierkegaard, the example par excellence of breaking through the universal.

Suggestions for Further Reading

Bretall, R., ed. *A Kierkegaard Anthology.* Princeton, Princeton University Press, 1949.

Collins, J. *The Mind of Kierkegaard.* Princeton, Princeton University Press, 1983.

Fear and Trembling, and Sickness Until Death. Tr. Lowrie, W. New York, Doubleday Anchor, 1954.

Lowrie, W. *A Short Life of Kierkegaard.* Princeton, Princeton University Press, 1942.

22

Friedrich Nietzsche
(1844–1900)

Although unlike Kierkegaard in many respects, especially regarding the ultimate meaning of individuality, Friedrich Nietzsche is very much like him in his intense personalism, in rejecting a systematic approach to man, in positioning the subject of man as the true object of philosophy, and in literary style.

The Path to Cultural Humanism

He was born in 1844 near Leipzig. His father was a Lutheran minister who died young, leaving his son to grow up in a society of women including his mother, sister, grandmother, and two aunts. After normal schooling at the local gymnasium, he briefly attended the University of Bonn, where he studied theology, but gave it up once he lost the faith he was born in, beginning a separation from religion which grew more entrenched over the years. From 1864 to 1869 he attended the University of Leipzig, where he gained a reputation as a brilliant student in classical philology. In a most unusual move, he was appointed professor of philology at the University of Basel, Switzerland, at the age of twenty-four, without having completed the formal requirement of the doctorate, whereupon the University of Leipzig conferred it on him without an examination. For a short time during the Franco-Prussian War, he served with the ambulance corps, but illness forced him to resign and return to his professorial duties.

While at Basel he developed a disciple-like friendship with the great composer Richard Wagner and helped him to establish the famous Bayreuth Festival. He accepted Wagner not only as a musical genius but also as a cultural hero who would become the longed-for messiah destined to save a retrograde German culture and lead it to new heights; these themes he put forward as early as 1872 in his first book, *The Birth of Tragedy*. After 1876, however, he broke with Wagner, becoming disillusioned with him not only for personal reasons but also because of what he felt was Wagner's abuse of the art of music. Along with this disillusionment went his despair at ever seeing the rescue of German culture. Offering ill health as a reason, he resigned his chair at Basel in 1879, but no doubt felt that continuing in an academic career would hamper his development as a writer. From then on he led a lonely life, but his writing increased apace until he had fairly well expended himself by 1889, when, having shown signs of mental instability and after being treated clinically, he lived out his remaining days with his sister at Weimar until he died in 1900. For most of his life, his work was not seriously received; ironically, acceptance and fame came in the last ten years of his life, at a time when he could not know, let alone enjoy, the reputation his works had finally won him. His main books include *Thus Spoke Zarathustra* (1883), *Beyond Good and Evil* (1886), *The Gay Science* (1882–87), *The Genealogy of Morals* (1887), and *Twilight of the Idols* (1888).

If it is not true that style makes the man, it at least announces who he is. Nietzsche's style is an immediate reflection of how human life is actually lived — personal, nonsystematic, emotionally charged, and full of peaks and valleys. He writes now in aphorisms and epigrams, now in story form, now in poetry, now in essays, but never in any methodical or scientific way; where necessary, he creates new words and phrases: His writing can never be more confined than his thought. His works reflect a lived existence, a style of flesh and blood, sometimes pungent and acidulous; it is not designed to persuade by charm, but by its direct, prophetic tone. It does, however, befit a philosopher who is disturbed about man's state and who is searching for new ways to arrive at a humanism without the constraints of the past that have, in his view, sorrowfully brought man to where he is today. Nietzsche punctured the membrane of contemporary life as often as possible in the hope of releasing the forces and energy of life, which could then be creatively reassembled into a new humanism.

As a young man, Nietzsche began to probe the possibilities of a renewed humanism through the dimension of culture. As we have stated, *The Birth of Tragedy* was his first book; in it he expressed an apprehension that in its culture, particularly German culture, Western man was headed for a new barbarism, and some way had to be found to divert it from the impending cataclysm. Greek culture was, for Nietzsche, the model of all cultures, and when he tried to resolve the elements that made it so, he discovered they were two, the Apollonian and the Dionysian. The Apollonian, after the god Apollo, whose prophetic voice was often heard in the oracle of Delphi, is the formal element, giving measure, restraint, form, and individuality to life, supplying the opportunity to share in the ideal world. In art form, it is expressed in the epic and the plastic arts. The Dionysian is the element of enthusiasm, after the god Dionysus (the Roman god Bacchus), in whose honor wild revelry was held at grape-gathering, wine-drinking time; this element is an unplanned, uncharted insertion into the stream of life without concern about where it might lead, the acceptance of dark and shadow as well as joy, the blind affirmation of existence; here the individual tends to dissolve and merge with primordial unity. In art form, the Dionysian is expressed in tragedy and music.

When either of these two elements gains the ascendancy and overrides the other, the imbalance spells the doom of culture and of the life of man. There is a clear need for a savior, for someone who, as a creative genius, can stave off the wild forces at work, transforming existence and giving it meaning. Though the original need for a creative genius stemmed mainly from a decaying culture, as time went on the role became more and more enlarged to involve every important aspect of life, thus developing a still greater demand for such a genius, now called *Superman* (Overman; *Übermensch*).

The Death of God and the Transformation of Values

The center of this transformation is the individual, who has to be free to create new values. In the moral sphere, for example, *universal* morality has to be rejected because it destroys the individual's freedom to act according to his own creative insights. Universal morality, compelling everyone to behave the same way, is absolute, closed—a torturous straightjacket preventing the individual from asserting himself. The same rigorous individualism occurs in Nietzsche's division of morality into *master morality* and *slave morality;* the former stressed independence, self-approbation, action flowing out of strength or power; the latter bespeaks a herd mentality, behavior unsure of itself, action born out of resentment, whence its emphasis on virtues like humility and patience. In these terms, morality has to be transformed from the self-defeating, absolute precepts of slave morality that, in the course of history invaded all of Europe into the independence of creative action characteristic of master morality.

The transformation of moral values is the first consequence of the longed-for renunciation of God—a confident proclamation that *God is dead.* Belief in God, as history abundantly shows, destroys man, closes in on him, denies him his freedom, and generates a morality inimical to human dignity. Only atheism, which pits man against all external powers, can encourage him to return to his inner strength, there to find the source of true moral values and indeed all human value. The transcendence of man can come only with the emergence of the individual, and not in any appeal to the cosmic evolution of Hegel or the biological evolution of Darwin or the mystical transcendence of the theologian. In the opening pages of *Thus Spoke Zarathustra,* Nietzsche proclaims the death of God, as well as the advent of the Superman. Having come down from his mountain, the prophet Zarathustra meets a holy man who has spent long years in the forest praising God in his prayers and songs, and then the prophet asks himself, "Could it be possible? This old saint in the forest has not yet heard anything of this, that *God is dead!*" More explicitly, it is the Christian God who is dead: "The greatest recent event—that 'God is dead', that the belief in the Christian god has become unbelievable—is already beginning to cast its first shadows over Europe." With the fall of God, values dependent on Him will also fall.

When the term *nihilism* is used of Nietzsche's philosophy, what is usually referred to is the destruction of values following the death of God. But the destruction of these God-dependent values does not mean for him the absolute destruction of value, for value as such seems to be a permanent given in human existence. Granted that it is not always easy to determine his meaning, by the *revaluation of values* or the *transvaluation of values,* Nietzsche looks forward primarily to the imminent obliteration of traditional values. Philosophers have to oppose their "today" while looking forward to their "tomorrow," and they have to be "the bad conscience of their time. By putting the vivisectionist's knife to the *virtues of their time,* they revealed their own secret: they knew a *new* magnitude of man, a new un-worn path to his magnification." It may be that Nietzsche, in his prophetic style, is simply calling for courage to stand up against accepted values, come what may, but a plain reading shows more; it shows that, even though he does not have in mind a whole spectrum of new values ready to take over once the old ones are gone, he passionately expects a new order of things without knowing its specifics. This is an integral part of the role of Superman, whose "strength of will, hardness, and ability to make far-reaching decisions" refer not only to putting down the intolerable present but also to the fearless charting of the unseen future.

The Embodiment of Human Perfection: Superman

With the death of God and the transvaluation of values, the task of Superman is huge. The word *super-man* appears several times in classical literature and in German literature before Nietzsche, but with him the concept of Superman becomes an essential part of his philosophy. He is that person (whether one person or a member of a class) who represents the high point of human existence, combining in himself the highest of human traits; in that sense, he is man beyond man. Zarathustra tells the people of a town gathered in the marketplace, "*I teach you the overman.* Man is something that shall be overcome. . . . All beings so far have created something beyond themselves; and do you want to be the ebb of this great flood and even go back to the beasts rather than overcome man?"

Because Superman is strong-willed, independent, and the apex of master morality, he becomes the force through whom values will be re-created; and because God is dead and expectations from the "otherworld" are futile, his nourishment comes from "this world"; "The overman is the meaning of the earth. Let your will say: the overman *shall be* the meaning of the earth. I beseech you, my brothers, remain faithful to the earth, and do not believe those who speak to you of otherworldly hopes!" Glimpses of Superman are given us in certain figures of history, such as Caesar, whom Nietzsche refers to as the "Roman Caesar with Christ's soul"; Napoleon, with whom he had a love–hate relationship; and Goethe. But there are no examples of the ideal Superman as the one who integrates all variations of human power under the free mastery of the will and faces the future with a sense of boundless time. Furthermore, because Nietzsche sees the meaning of humanity in terms of its "highest specimens," Superman is the value-creative genius who, savior-like, refracts the light of a new order for the rest of us.

Whether it is the primacy of the will, the revaluation of value, the death of God, or Superman, all of Nietzsche's thoughts are so interwoven that an insight into one is an insight into the others. This is particularly true of the concept of the *will to power*, which, in the view of some commentators on Nietzsche, is the central thought of his later writings. On first hearing the phrase, there is a suggestion of power for the sake of power, might as right, or naked force; however, this is far from Nietzsche's meaning, since his thought carries with it no sense of domination or hurt. Nietzsche himself became worried over the way some of his ideas were taken up and wanted to dissociate himself, for example, from the concept of Bismarck's *Reich*, a *Deutschland Über Alles*. Basically what Nietzsche had in mind was an extension of the very strength that made for Superman, the strength first and foremost of overcoming the fear one has of himself, of overcoming weakness, or simply of *self-overcoming*. In the chapter entitled "On Self-overcoming" in *Thus Spoke Zarathustra*, Nietzsche has the prophet say, "That is your whole will, you who are wisest: a will to power—when you speak of good and evil, too, and of valuations. You still want to create the world before which you can kneel: that is your ultimate hope and intoxication. . . . Whatever lives, obeys . . . he who cannot obey himself is commanded. That is the nature of the living. . . . Where I found the living, there I found will to power; and even in the will of those who serve I found the will to be master. . . . And life itself confided this secret to me. 'Behold', it said, 'I am *that which must always overcome itself*. Indeed, you call it a will to procreate or a drive to an end, to something higher, farther, more manifold: but all this is one, and one secret'." The will to power underlies all human activities—knowledge, politics, pursuit of virtue, emotions of pleasure and pain: "all driving force is will to power . . . there is no other physical, dynamic, or psychic force except this." Value is decisive for life, not truth. The will to power is life itself. It is no surprise, then, that for Superman it is the basis of his exhilaration.

But Superman's exhilaration requires one more test; otherwise, it would be short-lived. The test is a test of strength, of the final surge of the will to power in what Nietzsche calls *eternal recurrence*, a concept borrowed from Pythagoras. As previously indicated, Nietzsche's meaning is sometimes difficult to understand; the doctrine of eternal recurrence is one such difficulty, although its importance for Nietzsche is clear. Given the unlimited amount of time involved in eternity, and given the limited number of things in this world that exist in time, we can imaginatively suppose that amid the countless shufflings and reshufflings of the world's elements, there must be repeated configurations of things as they are at this moment. Eternal recurrence is the "unconditional and infinitely repeated circulations of all things." In *Thus Spoke Zarathustra* Nietzsche describes the present moment as a "gateway," and if the lane leading to it is eternal and the lane leading away is eternal, then "From this gateway, Moment, a long, eternal lane leads *backwards*: behind us lies an eternity. Must not whatever *can* walk have walked on this lane before? . . . And are not all things knotted together so firmly that this moment draws after it *all* that is to come? . . . whatever *can* walk—in this long lane out *there* too, it *must* walk once more."

Eternal recurrence seems to be a bleak doctrine for one who looks forward to eternal joy. Perhaps Nietzsche espoused it as a hypothesis fitting in nicely with his atheism which could not permit a deity to preside over the course of the world's events; a universe self-contained, self-enclosed, that always was and always will be, was the only answer. Also, Nietzsche saw in eternal recurrence the ultimate exercise of Superman's will to power, for it is the final trial in his saying "yes" to life regardless of where it would lead him; and it leads Superman, and in him all humanity, to the state where he would never again rest "in endless trust"; then he would have to say "yes" and rejoice in accepting it. Or, using the imagery of the poet Heinrich Heine, Nietzsche has a demon say, "This life as you now live it and have lived it, you have to live once more and innumerable times more; and there will be nothing new in it, but every pain and every joy and every thought and sigh and everything unutterably small or great in your life will have to return to you, all in the same succession . . . how well disposed would you have to become to yourself and to life *to crave nothing more fervently* than this ultimate confirmation and seal?" Therein lies the profound strength of Superman, for if eternal recurrence is true, the new world he fought so hard to create would be fated to go under and the entire scenario to be replayed as though it had never happened before. This is the paragon of the Dionysian man who throws himself gladly into the primal stream of life.

If the success of a philosophy is measured by the insights it opens up for others, Nietzsche has been truly successful. Philosophers, theologians, and psychologists have long since been pursuing the leads supplied by him; art critics have been given a new awareness of the subtleties of artistic expression and political scientists astringent lessons in politics and government. At least one of Nietzsche's recent admirers, in the person of Walter Kaufman, Nietzsche's competent translator and interpreter, feels that Nietzsche is the most creative mind since Plato.

READINGS

The Death of God and the Ascendancy of Superman

(from *Thus Spoke Zarathustra*)

1

When Zarathustra was thirty years old, he left his home and the lake of his home, and went into the mountains. There he enjoyed his spirit and his solitude, and for ten years did not weary of it. But at last his heart changed,–and rising one morning with the rosy dawn, he went before the sun, and spoke thus unto it:

You great star! What would be your happiness if you did not have those for whom you shine!

For ten years you have climbed here to my cave: you would have wearied of your light and of the journey, had it not been for me, my eagle, and my serpent.

But we awaited you every morning, took from you your overflow, and blessed you for it.

Lo! I am weary of my wisdom, like the bee that has gathered too much honey; I need hands outstretched to take it.

I would fain bestow and distribute, until the wise have once more become joyous in their folly, and the poor happy in their riches.

Therefore must I descend into the deep: as you do in the evening, when you go behind the sea, and give light also to the nether-world, you exuberant star!

Like you must I go down, as men say, to whom I shall descend.

Bless me, then, you tranquil eye that can behold even the greatest happiness without envy!

Bless the cup that is about to overflow, that the water may flow golden out of it, and carry everywhere the reflection of your bliss!

Lo! This cup is again going to empty itself, and Zarathustra is again going to be a man.

Thus began Zarathustra's down-going.

2

Zarathustra went down the mountain alone, no one meeting him. When he entered the forest, however, there suddenly stood before him an old man, who had left his holy cot to seek roots. And thus spoke the old man to Zarathustra:

"No stranger to me is this wanderer: many years ago he passed by. Zarathustra he was called; but he has changed.

Then you carried your ashes into the mountains: will you now carry your fire into the valleys? Do you not fear the arsonist's doom?

Yes, I recognize Zarathustra. Pure is his eye, and no loathing lurks about his mouth. Does he not move like a dancer?

Changed is Zarathustra; a child has Zarathustra become; an awakened one is Zarathustra: what will you do in the land of the sleepers?

As in the sea you lived in solitude, and it has borne you up. Alas, will you now go ashore? Alas, will you again drag your body by yourself?"

Zarathustra answered: "I love mankind."

"Why," said the saint, "did I go into the forest and the desert? Was it not because I loved men far too well?

Now I love God: men, I do not love. Man is a thing too imperfect for me. Love of man would be fatal to me."

Zarathustra answered: "Did I speak of love! I am bringing gifts to men."

"Give them nothing," said the saint. "Take rather part of their load, and carry it along with them—that will be most agreeable unto them: if only it be agreeable to you!

If, however, you insist on giving them something, give them no more than an alms, and let them beg for that too!"

"No," replied Zarathustra, "I give no alms. I am not poor enough for that."

The saint laughed at Zarathustra, and spoke thus: "Then see to it that they accept your treasures! They are distrustful of anchorites, and do not believe that we come with gifts.

The fall of our footsteps rings too hollow through their streets. And just as at night, when they are in bed and hear a man abroad long before sunrise, so they ask themselves concerning us: Where is the thief going?

Go not to men, but stay in the forest! Go rather to the animals! Why not be like me—a bear among bears, a bird among birds?"

"And what does the saint do in the forest?" asked Zarathustra.

The saint answered: "I make hymns and sing them; and in making hymns I laugh and weep and mumble: thus do I praise God.

With singing, weeping, laughing, and mumbling do I praise the God who is my God. But what do you bring us as a gift?"

When Zarathustra had heard these words, he bowed to the saint and said: "What should I have to give you! Let me rather hurry hence lest I take anything away from you!"- And thus they parted from one another, the old man and Zarathustra, laughing like schoolboys.

When Zarathustra was alone, however, he said to his heart: "Could it be possible! This old saint in the forest has not yet heard of it, that God is dead!"

3

When Zarathustra arrived at the nearest town which adjoins the forest, he found many people assembled in the market-place; for it had been announced that a rope-dancer would give a performance. And Zarathustra spoke thus unto the people:

I teach you the Superman. Man is something that is to be surpassed. What have you done to surpass man?

All beings hitherto have created something beyond themselves: and you want to be the ebb of that great tide, and would rather go back to the beast than surpass man?

What is the ape to man? A laughing-stock, a thing of shame. And just the same shall man be to the Superman: a laughing-stock, a thing of shame.

You have made your way from the worm to man, and much within you is still worm. Once you were apes, and even yet man is more of an ape than any of the apes.

Even the wisest among you is only a disharmony and hybrid of plant and phantom. But do I bid you become phantoms or plants?

Lo, I teach you the Superman!

The Superman is the meaning of the earth. Let your will say: The Superman shall be the meaning of the earth!

I adjure you, my brethren, remain true to the earth, and believe not those who speak unto you of superearthly hopes! Poisoners are they, whether they know it or not.

Despisers of life are they, decaying ones and poisoned ones themselves, of whom the earth is weary: so away with them!

Once blasphemy against God was the greatest blasphemy; but God died, and with him those blasphemers died too. To blaspheme the earth is now the most dreadful sin, and to rate the heart of the unknowable higher than the meaning of the earth!

Once the soul looked contemptuously on the body, and then that contempt was the supreme thing:—the soul wished the body meagre, ghastly, and famished. Thus it thought to escape from the body and the earth.

Oh, that soul was itself meagre, ghastly, and famished; and cruelty was the delight of that soul!

But you, also, my brethren, tell me: What does your body say about your soul? Is your soul not poverty and pollution and wretched self-complacency?

Verily, a polluted stream is man. One must be a sea, to receive a polluted stream without becoming impure.

Lo, I teach you the Superman: he is that sea; in him can your great contempt be submerged.

What is the greatest thing you can experience? It is the hour of great contempt. The hour in which even your happiness becomes loathsome unto you, and so also your reason and virtue.

The hour when you say: "What good is my happiness! It is poverty and pollution and wretched self-complacency. But my happiness should justify existence itself!"

The hour when you say: "What good is my reason! Does it long for knowledge as the lion for his food? It is poverty and pollution and wretched self-complacency!"

The hour when you say: "What good is my virtue! As yet it has not made me passionate. How weary I am of my good and my bad! It is all poverty and pollution and wretched self-complacency!"

The hour when you say: "What good is my justice! I do not see that I am fervour and fuel. The just, however, are fervour and fuel!"

The hour when you say: "What good is my pity! Is not pity the cross on which he is nailed who loves man? But my pity is not a crucifixion."

Have you ever spoken thus? Have you ever cried thus? Ah! would that I had heard you crying thus!

It is not your sin—it is your self-satisfaction that cries to heaven; your very sparingness in sin cries unto heaven!

Where is the lightning to lick you with its tongue? Where is the frenzy with which you should be inoculated?

Lo, I teach you the Superman: he is that lightning, he is that frenzy!—

When Zarathustra had spoken thus, one of the people called out: "We have now heard enough of the rope-dancer; it is time now for us to. see him!" And all the people laughed at Zarathustra. But the rope-dancer, who thought the words applied to him, began his performance.

(Trans. Thomas Common)

Anti-Christ and Revaluation
(from *The Anti-Christ*)

PREFACE
REVALUATION OF ALL VALUES

This book belongs to the most rare of men. Perhaps not one of them is yet alive. It is possible that they may be among those who understand my "Zarathustra": how *could* I confound myself with those who are now sprouting ears?—First the day after tomorrow must come for me. Some men are born posthumously.

The conditions under which any one understands me, and *necessarily* understands me—I know them only too well. Even to endure my seriousness, my passion, he must carry intellectual integrity to the verge of hardness. He must be accustomed to living on mountain tops—and to looking upon the wretched gabble of politics and nationalism as *beneath* him. He must have become indifferent; he must never ask of the truth whether it brings profit to him or a fatality to him . . . He must have an inclination, born of strength, for questions that no one has the courage for; the courage for the *forbidden;* predestination for the labyrinth. The experience of seven solitudes. New ears for new music. New eyes for what is most distant. A new conscience for truths that have hitherto remained unheard. *And* the will to economize in the grand manner—to hold together his strength, his enthusiasm . . . Reverence for self; love of self; absolute freedom of self. . . .

Very well, then! of that sort only are my readers, my true readers, my readers foreordained: of what account are the *rest?*—The rest are merely humanity.—One must make one's self superior to humanity, in power, in *loftiness* of soul,—in contempt.

1

—Let us look each other in the face. We are Hyperboreans—we know well enough how remote our place is. "Neither by land nor by water will you find the road to the Hyperboreans": even Pindar, in his day, knew *that* much about us. Beyond the North, beyond the ice, beyond *death*—*our* life, *our* happiness . . . We have discovered that happiness; we know the way; we got our knowledge of it from thousands of years in the labyrinth. Who *else* has found it?—The man of today?—"I don't know either the way out or the way in; I am whatever doesn't know either the way out or the way in"—so sighs the man of today . . . *This* is the sort of modernity that made us ill,—we sickened on lazy peace, cowardly compromise, the whole virtuous dirtiness of the modern Yea and Nay. This tolerance and *largeur* of the heart that "forgives" everything because it "understands" everything is a sirocco to us. Rather live amid the ice than among modern virtues and other such south-winds! . . . We were brave enough; we spared neither ourselves nor others; but we were a long time finding out *where* to direct our courage. We grew dismal; they called us fatalists. *Our* fate—it was the fulness, the tension, the *storing up* of powers. We thirsted for the lightnings and great deeds; we kept as far as possible from the happiness of the weakling, from "resignation" . . . There was thunder in our air; nature, as we embodied it, became overcast—*for we had not yet found the way.* The formula of our happiness: a Yea, a Nay, a straight line, a *goal* . . .

2

What is good?—Whatever augments the feeling of power, the will to power, power itself, in man.

What is evil?—Whatever springs from weakness.

What is happiness?—The feeling that power *increases*—that resistance is overcome.

Not contentment, but more power; not peace at any price, but war; *not* virtue, but efficiency (virtue in the Renaissance sense, *virtu,* virtue free of moral acid).

The weak and the botched shall perish: first principle of *our* charity. And one should help them to it.

What is more harmful than any vice?—Practical sympathy for the botched and the weak—Christianity . . .

3

The problem that I set here is not what shall replace mankind in the order of living creatures (—man is an end—): but what type of man must be *bred,* must be *willed,* as being the most valuable, the most worthy of life, the most secure guarantee of the future.

This more valuable type has appeared often enough in the past: but always as a happy accident, as an exception, never as deliberately *willed.* Very often it has been precisely the most feared; hitherto it has been almost *the* terror of terrors;—and out of that terror the contrary type has been willed, cultivated and *attained:* the domestic animal, the herd animal, the sick brute-man—the Christian . . .

4

Mankind surely does *not* represent an evolution toward a better or stronger or higher level, as progress is now understood. This "progress" is merely a modern idea, which is to say, a false idea. The European of today, in his essential worth, falls far below the European of the Renaissance; the process of evolution does *not* necessarily mean elevation, enhancement, strengthening.

True enough, it succeeds in isolated and individual cases in various parts of the earth and under the most widely different cultures, and in these cases a *higher* type certainly manifests itself; something which, compared to mankind in the mass, appears as a sort of superman. Such happy strokes of high success have always been possible, and will remain possible, perhaps, for all time to come. Even whole races, tribes and nations may occasionally represent such lucky accidents.

5

We should not deck out and embellish Christianity: it has waged a war to the death against this *higher* type of man, it has put all the deepest instincts of this type under its ban, it has developed its concept of evil, of the Evil One himself, out of these instincts—the strong man as the typical reprobate, the "outcast among men." Christianity has taken the part of all the weak, the low, the botched; it has made an ideal out of *antagonism* to all the self-preservative instincts of sound life; it has corrupted even the faculties of those natures that are intellectually most vigorous, by representing the highest intellectual values as sinful, as misleading, as full of temptation. The most lamentable example: the corruption of Pascal, who believed that his intellect had been destroyed by original sin, whereas it was actually destroyed by Christianity!—

6

It is a painful and tragic spectacle that rises before me: I have drawn back the curtain from the *rottenness* of man. This word, in my mouth, is at least free from one suspicion: that it involves a moral accusation against humanity. It is used— and I wish to emphasize the fact again—without any moral significance: and this is so far true that the rottenness I speak of is most apparent to me precisely in those quarters where there has been most aspiration, hitherto, toward "virtue" and "godliness." As you probably surmise, I understand rottenness in the sense of *decadence:* my argument is that all the values on which mankind now fixes its highest aspirations are *decadence*-values.

I call an animal, a species, an individual corrupt, when it loses its instincts, when it chooses, when it *prefers,* what is injurious to it. A history of the "higher feelings," the "ideals of humanity"—and it is possible that I'll have to write it— would almost explain why man is so degenerate. Life itself appears to me as an instinct for growth, for survival, for the accumulation of forces, for *power:* whenever the will to power fails there is disaster. My contention is that all the highest values of humanity have been emptied of this will—that the values of *decadence,* of *nihilism,* now prevail under the holiest names.

7

Christianity is called the religion of *pity.*—Pity stands in opposition to all the tonic passions that augment the energy of the feeling of aliveness: it is a depressant. A man loses power when he pities. Through pity that drain upon strength which suffering works is multiplied a thousandfold. Suffering is made contagious by pity; under certain circumstances it may lead to a total sacrifice of life and living energy—a loss out of all proportion to the magnitude of the cause (—the case of the death of the Nazarene).This is the first view of it; there is, however, a still more important one. If one measures the effects of pity by the gravity of the reactions it sets up, its character as a menace to life appears in a much clearer light. Pity thwarts the whole law of evolution, which is the law of natural selection. It preserves whatever is ripe for destruction; it fights on the side of those disinherited and condemned by life; by maintaining life in so many of the botched of all kinds, it gives life itself a gloomy and dubious aspect. Mankind has ventured to call pity a virtue (—in every *superior* moral system it appears as a weakness—); going still further, it has been called *the* virtue, the source and foundation of all other virtues—but let us always bear in mind that this was from the standpoint of a philosophy that was nihilistic, and upon whose shield *the denial of life* was inscribed. Schopenhauer was right in this: that by means of pity life is denied, and made *worthy of denial—pity* is the technic of nihilism. Let me repeat: this depressing and contagious instinct stands against all those instincts which work for the preservation and enhancement of life: in the role of *protector* of the miserable, it is a prime agent in the promotion of *decadence—pity* persuades to extinction. . . . Of course, one doesn't say "extinction": one says "the other world," or "God," or "the *true* life," or Nirvana, salvation, blessedness. . . . This innocent rhetoric, from the realm of religious-ethical balderdash, appears a *good deal less innocent* when one reflects upon the tendency that it conceals beneath sublime words: the tendency to *destroy life*. Schopenhauer was hostile to life: that is why pity appeared to him as a virtue. . . . Aristotle, as every one knows, saw in pity a sickly and dangerous state of mind, the remedy for which was an occasional purgative: he regarded tragedy as that purgative.The instinct of life should prompt us to seek some means of puncturing any such pathological and dangerous accumulation of pity as that appearing in Schopenhauer's case (and also, alack, in that of our whole literary *decadence,* from St. Petersburg to Paris, from Tolstoi to Wagner), that it may burst and be discharged . . . Nothing is more unhealthy, amid all our unhealthy modernism, than Christian pity. To be the doctors *here,* to be unmerciful *here,* to wield the knife here—all this is *our* business, all this is *our* sort of humanity, by this sign we are philosophers, we Hyperboreans!—

(Trans. by H. L. Mencken)

REVIEW QUESTIONS

1. Compare the notion of humanism in Nietzsche with that of Kierkegaard.
2. In what way is the cultural man the point of contact with human existence for Nietzsche?
3. Why is traditional morality found wanting by Nietzsche?
4. What does Nietzsche mean by his announcement that God is dead?
5. Is Nietzsche truly a nihilist? What does he mean by *transvaluation of values?*
6. What is the role of Overman (Superman) in evolving a new set of values?
7. What does Nietzsche mean by *eternal recurrence?*

SUGGESTIONS FOR FURTHER READING

Danto, A. *Nietzsche as Philosopher.* New York, Columbia University Press, 1980.

Danto, A. *Nietzsche as Philosopher,* updated version, New York, Columbia University Press, 2005.

Kaufman, W. *Nietzsche.* New York, Meridian, 1956.

The Portable Nietzsche. Tr. Kaufman, W. New York, Viking, 1968.

The Philosophy of Nietzsche. Intro. Wright, W. H. New York, Modern Library, 1954.

23

───── ◆ ─────

Karl Marx
(1816–1883)

❧

Kierkegaard and Nietzsche highlighted the direction taken by philosophy in the mid-nineteenth century by searching for the roots of a true humanism; Karl Marx did the same, but took as his starting point the experience of the laboring man, alienated by the demands put upon him in a capitalist society. His was a practical philosophy designed to resolve the tension between the capitalist and working classes, paving the way for the restoration of man to his true dignity.

Early Direction

Marx was born in Trier, Germany, in 1816, of Jewish descent, though he was baptized a Christian at the age of six, when his father, not unquestionably for religious reasons, was converted. For a short time he attended the University of Bonn, where he began the study of law, but left Bonn for Berlin, where he studied a variety of subjects, settling finally on philosophy; he was awarded a doctorate for his dissertation on the atomism of the Greek philosophers Democritus and Epicurus. After giving up his intention of teaching philosophy, he joined a group of young radical Hegelians in Berlin who believed that philosophy, conceived in terms of the dialectic, must have a practical political end; however, before long, Marx left the group, feeling that it was far too theoretical. He took on the editorship of the *Rheinische Zeitung,* an activist paper in Cologne that was soon discovered to be uncongenial to the public authorities, who clamped such tight censorship on it that Marx resigned. In one year, 1843, he got married, moved to Paris, helped to found the short-lived *Deutsch-Französische Jahrbücher,* joined an active socialist group, and took up a detailed study of political economy. Earlier he had met Friedrich Engels, the son of a wealthy industrialist living in England, who was actively involved in socialism; the two worked in close collaboration for the rest of their lives. Banished now from Paris, he went to Brussels, where he continued to deepen his affiliation with the Communist League and to collaborate with Engels, principally on the *Communist Manifesto,* published in 1848. One last government crackdown brought him to London, where he was allowed to remain. His dedication to his work resulted in poverty for himself and his family, who barely survived with help from Engels and from articles he wrote for the *New York Tribune.*

He carried on his research at the British Museum, where he became a familiar figure, and while he continued writing, he remained active in his support of the cause of the working man, founding, for example, the First International Working-men's Association in 1864. He had designed three volumes for his major work, *Das Kapital,* the first of which he published in 1867; though he never lived to complete it, Engels was able to do so from the extensive preparation already done. Marx died in 1883; his wife and two of his children predeceased him. In addition to the *Communist Manifesto* and *Das Kapital,* some of his other works include *The Holy Family* (with Engels, 1845), *German Ideology* (with Engels, 1846), *Poverty of Philosophy* (1847), and the *Critique of Political Economy* (1859); in addition to his books, he wrote a vast number of articles for various magazines and journals.

Alienation: Loss of Human Meaning

As pointed out in an earlier chapter, every segment of reality invites reflection and response; yet, though man had always been a laborer, man the laborer had never been brought to the forefront of human consciousness as it was by Marx. In one sense, the world of the Industrial Revolution that Marx saw, everyone saw; in another sense, no one did. Surrounding him were thousands of human beings who endured a life completely determined by an inhuman labor system. The worker rose before dawn, sweated out the day, had supper as the last event before sleep, and awoke to the same unbroken, day-by-day routine in a grind that made him behave like the machine he worked on. Often no meal, often no sleep, always squalid. The chapter on "The Working Day" in *Capital* is a catalog of the brutal conditions prevailing throughout the industrialized world—a system of exploitation, thought Marx, tantamount to slavery.

What chance, asked Marx, did such people or their families have for education, cultural growth, self-reliance, leisure, or the whole range of pursuits that enlarge one's humanity? How could they escape the feeling of being embattled? Of being strangers to life? Of alienation? Thoughts like these activated Marx, who, very early in life, appreciated the fact that if ideas are to live they should not remain idle but must be dressed in the clothes of practical action and enter the real world as living philosophy. In the phrase of Ernst Bloch, the young Marx developed a "*public* self-consciousness," and would never entertain any but a philosophy directed to action.

Marx touches on three main points: the loss of man's meaning, the philosophical framework of loss and gain, and the recovery of man's meaning. Every window Marx looked through opened on to a human landscape as frightful as the one previously described, and it seemed to him that all the forces that should have supported man—economy, politics, culture, religion—conspired to destroy him. Marx followed a fellow German philosopher, Ludwig Feuerbach, in his analysis of *alienation,* the loss of meaning for man. Take religion, for example; even though it may be argued that religion, in the beginning, was a revolt against human degradation, it gradually developed as a force in its own interest, to which it sacrificed the good of man. In a strangely psychological but understandable way, under the oppression of religion, man surrendered his own attributes, one by one, to an external divinity, and in the process lost them for himself. So man, in this state of alienation, accepted religion as a solace for his oppression, as a drug to deaden the pain from so much suffering, or, in Marx's oft-quoted phrase, as the opium of the people: "Religion is the sigh of the oppressed creature, the sentiment of a heartless world, and the soul of soulless conditions. It is the *opium* of the people." Man, as Marx sees it, has finally become conscious of this destructive relationship and owes it to his humanity to purge God radically from his life.

The situation is exactly the same in the social order, for man has alienated himself from *his own labor;* his *productive activity* is not for himself. In this he has become enslaved, with little hope for emancipation. If his needs as a human being are to be satisfied by his productive capacity, then truly he has been indentured by the capitalist, who, in defrauding him of his labor, defrauds him of his humanity. Though valuation will vary from age to age, in the age of capitalism human values are seen to be a function of labor; that is, a just return to the worker for his labor means a respect for him as a human being and an opportunity, as previously mentioned, to engage in humanizing pursuits; to the extent that justice is denied, human values are lessened or even extinguished. For Marx, inasmuch as labor endows a thing with value, value is crystallized human labor: "When looked at as crystals of this social substance (i.e. human labor), common to them all, they are—Values."

Dialectical Materialism and the Recovery of Man's Meaning

The framework of Marx's philosophy is most often referred to as *dialectical materialism,* a term that, though not used by Marx himself, aptly designates his meaning. It is an amalgam of the dialectic of Hegel and the materialism of Feuerbach. For Hegel, dialectical idealism is the process whereby the Idea, or Spirit, unfolds itself in the course of time. For Marx, consistent with his atheism, reality is not to be conceived of in terms of Idea, or Spirit, but in terms of matter, that is, in terms of a materialism that departs from the old "billiard ball" kind, as found in Democritus, whose luckless atoms enter into chance configurations, but of the kind that admits free will, mind, value, virtue—in short, all the attributes one would like to welcome in the name of what is "natural," though hitherto were spoken for in the name of the "supernatural." In comparing his use of the dialectic with that of Hegel, whom he regarded as a mighty thinker, Marx writes: "My dialectic method is not only different from the Hegelian, but is its direct opposite. To Hegel, the life-process of the human brain, i.e. the process of thinking, which, under the name of 'the Idea,' he even transforms into an independent subject, is the demiurgos of the real world, and the real world is only the external, phenomenal form of 'the Idea.' With me, on the contrary, the ideal is nothing else than the material world reflected by the human mind, and translated into forms of thought." In Hegel, the dialectic is "standing on its head" and has to be turned right side up again; this is accomplished by Marx in giving primacy to matter over mind rather than to mind over matter.

The philosophical path to be taken to recover man's meaning is now clear. In the course of history, society has always developed a class structure on the basis of productive activity, whether it be freeman and slave, lord and serf, or capitalist and worker. More than the social strata themselves, the forces of production govern the entire shape of society, determining its culture, morality, and indeed all social relations: "Social relations are closely bound up with productive forces. In acquiring new productive forces men change their mode of production; and in changing their mode of production, in changing the way of earning their living, they change all their social relations. The handmill gives you society with the feudal lord; the steam-mill, society with the industrial capitalist. The same men who establish their social relations in conformity with their material productivity, produce also principles, ideas and categories, in conformity with their social relations."

The recovery of man's meaning, therefore, takes on an inevitable social thrust in terms of the classes of society, which are, in the nature of social reality, subject to the dialectic and must resolve the tension between them. Using the terminology introduced in the discussion of Hegel, the capitalist (bourgeois) class as thesis necessarily contradicts and reacts to the proletariat class as antithesis, thus transforming a two-class society into a classless society as synthesis. A *social revolution* is underway and historically inevitable, and all the productive forces hitherto consigned to private property will meld into the common good as the communist society, the next stage in the process of human emancipation and recovery, emerges.

For Marx, man is determined by the social structure in which he lives, or, more precisely, the kind of productive–economic structure in which he exists creates his very existence. At times this idea is expressed in the terms *substructure* and *superstructure:* The substructure is the productive-economic structure, which serves as a foundation for the legal, political, and social superstructures. If the substructure is antipathetic to humanity, so is the superstructure, and the only way to make the superstructure sympathetic to humanity is to change the substructure radically. In Marx's own words: "In the social production of their life, men enter into definite relations that are indispensable and independent of their will, relations of production which correspond to a definite stage of development of their material productive forces. The sum total of these relations of production constitutes the economic structure of society, the real foundation, on which rises a legal, political superstructure and to which correspond definite forms of social consciousness. The mode of production of material life conditions the social, political and intellectual life process in general." This is followed by a single sentence that summarizes Marx's whole philosophy: "It is not the consciousness of men that determines their being, but, on the contrary, their social being that determines their consciousness."

With the transformation of economic and productive forces, values as a whole are transformed; they are transformed into a truly human configuration, for the expropriation of man's labor will be done away with and the recovery of man's dignity will be achieved: Communism is "the *positive* transcendence of *private property,* or human *self-estrangement,* and therefore . . . the real *appropriation of the human* essence by and for man; . . . the complete return of man to himself as a *social* (i.e. human) being—a return become conscious, and accomplished within the entire wealth of previous development."

It is true that ideas have consequences, and Marx's ideas have had immediate practical consequences for countless millions of people throughout the world living under a Marx-inspired social philosophy. However, without trying to evaluate Marxian philosophy quantitatively or politically, it must be seen as a personalist philosophy, in the guise of an ethical revolt, an attempt to discover a human life for human beings.

READINGS

A Chapter in the Exploitation of the Working Man
(from *Das Kapital*)

SECTION 3
BRANCHES OF ENGLISH INDUSTRY WITHOUT
LEGAL LIMITS TO EXPLOITATION

We have hitherto considered the tendency to the extension of the working day, the were-wolf's hunger for surplus-labour in a department where the monstrous exactions, not surpassed, says an English bourgeois economist, by the cruelties of the Spaniards to the American redskins, caused capital at last to be bound by the chains of legal regulations. Now, let us cast a glance at certain branches of production in which the exploitation of labour is either free from fetters to this day, or was so yesterday.

Mr. Broughton Charlton, country magistrate, declared as chairman of a meeting held at the Assembly Rooms, Nottingham, on the 14th of January, 1860, "that there was an amount of privation and suffering among that portion of the population connected with the lace trade, unknown in other parts of the kingdom, indeed, in the civilized world. . . . Children of nine or ten years are dragged from their squalid beds at two, three, or four o'clock in the morning and compelled to work for a bare subsistence until ten, eleven, or twelve at night, their limbs wearing away, their frames dwindling, their faces whitening, and their humanity absolutely sinking into a stone-like torpor, utterly horrible to contemplate. . . . We are not surprised that Mr. Mallett, or any other manufacturer, should stand forward and protest against discussion. . . . The system, as the Rev. Montagu Valpy describes it, is one of unmitigated slavery, socially, physically, morally, and spiritually. . . . What can be thought of a town which holds a public meeting to petition that the period of labour for men shall be diminished to eighteen hours a day? . . . We declaim against the Virginian and Carolina cotton-planters. Is their black-market, their lash, and their barter of human flesh more detestable than this slow sacrifice of humanity which takes place in order that veils and collars may be fabricated for the benefit of capitalists?"

William Wood, 9 years old, was 7 years and 10 months when he began to work. He "ran moulds" (carried ready-moulded articles into the drying room, afterwards bringing back the empty mould) from the beginning. He came to work every day in the week at 6 A.M., and left off about 9 P.M. "I work till 9 o'clock at night six days in the week. I have done so seven or eight weeks." Fifteen hours of labour for a child of 7 years old! J. Murray, 12 years of age, says: "I turn jigger, and run moulds. I come at 6. Sometimes I come at 4. I worked all last night, till 6 o'clock this morning. I have not been in bed since the night before last. There were eight or nine other boys working last night. All but one have come this morning. I get 3 shillings and sixpence. I do not get any more for working at night. I worked two nights last week." Fernyhough, a boy of ten: "I have not always an hour (for dinner). I have only half an hour sometimes; on Thursday, Friday, and Saturday."

From the report of the Commissioners in 1863, the following: Dr. J.T. Arledge, senior physician of the North Staffordshire Infirmary, says: "The potters as a class, both men and women, represent a degenerated population, both physically and morally. They are, as a rule, stunted in growth, ill-shaped, and frequently ill-formed in the chest; they become prematurely old, and are certainly short-lived; they are phlegmatic and bloodless, and exhibit their debility of constitution of obstinate attacks of dyspepsia, and disorders of the liver and kidneys, and by rheumatism. But of all diseases they are especially prone to chest-disease, to pneumonia, pythisis, bronchitis, and asthma. One form would appear peculiar to them, and is known as potter's asthma, or potter's consumption. Scrofula attacking the glands, or bones, or other parts of the body, is a disease of two-thirds or more of the potters . . . that the 'degenerescence' of the population of this district is not even greater than it is, is due to the constant recruiting from adjacent country, and intermarriage with more healthy races."

J. Leach deposes: "Last winter six out of nineteen girls were away from ill-health at one time from over-work. I have to bawl at them to keep them awake." W. Duffy: "I have seen when the children could none of them keep their eyes open for the work; indeed, none of us could." J. Lightbourne: "Am 13 . . . We worked last winter till 9 (evening), and the winter before till 10. I used to cry with sore feet every night last winter." G. Apsden: "That boy of mine . . . when he was 7 years old I used to carry him on my back to and from through the snow, and he used to have 16 hours a day . . . I have often knelt down to feed him as he stood by the machine, for he could not leave it or stop." Smith, the managing partner of a Manchester factory: "We (he means his "hands" who work for "us") work on, with no stoppage for meals, so that the day's work for 10½ hours is finished by 4:30 P.M., and all after that is overtime." (Does this Mr. Smith take no meals himself during 10½ hours?) "We (this same Smith) seldom leave off working before 6 P.M. (he means leave off the consumption of 'our' labour-power machines), so that we (iterum Crispinus) are really working overtime the whole year round. . . .

No branch of industry in England (we do not take into account the making of bread by machinery recently introduced) has preserved up to the present day a method of production so archaic, so—as we see from the poets of the Roman Empire—pre-christian, as baking. But capital, as was said earlier, is at first indifferent as to the technical character of the labour-process; it begins by taking it just as it finds it.

The incredible adulteration of bread, especially in London, was first revealed by the House of Commons Committee "on the adulteration of articles of food" (1855–56), and Dr. Hassall's work, "Adulterations detected." The consequence of these revelations was the Act of August 6th, 1860, "for preventing the adulteration of articles of food and drink," an inoperative law, as it naturally shows the tenderest consideration for every free-trader who determines by the buying or selling of adulterated commodities "to turn an honest penny." The Committee itself formulated more or less naively its conviction that free-trade meant essentially a trade with adulterated, or as the English ingeniously put it, "sophisticated" goods. In fact this kind of sophistry knows better than Protagoras how to make white black, and black white, and better than the Eleatics how to demonstrate *ad oculos* that everything is only appearance.

At all events the committee had directed the attention of the public to its "daily bread," and therefore to the baking trade. At the same time in public meetings and in petitions to Parliament rose the cry of the London journeymen bakers against their over-work, &c. The cry was so urgent that Mr. H. S. Tremenheere, also a member of the Commission of 1863 several times mentioned, was appointed Royal Commissioner of Inquiry. His report, together with the evidence given, roused not the heart of the public but its stomach. Englishmen, always well up in the Bible, knew well enough that man, unless by elective grace a capitalist, or landlord, or sinecurist, is commanded to eat his bread in the sweat of his brow, but they did not know that he had to eat daily in his bread a certain quantity of human perspiration mixed with the discharge of abscesses, cobwebs, dead black-beetles, and putrid German yeast, without counting alum, sand, and other agreeable mineral ingredients. Without any regard to his holiness, Freetrade, the free baking-trade was therefore placed under the supervision of the State inspectors (Close of the Parliamentary session of 1863), and by the same Act of Parliament, work from 9 in the evening to 5 in the morning was forbidden for journeymen bakers under 18. The last clause speaks volumes as to the over-work in this old-fashioned, homely line of business.

"The work of a London journeyman baker begins, as a rule, at about eleven at night. At that hour he 'makes the dough,'—a laborious process, which lasts from half-an-hour to three quarters of an hour, according to the size of the batch or the labour bestowed upon it. He then lies down upon the kneading-board, which is also the covering of the trough in which the dough is 'made'; and with a sack under him, and another rolled up as a pillow, he sleeps for about a couple of hours. He is then engaged in a rapid and continuous labour for about five hours—throwing out the dough, 'scaling it off,' moulding it, putting it into the oven, preparing and baking rolls and fancy bread, taking the batch bread out of the oven, and up into the shop, &c., &c. The temperature of a bakehouse ranges from about 75 to upwards of 90 degrees, and in the smaller bakehouses approximates usually to the higher rather than to the lower degree of heat. When the business of making the bread, rolls, &c., is over, that of its distribution begins, and a considerable proportion of the journeymen in the trade, after working hard in the manner described during the night, are upon their legs for many hours during the day, carrying baskets, or wheeling hand-carts, and sometimes again in the bakehouse, leaving off work at various hours between 1 and 6 P.M. according to the season of the year, or the amount and nature of their master's business; while others are again engaged in the bakehouse in 'bringing out' more batches until late in the afternoon. . . . During what is called 'the London season,' the operatives belonging to the 'full-priced' bakers at the West End of the town, generally begin work at 11 P.M., and are engaged in making the bread, with one or two short (sometimes very short) intervals of rest, up to 8 o'clock the next morning. They are then engaged all day long, up to 4, 5, 6, and as late as 7 o'clock in the evening carrying out bread, or sometimes in the afternoon in the bakehouse again, assisting in the biscuit-taking. They may have, after they have done their work, sometimes five or six, sometimes only four or five hours' sleep before they begin again. On Fridays they always begin sooner, some about ten o'clock, and continue in some cases, at work, either in making or delivering the bread up to 8 P.M. on Saturday night, but more generally up to 4 or 5 o'clock, Sunday morning. On Sundays the men must attend twice or three times during the day for an hour or two to make preparations for the next day's bread. . . . The men employed by the underselling masters (who sell their bread under the 'full price,' and who, as already point out, comprise three-fourths of the London bakers) have not only to work on the average longer hours, but their work is almost entirely confined to the bakehouse. The underselling masters generally sell their bread . . . in the shop. If they send it out, which is not common, except as supplying chandlers' shops, they usually employ other hands for that purpose. It is not their practice to deliver bread from house to house. Towards the end of the week . . . the men begin on Thursday night at 10 o'clock, and continue on with only slight intermission until late on Saturday evening."

Even the bourgeois intellect understands the position of the "underselling" masters. "The unpaid labour of the men was made the source whereby the competition was carried on." And the "full-priced" baker denounces his underselling competitors to the Commission of Inquiry as thieves of foreign labour and adulterators. "They only exist now by first defrauding the public, and next getting 18 hours work out of their men for 12 hours' wages."

The adulteration of bread and the formation of a class of bakers that sells the bread below the full price, date from the beginning of the 18th century, from the time when the corporate character of the trade was lost, and the capitalist in the form of the miller or flour-factor, rises behind the nominal master baker. Thus was laid the foundation of capitalistic production in this trade, of the unlimited extension of the working day and of night labour, although the latter only since 1824 gained a serious footing, even in London.

After what has just been said, it will be understood that the Report of the Commission classes journeymen bakers among the short-lived labourers, who, having by good luck escaped the normal decimation of the children of the working-class, rarely reach the age of 42. Nevertheless, the baking trade is always overwhelmed with applicants. The sources of the supply of these labour-powers to London are Scotland, the western agricultural districts of England, and Germany.

In the last week of June, 1863, all the London daily papers published a paragraph with the "sensational" heading "Death from simple over-work." It dealt with the death of the milliner, Mary Ann Walkley, 20 years of age, employed in a highly-respectable dressmaking establishment, exploited by a lady with the pleasant name of Elise. The old, often-told story, was once more recounted. This girl worked, on an average, $16\frac{1}{2}$ hours, during the season often 30 hours, without a break, whilst her failing labour-power was revived by occasional supplies of sherry, port, or coffee. It was just now the height of the season. It was necessary to conjure up in the twinkling of an eye the gorgeous dresses for the noble ladies bidden to the ball in honour of the newly-imported Princess of Wales. Mary Anne Walkley had worked without inter-mission for $26\frac{1}{2}$ hours, with 60 other girls, 30 in one room, that only afforded $\frac{1}{3}$ of the cubic feet of air required for them. At night, they slept in pairs in one of the sti-fling holes into which the bedroom was divided by partitions of board. And this was one of the best millinery establishments in London. Mary Anne Walkley fell ill on the Friday, died on Sunday, without, to the astonishment of Madame Elise, having previously completed the work in hand. The doctor, Mr. Keys, called too late to the death-bed, duly bore witness before the coroner's jury that "Mary Anne Walkley had died from long hours of work in an overcrowded workroom, and a too small and badly-ventilated bedroom." In order to give the doctor a lesson in good manners, the coroner's jury thereupon brought in a verdict that "the deceased had died of apoplexy, but there was reason to fear that her death had been accelerated by over-work in an overcrowded workroom, &c." "Our white slaves," cried the "Morning Star," the organ of the free-traders, Cobden and Bright, "our white slaves, who are toiled into the grave, for the most part silently pine and die."

"It is not in dressmakers' rooms that working to death is the order of the day, but in a thousand other places; in every place I had almost said, where 'a thriving business' has to be done. . . . We will take the blacksmith as a type. If the poets were true, there is no man so hearty, so merry, as the blacksmith; he rises early and strikes his sparks before the sun; he eats and drinks and sleeps as no other man. Working in moderation, he is, in fact, in one of the best of human positions, physically speaking. But we follow him into the city or town, and we see the stress of work on that strong man, and what then is his position in the death-rate of his country. In Marylebone, blacksmiths die at the rate of 31 per thousand per annum, or 11 above the mean of the male adults of the country in its entirety. The occupation, instinctive almost as a portion of human art, unobjectionable as a branch of human industry, is made by mere excess of work, the destroyer of the man. He can strike so many blows per day, walk so many steps, breathe so many breaths, produce so much work, and live an average, say of fifty years; he is made to strike so many more blows, to walk so many more steps, to breathe so many more breaths per day, and to increase altogether a fourth of his life. He meets the effort; the result is, that producing for a limited time a fourth more work, he dies at 37 for 50."

(From *Capital,* Vol. I, Chap. X, Sect. 3, translated from 3rd German edition by Samuel Moore and Edward Aveling, edited by Frederick Engels, 1887. Republished by Allen and Unwin, 1957.)

On the Alienation of Man
(from *Economic and Philosophical Manuscripts*)

We shall begin from a *contemporary* economic fact. The worker becomes poorer the more wealth he produces and the more his production increases in power and extent. The worker becomes an ever cheaper commodity the more goods he creates. The *devaluation* of the human world increases in direct relation with the *increase in value* of the world of things. Labour does not only create goods; it also produces itself and the worker as a *commodity,* and indeed in the same proportion as it produces goods.

This fact simply implies that the object produced by labour, its product, now stands opposed to it as an *alien being,* as a *power independent* of the producer. The product of labour which has been embodied in an object and turned into a physical thing; this product is an *objectification* of labour. The performance of work is at the same time its objectification. The performance of work appears in the sphere of political economy as a *vitiation* of the worker, objectification as a *loss* and as *servitude to the object,* and appropriation as *alienation*.

So much does the performance of work appear as vitiation that the worker is vitiated to the point of starvation. So much does objectification appear as loss of the object that the worker is deprived of the most essential things not only of life but also of work. Labour itself becomes an object which he can acquire only by the greatest effort and with unpredictable interruptions. So much does the appropriation of the object appear as alienation that the more objects the worker produces the fewer he can possess and the more he falls under the domination of his product, of capital.

All these consequences follow from the fact that the worker is related to the *product of his labour* as to an *alien* object. For it is clear on this presupposition that the more the worker expends himself in work the more powerful becomes the world of objects which he creates in face of himself, the poorer he becomes in his inner life, and the less he belongs to himself. It is just the same as in religion. The more of himself man attributes to God the less he has left in himself. The worker puts his life into the object, and his life then belongs no longer to himself but to the object. The greater his activity, therefore, the less he possesses. What is embodied in the product of his labour is no longer his own. The greater this product is, therefore, the more he is diminished. The *alienation* of the worker in his product means not only that his labour becomes an object, assumes an *external* existence, but that it exists independently, *outside himself,* and alien to him, and that it stands opposed to him as an autonomous power. The life which he has given to the object sets itself against him as an alien and hostile force. . . .

Let us now examine more closely the phenomenon of *objectification;* the worker's production and the *alienation* and *loss* of the object it produces, which is involved in it. The worker can create nothing without *nature,* without the *sensuous external world.* The latter is the material in which his labour is realized, in which it is active, out of which and through which it produces things.

But just as nature affords the *means of existence* of labour, in the sense that labour cannot *live* without objects upon which it can be exercised, so also it provides the *means of existence* in a narrower sense; namely the means of physical existence for the *worker* himself. Thus, the more the worker *appropriates* the external world of sensuous nature by his labour the more he deprives himself of *means of existence,* in two respects: first, that the sensuous external world becomes progressively less an object belonging to his labour or a means of existence of his labour, and secondly, that it becomes progressively less a means of existence in the direct sense, a means for the physical subsistence of the worker.

In both respects, therefore, the worker becomes a slave of the object; first, in that he receives an *object of work,* i.e. receives *work,* and secondly, in that he receives *means of subsistence.* Thus the object enables him to exist, first as a *worker* and secondly, as a *physical subject.* The culmination of this enslavement is that he can only maintain himself as a *physical subject* so far as he is a *worker,* and that it is only as a *physical subject* that he is a worker.

(The alienation of the worker in his object is expressed as follows in the laws of political economy: the more the worker produces the less he has to consume; the more value he creates the more worthless he becomes; the more refined his product the more crude and misshapen the worker; the more civilized the product the more barbarous the worker; the more powerful the work the more feeble the worker; the more the work manifests intelligence the more the worker declines in intelligence and becomes a slave of nature.)

Political economy conceals the alienation in the nature of labour in so far as it does not examine the direct relationship between the worker (work) and production. Labour certainly produces marvels for the rich but it produces privation for the worker. It produces palaces, but hovels for the worker. It produces beauty, but deformity for the worker. It replaces labour by machinery, but it casts some of the workers back into a barbarous kind of work and turns the others into machines. It produces intelligence, but also stupidity and cretinism for the workers.

The direct relationship of labour to its products is the relationship of the worker to the objects of his production. The relationship of property owners to the objects of production and to production itself is merely a *consequence* of this first relationship and confirms it. We shall consider this second aspect later.

Thus, when we ask what is the important relationship of labour, we are concerned with the relationship of the *worker* to production.

So far we have considered the alienation of the worker only from one aspect; namely, *his relationship with the products of his labour.* However, alienation appears not merely in the result but also in the *process of production,* within *productive activity* itself. How could the worker stand in an alien relationship to the product of his activity if he did not alienate himself in the act of production itself? The product is indeed only the résumé of activity, of production. Consequently, if the product of labour is alienation, production itself must be active alienation—the alienation of activity and the activity of alienation. The alienation of the object of labour merely summarizes the alienation in the work activity itself.

What constitutes the alienation of labour? First, that the work is *external* to the worker, that it is not part of his nature; and that, consequently, he does not fulfil himself in his work but denies himself, has a feeling of misery rather than well-being, does not develop freely his mental and physical energies but is physically exhausted and mentally debased. The worker, therefore, feels himself at home only during his leisure time, whereas at work he feels homeless. His work is not voluntary but imposed, *forced labour.* It is not the satisfaction of a need, but only a *means* for satisfying other needs. Its alien character is clearly shown by the fact that as soon as there is no physical or other compulsion it is avoided like the plague. External labour, labour in which man alienates himself, is a labour of self-sacrifice, of mortification. Finally, the external character of work for the worker is shown by the fact that it is not his own work but work for someone else, that in work he does not belong to himself but to another person.

Just as in religion the spontaneous activity of human fantasy, of the human brain and heart, reacts independently as an alien activity of gods or devils upon the individual, so the activity of the worker is not his own spontaneous activity. It is another's activity and a loss of his own spontaneity.

We arrive at the result that man (the worker) feels himself to be freely active only in his animal functions—eating, drinking and procreating, or at most also in his dwelling and in personal adornment—while in his human functions he is reduced to an animal. The animal becomes human and the human becomes animal.

Eating, drinking and procreating are of course also genuine human functions. But abstractly considered, apart from the environment of human activities, and turned into final and sole ends, they are animal functions.

We have now considered the act of alienation of practical human activity, labour, from two aspects: (1) the relationship of the worker to the *product of labour* as an alien object which dominates him. This relationship is at the same time the relationship to the sensuous external world, to natural objects, as an alien and hostile world; (2) the relationship of labour to the *act of production* within *labour.* This is the relationship of the worker to his own activity as something alien and not belonging to him, activity as suffering (passivity), strength as powerlessness, creation as emasculation, the *personal* physical and mental energy of the worker, his personal life (for what is life but activity?), as an activity which is directed against himself, independent of him and not belonging to him. This is *self-alienation* as against the above-mentioned alienation of the *thing.* . . . We have now to infer a third characteristic of *alienated labour* from the two we have considered.

Man is a species-being not only in the sense that he makes the community (his own as well as those of other things) his object both practically and theoretically, but also (and this is simply another expression for the same thing) in the sense that he treats himself as the present, living species, as a *universal* and consequently free being.

Species-life, for man as for animals, has its physical basis in the fact that man (like animals) lives from inorganic nature, and since man is more universal than an animal so the range of inorganic nature from which he lives is more universal. Plants, animals, minerals, air, light, etc. constitute, from the theoretical aspect, a part of human consciousness as objects of natural science and art; they are man's spiritual inorganic nature, his intellectual means of life, which he must first prepare for enjoyment and perpetuation. So also, from the practical aspect, they form a part of human life and activity. In practice man lives only from these natural products, whether in the form of food, heating, clothing, housing, etc. The universality of man appears in practice in the universality which makes the whole of nature into his inorganic body: (1) as a direct means of life; and equally (2) as the material object and instrument of his life activity. Nature is the inorganic body of man; that is to say nature, excluding the human body itself. To say that man *lives* from nature means that nature is his *body* with which he must remain in a continuous interchange in order not to die. The statement that the physical and mental life of man, and nature, are interdependent means simply that nature is interdependent with itself, for man is a part of nature.

Since alienated labour: (1) alienates nature from man; and (2) alienates man from himself, from his own active function, his life activity; so it alienates him from the species. It makes *species-life* into a means of individual life. In the first place it alienates species-life and individual life, and secondly, it turns the latter, as an abstraction, into the purpose of the former, also in its abstract and alienated form.

For labour, *life activity, productive life,* now appear to man only as *means* for the satisfaction of a need, the need to maintain his physical existence. Productive life is, however, species-life. It is life creating life. In the type of life activity resides the whole character of a species, its species-character; and free, conscious activity is the species-character of human beings. Life itself appears only as a *means of life.*

The animal is one with its life activity. It does not distinguish the activity from itself. It is *its activity.* But man makes his life activity itself an object of his will and consciousness. He has a conscious life activity. It is not a determination with which he is completely identified. Conscious life activity distinguishes man from the life activity of animals. Only for this reason is he a species-being. Or rather, he is only a species-being, i.e. his own life is an object for him, because he is a species-being. Only for this reason is his activity free activity. Alienated labour reverses the relationship, in that man because he is a self-conscious being makes his life activity, his *being,* only a means for his *existence.* . . .

We began with an economic fact, the alienation of the worker and his production. We have expressed this fact in conceptual terms as *alienated labour,* and in analysing the concept we have merely analysed an economic fact.

Let us now examine further how this concept of alienated labour must express and reveal itself in reality. If the product of labour is alien to me and confronts me as an alien power, to whom does it belong? If my own activity does not belong to me but is an alien, forced activity, to whom does it belong? To a being *other* than myself. And who is this being? The *gods?* It is apparent in the earliest stages of advanced production, e.g. temple building, etc. in Egypt, India, Mexico, and in the service rendered to gods, that the product belonged to the gods. But the gods alone were never the lords of labour. And no more was *nature.* What a contradiction it would be if the more man subjugates nature by his labour, and the more the marvels of the gods are rendered superfluous by the marvels of industry, the more he should abstain from his joy in producing and his enjoyment of the product for love of these powers.

The *alien* being to whom labour and the product of labour belong, to whose service labour is devoted, and to whose enjoyment the product of labour goes, can only be man himself. If the product of labour does not belong to the worker, but confronts him as an alien power, this can only be because it belongs to *a man other than the worker.* If his activity is a torment to him it must be a source of *enjoyment* and pleasure to another. Not the gods, nor nature, but only man himself can be this alien power over men.

Consider the earlier statement that the relation of man to himself is first *realized, objectified,* through his relation to other men. If he is related to the product of his labour, his objectified labour, as to an alien, hostile, powerful and independent object, he is related in such a way that another *alien,* hostile, powerful and independent man is the lord of this object. If he is related to his own activity as to unfree activity, then he is related to it as activity in the service, and under the domination, coercion and yoke, of another man.

Every self-alienation of man, from himself and from nature, appears in the relation which he postulates between other men and himself and nature. Thus religious self-alienation is necessarily exemplified in the relation between laity and priest, or, since it is here a question of the spiritual world, between the laity and a mediator. In the real world of practice this self-alienation can only be expressed in the real, practical relation of man to his fellow man. The medium through which alienation occurs is itself a *practical* one. Through alienated labour, therefore, man not only produces his relation to the object and to the process of production as to alien and hostile men; he also produces the relation of other men to his production and his product, and the relation between himself and other men. Just as he creates his own production as a vitiation, a punishment, and his own product as a loss, as a product which does not belong to him, so he creates the domination of the nonproducer over production and its product. As he alienates his own activity, so he bestows upon the stranger an activity which is not his own.

REVIEW QUESTIONS

1. Show how Marx's philosophy begins with the experience of the laboring man.
2. How does a philosophy centering on one class of mankind enlarge one's conception of humanity as a whole?
3. How is Marx's philosophy a foray against alienation?
4. Explain the phrase "dialectical materialism" and show how it differs from the "dialectic idealism" of Hegel.
5. Marx is dead set against religion. Why?
6. How is man, in our time, to recover his true meaning, according to Marx?

SUGGESTIONS FOR FURTHER READING

Berlin, I. *Karl Marx, His Life and Environment.* New York, Oxford University Press, 1978.

Mazlish, B. *The Meaning of Karl Marx.* New York, Oxford University Press, 1987.

Simon, L., ed. *Selected Writings of Karl Marx.* Indianapolis, Hackett, 1994.

24

Henri Bergson (1859–1941)

Science and Philosophy

At any given time, several traditions in the history of ideas exist side by side, and alongside the history of philosophy is that of science, a realm of fresh discovery that has expanded since the time of the Renaissance. The revolutionary view of the heavenly bodies created by Copernicus, Galileo, and Newton created not only a new understanding of the cosmos but also a new understanding of man. A new physics led to a new metaphysics because it moved to ever-broadening horizons in terms of which man's universe must be grasped. The advancing front of science disclosed another dimension—not in the direction of the infinite but in the direction of the infinitesimal; just as astronomy was taking man to measureless heights, chemistry, following the insights of Lavoisier, Priestly, and Dalton, was taking him to measureless depths, proclaiming that the irreducibility of matter was only apparent, not real. In actuality, matter too was an endless world of atoms, subatoms, and a dazzling array of interlocking energies just as exciting as the planets and stars. Add to this the increasing acceptance of evolution, as a result of Darwin's studies, and we have a picture of man as microcosm unimagined by the ancients.

As we have seen, the success of any discipline is its own burden, for it bears within itself the inevitable tendency to overreach and extend its method to other areas. Thus, it is to be expected that science would be offered by its enthusiasts as the ultimate arbiter of what man is really like and, postulating the machine as model, that man is to be understood in terms of scientific principles only. Henri Bergson's philosophy of human freedom at the turn of the century was a magnificent protest against such a view, though he stoutly maintained that truth required a friendly holding of hands between science and philosophy.

Bergson was born in Paris in 1859, of Jewish descent, the son of a Polish father and an English mother. As a young student he distinguished himself in mathematics and later, at the École Normale Supérieure, became a passionate reader in science and philosophy. At age twenty-two he began his teaching career at Angers and continued at other places until 1900, during which time he enjoyed a growing reputation, especially with the publication of his doctoral dissertation on the immediate data of consciousness. In 1900 he was invited to take the chair of modern philosophy at the Collège de France in Paris, where his prestige as a lecturer was steadily enhanced and filled the hall with avid students—a cross-section of men and women, even from the fashionable world, all eager to hear him defend the claims of human freedom and spirituality against scientific determinism. In the same year he published *Laughter,* on the role of the comic in human life. The best insight into his method is found in *An Introduction to Metaphysics,* published in 1903. On the strength of *Creative Evolution,* published in 1907, Bergson was recognized the world over not only as an outstanding philosopher, but as by far the most engaging stylist writing in any language; William James was prompted to call his book "a pure classic in point of form." At the peak of his reputation, Bergson's ill health forced him to retreat from teaching and finally to resign from academic life in 1921, and practically from public life, with the exception of his service as president of the League of Nations committee for intellectual cooperation for several years. In 1928 he won the Nobel Prize for literature. Just when it seemed that his writing years were over, Bergson astonished the intellectual world in 1932 with the publication of *The Two Sources of Morality and Religion,* in which he developed the concepts of open morality and dynamic religion as opposed to closed morality and static religion. Bergson's wondering years were wracked not only with pain but also with sorrow at the occupation of France early in World War II and the anti-Jewish measures of the regime. To declare his solidarity with the Jewish people, he refused to let his fame exempt him from the repressive laws against them, and for the same reason he postponed making public his wish to espouse Christianity until he knew he was dying in 1941.

Reality as a Whole

Bergson belongs to that group of philosophers who see reality as a whole, though not with the determinate wholeness of mathematics or science. Quite the contrary, Bergson's vision of wholeness comes from a living, undetermined reality whose universal impulse is to create human beings who are free to reach their full humanity by entering, beyond all rationality, into a mystical union with the ultimate. However, the mind in its relationship with reality begins its work almost with the reverse effect. When we say we know a thing, we abstract it or cut it out of its setting, thereby separating it from the whole in which it is presented. We call this thing a table, a chair, a dog, and in doing so sort out this parcel of sensible qualities from all others and give it a name. The sense of continuity, of oneness with all else, is not immediately seized and is, at least for the present, relegated to the sidelines. The same is true of the sciences, which, by analysis, pursue objects as though they were detached from a larger whole. Biology, for example, is concerned with organs, cells, tissues, and such like without once considering what life itself is in the whole living organism, thereby losing the sense of continuity.

Accordingly, Bergson makes a distinction between *intelligence* and *intuition.* Intelligence, which functions as analysis, separates or detaches the object from its setting; analysis "goes around" the object. Intuition, on the other hand, is the power of the mind to grasp a thing in its wholeness, to see it in its relatedness, and therefore to seize its meaning; it "gets inside" the object. Intelligence creates isolated parcels; it does not consider movement as a continuity, but measures it as "successive location"; intelligence is the faculty of "man as maker," *homo faber.* Intuition, in its vision of wholeness, is not satisfied with the piecemeal and seeks to lay hold of the unity and continuity in the stream of existence; intuition is the faculty of "man as wise," *homo sapiens.*

Duration and Creative Evolution

This notion of continuous existence, called *duration,* is the most important single notion in Bergson, for it involves the mysterious fact that things endure through time; they do not exist from moment to moment, as though moments are discrete measures of existence; no, their duration means their existence, not parceled out, but as one with the stream of becoming in which they are immersed. This is especially true of man, whose awareness of duration gives him the awareness of himself as a *self,* and as the ultimate goal of the larger duration of all living things under the grand movement of *creative evolution.*

The concept of creative evolution was born of Bergson's intensive studies in biology and of his firm belief that life is not subject to mechanical laws determining events beforehand, or to teleology in the sense of an already established evolutionary plan. If what we see around us is a great unfolding of life, such unfolding is possible because there is at the foundation of living things a throbbing surge to life that Bergson calls the *life impulse,* the *élan vital.* Reality, as recognized from ancient days on, is constantly becoming, and for Bergson there is more in becoming than there is in being. The *élan vital,* in this stream of reality, can move upward or downward, ascend or descend; as it ascends it creates more living, more consciousness, more freedom; as it descends, by becoming more and more tied to matter, life diminishes, exhausts itself. It is as though the *élan vital,* given in such profusion, is creatively experimenting, trying to discover how much less of an obstacle matter might become as it gropes for higher expressions of life. In the course of its evolution, as the *élan vital* fractioned off into the animal and plant worlds, it discovered a higher level of life in the former, and as it further probed its way through animal life, it pushed on to two yet higher levels, insect and human life, differentiated by the former's high development of instinct, particularly with regard to the use of certain of its organs as tools, and the latter's development of its own tools, characteristic of *homo faber.*

Morality and Sanctity

But man, now possessed not only of intellect but also of intuition, is the highest stage of life on our planet and lies open to further evolution *as a human being* on the basis of his own humanity, that is, of his consciousness and freedom. To "lie open" is the all-important factor. Man's moral life can be a closed affair, a *closed morality,* meaning an unfree social conformism, acting under pressure or stereotyped obligation; or an *open morality,* which stands for what is truly human and personal, and for the sensitivity with which a person becomes attuned to the boundaryless possibilities of his humanity, following the many examples given by moral heroes and saints. Religion, the second great arena of man's life, is the practical stance man takes toward the higher powers, or, in Bergson's words, "that element which, in beings endowed with reason, is called upon to make good any deficiency of attachment to life." Religion is *static* insofar as it is a defense against nature and its necessity, but it is *dynamic* when looked upon as springing forth from the depths of the life impulse in its struggle toward an unseen though strongly felt goal, exemplified in mysticism, whose ultimate end is "the establishment of a contact, consequently of a partial coincidence, with the creative efforts which life itself manifests. This effort is of God, if it is not God himself."

For Bergson, then, the living universe has brought about the phenomenon of man, who is phenomenon precisely because he expresses what is highest in the universe, because he is the culmination of the *élan vital*'s struggle to ascend from necessity to freedom. With increasing freedom comes increasing joy, "diffused throughout the world by an ever-spreading mystic intuition," and, yes, even by the "furtherance of scientific experiment." But freedom carries with it a charge and a hope: "Mankind lies groaning, half crushed beneath the weight of its own progress. Men do not sufficiently realize that their future is in their own hands. Theirs is the task of determining first of all whether they want to go on living or not. Theirs the responsibility, then, for deciding if they want merely to live, or intend to make just the extra effort required for fulfilling, even on their refractory planet, the essential function of the universe, which is a machine for the making of gods."

William James, quoted earlier in this section, had a very high opinion of Bergson's works, but the publication of *Two Sources* occurred long after James died. However, upon the publication of *Creative Evolution,* he wrote to Bergson, "And if your next book proves to be as great an advance on this one as this is on its two predecessors, your name will surely go down as one of the great creative names in philosophy." The future turned out to be true to his prophecy. Bergson's popularity today is hardly what it was when James wrote those words, but his works remain a permanent testimony to the legitimacy of metaphysics, a metaphysics, in his case, rooted in experience and expanded by the insight afforded him by science and mysticism; it enabled him to produce a philosophy in which we can seek the meaning of the universe, not among the dead, but among the living.

Readings

From Creative Evolution

1. CREATIVE EVOLUTION

The history of the evolution of life, incomplete as it yet is, already reveals to us how the intellect has been formed, by an uninterrupted progress, along a line which ascends through the vertebrate series up to man. It shows us in the faculty of understanding an appendage of the faculty of acting, a more and more precise, more and more complex and supple adaptation of the consciousness of living beings to the conditions of existence that are made for them. Hence should result this consequence that our intellect, in the narrow sense of the word, is intended to secure the perfect fitting of our body to its environment, to represent the relations of external things among themselves—in short, to think matter. Such will indeed be one of the conclusions of the present essay. We shall see that the human intellect feels at home among inanimate objects, more especially among solids, where our action finds its fulcrum and our industry its tools; that our concepts have been formed on the model of solids; that our logic is, pre-eminently, the logic of solids; that, consequently, our intellect triumphs in geometry, wherein is revealed the kinship of logical thought with unorganized matter, and where the intellect has only to follow its natural movement, after the lightest possible contact with experience, in order to go from discovery to discovery, sure that experience is following behind it and will justify it invariably.

But from this it must also follow that our thought, in its purely logical form, is incapable of presenting the true nature of life, the full meaning of the evolutionary movement. Created by life, in definite circumstances, to act on definite things, how can it embrace life, of which it is only an emanation or an aspect? . . .

In fact, we do indeed feel that not one of the categories of our thought—unity, multiplicity, mechanical causality, intelligent finality, etc.—applies exactly to the things of life: who can say where individuality begins and ends, whether the living being is one or many, whether it is the cells which associate themselves into the organism or the organism which dissociates itself into cells? In vain we force the living into this or that one of our moulds. All the moulds crack. They are too narrow, above all too rigid, for what we try to put into them. Our reasoning, so sure of itself among things inert, feels ill at ease on this new ground. It would be difficult to cite a biological discovery due to pure reasoning. And most often, when experience has finally shown us how life goes to work to obtain a certain result, we find its way of working is just that of which we should never have thought.

Yet evolutionist philosophy does not hesitate to extend to the things of life the same methods of explanation which have succeeded in the case of unorganized matter. It begins by showing us in the intellect a local effect of evolution, a flame, perhaps accidental, which lights up the coming and going of living beings in the narrow passage open to their action; and lo! forgetting what it has just told us, it makes of this lantern glimmering in a tunnel a Sun which can illuminate the world. Boldly it proceeds, with the powers of conceptual thought alone, to the ideal reconstruction of all things, even of life. . . .

Must we then give up fathoming the depths of life? Must we keep to that mechanistic idea of it which the understanding will always give us—an idea necessarily artificial and symbolical, since it makes the total activity of life shrink to the form of a certain human activity which is only a partial and local manifestation of life, a result or by-product of the vital process? We should have to do so, indeed, if life had employed all the psychical potentialities it possesses in producing pure understandings—that is to say, in making geometricians. But the line of evolution that ends in man is not the only one. On other paths, divergent from it, other forms of consciousness have been developed, which have not been able to free themselves from external constraints or to regain control over themselves, as the human intellect has done, but which, none the less, also express something that is immanent and essential in the evolutionary movement. Suppose these other forms of consciousness brought together and amalgamated with intellect: would not the result be a consciousness as wide as life? And such a consciousness, turning around suddenly against the push of life which it feels behind, would have a vision of life complete—would it not?—even though the vision were fleeting.

It will be said that, even so, we do not transcend our intellect, for it is still with our intellect, and through our intellect, that we see the other forms of consciousness. And this would be right if we were pure intellects, if there did not remain, around our conceptual and logical thought, a vague nebulosity, made of the very substance out of which has been formed the luminous nucleus that we call the intellect. Therein reside certain powers that are complementary to the understanding, powers of which we have only an indistinct feeling when we remain shut up in ourselves, but which will become clear and distinct when they perceive themselves at work, so to speak, in the evolution of nature. They will thus learn what sort of effort they must make to be intensified and expanded in the very direction of life.

This amounts to saying that *theory of knowledge* and *theory of life* seem to us inseparable. A theory of life that is not accompanied by a criticism of knowledge is obliged to accept, as they stand, the concepts which the understanding puts at its disposal: it can but enclose the facts, willing or not, in preexisting frames which it regards as ultimate. It thus obtains a symbolism which is convenient, perhaps even necessary to positive science, but not a direct vision of its object. On the other hand, a theory of knowledge which does not replace the intellect in the general evolution of life will teach us neither how the frames of knowledge have been constructed nor how we can enlarge or go beyond them. It is necessary that these two inquiries, theory of knowledge and theory of life, should join each other, and, by a circular process, push each other on unceasingly.

Together, they may solve by a method more sure, brought nearer to experience, the great problems that philosophy poses. For, if they should succeed in their common enterprise, they would show us the formation of the intellect, and thereby the genesis of that matter of which our intellect traces the general configuration. They would dig to the very root of nature and of mind. They would substitute for the false evolutionism of Spencer—which consists in cutting up present reality, already evolved, into little bits no less evolved, and then recomposing it with these fragments, thus positing in advance everything that is to be explained—a true evolutionism, in which reality would be followed in its generation and its growth.

But a philosophy of this kind will not be made in a day. Unlike the philosophical systems properly so called, each of which was the individual work of a man of genius and sprang up as a whole, to be taken or left, it will only be built up by the collective and progressive effort of many thinkers, of many observers also, completing, correcting and improving one another. So the present essay does not aim at resolving at once the greatest problems. It simply desires to define the method and to permit a glimpse, on some essential points, of the possibility of its application.

2. DURATION

The existence of which we are most assured and which we know best is unquestionably our own, for of every object we have notions which may be considered external and superficial, whereas, of ourselves, our perception is internal and profound. What, then, do we find? In this privileged case, what is the precise meaning of the word "exist"? Let us recall here briefly the conclusions of an earlier work.

I find, first of all, that I pass from state to state. I am warm or cold, I am merry or sad, I work or I do nothing, I look at what is around me or I think of something else. Sensations, feelings, volitions, ideas—such are the changes into which my existence is divided and which colour it in turns. I change, then, without ceasing. But this is not saying enough. Change is far more radical than we are at first inclined to suppose.

For I speak of each of my states as if it formed a block and were a separate whole. I say indeed that I change, but the change seems to me to reside in the passage from one state to the next: of each state, taken separately, I am apt to think that it remains the same during all the time that it prevails. Nevertheless, a slight effort of attention would reveal to me that there is no feeling, no idea, no volition which is not undergoing change every moment: if a mental state ceased to vary, its duration would cease to flow. Let us take the most stable of internal states, the visual perception of a motionless external object. The object may remain the same, I may look at it from the same side, at the same angle, in the same light; nevertheless the vision I now have of it differs from that which I have just had, even if only because the one is an instant older than the other. . . . The truth is that we change without ceasing, and that the state itself is nothing but change.

This amounts to saying that there is no essential difference between passing from one state to another and persisting in the same state. If the state which "remains the same" is more varied than we think, on the other hand the passing from one state to another resembles, more than we imagine, a single state being prolonged; the transition is continuous. But, just because we close our eyes to the unceasing variation of every psychical state, we are obliged, when the change has become so considerable as to force itself on our attention, to speak as if a new state were placed alongside the previous one. Of this new state we assume that it remains unvarying in its turn, and so on endlessly. The apparent discontinuity of the psychical life is then due to our attention being fixed on it by a series of separate acts: actually there is only a gentle slope; but in following the broken line of our acts of attention, we think we perceive separate steps. . . . Now, states thus defined cannot be regarded as distinct elements. They continue each other in an endless flow.

But, as our attention has distinguished and separated them artificially, it is obliged next to reunite them by an artificial bond. It imagines, therefore, a formless *ego,* indifferent and unchangeable, on which it threads the psychic states which it has set up as independent entities. . . . If our existence were composed of separate states with an impassive ego to unite them, for us there would be no duration. For an ego which does not change does not *endure,* and a psychic state which remains the same so long as it is not replaced by the following state does not *endure* either. Vain, therefore, is the attempt to range such states beside each other on the ego supposed to sustain them: never can these solids strung upon a solid make up that duration which flows. What we actually obtain in this way is an artificial imitation of the internal life, a static equivalent which will lend itself better to the requirements of logic and language, just because we have eliminated from it the element of real time. But, as regards the psychical life unfolding beneath the symbols which conceal it, we readily perceive that time is just the stuff it is made of.

3. CONTINUITY OF LIFE

But then, we must no longer speak of *life in general* as an abstraction, or as a mere heading under which all living beings are inscribed. At a certain moment, in certain points of space, a visible current has taken rise; this current of life, traversing the bodies it has organized one after another, passing from generation to generation, has become divided amongst species and distributed amongst individuals without losing anything of its force, rather intensifying in proportion to its advance. . . .

Regarded from this point of view, *life is like a current passing from germ to germ through the medium of a developed organism.* It is as if the organism itself were only an excrescence, a bud caused to sprout by the former germ endeavouring to continue itself in a new germ. The essential thing is the *continuous progress* indefinitely pursued, an invisible progress, on which each visible organism rides during the short interval of time given it to live.

Now, the more we fix our attention on this continuity of life, the more we see that organic evolution resembles the evolution of a consciousness, in which the past presses against the present and causes the upspringing of a new form of consciousness, incommensurable with its antecedents. . . . Of the future, only that is foreseen which is like the past or can be made up again with elements like those of the past. Such is the case with astronomical, physical and chemical facts, with all facts which form part of a system in which elements supposed to be unchanging are merely put together, in which the only changes are changes of position, in which there is no theoretical absurdity in imagining that things are restored to their place; in which, consequently, the same total phenomenon, or at least the same elementary phenomena, can be repeated. But an original situation, which imparts something of its own originality to its elements, that is to say, to the partial views that are taken of it, how can such a situation be pictured as given before it is actually produced? All that can be said is that, once produced, it will be explained by the elements that analysis will then carve out of it. . . . In this sense it might be said of life, as of consciousness, that at every moment it is creating something.

4. DIVERGENT TENDENCIES

The evolution movement would be a simple one, and we should soon have been able to determine its direction, if life had described a single course, like that of a solid ball shot from a cannon. But it proceeds rather like a shell, which suddenly bursts into fragments, which fragments, being themselves shells, burst in their turn into fragments destined to burst again, and so on for a time incommensurably long. We perceive only what is nearest to us, namely, the scattered movements of the pulverized explosions. From them we have to go back, stage by stage, to the original movement.

When a shell bursts, the particular way it breaks is explained both by the explosive force of the powder it contains and by the resistance of the metal. So of the way life breaks into individuals and species. It depends, we think, on two series of causes: the resistance life meets from inert matter, and the explosive force—due to an unstable balance of tendencies—which life bears within itself.

The resistance of inert matter was the obstacle that had first to be overcome. Life seems to have succeeded in this by dint of humility, by making itself very small and very insinuating, bending to physical chemical forces, consenting even to go a part of the way with them, like the switch that adopts for a while the direction of the rail it is endeavouring to leave. Of phenomena in the simplest forms of life, it is hard to say whether they are still physical and chemical or whether they are already vital. Life had to enter thus into the habits of inert matter, in order to draw it little by little, magnetized, as it were, to another track. The animate forms that first appeared were therefore of extreme simplicity. They were probably tiny masses of scarcely differentiated protoplasm, outwardly resembling the amoeba observable to-day, but possessed of the tremendous internal push that was to raise them even to the highest forms of life. That in virtue of this push the first organisms sought to grow as much as possible, seems likely. But organized matter has a limit of expansion that is very quickly reached; beyond a certain point it divides instead of growing. Ages of effort and prodigies of subtlety were probably necessary for life to get past this new obstacle. It succeeded in inducing an increasing number of elements, ready to divide, to remain united. By the division of labour it knotted between them an indissoluble bond. The complex and quasi-discontinuous organism is thus made to function as would a continuous living mass which had simply grown bigger.

But the real and profound causes of division were those which life bore within its bosom. For life is tendency, and the essence of a tendency is to develop in the form of a sheaf, creating, by its very growth, divergent directions among which its impetus is divided. . . .

So our study of the evolution movement will have to unravel a certain number of divergent directions, and to appreciate the importance of what has happened along each of them—in a word, to determine the nature of the dissociated tendencies and estimate their relative proportion. Combining these tendencies, then, we shall get an approximation, or rather an imitation, of the indivisible motor principle whence their impetus proceeds. Evolution will thus prove to be something entirely different from a series of adaptations to circumstances, as mechanism claims; entirely different also from the realization of a plan of the wholes, as maintained by the doctrine of finality.

5. ANIMAL AND HUMAN CONSCIOUSNESS

Radical therefore, also, is the difference between animal consciousness, even the most intelligent, and human consciousness. For consciousness corresponds exactly to the living being's power of choice; it is co-extensive with the fringe of possible action that surrounds the real action: consciousness is synonymous with invention and with freedom. Now, in the animal, invention is never anything but a variation on the theme of routine. Shut up in the habits of the species, it succeeds, no doubt, in enlarging them by its individual initiative; but it escapes automatism only for an instant, for just the time to create a new automatism. The gates of its prison close as soon as they are opened; by pulling at its chain it succeeds only in stretching it. With man, consciousness breaks the chain. In man, and man alone, it sets itself free. The whole history of life until man has been that of the effort of consciousness to raise matter, and of the more or less complete overwhelming of consciousness by the matter which has fallen back on it. The enterprise was paradoxical, if, indeed, we may speak here otherwise than by metaphor of enterprise and of effort. It was to create with matter, which is necessity itself, an instrument of freedom, to make a machine which should triumph over mechanism, and to use the determinism of nature to pass through the meshes of the net which this very determinism had spread. But, everywhere except in man, consciousness has let itself be caught in the net whose meshes it tried to pass through: it has remained the captive of the mechanisms it has set up. . . . But our brain, our society, and our language are only the external and various signs of one and the same internal superiority. They tell, each after its manner, the unique, exceptional success which life has won at a given moment of its evolution. They express the difference of kind, and not only of degree, which separates man from the rest of the animal world. They let us guess that, while at the end of the vast spring-board from which life has taken its leap, all the others have stepped down, finding the cord stretched too high, man alone has cleared the obstacle.

6. PHILOSOPHY AND THE LIFE OF THE SPIRIT

Philosophy introduces us thus into the spiritual life. And it shows us at the same time the relation of the life of the spirit to that of the body. The great error of the doctrines on the spirit has been the idea that by isolating the spiritual life from all the rest, by suspending it in space as high as possible above the earth, they were placing it beyond attack, as if they were not thereby simply exposing it to be taken as an effect of mirage! Certainly they are right to listen to conscience when conscience affirms human freedom; but the intellect is there, which says that the cause determines its effect, that like conditions like, that all is repeated and that all is given. They are right to believe in the absolute reality of the person and in his independence toward matter; but science is there, which shows the interdependence of conscious life and cerebral activity. They are right to attribute to man a privileged place in nature, to hold that the distance is infinite between the animal and man; but the history of life is there, which makes us witness the genesis of species by gradual transformation, and seems thus to reintegrate man in animality. When a strong instinct assures the probability of personal survival, they are right not to close their ears to its voice; but if there exist "souls" capable of an independent life, whence do they come? When, how and why do they enter into this body which we see arise, quite naturally, from a mixed cell derived from the bodies of its two parents? All these questions will remain unanswered, a philosophy of intuition will be a negation of science, will be sooner or later swept away by science, if it does not resolve to see the life of the body just where it really is, on the road that leads to the life of the spirit. . . .

Thus, to the eyes of a philosophy that attempts to reabsorb intellect in intuition, many difficulties vanish or become light. But such a doctrine does not only facilitate speculation; it gives us also more power to act and to live. For, with it, we feel ourselves no longer isolated in humanity, humanity no longer seems isolated in the nature that it dominates. As the smallest grain of dust is bound up with our entire solar system, drawn along with it in that undivided movement of descent which is materiality itself, so all organized beings, from the humblest to the highest, from the first origins of life to the time in which we are, and in all places as in all times, do but evidence a single impulsion, the inverse of the movement of matter and in itself indivisible. All the living hold together, and all yield to the same tremendous push. The animal takes its stand on the plant, man bestrides animality, and the whole of humanity, in space and time, is one immense army galloping beside and before and behind each of us in an overwhelming charge able to beat down every resistance and clear the most formidable obstacles, perhaps even death.

(From *Creative Evolution* by Henri Bergson. Trans. by Arthur Mitchell. Copyright © 1911, 1939 by Holt, Rinehart and Winston.)

Open Morality and Dynamic Religion
(from *The Two Sources of Morality and Religion*)

One of the results of our analysis has been to draw a sharp distinction, in the sphere of society, between the closed and the open. The closed society is that whose members hold together, caring nothing for the rest of humanity, on the alert for attack or defence, bound, in fact, to a perpetual readiness for battle. Such is human society fresh from the hands of nature. Man was made for this society, as the ant was made for the ant-heap. We must not overdo the analogy; we should note, however, that the hymenopterous communities are at the end of one of the two principal lines of animal evolution, just as human societies are at the end of the other, and that they are in this sense counterparts of one another. True, the first are stereotyped, whereas the others vary; the former obey instinct, the latter intelligence. But if nature, and for the very reason that she has made us intelligent, has left us to some extent with freedom of choice in our type of social organization, she has at all events ordained that we should live in society. A force of unvarying direction, which is to the soul what force of gravity is to the body, ensures the cohesion of the group by bending all individual wills to the same end. That force is moral obligation. We have shown that it may extend its scope in societies that are becoming open, but that it was made for the closed society. And we have shown also how a closed society can live, resist this or that dissolving action of intelligence, preserve and communicate to each of its members that confidence which is indispensable, only through a religion born of the myth-making function. This religion, which we have called the static, and this obligation, which is tantamount to a pressure, are the very substance of closed society.

Never shall we pass from the closed society to the open society, from the city to humanity, by any mere broadening out. The two things are not of the same essence. The open society is the society which is deemed in principle to embrace all humanity. A dream dreamt, now and again, by chosen souls, it embodies on every occasion something of itself in creations, each of which, through a more or less far-reaching transformation of man, conquers difficulties hitherto unconquerable. But after each occasion the circle that has momentarily opened closes again. Part of the new has flowed into the mould of the old; individual aspiration has become social pressure; and obligation covers the whole. . . .

This impetus is thus carried forward through the medium of certain men, each of whom thereby constitutes a species composed of a single individual. If the individual is fully conscious of this, if the fringe of intuition surrounding his intelligence is capable of expanding sufficiently to envelop its object, that is the mystic life. The dynamic religion which thus springs into being is the very opposite of the static religion born of the myth-making function, in the same way as the open society is the opposite of the closed society. But just as the new moral aspiration takes shape only by borrowing from the closed society its natural form, which is obligation, so dynamic religion is propagated only through images and symbols supplied by the myth-making function. There is no need to go back over these different points. I wanted simply to emphasize the distinction I have made between the open and the closed society. . . .

Joy indeed would be that simplicity of life diffused throughout the world by an ever-spreading mystic intuition; joy, too, that which would automatically follow a vision of the life beyond attained through the furtherance of scientific experiment. Failing so throughgoing a spiritual reform, we must be content with shifts and submit to more and more numerous and vexatious regulations, intended to provide a means of circumventing each successive obstacle that our nature sets up against our civilization. But, whether we go bail for small measures or great, a decision is imperative. Mankind lies groaning, half crushed beneath the weight of its own progress. Men do not sufficiently realize that their future is in their own hands. Theirs is the task of determining first of all whether they want to go on living or not. Theirs the responsibility, then, for deciding if they want merely to live, or intend to make just the extra effort required for fulfilling, even on their refractory planet, the essential function of the universe, which is a machine for the making of gods.

(From *The Two Sources of Morality and Religion.* Trans. by R. Ashley Audra and Cloudesley Brereton, London: Macmillan, 1935.)

Review Questions

1. Some philosophers rely heavily on the findings of science; show how this is true of Bergson.
2. Explain how Bergson's concern for totality is based on life.
3. Discuss Bergson's notion of *life impulse* together with his notion of *creative evolution.*
4. What is the meaning of intuition for Bergson?
5. If biological evolution is over, where does man go from here, according to Bergson?
6. What does Bergson mean by *open morality? dynamic religion?*

Suggestions for Further Reading

Creative Evolution. Tr. Mitchell, A. Lanham, MD, University Press of America, 1984.
Kolakowski, L. *Bergson.* New York, Oxford University Press, 1985.
Lacey, A. R. *Bergson.* New York, Routledge, Chapman and Hall, 1989.
Mullarkey, J. *Bergson and Philosophy.* Notre Dame, IN, University of Notre Dame Press, 2000.
The Two Sources of Morality and Religion. Tr. Audra, R. C. and Brereton, C. Notre Dame, University of Notre Dame Press, 1977.

25

William James
(1842–1910)

There are many affinities between the philosophies of Henri Bergson and William James: They are both firmly rooted in an empirical base, allow for the role of the nonrational in arriving at truth, and are totally centered on the value of human life. While Bergson, however, was emerging from a European matrix, James, although quite at home in the European tradition, was emerging from an American matrix: He knew the works of the early divines like Cotton Mather and Jonathan Edwards; through his father, a thinker in his own right, he came to know Ralph Waldo Emerson; he had, as colleagues or friends, Charles Sanders Peirce, Josiah Royce, and George Santayana; he respected the work of John Dewey; and, while lamenting America's huge defects, James could still write in 1882 that his recent experience made him "quieter with my home-lot and readier to believe that it is one of the chosen places of the Earth." In a sense, the study of James is the study of American philosophy in capsule form, which is borne out by the fact that the force already poised to produce pragmatism as a truly American contribution to philosophy did so in the philosopher whose name is most directly connected with it.

William James was born in 1842 in New York City into a family of four brothers and a sister. His father was a wealthy gentleman, widely traveled in Europe and a deeply religious person. His brother Henry was a famous novelist. His early schooling occurred both in America and abroad, giving him the opportunity to learn French and German fluently. He gave up the study of art to pursue science for the next eight years at Harvard University, first at the Lawrence Scientific School and then at the Medical School, interrupting his medical education in 1865 to accompany the famed Louis Agassiz in an expedition to the Amazon. Though frail in health, he continued his medical studies in Germany in 1867 and began to develop his deep interest in psychology, perhaps as a result of a long-standing internal conflict between freedom and religion on the one hand and science and mechanism on the other. At one point, he fell into a sudden depression at the "horrible fear of my own existence" and found comforting support in the writings of the French philosopher-psychologist Charles Renouvier, who reaffirmed for James the actuality of freedom and the strength of the will. In 1869 he received his medical degree from Harvard, which, after several years, appointed him as an instructor in physiology and later in psychology. He married in 1878. From the 1880s on, he taught and wrote in the fields of philosophy, religion, and ethics. He died in 1910. His chief works include *Principles of Psychology* (1891), *The Will to Believe* (1897), *Varieties of Religious Experience* (1902), *Pragmatism* (1907), *A Pluralistic Universe,* and *The Meaning of Truth* (1909), and posthumously *Essays in Radical Empiricism* (1912).

Experience: The Touchstone of Truth

We have seen several times that philosophical attitudes in human knowing reduce to two, empiricism and rationalism, and that even though pure empiricism or pure rationalism is hard to find, there is a wide range of mixtures between them, often with a tendency to lean in one direction or the other. In describing these two kinds of mental makeup, James uses vest-pocket terminology in referring to the first type as "tough-minded" and the second as "tender-minded"; the empirical mind "goes by facts," the rationalist mind "goes by principles." When James writes, "Never were as many men of a decidedly empiricist proclivity in existence as there are at the present day," he is not counting noses but expressing the temper of the time in which he lived and considering himself as an example. The touchstone of truth is experience, for only through experience can any position be verified; what is beyond experience can never enter into our consciousness and can never compel us to admit its existence. By prefixing the word *radical* to *empiricism,* James elaborates his own position as a "radical empiricist" and proclaims his brand of empiricism as going more to the root of things than even that of Hume, whose philosophy he criticized for not being radical enough. Yet, when surveyed, his empiricism seems to be more tender than Hume's, for Hume could only bring himself to see experiences as atomistic, mirroring an atomistic world where one fact had no connection with any other. For James, however, interrelation and interconnection are themselves *facts of experience,* so that the immense difficulty Hume had, for example, in managing causality is not a difficulty for James. This loosening up of empiricism, even though he calls it radical, helps James to achieve a more satisfactory posture regarding the universe than did Hume, whose hands were empty when the unifying questions were asked.

A further consideration shows that, for James, experience is the event in which mind and object hold together, so that there is no duality between them; prior to experience, there is no subject, as *knowing,* which exists independently, and no object, as *known,* which exists independently. No, they are two sides of the one experience, momentarily snatched from reality, which itself must be understood as the "immediate flux of life which furnishes the material to our later reflection with its conceptual categories." So, the distinction between knower and known, subject and object, mind and matter, consciousness and content is subsequent to experience.

Pragmatism

Empiricism, as an attitude, seeks the method best adapted to its nature and, for James, that method is *pragmatism.* Its characteristics existed long before James, even in Socrates and Aristotle, but only at the turn of the twentieth century, beginning with James and the group familiar with his work, did it "generalize itself" and "become conscious of a universal mission." Historically, though it was given its popular shape by James, pragmatism was actually introduced by Charles Peirce. It is a way of arriving at the meaning of a thought by determining the conduct or action it was "fitted to produce," a way of attaining as much clarity as possible in our ideas from the practical effects we believe them to have. Pragmatism for James represents the empiricist attitude, and "in a more radical and in a less objectionable form than it has ever yet assumed." It looks away from the fixity of things—from supposed necessities, tight categories, and stiff theories—which arrests the freely searching mind and it looks to consequences, action, fruits, facts. The pragmatist's interest is in how an idea can be converted into an empirical return, or in James's favorite expression, into "cash value." An idea has worth only insofar as it can be translated into the facts of experience; if it cannot be translated, it has no value. As a method, it can presumably be used by the scientist, the metaphysician, the ethician, or even by persons of opposite persuasion such as the theist and the atheist.

It is obvious that, if the disclosures of pragmatism are taken as true, pragmatism is more than a method; it is also a *theory of truth.* But it is a theory of truth with a difference. The popular notion of truth requires agreement between an idea and a thing, as though the idea were a copy of the thing, thus creating a static, fixed relationship between them. For the pragmatist, however, the agreement is not a copy but rather the harmonious entrance of an idea into the total fabric of one's life in response to the questions: What concrete difference will its being true make in anyone's life?, What is the truth's cash value in experiential terms? For James, "True ideas are those we can assimilate, validate, corroborate and verify. False ideas are those we can not."

Truth, then, is not a stagnant property inherent in an idea, nor a static relationship between subject and object, for the dynamics of experience account only for reality as flux. As a consequence, truth *happens;* truth is *made,* not discovered: "Truth *happens* to an idea. It *becomes* true, is *made* true by events. Its verity *is* in fact an event, a process: the process namely of its verifying itself, its veri-*fication.* Its validity is the process of its valid-*ation.*" Whether dealing with concrete objects or abstractions, matters of fact or mental ideas, the notion of verification by agreement still holds, with the expectation that the more abstract the idea, the more complicated the network into which the idea must successfully, and therefore, truthfully, *lead* us.

The work of James is, of course, replete with the *application* of pragmatism to a variety of questions. Reflection on the simple example of blackboard chalk shows that the so-called attributes of whiteness, friability, and insolubility indeed exist, but there is no practical consideration that points to the existence of a *substance* lying beneath them; the very coherence of the attributes themselves is sufficient to warrant calling the group *chalk,* without looking any further. Likewise in the matter of consciousness: Because experience itself is undivided, there is no need to invoke a faculty that, as subject, is conscious of another as object, so that consciousness as an "entity is fictitious, while thoughts in the concrete are fully real. But thoughts in the concrete are made of the same stuff as things are." To the question of whether the world is of one substance (monism) or of many substances (pluralism), which James felt was the most central of all philosophical questions because the designation "monist" or "pluralist" reveals more about a philosopher than any other label, pragmatism, by her criterion of practical differences, "must obviously range herself upon the pluralist side."

Morality and Religion

In concerns that come close to the center of life, namely, morality, religion, and God, James, without giving in to what he believed to be the presumptions of metaphysics, weighs the practical implications of all three in nurturing a personal life, and avers in page after page of broadening insights that, pragmatically, their role is indispensable for human meaning and value. Proceeding on a pragmatic basis, James finds no use whatsoever for the classical arguments for God's existence, which "are not solid enough to serve as religion's all-sufficient foundation." The arguments themselves prove nothing; they only strengthen one's "preexistent partialities": "If you have a God already whom you believe in, these arguments confirm you. If you are atheistic, they fail to set you right."

What then? Speaking in general terms, James writes: "On pragmatistic principles, if the hypothesis of God works satisfactorily in the widest sense of the word, it is true . . . but when I tell you that I have written a book on men's religious experience, which on the whole has been regarded as making for the reality of God, you will perhaps exempt my own pragmatism from the charge of being an atheistic system." So, belief in God changes the way a person looks at the world: "Theism always stands ready with the most practically rational solution it is possible to conceive. Not an energy of our active nature to which it does not authoritatively appeal, not an emotion of which it does not normally and naturally release the springs. At a single stroke, it changes the dead blank *it* of the world into a living *thou,* with whom the whole man may have dealings." Further, if it is true that the "need for an eternal moral order is one of the deepest needs of our breast," then religion takes the form of a living correspondence with the higher powers to bring about a world bettered by our actions, indeed, to bring about the salvation of the world.

Several years after writing these words, William James died—but not the philosopher, who has been inscribed in his works as a thinker of vision, of sensitivity, of learning, and of literary style. His broad interest in timeless themes makes him a permanent contemporary. No less a thinker than Alfred North Whitehead praises James as one of history's great "assemblers," along with Plato, Aristotle, and Leibniz.

The Meaning of Pragmatism
(from *What Is Pragmatism?*)

A glance at the history of the idea will show you still better what pragmatism means. The term is derived from the Greek word Greek πραγμα, meaning action, from which our words 'practice' and 'practical' come. It was first introduced into philosophy by Mr. Charles Peirce in 1878. In an article entitled 'How to Make Our Ideas Clear,' in the 'Popular Science Monthly' for January of that year Mr. Peirce, after pointing out that our beliefs are really rules for action, said that, to develop a thought's meaning, we need only determine what conduct it is fitted to produce: that conduct is for us its sole significance. And the tangible fact at the root of all our thought-distinctions, however subtle, is that there is no one of them so fine as to consist in anything but a possible difference of practice. To attain perfect clearness in our thoughts of an object, then, we need only consider what conceivable effects of a practical kind the object may involve—what sensations we are to expect from it, and what reactions we must prepare. Our conception of these effects, whether immediate or remote, is then for us the whole of our conception of the object, so far as that conception has positive significance at all.

This is the principle of Peirce, the principle of pragmatism. It lay entirely unnoticed by any one for twenty years, until I, in an address before Professor Howison's philosophical union at the University of California, brought it forward again and made a special application of it to religion. By that date (1898) the times seemed ripe for its reception. The word 'pragmatism' spread, and at present it fairly spots the pages of the philosophical journals. On all hands we find the 'pragmatic movement' spoken of, sometimes with respect, sometimes with contumely, seldom with clear understanding. It is evident that the term applies itself conveniently to a number of tendencies that hitherto have lacked a collective name, and that it has 'come to stay.'

To take in the importance of Peirce's principle, one must get accustomed to applying it to concrete cases. I found a few years ago that Ostwald, the illustrious Leipzig chemist, had been making perfectly distinct use of the principle of pragmatism in his lectures on the philosophy of science, though he had not called it by that name.

"All realities influence our practice," he wrote me, "and that influence is their meaning for us. I am accustomed to put questions to my classes in this way: In what respects would the world be different if this alternative or that were true? If I can find nothing that would become different, then the alternative has no sense."

That is, the rival views mean practically the same thing, and meaning, other than practical, there is for us none. Ostwald in a published lecture gives this example of what he means. Chemists have long wrangled over the inner constitution of certain bodies called 'tautomerous.' Their properties seemed equally consistent with the option that an instable hydrogen atom oscillates inside of them, or that they are instable mixtures of two bodies. Controversy raged, but never was decided. "It would never have begun," says Ostwald, "if the combatants had asked themselves what particular experimental fact could have been made different by one or the other view being correct. For it would then have appeared that no difference of fact could possibly ensue; and the quarrel was as unreal as if, theorizing in primitive times about the raising of dough by yeast, one party should have invoked a 'brownie,' while another insisted on an 'elf' as the true cause of the phenomenon."

It is astonishing to see how many philosophical disputes collapse into insignificance the moment you subject them to this simple test of tracing a concrete consequence. There can be no difference anywhere that doesn't make a difference elsewhere—no difference in abstract truth that doesn't express itself in a difference in concrete fact and in conduct consequent upon that fact, imposed on somebody, somehow, somewhere, and somewhen. The whole function of philosophy ought to be to find out what definite difference it will make to you and me, at definite instants of our life, if this world-formula or that world-formula be the true one.

There is absolutely nothing new in the pragmatic method. Socrates was an adept at it. Aristotle used it methodically. Locke, Berkeley, and Hume made momentous contributions to truth by its means. Shadworth Hodgson keeps insisting that realities are only what they are 'known as.' But these forerunners of pragmatism used it in fragments: they were precluders only. Not until in our time has it generalized itself, become conscious of a universal mission, pretended to a conquering destiny. I believe in that destiny, and I hope I may end by inspiring you with my belief.

Pragmatism represents a perfectly familiar attitude in philosophy, the empiricist attitude, but it represents it, as it seems to me, both in a more radical and in a less objectionable form than it has ever yet assumed. A pragmatist turns his back resolutely and once for all upon a lot of inveterate habits dear to professional philosophers. He turns away from abstraction and insufficiency, from verbal solutions, from bad *a priori* reasons, from fixed principles, closed systems, and pretended absolutes and origins. He turns towards concreteness and adequacy, towards facts, towards action and towards power. That means the empiricist temper regnant and the rationalist temper sincerely given up. It means the open air and possibilities of nature, as against dogma, artificiality, and the pretence of finality in truth.

At the same time it does not stand for any special results. It is a method only. But the general triumph of that method would mean an enormous change in what I called in my last lecture the 'temperament' of philosophy. Teachers of the ultra-rationalistic type would be frozen out, much as the courtier type is frozen out in republics, as the ultra-montane type of priest is frozen out in protestant lands. Science and metaphysics would come much nearer together, would in fact work absolutely hand in hand.

The Pragmatic Method Applied to the Problem of Substance

(from *What Is Pragmatism?*)

I am now to make the pragmatic method more familiar by giving you some illustrations of its application to particular problems. I will begin with what is driest, and the first thing I shall take will be the problem of *Substance*. Every one uses the old distinction between substance and attribute, enshrined as it is in the very structure of human language, in the difference between grammatical subject and predicate. Here is a bit of blackboard crayon. Its modes, attributes, properties, accidents, or affects,—use which term you will,—are whiteness, friability, cylindrical shape, insolubility in water, etc., etc. But the bearer of these attributes is so much *chalk,* which thereupon is called the substance in which they inhere. So the attributes of this desk inhere in the substance 'wood,' those of my coat in the substance 'wool,' and so forth. Chalk, wood and wool, show again, in spite of their differences, common properties, and in so far forth they are themselves counted as modes of a still more primal substance, *matter,* the attributes of which are space-occupancy and impenetrability. Similarly our thoughts and feelings are affections or properties of our several *souls,* which are substances, but again not wholly on their own right, for they are modes of the still deeper substance 'spirit.'

Now it was very early seen that all *we know* of the chalk is the whiteness, friability, etc., all *we know* of the wood is the combustibility and fibrous structure. A group of attributes is what each substance here is known as, they form its sole cash-value for our actual experience. The substance is in every case revealed through *them;* if we were cut off from *them* we should never suspect its existence; and if God should keep sending them to us in an unchanged order, miraculously annihilating at a certain moment the substance that supported them, we never could detect the moment, for our experiences themselves would be unaltered. Nominalists accordingly adopt the opinion that substance is a spurious idea due to our inveterate human trick of turning names into things. Phenomena come in groups—the chalk-group, the wood-group, etc.— and each group gets its name. The name we then treat as in a way supporting the group of phenomena. The low thermometer to-day, for instance, is supposed to come from something called the 'climate.' Climate is really only the name for a certain group of days, but it is treated as if it lay *behind* the day, and in general we place the name, as if it were a being, behind the facts it is the name of. But the phenomenal properties of things, nominalists say, surely do not really inhere in names, and if not in names then they do not inhere in anything. They *ad*here, or *cohere*, rather, *with each other,* and the notion of a substance inaccessible to us, which we think accounts for such cohesion by supporting it, as cement might support pieces of mosaic, must be abandoned. The fact of the bare cohesion itself is all that the notion of the substance signifies. Behind that fact is nothing.

The Pragmatic Method Applied to the Problem of Religion

(from *What Is Pragmatism?*)

I fear that my previous lectures, confined as they have been to human and humanistic aspects, may have left the impression on many of you that pragmatism means methodically to leave the superhuman out. I have shown small respect indeed for the Absolute, and I have until this moment spoken of no other super-human hypothesis but that. But I trust that you see sufficiently that the Absolute has nothing but its superhumanness in common with the theistic God. On prag-matistic principles, if the hypothesis of God works satisfactorily in the widest sense of the word, it is true. Now whatever its residual difficulties may be, experi-ence shows that it certainly does work, and that the problem is to build it out and determine it so that it will combine satisfactorily with all the other working truths. I can not start upon a whole theology at the end of this last lecture; but when I tell you that I have written a book on men's religious experience, which on the whole has been regarded as making for the reality of God, you will per-haps exempt my own pragmatism from the charge of being an atheistic system. I firmly disbelieve, myself, that our human experience is the highest form of expe-rience extant in the universe. I believe rather that we stand in much the same relation to the whole of the universe as our canine and feline pets do to the whole of human life. They inhabit our drawing-rooms and libraries. They take part in scenes of whose significance they have no inkling. They are merely tangent to curves of history the beginnings and ends and forms of which pass wholly beyond their ken. So we are tangent to the wider life of things. But, just as many of the dog's and cat's ideals coincide with our ideals, and the dogs and cats have daily living proof of the fact, so we may well believe, on the proofs that religious experience affords, that higher powers exist and are at work to save the world on ideal lines similar to our own.

You see that pragmatism can be called religious, if you allow that religion can be pluralistic or merely melioristic in type. But whether you will finally put up with that type of religion or not is a question that only you yourself can decide. Pragmatism has to postpone dogmatic answer, for we do not yet know certainly which type of religion is going to work best in the long run. The vari-ous overbeliefs of men, their several faith-ventures, are in fact what are needed to bring the evidence in. You will probably make your own ventures severally. If radically tough, the hurly-burly of the sensible facts of nature will be enough for you, and you will need no religion at all. If radically tender, you will take up with the more monistic form of religion: the pluralistic form, with its reliance on possibilities that are not necessities, will not seem to afford you security enough.

But if you are neither tough nor tender in an extreme and radical sense, but mixed as most of us are, it may seem to you that the type of pluralistic and moralistic religion that I have offered is as good a religious synthesis as you are likely to find.

Between the two extremes of crude naturalism on the one hand and transcendental absolutism on the other, you may find that what I take liberty in calling the pragmatistic or melioristic type of theism is exactly what you require.

The Will to Believe

I have brought with me to-night something like a sermon on justification by faith to read to you,—I mean an essay in justification *of* faith, a defence of our right to adopt a believing attitude in religious matters, in spite of the fact that our merely logical intellect may not have been coerced. 'The Will to Believe,' accordingly, is the title of my paper.

I have long defended to my own students the lawfulness of voluntarily adopted faith; but as soon as they have got well imbued with the logical spirit, they have as a rule refused to admit my contention to be lawful philosophically, even though in point of fact they were personally all the time chock-full of some faith or other themselves. I am all the while, however, so profoundly convinced that my own position is correct, that your invitation has seemed to me a good occasion to make my statements more clear. Perhaps your minds will be more open than those with which I have hitherto had to deal. I will be as little technical as I can, though I must begin by setting up some technical distinctions that will help us in the end.

I

Let us give the name of *hypothesis* to anything that may be proposed to our belief; and just as the electricians speak of live and dead wires, let us speak of any hypothesis as either *live* or *dead*. A live hypothesis is one which appeals as a real possibility to him to whom it is proposed. If I ask you to believe in the Mahdi, the notion makes no electric connection with your nature,—it refuses to scintillate with any credibility at all. As an hypothesis it is completely dead. To an Arab, however (even if he be not one of the Mahdi's followers), the hypothesis is among the mind's possibilities: it is alive. This shows that deadness and liveness in an hypothesis are not intrinsic properties, but relations to the individual thinker. They are measured by his willingness to act. The maximum of liveness in an hypothesis means willingness to act irrevocably. Practically, that means belief; but there is some believing tendency wherever there is willingness to act at all.

Next, let us call the decision between two hypothesis an *option*. Options may be of several kinds. They may be—1, *living* or *dead;* 2, *forced* or *avoidable;* 3, *momentous* or *trivial;* and for our purposes we may call an option a *genuine* option when it is of the forced, living, and momentous kind.

1. A living option is one in which both hypotheses are live ones. If I say to you: "Be a theosophist or be a Mohammedan," it is probably a dead option,

because for you neither hypothesis is likely to be alive. But if I say:"Be an agnostic or be a Christian," it is otherwise: trained as you are, each hypothesis makes some appeal, however small, to your belief.

2. Next, if I say to you: "Choose between going out with your umbrella or without it," I do not offer you a genuine option, for it is not forced. You can easily avoid it by not going out at all. Similarly, if I say, "Either love me or hate me," "Either call my theory true or call it false," your option is avoidable. You may remain indifferent to me, neither loving nor hating, and you may decline to offer any judgment as to my theory. But if I say, "Either accept this truth or go without it," I put on you a forced option, for there is no standing place outside of the alternative. Every dilemma based on a complete logical disjunction, with no possibility of not choosing, is an option of this forced kind.

3. Finally, if I were Dr. Nansen and proposed to you to join my North Pole expedition, your option would be momentous; for this would probably be your only similar opportunity, and your choice now would either exclude you from the North Pole sort of immortality altogether or put at least the chance of it into your hands. He who refuses to embrace a unique opportunity loses the prize as surely as if he tried and failed. *Per contra,* the option is trivial when the opportunity is not unique, when the stake is insignificant, or when the decision is reversible if it later prove unwise. Such trivial options abound in the scientific life. A chemist finds an hypothesis live enough to spend a year in its verification: he believes in it to that extent. But if his experiments prove inconclusive either way, he is quit for his loss of time, no vital harm being done.

It will facilitate our discussion if we keep all these distinctions well in mind.

II

The next matter to consider is the actual psychology of human opinion. When we look at certain facts, it seems as if our passional and volitional nature lay at the root of all our convictions. When we look at others, it seems as if they could do nothing when the intellect had once said its say. Let us take the latter facts up first.

Does it not seem preposterous on the very face of it to talk of our opinions being modifiable at will? Can our will either help or hinder our intellect in its perceptions of truth? Can we, by just willing it, believe that Abraham Lincoln's existence is a myth, and that the portraits of him in McClure's Magazine are all of some one else? Can we, by any effort of our will, or by any strength of wish that it were true, believe ourselves well and about when we are roaring with rheumatism in bed, or feel certain that the sum of the two one-dollar bills in our pocket must be a hundred dollars? We can say any of these things, but we are absolutely impotent to believe them; and of just such things is the whole fabric of the truths that we do believe in made up,—matters of fact, immediate or remote, as Hume said, and relations between ideas, which are either there or not there for us if we see them so, and which if not there cannot be put there by any action of our own.

In Pascal's Thoughts there is a celebrated passage known in literature as Pascal's wager. In it he tries to force us into Christianity by reasoning as if our concern with truth resembled our concern with the stakes in a game of chance. Translated freely his words are these: You must either believe or not believe that God is—which will you do? Your human reason cannot say. A game is going on between you and the nature of things which at the day of judgment will bring out either heads or tails. Weigh what your gains and your losses would be if you should stake all you have on heads, or God's existence: if you win in such case, you gain eternal beatitude; if you lose, you lose nothing at all. If there were an infinity of chances, and only one for God in this wager, still you ought to stake your all on God; for though you surely risk a finite loss by this procedure, any finite loss is reasonable, even a certain one is reasonable, if there is but the possibility of infinite gain. . . .

III

All this strikes one as healthy, even when expressed, as by Clifford, with somewhat too much of robustious pathos in the voice. Free-will and simple wishing do seem, in the matter of our credences, to be only fifth wheels to the coach. Yet if any one should thereupon assume that intellectual insight is what remains after wish and will and sentimental preference have taken wing, or that pure reason is what then settles our opinions, he would fly quite as directly in the teeth of the facts.

It is only our already dead hypotheses that our willing nature is unable to bring to life again. But what has made them dead for us is for the most part a previous action of our willing nature of an antagonistic kind. When I say 'willing nature,' I do not mean only such deliberate volitions as may have set up habits of belief that we cannot now escape from,—I mean all such factors of belief as fear and hope, prejudice and passion, imitation and partisanship, the circumpressure of our caste and set. As a matter of fact we find ourselves believing, we hardly know how or why. Mr. Balfour gives the name of 'authority' to all those influences, born of the intellectual climate, that make hypotheses possible or impossible for us, alive or dead. Here in this room, we all of us believe in molecules and the conservation of energy, in democracy and necessary progress, in Protestant Christianity and the duty of fighting for 'the doctrine of the immortal Monroe,' all for no reasons worthy of the name. We see into these matters with no more inner clearness, and probably with much less, than any disbeliever in them might possess. His unconventionality would probably have some grounds to show for its conclusions; but for us, not insight, but the *prestige* of the opinions, is what makes the spark shoot from them and light up our sleeping magazines of faith. Our reason is quite satisfied, in nine hundred and ninety-nine cases out of every thousand of us, if it can find a few arguments that will do to recite in case our credulity is criticised by some one else. Our faith is faith in some one else's faith, and in the greatest matters this is most the case. Our belief in truth itself, for instance, that there is a truth, and that our minds and it are made for each other,—what is it but a passionate affirmation of desire, in which our social system backs us up? We want to have a truth; we want to believe that our experiments and studies and discussions must put us in a continually better and better position towards it; and on this line we agree to fight out our thinking lives. But if a pyrrhonistic sceptic asks us *how we know* all this, can our logic find a reply? No! certainly it cannot. It is just one volition against another,—we willing to go in for life upon a trust or assumption which he, for his part, does not care to make. . . .

Evidently, then, our non-intellectual nature does influence our convictions. There are passional tendencies and volitions which run before and others which come after belief, and it is only the latter that are too late for the fair; and they are not too late when the previous passional work has been already in their own direction. Pascal's argument, instead of being powerless, then seems a regular clincher, and is the last stroke needed to make our faith in masses and holy water complete. The state of things is evidently far from simple; and pure insight and logic, whatever they might do ideally, are not the only things that really do produce our creeds.

IV

Our next duty, having recognized this mixed-up state of affairs, is to ask whether it be simply reprehensible and pathological, or whether, on the contrary, we must treat it as a normal element in making up our minds. The thesis I defend is, briefly stated, thus: *Our passional nature not only lawfully may, but must, decide an option between propositions, whenever it is a genuine option that cannot by its nature be decided on intellectual grounds; for to say, under such circumstances, "Do not decide, but leave the question open," is itself a passional decision,—just like deciding yes or no,—and is attended with the same risk of losing the truth.* The thesis thus abstractly expressed will, I trust, soon become quite clear. But I must first indulge in a bit more of preliminary work.

V

It will be observed that for the purposes of this discussion we are on 'dogmatic' ground—ground, I mean, which leaves systematic philosophical scepticism altogether out of account. The postulate that there is truth, and that it is the destiny of our minds to attain it, we are deliberately resolving to make, though the sceptic will not make it. We part company with him, therefore, absolutely, at this point. But the faith that truth exists, and that our minds can find it, may be held in two ways. We may talk of the *empiricist* way, and of the *absolutist* way of believing in truth. The absolutists in this matter say that we not only can attain to knowing truth, but we can *know when* we have attained to knowing it; while the empiricists think that although we may attain it, we cannot infallibly know when. To *know* is one thing, and to know for certain *that* we know is another. One may hold to the first being possible without the second; hence the empiricists and the absolutists, although neither of them is a sceptic in the usual philosophic sense of the term, show very different degrees of dogmatism in their lives.

If we look at the history of opinions, we see that the empiricist tendency has largely prevailed in science, while in philosophy the absolutist tendency has had everything its own way. The characteristic sort of happiness, indeed, which philosophers yield has mainly consisted in the conviction felt by each successive school or system that by it bottom-certitude had been attained. . . .

Scholastic orthodoxy, to which one must always go when one wishes to find perfectly clear statement, has beautifully elaborated this absolutist conviction in a doctrine which it calls that of 'objective evidence.' If, for example, I am unable to doubt that I now exist before you, that two is less than three, or that if all men are mortal than I am mortal too, it is because these things illumine my intellect irresistibly. . . . When the Cliffords tell us how sinful it is to be Christians on such 'insufficient evidence,' insufficiency is really the last thing they have in mind. For them the evidence is absolutely sufficient, only it makes the other way. They believe so completely in an anti-christian order of the universe that there is no living option: Christianity is a dead hypothesis from the start.

VI

But now, since we are all such absolutists by instinct, what in our quality of students of philosophy ought we to do about the fact? Shall we espouse and indorse it? Or shall we treat it as a weakness of our nature from which we must free ourselves, if we can?

I sincerely believe that the latter course is the only one we can follow as reflective men. Objective evidence and certitude are doubtless very fine ideals to play with, but where on this moonlit and dream-visited planet are they found? I am, therefore, myself a complete empiricist so far as my theory of human knowledge goes. I live, to be sure, by the practical faith that we must go on experiencing and thinking over our experience, for only thus can our opinions grow more true; but to hold any one of them—I absolutely do not care which—as if it never could be reinterpretable or corrigible, I believe to be a tremendously mistaken attitude, and I think that the whole history of philosophy will bear me out. There is but one indefectibly certain truth, and that is the truth that pyrrhonistic scepticism itself leaves standing,—the truth that the present phenomenon of consciousness exists. That, however, is the bare starting-point of knowledge, the mere admission of a stuff to be philosophized about. The various philosophies are but so many attempts at expressing what this stuff really is. And if we repair to our libraries what disagreement do we discover! Where is a certainly true answer found? Apart from abstract propositions of comparison (such as two and two are the same as four), propositions which tell us nothing by themselves about concrete reality, we find no proposition ever regarded by any one as evidently certain that has not either been called a falsehood, or at least had its truth sincerely questioned by some one else. . . .

No concrete test of what is really true has ever been agreed upon. Some make the criterion external to the moment of perception, putting it either in revelation, the *consensus gentium,* the instincts of the heart, or the systematized experience of the race. Others make the perceptive moment its own test,—Descartes, for instance, with his clear and distinct ideas guaranteed by the veracity of God; Reid with his 'common-sense'; and Kant with his forms of synthetic judgment *a priori.* The inconceivability of the opposite; the capacity to be verified by sense; the possession of complete organic unity or self-relation, realized when a thing is its own other—are standards which, in turn, have been used. The much lauded objective evidence is never triumphantly there; it is a mere aspiration or *Grenzbegriff,* marking the infinitely remote ideal of our thinking life. To claim that certain truths now possess it, is simply to say that when you think them true and they *are* true, then their evidence is objective, otherwise it is not. But practically one's conviction that the evidence one goes by is of the real objective brand, is only one more subjective opinion added to the lot. For what a contradictory array of opinions have objective evidence and absolute certitude been claimed! The world is rational through and through,—its existence is an ultimate brute fact; there is a personal God,—a personal God is inconceivable; there is an extra-mental physical world immediately known,—the mind can only know its own ideas; a moral imperative exists,—obligation is only the resultant of desires; a permanent spiritual principle is in every one,—there are only shifting states of mind; there is an endless chain of causes,—there is an absolute first cause; an eternal necessity,—a freedom, a purpose,—no purpose; a primal One,—a primal Many; a universal continuity,—an essential discontinuity in things; an infinity,—no infinity. There is this,—there is that; there is indeed nothing which some one has not thought absolutely true, while his neighbor deemed it absolutely false; and not an absolutist among them seems ever to have considered that the trouble may all the time be essential, and that the intellect, even with truth directly in its grasp, may have no infallible signal for knowing whether it be truth or no. When, indeed, one remembers that the most striking practical application to life of the doctrine of objective certitude has been the conscientious labors of the Holy Office of the Inquisition, one feels less tempted than ever to lend the doctrine a respectful ear.

But please observe, now, that when as empiricists we give up the doctrine of objective certitude, we do not thereby give up the quest or hope of truth itself. We still pin our faith on its existence, and still believe that we gain an ever better position towards it by systematically continuing to roll up experiences and think. Our great difference from the scholastic lies in the way we face. The strength of his system lies in the principles, the origin, the *terminus a quo* of his thought; for us the strength is in the outcome, the upshot, the *terminus ad quem.* Not where it comes from but what it leads to is to decide. It matters not to an empiricist from what quarter an hypothesis may come to him: he may have acquired it by fair means or foul; passion may have whispered or accident suggested it; but if the total drift of thinking continues to confirm it, that is what he means by its being true.

VII

One more point, small but important, and our preliminaries are done. There are two ways of looking at our duty in the matter of opinion,—ways entirely different, and yet ways about whose difference the theory of knowledge seems hitherto to have shown very little concern. *We must know the truth;* and *we must avoid error,*—these are our first and great commandments as would-be knowers; but they are not two ways of stating an identical commandment, they are two separable laws. Although it may indeed happen that when we believe the truth *A,* we escape as an incidental consequence from believing the falsehood *B,* it hardly ever happens that by merely disbelieving *B* we necessarily believe *A.* We may in escaping *B* fall into believing other false-hoods, *C* or *D,* just as bad as *B;* or we may escape *B* by not believing anything at all, not even *A.*

Believe truth! Shun error!—these, we see, are two materially different laws; and by choosing between them we may end by coloring differently our whole intellectual life. We may regard the chase for truth as paramount, and the avoid-ance of error as secondary; or we may, on the other hand, treat the avoidance of error as more imperative, and let truth take its chance. Clifford, in the instructive passage which I have quoted, exhorts us to the latter course. Believe nothing, he tells us, keep your mind in suspence forever, rather than by closing it on insuffi-cient evidence incur the awful risk of believing lies. You, on the other hand, may think that the risk of being in error is a very small matter when compared with the blessings of real knowledge, and be ready to be duped many times in your investigation rather than postpone indefinitely the chance of guessing true. I myself find it impossible to go with Clifford. . . .

IX

Moral questions immediately present themselves as questions whose solution cannot wait for sensible proof. A moral question is a question not of what sensi-bly exists, but of what is good, or would be good if it did exist. Science can tell us what exists; but to compare the *worth,* both of what exists and of what does not exist, we must consult not science, but what Pascal calls our heart. Science herself consults her heart when she lays it down that the infinite ascertainment of fact and correction of false belief are the supreme goods for man. Challenge the state-ment, and science can only repeat it oracularly, or else prove it by showing that such ascertainment and correction bring man all sorts of other goods which man's heart in turn declares. The question of having moral beliefs at all or not hav-ing them is decided by our will. Are our moral preferences true or false, or are they only odd biological phenomena, making things good or bad for *us,* but in themselves indifferent? How can your pure intellect decide? If your heart does not *want* a world of moral reality, your head will assuredly never make you believe in one. Mephistophelian scepticism, indeed, will satisfy the head's play-instincts much better than any rigorous idealism can. Some men (even at the stu-dent age) are so naturally cool-hearted that the moralistic hypothesis never has

for them any pungent life, and in their supercilious presence the hot young moralist always feels strangely ill at ease. The appearance of knowingness is on their
side, of *naïveté* and gullibility on his. Yet, in the inarticulate heart of him, he clings
to it that he is not a dupe, and that there is a realm in which (as Emerson says) all
their wit and intellectual superiority is no better than the cunning of a fox. Moral
scepticism can no more be refuted or proved by logic than intellectual scepticism can. When we stick to it that there *is* truth (be it of either kind), we do so
with our whole nature, and resolve to stand or fall by the results. The sceptic with
his whole nature adopts the doubting attitude; but which of us is the wiser, Omniscience only knows.

Turn now from these wide questions of good to a certain class of questions
of fact, questions concerning personal relations, states of mind between one
man and another. *Do you like me or not?*—for example. Whether you do or not
depends, in countless instances, on whether I meet you half-way, am willing to
assume that you must like me, and show you trust and expectation. The previous
faith on my part in your liking's existence is in such cases what makes your liking
come. But if I stand aloof, and refuse to budge an inch until I have objective
evidence, until you shall have done something apt, as the absolutists say, *ad
extorquendum assensum meum,* ten to one your liking never comes. How many
women's hearts are vanquished by the mere sanguine insistence of some man
that they *must* love him! he will not consent to the hypothesis that they cannot.
The desire for a certain kind of truth here brings about that special truth's existence; and so it is in innumerable cases of other sorts. Who gains promotions,
boons, appointments, but the man in whose life they are seen to play the part of
live hypotheses, who discounts them, sacrifices other things for their sake before
they have come, and takes risks for them in advance? His faith acts on the powers
above him as a claim, and creates its own verification.

A social organism of any sort whatever, large or small, is what it is because
each member proceeds to his own duty with a trust that the other members
will simultaneously do theirs. Wherever a desired result is achieved by
the co-operation of many independent persons, its existence as a fact is a
pure consequence of the precursive faith in one another of those immediately
concerned. A government, an army, a commercial system, a ship, a college, an
athletic team, all exist on this condition, without which not only is nothing
achieved, but nothing is even attempted. A whole train of passengers (individually brave enough) will be looted by a few highwaymen, simply because the
latter can count on one another, while each passenger fears that if he makes a
movement of resistance, he will be shot before any one else backs him up. If
we believed that the whole car-full would rise at once with us, we should each
severally rise, and train-robbing would never even be attempted. There are,
then, cases where a fact cannot come at all unless a preliminary faith exists in
its coming. *And where faith in a fact can help create the fact,* that would
be an insane logic which should say that faith running ahead of scientific
evidence is the 'lowest kind of immorality' into which a thinking being can fall.
Yet such is the logic by which our scientific absolutists pretend to regulate
our lives!

X

In truths dependent on our personal action, then, faith based on desire is certainly a lawful and possibly an indispensable thing.

But now, it will be said, these are all childish human cases, and have nothing to do with great cosmical matters, like the question of religious faith. Let us then pass on to that. Religions differ so much in their accidents that in discussing the religious question we must make it very generic and broad. What then do we now mean by the religious hypothesis? Science says things are; morality says some things are better than other things; and religion says essentially two things.

First, she says that the best things are the more eternal things, the overlapping things, the things in the universe that throw the last stone, so to speak, and say the final word. "Perfection is eternal,"—this phrase of Charles Secretan seems a good way of putting his first affirmation of religion, an affirmation which obviously cannot yet be verified scientifically at all.

The second affirmation of religion is that we are better off even now if we believe her first affirmation to be true.

Now, let us consider what the logical elements of this situation are *in case the religious hypothesis in both its branches be really true.* (Of course, we must admit that possibility at the outset. If we are to discuss the question at all, it must involve a living option. If for any of you religion be a hypothesis that cannot, by any living possibility be true, then you need go no farther. I speak to the 'saving remnant' alone.) So proceeding, we see, first, that religion offers itself as a *momentous* option. We are supposed to gain, even now, by our belief, and to lose by our non-belief, a certain vital good. Secondly, religion is a forced option so far as that good goes. We cannot escape the issue by remaining sceptical and waiting for more light, because although we do avoid error in that way *if religion be untrue,* we lose the good, *if it be true,* just as certainly as if we positively chose to disbelieve. It is as if a man should hesitate indefinitely to ask a certain woman to marry him because he was not perfectly sure that she would prove an angel after he brought her home. Would he not cut himself off from the particular angel-possibility as decisively as if he went and married some one else? Scepticism, then, is not avoidance of option; it is option of a certain particular kind of risk. *Better risk loss of truth than chance of error,*—that is your faith-vetoer's exact position. He is actively playing his stake as much as the believer is; he is backing the field against the religious hypothesis, just as the believer is backing the religious hypothesis against the field. To preach scepticism to us as a duty until 'sufficient evidence' for religion be found, is tantamount therefore to telling us, when in presence of the religious hypothesis, that to yield to our fear of its being error is wiser and better than to yield to our hope that it may be true. It is not intellect against all passions, then; it is only intellect with one passion laying down its law. And by what, forsooth, is the supreme wisdom of this passion warranted? Dupery for dupery, what proof is there that dupery through hope is so much worse than dupery through fear? I, for one, can see no proof; and I simply refuse obedience to the scientist's command to imitate his kind of option, in a case where my own stake is important enough to give me the right to choose my own form of risk. If religion be true and the evidence for it be still insufficient, I do not wish, by putting your extinguisher upon my nature (which feels to me as if it had after all some business of this matter), to forfeit my sole chance in life of getting upon the winning side,—that chance depending, of course, on my willingness to run the risk of acting as if my passional need of taking the world religiously might be prophetic and right.

All this is on the supposition that it really may be prophetic and right, and that, even to us who are discussing the matter, religion is a live hypothesis which may be true. Now, to most of us religion comes in a still further way that makes a veto in our active faith even more illogical. The more perfect and more eternal aspect of the universe is represented in our religions as having personal form. The universe is no longer a mere *It* to us, but a *Thou,* if we are religious; and any relation that may be possible from person to person might be possible here. For instance, although in one sense we are passive portions of the universe, in another we show a curious autonomy, as if we were small active centres on our own account. We feel, too, as if the appeal of religion to us were made to our own active good-will, as if evidence might be forever withheld from us unless we met the hypothesis half-way. To take a trivial illustration: just as a man who in a company of gentlemen made no advances, asked a warrant for every concession, and believed no one's word without proof, would cut himself off by such churlishness from all the social rewards that a more trusting spirit would earn,—so here, one who should shut himself up in snarling logicality and try to make the gods extort his recognition willy-nilly, or not get it at all, might cut himself off forever from his only opportunity of making the gods' acquaintance. This feeling, forced on us we know not whence, that by obstinately believing that there are gods (although not to do so would be so easy both for our logic and our life) we are doing the universe the deepest service we can, seems part of the living essence of the religious hypothesis. If the hypothesis *were* true in all its parts, including this one, then pure intellectualism, with its veto on our making willing advances, would be an absurdity; and some participation of our sympathetic nature would be logically required. I, therefore, for one, cannot see my way to accepting the agnostic rules for truth-seeking, or wilfully agree to keep my willing nature out of the game. I cannot do so for this plain reason, that *a rule of thinking which would absolutely prevent me from acknowledging certain kinds of truth if those kinds of truth were really there, would be an irrational rule.* That for me is the long and short of the formal logic of the situation, no matter what the kinds of truth might materially be.

I confess I do not see how this logic can be escaped. But sad experience makes me fear that some of you may still shrink from radically saying with me, *in abstracto,* that we have the right to believe at our own risk any hypothesis that is live enough to tempt our will. I suspect, however, that if this is so, it is because you have got away from the abstract logical point of view altogether, and are thinking (perhaps without realizing it) of some particular religious hypothesis which for you is dead. The freedom to 'believe what we will' you apply to the case of some patent superstition; and the faith you think of is the faith defined by the schoolboy when he said, "Faith is when you believe something that you know ain't true." I can only repeat that this is misapprehension. *In concerto,* the freedom to believe can only cover living options which the intellect of the individual cannot by itself resolve; and living options never seem absurdities to him who has them to consider. When I look at the religious question as it really puts itself to concrete men, and when I think of all the possibilities which both practically and theoretically it involves, then this command that we shall put a stopper on our heart, instincts, and courage, and *wait*—acting of course meanwhile more or less as if religion were *not* true*— till doomsday, or till such time as our intellect and senses working together may have raked in evidence enough,—this command, I say, seems to me the queerest idol ever manufactured in the philosophic cave. Were we scholastic absolutists, there might be more excuse. If we had an infallible intellect with its objective certitudes, we might feel ourselves disloyal to such a perfect organ of knowledge in not trusting to it exclusively, in not waiting for its releasing word. But if we are empiricists, if we believe that no bell in us tolls to let us know for certain when truth is in our grasp, then it seems a piece of idle fantasticality to preach so solemnly our duty of waiting for the bell. Indeed we *may* wait if we will,—I hope you do not think that I am denying that,—but if we do so, we do so at our peril as much as if we believed. In either case we *act,* taking our life in our hands. No one of us ought to issue vetoes to the other, nor should we bandy words of abuse. We ought, on the contrary, delicately and profoundly to respect one another's mental freedom: then only shall we bring about the intellectual republic; then only shall we have that spirit of inner tolerance without which all our outer tolerance is soulless, and which is empiricism's glory; then only shall we live and let live, in speculative as well as in practical things.

Review Questions

1. Explain what is meant by the *radical* empiricism of James.
2. In what way is pragmatism a method?
3. As a method for clarifying ideas, is pragmatism a totally new approach, or does it have some traditional forebears?
4. Show how, for example, James applies the pragmatic method to the notion of substance; to God.

---

*Since belief is measured by action, he who forbids us to believe religion to be true, necessarily forbids us to act as we should if we did believe it to be true. The whole defence of religious faith hinges upon action. If the action required or inspired by the religious hypothesis is in no way different from that dictated by the naturalistic hypothesis, then religious faith is a pure superfluity, better pruned away, and controversy about its legitimacy is a piece of idle trifling, unworthy of serious minds. I myself believe, of course, that the religious hypothesis gives to the world an expression which specifically determines our reactions, and makes them in a large part unlike what they might be on a purely naturalistic scheme of belief.

Suggestions for Further Reading

Barzun, J. *A Stroll with William James.* New York, Harper & Row, 1983.

McDermott, J., ed. *The Writings of William James.* New York, Random House, 1967.

Menand, L. *The Metaphysical Club.* NY, Farrar, Straus and Giroux, 1997.

Myers, G. E. *William James: His Life and Thought.* New Haven, CT, Yale University Press, 1986.

26

Edmund Husserl
(1859–1938)

In shifting our attention from the philosophy of William James to continental philosophy, we are shifting back to those philosophers who, like James, were prone to search the inner man for the key to understanding the self and the self's presence in the world. A huge effort was made in this direction by a group of philosophers in the early part of the twentieth century who advanced a philosophical method called *phenomenology* and are referred to under the general name of phenomenologists. The use of the words *phenomenon* or *phenomenology* did not begin with them, for we have already seen how Kant used the word *phenomenon* in contradistinction to *noumenon*, which stand to each other as sensible to beyond-the-sensible. We are also familiar with the word *phenomenology* from Hegel's account of the "phenomenology of the Mind" in which phenomenon, appearance, makes Mind knowable. So, there is a broad sense in which both phenomenon and phenomenology are used, but in its strict, or narrower, sense phenomenology refers to the philosophical movement already mentioned, finally becoming associated with the philosopher who gave it its present shape and whose name is most directly connected with it, Edmund Husserl.

Husserl was born in 1859 in Prostějov (Prossnitz), Moravia, and as a youth attended the University of Leipzig where he received a thorough education in the sciences, especially mathematics, in which, a few years later, he was awarded a doctorate; from then on he was launched on a lifelong career as an academician. In Vienna from 1884 to 1886 he attended the lectures of Franz Brentano, who was to have a formative role in his undertaking of philosophy as a life's vocation. He taught at the University of Halle for a few years, then at the University of Göttingen for sixteen years, which proved to be extremely productive years for him. At the same time Husserl immersed himself in the study of psychology, not in a contemporary experimental or clinical sense, nor Freudian, but in classical philosophical psychology, primarily Brentano's. In 1916 he accepted the invitation to become a full professor at the University of Freiburg, which post he held until retirement in 1929. He remained in Freiburg until he died in 1938. During the last five years of his life he was prohibited, because of his Jewish background, from engaging in any public, academic activities. Though invited by the University of Southern California to take up teaching there as a professor, he chose to stay in Germany. Among his published works, the following should be mentioned: *Ideas: General Introduction to Pure Phenomenology* (1913), *The Phenomenology of Internal Time Consciousness* (1928), *Formal and Transcendental Logic* (1929), *Cartesian Meditations* (1931), *Philosophy and the Crisis of European Man* (1936), and *The Crisis of European Sciences* (1937, unfinished). Husserl left an immense legacy of unpublished manuscripts, which gradually have been edited and published.

Search for Philosophy's Foundation

There is no possibility, in Husserl's view, of any philosophy worthy of the name unless it is built on a firm, unassailable foundation, and the search for such a foundation occupied his entire philosophical life. Besides philosophy there were two other claimants to this project of building such a foundation, one coming from the side of the natural sciences and the other from the side of psychology, whose claims he felt had to be rejected. Husserl had a tremendous respect for both areas of knowledge and had committed himself to several years of formal study in each of them; he was fully aware of their methods, their accomplishments, and indeed their shortcomings. As for the sciences, despite his admiration for their continued success, Husserl thought that in the end their very success was their undoing because their unbridled confidence led them to hold the position that all reality is to be understood in terms of the physical, thus foreclosing, in his view, the realm of the spirit, which defined the human being as human. Toward the end of his life, disturbed by what he saw as a malaise afflicting modern man, he wrote: "The exclusiveness with which the total world-view of modern man, in the second half of the nineteenth century, let itself be determined by the positive sciences and be blinded by the 'prosperity' they produced, meant an indifferent turning-away from the questions which are decisive for a genuine humanity. Merely fact-minded sciences make merely fact-minded people."

Psychology comes closer to the heart of phenomenology, for the act of consciousness lies open to the psychologist as the faculty of self-awareness and self-direction, which form the core of a person's wholeness and serve to integrate discrete activities into a single center. But here too there was a danger, as Husserl saw it, of the mystery of consciousness becoming entrapped in physical structures so that, at least from an epistemological point of view, a conscious act would have a severely limited knowledge function and would be absolutely incapable of a wider understanding: "To be sure, even after Hume and Kant it remained a great temptation . . . to want to deal psychologically with epistemological problems." The root of the problem, for all too many, lay in treating the psyche as though it were a physical object of science: "Psychology was burdened in advance with the task of being a science parallel to physics and with the conception that the soul—its subject matter—was something real in a sense similar to corporeal nature, the subject matter of natural sciences."

Consciousness: A Radical Beginning

So, with the philosophical claims of the sciences and psychology laid aside, the act of consciousness is, for Husserl, open to the philosopher who wants to find there knowledge of self and then the nexus between knowledge of self and other-than-self, an epistemological finding. So often it happens in the history of philosophy, when a philosopher sees himself hemmed in, the only option available is to strike out afresh and search for a new beginning. Husserl, integrating the exactness of science with the interiority of classical psychology, hoped to pioneer an approach in philosophy which would result in a new method of getting to the essences of things: "Anyone," he wrote in the *Paris Lectures,* "who seriously considers becoming a philosopher must once in his life withdraw into himself and then, from within, attempt to destroy and rebuild all previous learning." In this regard Husserl was never quite satisfied with what he had accomplished or tried to accomplish because he was always searching for new ways of introducing the enterprise of phenomenology; he was an eternal beginner. Toward the end of his life, Husserl wrote in the preface to the English edition of *Ideas* that his book ". . . does not claim to be anything more than an attempt that has been growing through the decades of meditation exclusively directed to this one end: to discover a *radical beginning* of a philosophy which, to repeat the Kantian phrase, 'will be able to present itself as science.'"

Common sense, whose presentations must be respected, would seem to be aligned with the traditional view that we are in direct contact with things which we first come to know through our experiences—the primary meaning of empirical. Yet, in reexamining the connection between *consciousness* and the *thing* one is conscious of, Husserl, along with all other phenomenologists of the time, insisted that phenomenology is a nonempirical science and that the phenomenon, which this science is the study of, is nonempirical as well. It looks at first as though Husserl is dealing with a vicious circle for, as he puts it in *The Idea of Phenomenology,* "But if . . . we accept nothing transcendent until we have established its possibility . . . then it seems that we are faced with the prospect of a circle, which makes phenomenology and the theory of knowledge impossible." Simply stated: we cannot know that this is a phenomenon until we know what one is, and we cannot know what one is until we know that this is a phenomenon. The ambiguity is deepened by Husserl's constant admonition, a kind of rallying cry, "To the things!" we must go, as though "things" enjoyed an independent existence and are "there" awaiting our attention, giving every impression that something like empiricism is at work. Husserl's agenda, however, spelled out over many years, called for the recognition that knowledge is an activity of the mind, so that the original datum is not found "out there" but precisely *in our consciousness:* Authentic philosophical inquiry is located in consciousness' contemplation of the datum it possesses. The knowing process at work, then, is *intuition,* a direct and immediate grasp of the given in an act of self-awareness on the part of consciousness, so that there is no "first" or "second" but an immediacy that dispenses with chronology. There is no vicious circle. We can also understand why Husserl, insisting on the nonempirical character of phenomenology, refers to it as *a priori,* for knowledge *begins* in consciousness with the very "things," or phenomena, held therein. Intuition itself is its own authority, its own source of knowledge justification, and is to be accepted for what it is; referring to this as his "principle or principles," Husserl writes, "every primordial . . . intuition is a source of authority for knowledge . . . whatever presents itself in 'intuition' in primordial form . . . is simply to be accepted as it gives itself out to be, though only within the limits in which it then presents itself."

Granted then that by Husserl's account phenomenology is nonempirical and is not involved in a vicious circle, another question arises: Does what the mind knows really exist, or is consciousness' grasp of the thing (phenomenon) a grasp of that thing's existence outside consciousness? We easily recognize the force of this question as it has often appeared in various guises in the history of philosophy, for example, in the extreme realism of Plato, in the moderate realism of Aristotle and Aquinas, or in the innate ideas of Anselm and Descartes. It appears again with Husserl as a fundamental epistemological problem which must be explored at the risk of extreme subjectivism, often called solipsism.

Intentionality as the guarantee of the truth of external objects

In following the direction taken by his teacher Franz Brentano, Husserl sees a solution in what he refers to as *intentionality.* Whenever we use the word *intend* or *intention,* as when the sportsman says, "I intend to go fishing," or the judge says, "It is my intention to see justice done," we mean that our actions have some object in view, that our awareness centers on some definite content, so that "intention" could never be empty of meaning. It is this character of intention that Husserl conveys to an act of consciousness, so that every act of consciousness necessarily refers to, is related to, has a bearing on, an object whether it be a thing, a principle, a problem, a moral value, or existence itself. The object, it can be said, is *presented* in consciousness, and when presented ushers it into the real world of time and space and life. "One thing," writes Husserl, "of the greatest, even decisive, importance remains . . . the expression *ego cogito* (I think) must be expanded by one term. Every *cogito* (I think) contains a meaning: its *cogitatum* (what is thought). . . . *The essence of consciousness, in which I live as my own self, is the so-called intentionality.*

Consciousness is always conscious of something." Again, common sense inclines us to a naive realism, so that its presentations are of a world "out there," but the world, for Husserl, is neither "out there" nor "in here" for what is given in our consciousness is seamless, without the dichotomies subjective-objective, within-without, in here-out there: That is, the pen on my desk is "out there in my consciousness" and is an example of *transcendental subjectivity.*

Given in intuition are both the singularity of the thing and its essence (its "ways of being," its *Wesen*), but because common sense presents singularity so intensely, our attention could lose sight of essentiality: To grasp the object in its fullness, that is, in its very essence, requires concentration on *what* the object is, as opposed to whether it exists or not—a concentration on "whatness" rather than "thatness." So, to help consciousness see the object, if the question of its existence could provisionally be set aside, the essence of the object, the phenomenon that is, would be laid bare to our contemplation. The process of methodologically setting existence aside is, for Husserl, putting existence into parentheses, or brackets, whence he refers to it as *bracketing,* or by its Greek name, *epoché;* since his aim is to "reduce" the object, or "bring it back," to its pure essence (*eidos*), he also calls the process *eidetic reduction.* If Husserl is right in his approach, then indeed the phenomenon, the object, becomes more transparent to the understanding; an opportunity for reflection has been made available, and we can more directly focus on the object in itself. In his own words, "This ubiquitous detachment from any point of view regarding the objective world we term the phenomenological epoché. It is the methodology through which I come to understand myself as the ego and life of consciousness in which and through which the entire objective world exists for me, and is for me precisely as it is."

Husserl puts to rest any questions that might have emerged from the interiority of consciousness: Has consciousness, so turned in on itself, now become incapable of an other-directed awareness? of certainty with regard to an objective world? of knowing anything other than itself? We have seen the problem Descartes faced with his *cogito,* a seeming impossibility to extricate himself from a throughgoing subjectivity because his line to the outside world was so tenuous. In his penetrating commentary on Descartes' method, although affirming many similarities between the phenomenological method and the Cartesian, and explicitly stating that "phenomenology must honor Descartes as its genuine patriarch," Husserl underscored the irreconcilable difference between his *epoché* and Descartes' *cogito,* for the former involves a mere suspension of belief in reality beyond the ego, whereas the latter doubts it. Indeed, Husserl relies on the dynamic of intentionality, which is never to be foreshortened in any phenomenon, and if that intentiality bears on external existence then, for Husserl, a real existent is disclosed, and far from there being any dichotomy to overcome, there is a perfect continuum between the internal and external, the subjective and objective.

The fact that, for Husserl, there is no breach between the subjective and objective, can be viewed another way, for he develops the notion that consciousness *constitutes* the world, not metaphysically as though cause and effect were at work, but phenomenologically, that is, consciousness makes the world exist for *me;*

were there no phenomena, I could never know the world, but given the phenomena, then in and through them I know that I am in the world, part of the world, living in the world, and moving in the flow of time. Husserl sometimes refers to this intrinsic connection between consciousness and the objects whose meanings are contained therein as "transcendental (or phenomenological) idealism," a term he did not hesitate to use even though it was redolent of the problems of objective reality associated with it in the past. He expresses his confidence in phenomenological idealism in the following words: "I become conscious (through what is phenomenologically accessible to me) . . . that I possess in myself an essential individuality, self-centered, and holding well together in itself . . . through whose agency the objective world is there for me in all its empirically confirmed facts." Once again, we see that for Husserl consciousness is a kind of epistemological reservoir which, on being tapped, immediately and naturally flows into the awareness of the realities of self and nonself in one continuous stream.

The enterprise of phenomenology was to be, for Husserl, a new and fresh beginning, based indeed on the contributions of the past, but still a new start at a critical time to place human knowledge on the unshakable foundation so many philosophers have dreamt of. We have noted that he thought of himself as an eternal beginner; it inspires confidence in a philosopher to know that he does not regard himself as having said the final word, or thought the final thought, and even though Husserl was sure of the main line of his new method, he expectantly welcomed the contributions others would certainly make in the future; he referred to it as the "promised land," on which he himself would never set foot.

Phenomenology is certainly a method, but if we constrain ourselves to a too narrow interpretation of method, we stand to miss its all-important feature as a way of looking at reality, as a perspective, as a mode of seeing; in a sense, Husserl tried to formalize the subjective, personal direction philosophy took in the nineteenth century, particularly with Kierkegaard and Nietzsche. As a movement, phenomenology has established itself in contemporary philosophy, entering into the mainstream chiefly in Europe where it has maintained a steady influence. Maurice Merleau-Ponty, Max Scheler, Martin Heidegger, and Jean-Paul Sartre are among those who, though they developed their own philosophies, did so on the strength of leading ideas from Husserl. Sartre was a student of Husserl's, and Heidegger was not only a student but also a close associate and friend.

R E A D I N G

Author's Preface to the English Edition
(from *Ideas: General Introduction to Pure Phenomenology*)

May the author of this work, which first appeared in the year 1913, be permitted to contribute to the English Edition certain explanations that may prove of use to the reader, both before and as he reads?

Under the title "A Pure or Transcendental Phenomenology," the work here presented seeks to found a new science—though, indeed, the whole course of philosophical development since *Descartes* has been preparing the way for it—a science covering a new field of experience, exclusively its own, that of "Transcendental Subjectivity." Thus Transcendental Subjectivity does not signify the outcome of any speculative synthesis, but with its transcendental experiences, capacities, doings, is an absolutely independent realm of direct experience, although for reasons of an essential kind it has so far remained inaccessible. Transcendental experience in its theoretical and, at first, descriptive bearing, becomes available only through a radical alteration of that same dispensation under which an experience of the natural world runs its course, a readjustment of viewpoint which, as the method of approach to the sphere of transcendental phenomenology, is called "phenomenological reduction."

In the work before us transcendental phenomenology is not founded as the empirical science of the empirical facts of this field of experience. Whatever facts present themselves serve only as examples similar in their most general aspect to the empirical illustrations used by mathematicians; much, in fact, as the actual intuitable dispositions of numbers on the abacus assist us, in their merely exemplary capacity, to grasp with insight, and in their pure generality the series 2, 3, 4 . . . as such, pure numbers as such, and the propositions of pure mathematics relative to these, the essential generalities of a mathematical kind. In this book, then, we treat of an *a priori* science ("eidetic," directed upon the universal in its original intuitability), which appropriates, though as pure possibility only, the empirical field of fact of transcendental subjectivity with its factual *(faktischen)* experiences, equating these with pure intuitable possibilities that can be modified at will, and sets out as its *a priori* the indissoluble essential structures of transcendental subjectivity, which persist in and through all imaginable modifications. Since the reduction to the transcendental and, with it, this further reduction to the Eidos is the method of approach to the field of work of the new science, it follows (and we stress the point in advance) that the proper starting-point for the systematic unravelling of this science lies in the chapters which treat of the reductions we have indicated. Only from this position can the reader, who follows with inner sympathy the indications proffered step by step, judge whether something characteristically new has really been worked out here—worked out, we say, and not constructed, drawn from real, general intuition of essential Being, and described accordingly.

Eidetic phenomenology is restricted in this book to the realm of pure eidetic "description," that is to the realm of essential structures of transcendental subjectivity immediately transparent to the mind. For this constitutes in itself already a systematically self-contained infinitude of essential characteristics. Thus no attempt is made to carry out systematically the transcendental knowledge that can be obtained through logical deduction. Here we have one difference (though not the only one) between the whole manner of this new *a priori* science and that of the mathematical disciplines. These are "deductive" sciences, and that means that in their scientifically theoretical mode of development mediate deductive knowledge plays an incomparably greater part than the immediate axiomatic knowledge upon which all the deductions are based. An infinitude of deductions rests on a very few axioms.

But in the transcendental sphere we have an infinitude of knowledge previous to all deduction, knowledge whose mediated connexions (those of intentional implication) have nothing to do with deduction, and being entirely intuitive prove refractory to every methodically devised scheme of constructive symbolism.

A note of warning may be uttered here against a misunderstanding that has frequently arisen. When, in an anticipatory vein, it is stated right from the start that, according to the author's views (to be established in those further portions of the whole work which are still to be published), all radically scientific philosophy rests on the basis of phenomenology, that in a further sense it is phenomenological philosophy right through, this does not mean to say that philosophy itself is an *a priori* science throughout. The task which this book was planned to carry out, that of establishing a science of the eidetic essence of a transcendental subjectivity, is as far as it can be from carrying the conviction with it that philosophy itself is entirely a science *a priori*. A glance at the mathematical sciences, these great logical instruments for corresponding sciences of fact, would already lead us to anticipate the contrary. The science of fact in the strict sense, the genuinely rational science of nature, has first become possible through the independent elaboration of a "pure" mathematics of nature. The science of pure possibilities must everywhere precede the science of real facts, and give it the guidance of its concrete logic. So is it also in the case of transcendental philosophy, even though the dignity of the service rendered here by a system of the transcendental *a priori* is more exalted.

The understanding, or at any rate the sure grasp, of the distinction between *transcendental phenomenology* and *"descriptive,"* or, as it is often called nowadays, *"phenomenological" psychology,* is a problem that as a rule brings great difficulties with it, which indeed are grounded in the very nature of the case. It has led to misunderstandings, to which even thinkers who subscribe to the phenomenological line of thought are subject. Some attempt to clarify the situation should prove useful.

The change of standpoint which in this work bears the name phenomenological reduction (transcendental-phenomenological we now say, to be more definite) is effected by me, as the actually philosophizing subject, from the natural standpoint as a basis, and I experience myself here in the first instance as "I" in the ordinary sense of the term, as this human person living among others in the world. As a psychologist, I take as my theme this I-type of being and life, in its general aspect, the human being as "psychical." Turning inwards in pure reflection, following exclusively "inner experience" (self-experience and "empathy," to be more precise), and setting aside all the psychophysical questions which relate to man as a corporeal being, I obtain an original and pure descriptive knowledge of the psychical life as it is in itself, the most original information being obtained from myself, because here alone is perception the medium. If, as is often done, descriptions of all sorts, which attach themselves purely and truly to the data of intuition, are referred to as phenomenological, there here grows up, on the pure basis of inner intuition, of the intuition of the soul's own essence, a phenomenological psychology. A right form of method (on this point we shall have something further to say) gives us in point of fact not only scanty, superficially classificatory descriptions, but a great self-supporting science; the latter, however, properly speaking, only when, as is possible also here, one first sets before oneself as goal a science which deals not with the factual data of this inner sphere of intuition, but with the essence, inquiring, that is, after the invariant, essentially characteristic structures of a soul, of a psychical life in general.

If we now perform this transcendental-phenomenological reduction, this transformation of the natural and psychologically inward standpoint whereby it is transcendentalized, the psychological subjectivity loses just that which makes it something real in the world that lies before us; it loses the meaning of the soul as belonging to a body that exists in an objective, spatio-temporal Nature. This transformation of meaning concerns myself, above all, the "I" of the psychological and subsequently transcendental inquirer for the time being. Posited as real *(wirklich),* I am now no longer a human Ego *in* the universal, existentially posited world, but exclusively a subject *for* which this world has being, and purely, indeed, *as* that which appears to me, is presented to me, and of which I am conscious in some way or other, so that the real being of the world thereby remains unconsidered, unquestioned, and its validity left out of account. Now if transcendental description passes no judgment whatsoever upon the world, and upon my human Ego as belonging to the world, and if, in this description, the transcendental Ego exists *(ist)* absolutely in and for itself prior to all cosmic being (which first wins in and through its existential validity), it is still at the same time evident that, at every conversion of meaning which concerns the phenomenological-psychological content of the soul as a whole, this very content by simply putting on another existential meaning *(Seinssinn)* becomes transcendental-phenomenological, just as conversely the latter, on reverting to the natural psychological standpoint, becomes once again psychological. Naturally this correspondence must still hold good if, prior to all interest in the development of psychological science, and of a "descriptive" or "phenomenological psychology" in particular, a transcendental phenomenology is set up under the leading of a philosophical idea, so that through phenomenological reduction the transcendental Ego is directly set up at the focus of reflexion, and made the theme of a transcendental description. We have thus a remarkable thoroughgoing parallelism between a (properly elaborated) phenomenological psychology and a transcendental phenomenology. To each eidetic or empirical determination on the one side there must correspond a parallel feature on the other. And yet this whole content as psychology, considered from the natural standpoint as a positive science, therefore, and related to the world as spread before us, is entirely non-philosophical, whereas "the same" content from the transcendental standpoint, and therefore as transcendental phenomenology, is a philosophical science—indeed, on closer view, *the* basic philosophical science, preparing on descriptive lines the transcendental ground which remains henceforth the exclusive ground for all philosophical knowledge. Here in fact lie the chief difficulties in the way of an understanding, since it must be felt at first as a most unreasonable demand that such a "nuance" springing from a mere change of standpoint should possess such great, and indeed, for all genuine philosophy, such decisive significance. The wholly unique meaning of this "nuance" can be clearly appreciated only when he who philosophizes has reached a radical understanding with himself as to what he proposes to bring under the title "philosophy," and only in so far as he is constrained to look for something differing in principle from positive science: the theoretic control, that is, of something other than the world ostensibly given to us through experience. From such understanding with one's own self, carried out in a really radical and consistent way, there springs up of necessity a motivation which compels the philosophizing Ego to reflect back on that very subjectivity of his, which in all his experience and knowledge of the natural world, both real and possible, is in the last resort the Ego that experiences and knows, and is thus already presupposed in all the natural self-knowledge of the "human Ego who experiences, thinks, and acts naturally in the world." In other words: from this source springs the phenomenological transposition as an absolute requirement, if philosophy generally is to work out its distinctive purposes upon a basis of original experience, and so contrive to begin at all. It can make a beginning, and generally speaking develop all its further philosophical resources, only as a science working from the transcendental-philosophical standpoint. For this very reason the immediate *a priori* phenomenology (portrayed in this work in its actual functioning as that which directly prepares the transcendental basis) is the "first philosophy" in itself, the philosophy of the Beginning. Only when this motivation (which stands in need of a very minute and comprehensive analysis) has become a vital and compelling insight, does it become clear that the "change in shading," which at first appears so strange, transforming as it does a pure psychology of the inner life into a self-styled transcendental phenomenology, determines the being and non-being of philosophy—of a philosophy which knows with thoroughgoing scientific assurance what its own distinctive meaning calls for as the basis and the method of its inquiry. In the light of such self-comprehension, we understand for the first time that deepest and truly radical meaning of "psychologism" (that is, of transcendental psychologism) as the error that perverts the pure meaning of philosophy, proposing as it does to found philosophy on psychology, on the positive science of the life of the soul. This perversion persists unmodified when, in sympathy with our own procedure, the pure psychology of the inner life is set up also as an *a priori* science; even then it remains a positive science, and can provide a basis for positive science only, never for philosophy.

In the course of many years of brooding over these matters, the author has followed up different lines of inquiry, all equally possible, in the attempt to exhibit in an absolutely transparent and compelling way the nature of such motivation as propels beyond the natural positive realism of life and science, and necessitates the transcendental transposition, the "phenomenological Reduction." They are the ways of reaching the starting-point of a serious philosophy, and as they must be thought out in conscious reflexion, they themselves belong properly to the Beginning, as is possible, indeed, only within the beginner as he reflects upon himself. For each of these ways the point of departure is, of course, the natural unsophisticated standpoint of positive reality *(Positivität)* which the world of experience has as the basis of its being, and is confessedly "taken for granted" (the nature of such Being never having been questioned). In the work here presented (Second Section, second chapter, § 33 f.), the author selected that way of approach, which then appeared to him the most effective. It develops as a course of self-reflexion taking place in the region of the pure psychological intuition of the inner life, or, as we might also say, as a "phenomenological" reflexion in the ordinary psychological sense. It leads eventually to the point that I, who am here reflecting upon myself, become conscious that under a consistent and exclusive focusing of experience upon that which is purely inward, upon what is "phenomenologically" accessible to me, I possess in myself an essential individuality, self-contained, and holding well together in itself, to which all real and objectively possible experience and knowledge belongs, through whose agency the objective world is there for me with all its empirically confirmed facts, in and through which it has for me at any rate trustworthy (even if never scientifically authorized) essential validity. This also includes the more special apperceptions through which I take myself to be a man with body and soul, who lives in the world with other men, lives the life of the world, and so forth. Continuing this self-reflexion, I now also become aware that my own phenomenologically self-contained essence can be posited in an *absolute* sense, as I am the Ego who invests the being of the world which I so constantly speak about the existential validity, as an existence *(Sein)* which wins for me from my own life's pure essence meaning and substantiated validity. I myself as this individual essence, posited absolutely, as the open infinite field of pure phenomenological data and their inseparable unity, am the "transcendental Ego"; the absolute positing means that of world is no longer "given" to me advance, its validity that of a simple existent, but that henceforth it is exclusively my Ego that is given (given from my new standpoint), given purely as that which has being in itself, in itself experiences a world, confirms the same, and so forth.

Review Questions

1. Give a brief account of what Husserl means by phenomenology.
2. What is meant by intentionality?
3. How does the Husserlian *epoché* differ from the Cartesian *cogito?*
4. What is meant by consciousness "constituting" the world?
5. Is Husserl successful in avoiding extreme subjectivism?

Suggestions for Further Reading

Ideas: General Introduction to Pure Phenomenology. Tr. Gibson, W. R. London, George Allen and Unwin, 1931.

Kohàk, Erazim. *Idea and Experience: Edmund Husserl's Project of Phenomenology in "Ideas I."* Chicago, University of Chicago Press, 1978.

Smith, B. and Smith, D. W., ed. *The Cambridge Companion to Husserl.* New York, Cambridge University Press, 1994.

Welton, D. *The Essential Husserl.* Bloomington, Indiana University Press, 1999.

27

Martin Heidegger (1889–1976)

The "human condition"

Though in modern times the emphasis given to consciousness as the starting point of philosophy began with Descartes, in the last chapter we saw the immense contribution made by Husserl in the same vein. When this is coupled with the intense focus on the subjective initiated by Kierkegaard, we can readily understand how the human person defined in the drama of the "human condition" emerges as one of the consuming themes of contemporary philosophy. Reflection on the life of human beings immersed in all the vagaries of a day-by-day existence gave rise, in the philosopher's lexicon, to words and phrases like *absurdity, anguish, dread, self, the other, value, freedom, consciousness, finitude, responsibility, transcendence, hate, love, death,* and *God,* all of which signify the personal direction such a philosophy took. We shall see in the following chapter on Jean-Paul Sartre how this development affected a style of philosophy called *existentialism,* within which category historians almost always include the philosophy of Martin Heidegger. For his part, Heidegger rejects this categorization and emphatically distances himself from Sartre on the meaning of humanism. Though the wellsprings of Heidegger's philosophy run deep—with his studies in ancient philosophy, especially Aristotle; in medieval philosophy, especially Augustine and Scotus; and in modern philosophy, especially Kant and Nietzsche—his immediate preparation was phenomenological and flowed naturally from his association with Husserl, his revered mentor and sometime friend.

Heidegger's Philosophical Development and Political Involvement

Martin Heidegger was born in Messkirch, Baden-Württemberg, in 1889 and received his early education until the age of fourteen in the local schools, after which, for his secondary education, he attended Jesuit schools for the next six years where he "acquired everything that was to be of lasting value." Here he received a thorough grounding in classical studies. His devotion to the classical period rooted him for the rest of his life in Greek culture and the Greek language, opening up a constant stream of fresh philosophical insights together with the language in which to express them. For a short time he was a Jesuit novice before he entered the diocesan seminary at Freiburg. However, after several years he left the seminary to devote himself entirely to the study of philosophy, for which purpose he enrolled at the University of Freiburg. This worked out providentially for Heidegger because in 1916 Edmund Husserl, who by now had received wide recognition as a profound and creative philosopher, was appointed professor. Heidegger studied with him and became so thoroughly immersed in phenomenology that several years later his mentor astonished his student with the words "you and I *are* phenomenology."

In an atmosphere of friendship, Husserl encouraged and aided Heidegger in the writing of *Being and Time,* which established Heidegger's reputation as a brilliant philosopher and original thinker; Heidegger dedicated it to Husserl but years later, owing to his departure from the direction his mentor's philosophical development was taking, he withdrew the dedication. With Husserl's help, Heidegger assumed the professorship of philosophy at Marburg, and after a few years, when Husserl retired from Freiburg, his former student was appointed to replace him in 1928.

In the early thirties the Nazi party, promising so much to a Germany in shambles and winning so many enthusiastic adherents to its cause, even among university professors and administrators, proved to be a wrenching experience for some who tried to hold out for the independence and freedom of the university. When the rector of the University of Freiburg was forced to step down as a result of this initial turbulence, Heidegger was elected rector in April of 1933. After refusing, like his predecessor, to permit anti-Jewish posters from being displayed, Heidegger tried to settle into an accommodating posture with the new regime to protect the university from political interference. To this end, he became a member of the Party and delivered several addresses carefully upholding the priority of teaching and learning, while at the same time asking universities to undertake "the education and training of the leaders and guardians of the destiny of the German people." But Heidegger's subsequent activities, unsympathetic and even hostile to the Nazi cause, precipitated his resignation ten months later. Heidegger's conduct during these trying times has been the subject of agonizing reevaluation by some historians who feel that he was in reality sympathetic to the Nazi regime, never really renouncing his questionable activities, and by his supporters who feel that he, like many Germans early on, could not have foreseen the evils latent in Nazism and therefore it would be grossly unfair to judge his activity as rector retroactively from the final state of affairs. At the end of the war, the French occupation forces in their de-Nazification program, considered his behavior sufficient warrant to ban him from teaching, which lasted for five years until 1951, after which he was allowed to return a year away from retirement. From the early fifties on he lived at Freiburg, Messkirch, and in his ski hut in the Black Forest, giving himself unhurried time and space to ponder, study, write, and publish. He also traveled to France and Greece, and maintained a close relationship with his many friends. He died in 1976.

More than with any other area of philosophy, Heidegger's name is associated with the study of being. It was his lifelong preoccupation, going back to his youth when a clerical friend of the family put into his hands a copy of a doctoral dissertation on the many meanings of being in the philosophy of Aristotle. As a result, Heidegger eventually committed himself to the philosophical goal of rethinking the meaning of being, convinced that, once you understand the distinction between beings as individuals and being itself, you understand how metaphysics in the West invested so much in the individual that it *forgot* "being itself," and the phrase "the forgetting of being" has become a Heideggerian logo standing for the decline of the West and the advent of nihilism.

When the young Heidegger turned to Aristotle's *Metaphysics,* he observed that indeed the meaning of "being" is manifold, inasmuch as it variously means substance, accident, that which is, actuality, potentiality, truth, becoming. However, in speaking thus of the many meanings of being, Aristotle holds that we always have *One* ultimate meaning in mind, just as when we speak of many things as "healthy," we have only one "health" in mind; so, just as there is one science of health there must be one science of being. For Heidegger, then, if "being" can be said of many things, precisely what is its most fundamental meaning? What does "Being" mean? To answer this question, having already acquired a reputation for philosophical originality and for his fresh insights into Aristotle, Heidegger published *Being and Time* in 1927, hailed by some to be the most important work in philosophy of the century; in it he made an immense effort to set the study of being on an entirely new path.

The Primacy of Being

But how to make a start? Is it possible to "get inside" the vast array of individual beings for a firsthand look as to what "Being" might mean? This, of course, could not be done, save for one exception, to get inside the human being or, better, inside oneself. This is the path Heidegger took to inquire into what the *human*-being would reveal about *being*-human, and the method he used was the method of phenomenology which, as we saw in the last chapter, calls for focusing on the object as presented in our consciousness, from a point where there is nothing but the object itself, so that a pure description, without explanation or theory, becomes available. With this beginning, the higher reaches of being may be achieved so that, for Heidegger, it becomes possible to discover what is hidden through the disclosures a thing makes of itself, and one who has fine-tuned himself to the task is able to recognize these disclosures and come to an understanding of what-is.

An adventure of this kind, bound to encounter a new vision of things, will demand new words, phrases, or usages to express them. Such a word is had in what, for Heidegger, is the basic meaning of truth; he retrieves an ancient Greek usage by stating that a thing "unconceals" itself, or that the "hiddenness" of a thing is "overcome" by its "unconcealment." The first "unconcealment," the first truth, or the first understanding man has of himself is the fact that he is *there* in the world; not merely in a physical sense but in the sense of the context where the "human" takes shape. It is the everyday existence of man, dependent, contingent, without given meaning or sense. It is as if man were "thrown-down" in the world; it is the "facticity" of man. This "being-in-the-world," the fact of being simply "there," Heidegger refers to as "there-being," or, in German, *Dasein* (better, *Da-sein*), a word that has been taken over directly into English.

Getting to the Meaning of the Human Be-ing

The meaning of human existence, insofar as it can be ascertained at all, must come from the "being-in-the-world." It cannot come from any other context than the one man finds himself in; the moment the context possesses anything other than "thereness," it becomes a different context and disallowed if we are trying to get a pure description of human existence. If, for example, we invoke an infinite Being as the explanation of "thereness," then the stripped-down immediacy of being-there is lost. So the meaning of human existence must come from the existential fact of man's "thereness," from his "existentiality." From this fundamental self-understanding, man can proceed to the other elements of his immersion in existence, and he does so on the basis of concern, or care. Concern is one of the various modes of awareness Heidegger describes that harvest for us the meaning of being-in-the-world, and the more I, as Dasein, harvest these hitherto undisclosed elements of existence, the more I appropriate existence for myself and pave the way to what Heidegger will refer to later on as "freedom."

One of these further elements of existential immersion has to do with what Heidegger calls *temporality*. The problem of time has been a constant concern for philosophers in the West, seen now as the opposite of eternity, or again as the measure of change, or again as a human imperfection calling for redemption. But, ever since Aristotle's description of time in terms of "before" and "after," or St. Augustine's puzzling over the "length" of time, or Kant's casting of time as an epistemological absolute, there has not been significant advance in the understanding of the meaning of time because of a too literal adherence to the notion of chronology. The mystery of time has even been trivialized over the centuries with emphasis being given to the speed in which things can be done, with the inevitable consequence that the mystery of being has also been trivialized. Past, present, and future are indeed factors in Heidegger's account of temporality, but they are considerations of metaphysics and not chronology; temporality has more to do with meaning than it has with the calendar. The kind of time Heidegger is striving for is "existential" time; it is *my* time, *my* life, that is at stake. Temporality must be grasped as constituting our very life, and the ultimate reason for this is had, in Heidegger's early writings, in what he calls the "horizon," a concept borrowed from Husserl. The horizon, with its obvious imagery of the togetherness of things mysteriously meeting in the distance and whose very sight gives one a sense of location, allows a thing to be what it is; for man the horizon constitutes his life, his Dasein, and though he realizes that the horizon can never be known in itself, he also realizes that he can only know himself within the "horizonal" context. We can understand that our life is linked to an unknown future, to which death is a poignant witness, and that the future, though chronologically not yet here, is existentially here, already present to us at every moment, creating in us the mood of dread, a sense of the nothingness of being-in-the-world. For Heidegger, man has been "pro-jected" through an uncharted present into an uncertain future, and however agonizing the effort might be to understand this, only by understanding is one able to transcend it.

The third element of human existence besides "being-there" and "temporality" is the response the human being gives to his condition, a condition of apparent aimlessness, *anguish*, fragility, and unease, all reminiscent of Kierkegaard's description of the human condition. Heidegger recognizes, as does Kierkegaard, the critical character of death for human existence, but, whereas Kierkegaard sees death as an event to be overcome by a deeper engagement with the transcendental dimension of one's individuality, Heidegger sees death as a prism through which our being-in-the-world is refracted as being-toward-death. Death, for Dasein, brings into question all relations in human existence, indeed, even though death is in the future, "all relations in it to other Daseins are dissolved." More than any other event, death reveals temporality as pertaining to the very structure of human existence, for death is precisely the future thrusting itself into the present. Man can ignore death by losing himself in the swirl of daily busyness, and thus risk his authenticity; however, in recognizing our tendency toward nothingness, toward death, and accepting it, is the beginning of authentic freedom for the human being.

Reversal: to know Man Through Being, not Being Through Man

In working out his scheme of metaphysics, especially in *Being and Time,* if we can speak of the direction in which he was going, Heidegger was working toward the discovery of Being through man, through Dasein. Though he never completed *Being and Time* as he had hoped, in lectures and papers on various occasions he did give some indication of the new direction he wanted to take, and that was to get at man through Being, rather than to get at Being through man, just the reverse of his earlier direction; whence the title of the work, never published, as *Time and Being,* a complement to *Being and Time.* This change of focus, or direction, is referred to simply as "the reversal," or the "turn." Heidegger developed this line of thought in a series of responses to a number of questions on existence, taking the occasion to differentiate his philosophy from that of the so-called existentialists, particularly Jean-Paul Sartre. As we shall observe in the next chapter, Sartre held that "existence precedes essence" in that there is no absolute human nature equipped with an internal direction or purpose, no way to say "in accordance with nature," no standard or norm against which our actions are to be measured as right or wrong, no essence to appeal to. It matters profoundly, however, how man acts, for man *is* how he acts—the very reality of man is constituted by his activity so that "essence" is shaped "existentially" by the choices he makes. Sartre's intense centering on the human subject, "subjectivity" therefore, is the reason he refers to "existentialism" as a "humanism."

But for Heidegger, even though Sartre's view of existence is a marked departure from the traditional view and represents the limits to which his conception of a philosophy of existence can bring us, it is still not radical enough. Heidegger feels that his own approach to existence is *outside* any other approach ever taken, including Sartre's. For him, the existence of man is not the totality of existence, as it is for Sartre; it is rather one manifestation, one epiphany, one thrusting-out of Being. That is why Heidegger at times rewrites "existence" as "ek-sistence": man "ek-sists," that is, stands forth, or "stands out into the truth of Being." The truth of Being can be made known, or identified, to us only ". . . when it dawns on us that man is in that he ek-sists. Were we now to say this in the language of tradition, it would run: the ek-sistence of man is his substance." So if we are looking for an identification of man, in Heidegger's own words, "Ek-sistence identifies the determination of what man is in the destiny of truth." Dasein therefore is described in its "thrown" character, thrown by Being as on a "fateful sending" to its destiny.

In any other philosophy of existence the role of action is to produce an effect, so it could be argued that the meaning of "humanism" depends on the kind of action in question, or on the kind of engagement the action represents for the human being. For a variety of historical reasons, Heidegger would have been happy to drop the word *humanism,* but for reasons rooted in his philosophy of being he could never hold to a humanism based on an effect-producing action: he maintains that the activity of thinking, a kind of meditation as opposed to ratiocination, is the high point of being human and is an action for which producing an effect has no meaning; thinking is an engagement by and for the truth of Being.

Further Implications

This introduction has been an attempt to convey the ethos of Heidegger's work and the spirit of his method of philosophizing. His many years of meditation and writing brought him to a vast array of explorations including those on the essence of truth, on poetry, on language, on art, and on the sciences, but none of these explorations were undertaken with the idea of developing a "practical" body of philosophy; no, he was much too remote, for he attempted only to analyze these questions in light of Being. In his early years, his original plan seemed to be to proceed from the being of the human being to Being in general, but in vain do we look for a "conclusion" to his philosophy, or a final statement. Indeed, as time went on, it became clear that his vocation was simply to follow the path he was on and, based on his experience as a hiker, to take the sudden and unexpected "turn" in the path and follow it wherever it would happen to lead.

The philosophy of being is richer for Heidegger's philosophizing presence. Moved by all the great philosophers of being, beginning with Parmenides, Heidegger saw that much more had to be said. The mystery of being is contained, both in its hiddenness and disclosure, in every single thing: the tree, the dog, the word, the thought, the star, the painting, the sonata, the human being. How then can being be so multiple, so varied, so fruitful without at the same time opening our minds, and perhaps our hearts, to the oneness of Being? The vast array of questions raised by Heidegger and the continual flow of fresh insights running through all his works had a profound influence not only on philosophy but also on the meaning of language, on art and poetry, and finally on theology striving to articulate the saving truths of faith. Though there have been many critics of Heidegger, accusing him of destroying reason or writing mere jargon, the judgment of Hans-Georg Gadamer, one of his well-known students, seems more dispassionate: ". . . his place in our troubled century is . . . beyond dispute."

READINGS

The Fundamental Question of Metaphysics
(from *An Introduction to Metaphysics*)

Why are there essents[1] rather than nothing? That is the question. Clearly it is no ordinary question. "Why are there essents, why is there anything at all, rather than nothing?"—obviously this is the first of all questions, though not in a chronological sense. Individuals and peoples ask a good many questions in the course of their historical passage through time. They examine, explore, and test a good many things before they run into the question "Why are there essents rather than nothing?" Many men never encounter this question, if by encounter we mean not merely to hear and read about it as an interrogative formulation but to ask the question, that is, to bring it about, to raise it, to feel its inevitability.

And yet each of us is grazed at least once, perhaps more than once, by the hidden power of this question, even if he is not aware of what is happening to

---

[1]The translator uses the newly coined word *essents* for "existence," or "things that are."

him. The question looms in moments of great despair, when things tend to lose all their weight and all meaning becomes obscured. Perhaps it will strike but once like a muffled bell that rings into our life and gradually dies away. It is present in moments of rejoicing, when all the things around us are transfigured and seem to be there for the first time, as if it might be easier to think they are not than to understand that they are and are as they are. The question is upon us in boredom, when we are equally removed from despair and joy, and everything about us seems so hopelessly commonplace that we no longer care whether anything is or is not—and with this the question "Why are there essents rather than nothing?" is evoked in a particular form.

But this question may be asked expressly, or, unrecognized as a question, it may merely pass through our lives like a brief gust of wind; it may press hard upon us, or under one pretext or another, we may thrust it away from us and silence it. In any case it is never the question that we ask first in point of time.

But it is the first question in another sense—in regard to rank. This may be clarified in three ways. The question "Why are there essents rather than nothing?" is first in rank for us first because it is the most far reaching, second because it is the deepest, and finally because it is the most fundamental of all questions.

It is the widest of all questions. It confines itself to no particular essent of whatever kind. The question takes in everything, and this means not only everything that is present in the broadest sense but also everything that ever was or will be. The range of this question finds its limit only in nothing, in that which simply is not and never was. Everything that is not nothing is covered by this question, and ultimately even nothing itself; not because it is *something,* since after all we speak of it, but because it *is* nothing. Our question reaches out so far that we can never go further. We do not inquire into this and that, or into each essent in turn, but from the very outset into the essent as a whole, or, as we say for reasons to be discussed below: into the essent as such in its entirety.

This broadest of questions is also the deepest: Why are there essents . . .? Why, that is to say, on what ground? from what source does the essent derive? on what ground does it stand? The question is not concerned with particulars, with what essents are and of what nature at any time, here and there, with how they can be changed, what they can be used for, and so on. The question aims at the ground of what is insofar as it is. To seek the ground is to try to get to the bottom; what is put in question is thus related to the ground. However, since the question is a question, it remains to be seen whether the ground arrived at is really a ground, that is, whether it provides a foundation; whether it is a primal ground (Ur-gund); or whether it fails to provide a foundation and is an abyss (Ab-grund); or whether the ground is neither one nor the other but presents only a perhaps necessary appearance of foundation—in other words, it is a non-ground (Un-grund). Be that as it may, the ground in question must account for the being of the essent as such. This question "why" does not look for causes that are of the same kind and on the same level as the essent itself. This "why" does not move on any one plane but penetrates to the "underlying" ("zu-grunde" liegend) realms and indeed to the very last of them, to the limit; turning away from the surface, from all shallowness, it strives toward the depths; this broadest of all questions is also the deepest.

Finally, this broadest and deepest question is also the most fundamental. What do we mean by this? If we take the question in its full scope, namely the essent as such in its entirety, it readily follows that in asking this question we keep our distance from every particular and individual essent, from every this and that. For we mean the essent as whole, without any special preference. Still, it is noteworthy that in this questioning *one* kind of essent persists in coming to the fore, namely the men who ask the question. But the question should not concern itself with any particular essent. In the spirit of its unrestricted scope, all essents are of equal value. An elephant in an Indian jungle "is" just as much as some chemical combustion process at work on the planet Mars, and so on.

Accordingly, if our question "Why are there essents rather than nothing?" is taken in its fullest sense, we must avoid singling out any special, particular essent, including man. For what indeed is man? Consider the earth within the endless darkness of space in the universe. By way of comparison it is a tiny grain of sand; between it and the next grain of its own size there extends a mile or more of emptiness; on the surface of this grain of sand there lives a crawling, bewildered swarm of supposedly intelligent animals, who for a moment have discovered knowledge. And what is the temporal extension of a human life amid all the millions of years? Scarcely a move of the second hand, a breath. Within the essent as a whole there is no legitimate ground for singling out this essent which is called mankind and to which we ourselves happen to belong.

But whenever the essent as a whole enters into this question, a privileged, unique relation arises between it and the act of questioning. For through this questioning the essent as a whole is for the first time opened up *as such* with a view to its possible ground, and in the act of questioning it is kept open. In relation to the essent as such in its entirety the asking of the question is not just any occurrence within the realm of the assent, like the falling of raindrops for example. The question "why" may be said to confront the essent as a whole, to break out of it, though never completely. But that is exactly why the act of questioning is privileged. Because it confronts the essent as a whole, but does not break loose from it, the content of the question reacts upon the questioning itself. Why the why? What is the ground of this question "why" which presumes to ask after the ground of the assent as a whole? Is the ground asked for in *this* why not merely a foreground—which would imply that the sought-for ground is again an essent? Does not the "first" question nevertheless come first in view of the intrinsic rank of the question of being and its modulations?

(From *An Introduction to Metaphysics,* Trans. R. Manheim, New Haven: Yale University Press, 1959.)

Selections from Being and Time

4. THE ONTICAL PRIORITY OF THE QUESTION OF BEING

Science in general may be defined as the totality established through an interconnection of true propositions. This definition is not complete, nor does it reach the meaning of science. As ways in which man behaves, sciences have the manner of Being which this entity—man himself—possesses. This entity we denote by the term *"Dasein"*. Scientific research is not the only manner of Being which this entity can have, nor is it the one which lies closest. Moreover, Dasein itself has a special distinctiveness as compared with other entities, and it is worth our while to bring this to view in a provisional way. Here our discussion must anticipate a later analysis, in which our results will be authentically exhibited for the first time.

Dasein is an entity which does not just occur among other entities. Rather it is ontically distinguished by the fact that, in its very Being, that Being is an *issue* for it. But in that case, this is a constitutive state of Dasein's Being, and this implies that Dasein, in its Being, has a relationship towards that Being—a relationship which itself is one of Being. And this means further that there is some way in which Dasein understands itself in its Being, and that to some degree it does so explicitly. It is peculiar to this entity that with and through its Being, this Being is disclosed to it. *Understanding of Being is itself a definite characteristic of Dasein's Being.* Dasein is ontically distinctive in that it *is* ontological.

Here "Being-ontological" is not yet tantamount to "developing an ontology". So if we should reserve the term "ontology" for that theoretical inquiry which is explicitly devoted to the meaning of entities, then what we have had in mind in speaking of Dasein's "Being-ontological" is to be designated as something "pre-ontological". It does not signify simply "being-ontical", however, but rather "being in such a way that one has an understanding of Being."

That kind of Being towards which Dasein can comport itself in one way or another, and always does comport itself somehow, we call *"existence" [Existenz]*. And because we cannot define Dasein's essence by citing a "what" of the kind that pertains to a subject-matter, and because its essence lies rather in the fact that in each case it has its Being to be, and has it as its own, we have chosen to designate this entity as "Dasein", a term which is purely an expression of its Being.

Dasein always understands itself in terms of its existence—in terms of a possibility of itself: to be itself or not itself. Dasein has either chosen these possibilities itself, or got itself into them, or grown up in them already. Only the particular Dasein decides its existence, whether it does so by taking hold or by neglecting. The question of existence never gets straightened out except through existing itself. The understanding of oneself which leads *along this way* we call *"existentiell."* The question of existence is one of Dasein's ontical 'affairs'. This does not require that the ontological structure of existence should be theoretically transparent. The question about that structure aims at the analysis of what constitutes existence. The context of such structures we call *"existentiality."* Its analytic has the character of an understanding which is not existentiell, but rather *existential*. The task of an existential analytic of Dasein has been delineated in advance, as regards both its possibility and its necessity, in Dasein's ontical constitution.

12. A PRELIMINARY SKETCH OF BEING-IN-THE-WORLD, IN TERMS OF AN ORIENTATION TOWARDS BEING-IN AS SUCH

In our preparatory discussions we have brought out some characteristics of Being which will provide us with a steady light for our further investigation, but which will at the same time become structurally concrete as that investigation continues. Dasein is an entity which, in its very Being, comports itself understandingly towards that Being. In saying this, we are calling attention to the formal concept of existence. Dasein exists.

Furthermore, Dasein is an entity which in each case I myself am. Mineness belongs to any existent Dasein, and belongs to it as the condition which makes authenticity and inauthenticity possible. In each case Dasein exists in one or the other of these two modes, or else it is modally undifferentiated.

But these are both ways in which Dasein's Being takes on a definite character, and they must be seen and understood *a priori* as grounded upon that state of Being which we have called *"Being-in-the-world"*. An interpretation of this constitutive state is needed if we are to set up our analytic of Dasein correctly.

The compound expression 'Being-in-the-world' indicates in the very way we have coined it, that it stands for a *unitary* phenomenon. This primary datum must be seen as a whole. But while Being-in-the-world cannot be broken up into contents which may be pieced together, this does not prevent it from having several constitutive items in its structure. Indeed the phenomenal datum which our expression indicates is one which may, in fact, be looked at in three ways. If we study it, keeping the whole phenomenon firmly in mind beforehand, the following items may be brought out for emphasis:

First, *'in-the-world'*. With regard to this there arises the task of inquiring into the ontological structure of the 'world' and defining the idea of *worldhood* as such.

Second, that *entity* which in every case has Being-in-the-world as the way in which it is. Here we are seeking that which one inquires into when one asks the question 'Who?' By a phenomenological demonstration we shall determine who is in the mode of Dasein's average everydayness.

Third, *Being-in [In-sein]* as such. We must set forth the ontological Constitution of inhood [Inheit] itself. Emphasis upon any one of these constitutive items signifies that the others are emphasized along with it; this means that in any such case the whole phenomenon gets seen. Of course Being-in-the-world is a state of Dasein which is necessary *a priori*, but it is far from sufficient for completely determining Dasein's Being. . . .

14. THE IDEA OF THE WORLDHOOD OF THE WORLD IN GENERAL

Being-in-the-world shall first be made visible with regard to that item of its structure which is the 'world' itself. To accomplish this task seems easy and so trivial as to make one keep taking for granted that it may be dispensed with.

What can be meant by describing 'the world' as a phenomenon? It means to let us see what shows itself in 'entities' within the world. Here the first step is to enumerate the things that are 'in' in the world: houses, trees, people, mountains, stars. We can *depict* the way such entities 'look', and we can give an *account* of occurrences in them and with them. This, however, is obviously a pre-phenomenological 'business' which cannot be at all relevant phenomenologically. Such a description is always confined to entities. It is ontical. But what we are seeking is Being. And we have formally defined 'phenomenon' in the phenomenological sense as that which shows itself as Being and as a structure of Being. . . .

'Worldhood' is an ontological concept, and stands for the structure of one of the constitutive items of Being-in-the-world. But we know Being-in-the-world as a way in which Dasein's character is defined existentially. Thus worldhood itself is an *existentiale*. If we inquire ontologically about the 'world', we by no means abandon the analytic of Dasein as a field for thematic study. Ontologically, 'world' is not a way of characterizing those entities which Dasein essentially is *not;* it is rather a characteristic of Dasein itself. This does not rule out the possibility that when we investigate the phenomenon of the 'world' we must do so by the avenue of entities within-the-world and the Being which they possess. The task of 'describing' the world phenomenologically is so far from obvious that even if we do no more than determine adequately what form it shall take, essential ontological clarifications will be needed.

This discussion of the word 'world', and our frequent use of it have made it apparent that it is used in several ways. By unravelling these we can get an indication of the different kinds of phenomena that are signified, and of the way in which they are interconnected.

1. "World" is used as an ontical concept, and signifies the totality of those entities which can be present-at-hand within the world.

2. "World" functions as an ontological term, and signifies the Being of those entities which we have just mentioned. And indeed 'world' can become a term for any realm which encompasses a multiplicity of entities: for instance, when one talks of the 'world' of a mathematician, 'world' signifies the realm of possible objects of mathematics.

3. "World" can be understood in another ontical sense—not, however, as those entities which Dasein essentially is not and which can be encountered within-the-world, but rather as that *'wherein'* a factical Dasein as such can be said to 'live'. "World" has here a pre-ontological existentiell signification. Here again there are different possibilities: "world" may stand for the 'public' we-world, or one's 'own' closest (domestic) environment.

4. Finally, "world" designates the ontologico-existential concept of *worldhood*. Worldhood itself may have as its modes whatever structural wholes any special 'worlds' may have at the time; but it embraces in itself the *a priori* character of worldhood in general. We shall reserve the expression "world" as a term for our third signification. If we should sometimes use it in the first of these senses, we shall mark this with single quotation marks.

The derivative form 'worldly' will then apply terminologically to a kind of Being which belongs to Dasein, never to a kind which belongs to entities present-at-hand 'in' the world. We shall designate these latter entities as "belonging to the world" or "within-the-world". . . .

The theme of our analytic is to be Being-in-the-world, and accordingly the very world itself; and these are to be considered within the horizon of average everydayness—the kind of Being which is *closest* to Dasein. We must make a study of everyday Being-in-the-world; with the phenomenal support which this gives us, something like the world must come into view.

40. THE BASIC STATE-OF-MIND OF ANXIETY AS A DISTINCTIVE WAY IN WHICH DASEIN IS DISCLOSED

One of Dasein's possibilities of Being is to give us ontical 'information' about Dasein itself as an entity. Such information is possible only in that disclosedness which belongs to Dasein and which is grounded in state-of-mind and understanding. How far is anxiety a state-of-mind which is distinctive? How is it that in anxiety Dasein gets brought before itself through its own Being, so that we can define phenomenologically the character of the entity disclosed in anxiety, and define it as such in its Being, or make adequate preparations for doing so?

Since our aim is to proceed towards the Being of the totality of the structural whole, we shall take as our point of departure the concrete analyses of falling which we have just carried through. Dasein's absorption in the "they" and its absorption in the 'world' of its concern, make manifest something like a *fleeing* of Dasein in the face of itself—of itself as an authentic potentiality-for-Being-its-Self. This phenomenon of Dasein's fleeing *in the face of itself* and in the face of its authenticity, seems at least a suitable phenomenal basis for the following investigation. But to bring itself face to face with itself, is precisely what Dasein does *not* do when it thus flees. It turns *away from* itself in accordance with its ownmost inertia of falling. In investigating such phenomena, however, we must be careful not to confuse ontico-existentiell characterization with ontologico-existential Interpretation nor may we overlook the positive phenomenal bases provided for this Interpretation by such a characterization. . . .

To understand this talk about Dasein's fleeing in the face of itself in falling, we must recall that Being-in-the-world is a basic state of Dasein. *That in the face of which one has anxiety is Being-in-the-world as such.* . . .

Accordingly, when something threatening brings itself close, anxiety does not 'see' any definite 'here' or 'yonder' from which it comes. That in the face of which one has anxiety is characterized by the fact that what threatens is *nowhere.* Anxiety 'does not know' what that in the face of which it is anxious is. 'Nowhere', however, does not signify nothing: this is where any region lies, and there too lies any disclosedness of the world for essentially spatial Being-in. Therefore that which threatens cannot bring itself close from a definite direction within what is close by; it is already 'there', and yet nowhere; it is so close that it is oppressive and stifles one's breath, and yet it is nowhere. . . .

Anxiety makes manifest in Dasein in its *Being towards* its ownmost potentiality-for-Being—that is, its *Being-free for* the freedom of choosing itself and taking hold of itself. Anxiety brings Dasein face to face with its *Being-free for (propensio in . . .)* the authenticity of its Being, and for this authenticity as a possibility which it always is. But at the same time, this is the Being to which Dasein as Being-in-the-world has been delivered over.

51. BEING-TOWARDS-DEATH AND THE EVERYDAYNESS OF DASEIN

In setting forth average everyday Being-towards-death, we must take our orientation from those structures of everydayness at which we have earlier arrived. In Being-towards-death, Dasein comports itself *towards itself* as a distinctive potentiality-for-Being. But the Self of everydayness is the "they". The "they" is constituted by the way things have been publicly interpreted, which expresses itself in idle talk. Idle talk must accordingly make manifest the way in which everyday Dasein interprets for itself its Being-towards-death. The foundation of any interpretation is an act of understanding, which is always accompanied by a state-of-mind, or, in other words, which has a mood. So we must ask how Being-towards-death is disclosed by the kind of understanding which, with its state-of-mind, lurks in the idle talk of the "they". How does the "they" comport itself understandingly towards that ownmost possibility of Dasein, which is non-relational and is not to be outstripped? What state-of-mind discloses to the "they" that it has been delivered over to death, and in what way?

In the publicness with which we are with one another in our everyday manner, death is 'known' as a mishap which is constantly occurring—as a 'case of death'. Someone or other 'dies', be he neighbour or stranger. People who are no acquaintances of ours are 'dying' daily and hourly. 'Death' is encountered as a well-known event occurring within-the-world. As such it remains in the inconspicuousness characteristic of what is encountered in an everyday fashion. The "they" has already stowed away an interpretation for this event. It talks of it in a 'fugitive' manner, either expressly or else in a way which is mostly inhibited, as if to say, "One of these days one will die too, in the end; but right now it has nothing to do with us."

The analysis of the phrase 'one dies' reveals unambiguously the kind of Being which belongs to everyday Being-towards-death. In such a way of talking, death is understood as an indefinite something which, above all, must duly arrive from somewhere or other, but which is proximally *not yet present-at-hand* for oneself, and is therefore no threat. The expression 'one dies' spreads abroad the opinion that what gets reached, as it were, by death, is the "they". In Dasein's public way of interpreting, it is said that 'one dies', because everyone else and oneself can talk himself into saying that "in no case is it I myself", for this "one" is *the "nobody"*. 'Dying' is levelled off to an occurrence which reaches Dasein, to be sure, but belongs to nobody in particular. If idle talk is always ambiguous, so is this manner of talking about death. Dying, which is essentially mine in such a way that no one can be my representative, is perverted into an event of public occurrence which the "they" encounters. In the way of talking which we have characterized, death is spoken of as a 'case' which is constantly occurring. Death gets passed off as always something 'actual'; its character as a possibility gets concealed, and so are the other two items that belong to it—the fact that it is non-relational and that it is not to be outstripped. By such ambiguity, Dasein puts itself in the position of losing itself in the "they" as regards a distinctive potentiality-for-Being which belongs to Dasein's ownmost Self. The "they" gives its approval, and aggravates the *temptation* to cover up from oneself one's ownmost Being-towards-death. This evasive concealment in the face of death dominates everydayness so stubbornly that, in Being with one another, the 'neighbours' often still keep talking the 'dying person' into the belief that he will escape death and soon return to the tranquillized everydayness of the world of his concern. Such 'solicitude' is meant to 'console' him. It insists upon bringing him back into Dasein, while in addition it helps him to keep his ownmost non-relational possibility-of-Being completely concealed. In this manner the "they" provides a *constant tranquillization about death.* At bottom, however, this is a tranquillization not only for him who is 'dying' but just as much for those who 'console' him. And even in the case of a demise, the public is still not to have its own tranquillity upset by such an event, or be disturbed in the carefreeness with which it concerns itself. Indeed the dying of Others is seen often enough as a social inconvenience, if not even a downright tactlessness, against which the public is to be guarded....

But temptation, tranquillization, and alienation are distinguishing marks of the kind of Being called *"falling".* As falling, everyday Being-towards-death is a constant *fleeing in the face of death.* Being-*towards*-the-end has the mode of *evasion in the face of it*—giving new explanations for it, understanding it inauthentically, and concealing it. Factically one's own Dasein is always dying already; that is to say, it is in a Being-towards-its-end. And it hides this Fact from itself by recoining "death" as just a "case of death" in Others—an everyday occurrence which, if need be, gives us the assurance still more plainly that 'oneself' is still 'living'. But in thus falling and fleeing *in the face of* death, Dasein's everydayness attests that the very "they" itself already has the definite character of *Being-towards-death,* even when it is not explicitly engaged in 'thinking about death'. *Even in average everydayness, this ownmost potentiality-for-Being, which is non-relational and not to be outstripped, is constantly an issue for Dasein. This is the case when its concern is merely in the mode of an untroubled indifference* towards *the uttermost possibility of existence.*

81. WITHIN-TIME-NESS AND THE GENESIS OF THE ORDINARY CONCEPTION OF TIME

How does something like 'time' first show itself for everyday circumspective concern? In what kind of concernful equipment-using dealings does it become *explicitly* accessible? If it has been made public with the disclosedness of the world, if it has always been already a matter of concern with the discoveredness of entities within-the-world—a discoveredness which belongs to the world's disclosedness—and if it has been a matter of such concern in so far as Dasein calculates time in reckoning with *itself,* then the kind of behaviour in which 'one' explicitly regulates oneself *according to time,* lies in the use of clocks. The existential-temporal meaning of this turns out to be a making-present of the travelling pointer. By *following* the positions of the pointer in a way which makes present, one *counts* them. This making-present temporalizes itself in the ecstatical unity of a retention which awaits. To *retain* the 'on that former occasion' and to retain it by *making it present,* signifies that in saying "now" one is open for the horizon of the earlier—that is, of the "now-no-longer". To *await* the 'then' by *making it present,* means that in saying "now" one is open for the horizon of the later—that is, of the "now-not-yet". *Time is what shows itself in such a making-present.* How then, are we to define the *time* which is manifest within the horizon of the circumspective concernful clock-using in which one takes one's time? *This time is that which is* counted *and which shows itself when one follows the travelling pointer, counting and making present in such a way that this making-present temporalizes itself in an ecstatical unity with the retaining and awaiting which are horizonally open according to the "earlier" and "later".* This, however, is nothing else than an existential-ontological interpretation of Aristotle's definition of "time": τουτο γάρέφστιν ὁ χρόνος, ἀριθμὸς κινήσεως κατὰ; τό πρότερον και; ὕστερον. "For this is time: that which is counted in the movement which we encounter within the horizon of the earlier and later." This definition may seem strange at first glance; but if one defines the existential-ontological horizon from which Aristotle has taken it, one sees that it is 'obvious' as it at first seems strange, and has been genuinely derived. The source of the time which is thus manifest does not become a problem for Aristotle. His Interpretation of time moves rather in the direction of the 'natural' way of understanding Being. Yet because this very understanding and the Being which is thus understood have in principle been made a problem for the investigation which lies before us, it is only *after* we have found a solution for the question of Being that the Aristotelian analysis of time can be Interpreted thematically in such a way that it may indeed gain some signification in principle, if the formulation of this question in ancient ontology, with all its critical limitations, is to be appropriated in a positive manner.

Ever since Aristotle all discussions of the concept of time have clung *in principle* to the Aristotelian definitions; that is, in taking time as their theme, they have taken it as it shows itself in circumspective concern. Time is what is 'counted'; that is to say, it is what is expressed and what we have in view, even if unthematically, when the *travelling* pointer (or the shadow) is made present. . . .

(From *Being and Time,* Trans. by J. Macquarrie and E. Robinson. New York: Harper & Row, 1962.)

Review Questions

1. How does Heidegger's view on metaphysics differ from the "traditional" view?
2. What does Heidegger mean by "unconcealment"?
3. Explain Heidegger's thought on Dasein.
4. Compare Heidegger's understanding of "temporality" with the common-sense understanding.
5. What does the event of death reveal to man about himself?

SUGGESTIONS FOR FURTHER READING

Dreyfus, H. L. and Hall, H., ed. *Heidegger: A Critical Reader.* New York, Oxford University Press, 1992.

Inword, M. *Heideppet, A very Short Introduction.* New York, Oxford University Press, 2002.

Langan, Thomas D. *The Meaning of Heidegger.* New York, Columbia University Press, 1989.

Poit, P. *Heidegger, An Introduction.* Itheca, Cornill University Press, 1998.

28

Jean-Paul Sartre (1905–1980)

Existentialism

Dismay with man's low self-esteem is what prompted Kierkegaard, Nietzsche, and Marx to call for the destruction of all constraints, institutional or social, which barricaded man against himself. As a result, their philosophies, especially Kierkegaard's and Nietzsche's, personalist to the core, established themselves as the source of the age of *existentialism*. The movement, numbering among its better-known representatives Jean-Paul Sartre, Albert Camus, Gabriel Marcel, Karl Jaspers, and Martin Heidegger (who, as we have observed, rejected the term *existentialist* as applicable to himself), emerged between the two world wars and achieved widespread popularity shortly after World War II. These philosophers all speak of the precarious condition of man, subject as he is to an existence full of unanswered or unanswerable questions, fearful of death and nullity, vulnerable to the ravages of disease and chance, in danger of the thoughtless employment of scientific technology, and liable therefore to lose freedom as the essential human gift. For Sartre and Camus, there is no way to liberate man from this dead end, no way to redeem him, not from without, for God does not exist, nor from within, for man is condemned to his own absurdity. For Jaspers and Marcel, the same humanity longs for redemptive meaning, and the same human condition evidences hope in the actual presence of God. Stylistically, when such philosophers as Plato, Augustine, Kierkegaard, or Nietzsche want to make a personal or personalist statement, they forsake academic treatises and fall back on dialogue, metaphor, exhortation, or some style using the language of life situations. So, among the existentialists, we find a richness of literary forms including novels, short stories, plays, and even, as in the case of Marcel, music—all for the purpose of touching the center of life, which academic treatises are ill-suited to do.

The name that springs to mind immediately when existentialism is mentioned, and the only one who accepts the designation of himself as an existentialist, is Sartre. We can turn to him as a striking example of the philosophic mood of the time.

Philosophical Formation

Jean-Paul Sartre was born in Paris in 1905. His life's dedication to words was made early, for as a child he became fascinated with the world of books, and his imagination ran free as he established his real, living world therein. His native curiosity was enhanced by his grandfather, who opened up for him the whole horizon of literature, so that Sartre says, "I had found my religion: nothing seemed to me more important than a book. I regarded the library as a temple." During his years as a lycée student, his "religion" of books nullified the hold any other religion had on him. He was brought up half Protestant, half Catholic, but as a youngster of twelve or thirteen the image of God was already becoming clouded, and he writes of the time he was awaiting the arrival of some school-mates who were late in coming: "After a while, not knowing what else to do to occupy my mind, I decided to think of the Almighty. Immediately He tumbled into the blue and disappeared without giving any explanation. He doesn't exist, I said to myself with polite surprise, and I thought the matter was settled. In a way, it was, since never have I had the slightest temptation to bring Him back to life." Yet, the idea of God was not thereby eradicated, for "traces of God" or "ele-ments of the idea of God" remained with Sartre for a long time. Toward the end of his life, in an interview with Simone de Beauvoir over the course of several months, when asked what he meant by saying that atheism was a long-term task, Sartre responded: ". . . moving on from idealist atheism to materialist athe-ism was difficult. It implied long-drawn-out work. I've told you what I meant by idealist atheism. It's the absence of an *idea,* the idea of God. Whereas materialist atheism is the world seen without God, and obviously it's a very long-term affair, passing from that absence of an idea to this new conception of the being—of the being that is left among things and is not set apart from them by a divine consciousness that contemplates them and causes them to exist."

He enrolled as a student at the École Normale Supérieure and received an academic training in philosophy. Later, after studying in Berlin in 1934–35, he taught philosophy for several years at Le Havre and Paris, choosing finally to give up academic teaching to devote himself to writing.

Sartre was in the army in World War II, was captured, made a prisoner, and then escaped to become a leader in the resistance against the occupying forces. Earlier, in 1938, he had written his first novel, *Nausea,* and during the occupation he wrote two plays, *The Flies* and *No Exit.* In formal style, his work in philosophy was done in 1936 as a historical study of the imagination; in 1943 his *Being and*

Nothingness appeared; it has become a classic in philosophy. With the war over, Sartre became increasingly influential as a philosopher, literary figure, and political commentator, particularly after founding the journal *Les Temps Modernes.* His renewed interest in Marx culminated in the *Critique of Dialectical Reason,* in which he tries to impregnate classical Marxism with the insights of existentialism. His autobiography, *The Words,* was begun in 1964, the same year in which he declined the Nobel Prize for literature because he felt it would hamper his freedom to write. Since that time, he wrote a seemingly endless stream of works on esthetics, freedom, literature, and a host of other topics that made him a literary monument of his time. He died in 1980.

"Ontology," not "Metaphysics"

Toward the end of *The Words,* Sartre tells us that he was in fact Antoine Roquentin, the central figure of the novel *Nausea:* "I *was* Roquentin; I used him to show, without complacency, the texture of my life." In the story, Roquentin is seated on a park bench when, in a reflective mood, he notices the roots of an old chestnut tree in their huge, gnarled intertwining; in a flash, beyond the massive pressure of the roots on each other, he sees reality for what it truly is, shapeless, senseless, just *there,* and he reacts with a feeling of loathing and disgust at the absurdity of existence. Roquentin is the fictionalized personification of the philosophy Sartre explores in *Being and Nothingness,* a work so systematically detailed that it shows a Germanic intellect hovering over the Gallic emotions evident in his other works. Sartre's analysis of being is thorough, but he takes care to call it an *ontology* rather than a *metaphysics,* for ontology, even though it denotes the study of being, does not revive the ghosts of substance, soul, and God. His brand of ontology, saturated with themes adapted from Hegel and Husserl, is *phenomenological*—the study of being through its phenomena, or appearances; thus, an ontology without metaphysics.

Sartre distinguished between two categories of being, *being-in-itself (l'en-soi)* and *being-for-itself (le pour-soi).* Particular things, like Roquentin's chestnut tree, are presented to us with all their particularities, their determinate characteristics. Getting beyond these appearances *(transphenomenal)* reveals being as neither active nor passive; it does not acquire being, it does not have it, it just *is.* It harbors no potentiality, no possibility. *Being-in-itself* is completely unrelated to anything else, and without relation it is without meaning. So described, being-in-itself is reminiscent of the being of Parmenides, monolithic and unmoving, offered with the announcement that "whatever is, *is.*" The second category of being, *being-for-itself,* stands in sharp contrast to the first and, in a sense, rejects it. It is the realm of the *human* being, characterized by consciousness and freedom, which enable man to decide meaning for himself by the choices he makes. By nurturing his own meaning, man gives himself his own *existence;* hence, the term *existential* pertains to the being of man, and *existentialism* to the philosophy of human existence.

Freedom and Responsibility

Sartre's terminology often requires a readjustment in the way we normally use certain words. When, for example, he calls man "nothing," he wants to show that consciousness and freedom are open and indeterminate, the complete *opposite* of being-in-itself, which is closed and determinate; man, therefore, is nothing. Consciousness, on the same philosophical axis as freedom, is characterized by the distance it creates from being-in-itself by overcoming its passivity; in that sense, consciousness "negates" or "nihilates" being-in-itself. Freedom, however, is Sartre's main key to the understanding of man: Through freedom *meaning* enters the world. Freedom brings into the zone of the real the objects man chooses or the projects (pro-jects) man sets for himself as the course for the future. Thus, man gives meaning to himself, builds up his own existence; his *ex-sistence* is the way he stands out from the meaninglessness of being-in-itself. Existence, in its ongoing creation by freedom, precedes the essence of man and therefore defines it. In page after page of his writings, Sartre never lets the notion of freedom get out of sight. Whether in his strictly philosophical essays or in his novels and plays, freedom is always seen as the meaningful force declaring the glory and misery of man.

Indeed, glory and misery, for the student of Sartre's philosophy, hurtles between optimism and pessimism; he no sooner reaches the crest of the wave than he is pulled down to the trough. Man is "condemned to freedom!" Take the fact of relationship to others. It has to be. Being-for-another belongs to the very being of man. Yet the moment this relationship is analyzed, it is seen that the Other pushes against my freedom, circumscribes it. At one and the same time, the Other, who helps establish my freedom, also destroys it; being-for-itself and being-for-another shatter each other. The last line of Sartre's play *No Exit* is "Hell is other people."

There is another level that shows much more profoundly how human freedom is encircled with impossibility, so that man is truly condemned to futility. If being-for-itself seeks being, it seeks it totally and has as its "project" to become being-in-*and*-for-itself; man desires to become God: "This is why the possible is projected in general as what the for-itself lacks in order to become in-itself-for-itself. The fundamental value which presides over this project is exactly the in-itself-for-itself; that is, the ideal of a consciousness which would be the foundation of its own being-in-itself by the pure consciousness which it would have of itself. It is this ideal which can be called God. Thus the best way to conceive of the fundamental project of human reality is to say that man is the being whose project is to be God. . . . To be man means to reach toward being God. Or if you prefer, man fundamentally is the desire to be God." But the project is *impossible* because God does not exist. Like Sisyphus, man always fails. Life is irrational; being is absurd. And the human being? In an oft-quoted phrase, "Man is a useless passion."

Though Sartre never wrote a complete theory of morality, there is a distinct moral tone—better, a moral imperative—to his writings. Despite the futility that saturates man's being, *responsibility* is the correlative of freedom and therefore an indispensable ingredient of human activity. The avoidance of responsibility is Sartre's main reason for rejecting Freudian psychoanalysis: I must take seriously the fact that my being involves being-for-another. My involvement is not exhausted by this one action toward this one person, for my action has *universal* meaning and significance. There is no single activity of an atom but what affects the entire cosmos, and there is no single human activity but what affects all mankind; indeed, responsibility "extends to the entire world as a peopled-world."

Commitment

Responsibility is translated into commitment. A writer, for example, has the responsibility to write for his time, to be committed to change, not to "preservation." His commitment calls for an involvement with his age; no retreat, no seclusion, no withdrawal. A philosopher's commitment must be to moral and political action, a commitment clearly exemplified in Sartre's own life and the active concern he showed toward many of humane and political causes. Expressed throughout his works, the notion of commitment reaches a final philosophical statement in one of his last and uncompleted works, *Critique of Dialectical Reason.* Here he espouses the view, presented earlier in an essay on method, that a philosophy is true only insofar as it speaks for the rising class, that is, for the proletariat. Though Marxism, for Sartre, is the only philosophy of the twentieth century, something has gone amiss with it; what it requires is an updating, a renewal in which the insights of existentialism are to be assimilated by the Marxian dialectic. In contemporary Marxism, there is still too much acceptance of the inevitability of the dialectic working itself out, disregarding the concrete situation in actual praxis. In this matter, existentialism, alive to the demands of the existential situation, can make enormous contributions to the renewal of Marxism in meeting the needs of men in their present-day struggle. Underscored here is the word *need,* or *scarcity,* which Marxism today, and even Marx himself, somehow fails to see is the basis of all human relations, and therefore of the struggle men are engaged in: "The origin of struggle always lies, in fact, in some concrete antagonism whose material condition is scarcity." The only way to understand scarcity, to understand man, is to see it against the background of *all* history, history taken as the *total* precedent to present time. So, when Sartre speaks of the *totalization* of human history, he is speaking of *all of history* seen at once as *interiorized* in me, thus explaining the scarcity in me as a "fundamental relation" of history, which in turn serves as my launching pad into the future. Thus, Sartre enrolls himself in the camp of Marx, which requires a philosophical commitment to political action to be undertaken to advance the cause of the proletariat.

The Enigma of God

At the very end of the *Critique,* Sartre again hints at the problem that lingered with him from the very beginning of his philosophical journey: the problem of God. He sees the problem in the context of history when we, in effect, ask how the vast and diverse multiplicities of history can be added up without someone to add them; totalled up without someone to total them; or, to use his terminology, how can there be totalization without a totalizer? Sartre quickly closes off the open end of his question lest he admit the need to transcend history; rather than do that, he sees history as self-enclosed so that it *totalizes itself.* Sartre is a God-conscious philosopher. This does not mean that in some inscrutable way he is "taking back" his atheism; rather, it means that, like Nietzsche, he has *consciously* organized his philosophy outside God to see what happens to man in His absence. After all, postulating that God does not exist is just as valid as postulating that He does. In company with his predecessors, Nietzsche and Marx, the denial of God is polarized by the affirmation of man: "But the being toward which human reality surpasses itself is not a transcendent God; it is at the heart of human reality; it is only human reality itself as totality." Sartre's view of man, then, is both pessimistic and optimistic. It is pessimistic inasmuch as it sees man pathetically feeling his way to the bright promise of tomorrows that never come; optimistic inasmuch as "man's destiny is within himself." This dualism is captured in the conclusion of *The Words:* "My sole concern has been to save myself—nothing in my hands, nothing up my sleeve—by work and faith. Without equipment, without tools, I set all of me to work in order to save all of me. If I relegate impossible Salvation to the prop room, what remains? A whole man, composed of all men and as good as all of them and no better than any."

READINGS

The Meaning of Existentialism
(from *Existentialism and Humanism*)

What then is . . . existentialism?

The question is only complicated because there are two kinds of existentialists. There are, on the one hand, the Christians, amongst whom I shall name Jaspers and Gabriel Marcel, both professed Catholics; and on the other the existential atheists, amongst whom we must place Heidegger as well as the French existentialists and myself. What they have in common is simply the fact that they believe that *existence* comes before *essence*—or, if you will, that we must begin from the subjective. What exactly do we mean by that?

If one considers an article of manufacture—as, for example, a book or a paper-knife—one sees that it has been made by an artisan who had a conception of it; and he has paid attention, equally, to the conception of a paper-knife and to the pre-existent technique of production which is a part of that conception and is, at bottom, a formula. Thus the paper-knife is at the same time an article producible in a certain manner and one which, on the other hand, serves a definite purpose, for one cannot suppose that a man would produce a paper-knife without knowing what it was for. Let us say, then, of the paper-knife that its essence—that is to say the sum of the formulae and the qualities which made its production and its definition possible—precedes its existence. The presence of such-and-such a paper-knife or book is thus determined before my eyes. Here, then, we are viewing the world from a technical standpoint, and we can say that production precedes existence.

When we think of God as the creator, we are thinking of him, most of the time, as a supernal artisan. Whatever doctrine we may be considering, whether it be a doctrine like that of Descartes, or of Leibnitz himself, we always imply that the will follows, more or less, from the understanding or at least accompanies it, so that when God creates he knows precisely what he is creating. Thus, the conception of man in the mind of God is comparable to that of the paper-knife in the mind of the artisan: God makes man according to a procedure and a conception, exactly as the artisan manufactures a paper-knife, following a definition and a formula. Thus each individual man is the realisation of a certain conception which dwells in the divine understanding. In the philosophic atheism of the eighteenth century, the notion of God is suppressed, but not, for all that, the idea that essence is prior to existence; something of that idea we still find everywhere, in Diderot, in Voltaire and even in Kant. Man possesses a human nature; that "human nature," which is the conception of human being, is found in every man; which means that each man is a particular example of an universal conception, the conception of Man. In Kant, this universality goes so far that the wild man of the woods, man in the state of nature and the bourgeois are all contained in the same definition and have the same fundamental qualities. Here again, the essence of man precedes that historic existence which we confront in experience.

Atheistic existentialism, of which I am a representative, declares with greater consistency that if God does not exist there is at least one being whose existence comes before its essence, a being which exists before it can be defined by any conception of it. That being is man or, as Heidegger has it, the human reality. What do we mean by saying that existence precedes essence? We mean that man first of all exists, encounters himself, surges up in the world—and defines himself afterwards. If man as the existentialist sees him is not definable, it is because to begin with he is nothing. He will not be anything until later, and then he will be what he makes of himself. Thus, there is no human nature, because there is no God to have a conception of it. Man simply is. Not that he is simply what he conceives himself to be, but he is what he wills, and as he conceives himself after already existing—as he wills to be after that leap towards existence. Man is nothing else but that which he makes of himself. That is the first principle of existentialism. And this is what people call its "subjectivity," using the word as a reproach against us. But what do we mean to say by this, but that man is of a greater dignity than a stone or a table? For we mean to say that man primarily exists—that man is, before all else, something which propels itself towards a future and is aware that it is doing so.

This may enable us to understand what is meant by such terms—perhaps a little grandiloquent—as anguish, abandonment and despair. As you will soon see, it is very simple. First, what do we mean by anguish? The existentialist

frankly states that man is in anguish. His meaning is as follows—When a man
commits himself to anything, fully realising that he is not only choosing what he
will be, but is thereby at the same time a legislator deciding for the whole of
mankind—in such a moment a man cannot escape from the sense of complete
and profound responsibility. There are many, indeed, who show no such anxiety.
But we affirm that they are merely disguising their anguish or are in flight from
it. Certainly, many people think that in what they are doing they commit no one
but themselves to anything: and if you ask them, "What would happen if everyone did so?" they shrug their shoulders and reply, "Everyone does not do so." But
in truth, one ought always to ask oneself what would happen if everyone did as
one is doing; nor can one escape from that disturbing thought except by a kind
of self-deception. The man who lies in self-excuse, by saying "Everyone will not
do it" must be ill at ease in his conscience, for the act of lying implies the universal value which it denies. By its very disguise his anguish reveals itself. This is
the anguish that Kierkegaard called "the anguish of Abraham." You know the
story: An angel commanded Abraham to sacrifice his son: and obedience was
obligatory, if it really was an angel who had appeared and said, "Thou, Abraham,
shalt sacrifice thy son." But anyone in such a case would wonder, first, whether
it was indeed an angel and secondly, whether I am really Abraham. Where are
the proofs? . . . There is nothing to show that I am Abraham: nevertheless I also
am obliged at every instant to perform actions which are examples. Everything
happens to every man as though the whole human race had its eyes fixed upon
what he is doing and regulated its conduct accordingly. So every man ought to
say, "Am I really a man who has the right to act in such a manner that humanity
regulates itself by what I do." If a man does not say that, he is dissembling his
anguish. Clearly, the anguish with which we are concerned here is not one that
could lead to quietism or inaction. It is anguish pure and simple, of the kind
well known to all those who have borne responsibilities. When, for instance, a
military leader takes upon himself the responsibility for an attack and sends a
number of men to their death, he chooses to do it and at bottom he alone
chooses. No doubt he acts under a higher command, but its orders, which are
more general, require interpretation by him and upon that interpretation
depends the life of ten, fourteen or twenty men. In making the decision, he cannot but feel a certain anguish. All leaders know that anguish. It does not prevent
their acting, on the contrary it is the very condition of their action, for the
action presupposes that there is a plurality of possibilities, and in choosing one
of these, they realise that it has value only because it is chosen. Now it is
anguish of that kind which existentialism describes, and moreover, as we shall
see, makes explicit through direct responsibility towards other men who are
concerned. Far from being a screen which could separate us from action, it is a
condition of action itself.

 And when we speak of "abandonment"—a favourite word of Heidegger—
we only mean to say that God does not exist, and that it is necessary to draw
the consequences of his absence right to the end. The existentialist is strongly
opposed to a certain type of secular moralism which seeks to suppress God
at the least possible expense. Towards 1880, when the French professors

endeavoured to formulate a secular morality, they said something like this:—
God is a useless and costly hypothesis, so we will do without it. However, if we
are to have morality, a society and a law-abiding world, it is essential that certain values should be taken seriously; they must have an *a priori* existence
ascribed to them. It must be considered obligatory *a priori* to be honest, not to
lie, not to beat one's wife, to bring up children and so forth; so we are going to
do a little work on this subject, which will enable us to show that these values
exist all the same, inscribed in an intelligible heaven although, of course, there
is no God. In other words—and this is, I believe, the purport of all that we in
France call radicalism—nothing will be changed if God does not exist; we shall
rediscover the same norms of honesty, progress and humanity, and we shall
have disposed of God as an out-of-date hypothesis which will die away quietly
of itself. The existentialist, on the contrary, finds it extremely embarrassing that
God does not exist, for there disappears with Him all possibility of finding values in an intelligible heaven. There can no longer be any good *a priori,* since
there is no infinite and perfect consciousness to think it. It is nowhere written
that "the good" exists, that one must be honest or must not lie, since we are
now upon the plane where there are only men. Dostoievsky once wrote "If
God did not exist, everything would be permitted"; and that, for existentialism,
is the starting point. Everything is indeed permitted if God does not exist, and
man is in consequence forlorn, for he cannot find anything to depend upon
either within or outside himself. He discovers forthwith, that he is without
excuse. For if indeed existence precedes essence, one will never be able to
explain one's action by reference to a given and specific human nature; in
other words, there is no determinism—man is free, man *is* freedom. Nor, on the
other hand, if God does not exist, are we provided with any values or commands that could legitimise our behaviour. Thus we have neither behind us,
nor before us in a luminous realm of values, any means of justification or
excuse. We are left alone, without excuse. That is what I mean when I say that
man is condemned to be free. Condemned, because he did not create himself,
yet is nevertheless at liberty, and from the moment that he is thrown into this
world he is responsible for everything he does. The existentialist does not
believe in the power of passion. He will never regard a grand passion as a
destructive torrent upon which a man is swept into certain actions as by fate,
and which, therefore, is an excuse for them. He thinks that man is responsible
for his passion. Neither will an existentialist think that a man can find help
through some sign being vouchsafed upon earth for his orientation: for he
thinks that the man himself interprets the sign as he chooses. He thinks that
every man, without any support or help whatever, is condemned at every
instant to invent man.

As for "despair," the meaning of this expression is extremely simple. It merely
means that we limit ourselves to a reliance upon that which is within our wills, or
within the sum of the probabilities which render our action feasible. Whenever
one wills anything, there are always these elements of probability. If I am counting upon a visit from a friend, who may be coming by train or by tram, I presuppose that the train will arrive at the appointed time, or that the tram will not be

derailed. I remain in the realm of possibilities; but one does not rely upon any possibilities beyond those that are strictly concerned in one's action. Beyond the point at which the possibilities under consideration cease to affect my action, I ought to disinterest myself. For there is no God and no prevenient design, which can adapt the world and all its possibilities to my will. When Descartes said, "Conquer yourself rather than the world," what he meant was, at bottom, the same— that we should act without hope.

(Tr. P. Mairet)

Reflections on Being and Nothingness
(from *Being and Nothingness*)

1. CONSCIOUSNESS

Consciousness is consciousness of something. This means that transcendence is the constitutive structure of consciousness; that is, that consciousness is born *supported by* a being which is not itself. This is what we call the ontological proof. No doubt someone will reply that the existence of the demand of consciousness does not prove that this demand ought to be satisfied. But this objection can not hold up against an analysis of what Husserl calls intentionality, though, to be sure, he misunderstood its essential character. To say that consciousness is consciousness of something means that for consciousness there is no being outside of that precise obligation to be a revealing intuition of something—*i.e.,* of a transcendent being. Not only does pure subjectivity, if initially given, fail to transcend itself to posit the objective; a "pure" subjectivity disappears. What can properly be called subjectivity is consciousness (of) consciousness. But this consciousness (of being) consciousness must be qualified in some way, and it can be qualified only as revealing intuition or it is nothing. Now a revealing intuition implies something revealed. Absolute subjectivity can be established only in the face of something revealed; immanence can be defined only within the apprehension of a transcendent. It might appear that there is an echo here of Kant's refutation of problematical idealism. But we ought rather to think of Descartes. We are here on the ground of being, not of knowledge. It is not a question of showing that the phenomena of inner sense imply the existence of objective spatial phenomena, but that consciousness implies in its being a non-conscious and transphenomenal being. In particular there is no point in replying that in fact subjectivity implies objectivity and that it constitutes itself in constituting the objective; we have seen that subjectivity is powerless to constitute the objective. To say that consciousness is consciousness of something is to say that it must produce itself as a revealed-revelation of a being which is not it and which gives itself as already existing when consciousness reveals it.

Thus we have left pure appearance and have arrived at full being. Consciousness is a being whose existence posits its essence, and inversely it is consciousness of a being, whose essence implies its existence; that is, in which appearance lays claim to *being.* Being is everywhere. Certainly we could apply to consciousness the definition which Heidegger reserves for *Dasein* and say that it is a being such that in its being, its being is in question. But it would be necessary to complete the definition and formulate it more like this: *consciousness is a being such that in its being, its being is in question in so far as this being implies a being other than itself.*

We must understand that this being is no other than the transphenomenal being of phenomena and not a noumenal being which is hidden behind them. It is the being of this table, of this package of tobacco, of the lamp, more generally the being of the world which is implied by consciousness. It requires simply that the being of that which *appears* does not exist *only* in so far as it appears. The transphenomenal being of what exists *for consciousness* is itself in itself (*lui-même en soi*).

2. BEING-IN-ITSELF

A clear view of the phenomenon of being has often been obscured by a very common prejudice which we shall call "creationism." Since people supposed that God had given being to the world, being always appeared tainted with a certain passivity. But a creation *ex nihilo* can not explain the coming to pass of being; for if being is conceived in a subjectivity, even a divine subjectivity, it remains a mode of intra-subjective being. Such subjectivity can not have even the *representation* of an objectivity, and consequently it can not even be affected with the *will* to create the objective. Furthermore being, if it is suddenly placed outside the subjective by the fulguration of which Leibniz speaks, can only affirm itself as distinct from and opposed to its creator; otherwise it dissolves in him. The theory of perpetual creation, by removing from being what the Germans call *Selbständigkeit,* makes it disappear in the divine subjectivity. If being exists as over against God, it is its own support; it does not preserve the least trace of divine creation. In a word, even if it had been created, being-in-itself would be *inexplicable* in terms of creation; for it assumes its being beyond the creation.

This is equivalent to saying that being is uncreated. But we need not conclude that being creates itself, which would suppose that it is prior to itself. Being can not be *causa sui* in the manner of consciousness. Being is *itself.* This means that it is neither passivity nor activity. Both of these notions are *human* and designate human conduct or the instruments of human conduct. There is activity when a conscious being uses means with an end in view. And we call those objects passive on which our activity is exercised, in as much as they do not spontaneously aim at the end which we make them serve. In a word, man is active and the means which he employs are called passive. These concepts, put absolutely, lose all meaning. In particular, being is not active; in order for there to be an end and means, there must be being. For an even stronger reason it can not be passive, for in order to be passive, it must be. The self-consistency of being is beyond the active as it is beyond the passive.

Being is equally beyond negation as beyond affirmation. Affirmation is always affirmation of something; that is, the act of affirming is distinguished from the thing affirmed. But if we suppose an affirmation in which the affirmed comes to fulfill the affirming and is confused with it, this affirmation can not be affirmed—owing to too much of plenitude and the immediate inherence of the noema in the noesis. It is there that we find being—if we are to define it more clearly—in connection with consciousness. It is the noema in the noesis; that is, the inherence in itself without the least distance. From this point of view, we should not call it "immanence," for immanence in spite of all *connection* with self is still that very slight withdrawal which can be realized—away from the self. But being is not a connection with itself. It is *itself.* It is an immanence which can not realize itself, an affirmation which can not affirm itself, an activity which can not act, because it is glued to itself. Everything happens as if, in order to free the affirmation of self from the heart of being, there is necessary a decompression of being. Let us not, however, think that being is merely *one* undifferentiated self-affirmation; the undifferentiation of the in-itself is beyond an infinity of self-affirmations, inasmuch as there is an infinity of modes of self-affirming. We may summarize these first conclusions by saying that being is in itself.

But if being is in itself, this means that it does not refer to itself as self-consciousness does. It is this self. It is itself so completely that the perpetual reflection which constitutes the self is dissolved in an identity. That is why being is at bottom beyond the *self,* and our first formula can be only an approximation due to the requirements of language. In fact being is opaque to itself precisely because it is filled with itself. This can be better expressed by saying that *being is what it is.* This statement is in appearance strictly analytical. Actually it is far from being reduced to that principle of identity which is the unconditioned principle of all analytical judgments. First the formula designates a particular region for being, that of *being-in-itself.* We shall see that the being of *for-itself* is defined, on the contrary, as being what it is not and not being what it is. The question here then is of a regional principle and is as such synthetical. Furthermore it is necessary to oppose this formula—being in-itself is what it is—to that which designates the being of consciousness. The latter in fact, as we shall see, *has to be* what it is.

3. ANGUISH

Kierkegaard describing anguish in the face of what one lacks characterizes it as anguish in the face of freedom. But Heidegger, whom we know to have been greatly influenced by Kierkegaard, considers anguish instead as the apprehension of nothingness. These two descriptions of anguish do not appear to us contradictory; on the contrary the one implies the other.

First we must acknowledge that Kierkegaard is right; anguish is distinguished from fear in that fear is fear of beings in the world whereas anguish is anguish before myself. Vertigo is anguish to the extent that I am afraid not of falling over the precipice, but of throwing myself over. A situation provokes fear if there is a possibility of my life being changed from without; my being provokes anguish to the extent that I distrust myself and my own reactions in that situation. The artillery preparation which precedes the attack can provoke fear in the soldier who undergoes the bombardment, but anguish is born in him when he tries to foresee the conduct with which he will face the bombardment, when he asks himself if he is going to be able to "hold up." Similarly the recruit who reports for active duty at the beginning of the war can in some instances be afraid of death, but more often he is "afraid of being afraid"; that is, he is filled with anguish before himself. Most of the time dangerous or threatening situations present themselves in facets; they will be apprehended through a feeling of fear or of anguish according to whether we envisage the situation as acting on the man or the man as acting on the situation. The man who has just received a hard blow—for example, losing a great part of his wealth in a crash—can have the fear of threatening poverty. He will experience anguish a moment later when nervously wringing his hands (a symbolic reaction to the action which is imposed but which remains still wholly undetermined), he exclaims to himself: "What am I going to do? But what am I going to do?" In this sense fear and anguish are exclusive of one another since fear is unreflective apprehension of the transcendent and anguish is reflective apprehension of the self; the one is born in the destruction of the other. The normal process in the case which I have just cited is a constant transition from the one to the other. But there exist also situations where anguish appears pure; that is, without ever being preceded or followed by fear. If, for example, I have been raised to a new dignity and charged with a delicate and flattering mission, I can feel anguish at the thought that I will not be capable perhaps of fulfilling it, and yet I will not have the least fear in the world of the consequences of my possible failure.

What is the meaning of anguish in the various examples which I have just given? Let us take up again the example of vertigo. Vertigo announces itself through fear; I am on a narrow path—without a guard-rail—which goes along a precipice. The precipice presents itself to me *as to be avoided;* it represents a danger of death. At the same time I conceive of a certain number of causes, originating in universal determinism, which can transform that threat of death into reality; I can slip on a stone and fall into the abyss; the crumbling earth of the path can give way under my steps. Through these various anticipations, I am given to myself as a thing; I am passive in relation to these possibilities; they come to me from without; in so far as I am also an object in the world, subject to gravitation, they are *my* possibilities. At this moment *fear* appears, which in terms of the situation is the apprehension of myself as a destructible transcendent in the midst of transcendents, as an object which does not contain in itself the origin of its future disappearance. My reaction will be of the reflective order; I will pay attention to the stones in the road; I will keep myself as far as possible from the edge of the path. I realize myself as pushing away the threatening situation with all my strength, and I project before myself a certain number of future conducts destined to keep the threats of the world at a distance from me. These conducts are *my* possibilities. I escape fear by the very fact that I am placing myself on a plane where *my own* possibilities are substituted for the transcendent probabilities where human action had no place.

4. BEING-FOR-ITSELF

. . . In truth the *cogito* must be our point of departure, but we can say of it, parodying a famous saying, that it leads us only on condition that we get out of it. Our preceding study, which concerned the conditions for the possibility of certain types of conduct, had as its goal only to place us in a position to question the *cogito* about its being and to furnish us with the dialectic instrument which would enable us to find in the *cogito* itself the means of escaping from instantaneity toward the totality of being which constitutes human reality. Let us return now to description of non-thetic self-consciousness; let us examine its results and ask what it means for consciousness that it must necessarily be what it is not and not be what it is.

"The being of consciousness," we said in the Introduction, "is a being such that in its being, its being is in question." This means that the being of consciousness does not coincide with itself in a full equivalence. Such equivalence, which is that of the in-itself, is expressed by this simple formula: being is what it is. In the in-itself there is not a particle of being which is not wholly within itself without distance. When being is thus conceived there is not the slightest suspicion of duality in it; this is what we mean when we say that the density of being of the in-itself is infinite. It is a fullness. The principle of identity can be said to be synthetic not only because it limits its scope to a region of definite being, but in particular because it masses within it the infinity of density. "A is A" means that A exists in an infinite compression with an infinite density. Identity is the limiting concept of unification: it is not true that the in-itself has any need of a synthetic unification of its being; at its own extreme limit, unity disappears and passes into identity. Identity is the ideal of "one," and "one" comes into the world by human reality. The in-itself is full of itself, and no more total plenitude can be imagined, no more perfect equivalence of content to container. There is not the slightest emptiness in being, not the tiniest crack through which nothingness might slip in.

This presence of itself has often been taken for a plenitude of existence, and a strong prejudice prevalent among philosophers causes them to attribute to consciousness the highest rank in being. But this postulate can not be maintained after a more thorough description of the notion of presence. Actually *presence to* always implies duality, at least a virtual separation. The presence of being to itself implies a detachment on the part of being in relation to itself. The coincidence of identity is the veritable plenitude of being exactly because in this coincidence there is left no place for any negativity. Of course the principle of identity can involve the principle of noncontradiction as Hegel has observed. The being which is what it is must be able to be the being which is not what it is not. But in the first place this negation, like all others, comes to the surface of being through human reality, as we have shown, and not through a dialectic appropriate just to being. In addition this principle can denote only the relations of being with the *external,* exactly because it presides over the relations of being with what it is not. We are dealing then with a principle constitutive of *external relations* such that they can appear to a human reality present to being-in-itself and engaged in the world. This principle does not concern the internal relations of being; these relations, inasmuch as they would posit an otherness, do not exist. The principle of identity is the negation of every species of relation at the heart of being-in-itself.

This negative which is the nothingness of being and the nihilating power both together, is *nothingness.* Nowhere else can we grasp it in such purity. Everywhere else in one way or another we must confer on it being-in-itself as nothingness. But the nothingness which arises in the heart of consciousness is *not.* It is *made-to-be.* Belief, for example, is not the contiguity of one being with another being; it is its *own* presence to itself, its own decompression of being. Otherwise the unity of the for-itself would dissolve into the duality of two in-itselfs. Thus the for-itself must be its own nothingness. The being of consciousness qua consciousness is to exist at *a distance from itself* as a presence to itself, and this empty distance which being carries in its being is Nothingness. Thus in order for a *self* to exist, it is necessary that the unity of this being include its own nothingness as the nihilation of identity. For the nothingness which slips into belief is *its* nothingness, the nothingness of belief as belief in itself, as belief blind and full, as "simple faith." The for-itself is the being which determines itself to exist inasmuch as it can not coincide with itself.

5. FREEDOM

Since the intention is a choice of the end and since the world reveals itself across our conduct, it is the intentional choice of the end which reveals the world, and the world is revealed as this or that (in this or that order) according to the end chosen. The end, illuminating the world, is a state of the world to be obtained and not yet existing. The intention is a thetic consciousness of the end. But it can be so only by making itself a non-thetic consciousness of its own possibility. Thus my end can be a good meal if I am hungry. But this meal which beyond the dusty road on which I am traveling is projected as the *meaning* of this road (it goes *toward* a hotel where the table is set, where the dishes are prepared, where I am expected, *etc.*) can be apprehended only correlatively with my non-thetic project toward my own possibility of eating this meal. Thus by a double but unitary upsurge the intention illuminates the world in terms of an end not yet existing and is itself defined by the choice of its possible. My end is a certain objective state of the world, my possible is a certain structure of my subjectivity; the one is revealed to the thetic consciousness, the other flows back over the non-thetic consciousness in order to characterize it.

The free project is fundamental, for it is my being. Neither ambition nor the passion to be loved nor the inferiority complex can be considered as fundamental projects. On the contrary, they of necessity must be understood in terms of a primary project which is recognized as the project which can no longer be interpreted in terms of any other and which is total. A special phenomenological method will be necessary in order to make this initial project explicit. This is what we shall call existential psychoanalysis. We shall speak of this in the next chapter. For the present we can say that the fundamental project which I am is a project concerning not my relations with this or that particular object in the world, but my total being-in-the-world; since the world itself is revealed only in the light of an end, this project posits for its end a certain type of relation to being which the for-itself wills to adopt. This project is not instantaneous, for it can not be "in" time. Neither is it non-temporal in order to "give time to itself" afterwards. This is why we reject Kant's "choice of intelligible character." The structure of the choice necessarily implies that it be a choice in the world. A choice which would be a choice in *terms of nothing,* a choice *against nothing* would be a choice of nothing and would be annihilated as choice. There is only phenomenal choice, provided that we understand that the phenomenon is here the absolute. But in its very upsurge, the choice is temporalized since it causes a future to come to illuminate the present and to constitute it as a present by giving the meaning of *pastness* to the in-itself "data." However we need not understand by this that the fundamental project is coextensive with the entire "life" of the for-itself. Since freedom is a being-without-support and without-a-springboard, the project in order to be must be constantly renewed. I choose myself perpetually and can never be merely by virtue of having-been-chosen; otherwise I should fall into the pure and simple existence of the in-itself. The necessity of perpetually choosing myself is one with the pursued-pursuit which I am. But precisely because here we are dealing with a *choice,* this choice as it is made indicates in general other choices as possibles. The possibility of these other choices is neither made explicit nor posited, but it is lived in the feeling of unjustifiability; and it is this which is expressed by the fact of the *absurdity* of my choice and consequently of my being. Thus my freedom eats away my freedom. Since I am free, I project my total possible, but I thereby posit that I am free and that I can always nihilate this first project and make it past.

(From *Being and Nothingness.* Trans. Hazel E. Barnes. New York: Philosophical Library, 1956. Reprinted by permission of Philosophical Library.)

Review Questions

1. In Sartre's view, what is existentialism?
2. Is there a distinction between *personalist* and *individual?*
3. Why does Sartre speak of *ontology* rather than *metaphysics?*
4. Distinguish between being-in-itself and being-for-itself.

5. Explain the notion of freedom for Sartre.
6. What is the meaning of a *critique* of dialectical reason?
7. Are there any values in the philosophy of Sartre?
8. Is atheism an active commitment for Sartre?

SUGGESTIONS FOR FURTHER READING

Caws, P. *Sartre.* New York, Routledge, Chapman and Hall, 1984.
Existentialism and Humanism. Tr. Mairet, P. London, Metheun, 1948.
Murdock, I. *Sartre, Romantic Rationalist.* New York, Viking Penguin, 1987.

29

Bertrand Russell
(1872–1970)

Toward the Philosophy of Language

The idealist philosophy of Hegel was, as we have seen, extremely influential in the latter nineteenth and early twentieth centuries. It even made a substantial inroad in England, where philosophy seemed to have taken temporary leave of its empirical and scientific tradition. Francis H. Bradley, Bernard Bosanquet, and John M. E. McTaggart were a trio of outstanding and persuasive idealists who would have liked to create in a generation of budding philosophers a sympathy for idealism—for a world in which the Absolute reigned supreme and the particular did not gain easy admittance. But this adventure in idealism was short-lived because the new generation, counting among its members George E. Moore, Bertrand Russell, and Samuel Alexander, reacted strongly against it in favor of a realism that hewed closely to the main line of British empiricism. At first, this reaction took the form of a "commonsense" appeal made by Moore, to the effect that I, by common sense, am able to formulate statements or propositions concerning my own existence and the existence of sense objects. However, his emphasis on propositions resulted in the propositions themselves becoming the object of succeeding British philosophers. This began with Russell's treatment of propositions, called *analysis,* and continued with Ludwig Wittgenstein's fascinating approach to philosophical language, followed by the school of *logical positivism* with its concern for the problem of meaning as empirical verifiability. The figure, then, who stands out at the critical juncture, bidding farewell to idealism and welcome to the logical-language path to realism, was Bertrand Russell.

Philosophical Background

He was born in 1872 in Monmouthshire, England, the son of Lord and Lady Amberley, both of whom died when he was a child. He was brought up by his grandmother and his grandfather, Lord John Russell. His parents had been liberal thinkers—John Stuart Mill was his informal godfather—but his grandparents had a sternly religious home. As a young man, however, he abandoned the basic beliefs of religion, namely, free will, immortality, and God. At Cambridge University, which he entered in 1890, he took up the study of mathematics and philosophy, becoming an early devotee of Hegel through Bradley's influence. Upon leaving Cambridge, he became attached to the British Embassy in Paris for a year before going on to Berlin for the purpose of studying economics and German political science; this experience resulted in his first book, *German Social Democracy,* in 1896. In 1898 he rejected Hegelianism and every kind of idealism, being led by his friend Moore to the position that whatever common sense held to be real *is* real. In 1900 he wrote a book on Leibniz, considering areas of that thinker's logic hitherto neglected. In the same year, his attendance at the International Congress of Philosophy gave him the impetus to pursue his interest in the foundation of mathematics, which brought him to the publication of *The Principles of Mathematics* in 1903, and, years later, to his epoch-making opus with Alfred North Whitehead, *Principia Mathematica* (1910–13).

From 1910 to 1916 he lectured at Cambridge, having Wittgenstein as one of his students. Wittgenstein, in his turn, influenced Russell in several important aspects of the philosophy of language and the nature of mathematics. Russell thought so much of Wittgenstein's innovative ideas that he offered to write the introduction to his now famous work *Tractatus Logico-Philosophicus* (1922). During this time Russell became involved in social issues, mainly as a result of World War I, and embraced a pacifism that made him exceedingly unpopular and caused the university to dismiss him; he maintained his record of pacifism, with the exception of his approval of World War II as the only means of repelling Nazi aggression. After the war he resumed his pacifism, highlighted by the position he assumed against the nuclear bomb and the activities of the United States in Vietnam. From 1938 on, he taught at several places in the United States but had an appointment to the City College of New York canceled after a stormy and discreditable reaction to his liberal views on sexual morality. In 1950 he was awarded the Nobel Prize for literature.

Despite his extremely active life of traveling and of espousing social causes, his literary output never abated; he wrote many articles, pamphlets, and books, ranging from the popular to the professional. He died in 1970. Among his chief works, besides those mentioned already, are *The Problems of Philosophy* (1912), *Our Knowledge of the External World* (1914), *The Analysis of Mind* (1921), *An Inquiry into Meaning and Truth* (1940), *A History of Western Philosophy* (1945), and *My Philosophical Development* (1959).

Analysis

In the context of Russell's belief that philosophy should be scientific, and perhaps even more rigorous than the sciences themselves, his philosophical method, which, as previously noted, is called *analysis,* is addressed first of all to the analysis of empirical data, that is, to an analysis of things as they are given in experience; sense data are realities, they are trans-subjective. But things of the outside world are not given to us directly; they are given to us through their properties and their relations to each other, which Russell refers to as *facts,* so that analysis is principally a method for evaluating facts. Adopting as a basic part of his method, a principle adopted from the fourteenth-century philosopher William of Ockham, which states that "entities are not to be multiplied without necessity"—appropriately called *Ockham's razor*—Russell attempts to eliminate as many complexities, postulates, and entities as possible to arrive at the "last residue" of what is "uneliminable." We therefore cannot *infer* the existence of entities not known empirically to exist, and because the mind constructs *logical* relations within the sense field in which facts are given, "wherever possible logical constructions are to be substituted for inferred entities."

The most fruitful source of logical construction is *language,* and it is by the *analysis of language* that we are brought to a knowledge of the reality beyond it. Although he does not try to state precisely why there is a connection between language and reality, it is essential for him to hold that there is some kind of connection between the way the mind *works* and the way reality *is,* or between "the laws of syntax and the laws of physics."

Facts are stated in the form of propositions, and, by analysis, the simplest proposition would be one like "John is tall," that is, a proposition composed of a proper name and a simple predicate; or, because we do not assign proper names to every single thing, a similar proposition would be "This is red." These propositions Russell calls *atomic propositions;* they signify *atomic facts.* Where several atomic propositions are put together, as in "This is red and sweet" (i.e., "This is red" and "This is sweet"), the proposition is called a *molecular proposition.* But, by the application of Ockham's razor, molecular propositions do not signify *molecular facts* because the truth of a molecular proposition depends on, or is a function of, the atomic propositions it is composed of; therefore, the atomic fact is all that is necessary. This is true even of a fact that refers to an entire class, such as "All trees are green"; even if it is a *general* fact, it is still atomic because it is irreducible. Russell refers to this view of things—a view very much in keeping with the British tradition of analyzing the given down to its simplest elements—as *logical atomism,* although he disagrees in several important respects with the views of Locke and Hume.

Mathematical Logic as the Perfect Language

The enormous contribution Russell, together with Whitehead, made to the study of the nature of mathematics can be left to mathematicians. Here we simply want to point out that Russell's interest in making language as precise an instrument as possible urged him to develop a vehicle that would avoid the limitations of ordinary language. A new language, to be logically perfect, would use symbols and symbolic expressions, transcend national languages, avert the pitfalls of grammar, and make it easier to deal with abstractions and deductions than words allow. Accordingly, Russell and Whitehead, furthering the work of their predecessors, fine-tuned mathematical or symbolic logic to such an extent that serious students in this field must familiarize themselves with *Principia Mathematica,* "one of the most influential works of European thought in the twentieth century."

It is not difficult to see how logical atomism inclines favorably toward the sciences and, because philosophy is to be built on an empirical foundation, the obvious source of hard knowledge is the natural sciences. It is sometimes difficult to see how, for Russell, philosophy differs from the sciences, for philosophy consists of learning "principles and methods and general conceptions" from science. Philosophy, even though it is focused more on organizing principles and less on detail, still has the same objective as science: "Philosophy involves a criticism of scientific knowledge, not from a point of view ultimately different from that of science, but from a point of view less concerned with details and more concerned with the harmony of the whole body of special sciences." The laws and language of the sciences must themselves be subject to logical analysis in order to clarify their meaning, which becomes one of the major tasks of philosophy.

Even with his complete devotion to the sciences, Russell does not come down as heavily on metaphysics as most of his empiricist predecessors. It is true that he sees no compelling reason for substance, self, soul, immortality, and God, yet the fact that he was looking for "harmony," or trying to find out what is "ultimate" in the universe, is a clear indication that he is not eschewing metaphysics altogether. And as previously indicated, though he did not elaborate on the link between language and things, he writes, "I am inclined to think that quite important metaphysical conclusions, of a more or less skeptical kind, can be drawn from simple considerations as to the relation between language and things."

Ambiguity in metaphysics in no way deterred Russell from holding that one of the goals of philosophy is to give an account of "daily life." This statement is borne out in a practical way, by his ardent and personal commitment to social causes for most of his life, but particularly after World War I, which he saw as a cataclysm crystallizing the evil forces in man and paving the way for endless suffering in the future. The principles behind the activities of daily life pertain to ethics, the province of general maxims and not of specific applications in specific circumstances. Morality derives meaning in a social context; as such, the common good or happiness is the fundamental consideration, so that a person's actions, "inspired by love and guided by knowledge," ought to proceed from a desire for harmony in the whole of a society. Imitating Kant's mode of formulation, Russell states the supreme moral rule as follows: "*Act so as to produce harmonious rather than discordant desires.*"

Russell tells us that it was his interest in religion that urged him, as a young man, to take up the study of philosophy; he wanted "to find some satisfaction for religious impulses." In anticipation, he moved on to one philosophical system after another, seeking its religious tone, but he never found "religious satisfaction in any philosophical doctrine" he could accept. However, he attests to the agony of the philosopher whose emotions go one way while his intellect goes another:"Those who attempt to make a religion of humanism, which recognizes nothing greater than man, do not satisfy my emotions.And yet I am unable to believe that, in the world as known, there is anything that I can value outside human beings, and, to a much lesser extent, animals."

A beautiful testimony by Russell as to what life is finally all about is worth giving in full:"Three passions, simple but overwhelmingly strong, have governed my life: the longing for love, the search for knowledge, and unbearable pity for the suffering of mankind.These passions, like great winds, have blown me hither and thither in a wayward course over a deep ocean of anguish, reaching to the very verge of despair.

"I have sought love, first, because it brings ecstasy—ecstasy so great that I would often have sacrificed all the rest of life for a few hours of this joy. I have sought it, next, because it relieves loneliness—that terrible loneliness in which one shivering consciousness looks over the rim of the world into the cold unfathomable lifeless abyss. I have sought it, finally, because in the union of love I have seen, in a mystic miniature, the prefiguring vision of the heaven that saints and poets have imagined. This is what I sought, and though it might seem too good for human life, this is what—at last—I have found.

"With equal passion I have sought knowledge. I have wished to understand the hearts of men. I have wished to know why the stars shine.A little of this, but not much, I have achieved.

"Love and knowledge, so far as they were possible, led upward toward the heavens. But always pity brought me back to earth. Echoes of cries of pain reverberate in my heart. Children in famine, victims tortured by oppressors, helpless old people a hated burden to their sons, and the whole world of loneliness, poverty, and pain make a mockery of what human life should be. I long to alleviate the evil, but I cannot, and I too suffer.

"This has been my life. I have found it worth living, and would gladly live it again if the chance were offered me."

READINGS

Man's Place in the Universe
(from *An Outline of Philosophy*)

I want to end with a few words about man's place in the universe. It has been customary to demand of a philosopher that he should show that the world is good in certain respects. I cannot admit any duty of this sort. One might as well demand of an accountant that he should show a satisfactory balance-sheet. It is just as bad to be fraudulently optimistic in philosophy as in money matters. If the world is good, by all means let us know it; but if not, let us know that. In any case, the question of the goodness or badness of the world is one for science rather than for philosophy. We shall call the world good if it has certain characteristics that we desire. In the past philosophy professed to be able to prove that the world had such characteristics, but it is now fairly evident that the proofs were invalid. It does not, of course, follow that the world does not have the characteristics in question; it follows only that philosophy cannot decide the problem. Take for example the problem of personal immortality. You may believe this on the ground of revealed religion, but that is a ground which lies outside philosophy. You may believe it on the ground of the phenomena investigated by psychical research, but that is science, not philosophy. In former days, you could believe it on a philosophical ground, namely, that the soul is a substance and all substances are indestructible. You will find this argument, sometimes more or less disguised, in many philosophers. But the notion of substance, in the sense of permanent entity with changing states, is no longer applicable to the world. It may happen, as with the electron, that a string of events are so interconnected causally that it is practically convenient to regard them as forming one entity, but where this happens it is a scientific fact, not a metaphysical necessity. The whole question of personal immortality, therefore lies outside philosophy, and is to be decided, if at all, either by science or by revealed religion.

I will take up another matter in regard to which what I have said may have been disappointing to some readers. It is sometimes thought that philosophy ought to aim at encouraging a good life. Now, of course, I admit that it should have this effect, but I do not admit that it should have this as a conscious purpose. To begin with, when we embark upon the study of philosophy we ought not to assume that we already know for certain what the good life is; philosophy may conceivably modify our views as to what is good, in which case it will seem to the non-philosophical to have had a bad moral effect. That, however, is a secondary point. The essential thing is that philosophy is part of the pursuit of knowledge, and that we cannot limit this pursuit by insisting that the knowledge obtained shall be such as we should have thought edifying before we obtained it. I think it could be maintained with truth that *all* knowledge is edifying, provided we have a right conception of edification. When this appears to be not the case, it is because we have moral standards based upon ignorance. It may happen by good fortune that a moral standard based upon ignorance is right, but if so knowledge will not destroy it; if knowledge can destroy it, it must be wrong. The conscious purpose of philosophy, therefore, ought to be solely to *understand* the world as well as possible, not to establish this or that proposition which is thought morally desirable. Those who embark upon philosophy must be prepared to question all their preconceptions, ethical as well as scientific; if they have a determination never to surrender certain philosophic beliefs, they are not in the frame of mind in which philosophy can be profitably pursued.

But although philosophy ought not to have a moral purpose, it ought to have certain good moral effects. Any disinterested pursuit of knowledge teaches us the limits of our power, which is salutary; at the same time, in proportion as we succeed in achieving knowledge, it teaches the limits of our impotence, which is equally desirable. And philosophical knowledge, or rather philosophical thought, has certain special merits not belonging in an equal degree to other intellectual pursuits. By its generality it enables us to see human passions in their just propositions, and to realise the absurdity of many quarrels between individuals, classes, and nations. Philosophy comes as near as possible for human beings to that large, impartial contemplation of the universe as a whole which raises us for the moment above our purely personal destiny. There is a certain asceticism of the intellect which is good as a part of life, though it cannot be the whole so long as we have to remain animals engaged in the struggle for existence. The asceticism of the intellect requires that, while we are engaged in the pursuit of knowledge, we shall repress all other desires for the sake of the desire to know. While we are philosophising, the wish to prove that the world is good, or that the dogmas of this or that sect are true, must count as weaknesses of the flesh— they are temptations to be thrust on one side. But we obtain in return something of the joy which the mystic experiences in harmony with the will of God. This joy philosophy can give, but only to those who are willing to follow it to the end, through all its arduous uncertainties. . . .

Philosophy should make us know the ends of life, and the elements in life that have value on their own account. However, our freedom may be limited to the causal sphere, we need admit no limitations to our freedom in the sphere of values: what we judge good on its own account we may continue to judge good, without regard to anything but our own feeling. Philosophy cannot itself determine the ends of life, but it can free us from the tyranny of prejudice and from distortions due to a narrow view. Love, beauty, knowledge, and joy of life: these things retain their lustre however wide our purview. And if philosophy can help us to feel the value of these things, it will have played its part in man's collective work of bringing light into the world of darkness.

(From Bertrand Russell, *An Outline of Philosophy.* London: Allen & Unwin, 1927. Reprinted by permission of Allen & Unwin.)

The Value of Philosophy

(from *The Problems of Philosophy*)

Having now come to the end of our brief and very incomplete review of the problems of philosophy, it will be well to consider, in conclusion, what is the value of philosophy and why it ought to be studied. It is the more necessary to consider this question, in view of the fact that many men, under the influence of science or of practical affairs, are inclined to doubt whether philosophy is anything better than innocent but useless trifling, hair-splitting distinctions, and controversies on matters concerning which knowledge is impossible.

This view of philosophy appears to result, partly from a wrong conception of the ends of life, partly from a wrong conception of the kind of goods which philosophy strives to achieve. Physical science, through the medium of inventions, is useful to innumerable people who are wholly ignorant of it; thus the study of physical science is to be recommended, not only, or primarily, because of the effect on the student, but rather because of the effect on mankind in general. Thus utility does not belong to philosophy. If the study of philosophy has any value at all for others than students of philosophy, it must be only indirectly, through its effects upon the lives of those who study it. It is in these effects, therefore, if anywhere, that the value of philosophy must be primarily sought.

But further, if we are not to fail in our endeavour to determine the value of philosophy, we must first free our minds from the prejudices of what are wrongly called "practical" men. The "practical" man, as this word is often used, is one who recognizes only material needs, who realizes that men must have food for the body, but is oblivious of the necessity of providing food for the mind. If all men were well off, if poverty and disease had been reduced to their lowest possible point, there would still remain much to be done to produce a valuable society; and even in the existing world the goods of the mind are at least as important as the goods of the body. It is exclusively among the goods of the mind that the value of philosophy is to be found; and only those who are not indifferent to these goods can be persuaded that the study of philosophy is not a waste of time.

Philosophy, like all other studies, aims primarily at knowledge. The knowledge it aims at is the kind of knowledge which gives unity and system to the body of sciences, and the kind which results from a critical examination of the grounds of our convictions, prejudices, and beliefs. But it cannot be maintained that philosophy has had any very great measure of success in its attempts to provide definite answers to its questions. If you ask a mathematician, a mineralogist, a historian, or any other man of learning, what definite body of truths has been ascertained by his science, his answer will last as long as you are willing to listen. But if you put the same question to a philosopher, he will, if he is candid, have to confess that his study has not achieved positive results such as have been achieved by other sciences. It is true that this is partly accounted for by the fact that, as soon as definite knowledge concerning any subject becomes possible, this subject ceases to be called philosophy, and now becomes a separate science. The whole study of the heavens, which now belongs to astronomy, was once included in philosophy; Newton's great work was called 'the mathematical principles of natural philosophy'. Similarly, the study of the human mind, which was a part of philosophy, has now been separated from philosophy and has become the science of psychology. Thus, to a great extent, the uncertainty of philosophy is more apparent than real: those questions which are already capable of definite answers are placed in the sciences, while those only to which, at present, no definite answer can be given, remain to form the residue which is called philosophy.

This is, however, only a part of the truth concerning the uncertainty of philosophy. There are many questions—and among them those that are of the profoundest interest to our spiritual life—which, so far as we can see, must remain insoluble to the human intellect unless its powers become of quite a different order from what they are now. Has the universe any unity of plan or purpose, or is it a fortuitous concourse of atoms? Is consciousness a permanent part of the universe, giving hope of indefinite growth in wisdom, or is it a transitory accident on a small planet on which life must ultimately become impossible? Are good and evil of importance to the universe or only to man? Such questions are asked by philosophy, and variously answered by various philosophers. But it would seem that, whether answers be otherwise discoverable or not, the answers suggested by philosophy are none of them demonstrably true. Yet, however slight may be the hope of discovering an answer, it is part of the business of philosophy to continue the consideration of such questions, to make us aware of their importance, to examine all the approaches to them, and to keep alive that speculative interest in the universe which is apt to be killed by confining ourselves to definitely ascertainable knowledge.

Many philosophers, it is true, have held that philosophy could establish the truth of certain answers to such fundamental questions. They have supposed that what is of most importance in religious beliefs could be proved by strict demonstration to be true. In order to judge of such attempts, it is necessary to take a survey of human knowledge, and to form an opinion as to its methods and its limitations. On such a subject it would be unwise to pronounce dogmatically; but if the investigations of our previous chapters have not led us astray, we shall be compelled to renounce the hope of finding philosophical proofs of religious beliefs. We cannot, therefore, include as part of the value of philosophy any definite set of answers to such questions. Hence, once more, the value of philosophy must not depend upon any supposed body of definitely ascertainable knowledge to be acquired by those who study it. . . .

The mind which has become accustomed to the freedom and impartiality of philosophic contemplation will preserve something of the same freedom and impartiality in the world of action and emotion. It will view its purposes and desires as parts of the whole, with the absence of insistence that results from seeing them as infinitesimal fragments in a world of which all the rest is unaffected by any one man's deeds. The impartiality which, in contemplation, is the unalloyed desire for truth, is the very same quality of mind which, in action, is justice, and in emotion is that universal love which can be given to all, and not only to those who are judged useful or admirable. Thus contemplation enlarges not only the objects of our thoughts, but also the objects of our actions and our affections: it makes us citizens of the universe, not only of one walled city at war with all the rest. In this citizenship of the universe consists man's true freedom, and his liberation from the thraldom of narrow hopes and fears.

Thus, to sum up our discussion of the value of philosophy; Philosophy is to be studied, not for the sake of any definite answers to its questions, since no definite answers can, as a rule, be known to be true, but rather for the sake of the questions themselves; because these questions enlarge our conception of what is possible, enrich our intellectual imagination and diminish the dogmatic assurance which closes the mind against speculation; but above all because, through the greatness of the universe which philosophy contemplates, the mind also is rendered great, and becomes capable of that union with the universe which constitutes its highest good.

Review Questions

1. Explain how Russell arrived at the analysis of language as the focal point of his philosophy.
2. What is the nature of a proposition for Russell?
3. For Russell, does philosophy have any role beyond that of establishing a language for science?
4. How ought we evaluate moral action, according to Russell?
5. What relationship does Russell see between mathematics and logic?
6. What is the meaning of Russell's propositional logic?

Suggestions for Further Reading

Ayer, A. J. *Bertrand Russell.* Chicago, University of Chicago Press, 1988.

Egner, R. E. and Dennon, L. E., ed. *The Basic Writings of Bertrand Russell.* New York, Touchstone Books, 1967.

Ryan, Alan. *Bertrand Russell, A Political Life.* New York, Oxford University Press, 1993.

30

Ludwig Wittgenstein (1889–1951)

Viennese Background

Preoccupation with the problem of language in Cambridge was paralleled by a similar preoccupation in Vienna, but whereas in Cambridge the problem had a narrow setting in that it was treated by philosophers apart from the rest of the intellectual community, in Vienna the problem was considered by thinkers of diverse intellectual interests. Musicians, painters, architects, physicists, psychologists, and journalists, as well as philosophers, were all concerned with the power of language and were moved to inquire into its structure as it was employed in art, literature, and science. They tried to get inside language, inside expression, to map it from within. And so we find people like Arnold Schönberg the composer, Oskar Kokoschka the painter, Adolf Loos the architect, Ernst Mach the physicist, Karl Kraus the journalist, and Moritz Schlick the philosopher, each trying to discover the essence of expression in his own field; they were engaged in what Fritz Mauthner, the philosopher-journalist, called the "critique of language."

It is not surprising, then, that Ludwig Wittgenstein, who was thoroughly Viennese, was already caught up in the problem of language—especially the language of physics as it relates to the real world—long before he became acquainted with the work of Bertrand Russell at Cambridge.

He was born in 1889 into a family that was very much a part of the cultural life of Vienna—indeed, located at its center. Karl Wittgenstein, his father, by a combination of engineering know-how and marketing sense, developed a steel company second to none in Austria. His immense wealth enabled him to foster cultural pursuits, especially in music, so that his household became a veritable conservatory and haven for every musician in Vienna. With his father a violinist, his mother a pianist, and his older four brothers and three sisters musically or otherwise artistically talented, Ludwig was bound to play his clarinet like a virtuoso; beyond his instrumental ability, he developed a profound love of music and saw in it the epitome of nonverbal communication. From a religious point of view, though he was baptized a Roman Catholic, his heritage was Jewish, albeit for several generations of the recent past, for many reasons peculiar to central Europe, it was Jewish turned Protestant.

Educated at home until age fourteen and unattracted by a classical education, Ludwig enrolled at the *Realschule* in Linz (just as a young student named Adolph Hitler was leaving) to study mathematics and physics. This was followed by two years of study in mechanical engineering in Berlin. In 1908 he continued his studies in engineering in England at the University of Manchester. But more and more he was being drawn to pure mathematics, and as his interests began to gravitate toward the foundations of mathematics he was directed to the work of Bertrand Russell, whose *Principles of Mathematics* he devoured; he then decided to study with him at Cambridge in 1912–13 and was so swept up by Russell's analysis of language that in later years he occasionally referred to Russell as his "salvation." He made tremendous strides in his new undertaking and was soon able to take his own philosophical path and to discuss his ideas with Russell on equal terms.

Wittgenstein, in a situation often found among artists and intellectuals, fluctuated between a need for friendship and a need for seclusion, which reflected, on the one hand, his cheerful and sometimes charming disposition and, on the other, his depressive state of mind, which resulted in several brushes with suicide, a not uncommon situation in his family. Life was not made easier for him by his total rejection of sham and hypocrisy and his awareness that his demeanor often irritated others. At about this time, he divested himself of his portion of the fortune inherited from his father so that he could live as simple and unaffected a life as possible. A crude hut on a remote farm in Norway was congenial to his spirit, and for a time he lived there enjoying the leisure he required to work out his thoughts.

"*Tractatus Logico-Philosophicus*": *Proposition as Picture*

But it was not long before World War I broke out, and Wittgenstein volunteered for the Austrian army and served on the eastern front. Wherever he went he backpacked his notebooks, and from a prison camp in Italy in 1918 he completed the manuscript for the first of the two books on which his reputation rests, the *Tractatus Logico-Philosophicus.*

When the only publisher to whom he submitted the manuscript rejected it, he sent it off to Russell and, in characteristic style, told him to do whatever he wanted with it; yet when Russell offered to present it publicly with his own introduction, Wittgenstein demurred because he now had misgivings as to whether Russell really understood his main ideas. Nevertheless, it was published, first in German in 1921 and then in English/German a year later, with Russell's introduction.

The *Tractatus,* an "important event in the philosophical world," as Russell called it, is stylistically like its author—lean and reclusive; its terse, laconic form is reminiscent of Heraclitus, but its tight, mathematical-logical shape is reminiscent of Spinoza. It is a series of propositions that are the result of Wittgenstein's thinking, but the working out of the propositions, the explanation, was never put into writing except in the notebooks, previously mentioned, which he kept with him at all times and which, for the most part, were destroyed on his orders. As a result, students are forced to think through the problems for themselves and, in a sense, to retrace the steps the author himself had taken.

In the preface, Wittgenstein tells us that he is going to deal with the problems of philosophy; the reason why there are problems in the first place is that "the logic of our language is misunderstood." So, clarification of language is his main purpose and is formulated in words that have become well known: "what can be said at all can be said clearly."

Let us recall that criticism has been the concern of epistemology since Locke, and that, since Kant, the very term *critique* has meant "the exploration of the limits of"; for example, the critique of pure reason announces Kant's inquiry into the limits of that faculty. Wittgenstein, attempting a critique of language, has a similar goal in the *Tractatus,* that is, to draw a *limit to language* as the expression of thought. If such a limit can be drawn, then what lies within that limit is "sense" and what lies "on the other side of the limit" is "nonsense."

The vehicle of expression in the *Tractatus* is the *proposition,* which, as Wittgenstein puts it, is a statement of fact, and the totality of propositions—how they relate to facts and how they are interrelated among themselves—constitutes language. *How* a proposition relates to facts (i.e., combinations of things in reality, or a "state of affairs") is the key question. Wittgenstein's response to this question is that a *proposition is a picture* of reality, a "picture" of the fact it is destined to stand for, or symbolize. He did not use *picture* in the sense of a duplicate of reality, as might be found in a photograph, diagram, sketch, or image; yet there must be something in common—a kind of literalness—between the picture and the fact: "There must be something identical in a picture and what it depicts, to enable the one to be a picture of the other at all." Perhaps a better word for *picture (Bild)* is simply *representation,* which allows for a departure from literalness in how a fact is modeled by us in forming a proposition, while holding to a certain determinateness in the way a verbal picture actually represents: "The fact that the elements of a picture are related to one another in a determinate way represents that things are related to one another in the same way."

A discernible pattern in the way we use words enables language to be rendered in abstract form, thus making it possible to see more clearly what relationships occur among constituents of a proposition and among propositions themselves—the idea of *propositional logic,* for which Wittgenstein was indebted to Bertrand Russell. Wittgenstein then inventories *all* of the imaginable connections propositions can have: to reality, to thought, to possible states of affairs; within themselves, and to each other; and the connections they must have to be designated as true or false, meaningful or meaningless, or tautological. This inventory would reveal all the ways in which we can actually *say* something or the ways in which we can *possibly* say something. And if, as previously suggested, a proposition stands midway between thought and reality, then clarifying propositions is also clarifying thought, for "a thought is a proposition with a sense," to which Wittgenstein adds his own comment that philosophy itself is an activity that "aims at the logical clarification of thought."

Two clarifications stand out as basic to Wittgenstein's project. First, propositions are true or false and sensical or nonsensical. A proposition is true if things are the way a proposition says they are; if not, it is false: "A proposition can be true or false only in virtue of being a picture of reality." That is, a proposition, as a picture, is "attached to reality; it reaches right out to it" and "is laid against reality like a measure." Second, a proposition is sensical (has sense, makes sense) if it logically holds together and depicts a possible state of affairs; otherwise it is nonsensical (has no sense, makes no sense, is nonsense).

The tone of these distinctions is typical of much of the *Tractatus* because propositions, or thoughts, or indeed knowledge appear to be concerned solely with physical reality, without allowing a viable option for the metaphysical. Statements like "The totality of true propositions is the whole of natural science" and "Superstition is nothing but belief in the causal nexus" lend some plausibility to this view, at least in the minds of the Viennese logical positivists, who regarded philosophy's role as the analysis of scientific statements in which the metaphysical had no part; indeed, when the *Tractatus* was first issued, some of them felt that they had finally found their long-sought manual of operation.

Wittgenstein, always afraid of being misunderstood or misrepresented, took pains to distance himself from this narrow interpretation of his work, and the reason why he did so is to be found in a closer look at the *Tractatus* itself. Wittgenstein consistently made the distinction between what can be *shown* and what can be *said;* the entire book is built around it. What can be said is what can be formulated in propositions, that is, what can be pictured or represented in verbal signs. However, what can be shown can never be said because it lies outside the domain of the picturable or representable. It is quite possible, then, for us to lay hold of, to "feel," to grasp, or simply to know things that cannot be said, but that show themselves: values in general, ethical values in particular, the meaning of life, soul, God—these are among the things that "cannot be put into words. They *make themselves manifest.* They are what is mystical."

The distinction between "show" and "say" shares a common thread with similar distinctions made before Wittgenstein, such as that between "to know" and "to postulate," to know through "proof" and to know through "self-evidence," to "demonstrate" and to "intuit," but in Wittgenstein's case, though it was there all along, the distinction comes with surprising force at the end of the treatise. He himself seems to have preferred the word *mystical* to refer to the domain of what cannot be shown, the nonsensical domain, and in this he is followed by Russell; others, not at all in disagreement, prefer to call the *Tractatus* a "metaphysical" or even an "ethical" work. However it is styled, its transcendental intent is clear, and the fact that "The solution of the riddle of life in space and time lies *outside* space and time" is the foundation for the remarkable conclusion to the *Tractatus:* "My propositions serve as elucidations in the following way: anyone who understands me eventually recognizes them as nonsensical, when he has used them—as steps—to climb up beyond them. (He must, so to speak, throw away the ladder after he has climbed up it.) He must transcend these propositions, and then he will see the world aright." And the very last proposition, standing there without any comment, not only summarizes the book but also states the agenda operative from the outset: "What we cannot speak of we must pass over in silence."

With the *Tractatus* behind him, Wittgenstein, believing he had solved the problems of philosophy by drawing the limits of language, turned to other pursuits—pursuits that fitted his unpretentious nature and his idea of the simpleness of truly human things. He was a schoolteacher for several years in Austria, having as his charges youngsters aged nine to ten. Later, after being dissuaded by the abbot of a monastery near Vienna from becoming a monk, he served as a gardener in the monastery for a time. Meanwhile, he designed a house for one of his sisters, did some sculpting, and occasionally carried on philosophical conversations with Moritz Schlick and Friedrich Waismann.

In 1929 Wittgenstein returned to Cambridge, was awarded a doctorate on the strength of the *Tractatus,* gave lectures from 1930 to 1936, repaired for a year to his retreat in Norway, and in 1937 succeeded G. E. Moore in the chair of philosophy. He never took to the formalities of academic life and withdrew from them whenever he could. He would teach mainly in his own rooms, using no notes, and would proceed, not so much as though he were teaching, but rather "philosophizing" aloud, trying to create something new with each lecture. Between this period and the time of his death, he wrote or dictated extensively; though much of what he put down was circulated among his students, he expressly forbade the publication of his works, at least during his lifetime.

When World War II broke out, he worked as a hospital orderly and laboratory assistant. He taught at Cambridge for several more years, but in 1947 he resigned his chair and went into seclusion in Ireland. Here he tried to rework his manuscripts, but gave up his hope of reorganizing them into a whole with which he was satisfied.

The book he so struggled with appeared under the title of *Philosophical Investigations* in 1953, two years after his death; it brought together the thoughts that had occupied him for sixteen years: "the concepts of meaning, of understanding, of a proposition, of logic, the foundation of mathematics, states of consciousness, and other things." It is written in his idiosyncratic style, but is far less laconic than the *Tractatus,* and full of analogies, stories, and life situations. It is an assemblage of "remarks," or an album of "sketches of landscapes" made in the course of the long and involved journeys of thought.

During the years after the *Tractatus,* Wittgenstein was becoming gradually disenchanted with the notion of picture, which had been its mainstay, as well as with its severe logical demands. Reminiscent of the frankness displayed toward his early works by St. Augustine—the first author quoted in *Philosophical*

Investigations—Wittgenstein writes, "I have been forced to recognize grave mistakes in what I wrote" in the *Tractatus*. That his mistakes were grave may not be anyone else's judgment, but it was certainly his. A key to his changing mood was given in an observation he made to Waismann in 1932: "I used to think that there was a direct link between Language and Reality." Wittgenstein highlights his new direction by a quotation from the *Confessions* in which St. Augustine describes his efforts as a child to reproduce the sounds repeatedly made by his parents to designate an object, and "I gradually learnt to understand what objects they signified." On reflection, Wittgenstein comments that Augustine is describing only *one* system of communication, but "not everything we call language is this system." So, Wittgenstein is not rejecting pictorial representation entirely, merely limiting it to one use of language.

"Philosophical Investigation": Proposition as Family Resemblance

There are, then, *many other* uses of language—ordinary language put to human use, so that meanings come from the way expressions are used in real-life situations. This view was already adumbrated in the *Tractatus* when Wittgenstein observed that "The tacit conventions on which the understanding of everyday language depends are enormously complicated." The whole of language cannot therefore be discovered in any one proposition, as maintained in the *Tractatus,* but rather in the pluralism of uses discovered in the social settings of mankind, in tribal and cultural and scientific milieus, in jobs to be done, in the simple and everyday demands of language, and in psychological contexts. The refrain is found throughout the *Philosophical Investigations* that "the meaning of a word is its use in the language." Alternatively, as another method of reaching the same goal, Wittgenstein tells us to see his remarks in light of anthropology, "as remarks in the natural history of human beings"; or more specifically, "Commanding, questioning, recounting, chatting, are as much a part of our natural history as walking, eating, drinking, playing."

The analogy that most recommends itself to Wittgenstein to cover his new concept of language comes from his insight into the way we play games, and is therefore referred to simply as the idea of *language-games*. The shift from the *Tractatus* to the *Philosophical Investigations* is a shift from the picture notion of language to the use notion of language. A game, in Wittgenstein's explanation, is played according to the rules, yet the rules change from one kind of game to another. Given an indefinite number of games, there is also an indefinite number of rules to be used, for every game is played according to its own rules, and it becomes difficult, if not impossible, to settle on a common denominator identifying all of these activities as games, which indeed they are. Some games feature competition, others do not; some are amusing, others are not; some require skill, others do not; some are played by one person, others are not. In Wittgenstein's own words: "Consider for example the proceedings that we call 'games'. I mean board-games, card-games, ball-games, Olympic games, and so on. What is common to them all?—Don't say:"There *must* be something common, or they would not be called 'games'—but *look and see* whether there is anything common to all.—For if you look at them you will not see something that is common to *all,* but similarities, relationships, and a whole series of them at that."

Given that nothing can be stated as common to all games, there are still similarities that "overlap" and "criss-cross"; from these Wittgenstein develops the notion of *family resemblances:* "I can think of no better expression to characterize these similarities than 'family resemblances'; for the various resemblances between members of a family: build, features, colour of eyes, gait, temperament, etc. overlap and criss-cross in the same way.—And I shall say: 'games' form a family." So with language. There are so many different life situations in which language is used, and used differently in each case, that the rules of language vary with each life event just as the rules of the game vary with each game event: Language is a family too.

In certain ways, the *Tractatus* and the *Philosophical Investigations* are markedly different works, moving as they do from the pictorial to the descriptive, from logical atomism to linguistic pluralism. The rational certainty the mathematician-logician finds in matching pieces exactly is surrendered to the excitement of discovery the psychologist-anthropologist finds in the unshaped ways of human living. In his later book, Wittgenstein came close to adopting a position in language criticism, that of Mauthner, which he had rejected in the earlier one.

Despite the differences, there is a continuity between the earlier and the later Wittgenstein. Language is still his main concern, and the limits of language—the critique of language—is still his main goal. The work of philosophy remains constant throughout; it is, in the words of the later book, the "battle against the bewitchment of our intelligence by means of language"; it is the seeking of clarity—to show "the fly the way out of the fly-bottle."

Commitment to Life

But underlying it all is Wittgenstein's commitment to life, a commitment seen in and through himself, not unlike what he found in Kierkegaard's individualism. In his works he tried to secure the claims of the unsayable against the sayable; he kept value separate from fact, so that the meaning of life for him cannot be discovered in the realm of the rational, the scientific, or the fact-bound world—and yet it can be discovered, which is precisely what we must be "silent" about. This attitude can be summed up in the final words of a lecture on ethics Wittgenstein gave to a Cambridge society in 1929–30: "My whole tendency and I believe the tendency of all men who ever tried to write or talk on Ethics or Religion was to run against the boundaries of language. This running against the walls of our cage is perfectly, absolutely hopeless. Ethics so far as it springs from the desire to say something about the ultimate meaning of life, the absolute good, the absolute value, can be no science. What it says does not add to our knowledge in any sense. But it is a document of a tendency in the human mind which I personally cannot help respecting deeply and I would not for my life ridicule it."

Although his influence is not as strong as it used to be it is understandable why Wittgenstein, having given the philosophy of language a decisive turn, was the vogue for a generation after the appearance of *Philosophical Investigations* and why he will be remembered as one of the dominant voices of the twentieth century.

READINGS

Preface to Tractatus Logico-Philosophicus

Perhaps this book will be understood only by someone who has himself already had the thoughts that are expressed in it—or at least similar thoughts.—So it is not a textbook.—Its purpose would be achieved if it gave pleasure to one person who read and understood it.

The book deals with the problems of philosophy, and shows, I believe, that the reason why these problems are posed is that the logic of our language is misunderstood. The whole sense of the book might be summed up in the following words: what can be said at all can be said clearly, and what we cannot talk about we must pass over in silence.

Thus the aim of the book is to draw a limit to thought, or rather—not to thought, but to the expressing of thoughts: for in order to be able to draw a limit to thought, we should have to find both sides of the limit thinkable (i.e. we should have to be able to think what cannot be thought).

It will therefore only be in language that the limit can be drawn, and what lies on the other side of the limit will simply be nonsense.

I do not wish to judge how far my efforts coincide with those of other philosophers. Indeed, what I have written here makes no claim to novelty in detail, and the reason why I give no sources is that it is a matter of indifference to me whether the thoughts that I have had have been anticipated by someone else.

I will only mention that I am indebted to Frege's great works and to the writings of my friend Mr. Bertrand Russell for much of the stimulation of my thoughts.

If this work has any value, it consists in two things: the first is that thoughts are expressed in it, and on this score the better the thoughts are expressed—the more the nail has been hit on the head—the greater will be its value.—Here I am conscious of having fallen a long way short of what is possible. Simply because my powers are too slight for the accomplishment of the task.—May others come and do it better.

On the other hand the *truth* of the thoughts that are here communicated seems to me unassailable and definitive. I therefore believe myself to have found, on all essential points, the final solution of the problems. And if I am not mistaken in this belief, then the second thing in which the value of this work consists is that it shows how little is achieved when these problems are solved.

Language as Picture

(from *Tractatus Logico-Philosophicus*)

1¹   The world is all that is the case.

1.1   The world is the totality of facts, not of things.

1.11   The world is determined by the facts, and by their being *all* the facts.

1.12   Totality of facts determines what is the case, and also whatever is not the case.

1.13   The facts in logical space are the world.

1.2   The world divides into facts.

1.21   Each item can be the case or not the case while everything else remains the same.

2   What is the case—a fact—is existence of states of affairs.

2.01   A state of affairs (a state of things) is a combination of objects (things).

2.011   It is essential to things that they should be possible constituents of states of affairs.

2.012   In logic nothing is accidental: if a thing can occur in a state of affairs, the possibility of the state of affairs must be written into the thing itself.

2.0121   It would seem to be a sort of accident, if it turned out that a situation would fit a thing that could already exist entirely on its own.

          If things can occur in states of affairs, this possibility must be in them from the beginning.

          (Nothing in the province of logic can be merely possible. Logic deals with every possibility and all possibilities are its facts.)

          Just as we are quite unable to imagine spatial objects outside space or temporal objects outside time, so too there is no object that we can imagine excluded from the possibility of combining with others.

          If I can imagine objects combined in states of affairs, I cannot imagine them excluded from the *possibility* of such combinations.

2.0122   Things are dependent in so far as they can occur in all *possible* situations, but this form of independence is a form of connexion with states of affairs, a form of dependence. (It is impossible for words to appear in two different roles: by themselves, and in propositions.)

2.0123   If I know an object I also know its possible occurrences in states of affairs.

---

¹The decimal numbers assigned to the individual propositions indicate the logical importance of the propositions, the stress laid on them in my exposition. The propositions *n*.1, *n*.2, *n*.3, etc. are comments of proposition no.*n;* the propositions *n*.*m*1, *n*.*m*2, etc. are comments on proposition no. *n.m;* and so on.

(Every one of these possibilities must be part of the nature of the object.)

A new possibility cannot be discovered later.

2.01231   If I am to know an object, though I need not know its external properties, I must know all its internal properties.

2.0124   If all objects are given, then at the same time all *possible* states of affairs are also given.

2.013   Each thing is, as it were, in a space of possible states of affairs. This space I can imagine empty, but I cannot imagine the thing without the space.

2.0131   A spatial object must be situated in infinite space. (A spatial point is an argument-place.)

A speck in the visual field, though it need not be red, must have some colour: it is, so to speak, surrounded by colour-space. Notes must have *some* pitch, objects of the sense of touch *some* degree of hardness, and so on.

2.014   Objects contain the possibility of all situations.

2.0141   The possibility of its occurring in states of affairs is the form of an object.

2.02   Objects are simple.

2.0201   Every statement about complexes can be resolved into a statement about their constituents and into the propositions that describe the complexes completely.

2.021   Objects make up the substance of the world. That is why they cannot be composite.

2.0211   If the world had no substance, then whether a proposition had sense would depend on whether another proposition was true.

2.0212   In that case we could not sketch any picture of the world (true or false).

2.022   It is obvious that an imagined world, however different it may be from the real one, must have *something*—a form—in common with it.

2.023   Objects are just what constitute this unalterable form.

2.0231   The substance of the world *can* only determine a form, and not any material properties. For it is only by means of propositions that material properties are represented—only by the configuration of objects that they are produced.

2.0232   In a manner of speaking, objects are colourless.

2.0233   If two objects have the same logical form, the only distinction between them, apart from their external properties, is that they are different.

2.02331   Either a thing has properties that nothing else has, in which case we can immediately use a description to distinguish it from the others and refer to it; or, on the other hand, there are several things that have the whole set of their properties in common, in which case it is quite impossible to indicate one of them.

> For if there is nothing to distinguish a thing, I cannot distinguish it, since otherwise it would be distinguished after all.

2.024   Substance is what subsists independently of what is the case.

2.025   It is form and content.

2.0251   Space, time, and colour (being coloured) are forms of objects.

2.026   There must be objects, if the world is to have an unalterable form.

2.027   Objects, the unalterable, and the subsistent are one and the same.

2.0271   Objects are what is unalterable and subsistent; their configuration is what is changing and unstable.

2.0272   The configuration of objects produces states of affairs.

2.03   In a state of affairs objects fit into one another like the links of a chain.

2.031   In a state of affairs objects stand in a determinate relation to one another.

2.032   The determinate way in which objects are connected in a state of affairs is the structure of the state of affairs.

2.033   Form is the possibility of structure.

2.034   The structure of a fact consists of the structures of states of affairs.

2.04   The totality of existing states of affairs is the world.

2.05   The totality of existing states of affairs also determines which states of affairs do not exist.

2.06   The existence and non-existence of states of affairs is reality.

> (We also call the existence of states of affairs a positive fact, and their non-existence a negative fact.)

2.061   States of affairs are independent of one another.

2.062   From the existence or non-existence of one state of affairs it is impossible to infer the existence or non-existence of another.

2.063   The sum-total of reality is the world.

2.1   We picture facts to ourselves.

2.11   A picture presents a situation in logical space, the existence and non-existence of states of affairs.

2.12   A picture is a model of reality.

2.13   In a picture objects have the elements of the picture corresponding to them.

2.131   In a picture the elements of the picture are the representatives of objects.

2.14   What constitutes a picture is that its elements are related to one another in a determinate way.

2.141   A picture is a fact.

2.15   The fact that the elements of a picture are related to one another in a determinate way represents that things are related to one another in the same way.

> Let us call this connexion of its elements the structure of the picture, and let us call the possibility of this structure the pictorial form of the picture.

2.151	Pictorial form is the possibility that things are related to one another in the same way as the elements of a picture.
2.1511	*That* is how a picture is attached to reality; it reaches right out to it.
2.1512	It is laid against reality like a measure.
2.15121	Only the end-points of the graduating lines actually *touch* the object that is to be measured.
2.1513	So a picture, conceived in this way, also includes the pictorial relationship, which makes it into a picture.
2.1514	The pictorial relationship consists of the correlations of the picture's elements with things.
2.1515	These correlations are, as it were, the feelers of the picture's elements, with which the picture touches reality.
2.16	If a fact is to be a picture, it must have something in common with what it depicts.
2.161	There must be something identical in a picture and what it depicts, to enable the one to be a picture of the other at all.
2.17	What a picture must have in common with reality, in order to be able to depict it—correctly or incorrectly—in the way it does, is its pictorial form.
2.171	A picture can depict any reality whose form it has. A spatial picture can depict anything spatial, a coloured one any-thing coloured, etc.
2.172	A picture cannot, however, depict its pictorial form: it displays it.
2.173	A picture represents its subject from a position outside it. (Its standpoint is its representational form.) That is why a picture represents its subject correctly or incorrectly.
2.174	A picture cannot, however, place itself outside its representational form.
2.18	What any picture, of whatever form, must have in common with reality, in order to be able to depict it—correctly or incorrectly—in any way at all, is logical form, i.e., the form of reality.
2.181	A picture whose pictorial form is logical form is called logical picture.
2.182	Every picture is *at the same time* a logical one. (On the other hand, not every picture is, for example, a spatial one.)
2.19	Logical pictures can depict the world.
2.2	A picture has logico-pictorial form in common with what it depicts.
2.201	A picture depicts reality by representing a possibility of existence and non-existence of states of affairs.
2.202	A picture represents a possible situation in logical space.
2.203	A picture contains the possibility of the situation that it represents.
2.21	A picture agrees with reality or fails to agree; it is correct or incorrect, true or false.
2.22	What a picture represents it represents independently of its truth or falsity, by means of its pictorial form.
2.221	What a picture represents is its sense.

2.222   The agreement or disagreement of its sense with reality constitutes its truth or falsity.

2.223   In order to tell whether a picture is true or false we must compare it with reality.

2.224   It is impossible to tell from the picture alone whether it is true or false.

2.225   There are no pictures that are true a priori.

Beyond the Limits of Language
(from *Tractatus Logico-Philosophicus*)

6.4   All propositions are of equal value.

6.41   The sense of the world must lie outside the world. In the world everything is as it is, and everything happens as it does happen: *in* it no value exists—and if it did exist, it would have no value.

        If there is any value that does have values, it must lie outside the whole sphere of what happens and is the case. For all that happens and is the case is accidental.

        What makes it non-accidental cannot lie *within* the world, since if it did it would itself be accidental.

        It must lie outside the world.

6.42   So too it is impossible for there to be propositions of ethics.

        Propositions can express nothing that is higher.

6.421   It is clear that ethics cannot be put into words.

        Ethics is transcendental.

        (Ethics and aesthetics are one and the same.)

6.422   When an ethical law of the form, 'Thou shalt . . .', is laid down, one's first thought is, 'And what if I do not do it?' It is clear, however, that ethics has nothing to do with punishment and reward in the usual sense of the terms. So our question about the *consequences* of an action must be unimportant.—At least those consequences should not be events. For there must be something right about the question we posed. There must indeed be some kind of ethical reward and ethical punishment, but they must reside in the action itself.

        (And it is also clear that the reward must be something pleasant and the punishment something unpleasant.)

6.423   It is impossible to speak about the will in so far as it is the subject of ethical attributes.

        And the will as a phenomenon is of interest only to psychology.

6.43   If the good or bad exercise of the will does alter the world, it can alter only the limits of the world, not the facts—not what can be expressed by means of language.

In short the effect must be that it becomes an altogether different world. It must, so to speak, wax and wane as a whole.

The world of the happy man is a different one from that of the unhappy man.

6.431   So too at death the world does not alter, but comes to an end.

6.4311   Death is not an event in life: we do not live to experience death.

If we take eternity to mean not infinite temporal duration but timelessness, then eternal life belongs to those who live in the present.

Our life has no end in just the way in which our visual field has no limits.

6.4312   Not only is there no guarantee of the temporal immortality of the human soul, that is to say of its eternal survival after death; but, in any case, this assumption completely fails to accomplish the purpose for which it has always been intended. Or is some riddle solved by my surviving for ever? Is not this eternal life itself as much of a riddle as our present life? The solution of the riddle of life in space and time lies *outside* space and time.

(It is certainly not the solution of any problems of natural science that is required.)

6.432   *How* things are in the world is a matter of complete indifference for what is higher. God does not reveal himself *in* the world.

6.4321   The facts all contribute only to settling the problem, not to its solution.

6.44   It is not *how* things are in the world that is mystical, but *that* it exists.

6.45   To view the world sub specie aeterni is to view it as a whole—a limited whole.

Feeling the world as a limited whole—it is this that is mystical.

6.5   When the answer cannot be put into words, neither can the question be put into words.

The riddle does not exist.

If a question can be framed at all, it is also *possible* to answer it.

6.51   Scepticism is *not* irrefutable, but obviously nonsensical when it tries to raise doubts where no questions can be asked.

For doubt can exist only where a question exists, a question only where an answer exists, and an answer only where something *can be said.*

6.52   We feel that even when all *possible* scientific questions have been answered, the problems of life remain completely untouched. Of course there are then no questions left, and this itself is the answer.

6.521   The solution of the problem of life is seen in the vanishing of the problem.

(Is not this the reason why those who have found after a long period of doubt that the sense of life became clear to them have then been unable to say what constituted sense?)

6.522   There are, indeed, things that cannot be put into words. They *make themselves manifest.* They are what is mystical.

6.53   The correct method in philosophy would really be the following: to say nothing except what can be said, i.e. propositions of natural science—i.e. something that has nothing to do with philosophy—and then, whenever someone else wanted to say something metaphysical, to demonstrate to him that he had failed togive a meaning to certain signs in his propositions. Although it would not be satisfying to the other person—he would not have the feeling that we were teaching him philosophy—*this* method would be the only strictly correct one.

6.54   My propositions serve as elucidations in the following way: anyone who understands me eventually recognizes them as nonsensical, when he has used them—as steps—to climb up beyond them. (He must, so to speak, throw away the ladder after he has climbed up it.)

He must transcend these propositions, and then he will see the world aright.

7   What we cannot speak about we must pass over in silence.

(From *Tractatus Logico-Philosophicus.* Trans. by D. F. Pears and B. F. McGuiness. London: Routledge & Kegan Paul PLC, 1972. New York: Humanities Press, 1972. Reprinted by permission of Routledge & Kegan Paul.)

Language as Language-Games
(from *Philosophical Investigations*)

65. Here we come up against the great question that lies behind all these considerations.—For someone might object against me:"You take the easy way out! You talk about all sorts of language-games, but have nowhere said that the essence of a language-game, and hence of language, is: what is common to all these activities, and what makes them into language or parts of language. So you let yourself off the very part of the investigation that once gave you yourself most headache, the part about the *general form of propositions and of language.*"

And this is true.—Instead of producing something common to all that we call language, I am saying that these phenomena have no one thing in common which makes us use the same word for all,—but that they are *related* to one another in many different ways. And it is because of this relationship, or these relationships, that we call them all "language." I will try to explain this.

66. Consider for example the proceedings that we call "games". I mean board-games, card-games, ball-games, Olympic games, and so on. What is common to them all?—Don't say:"There *must* be something common, or they would not be called 'games'—but *look and see* whether there is anything common to all.—For if you look at them you will not see something that is common to *all,* but similarities, relationships, and a whole series of them at that. To repeat: don't think, but look!—Look for example at board-games, with their multifarious relationships.

Now pass to card-games; here you find many correspondences with the first group, but many common features drop out, and others appear. When we pass next to ball-games, much that is common is retained, but much is lost.—Are they all 'amusing'? Compare chess with noughts and crosses. Or is there always winning and losing, or competition between players? Think of patience. In ball games there is winning and losing; but when a child throws his ball at the wall and catches it again, this feature has disappeared. Look at the parts played by skill and luck; and at the difference between skill in chess and skill in tennis. Think now of games like ring-a-ring-a-roses; here is the element of amusement, but how many other characteristic features have disappeared! And we can go through the many, many other groups of games in the same way; can see how similarities crop up and disappear.

And the result of this examination is: we see a complicated network of similarities overlapping and criss-crossing: sometimes overall similarities, sometimes similarities of detail.

67. I can think of no better expression to characterize these similarities than "family resemblances"; for the various resemblances between members of a family: build, features, colour of eyes, gait, temperament, etc. etc. overlap and criss-cross in the same way.—And I shall say: 'games' form a family.

And for instance the kinds of number form a family in the same way. Why do we call something a "number"? Well, perhaps because it has a—direct—relationship with several things that have hitherto been called number; and this can be said to give it an indirect relationship to other things we call the same name. And we extend our concept of number as in spinning a thread we twist fibre on fibre. And the strength of the thread does not reside in the fact that some one fibre runs through its whole length, but in the overlapping of many fibres.

But if someone wished to say: "There is something common to all these constructions—namely the disjunction of all their common properties"—I should reply: Now you are only playing with words. One might as well say: "Something runs through the whole thread—namely the continuous overlapping of those fibres".

68. "All right: the concept of number is defined for you as the logical sum of these individual interrelated concepts: cardinal numbers, rational numbers, real numbers, etc.; and in the same way the concept of a game as the logical sum of a corresponding set of sub-concepts."—It need not be so. For I *can* give the concept "number" rigid limits in this way, that is, use the word "number" for a rigidly limited concept, but I can also use it so that the extension of the concept is *not* closed by a frontier. And this is how we do use the word "game". For how is the concept of a game bounded? What still counts as a game and what no longer does? Can you give the boundary? No. You can *draw* one; for none has so far been drawn. (But that never troubled you before when you used the word "game".)

"But when the use of the word is unregulated, the 'game' we play with it is unregulated."—It is not everywhere circumscribed by rules; but no more are there any rules for how high one throws the ball in tennis, or how hard; yet tennis is a game for all that and has rules too.

69. How should we explain to someone what a game is? I imagine that we should describe *games* to him, and we might add: "This *and similar things* are

called 'games'." And do we know any more about it ourselves? Is it only other people whom we cannot tell exactly what a game is?—But this is not ignorance. We do not know the boundaries because none have been drawn. To repeat, we can draw a boundary—for a special purpose. Does it take that to make the concept usable? Not at all! (Except for that special purpose.) No more than it took the definition: 1 pace = 75 cm. to make the measure of length 'one pace' usable. And if you want to say "But still, before that it wasn't an exact measure", then I reply: very well, it was an inexact one.—Though you still owe me a definition of exactness.

70. "But if the concept 'game' is uncircumscribed like that, you don't really know what you mean by a 'game'."—When I give the description: "The ground was quite covered with plants"—do you want to say I don't know what I am talking about until I can give a definition of a plant?

My meaning would be explained by, say, a drawing and the words "The ground looked roughly like this." Perhaps I even say "it looked *exactly* like this."—Then were just *this* grass and *these* leaves there, arranged just like this? No, that is not what it means. And I should not accept any picture as exact in *this* sense.

> Someone says to me: "Shew the children a game." I teach them gaming with dice, and the other says "I didn't mean that sort of game." Must the exclusion of the game with dice have come before his mind when he gave me the order? (Note added by Wittgenstein—ed.)

71. One might say that the concept 'game' is a concept with blurred edges.—"But is a blurred concept a concept at all?—Is an indistinct photograph a picture of a person at all? Is it even always an advantage to replace an indistinct picture by a sharp one? Isn't the indistinct one often exactly what we need?

Frege compares a concept to an area and says that an area with vague boundaries cannot be called an area at all. This presumably means that we cannot do anything with it.—But is it senseless to say: "Stand roughly there?" Suppose that I were standing with someone in a city square and said that. As I say it I do not draw any kind of boundary, but perhaps point with my hand—as if I were indicating a particular *spot*. And this is just how one might explain to someone what a game is. One gives examples and intends them to be taken in a particular way.—I do not, however, mean by this that he is supposed to see in those examples that common thing which I—for some reason—was unable to express; but that he is now to *employ* those examples in a particular way. Here giving examples is not an *indirect* means of explaining—in default of a better. For any general definition can be misunderstood too. The point is that *this* is how we play the game. (I mean the language-game with the word "game".)

In such a difficulty always ask yourself: How did we learn the meaning of this word ("good" for instance)? From what sort of examples? in what language-games? Then it will be easier for you to see that the word must have a family of meanings.

Review Questions

1. What is the meaning of critique as applied to the use of language?
2. Discuss the earlier position of Wittgenstein on language as picture.
3. Why did he change his position to that of language as language-games?
4. In what way can the *Tractatus* be thought of as metaphysical?
5. What significance do you attach to the exhortation that what we cannot speak about we should be silent about?

Suggestions For Further Reading

Grayling, A. C. *Wittgenstein.* New York, Oxford University Press, 1988.
Monk, Ray. *Ludwig Wittgenstein: The Duty of Genius.* New York, Free Press, 1990.
Philosophical Investigations. Tr. Anscombe, G. E. M. Oxford, Oxford University Press, 1953.
Tractatus Logico-Philosophicus. Tr. Pears, D. F. and McGuiness, B. F. London, Routledge & Kegan Paul, 1961.

31

Current Dimensions

1. Women Philosophers:
Susanne K. Langer

As we move into the last chapter of our introduction to philosophy, we are entering the time we live in, facing thereupon newly emerging problems as well as a number of older problems resurfacing in a fresh context. Since the spectrum is broad and the number of such questions has reached dizzying proportions, it would be impossible to give attention to every current philosophical question, but we can take a look at several to help us appreciate the state of affairs. This chapter, then, is a samples of current thought.

In a book like this, in which profiles of individuals serve to introduce the several chapters, it may seem odd that no women philosophers are to be found among them. Some students may well ask where the women philosophers are. The question is complex, but one answer may lie in acknowledging that in fact they have been there all along; however, for a skein of historical, sociocultural, and even prejudicial reasons, they have only recently entered the mainstream of academic philosophy. It could also be that, whatever exclusionary forces were at work, an artificial division was introduced between "masculine" and "feminine" areas of knowledge, resulting in the conclusion that philosophical insight was thought to be the proprietary domain of the former over the latter. Leaving the question aside as to whether there is a way that women experience the world not possessed by men, philosophy would remain woefully impoverished if it did not welcome everything the human mind can collectively bring to its understanding of reality.

"Women in philosophy" signifies that there *are* women engaged in philosophy and that this intellectual pursuit is not the domain of the male mind, but of the human mind. "Philosophy of woman" signifies commitment to a *particular* issue, that is, the right understanding of woman. It seeks the equal acceptance of woman alongside man as a natural right, and inasmuch as this equality still involves a struggle in our time, the lexicon of the philosophy of woman is assertive, as it has to be, to combat the notion of inferior status and to seek the "liberation" of woman from historic oppression. It is a legitimate philosophical goal, for it's trying to unmask a condition intolerable on every count. Karl Marx saw the condition of the working poor as oppression, as real alienation, and explored the foundations of their rehumanization. Likewise the philosopher today, in seeing the status of women as oppressed will also seek liberation in a similar humanizing undertaking.

To the earlier names of Mary Wollstonecraft and Harriet Taylor, whom we have already seen as the alter ego of John Stuart Mill, can be added the names of Mary Whiton Calkins and Susan Stebbing from the late nineteenth and early twentieth centuries, and from the mid- to late twentieth century an abundance of names like Susanne K. Langer, Hannah Arendt, Simone de Beauvoir, Edith Stein, Simone Weil, Iris Murdoch, Mary Midgely, G. E. M. Anscombe, Judith Jarvis Thomson, Susan Haack, and a sizable number of authors writing on the edge of feminist epistemology, among whom Alison Jagger is a reputed figure. For the most part, these women philosophers have made their way in academia owing to the gradual overcoming of insensitivity to the equality of education for women in the Western world. Their scholarly contributions augur prosperously for achieving a goal long overdue, the hearing of different voices.

As representative of a different voice, the name of Susanne K. Langer (†1985) should surely be counted among original thinkers of our time. She studied philosophy at Harvard and spent a life teaching in the academy as a professor of philosophy. Her major works, beginning with *Philosophy in a New Key,* through *Feeling and Form,* and *Mind: An Essay on Human Feeling,* explore one of the misunderstood dimensions of human life, that of feeling and emotion. Feeling, she holds, is of the very essence of the human being, and though ordinarily we may, in prizing humans, say they are essentially rational but also have feeling, we should rather prize them by saying they are essentially feeling but also have rationality. As Langer herself puts it, feeling ". . . is the starting-point of a philosophy of mind. The study of feeling—its sources, its forms, its complexities—leads one down into biological structures and process . . . and upward to the purely human sphere known as 'culture.'"

The direction of Langer's philosophical outlook, detailed in her extremely well-received book *Philosophy in a New Key,* is founded on the concept of the symbol, which she looks upon as the unique contribution of our age to the ongoing evolution of philosophy. Every philosophical era is an outgrowth of fundamental notions proper to it in the form of *generative ideas;* ideas, that is, that create a "whole new way of thinking," prompting questions which will shape the handling of problems of the time. Ancient Greek philosophy saw a rich succession of such ideas, beginning with the questions raised by the Ionians regarding the primacy of matter in the cosmos, to the question of value in Socrates and, with Plato and Aristotle, to questions like the purpose of political life, the nature of truth, knowledge, and the highest good. With the end of Hellenism, medieval Christianity was bent on interpreting the generative ideas of sin and salvation, nature and grace, unity, and infinity. The advent of Cartesianism in the seventeenth century brought with it yet another appearance of the mind-body problem accompanied by a radical division of all reality into "inner experience and outer world" followed by a host of new areas opening up to questioning. In time, there is a successor to Cartesianism in science and technology, and the bright savior of all "exhausted philosophical systems," the scientific method. But even the scientific method, under the questioning of fact and sense-data, yields the "surprising truth" that sense data are "primarily symbols." And thus, for Langer, with the concept of symbol as the key to all that is new in philosophy since the time of Kant, an astounding fresh horizon is disclosed and "in the fundamental notion of symbolization we have the keynote of all humanistic problems."

We are so used to the notion that the activity of intellect resides only in the act of reasoning, in thinking things through step-by-step and expressing it grammatically word-by-word, that intelligence has no other grasp on reality but a "discursive" grasp. Langer, however, contends that all intelligence, all our thinking activity, is based on symbolism: ". . . wherever a symbol operates, there is meaning; and conversely, different classes of experience—say, reason, intuition, appreciation—correspond to different types of symbolic mediation." It's clear that if intelligence, or rationality, were to be restricted to *discursive symbolism*," or discursive reasoning, then there would be no room for anything else knowable under another kind of symbolism. But such room *is* found in our experience: "there are things which do not fit the grammatical scheme of expression . . . language is by no means our only articulate product." Langer therefore contends that alongside of discursive symbolism a place must be found for *presentational symbolism*."

Symbolism in its discursive form is sequential in nature, and the whole is not seen until all its particular elements are in place. Symbolism in its presentational form gives, or presents, the whole in which its particular elements are seen to have meaning, not in sequence but simultaneously with the whole. In discursive form, the meanings of its several parts "given through language are successively understood, and gathered into a whole by the process called discourse," but in presentational form, it is the meaning of the whole that gives meaning to its several parts because "they are involved in a simultaneous, integral presentation."

Relying on this distinction, Langer husbands the vast abundance of symbols into four main types—language, ritual, myth, music—and analyzes how they relate to the human mind as the means for getting a deeper grasp on reality or for satisfying the innate "tendency to a symbolic transformation of experience" in expressing human feeling. Thus, language helps us to "hold on to the object" by means of its symbols; ritual and myth, emerging from the matrix of life, are the symbols thereof; and art, especially music, touch a deeper level of insight in a new mode of understanding. This insight and understanding are brought about by the arts in general on the plane of feeling and emotion, whence "art is the creation of forms symbolic of human feeling." But music in particular is the presentational form par excellence, for its "tonal structures . . . bear a close logical similarity to the forms of human feeling." This analysis, begun in *Philosophy in a New Key,* is extended in Langer's later work, *Feeling and Form.*

For Langer, then, the human being is both receiver and communicator. In both capacities humans are thoroughgoingly corporeal, and the reciprocal passing between them and the world begins and ends with the sensible interface of sound, color, and touch. She underscores the importance of this fact by insisting that what humans have received in their living embodiment they must communicate in the same way. This, then, becomes the primary role of art, to express an insight in some kind of tangible, sensible, corporeal form which, in its presentation, tends to impart the idea of wholeness lying beyond the sum of its parts.

Reading

From Philosophy in a New Key

CHAPTER 1
THE EMERGENCE OF SYMBOL

When we speak of fashions in thought, we are treating philosophy lightly. There is disparagement in the phrases, "a fashionable problem," "a fashionable term." Yet it is the most natural and appropriate thing in the world for a new problem or a new terminology to have a vogue that crowds out everything else for a little while. A word that everyone snaps up, or a question that has everybody excited, probably carries a generative idea—the germ of a complete reorientation in metaphysics, or at least the "Open Sesame" of some new positive science. The sudden vogue of such a key-idea is due to the fact that all sensitive and active minds turn at once to exploiting it; we try it in every connection, for every purpose, experiment with possible stretches of its strict meaning, with generalizations and derivatives. When we become familiar with the new idea our expectations do not outrun its actual uses quite so far, and then its unbalanced popularity is over. We settle down to the problems that it has really generated, and these become the characteristic issues of our time.

The rise of technology is the best possible proof that the basic concepts of physical science, which have ruled our thinking for nearly two centuries, are essentially sound. They have begotten knowledge, practice, and systematic understanding; no wonder they have given us a very confident and definite *Weltanshchauung*. They have delivered all physical nature into our hands. But strangely enough, the so-called "mental sciences" have gained very little from the great adventure. One attempt after another has failed to apply the concept of causality to logic and aesthetics, or even sociology and psychology. Causes and effects could be found, of course, and could be correlated, tabulated, and studied; but even in psychology, where the study of stimulus and reaction has been carried to elaborate lengths, no true science has resulted. No prospects of really great achievement have opened before us in the laboratory. If we follow the methods of natural science our psychology tends to run into physiology, histology, and genetics; we move further and further away from those problems which we ought to be approaching. That signifies that the generative idea which gave rise to physics and chemistry and all their progeny— technology, medicine, biology—does not contain any vivifying concept for the humanistic sciences. The physicist's scheme, so faithfully emulated by generations of psychologists, epistemologists, and aestheticians, is probably blocking their progress, defeating possible insights by its prejudicial force. The scheme is not false—it is perfectly reasonable—but it is bootless for the study of mental phenomena. It does not engender leading questions and excite a constructive imagination, as it does in physical researches. Instead of a method, it inspires a militant methodology.

Now, in those very regions of human interest where the age of empiricism has caused no revolution, the preoccupation with symbols has come into fashion. It has not sprung directly from any canon of science. It runs at least two distinct and apparently incompatible courses. Yet each course is a river of life in its own field, each fructifies its own harvest; and instead of finding mere contradiction in the wide difference of forms and uses to which this new generative idea is put, I see in it a promise of power and versatility, and a commanding philosophical problem. One conception of symbolism leads to logic, and meets the new problems in theory of knowledge; and so it inspires an evaluation of science and a quest for certainty. The other takes us in the opposite direction—to psychiatry, the study of emotions, religion, fantasy, and everything but knowledge. Yet in both we have a central theme: the *human response,* as a constructive, not a passive thing. Epistemologists and psychologists agree that symbolization is the key to that constructive process, though they may be ready to kill each other over the issue of what a symbol is and how it functions. One studies the structure of science, the other of dreams; each has his own assumptions—that is all they are—regarding the nature of symbolism itself. Assumptions, generative ideas, are what we fight for. Our conclusions we are usually content to demonstrate by peaceable means. Yet the assumptions are philosophically our most interesting stock-in-trade.

In the fundamental notion of symbolization—mystical, practical, or mathematical, it makes no difference—we have the keynote of all humanistic problems. In it lies a new conception of "mentality," that may illumine questions of life and consciousness, instead of obscuring them as traditional "scientific methods" have done. If it is indeed a generative idea, it will beget tangible methods of its own, to free the deadlocked paradoxes of mind and body, reason and impulse, autonomy and law, and will overcome the checkmated arguments of an earlier age by discarding their very idiom and shaping their equivalents in more significant phrase. The philosophical study of symbols is not a technique borrowed from other disciplines, not even from mathematics; it has arisen in the fields that the great advance of learning has left fallow. Perhaps it holds the seed of a new intellectual harvest, to be reaped in the next season of the human understanding.

CHAPTER IV
DISCURSIVE AND PRESENTATIONAL FORMS

It appears, then, that although the different media of non-verbal representation are often referred to as distinct "languages," this is really a loose terminology. Language in the strict sense is essentially discursive; it has permanent units of meaning which are combinable into larger units; it has fixed equivalences that make definition and translation possible; its connotations are general, so that it requires nonverbal acts, like pointing, looking, or emphatic voice-inflections, to assign specific denotations to its terms. In all these salient characters it differs from wordless symbolism, which is nondiscursive and untranslatable, does not allow of definitions within its own system, and cannot directly convey generalities. The meanings given through language are successively understood, and gathered into a whole by the process called discourse; the meanings of all other symbolic elements that compose a larger, articulate symbol are understood only through the meaning of the whole, through their relations within the total structure. Their very functioning as symbols depends on the fact that they are involved in a simultaneous, integral presentation. This kind of semantic may be called "presentational symbolism," to characterize its essential distinction from discursive symbolism, or "language" proper.

The recognition of presentational symbolism as a normal and prevalent vehicle of meaning widens our conception of rationality far beyond the traditional boundaries, yet never breaks faith with logic in the strictest sense. Wherever a symbol operates, there is a meaning; and conversely, different classes of experience—say, reason, intuition, appreciation—correspond to different types of symbolic mediation. No symbol is exempt from the office of logical formulation, of *conceptualizing* what it conveys; however simple its import, or however great, this import is a *meaning,* and therefore an element for understanding. Such reflection invites to tackle anew, and with entirely different expectations, the whole problem of the limits of reason, the much-disputed life of feeling, and the great controversial topics of fact and truth, knowledge and wisdom, science and art. It brings within the compass of reason much that has been traditionally relegated to "emotion," or to that crepuscular depth of the mind where "intuitions" are supposed to be born, without any midwifery of symbols, without due process of thought, to fill the gaps in the edifice of discursive, or "rational," judgment.

2.
W. V. Quine

Many current or recent names like Donald Davidson (+2003), Alonzo Church (+1995), Nelson Goodman (+1998), David Kaplan, Hilary Putnam, Noam Chomsky, and Saul Kripke are associated with the wave of interest in mathematical logic and philosophy of language begun by Bertrand Russell several generations ago. Yet the one that stands out as the dean among them is Willard Van Orman Quine. W. V. Quine, as he is usually referred to, circulated with the movers and shakers in modern philosophy to extend his studies in mathematics, logic, mathematical logic, language analysis, and the philosophy of science. Though his writings are not numerous, they have been profoundly influential, with *Word and Object* (1960) recognized as his most influential. He died in 2000 at the age of ninety-two.

We have seen, under the rubric of the one and the many, that every philosopher, at the risk of not being a philosopher at all, has, explicitly or implicitly, a view of reality *as a whole* in which particular, individual things are seen to make sense. Some philosophers begin with totality as the primary given, that is, that reality means all that is, and that what we perceive as particulars are metaphysical instances of the whole; others begin with particulars and on the demand for relationships among them, build out larger and larger wholes to sustain them. In their abstract moments, science and philosophy complement each other in seeking the explanation for the world's unity. With Quine too there is the pervasive sentiment that, though absolutely determinate meaning is impossible, we must work toward larger considerations in the attempt to "round out," as he puts it, "the system of the world"—reality taken as a whole; this is the precise role of philosophy. Whether he is speaking of physical objects, abstract objects, mind, free will, mathematics, logic, or language, they are all seen as interlocking considerations of that whole.

But the world presents itself first and foremost as physical and, because there is no reason to depart from the physical, the world reveals itself exclusively to the approach befitting its physicality, that is, to science. Quine's commitment to science is thoroughgoing. Science does not deal with questions like why the world began, or life; these are "pseudo questions" inasmuch as "I can't imagine what an answer would look like." Mind–body duality is not a real problem because mind exists only as an "activity on the part of physical objects, mainly persons." Further, a physical explanation for feelings, desires, and thoughts will ultimately be had in the study of behavior, whose basis is neurology but, for the time being, "we materialists" are not able to "translate our mentalistic talk into the language of neurology."

Physical objects are not objects in the ordinary sense of the word, but are a device, or a "myth," by which we configure "myriad scattered sense events" and call the resulting configurations "objects." In direct contact with physical objects are *abstract objects* like animal, roundness, triangle, virtue, whose status as entities is justified by the contribution they make to the system of the world. That is, just as physical objects are required for bringing together scattered sense events, so abstract objects are required for bringing together physical objects into larger wholes to hold reality together; otherwise, in W. B. Yeats' phrase, "Things fall apart; the center cannot hold."

It's at this point that the importance of *mathematics* and *logic* are seen because they enable us to lift statements on the experiential level to the level of the abstract, the philosophical level, and thus there is a "kinship," as he calls it, between logic and mathematics on the one hand and natural science on the other, and this allows for the "semantic ascent" to widening wholes. The third element in our getting inside reality is *language analysis,* justified again because language arises immediately from our personal contact with reality. But the use of language will always remain indeterminate, or relative, because the whole of reality in which language must find its reference, has no fixed nature, thus forming the basis of two of Quine's well-known phrases, "indeterminacy of translation" and "inscrutability of reference." In such a fashion, then, mathematics, logic, and language analysis are, for Quine, the trifocal lenses through which we read reality.

READING

Interview with W. V. Quine
(from *Men of Ideas* with Bryan Magee)

INTRODUCTION

MAGEE: If we took a poll among professional teachers of philosophy on the question 'Who is the most important living philosopher?' it is not at all obvious to me who would get the most votes. But we could predict with confidence that certain names would be in the top half dozen: Quine, Popper, Jean-Paul Sartre, Chomsky probably (though strictly speaking he is not exactly a philosopher). The first of those names is that of Willard van Orman Quine, a Professor of Philosophy at Harvard—who has been described by Stuart Hampshire, for example, as 'the most distinguished living systematic philosopher'. He was born in 1908, and is still highly productive; so he has had a long career, and it is by no means over yet. He has published innumerable articles, and more than a dozen books, the best known of which are *From a Logical Point of View* (1953) and *Word and Object* (1960). First and foremost he is a logician. The original contributions of logic which made him famous are for the most part highly technical, and not really accessible to the layman, though they always had their ultimate roots in problems fundamental to philosophy. However, in the latter part of his career he has become more overtly interested in philosophy in a more general sense. I thought it would be uniquely valuable in this series of dialogues to have a philosopher at the very summit of world reputation talking about the very basics of philosophy, and of his own activity.

DISCUSSION

MAGEE: What do you regard as the central task, or tasks, of philosophy?

QUINE: I think of philosophy as concerned with our knowledge of the world and the nature of the world. I think of philosophy as attempting to round out 'the system of the world', as Newton put it. There have been philosophers who thought of philosophy as somehow separate from science, and as providing a firm basis on which to build science, but this I consider an empty dream. Much of science is firmer than philosophy is, or can ever perhaps aspire to be. I think of philosophy as continuous with science, even as a part of science.

MAGEE: Well, if it's continuous with science, and even part of science, how does it differ from the rest of science?

QUINE: Philosophy lies at the abstract and theoretical end of science. Science, in the broadest sense, is a continuum that stretches from history and engineering at one extreme to philosophy and pure mathematics at the other. Philosophy is abstract through being very general. A physicist will tell us about causal connections between events of certain sorts; a biologist will tell us about causal connections between events of other sorts; but the philosopher asks about causal connection in general—what is it for one event to cause another? Or again a physicist or zoologist will tell us that there are electrons, that there are wombats; a mathematician will tell us that there are no end of prime numbers; but the philosopher wants to know, in more general terms, what sorts of things there are altogether. Philosophy seeks the broad outlines of the whole system of the world.

MAGEE: Do you include in its field of concern, or do you exclude from it, the age-old questions about how the world got here in the first place, and how life began?

QUINE: I exclude these from philosophy. How the world began is a problem for the physicist and astronomer, and of course there have been conjectures from that quarter. How life began is a problem for the biologist, on which he's made notable progress in recent years. Why the world began, or why life began—on the other hand—I think are pseudo questions, because I can't imagine what an answer would look like.

MAGEE: You think that, because there is no conceivable answer to these questions, they are meaningless questions?

QUINE: Yes.

MAGEE: Do you think that the most important questions philosophers have to deal with can be grouped under any particular headings?

QUINE: There are two headings which I think provide an important classification to begin with. There are the ontological questions, as they might be called: general questions as to what sorts of things there are, as well as what it means to exist, for there to be something. And there are the predicative questions: questions as to what sorts of things can meaningfully be asked about what there is. Epistemology would be included in the latter.

MAGEE: Since you've made this distinction, let's cling to it for clarity's sake, and discuss the two groups of questions one at a time. First, the whole group of questions about what there is. Although there are innumerable theories about this, it's fair to say that throughout the history of philosophy there have been two broadly opposing views in the matter of ontology. The argument is between what you might very roughly call materialists and what you might equally roughly call idealists; and although there are innumerable different versions of both doctrines, you have on the one hand the view that reality consists of material objects in spatial and temporal relationships which exist independently of anyone's experience of them, and on the other hand the view that reality consists ultimately of spirits, or minds, or exists in the mind of God, or is put together by our minds. Can I put a crude question to you? Which side are you on?

QUINE: I'm on the materialists' side. I hold that physical objects are real, and exist externally and independently of us. I don't hold that there are only these physical objects. There are also abstract objects: objects of mathematics that seem to be needed to fill out the system of the world. But I don't recognize the existence of minds, of mental entities, in any sense other than as attributes or activities on the part of physical objects, mainly persons.

MAGEE: Obviously that means not only that you reject idealism but also that you reject dualism. And dualism is, of course, the common-sense view—throughout history most human beings have believed that reality consisted ultimately of two categorically different kinds of entity: bodies and minds, or bodies and spirits.

QUINE: It's true, I do reject this view. The dualistic view presents problems, creates problems, which are neither soluble nor, it seems to me, necessary. It is clear that an individual's decisions will affect his movements, will determine his movements; in many cases his movements, in turn, will have consequences in the movements of other physical objects. At the same time the natural scientist, the physicist, insists on a closed system, on there being physical causes, physical explanations in principle, for the physical events. He allows no place for the incursion of influences from outside the physical world. Given all this, it would seem that a person's decisions must themselves be activity on the part of a physical object. It is a basic principle of physical science that there is no change without a change in the distribution of microphysical properties over space. Rejection of this principle I would find uncongenial, because the successes in natural science have been such that we must take its presuppositions very seriously.

MAGEE: What you are saying is that wishes, emotions, feelings, decisions, thoughts, and so on, are all processes which take place in, or are propensities of, certain physical objects, namely people, and that not only are they always accompanied by microphysical changes—changes in our brains and our central nervous systems, and so on—but they *are* those microphysical changes.

QUINE: Exactly.

MAGEE: Before I go on to raise some of the difficulties inherent in this view I wonder if you have any explanation of how it is that almost all of mankind disagrees, and always has disagreed, with you about this—why people in general take a dualist view of reality? If I were to put that question to almost anyone else he could say: 'But it's obvious why people think like that: it's because dualism corresponds to directly experienced reality—that is simply how we experience things.' But you can't say that. You don't think it is how we experience things. So what would your answer be?

QUINE: I recognize a profound difference between so-called mental events and externally observable physical ones, in spite of construing these mental events as themselves events, states, activity, on the part of a physical object. As for the traditional dualistic attitude, certainly this goes back to primitive times. I think one cause of it—one partial explanation— may be the experience of dreams and the seeming separation of the mind from the body in that state. Certainly animism antedated science. Thales, the first of the Greek philosophers, is said to have said that all things are full of gods. Primitive peoples today are said to be animists very largely, and to believe that what we call inanimate objects are animated by spirits. One can even imagine traces of animism in the basic concepts of science itself. The notion of cause, I suspect, began with the feeling of effort, of pushing; also the notion of force surely had that sort of origin; but as time has gone on, and as science has progressed in recent centuries, the dissociation of these concepts from their original mental context seems to have been conducive to great scientific progress. I think of physicalism as a departure, a product of latter-day science, which, of course, is a phenomenon that's very uncharacteristic of the history of mankind.

MAGEE: But, if I may say so, I don't think the chief reason why most people take a dualist view of reality has to do with dreams, or with the other things you mentioned. I think it's chiefly due to the fact that we all have direct experience of an internal flow of thoughts, emotions, responses, desires, fantasies, memories, and so on, which is going on all the time we're awake, and which is extremely complex, not only in the sense that it may be *about* complicated things, but also in the sense that there may be several different activities going on at once. As I say, we're all directly aware of this going on inside ourselves, and since none of it need manifest itself in observable behaviour, i.e. in bodily movement, it leads us naturally to think that this is an aspect of our existence which is non-bodily. Hence dualism.

QUINE: We are aware of these things, and I'm not denying their existence; but I'm construing them or reconstruing them, as activities on the part of physical objects, namely on our part. The fact that they are not observable, on the whole, from the outside does not distinguish them from much that the physicist assumes in the way of internal microscopic or sub-microscopic structure of inanimate objects. A great deal goes on that we do not observe from the outside. We have to account for it conjecturally. The important reason for construing all this activity as activity on the part of bodies is to preserve the closed character of the system of the physical world.

MAGEE: Does this mean that you deny the existence of the age-old problem about whether or not we have free will?

QUINE: Clearly we have free will. The supposed problem comes of a confusion, indeed a confusing turn of phrase. Freedom of the will means that *we* are free to *do* as we will; not that our will is free to will as it will, which would be nonsense. We *are* free to do as we will, unless someone holds us back, or unless we will something beyond our strength or talent. Our actions count as free insofar as our will is a cause of them. Certainly the will has its causes in turn; no one could wish otherwise. If we thought wills could not be caused, we would not try to train our children; you would not try to win votes; we would not try to sell things, or to deter criminals.

MAGEE: Given that you hold these views, how do you see the traditional body–mind problem? Do you simply by-pass it altogether?

QUINE: The body-mind problem that confronted the dualist was the problem of how mind and body could interact, and how such interaction could be reconciled with physical determinism. This problem is cleared up by dropping dualism and accepting materialism. But this move leaves us with another body-mind problem: the problem, now, of how we can ever hope to get along without talking of minds and mental processes, how we can make do just with bodies. Even if all sensation and all emotion and all thought are just a matter of nerves, as we materialists suppose, we don't know the details of all that mechanism; we cannot translate our mentalist talk into the language of neurology. We are evidently left talking of minds and mental processes in the same old way. There is an easy preliminary solution. We simply keep the old mentalistic terms, but understand them hereafter as applying to people as bodies. A man senses and feels and thinks, and he believes this and that, but the man who is doing all this is a body, a living body, and not something else called a mind or soul. Thus we keep our easy old mentalistic way of talking, while yet subscribing to materialism.

    Now this is alarmingly easy; too easy. For the fact is that the mentalistic way of talking suffers from a serious weakness that we haven't yet talked about. It is subjective; it is introspective; it reports events that outsiders have no way of verifying. It lacks the objectivity, or inter-subjectivity, that is the strength of materialism and has made physical science so successful. If we take the lazy course of keeping the whole mentalistic idiom and merely declaring that it applies to bodies, we are gaining none of the advantages of objective checks and intersubjective verification.

    Here, finally, is the proper place for behaviourism. For behaviourism, at its best, is the insistence on external, intersubjective criteria for the control of mentalistic terms. Behaviourism, mine anyway, does not say that the mental states and events *consist* of observable behaviour, nor that they are *explained* by behaviour. They are *manifested* by behaviour. Neurology is the place for the explanations, ultimately. But it is in terms of outward behaviour that we specify what we want explained.

MAGEE: And that would include verbal behaviour.

QUINE: Including verbal behaviour, yes. And, in so far as such criteria are available, we do have the benefits of materialism, after all, and even without full neurological explanation. So the extent to which I am a behaviourist is in seeing behaviourism as a way of making objective sense of mentalistic concepts.

MAGEE: What you're really saying is that behaviourism is not a solution to the kind of problems with which the psychologist deals, but a way of formulating them. It's a kind of model in terms of which the problems should be couched before we go on to seek solutions.

QUINE: Yes.

MAGEE: Can I now chart our present position in this whole discussion? I started by asking you what you regarded as the central tasks of philosophy, and you said not only what you thought philosophers ought to be doing, you said also what you thought they ought not to be doing; you ruled out a number of questions. You then grouped the questions you thought philosophers ought to concern themselves with under two main heads, the first being questions about what exists, the second being questions about what we can know (or say, or ask) about what exists. From that point onward we have been considering the first of those two groups of questions. You have said that your view of what there is is physicalist: you think that all reality consists of physical entities; that there are not minds separate from physical entities; and that the notion that there *are* leads us into all sorts of conceptual confusions which you think a behaviourist analysis liberates us from.

QUINE: Good. One correction I would make, though. My position is not that there are only physical objects—there are also abstract objects.

MAGEE: But these abstract objects are not mental—it's important to make that distinction, is it not?

QUINE: That they're not mental? That's it.

MAGEE: In other words, you don't believe in the existence of minds as separate from physical things, but you do believe in the existence of certain abstract non-mental entities.

QUINE: Yes, numbers notably.

MAGEE: I think you need to explain that a bit. If you are a physicalist, how can you justify belief in the existence of abstract entities at all?

QUINE: The justification lies in the indirect contribution that they make to natural science. They contribute already in a minor way when we speak of zoological species and genera; these are classes. They contribute also in more complex ways. We all know how important numbers are to natural science, and how important mathematical functions are, and other abstract mathematical objects; the scientific system of the world would collapse without them. But mathematicians have established in the past hundred years that classes, or sets, are enough for all these purposes: they can be made to do the work of numbers, functions, and the rest. This, then, is why I recognize sets: to meet the mathematical needs of our system of the natural world. Assuming sets, or classes, is on an equal footing with assuming molecules, atoms, electrons, neutrons, and the rest; all these are objects, concrete and abstract, that are assumed by the network of hypotheses by which we predict and explain our observations of nature. I see natural science as continuous with the mathematics that it uses, just as I see all this as continuous with philosophy. It all goes to make up our inclusive system of the world.

MAGEE: You say 'on an equal footing', but it seems to me there is a very important difference between the sense in which sub-atomic particles are unobservable and the sense in which numbers are unobservable. Sub-atomic particles are bits of material, bits of stuff. It so happens—perhaps because of the accident of our optical apparatus—that they are too small for us to see, but if we had super-microscopic eyes perhaps we could see them; and if we had different kinds of fingers perhaps we could pick them up. Numbers, on the other hand, are not material in any sense. They are abstract through and through—there is *nothing but* abstraction to them.

QUINE: It's true. There is this discontinuity. However, even the continuity of ordinary observable objects with the elementary particles is rather more tenuous than had once been supposed, because an elementary particle is too small, for instance, even in principle, to be detected by light, because it's smaller than any wavelength. Furthermore, the behaviour of the elementary particles is basically unlike that of bodies; so much so that it's, I think, only by courtesy that they're called material. The indeterminacy with respect to whether two segments of paths of electrons are segments of the path of one electron or of two different ones; indeterminacies of position; the antithesis between wave and corpuscle in the interpretation of light; these and other anomalies—notably something called the Bose–Einstein statistic—all suggest that the analogy of body is an analogy that was useful for extrapolation only up to a point. The evolution of hypotheses in the light of further experimentation and further refutations has finally carried us to the point where the continuity is no longer so evident.

MAGEE: I would like, if I may, to go back in our discussion to the point where you were saying that the adoption of a physicalist approach to reality and a behaviourist way of formulating problems liberates us from the spell of certain entrenched ways of looking at things which, though they may appear to be commonsensical, are nevertheless mistaken. Can you say what some of these entrenched ideas are?

QUINE: Good—liberation is one way of looking at it. A sterner discipline is another way of looking at behaviourism. But at any rate a major example is the notion of meaning. There's the common-sense notion that words somehow convey meanings. How do we know that the same words convey the same meaning to two speakers? We can see that the speakers react in the same way. All this is describable in behavioural terms, but might the meanings themselves be different? What behavioural sense can be made of the question? No behavioural sense, no adequate behavioural sense has been made of it. There are other notions that come similarly into question: translation: Once the notion of meaning is questioned, the notion of translation becomes more complex. We can no longer say it's simply a matter of producing another sentence that has the same meaning as the sentence that's being translated. The notion of necessity, again, comes into question.

MAGEE: Well, there are two kinds of necessity, aren't there, the logical and the causal.

QUINE: Yes. Some truths that are called necessary are said to hold true because of the meanings of their words. This sort of necessity goes dim along with the notion of meaning itself. Other truths that might be called necessary are the laws of nature. Necessity of this sort is a dubious notion too—not because of behaviourist strictures exactly, but because of similar scruples. Appreciation of this point goes back two centuries and more, to David Hume. People think necessity must make good sense because the adverb 'necessarily' is so frequent and useful. But if you examine the ordinary use of this adverb, you find that it has nothing to do with any enduring division of statements into necessary ones and contingent ones. When someone attaches the adverb 'necessarily' to some statement that he makes, he is apt merely to be predicting, in the light of the other speaker's statements, that the other speaker will agree that the statement is true. But necessity and possibility are interdefinable: 'necessary' means 'not possible not', and vice versa. So to drop the notion of necessity is to drop that of possibility as well. There is a fashionable philosophy of possible worlds, but it is something undreamed of in my philosophy.

MAGEE: How, on the basis of what you have been saying, are you able to provide an explanation of laws of nature, and of how we get to know them?

QUINE: I recognize no distinction in principle between laws of nature and other true statements about the world. What are called laws are usually general, but I would not distinguish them from other general truths. As for our method of knowing them, it can be and is summed up in a word, albeit a double-barrelled word: hypothetico-deductive. First we think up a theory, a set of hypotheses. Actually it will have been handed down to us, mostly, by our predecessors; we may have just changed a hypothesis, or added one. From this theory we then deduce what observations to expect under various observable conditions. If such an expectation is disappointed, we look to the theory for possible revisions. If not, we go on believing it.

MAGEE: You've called into question such fundamental elements in our thinking as causal necessity, logical necessity, the idea of a law, the notion of meaning. . . . The ground is beginning to disappear from under our feet. What kind of view of the world are you coming out with?

QUINE: My tentative ontology includes physical objects, in a generous sense. The content of any portion of space-time, however scattered, is for me a physical object. In addition my ontology includes, as I said, the abstract hierarchy of classes based on those objects. But the doubts about meaning that behaviourism imposes make me unreceptive to others of the commonly accepted abstract objects: to properties and to propositions. The trouble comes in identification. Thus, consider two expressions written out, two predicates, and suppose they are true of just the same objects. Perhaps one of them says 'equilateral triangle' and the other says 'equiangular triangle'; or suppose one of them says 'has a heart' and the other says 'has kidneys'. The two predicates are true of just the same individual, but shall we say they ascribe the *same* property? How do we decide? We are told that they ascribe the same property only if they are not only true of the same things but also are alike in meaning. The doubts about meaning thus induce doubts about the very notion of a property. Propositions are in the same trouble, for two sentences supposedly express the same proposition only if they are alike in meaning. So I reject propositions as well as properties, while keeping classes.

So much for the ontological side. On the predicative side my view is rather negative. I reject predicates that have too little in the way of inter-subjectively observable criteria, unless they compensate for that defect by contributing substantially to a well-knit system of the world which expedites prediction. I would insist, not that predicates have necessary and sufficient conditions in observation, but that they have a good share of observable criteria, symptoms of application, *or* that they play quite a promising role in theoretical hypotheses.

MAGEE: One thing that pleases me about the discussion we've had is that almost none of it has been about language or the use of words. I say this because a lot of intelligent laymen who take an interest in philosophy are put off by what they take to be the discovery that modern philosophers are doing nothing but talking about words, analysing sentences and so on—and you haven't talked in that way at all. It's clear that the problems you are concerned with are not problems about language. Nevertheless anyone opening your books or coming to study with you at Harvard would find that a great deal of your technique of approaching these problems *is* via the analysis of concepts, and therefore careful attention to words, elucidation of sentences, statements, and so on. Why is it that you and other contemporary philosophers adopt this linguistic approach—to what are, after all, essentially nonlinguistic problems?

QUINE: One reason is a strategy that I call semantic ascent. Philosophical issues often challenge the basic structure of our system of the world. When this happens, we cannot easily dissociate ourselves from our system so as to think about our opponent's alternative. The basic structure of our system inheres in our very way of thinking. Thus the discussion can degenerate into question-begging, each party stubbornly reiterating his own basic principles, the very principles that are at issue. But we can rise above this predicament by talking about our theories, as systems of sentences; talking *about* the sentences instead of just stubbornly asserting them. We can compare the rival systems of sentences in respect of structural simplicity. We can examine them for hidden equivalence, by seeing whether one can be converted into the other by redefinition of terms. We can find a common ground on which to join issues instead of begging the question. This is one reason philosophers talk of language. There are also others. For a deep understanding of our conceptual scheme, our system of the world, we do well to consider how it is acquired: how the individual learns it, and how the race may have developed it. The individual acquires the system mainly in the process of learning the language itself, and likewise the development of our basic conceptual scheme down the ages is bound up with the evolution of the language. The philosopher thus has good reason to be deeply concerned with the workings of language.

MAGEE: We're approaching the end of our discussion. Before we do finish, can I ask you to say something—perhaps in the light of what we've said so far—about the original work you're doing at this moment?

QUINE: In the few years since my book *The Roots of Reference* came out, all I have done is produce numerous short pieces intended to clarify or defend or improve my philosophy at a variety of points. But let me just indicate three sectors where I should like to see breakthroughs, by me or by others. One is semantics, or the theory of meaning. Since we can no longer put up with the uncritical old notion of meaning, we need to devise some systematic theories of translation and of lexicography that respond to behavioural criteria. This sounds like business for linguists, and in large measure it is. But it is closely bound up with philosophical interests and scruples. Anyway, I set little store by boundaries between philosophy and the rest of science. A second sector is the theory of the so-called propositional attitudes, which are expressed by sentences containing subordinate sentences: thus x believes that p, x hopes that p, x fears that p, x rejoices that p. These constructions involve certain subtle difficulties of a logical kind. Also they present grave problems in respect to behavioural criteria. I should like to see a new conceptual apparatus of a logically and behaviourally straightforward kind of which to formulate, for scientific purposes, the sort of psychological information that is conveyed nowadays by idioms of propositional attitude.

So the first of the three sectors that I have in mind is on the border of linguistics, and the second is on the border of psychology. The third is on the border of mathematics. What justifies pure mathematics, with its ontology of abstract objects, is the indispensable part it plays as an adjunct of natural science. I should like to see this apparatus pared down to the weakest and most natural set of assumptions that might still provide an adequate foundation for the scientific applications. One effect to be hoped for, in such a minimization, is a more natural and conclusive solution than we now have for the antinomies of set theory. Some of the people following our discussion are no doubt familiar with one of those antinomies under the name of Russell's paradox. But others are probably not familiar with them at all. So perhaps I'd better stop here.

(From Brian Magee, *Men of Ideas*, New York: Viking Press, 1979.)

3.
John Searle

Mathematics has been indispensable in the mind's effort to understand reality. Pythagoras, we saw, relied on it to give him a sense of cosmic unity, Descartes to give him a footing for certitude, Newton to furnish him with a means for expressing the physics of gravity. Science in general, and the would-be sciences, look to mathematics as a vehicle for quantifying their findings. Even though the past gives us every reason not to be surprised at the domain of mathematics, we still stand in awe at what its higher reaches, along with logic, can do. Today we are witnessing the awesome versatility of mathematical logic in the computer whose computational power staggers the imagination and sometimes enthralls the intellect.

The computer is a machine for all seasons. From the youngster playing his first computer game to the world champion chess player combating IMB's Deep Blue, from the design of livingroom furniture to the nation's outstanding architect, from the supermarket's simple arithmetic to the top physicist's theory of the ultimate unifying principle, the computer is there. Is it any wonder that so many are inclined to predicate human qualities of such a machine and call it *intelligent*, with an *artificial intelligence*, to be sure, but intelligence just the same? When the word *virtual* is used, as in *virtual explosion, virtual skiing, virtual car racing*, we all know it's unreal, but there's a comfort in thinking it's "just as good as." So with artificial, or virtual, intelligence. Some thinkers are bent on holding the position that if the computer can duplicate what the human mind can do, and do it even better, then the computer bids fair to be called a mind; and in reverse, it's clear to them that the human brain, and therefore the mind, is a computer too and that the machine computer is a better mind than the natural one.

The philosopher today who has assailed this point of view most successfully is John Searle. Over several decades he has stoutly maintained that, though we are tempted to say the computer "knows" how to work its way through a complicated problem, it doesn't really know how to because it doesn't know at all. What a computer does, like any tool made by man, is to "simulate," not "duplicate," what the human does without becoming human thereby. The cook knows that the ingredients are being mixed together to make bread but the blender doesn't. The waitress knows she's adding up the check but the calculator doesn't. Gary

Kasparov knows he's playing chess but Deep Blue doesn't. The engineer knows he's computing but the computer doesn't. What the computer does is to run the steps programmed for it by the programmer; only he knows the meaning of the symbols used, the computer doesn't. Over and above the commonsense objection that the computational model of the mind cannot account for essential constituents like consciousness, Searle, for the past two decades, has used the image of the "Chinese room" as a powerful argument against the exaggerated claims of artificial intelligence. Imagine, he says, a person who knows no Chinese is locked in a room with a stock of Chinese characters and that he has at his disposal a computer program for answering in Chinese questions put in Chinese. Chinese answers will then be given to Chinese questions without any knowledge of Chinese to be found in the system. "Any attempt," therefore, "to produce a mind purely with computer programs leaves out the essential features of the mind."

The computer-mind considerations so far discussed coalesce in the mind-body problem, a problem we have seen, that has ancient roots in pre-Socratic times and has been passed on in either the Platonic or Aristotelian tradition clear down to our own times. It was, however, given its modern cast by Descartes who held for an absolute separation between mind and body, with mind referred to, in various contexts, as spiritual, mental, immaterial, incorporeal, and body referred to as quantitative, nonmental, material, corporeal. Shortly after Descartes, extreme positions favoring either side were developed so that all human activity was considered only mind or only body. In our time, when the existence of soul, or spirit, has been having very rough sledding and therefore been virtually ignored, the question has become "Are all mental phenomena reducible to matter?" or, rephrased, "Are all activities of the 'mind' really activities of 'brain' only?" The scientific bias naturally says "yes" to both formulations. Even John Searle, who refuses to yield on the uniqueness of consciousness, holds that it is caused by "brain processes" of a higher order. He remains a defender of consciousness but without seeing any need for it to be of a higher order than matter. And so the mind-body problem continues to be high on the list of nature's mysteries.

READINGS

From The Rediscovery of the Mind (chap. 1 and 2)

I. THE SOLUTION TO THE MIND–BODY PROBLEM AND WHY MANY PREFER THE PROBLEM TO THE SOLUTION

The famous mind-body problem, the source of so much controversy over the past two millennia, has a simple solution. This solution has been available to any educated person since serious work began on the brain nearly a century ago, and, in a sense, we all know it to be true. Here it is: Mental phenomena are caused by neurophysiological processes in the brain and are themselves features of the brain. To distinguish this view from the many others in the field, I call it "biological naturalism." Mental events and processes are as much part of our biological natural history as digestion, mitosis, meiosis, or enzyme secretion.

Biological naturalism raises a thousand questions of its own. What exactly is the character of the neurophysiological processes and how exactly do the elements of the neuroanatomy—neurons, synapses, synaptic clefts, receptors, mitochondria, glial cells, transmitter fluids, etc.—produce mental phenomena? And what about the great variety of our mental life—pains, desires, tickles, thoughts, visual experiences, beliefs, tastes, smells, anxiety, fear, love, hate, depression, and elation? How does neurophysiology account for the range of our mental phenomena, both conscious and unconscious? Such questions form the subject matter of the neurosciences, and as I write this, there are literally thousands of people investigating these questions. But not all the questions are neurobiological. Some are philosophical or psychological or part of cognitive science generally. Some of the philosophical questions are: What exactly is consciousness and how exactly do conscious mental phenomena relate to the unconscious? What are the special features of the "mental," features such as consciousness, intentionality, subjectivity, mental causation; and how exactly do they function? What are the causal relations between "mental" phenomena and "physical" phenomena? And can we characterize those causal relations in a way that avoids epiphenomenalism?

I will try to say something about some of these questions later, but at this point I want to note a remarkable fact. I said that the solution to the mind-body problem should be obvious to any educated person, but at present in philosophy and cognitive science many, perhaps most, of the experts claim to find it not at all obvious. In fact, they don't even think the solution I have proposed is true. If one surveys the field of the philosophy of mind over the past few decades, one finds it occupied by a small minority who insist on the reality and irreducibility of consciousness and intentionality and who tend to think of themselves as property dualists, and a much larger mainstream group who think of themselves as materialists of one type or another. The property dualists think that the mind-body problem is frightfully difficult, perhaps altogether insoluble. The materialists agree that if intentionality and consciousness really do exist and are irreducible to physical phenomena, then there really would be a difficult mind-body problem, but they hope to "naturalize" intentionality and perhaps consciousness as well. By "naturalizing" mental phenomena, they mean reducing them to physical phenomena. They think that to grant the reality and irreducibility of consciousness and other mental phenomena commits one to some form of Cartesianism, and they do not see how such a view can be made consistent with our overall scientific world picture.

I believe that both sides are profoundly mistaken. They both accept a certain vocabulary and with it a set of assumptions. I intend to show that the vocabulary is obsolete and the assumptions are false. It is essential to show that both dualism and monism are false because it is generally supposed that these exhaust the field, leaving no other options. Most of my discussion will be directed at the various forms of materialism because it is the dominant view. Dualism in any form is today generally regarded as out of the question because it is assumed to be inconsistent with the scientific world view.

VI. STRONG ARTIFICIAL INTELLIGENCE

At this point there occurred one of the most exciting developments in the entire two-thousand-year history of materialism. The developing science of artificial intelligence provided an answer to this question: different material structures can be mentally equivalent if they are different hardware implementations of the same computer program. Indeed, given this answer, we can see that the mind just is a computer program and the brain is just one of the indefinite range of different computer hardwares (or "wetwares") that can have a mind. The mind is to the brain as the program is to the hardware (Johnson-Laird 1988). Artificial intelligence and functionalism coalesced, and one of the most stunning aspects of this union was that it turned out that one can be a thoroughgoing materialist about the mind and still believe, with Descartes, that the brain does not really matter to the mind. Because the mind is a computer program, and because a program can be implemented on any hardware whatever (provided only that the hardware is powerful and stable enough to carry out the steps in the program), the specifically mental aspects of the mind can be specified, studied, and understood without knowing how the brain works. Even if you are a materialist, you do not have to study the brain to study the mind.

This idea gave birth to the new discipline of "cognitive science." I will have more to say about it later (in chapters 7, 9, and 10); at this point I am just tracing the recent history of materialism. Both the discipline of artificial intelligence and the philosophical theory of functionalism converged on the idea that the mind was just a computer program. I have baptized this view "strong artificial intelligence" (Searle 1980a), and it was also called "computer functionalism" (Dennett 1978).

Objections to strong AI seem to me to exhibit the same mixture of commonsense objections and more or less technical objections that we found in the other cases. The technical difficulties and objections to artificial intelligence in either its strong or weak version are numerous and complex. I will not attempt to summarize them. In general, they all have to do with certain difficulties in programming computers in a way that would enable them to satisfy the Turing test. Within the AI camp itself, there were always difficulties such as the "frame problem" and the inability to get adequate accounts of "nonmonotonic reasoning" that would mirror actual human behavior. From outside the AI camp, there were objections such as those of Hubert Dreyfus (1972) to the effect that the way the human mind works is quite different from the way a computer works.

The commonsense objection to strong AI was simply that the computational model of the mind left out the crucial things about the mind such as consciousness and intentionality. I believe the best-known argument against strong AI was my Chinese room argument (Searle 1980a) that showed that a system could instantiate a program so as to give a perfect simulation of some human cognitive capacity, such as the capacity to understand Chinese, even though that system had no understanding of Chinese whatever. Simply imagine that someone who understands no Chinese is locked in a room with a lot of Chinese symbols and a computer program for answering questions in Chinese. The input to the system consists in Chinese symbols in the form of questions; the output of the system consists in Chinese symbols in answer to the questions. We might suppose that the program is so good that the answers to the questions are indistinguishable from those of a native Chinese speaker. But all the same, neither the person inside nor any other part of the system literally understands Chinese; and because the programmed computer has nothing that this system does not have, the programmed computer, qua computer, does not understand Chinese either. Because the program is purely formal or syntactical and because minds have mental or semantic contents, any attempt to produce a mind purely with computer programs leaves out the essential features of the mind.

(From John Searle, *The Rediscovery of the Mind.* Reprinted with permission of Bradford Books, MIT Press.)

The Other Me
(Review of Ray Kurzweil, *The Age of Spiritual Machines*)

So what, according to Kurzweil and Moore's Law, does the future hold for us? We will very soon have computers that vastly exceed us in intelligence. Why does increase in computing power automatically generate increased intelligence? Because intelligence, according to Kurzweil, is a matter of getting the right formulas in the right combination and then applying them over and over, in his sense "recursively," until the problem is solved. With sheer computational brute force, he thinks, you can solve any solvable problem. It is true, Kurzweil admits, that computational brute force is not enough by itself, and ultimately you will need "the complete set of unifying formulas that underlie intelligence." But we are well on the way to discovering these formulas: "Evolution determined an answer to this problem in a few billion years. We've made a good start in a few thousand years. We are likely to finish the job in a few more decades."

Let us suppose for the sake of argument that we soon will have computers that are more "intelligent" than we are. Then what? This is where Kurzweil's book begins to go over the edge. First off, according to him, living in this slow, wet, messy hardware of our own neurons may be sentimentally appealing, like living in an old shack with a view of the ocean, but within a very few decades, sensible people will get out of neurons and have themselves, "downloaded" onto some decent hardware. How is this to be done? You will have your entire brain and nervous system scanned, and then, when you and the experts you consult have figured out the programs exactly, you reprogram an electronic circuit with your programs and database. The electronic circuit will have more "capacity, speed, and reliability" than neurons. Furthermore, when the parts wear out they permit of much easier replacement than neurons do.

So that is the first step. You are no longer locked into wet, slow, messy, and above all decaying hardware; you are upgraded into the latest circuitry. But it would be no fun just to spend life as a desktop in the office, so you will need a new body. And how is that to be done? Nanotechnology, the technology of building objects atom by atom and molecule by molecule, comes to the rescue. You replace your old body atom by atom. "We will be able to reconstruct any or all of our bodily organs and systems, and do so at the cellular level. . . . We will then be able to grow stronger, more capable organs by redesigning the cells that constitute them and building them with far more versatile and durable materials." Kurzweil does not tell us anything at all about what these materials might be, but they clearly will not be flesh and blood, calcium bones and nucleoproteins.

Evolution will no longer occur in organic carbon-based materials but will pass to better stuff. However, though evolution will continue, we as individuals will no longer suffer from mortality. Even if you do something stupid like get blown up, you still keep a replacement copy of your programs and database on the shelf so you can be reconstructed at will. Furthermore, you can change your whole appearance and other characteristics at will, "in a split second." You can look like Marlon Brando at one minute and like Marlene Dietrich the next.

In Kurzweil's vision, there is no conflict between human beings and machines, because we will all soon, within the lifetimes of most people alive today, become machines. Strictly speaking we will become software. As he puts it, "*We will be software, not hardware*" (italics his) and can inhabit whatever hardware we like best. There will not be any difference between us and robots. "What, after all, is the difference between a human who has upgraded her body and brain using new nanotechnology, and computational technologies and a robot who has gained an intelligence and sensuality surpassing her human creators?" What, indeed? Among the many advantages of this new existence is that you will be able to read any book in just a few seconds. You could read Dante's *Divine Comedy* in less time than it takes to brush your teeth.

Kurzweil recognizes that there are some puzzling features of this utopian dream. If I have my programs downloaded onto a better brain and hardware but leave my old body still alive, which one is really me? The new robot or the old pile of junk? A problem he does not face: Suppose I make a thousand or a million copies of myself. Are they all me? Who gets to vote? Who owns my house? Who is my spouse married to? Whose driver's license is it, anyhow?

What will sex life be like in this brave new world? Kurzweil offers extended, one might even say loving, accounts. His main idea is that virtual sex will be just as good as, and in many ways better than, old-fashioned sex with real bodies. In virtual sex your computer brain will be stimulated directly with the appropriate signal without the necessity of any other human body, or even your own body.

(From "I Married a Computer," a review of Ray Kurzweil's *The Age of Spiritual Machines: When Computers Exceed Human Intelligence,* in New York Review, April 8, 1999. Reprinted with permission from The New York Review of Books.)

4.

John Rawls

We have seen in the early Pre-Socratics, how large the feature of the one and the many loomed in their understanding of the cosmos and how they sought to maintain a balance between individuality and plurality so that neither side surrendered itself to the other. Unity in plurality extends to every aspect of the real world, to the many elements united, for example, to make one painting, one symphony, one personality, one clock, or one drama. There is a polarity between the one and the many such that neither pole is lost if an ordered balance is maintained between them, or that either one can be lost by placing inordinate value on the other. The one and the many can serve as a template for the philosophy of society inasmuch as society is seen as the one, and the individual members are seen as the many, laying the groundwork thereby of our understanding that no theory of society can be entertained that brings about the destruction of either dimension. It's clear enough that no person can achieve life's ends by himself, or to put it as Rawls does, "We need one another as partners in ways of life that are engaged in for their own sake, and the successes and enjoyments of others are necessary for and complementary to our own good."

But what kind of society? How do we determine the society that fits the needs and aspirations of human beings? Anyone embarking on such a quest must seek to found a basic structure for such a society and must do so by constructing an ideal society that cuts across time. This was true of Plato, of Thomas Hobbes, of John Stuart Mill, and is true today of John Rawls, who has made one of the most engaging presentations of political philosophy in recent times and has provoked a cascade of reaction both supporting and attacking his position. His primary works are *A Theory of Justice* in 1971 and *Political Liberalism* in 1993.

In elaborating his theory on the philosophy of society, Rawls feels that he cannot subscribe to either of the two philosophies of society favored in the Anglo American tradition drawn from utilitarianism or intuitionism. We'll recall the identifying phrase of *utilitarianism*, the greatest happiness principle, that lies behind Rawls' summary statement of the doctrine: "The main idea is that society is rightly ordered, and therefore just, when its major institutions are arranged so as to achieve the greatest net balance of satisfaction over all the individuals belonging to it." That an individual could be called upon to sacrifice his own happiness to the general happiness is an insurmountable problem for Rawls who would have society look to the happiness of each and every one of its members: The relationship of the one and the many is reciprocal, not unilateral. In sum, "Utilitarianism does not take seriously the distinction between persons." Though sympathetic to *intuitionism*, Rawls feels that it is wanting as a doctrine for establishing the basic structure of society because, while it admits a "plurity of first principles," it advances no "explicit method, no priority rules, for weighing these principles against one another"; we simply have to strike a balance by "intuition." The rigors of rationality are not the prime focus of intuitionism.

Since the ideal basic structure of society is not discoverable historically—that is, not within any historical situation in which it was thought to be realized—it must be discoverable elsewhere. This is why Rawls has to turn to an imagined situation, to an *idea* of a position in which reasonable human beings can think through the kind of society they can all agree on, in which their own self-interests are met, and in which the common good of all is the personal good of each. In doing so, he is reviving an older political philosophy based on the *social contract,* a view put forth by Hobbes, Locke, Rousseau, and Kant, and adopted by Rawls to refashion as his own. Imagine, then, in what Rawls calls the *original position,* an assembly, or convention, of human beings, prompted by good faith and motivated by reasonable self-interest so that no one gets an upper hand over another, striving by argument, bargaining, and rational persuasion, to develop the basic principles of society as a *common* and binding foundation for all, still leaving scope for each member to exercise his own personal liberty. To insure that the participants in this original position argue impartially, Rawls assumes a *veil of ignorance;* that is, the participants know nothing of the relative wealth, status, or natural abilities of the others, and can move forward on general considerations only. "They do not know," states Rawls, "how the various alternatives will affect their own particular case and they are obliged to evaluate principles solely on the basis of general considerations."

It's important to observe that, for Rawls' overarching theory, the dialectics of give and take can be resolved only on the basis of *fairness* because this conception leads him to the doctrine that, in the last analysis, fairness is the main ingredient of justice, whence, one of his earlier magisterial papers is entitled "Justice as Fairness." What is fair in business matters, in the playing of games, in judging others, in the sharing of duties, is a concept we seem to possess early in life, so much so that Rawls refers to the idea of justice as fairness as intuitive. Lest we think of justice and fairness as the same, as tautological, Rawls assures us that the phrase "justice as fairness" does not mean "that the concepts of justice and fairness are the same, any more than the phrase 'poetry as metaphor' means that the concepts of poetry and metaphor are the same."

Given this theoretical foundation, or model, in which he has delineated the principles of justice, Rawls is able to illustrate, by means of constitutional democracy as his example, how they can be satisfied in the building up of basic political structures, and to show how the equality of liberty is to be maintained, how economy is to be shared, and how duties and obligations are to be distributed so that the ends of a well-ordered society can be achieved.

READINGS

The Main Idea of A Theory of Justice

My aim is to present a conception of justice which generalizes and carries to a higher level of abstraction the familiar theory of the social contract as found, say, in Locke, Rousseau, and Kant. In order to do this we are not to think of the original contract as one to enter a particular society or to set up a particular form of government. Rather, the original idea is that the principles of justice for the basic structure of society are the object of the original agreement. They are the principles that free and rational persons concerned to further their own interests would accept in an initial position of equality as defining the fundamental terms of their association. These principles are to regulate all further agreements; they specify the kinds of social cooperation that can be entered into and the forms of government that can be established. This way of regarding the principles of justice I shall call justice as fairness.

Thus we are to imagine that those who engage in social cooperation choose together, in one joint act, the principles which are to assign basic rights and duties and to determine the division of social benefits. Men are to decide in advance how they are to regulate their claims against one another and what is to be the foundation charter of their society. Just as each person must decide by rational reflection what constitutes his good, that is, the system of ends which it is rational for him to pursue, so a group of persons must decide once and for all what is to count among them as just and unjust. The choice which rational men would make in this hypothetical situation of equal liberty, assuming for the present that this choice problem has a solution, determines the principles of justice.

In justice as fairness the original position of equality corresponds to the state of nature in the traditional theory of the social contract. This original position is not, of course, thought of as an actual historical state of affairs, much less as a primitive condition of culture. It is understood as a purely hypothetical situation characterized so as to lead to a certain conception of justice. Among the essential features of this situation is that no one knows his place in society, his class position or social status, nor does any one know his fortune in the distribution of natural assets and abilities, his intelligence, strength, and the like. I shall even assume that the parties do not know their conceptions of the good or their special psychological propensities. The principles of justice are chosen behind a veil of ignorance. This ensures that no one is advantaged or disadvantaged in the choice of principles by the outcome of natural chance or the contingency of social circumstances. Since all are similarly situated and no one is able to design principles to favor his particular condition, the principles of justice are the result of a fair agreement or bargain. For given the circumstances of the original position, the symmetry of everyone's relations to each other, this initial situation is fair between individuals as moral persons, that is, as rational beings with their own ends and capable, I shall assume, of a sense of justice. The original position is, one might say, the appropriate initial status quo, and thus the fundamental agreements reached in it are fair. This explains the propriety of the name "justice as fairness": it conveys the idea that the principles of justice are agreed to in an initial situation that is fair. The name does not mean that the concepts of justice and fairness are the same, any more than the phrase "poetry as metaphor" means that the concepts of poetry and metaphor are the same.

Justice as fairness begins, as I have said, with one of the most general of all choices which persons might make together, namely, with the choice of the first principles of a conception of justice which is to regulate all subsequent criticism and reform of institutions. Then, having chosen a conception of justice, we can suppose that they are to choose a constitution and a legislature to enact laws, and so on, all in accordance with the principles of justice initially agreed upon. Our social situation is just if it is such that by this sequence of hypothetical agreements we would have contracted into the general system of rules which defines it. Moreover, assuming that the original position does determine a set of principles (that is, that a particular conception of justice would be chosen), it will then be true that whenever social institutions satisfy these principles those engaged in them can say to one another that they are cooperating on terms to which they would agree if they were free and equal persons whose relations with respect to one another were fair. They could all view their arrangements as meeting the stipulations which they would acknowledge in an initial situation that embodies widely accepted and reasonable constraints on the choice of principles. The general recognition of this fact would provide the basis for a public acceptance of the corresponding principles of justice. No society can, of course, be a scheme of cooperation which men enter voluntarily in a literal sense; each person finds himself placed at birth in some particular position in some particular society, and the nature of this position materially affects his life prospects. Yet a society satisfying the principles of justice as fairness comes as close as a society can to being a voluntary scheme, for it meets the principles which free and equal persons would assent to under circumstances that are fair. In this sense its members are autonomous and the obligations they recognize self-imposed.

One feature of justice as fairness is to think of the parties in the initial situation as rational and mutually disinterested. This does not mean that the parties are egoists, that is, individuals with only certain kinds of interests, say in wealth, prestige, and domination. But they are conceived as not taking an interest in one another's interests. They are to presume that even their spiritual aims may be opposed, in the way that the aims of those of different religions may be opposed. Moreover, the concept of rationality must be interpreted as far as possible in the narrow sense, standard in economic theory, of taking the most effective means to given ends. I shall modify this concept to some extent, as explained later (§25), but one must try to avoid introducing into it any controversial ethical elements. The initial situation must be characterized by stipulations that are widely accepted.

In working out the conception of justice as fairness one main task clearly is to determine which principles of justice would be chosen in the original position. To do this we must describe this situation in some detail and formulate with care the problem of choice which it presents. These matters I shall take up in the immediately succeeding chapters. It may be observed, however, that once the principles of justice are thought of as arising from an original agreement in a situation of equality, it is an open question whether the principle of utility would be acknowledged. Offhand it hardly seems likely that persons who view themselves as equals, entitled to press their claims upon one another, would agree to a principle which may require lesser life prospects for some simply for the sake of a greater sum of advantages enjoyed by others. Since each desires to protect his interests, his capacity to advance his conception of the good, no one has a reason to acquiesce in an enduring loss for himself in order to bring about a greater net balance of satisfaction. In the absence of strong, and lasting, benevolent impulses, a rational man would not accept a basic structure merely because it maximized the algebraic sum of advantages irrespective of its permanent effects on his own basic rights and interests. Thus it seems that the principle of utility is incompatible with the conception of social cooperation among equals for mutual advantage. It appears to be inconsistent with the idea of reciprocity implicit in the notion of a well-ordered society. Or, at any rate, so I shall argue.

I shall maintain instead that the persons in the initial situation would choose two rather different principles: the first requires equality in the assignment of basic rights, and duties, while the second holds that social and economic inequalities, for example inequalities of wealth and authority, are just only if they result in compensating benefits for everyone, and in particular for the least advantaged members of society. These principles rule out justifying institutions on the grounds that the hardships of some are offset by a greater good in the aggregate. It may be expedient but it is not just that some should have less in order that others may prosper. But there is no injustice in the greater benefits earned by a few provided that the situation of persons not so fortunate is thereby improved. The intuitive idea is that since everyone's well-being depends upon a scheme of cooperation without which no one could have a satisfactory life, the division of advantages should be such as to draw forth the willing cooperation of everyone taking part in it, including those less well situated. Yet this can be expected only if reasonable terms are proposed. The two principles mentioned seem to be a fair agreement on the basis of which those better endowed, or more fortunate in their social position, neither of which we can be said to deserve, could expect the willing cooperation of others when some workable scheme is a necessary condition of the welfare of all. Once we decide to look for a conception of justice that nullifies the accidents of natural endowment and the contingencies of social circumstance as counters in quest for political and economic advantage, we are led to these principles. They express the result of leaving aside those aspects of the social world that seem arbitrary from a moral point of view.

Two Principles of Justice

I shall now state in a provisional form the two principles of justice that I believe would be chosen in the original position. In this section I wish to make only the most general comments, and therefore the first formulation of these principles is tentative. As we go on I shall run through several formulations and approximate step by step the final statement to be given much later. I believe that doing this allows the exposition to proceed in a natural way.

The first statement of the two principles reads as follows.

First: each person is to have an equal right to the most extensive basic liberty compatible with a similar liberty for others.

Second: social and economic inequalities are to be arranged so that they are both (a) reasonably expected to be to everyone's advantage, and (b) attached to positions and offices open to all. . . .

These principles primarily apply, as I have said, to the basic structure of society and govern the assignment of rights and duties and regulate the distribution of social and economic advantages. Their formulation presupposes that, for the purposes of a theory of justice, the social structure may be viewed as having two more or less distinct parts, the first principle applying to the one, the second principle to the other. Thus we distinguish between the aspects of the social system that define and secure the equal basic liberties and the aspects that specify and establish social and economic inequalities. Now it is essential to observe that the basic liberties are given by a list of such liberties. Important among these are political liberty (the right to vote and to hold public office) and freedom of speech and assembly; liberty of conscience and freedom of thought; freedom of the person, which includes freedom from psychological oppression and physical assault and dismemberment (integrity of the person); the right to hold personal property and freedom from arbitrary arrest and seizure as defined by the concept of the rule of law. These liberties are to be equal by the first principle.

The second principle applies, in the first approximation, to the distribution of income and wealth and to the design of organizations that make use of differences in authority and responsibility. While the distribution of wealth and income need not be equal, it must be to everyone's advantage, and at the same time, positions of authority and responsibility must be accessible to all. One applies the second principle by holding positions open, and then, subject to this constraint, arranges social and economic inequalities so that everyone benefits.

(From John Rawls, *A Theory of Justice*. Cambridge, MA: The Belknap Press of Harvard University Press. Copyright © 1971 by the President and Fellows of Harvard College. Reprinted by permission of the publisher.)

5.

Peter Singer

The present time is no exception to the historical fact that certain questions, though entertained for centuries in one way or another, emerge in a new context, giving them an exigency they did not possess before. Such is the case today with the question of animal life. Life in general is the prime and wondrous face of reality, whose value is the ground for our endless efforts to understand the meaning of it all. The gradation of life in the natural world around us is all too obvious to deny, and it would take extraordinary mental acrobatics to deny as well that the human being is at the head of that gradation as the fullest expression of life as we know it. Saying so is not saying that lesser than human forms of life have no value in themselves and are not to be respected for what they are. Even those who maintain the tradition that non-human life subserves the human are bound to maintain that human beings must not maltreat lesser than human forms of life and must take all reasonable measures to respect them.

But the notion that animals, or at least some, have "rights," hitherto associated only with human beings, is a comparatively recent notion that has given the question of animal life a new urgency, and there is no name better known in this regard than that of Peter singer. Though it may be, as some say, that Singer is not a pro-found thinker or that he is too prone to sacrifice human relationships to cold reason, he is doubtless one of the most influential moral philosophers writing today, largely in virtue of his boldly raising life questions where others are too timid or cautious by comparison. He has written a great deal on the life of the embryo, abortion, infanticide, the ethical use of money, the environment, and other life questions, but his name has become permanently attached to "animal liberation" which is our main consideration here.

Animal liberation is an ethical stance holding that an openly fresh look at the life of animals reveals sentient life as a compelling call for the liberation of animals from the traditional view of their service to human life, and for the recognition of the rights they have as *conscious* beings. The key to determining whether a being is conscious or not is its sentiency, that is, the ability it has to feel, or to sense, pleasure and pain; to do so entails that it is *aware,* or conscious, of what is happening. Pain especially, because it is an unequivocal sign of suffer-ing. To permit, or to tolerate, suffering in animals is (though Singer doesn't use the phrase) self-evidently immoral: "If a being suffers, there can be no moral justifica-tion for refusing to take that suffering into consideration." Insofar as the respect for life is concerned, no scheme requiring the subservience of animal life to human life is acceptable, despite the claim of supposed needs on the part of human beings as a higher species. Whence, "The belief in human superiority," Singer writes, "is a very fundamental one, and it underlies our thinking in many sensitive areas. To challenge it is no trivial matter, and that such a challenge should provoke a strong reaction ought not to surprise us." Singer proceeds to invent a name to signify the rejection of equality among all beings possessing conscious-ness: *speciesism.* The word, modeled after *racism,* verbalizes the wrongness involved in evaluating one species as lower than any other and in justifying actu-al practices against a lower thought to fulfill the purposes of a higher. Speciesism is to species as racism is to race.

Respect for life is most dramatically seen in the taking of it and, for Singer, since there is such a diverse range of lives, no one principle can apply to all. It helps to use the word *person* as long as it is divested of an exclusively human use and to use it instead to designate the rational, self-conscious animal; applicable therefore to human beings, but not all (e.g., the unborn, infants, the hopelessly deranged) and to some nonhuman animals, but not all (e.g., chimpanzees, gorillas, orangutans). One, then, cannot categorically aver that it is always worse to kill humans who are not persons than nonhumans who are. "So," he writes, "it seems that killing, say, a chimpanzee is worse than killing of a human being who, because of a congenital intellectual disability, is not and can never be a person."

Within this context, Singer's case for vegetarianism, persuasive for many adherents, automatically follows, and "it would be better to reject altogether the killing of animals for food, unless one must do so to survive. . . . To foster the right attitude of consideration for animals, including non-self-conscious ones, it may be best to make it a simple principle to avoid killing them for food."

In searching for a foundation for ethical judgment, Singer follows a utilitarian course. We'll recall John Stuart Mill's ultimate hope of ameliorating the "condition of mankind" by constructing his version of *utilitarianism,* which holds that *utility,* or *the greatest happiness principle,* is the foundation of morals and that ". . . actions are right in proportion as they tend to promote happiness" and wrong if they do not. Singer does not deny that there are other moral positions worth considering or that there are many practical problems attached to the working out of the utilitarian principle, but it is still the best bet, in his view, for bringing reasoned argumentation to the service of ethics. "I am inclined to hold a utilitarian position" and attempt "to indicate how a consistent utilitarianism will deal with a number of controversial problems."

Readings

A Broadly Utilitarian Position
From *Practical Ethics*
(second edition, chap. 1 and 2)

From ancient times, philosophers and moralists have expressed the idea that ethical conduct is acceptable from a point of view that is somehow universal. The 'Golden Rule' attributed to Moses, to be found in the book of Leviticus and subsequently repeated by Jesus, tells us to go beyond our own personal interests and 'love thy neighbour as thyself'—in other words, give the same weight to the interests of others as one gives to one's own interests. The same idea of putting oneself in the position of another is involved in the other Christian formulation of the commandment, that we do to others as we would have them do to us. The Stoics held that ethics derives from a universal natural law. Kant developed this idea into his famous formula: 'Act only on that maxim through which you can at the same time will that it should become a universal law.' Kant's theory has itself been modified and developed by R. M. Hare, who sees universalisability as a logical feature of moral judgments.

The eighteenth-century British philosophers Hutcheson, Hume, and Adam Smith appealed to an imaginary 'impartial spectator' as the test of a moral judgment, and this theory has its modem version in the Ideal Observer theory. Utilitarians, from Jeremy Bentham to J. J. C. Smart, take it as axiomatic that in deciding moral issues 'each counts for one and none for more than one'; while John Rawls, a leading contemporary critic of utilitarianism, incorporates essentially the same axiom into his own theory by deriving basic ethical principles from an imaginary choice in which those choosing do not know whether they will be the ones who gain or lose by the principles they select. Even Continental European philosophers like the existentialist Jean-Paul Sartre and the critical theorist Jürgen Habermas, who differ in many ways from their English-speaking colleagues—and from each other—agree that ethics is in some sense universal.

One could argue endlessly about each of these characterisations of the ethical; but what they have in common is more important than their differences. They agree that an ethical principle cannot be justified in relation to any partial or sectional group. Ethics takes a universal point of view. This does not mean that a particular ethical judgment must be universally applicable. Circumstances alter causes, as we have seen. What it does mean is that in making ethical judgments we go beyond our own likes and dislikes. From an ethical point of view, the fact that it is I who benefit from, say, a more equal distribution of income and you who lose by it, is irrelevant. Ethics requires us to go beyond 'I' and 'you' to the universal law, the universalisable judgment, the standpoint of the impartial spectator or ideal observer, or whatever we choose to call it.

Can we use this universal aspect of ethics to derive an ethical theory that will give us guidance about right and wrong? Philosophers from the Stoics to Hare and Rawls have attempted this. No attempt has met with general acceptance. The problem is that if we describe the universal aspect of ethics in bare, formal terms, a wide range of ethical theories, including quite irreconcilable ones, are compatible with this notion of universality; if, on the other hand, we build up our description of the universal aspect of ethics so that it leads us ineluctably to one particular ethical theory, we shall be accused of smuggling our own ethical beliefs into our definition of the ethical—and this definition was supposed to be broad enough, and neutral enough, to encompass all serious candidates for the status of 'ethical theory'. Since so many others have failed to overcome this obstacle to deducing an ethical theory from the universal aspect of ethics, it would be foolhardy to attempt to do so in a brief introduction to a work with a quite different aim. Nevertheless I shall propose something only a little less ambitious. The universal aspect of ethics, I suggest, does provide a persuasive, although not conclusive, reason for taking a broadly utilitarian position.

My reason for suggesting this is as follows. In accepting that ethical judgments must be made from a universal point of view, I am accepting that my own interests cannot, simply because they are my interests, count more than the interests of anyone else. Thus my very natural concern that my own interests be looked after must, when I think ethically, be extended to the interests of others. Now, imagine that I am trying to decide between two possible courses of action—perhaps whether to eat all the fruits I have collected myself, or to share them with others. Imagine, too, that I am deciding in a complete ethical vacuum, that I know nothing of any ethical considerations—I am, we might say, in a pre-ethical stage of thinking. How would I make up my mind? One thing that would be still relevant would be how the possible courses of action will affect my interests. Indeed, if we define 'interests' broadly enough, so that we count anything people desire as in their interests (unless it is incompatible with another desire or desires), then it would seem that at this pre-ethical stage, *only* one's own interests can be relevant to the decision.

Suppose I then begin to think ethically, to the extent of recognising that my own interests cannot count for more, simply because they are my own, than the interests of others. In place of my own interests, I now have to take into account the interests of all those affected by my decision. This requires me to weigh up all these interests and adopt the course of action most likely to maximise the interests of those affected. Thus at least at some level in my moral reasoning I must choose the course of action that has the best consequences, on balance, for all affected. (I say 'at some level in my moral reasoning' because, as we shall see later, there are utilitarian reasons for believing that we ought not to try to calculate these consequences for every ethical decision we make in our daily lives, but only in very unusual circumstances, or perhaps when we are reflecting on our choice of general principles to guide us in future. In other words, in the specific example given, at first glance one might think it obvious that sharing the fruit that I have gathered has better consequences for all affected than not sharing them. This may in the end also be the best general principle for us all to adopt, but before we can have grounds for believing this to be the case, we must also consider whether the effect of a general practice of sharing gathered fruits will benefit all those affected, by bringing about a more equal distribution, or whether it will reduce the amount of food gathered, because some will cease to gather anything if they know that they will get sufficient from their share of what others gather.)

Equality for Animals?

If a being suffers, there can be no moral justification for refusing to take that suffering into consideration. No matter what the nature of the being, the principle of equality requires that the suffering be counted equally with the like suffering—in so far as rough comparisons can be made—of any other being. If a being is not capable of suffering, or of experiencing enjoyment or happiness, there is nothing to be taken into account. This is why the limit of sentience (using the term as a convenient, if not strictly accurate, shorthand for the capacity to suffer or experience enjoyment or happiness) is the only defensible boundary of concern for the interests of others. To mark this boundary by some characteristic like intelligence or rationality would be to mark it in an arbitrary way. Why not choose some other characteristic, like skin colour?

Racists violate the principle of equality by giving greater weight to the interests of members of their own race when there is a clash between their interests and the interests of those of another race. Racists of European descent typically have not accepted that pain matters as much when it is felt by Africans, for example, as when it is felt by Europeans. Similarly those I would call 'speciesists' give greater weight to the interests of members of their own species when there is a clash between their interests and the interests of those of other species. Human speciesists do not accept that pain is as bad when it is felt by pigs or mice as when it is felt by humans.

That, then, is really the whole of the argument for extending the principle of equality to nonhuman animals; but there may be some doubts about what this equality amounts to in practice. In particular, the last sentence of the previous paragraph may prompt some people to reply: 'Surely pain felt by a mouse just is not as bad as pain felt by a human. Humans have much greater awareness of what is happening to them, and this makes their suffering worse. You can't equate the suffering of, say, a person dying slowly from cancer, and a laboratory mouse undergoing the same fate.'

I fully accept that in the case described the human cancer victim normally suffers more than the nonhuman cancer victim. This in no way undermines the extension of equal consideration of interests to nonhumans. It means, rather, that we must take care when we compare the interests of different species. In some situations a member of one species will suffer more than a member of another species. In this case we should still apply the principle of equal consideration of interests but the result of so doing is, of course, to give priority to relieving the greater suffering. A simpler case may help to make this clear.

If I give a horse a hard slap across its rump with my open hand, the horse may start, but it presumably feels little pain. Its skin is thick enough to protect it against a mere slap. If I slap a baby in the same way, however, the baby will cry and presumably does feel pain, for the baby's skin is more sensitive. So it is worse to slap a baby than a horse, if both slaps are administered with equal force. But there must be some kind of blow—I don't know exactly what it would be, but perhaps a blow with a heavy stick—that would cause the horse as much pain as we cause a baby by a simple slap. That is what I mean by 'the same amount of pain' and if we consider it wrong to inflict that much pain on a baby for no good reason then we must, unless we are speciesists, consider it equally wrong to inflict the same amount of pain on a horse for no good reason.

There are other differences between humans and animals that cause other complications. Normal adult human beings have mental capacities that will, in certain circumstances, lead them to suffer more than animals would in the same circumstances. If, for instance, we decided to perform extremely painful or lethal scientific experiments on normal adult humans, kidnapped at random from public parks for this purpose, adults who entered parks would become fearful that they would be kidnapped. The resultant terror would be a form of suffering additional to the pain of the experiment. The same experiments performed on nonhuman animals would cause less suffering since the animals would not have the anticipatory dread of being kidnapped and experimented upon. This does not mean, of course, that it would be *right* to perform the experiment on animals, but only that there is a reason, and one that is not speciesist, for preferring to use animals rather than normal adult humans, if the experiment is to be done at all. Note, however, that this same argument gives us a reason for preferring to use human infants—orphans perhaps—or severely intellectually disabled humans for experiments, rather than adults, since infants and severely intellectually disabled humans would also have no idea of what was going to happen to them. As far as this argument is concerned, nonhuman animals and infants and severely intellectually disabled humans are in the same category; and if we use this argument to justify experiments on nonhuman animals we have to ask ourselves whether we are also prepared to allow experiments on human infants and severely intellectually disabled adults. If we make a distinction between animals and these humans, how can we do it, other than on the basis of a morally indefensible preference for members of our own species?

There are many areas in which the superior mental powers of normal adult humans make a difference: anticipation, more detailed memory, greater knowledge of what is happening, and so on. These differences explain why a human dying from cancer is likely to suffer more than a mouse. It is the mental anguish that makes the human's position so much harder to bear. Yet these differences do not all point to greater suffering on the part of the normal human being. Sometimes animals may suffer more because of their more limited understanding. If, for instance, we are taking prisoners in wartime we can explain to them that while they must submit to capture, search, and confinement they will not otherwise be harmed and will be set free at the conclusion of hostilities. If we capture wild animals, however, we cannot explain that we are not threatening their lives. A wild animal cannot distinguish an attempt to overpower and confine from an attempt to kill; the one causes as much terror as the other.

It may be objected that comparisons of the sufferings of different species are impossible to make, and that for this reason when the interests of animals and humans clash, the principle of equality gives no guidance. It is true that comparisons of suffering between members of different species cannot be made precisely. Nor, for that matter, can comparisons of suffering between different human beings be made precisely. Precision is not essential. As we shall see shortly, even if we were to prevent the infliction of suffering on animals only when the interests of humans will not be affected to anything like the extent that animals are affected, we would be forced to make radical changes in our treatment of animals that would involve our diet, the farming methods we use, experimental procedures in many fields of science, our approach to wildlife and to hunting, trapping and the wearing of furs, and areas of entertainment like circuses, rodeos, and zoos. As a result, the total quantity of suffering caused would be greatly reduced; so greatly that it is hard to imagine any other change of moral attitude that would cause so great a reduction in the total sum of suffering in the universe.

(From Peter Singer, *Practical Ethics* 2/E. Reprinted with the permission of Cambridge University Press.)

6.
Jacques Derrida

To designate the intellectual climate of our time, the term *postmodern* appears to be the term of choice, though it's much too early to tell whether it is only a term of fashion or whether it will take hold just as "modern" has and thus come to be used anachronistically in referring to a time gone by. Chronologically "postmodern" refers to the period following the usual sequence of ancient, medieval and modern, and in that sense it stands for contemporary, but with regard to its actual use it means "antimodern," for it constitutes a severe judgment on the past. Postmodern purports to hold that all, or most, of philosophy in the past has developed rigid pathways of thought impossible to get out of; it has generated systems uncongenial to new ways of thinking and is impervious to fresh insights; it has allowed institutions, interpretations, and styles to take on lives of their own; it has built constructions resistant to change. For these reasons some kind of attack on such constructions is always welcome, whence the term *deconstruction* moved to the foreground as the operative mode of doing so.

Deconstruction, in the past number of years, more so during the seventies and eighties, has proven itself to be an active force. For some it is a genuine, if not brilliant, contribution to current philosophy, while for others it is nothing more than traditional critical analysis decked out in newly coined words, neologisms, to give it the mystique of fresh discovery; it is a "buzzword" and will pass when the fashion passes. The name of *Jacques Derrida,* more than any other, is associated with the movement for he is not only the coiner of the term "deconstruction" but also a tireless and intriguing author committed to developing paths of deconstruction in a wide variety of disciplines, though he himself has said he has trouble recognizing the vast number of programmes undertaken in its name.

He was born in Algeria in 1930 but as a young man he attended the École Normale Supérieure in Paris; from 1960–84, he taught philosophy at the Sorbonne and then later at the École. He has had a vast experience in teaching and lecturing in the United States where he has enjoyed a devoted following, including the literary critics of the "Yale school", Harold Bloom, Paul de Man, Geoffrey Hartman, and J. Hillis Miller. He died in 2004.

To fit Derrida into the larger picture, let's recall the huge problem attached to the dichotomy of *saying* what we *know.* How do we put into words what we know? What is the relationship between what we say and what is? The understanding of reality takes on many aspects and to make life livable we naturally accustom ourselves to those we hold as common sense. But any understanding can be entered into more profoundly, becoming more intricate as deeper linkages open up to reflection. Our study has shown any number of such examples. Take the earliest, that of Thales and Pythagoras both *knowing* the cosmos as one and many but *saying* it differently, with Thales learning toward the physical and

Pythagoras toward the mathematical. Or, Aristotle, while holding with Plato that ideas are vehicles by which we *know*, chides him for *saying* that they refer to universal existences outside the mind when, in truth, only individuals exist. Or, as it has again been asked poignantly by Wittgenstein, how can the same one word be used to refer to many individuals, that is, how can we *say* in one word what we *know* to be many? The point here, in our discussion of Derrida, is that there is indeed a gap in the relationship between "saying" and "knowing", and because there is, there can also be objections to the way things are said, or there can be flaws, or inexactness, or insufficiencies, or the possibility that more is being said than the writer himself realizes.

Reducing that gap has been the background of the Anglo–American tradition, especially in the initial work of Bertrand Russell who felt, along the English empirical line, that philosophy would become more rigorous as it became more "scientific," as was also true of the American W. V. Quine. There would be then nothing more fruitful than scientifically analyzing the language we use in expressing what's in our minds,—the burden of *language analysis*. But in doing so Russell began to see the need of moving away from the porous nature of verbal language toward the solid and stern demands of *symbolic logic* in the hope of making expression more precise than words could do. Wittgenstein too tried to clarify the meaning of language, first in his view that propositions are "pictures" of objects, and later that words have a common meaning in their "family resemblance" to one another. Still, he said, language has a way of "bewitching our intelligence," making it extremely difficult to arrive at the clarity we need "to show the fly the way out of the fly-bottle." There are things that simply remain unsayable.

But the focus changes considerably when you look at the philosophical landscape of continental Europe with the analysis of language coming out of Vienna, the towering influence of Husserl and Heidegger, and the history and anthropology of language offered by Ferdinand de Saussure and Claude Levi-Strauss. Saussure (+1913) is held to be the founder of modern linguistics inasmuch as he underwrote the view that deep-level *structures* are accountable for the way human beings use language and that there are similar deep-level structures at the basis of all human activity, which anthropologists must explore in their search for the foundations of social phenomena. Hence the word *structuralism*. This theme was employed by Levi-Strauss in his own work in anthropology, particularly as presented in *Tristes tropiques,* an account of a trip he made to Brazil, several sections of which were subjected to minute criticism by Derrida in one of his early works, *On Grammatology,* 1967. Levi-Strauss narrated an incident in which the illiterate tribal chief, from a few scribbles on a piece of paper, made believe he was reading to the just as illiterate members of the tribe, perhaps mistakenly believing that he would advance his own standing with them. Levi-Strauss then proceeds to deploy the incident as proof from anthropology that speech always possessed a privileged place over writing because it is authentic, personal, and more subtly fitted to shaping one's meaning. According to Derrida, both Saussure and Levi-Strauss deny that writing plays any part in linguistics and, on the contrary, undermines genuine discourse. Against this view Derrida argues to the priority of writing in that it is the condition, or precondition, for speech because it allows for the "free play" of language—the floating nature of meaning—impossible in "authentic" speech. The point here is not who's right or wrong but to show how Derrida, having determined that in certain critical cases a "construction" built to defend a view can be "deconstructed" to nullify it. That's why, for him, we must always be ready to go beyond the given, beyond the text, beyond the construction to find what has been overlooked, overdone, or overvalued. It is this aspect of "deconstruction" that has made it a tool applicable to disciplines across the board, not least of which is philosophy. If language is the vehicle for saying what you know, and something is amiss with the language, it follows that something is also amiss with the correspondence between what you say and what you know. So philosophical texts are candidates for deconstruction as much as literary texts. A philosophical text is presumed to have bearing on what is *presented* to you, that is, it is a re*present*ation in language. But representations, or interpretations, can vary from individual to individual, giving us many representations or interpretations of the same thing, or the thing presumed to be the same. A gap then exists between word (language) and object (reality), thus affording the opportunity for deconstructing the presentation without necessarily replacing it. This readily paves the way to circumvent metaphysics altogether, leaving us perhaps with a deflated allegiance to western philosophy in the form of truth as myth and well on the road to a revived skepticism.

READING

Letter to a Japanese Friend

10 July 1983

Dear Professor Izutsu,

At our last meeting I promised you some schematic and preliminary reflections on the word "deconstruction." What we discussed were prolegomena to a possible translation of this word into Japanese, one which would at least try to avoid, if *possible,* a negative determination of its significations or connotations. The question would be therefore what deconstruction is not, or rather *ought* not to be. I underline these words "possible" and "ought." For if the difficulties of translation can be anticipated (and the question of deconstruction is also through and through *the* question of translation, and of the language of concepts, of the conceptual corpus of so-called Western metaphysics), one should not begin by naively believing that the word "deconstruction" corresponds in French to some clear and univocal signification. There is already in "my" language a serious *[sombre]* problem of translation between what here or there can be envisaged for the word and the usage itself, the reserves of the word. And it is already clear that even in French, things change from one context to another. More so in the German, English, and especially American contexts, where the *same* word is already attached to very different connotations, inflections, and emotional or affective values. Their analysis would be interesting and warrants a study of its own.

When I choose this word, or when it imposed itself upon me—I think it was in *Of Grammatology*—I little thought it would be credited with such a central role in the discourse that interested me at the time. Among other things I wished to translate and adapt to my own ends the Heideggerian word *Destruktion* or *Abbau*. Each signified in this context an operation bearing on the structure or traditional architecture of the fundamental concepts of ontology or of Western metaphysics. But in French "destruction" too obviously implied an annihilation or a negative reduction much closer perhaps to Nietzschean "demolition" than to the Heideggerian interpretation or to the type of reading that I proposed. So I ruled that out. I remember having looked to see if the word "deconstruction" (which came to me it seemed quite spontaneously) was good French. I found it in the *Littré:* The grammatical, linguistic, or rhetorical senses *[portées]* were found bound up with a "mechanical" sense *[portée* "machinique"]. This association appeared very fortunate and fortunately adapted to what I wanted at least to suggest. Perhaps I could cite some of the entries from the *Littré.* "*Déconstruction:* action of deconstructing. Grammatical term. Disarranging the construction of words in a   sentence. 'Of deconstruction, common way of saying construction,' Lemare, *De la manière d'apprendre les langues.* chap. 17, in *Cours de langue Latine. Déconstruire.* 1. To disassemble the parts of a whole. To deconstruct a machine to transport it elsewhere. 2. Grammatical term. . . . To deconstruct verse, rendering it, by the suppression of meter, similar to prose. Absolutely. ('In the system of prenotional sentences, one also starts with translation and one of its advantages is never needing to deconstruct,' Lemare, ibid., 3. *Se déconstruire* [to deconstruct itself] . . . to lose its construction. 'Modern scholarship has shown us that in a region of the timeless East, a language reaching its own state of perfection is deconstructed *[s'est déconstruite]* and altered from within itself according to the single law of change, natural to the human mind,' Villemain, *Préface du Dictionnaire de l'Académie.*"

Naturally it will be necessary to translate all of this into Japanese but that only postpones the problem. It goes without saying that if all the significations enumerated by the *Littré* interested me because of their affinity with what I "meant" *["voulais-dire"],* they concerned, metaphorically, so to say, only models or regions of meaning and not the totality of what deconstruction aspires to at its most ambitious. This is not limited to a linguistico-grammatical model, nor even a semantic model, let alone a mechanical model. These models themselves ought to be submitted to a deconstructive questioning. It is true then that these "models" have been behind a number of misunderstandings about the concept and word of "deconstruction" because of the temptation to reduce it to these models.

It must also be said that the word was rarely used and was largely unknown in France. It had to be reconstructed in some way, and its use value had been determined by the discourse that was then being attempted around and on the basis of *Of Grammatology*. It is to this use value that I am now going to try to give some precision and not some primitive meaning or etymology sheltered from or outside of any contextual strategy.

A few more words on the subject of "the context." At that time structuralism was dominant. "Deconstruction" seemed to be going in the same direction since the word signified a certain attention to structures (which themselves were neither simply ideas, nor forms, nor syntheses, nor systems). To deconstruct was also a structuralist gesture or in any case a gesture that assumed a certain need for the structuralist problematic. But it was also an antistructuralist gesture, and its fortune rests in part on this ambiguity. Structures were to be undone, decomposed, desedimented (all types of structures, linguistic, "logocentric," "phonocentric"—structuralism being especially at that time dominated by linguistic models and by a so-called structural linguistics that was also called Saussurian—socio-institutional, political, cultural, and above all and from the start philosophical). This is why, especially in the United States, the motif of deconstruction has been associated with "poststructuralism" (a word unknown in France until its "return" from the United States). But the undoing, decomposing, and desedimenting of structures, in a certain sense more historical than the structuralist movement it called into question, was not a negative operation. Rather than destroying, it was also necessary to understand how an "ensemble" was constituted and to reconstruct it to this end. However, the negative appearance was and remains much more difficult to efface than is suggested by the grammar of the word (de-), even though it can designate a genealogical restoration *[remonter]* rather than a demolition. That is why this word, at least on its own, has never appeared satisfactory to me (but what word is), and must always be girded by an entire discourse. It is difficult to effect it afterward because, in the work of deconstruction, I have had to, as I have to here, multiply the cautionary indicators and put aside all the traditional philosophical concepts, while reaffirming the necessity of returning to them, at least under erasure. Hence, this has been called, precipitously, a type of negative theology (this was neither true nor false but I shall not enter into the debate here).

All the same, and in spite of appearances, deconstruction is neither an *analysis* nor a *critique* and its translation would have to take that into consideration. It is not an analysis in particular because the dismantling of a structure is not a regression toward a *simple element*, toward an *indissoluble origin*. These values, like that of analysis, are themselves philosophemes subject to deconstruction. No more is it a critique, in a general sense or in a Kantian sense. The instance of *krinein* or of *krisis* (decision, choice, judgment, discernment) is itself, as is all the apparatus of transcendental critique, one of the essential "themes" or "objects" of deconstruction.

I would say the same about *method*. Deconstruction is not a method and cannot be transformed into one. Especially if the technical and procedural significations of the words are stressed. It is true that in certain circles (university or cultural, especially in the United States) the technical and methodological "metaphor" that seems necessarily attached to the very word "deconstruction" has been able to seduce or lead astray. Hence the debate that has developed in these circles: Can deconstruction become a methodology for reading and for interpretation? Can it thus let itself be reappropriated and domesticated by academic institutions?

It is not enough to say that deconstruction could not be reduced to some methodological instrumentality or to a set of rules and transposable procedures. Nor will it do to claim that each deconstructive "event" remains singular or, in any case, as close as possible to something like an idiom or a signature. It must also be made clear that deconstruction is not even an *act* or an *operation*. Not only because there would be something "patient" or "passive" about it (as Blanchot says, more passive than passivity, than the passivity that is opposed to activity). Not only because it does not return to an individual or collective *subject* who would take the initiative and apply it to an object, a text, a theme, etc. Deconstruction takes place, it is an event that does not await the deliberation, consciousness, or organization of a subject, or even of modernity. *It deconstructs it-self. It can be deconstructed. [Ça se déconstruit.]* The "it" *[ça]* is not here an impersonal thing that is opposed to some egological subjectivity. *It is in deconstruction* (the *Littré* says, "to deconstruct it-self *[se déconstruire]* . . . to lose its construction"). And the "se" of "se déconstruire," which is not the reflexivity of an ego or of a consciousness, bears the whole enigma. I recognize, my dear friend, that in trying to make a word clearer so as to assist its translation, I am only thereby increasing the difficulties: "the impossible task of the translator" (Benjamin). This too is what is meant by "deconstructs."

If deconstruction takes place everywhere it *[ça]* takes place, where there is something (and is not therefore limited to meaning or to the text in the current and bookish sense of the word), we still have to think through what is happening in our word, in modernity, at the time when deconstruction is becoming a motif, with its word, its privileged themes, its mobile strategy, etc. I have no simple and formalizable response to this question. All my essays are attempts to have it out with this formidable question. They are modest symptoms of it, quite as much as tentative interpretations. I would not even dare to say, following a Heideggerian schema, that we are in an "epoch" of being-in-deconstruction, of a being-in-deconstruction that would manifest or dissimulate itself at one and the same time in other "epochs." This thought of "epochs" and especially that of a gathering of the destiny of being and of the unity of its destination or its dispersions *(Schicken, Geschick)* will never be very convincing.

To be very schematic I would say that the difficulty of *defining* and therefore also of *translating* the word "deconstruction" stems from the fact that all the predicates, all the defining concepts, all the lexical significations, and even the syntactic articulations, which seem at one moment to lend themselves to this definition or to that translation, are also deconstructed or deconstructible, directly or otherwise, etc. And that goes for the *word*, the very unity of the *word* deconstruction, as for every *word. Of Grammatology* questioned the unity "word" and all the privileges with which it was credited, especially in its *nominal* form. It is therefore only a discourse or rather a writing that can make up for the incapacity of the word to be equal to a "thought." All sentences of the type "deconstruction is X" or "deconstruction is not X" *a priori* miss the point, which is to say that they are at least false. As you know, one of the principal things at stake in what is called in my texts "deconstruction" is precisely the delimiting of ontology and above all of the third person present indicative: S *is* P.

The word "deconstruction," like all other words, acquires its value only from its inscription in a chain of possible substitutions, in what is too blithely called a "context." For me, for what I have tried and still try to write, the word has interest only within a certain context, where it replaces and lets itself be determined by such other words as "écriture," "trace," "differance," "supplement," "hymen," "pharmakon," "marge," "entame," "parergon," etc.[3] By definition, the list can never be closed, and I have cited only names, which is inadequate and done only for reasons of economy. In fact, I should have cited the sentences and the interlinking of sentences which in their turn determine these names in some of my texts.

What deconstruction is not? everything of course!

What is deconstruction? nothing of course!

I do not think, for all these reasons, that it is a *good word [un bon mot]*. It is certainly not elegant *[beau]*. It has definitely been of service in a highly determined situation. In order to know what has been imposed upon it in a chain of possible substitutions, despite its essential imperfection, this "highly determined situation" will need to be analyzed and deconstructed. This is difficult and I am not going to do it here.

One final word to conclude this letter, which is already too long. I do not believe that translation is a secondary and derived event in relation to an original language or text. And as "deconstruction" is a word, as I have just said, that is essentially replaceable in a chain of substitution, then that can also be done from one language to another. The chance, first of all the chance of (the) "deconstruction," would be that another word (the same word and an other) can be found in Japanese to say the same thing (the same and an other), to speak of deconstruction, and to lead elsewhere to its being written and transcribed, in a word which will also be more beautiful.

When I speak of this writing of the other which will be more beautiful, I clearly understand translation as involving the same risk and chance as the poem. How to translate

"poem"? a "poem"? . . .

> With my best wishes,
> Jacques Derrida

—*(Trans. by David Wood and Andrew Benjamin)*

Suggestions for Further Reading

Danto, Arthur. *Mind: An Essay on Human Feeling,* abridged ed. Baltimore, Johns Hopkins, 1988.

Langer, Susanne K. *Philosophy in a New Key.* Cambridge, MA, Harvard University Press, 1979 (also editions by Mentor Books and Penguin).

Hahn, Lewis E. and Schilpp, Paul A. *The Philosophy of W. V. Quine.* LaSalle, IL, Open Court, 1986.

Hookway, Christopher. *Quine: Language, Experience and Reality.* Stanford, CA, Stanford University Press, 1988.

Quine, W. V. *The Time of my Life, An Autobiography.* Cambridge, MA, MIT Press, 1985.

Lepore, E. and van Gulich, R. *John Searle and His Critics.* Cambridge, MA, Basil Blackwell, 1991.

Searle, John R. *The Rediscovery of the Mind.* Cambridge, MA, MIT Press, 1992.

Searle, John R. Mind. NY, Oxford University Press, 2004.

Davion, V. and Wolf, C., ed. *The Idea of Political Liberalism: Essays on Rawls.* Lanham, MD, Roman and Littlefield, 1998.

Rawls, John. *A Theory of Justice,* revised ed. Cambridge, MA, Belknap Press of Harvard University Press, 1999.

Singer, Peter. *Animal Liberation.* New York, NY, Avon, 1991.

Singer, Peter. *Practical Ethics.* Cambridge University Press, 1993.

A Derrida Reader, P. Kamuf, ed. New York, Columbia University Press, 1991.

Norris, C., *Derrida.* Cambridge, Mass., Harvard Universty Press, 1987

Barradori. G., *Philosophy in a Time of Terror, Dialogues with Jürgen Habermas and Jacques Derrida.* Chicago, University of Chicago Press, 2003.

Epilogue

Past, Present, Future: Philosophy as Perennial

We have come to the end of our historical introduction to philosophy in the Western tradition. We now have a fuller appreciation of philosophy as the love of wisdom. The pre-Socratic philosophers expressed their wonder at the unity of the cosmos, Plato and Aristotle addressed a complex of problems from the good life to the mystery of being, and the Epicureans and Stoics championed a temperate judgment in all things. We observed the broad spectrum of medieval philosophers who, though with profound differences in style, sought to revisit reality with insights gained from faith. Then we moved on to the modern philosophers who, heirs to the exciting explosion of the natural sciences, initiated inquiries into the problem of knowledge, and finally we looked at the radical change wrought by the humanist philosophers of the late nineteenth century as they ushered in the contemporary period with its emphasis on the person, logic, and language analysis. This text provides an introduction to philosophy by attending to its principal themes as presented in the profiles of philosophers at work as opposed to a history of philosophical thought.

With these philosophers as our lead, we attempted to think through a host of problems confronting the human mind, for example, the meaning of knowledge, truth, and wisdom; the finite and the infinite; the one and the many; being and becoming; contradiction; causality; created and uncreated; the existence of God; time, timelessness, and eternity; the material, immaterial, and spiritual; virtue and vice; good and evil; life, death, and immortality; happiness; the meaning of man; the genesis of ideas; sense and intellect; certainty; skepticism; logic; the analysis of language; the existence of the soul; the meaning of substance and quality; the role of the natural sciences; free will and determinism; human alienation; the exploitation of man; the meaning of value; the human condition; the governance of man; symbolism; the philosophy of art; artificial intelligence. The number of concepts we touched on is a striking demonstration that the pursuit of truth never comes to an end. The joy and the pain of the search for truth lie in the paradox of the mind's wondrous ability to advance the horizon of knowledge, and at the same time to endure its fate of inevitable ignorance. Our experience is that one problem solved begets two more unsolved.

If there ever was a temptation for us to circumvent past philosophy as having only an antiquarian interest, that temptation has perhaps been put to rest by our realizing the perennial newness of philosophy; indeed it would take a rash mind to say that the thoughts of the ancients, though past, are passé. Plato and Aristotle always yield new insights; St. Augustine and St. Thomas are thinkers for all seasons. Yet all philosophers we have studied would have rejoiced in the ongoing pursuit of knowledge since their time, for it is precisely this pursuit that makes philosophy "perennial."

Who, 2,500 years ago, could have hazarded a guess as to what philosophy would be like today? And who could possibly hazard a guess today as to what philosophy will be like 2,500 years from now? There are questions we are dealing with today the ancients could never have dealt with, for mankind's experience gets wider and wider in the course of passing centuries. There are present-day problems, present-day methodologies, and present-day probings of nature with which philosophy must be engaged.

We've seen how, from time to time, an effort to engage the present meant a sweeping away of the past in order to clear the way for a new method of arriving at certainty. So with deconstruction as we saw earlier on, once it came to be appreciated as a productive tool, it enjoyed widespread popularity, for it was seen as applicable, not only to philosophy, but also to theology, to literary criticism, to biography, to language use, to psychology, and to political analysis. It's clear that, for many, deconstruction is considered to be the saving device of thought in our time, but it's also clear that for many others it is the newest form of skepticism and as such it can only destroy philosophy; given sufficient play, it will, as with all skepticisms, self-destruct. Our own study, however, has shown us how often it happens that an action produces an overreaction and that an overreaction does not necessarily mean unacceptable; an overreaction often highlights an important truth that has been bypassed by the singular onrush of events. It may be more like a pendulum, having swung past the center, swings back from the extreme to seek its center again; if the pendulum were to stop swinging altogether, it might well portend that change is over and end-time has been reached.

In that sense, deconstruction can be seen as another manifestation that there is no *one* way of understanding all reality, no one way of knowing all things knowable. If, as indicated earlier, the horizon of our experience gets wider and wider in the course of time, it means that more and more new things are emerging, more and more new experiences being generated for us to wonder at and reflect on. They are brought about by a universe in process, by scientific discovery, by meditation, by research, by invention, by creation, and by the simple fact of living in which we respond to the rhythms of life.

A cursory look at a few examples of new problems, or of long-standing ones in a new context, will be helpful in giving us some idea as to what philosophy is called upon to deal with, and how varied they can be.

Though historical considerations have always been part and parcel of the study of man, some thinkers feel that the designation of man as "rational animal" or "image of God" begs the question of man's true nature because it seems to be saying that, though subject to variations in time, the human being is the *same* person throughout, which does not do justice to the fact that the *very* person *is* his historicity, fashioned by change and defined as being-in-time.

From an entirely different quarter, the meaning of person has gained close attention in the question of abortion inasmuch as a difference is discerned between the human being and the human person, which difference, it is said, does not pertain to the science of biology but the philosophy of relationship.

Another sounding as to the meaning of human nature is made possible in our time by the astonishing movement of science in two opposing directions, one toward the infinite and the other toward the infinitesimal. Though the stars and planets are still there as of old to amaze us, the astronaut's pilgrimage among them has opened up a new dimension for man's self-understanding as he sees his meaning expand along with the universe: The astronaut's every trip for exploring the world's outer space is also a trip for exploring man's inner space. In similar fashion, the probings of the biologist into the never-ending inwardness of man beggars the mind in thinking upon human nature as seamlessly one from the infinitesimal to the infinite.

The computer, though the science is still in its infancy, came to the forefront so quickly that it seems to have required no period of gestation although it was early in the making ever since Leibniz put together the first calculator. There is no end in sight as to what the computer can do and how it can serve human needs, but it has already spawned many questions of philosophical interest. How will it affect human relationships? Will it supply a new dimension on the person-to-person level? Will it give us, not only a model of how the brain functions, but an extended understanding of cognition itself? Will it reduce the mysterious gap between the physical and nonphysical spheres of knowledge? Can it ever do more than simulate human intelligence? Will it ever have the creativity of an artist? Are we, with computer help, any closer to creating life out of an assemblage of physical constituents than we were a thousand years ago? If so, are we poised to erase the border between material and immaterial?

Evil has always been a soul-searing aspect of human life and has tested the best of saints and scholars, but does it have a new face in our time—not the physical evils of natural disaster or infectious disease, but the evils that proceed from a willed disregard for the sacredness of man? What do we see in the horrors of genocide, of engines of mass destruction, of thoughtless use of drugs, of human exploitation, of unconcern in the marketplace? On a more day-by-day level, do people seem less gentle, kind, and thoughtful of others than they were in the past? Has the individualistic aggressiveness of the 1980s taken such hold on us that we don't recognize it anymore? Do we see a latter-day confirmation of Hobbes' view of human life as nasty, brutish, and short?

Social philosophy is a practical and influential arena of thought and though, since the utopianism of Plato and the politics of Aristotle, treatises on state, citizenship, civic community, governance, and economy have never been wanting, there have been several times in the modern period when social thought reached a critical stage. Once such time was the seventeenth century with its revolution in empowerment as elaborated by Hobbes and Locke; another was the nineteenth century with the Marxian manifesto on economy and human alienation, destined to become the philosophical underpinning of social-political movements that have dominated the lives of more human beings than any other philosophy in history.

Thinking afresh on the reciprocity between community and individual can never be abandoned and will appear in various guises in the contexts history supplies. In South America, for example, where millions have been marginalized for centuries, a deepening sensitivity to human rights has crystallized around a renewed philosophy of human worth called "liberation philosophy," after a similar renewal nurtured by liberation theology. And in the United States, where millions are suffering from poverty, not only must further thought be given to the moral and practical aspects of alleviating poverty but also to the very meaning of impoverishment itself.

An integral part of social philosophy in our time has been signalized in a deepening appreciation of the nature of woman, whose definition historically has been determined for the most part by a male-dominated society. One can point, sociologically, to the increasing successful claims made by western women in recent decades in areas hitherto thought of as male domains, in business, in medicine, in law, in the ministry, in education, in sports, and so on, all of which are latter-day consequences of the struggle for equality. That equality, from a philosophical perspective, speaks to the common nature found in male and female, recognition of which compelled a long and arduous journey from Aristotle's view that the female, as a misbegotten male, is inferior in nature to the male. Given a common human nature and a common grasp of reality, it being true that the "human mind knows no gender," could it not still be an open question whether there are some insights into the real world that the woman has and the man does not, and the other way around, so that in those respects, male and female epistemologies are complementary? Plato touched on the notion of the male/female complementarity of human nature in his *Symposium* when he had Aristophanes, in a comic vein, account for the love men and women have for each other by saying that, whereas in the beginning they formed one sex together, Zeus split them in half and since then the two sexes have been trying to reunite.

A whole range of new moral problems have been created by medical and biological technology like in vitro fertilization, surrogate motherhood, indefinite life-support systems, frozen embryos, the nonresponding comatose, and other issues arising from the unstable margin between life and death. Questions on the right to life have been raised by a number of philosophers who ask whether an inviolable right to life can be predicated of animal life as it can of human. And in the matter of ecology, human care for the planet makes moral sense only in the renewed awareness of our oneness with nature overall.

These few examples give us some idea as to how new philosophical problems emerge and how they disclose new aspects of reality that the human mind must face. But trying to rethink the thoughts of the philosophers we've studied and to develop a deeper sense of "what is," two features emerged as the benchmarks of the philosophical venture: that reality is one and that it is moral. We long ago concluded that the main ingredient of wisdom is the seeing of things in unity, grasping them in their relationships with one another. A chair has meaning as a chair only when seen in relationship with the human anatomy; slate in front of the classroom is a blackboard, on the top of the building it is a roof, on the ground it is a sidewalk; a husband is a man with a specific relationship to a specific woman, and a band of gold is a band of gold until, on the finger, it becomes a sign of spousal relationship; the sun is sun only to what it shines on; the eye is an eye only because it serves a function in the bodily whole; the chemist seeks an understanding of how matter is composed; the nuclear biologist and the quantum physicist, in their endless probings into the infinitesimal, want to know how the smallest relates to the largest; the psychologist hopes to corral the random thoughts of his patient into an integrated personality; we praise Newton and Einstein in their accomplishments of reducing disparate cosmic forces to unity. Just try the mental experiment of imagining a universe with only one thing in it. Can that one thing, solitary and unrelated, be known? Now add some furniture to that vast emptiness, first inanimate things, then animate, then human beings; with these successive additions, the one thing becomes knowable, knowable to the extent of its relatedness to others; relatedness means unity.

As we look back, we can see this urge for unity as the foundation of every philosopher's work. It makes no difference whether a philosopher is a "top-down" thinker to begin with, or a "bottom-up" thinker; it's the drive for unity that motivates them. The top-down thinker, like Plato, takes the higher as the prime given and inquires how particulars fit in; the bottom-up thinker, like Aristotle, begins with the vast field of particulars, and seeks the unity they summon him to. The difference is artistically portrayed for us in Raphael's "School of Athens," in which the master's finger pointing upward admonishes us to look above first, and the student's finger pointing downward to look below.

What holds for the golden age of Greek philosophy holds as well for the pre-Socratic age before it and for the Epicureans and Stoics after it. No pre-Socratic philosopher (like Thales, Pythagoras, Heraclitus, or Parmenides) could have been happy with a chaotic reality; quite the contrary, in widely divergent paradigms, they left us a rich legacy of unity-in-plurality. The Epicure-ans reduced all activity to matter, and whether or not we are partial to a project of this kind, such reductionism is an effort at unity; and for the Stoics, the search for a unifying principle of human behavior was how it lay in the larger unity of the universe. The vision of unity for the medieval philosopher-theologian was the drawing of all creation into unity with the Creator, and though the clear distinction between Creator and created was maintained at all times, so was the more mysterious unity-in-distinction. As we come to modern and contempo-rary times, the essays toward unity are wonderfully varied, from the dream of Descartes to the logic–language unities of Russell and Wittgenstein, despite himself, and Quine's system of the world; to the new dimensions in epistemo-logical and metaphysical unity as propounded by Hegel, Bergson, Husserl, and Heidegger. These examples illustrate the direction of the inquiring mind: no unity, no meaning; no meaning, no philosophy.

The second main feature of reality (universe, world, cosmos) is its moral character, which is an aspect of unity specifically pertinent to the human being. We use the word *ought* in many different contexts. When we say, for example, the stone ought to fall, or the flower ought to turn to the sun, we are referring to the physical or chemical principles controlling the activity. When we refer to one construction engineer who maintains the bridge ought to be built of steel, and to another who says it ought to be built of concrete, the meaning of *ought* comes from discourse proper to engineers. When doctors talk of the medicine they ought to use, they are employing medical discourse. But there is a kind of discourse concerning oughtness that is radically differ-ent from the examples just given, as when we say teachers ought to educate their students, merchants ought to give honest weight, or a parent ought not demean a child. Here we are using ought in the way tradition has recognized it in the word *moral*. It is radically different because it touches the very heart of what it means to be a human being; it is "right" to do what one ought and "wrong" to do what one ought not. The choice of the right construction mate-rial makes for a good engineer, and the right medicine a good doctor; though, in these connections, the right choice is a form of practical wisdom, a good engineer or a good doctor is not thereby a good person. The "good" of a good person has moral significance. It embraces a person's sensitivity as to how his behavior resonates with his own humanness and how it impinges on the life and well-being of others; it looks to a continuum between what a person knows ought to be done and what he actually does; it expects a consonance of action so that it fits the human context in which it is placed. It is this kind of knowledge, called wisdom by Socrates, that leads to the doing of the human thing.

We have cautioned ourselves from time to time against believing the intellect to be a mere fact-gatherer and the pursuit of truth a muscular stock-piling of information. Wisdom means more. It means that truth, with every particular truth having its part to play in the totality of truth, is ultimately life-imparting. It demands to-be-lived. Truth is personal and is catastrophically incomplete unless it has within itself the promise of human fulfillment, the happiness of man. What form fulfillment might take varies from philosopher to philosopher, with some holding to man's destiny to be embedded in the very physicality of the world, and others holding, not that man transcends himself, whatever that might mean, but that human nature itself is at one and the same time immanent and transcendent, physical and transphysical, material and spiritual, temporal and eternal.

Glossary

Absolutism A rigorously held position brooking no opposition; opposed to relativism; truth is "there" to be discovered and is not "relative" to the individual.

Abstraction The mental process of separating one or several aspects of an object from all the others actually found in the object. The process whereby the mind, by leaving aside individuating differences, moves beyond individuals to a more inclusive level, class, or category; the results thereof, for example, humanity, animal, whiteness.

Accident In the Aristotelian-Thomistic tradition, that which exists but only in another; exists in and through the substance of which it is a quality.

Agnosticism The belief that it is impossible to attain certain knowledge, particularly as to God's existence.

A posteriori Pertains to things known through experience, primarily sense experience; therefore, "based on experience."

A priori Pertains to things known independently of experience; therefore, "prior to experience."

Argument The total force of reasons bearing on a conclusion; another name for "reasoning."

Atheism The belief that God does not exist.

Atomism The view that there are small, indivisible, and irreducible quantities called atoms, and that they comprise all reality.

Becoming Change; the process of going from one state to another, from one being to another.

Cause   That which in some way brings about the being or becoming of a thing; correlative with effect.

Concept   A term that usually refers to a general idea, or universal; that is, "man," or "humanity" as opposed to the concrete individual, Socrates.

Conclusion   The proposition in which an argument ends.

Contradiction   The difference between two terms or two propositions that are diametrically opposed to each other, so that if one stands or is true the other does not stand or is false.

Cosmology   The study of physical reality, especially of the world as "cosmos," or unified whole.

Deconstruction   An active search open to the possibility of revealing what is unsaid in what is said, what lies beyond the given, beyond the text, beyond the construction. (Derrida)

Deduction   The act of reasoning from what is given to what necessarily follows, or from the premises to a conclusion that necessarily follows.

Determinism   The view that every event is necessarily brought about by preexisting conditions; as a corollary, the human will is not free.

Dialectic   In its original Greek usage, a back and forth movement, as in dialogue, debate, or simple question and answer; later, the interplay among ideas, judgments, propositions in the act of reasoning; in Hegel and others, a metaphysical interplay of real opposites.

Dogmatism   The readiness to make assertions without support of proof or evidence.

Dualism   In general, the belief that there are but two substances, entities, or principles which are independent and mutually irreducible, such as, body and soul, matter and spirit, good and evil, sense and intellect, noumenal and phenomenal, actual and possible.

Empiricism   The view that all knowledge originates, and is somehow coterminous with, experience, especially sensation; opposed to rationalism.

Epistemology   The study of knowledge; the branch of philosophy dealing with the origin, nature, and scope of knowledge.

Essence   That which makes a thing what it is; it answers the question, "What kind of thing is it?"

Esthetics (aesthetics)   The philosophy of art; the study of what it is that makes a work a work of art.

Ethics   The study of moral conduct; the branch of philosophy dealing with oughtness, right and wrong, good and bad, moral value. *See* Moral philosophy.

Existentialism   A recent movement in philosophy concerned with human beings in their actual life situation, in the "human condition" of daily life in its anguish, problems, and individual choices.

Humanism   Any view that sees human dignity and values as paramount; Renaissance humanism centered on classical literature; contemporary humanism centers on human concerns apart from religious considerations.

Idealism   A term with many meanings that must be seen in context, but in general it refers to the view that reality consists mainly, or only, of ideas, spirit, mind or thought; opposed chiefly to realism, or at times, to materialism; different from its popular usage as "perfectionism."

Induction   The act of reasoning from what is given to what probably follows, or from the premises to a conclusion that probably follows.

Infinite   Not finite; without end; unlimited or unbounded in some way.

Innate   Inborn; pertains to that which is given in some way, or found in the very nature of a thing.

Intuition   Knowledge that is direct and immediate, that is, grasped without any intermediary.

Logic   The study of reasoning correctly.

Logical positivism   The view that sentences have cognitive meaning (as opposed, say, to either emotive or persuasive meaning) only when what they express is verifiable through sense-experience or is either a tautology or self-contradictory; sentences having cognitive meaning are deemed to express statements or propositions; sometimes referred to as logical empiricism.

Materialism   The view that emphasizes the priority of matter as the chief or only substance in reality.

Mechanism   The view that physical (mechanical) principles govern all activity.

Metaphysics   The science of being; the study of the ultimate reasons as to why things are the way they are; the study of those things which lie "beyond physics" or "beyond the senses," traditionally, God, soul, and substance. In some recent analytical philosophy, the study of the general conceptual structure of human thought and language.

Monism   The belief that there is only one substance in reality, usually either spiritual or physical.

Moral philosophy   The branch of philosophy dealing with the irreducible aspect of human acts touching on oughtness, good or bad, right or wrong, do-able or not do-able; values of a unique nature called "moral values." In most respects, the same as ethics, but differs in that some actions may be unethical without being immoral. *See* Ethics.

Naturalism   The view that all reality can be understood in terms of what is "natural" as opposed to what is "supernatural," which it rejects; what cannot be experienced cannot be real; often associated with scientific empiricism.

Nihilism   The tendency to reject values as real, or at least the present structure of values.

Nominalism   The view that only particular things are real, for example, only individuals exist; therefore, universal words or terms are but "names" (*nomina*) that we use only for convenience; they do not refer to anything real; opposed to "realism."

Objective   Pertaining to the object, that is, independent of the person and personal views; opposed to subjective.

Ontological argument   The argument for God's existence which moves from the Idea of the All Perfect to the existence of the All Perfect. (Anselm and Descartes.)

Ontology   The study of being, a word formerly used as synonomous with metaphysics; preferred by, for example, Sartre, to avoid the overtones of God, soul, and substance as found in traditional metaphysics.

Phenomenology   In Hegelian usage, the study of Mind in its dialectical manifestations, or epiphanies. In Husserl, the method whereby the object is held to be disclosed in the very act of consciousness.

Phenomenon   A Greek word meaning "appearance"; thus, that which appears; the appearance itself; a manifestation of a thing; that which appears to consciousness. In Kantian terms, opposed to *noumenon,* the thing itself that does not appear.

Pluralism   As opposed to either monism (one substance) or dualism (two substances), the view that there are many ultimate substances comprising reality.

Positivism   Usually refers to the view that our knowledge of reality is limited to what we can know "positively," that is, by concrete experience, mainly sensory or scientific.

Pragmatism   The method advanced by Peirce and James as a means of clarifying our ideas; the content, or truth, of an idea is measured by its practical references or consequences.

Premise   A proposition on which a conclusion is based; from which a conclusion is inferred.

Proposition   A statement; a sentence in which the predicate is affirmed or denied of the subject.

Rationalism   The belief that we can come to knowledge of the basic truths or reality first, and perhaps only, by an examination of our ideas; in this sense, opposed to empiricism.

Realism   The view that tends to hold that objects have an existence independent of the mind, or sense objects independent of the sense; opposed to idealism. In a stricter sense, opposed to nominalism; among the objects in which reality is deemed by some to be independent of mind are abstractions, universals, and numbers. Differs from the popular use of "realism" as facing facts as they are, or hard-hitting.

Relativism   The view that there is no such thing as absolute truth, for truth varies from person to person, or age to age.

Scepticism   Uncertainty or doubt concerning the very possibility of knowledge, or particular kinds of knowledge.

Scholasticism   Generally speaking, the process of education obtaining in "schools" during the Middle Ages; special reference to the philosophy taught.

Subjective   Pertaining to the subject, that is, to the person as individual; opposed to objective.

Substance   In traditional metaphysics, that which exists independently, or on its own, unlike accidents; it is not perceived by the senses but is concluded to.

Teleology   The study of purpose (end, goal, *telos* in Greek) in reality.

Transcendent   That which, or pertaining to that which, exists beyond what is given; opposed to immanent, though taken correlatively with immanent when speaking of God who is at the same time transcendent-immanent.

Utilitarianism   The view that an action is good or right or "useful" if it produces an increase of happiness or pleasure.

Voluntarism   From the Latin *voluntas,* meaning "will." Refers to the notion that the will is endowed with a power of its own and to that extent is independent of the intellect, or, at least, is a higher power than the intellect. In its medieval context, especially Ockhamist, it means that the will of God is supreme so that the nature of a created thing is precisely what God wills it to be.

Index